RUDOLF II
AND HIS WORLD

RUDOLF II
AND HIS WORLD

A STUDY IN
INTELLECTUAL HISTORY
1576–1612

BY

R. J. W. EVANS

OXFORD
AT THE CLARENDON PRESS

Oxford University Press, Walton Street, Oxford OX2 6DP
London New York Toronto
Delhi Bombay Calcutta Madras Karachi
Kuala Lumpur Singapore Hong Kong Tokyo
Nairobi Dar es Salaam Cape Town
Melbourne Auckland
and associated companies in
Beirut Berlin Ibadan Mexico City Nicosia

Oxford is a trade mark of Oxford University Press

Published in the United States
by Oxford University Press, New York

© Oxford University Press 1973

First published 1973
Corrected paperback edition published 1984

British Library Cataloguing in Publication Data
Evans, R. J. W.
Rudolf II and his world.
1. Rudolf II, Holy Roman Emperor
2. Holy Roman Empire—Kings and rulers
—Biography
I. Title
943'.034'0924   DD187
ISBN 0-19-821961-X

Printed in Great Britain by
Billings Ltd
Guildford

PREFACE

MANY people have helped me in the course of preparing this book and I am grateful to them all. Especial thanks must go to Professor John Elliott, late of Cambridge, now of King's College, London, for his constant advice and encouragement. I have benefited much from the kindness and erudition of Professor J. V. Polišenský in Prague, Professor Hugh Trevor-Roper in Oxford, and Dr. Frances Yates of London's Warburg Institute. Dr. Ivo Kořán, who is a member of the Czechoslovak Institute for the History of Art, gave generously of his time and offered many valuable suggestions. I have received great courtesy from libraries and archives throughout Central Europe, and should like to place on record my particular debt to the Strahov Library, the district archive of Litoměřice, the office of the Cathedral Chapter of St. Vitus in Prague, and the National Széchenyi Library in Budapest. Not least am I beholden to the staff of the Clarendon Press for their thoroughness and great expertise.

All translations in the text are my own, unless specifically indicated otherwise. I have, however, left a number of quotations in their original form. In particular, I have deliberately refrained from emending the charming inconsistencies of sixteenth-century German; these are some compensation for the labour expended in deciphering the handwritten originals. The wider problem of rendering Central European names— either contemporary or modern—into English cannot be resolved with complete satisfaction. The adoption of a Czech spelling rather than a German one, or vice versa, can always convey an unintended nuance, while it is often no simple matter to balance the claims of a more familiar form against those of one more strictly correct. Such matters have their significance, but in a book whose chief character might equally have been styled *Rudolph* of *Hapsburg* (or even, in Czech style: *Habsburk*) they should not be allowed to weigh unduly.

The following have kindly given their consent to the use of illustrations: Budapest: Museum of Fine Arts (Plate 8*a*), National Museum (Plate 15*c*); Cambridge: the Fitzwilliam Museum (Plate 9*b*); London: the Trustees of the British Museum (Plate 16), the Victoria and Albert Museum (Plate 5); Oxford: the Ashmolean Museum (Plate 14); Prague: National Gallery (Plate 9*a*), National Museum (Plate 15*b*); Uppsala:

Skokloster Castle (Plate 1); Vienna: Art-Historical Museum (Plates 2, 3, 6, 8*b*, 10, 11, 12), National Library of Austria (Plate 15*a*). Plate 4 is reproduced by gracious permission of Her Majesty the Queen.

PREFACE TO THE CORRECTED PAPERBACK
EDITION

This book originally appeared in 1973; research for it was completed in 1971. Since then I have profited both from discussion with friends and colleagues and from a heartening volume of new literature on many aspects of its subject-matter. If I were writing now, I should place a number of new accents. Here I can offer only a summary indication of recent writing (along with a few contributions overlooked earlier) which bears directly on Rudolfine issues.

I have myself, in *The Making of the Habsburg Monarchy* (Oxford 1979), expanded on the political and religious background to the age of Rudolf (chapter one below). Two books by W. Schulze, *Landesdefension und Staatsbildung* (Vienna 1973), on Inner Austria, and especially *Reich und Türkengefahr im späten 16. Jahrhundert* (Munich 1978), represent the most important work on the imperial resources available to the emperor; compare also G. Benecke, *Society and politics in Germany 1500–1750* (London 1974). K. J. Dillon, *King and estates in the Bohemian lands 1526–1564* (Brussels 1976), and J. Pánek, in a series of articles and in *Stavovská opozice a její zápas s Habsburky 1547–77* (Prague 1982), examine the Bohemian political scene, laying perhaps too much stress on confrontation. W. Eberhart, *Konfessionsbildung und Stände in Böhmen 1478–1530* (Munich–Vienna 1981), reassesses the Utraquist heritage, though R. Kalivoda, in *Studia Comeniana et Historica* xxv (1983), 3–44, remains convinced of the progressive nature of sixteenth-century Hussitism as expounded before in his *Husitská ideologie* (Prague 1961). The first two volumes of *Documenta Bohemica, Bellum Tricennale illustrantia*, ed. J. V. Polišenský et al. (Prague 1971–4), are also relevant; so is L. Bazylow, *Polska a Siedmiogród 1576–1613* (Warsaw 1967).

The largest study of court politics in Rudolfine Prague (chapter two) has been K. Vocelka, *Die politische Propaganda Rudolfs II* (Vienna 1981), whose assumptions about 'propaganda' beg many questions. Vocelka's pupil, M. Altfahrt, adopts the same approach to the ideological milieu of Rudolf's father, Maximilian, in *MIÖG* lxxxviii (1980), 283–312; lxxxix (1981), 53–92. There is important information, some hard, some anecdotal, in Hans Khevenhüller's *Geheimes Tagebuch 1548–1605*, ed. G. Probszt-Ohstorff (Graz 1971) (cf. below, p. 50, n. 3). The letters of the cultured secretary Milner (J. Müldner, *Jan Myllner z Milhauzu* (Prague 1934), ii) are likewise revealing. Smaller contributions on the imperial entourage include K. Jaitner in *Zeitschrift für Historische Forschung* iv (1977), 253—reviewing this book—and earlier J. Svátek in *Sborník Historický* (ed. A. Rezek) ii (1884), 231–9, and L. Schönach in *MVGDB* xliv (1905), 378–400. Considerable work is being done on aspects of the Habsburg–Ottoman antagonism. A. Randa, *Pro Republica Christiana: die Walachei im 'langen' Türkenkrieg* . . . (Munich 1964), has valuable material from Simancas, set in a peculiar Daco-Romanian and visionary matrix; W. Leitsch in *East European Quarterly* vi (1972), 301–20, covers similar ground more soberly. P. Bartl, *Der Westbalkan zwischen spanischer Monarchie und Osmanischem Reich* (Wiesbaden 1974), and E. Springer in *Mitteilungen des Österreichischen Staatsarchivs* xxxiii (1980), 77–105, help to explain Balkan issues. G. Bayerle in *Archivum Ottomanicum* vi (1980), 5–53, and K. Nehring (Munich 1982) have reassessed the intricate details of the peace (not really Rudolf's peace) signed at Zsitvatorok. The report of Warkotsch's mission to Muscovy has been published by J. V. Polišenský: *Poselství z Prahy do Moskvy roku 1589* (Prague 1974); P. Bushkovitch, *The merchants of Moscow 1580–1650* (Cambridge 1980), 153, indicates the extraordinary sumptuousness of the tsarist response.

Several substantial works throw light on Rudolfine religious issues (chapter three). Most directly relevant is the heavyweight edition by N. Mosconi of *La nunziatura di Praga di Cesare Speciano*, i–iv (Brescia 1966), though it covers only the years 1592–3 and 1597. L. Lukács (ed.), *Monumenta Antiquae Hungariae*, i–iii (Rome 1969–81), is a treasure-trove of documentation for Hungary, resting on Jesuit archives. J. Köhler, *Das Ringen um die tridentinische Erneuerung im Bistum Breslau* (Cologne–Vienna 1973), thoroughly investigates the clash between Roman and Habsburg interests in Silesia, while my suggestion of tensions between Rudolf and Counter-Reformation forces in Austria could have been underpinned by reference to the scathing correspondence between Georg Eder and the duke of Bavaria, published by V. Bibl in *Jahrbuch für Landeskunde von Niederösterreich*, N. F. viii (1909), 67–154. The conciliatory personality of Archbishop Brus is confirmed by A. Skýbová's analysis of his library in *Knihtisk a kniha od husitství do Bílé Hory*, ed. F. Šmahel (Prague 1971), 241–56, and by the letters ed. S. Steinherz (Prague 1907). Research into Antitrinitarian ideas in Central and Eastern Europe continues apace. D. Caccamo, *Eretici Italiani in Moravia, Polonia, Transilvania* (Florence–Chicago 1970) has important evidence, especially for Moravia and for the circle around Dudith (whose whole correspondence is to be published by the Hungarian and Polish Academies of Science, ed. L. Szczucki and T. Szepessy). Some of the latest work can be found in two collections of 1979 conference papers: *Antitrinitarianism in the second half of the 16th century*, ed. R. Dán and A. Pirnát (Budapest–Leiden 1982), and *Socinianism and its role in the culture of the 16th–18th centuries*, ed. L. Szczucki et al. (Warsaw 1983).

Two important collections of materials have now been made available to the student of Central European and especially Bohemian culture in this period (chapter four). The monumental *Rukovĕt'* (cf. below, p. 147, n. 1) was completed in 1982 in five volumes; the bulk of its entries relate to the Rudolfine years, and they seem to represent a more authoritative statement about the literary priorities of that time than the approach adopted by M. Kopecký, *Pokrokové tendence v české literatuře od konce husitství do Bílé Hory* (Brno 1979). Fr. Hrubý (ed.), *Étudiants tchèques aux écoles protestantes de l'Europe occidentale . . .* (Brno 1970), op. posth., documents university travels from Bohemia and Moravia around 1600; compare the work of G. Heiss and A. Kohler for Austria in *Wiener Beiträge zur Geschichte der Neuzeit* v (1978), 13–123; viii (1981), 139–57. On the Catholic side M. Truc, *Album Academiae Pragensis S.J. 1573–1617* (Prague 1968), should be noted. M. E. H. N. Mout, *Bohemen en de Nederlanden in de zestiende eeuw* (Leiden 1975), examines various kinds of cultural connection between Bohemia and the Low Countries; and for an interpretation of learned links between the Habsburg lands and the Rhineland see R. J. W. Evans, *The Wechel Presses* (Oxford 1975). There is interesting evidence of some private libraries in Prague from J. Pešek in *Documenta Pragensia* i (1980), 77–101, and in *Folia Historica Bohemica* ii (1980), 247–77. L. Brummel, *Twee ballingen 's lands tijdens onze opstand tegen Spanje* (The Hague 1972), covers Blotius (though mainly his earliest career); R. von Busch, *Studien zu deutschen Antikensammlungen des 16. Jahrhunderts* (Tübingen 1973), treats Jacopo Strada, as does D. J. Jansen in *Leids Kunsthistorisch Jaarboek* i (1982), 57–69. (Jansen has also discovered that Rudolf's mistress, far from being a daughter of Jacopo called Katharina, was really an illegitimate child of Octavio Strada called Anna Maria.) L. Ruttkay, *Jeszenszky (Jessenius) János és kora* (Budapest 1971) is mostly misguided. K. E. Ehrlicher adds to our knowledge of the family Hofmann von Grünpichl in *Bohemia, Jahrbuch des Collegium Carolinum* xxi (1980), 59–83. Significant additions to the literature on Tycho Brahe and Kepler are R. S. Westman in *The Copernican achievement*, ed. Westman (Berkeley–London 1975), 285–345, and *Johannes Kepler 1571–1971: Gedenkschrift*, ed. P. Urban & B. Sutter (Graz 1975). Important for Hungarians' experiences of Prague are J. L. Kovács, *Lackner Kristóf és kora* (Sopron 1972), and *Szenci Molnár Albert és a magyar késő-renesánsz* (Szeged 1978); while the latest discussion of János Rimay is in *Irodalomtörténeti Közlemények* lxxxvi (1982), 589–685.

New surveys of the Rudolfine period in art and architecture (chapter five) are available in J. Hořejší et al., *Renaissance art in Bohemia* (Prague–London 1979), and J. Białostocki, *The art of the Renaissance in Eastern Europe* (Oxford 1976). The *Leids Kunsthistorisch Jaarboek* i (1982) contains valuable specialist articles. So also does the Czech journal *Umění*: note especially M. Lejsková-Matyášová in xxi (1973), 1–17, on the castle of Bechyně; E. Fučíková in xx (1972), 149–63 (on Fröschl), and in xxvii (1979), 489–511. Fučíková has also produced the catalogue *Rudolfínská kresba* (Prague 1978). T. DaC. Kaufmann, *The imperial theme in the age of Maximilian II and Rudolf II* (New York–London 1978), considers new aspects of Arcimboldo; monographs on Aachen and Savery are forthcoming from Fučíková and J. Spicer respectively. The important, albeit incomplete, inventory of Rudolf's collections noted below, p. 180, n. 2, has since been published by R. Bauer and H. Haupt as *Jahrbuch* lxxii (N.S. 36) (1976). A Venturi in *Repertorium für Kunstwissenschaft* viii (1885), 1–23, brings some interesting details. N. von Holst, *Creators, collectors and connoisseurs* (London 1967), and E. Scheicher, *Die Kunst- und Wunderkammern der Habsburger* (Vienna [1979]), examine the larger phenomenon. There is more on Rudolfine architecture in J. Krčálová, *Centrální stavby české renesance* (Prague 1974), and from K. Merten in *Bohemia* (as above) viii (1967), 144–62. J. Racek, *Kryštof Harant z Polžie a jeho doba*, ii (Brno 1972), provides much information (some naive) on Harant's life and music. W. Eckhardt in *Jahrbuch der Hamburger Kunstsammlungen* xxi (1976), 55–92, and xxii (1977), 13–74, surveys the career and works of Erasmus Habermel (though some historians of science now suspect many of his instruments to be nineteenth-century forgeries).

The occult world of the Prague court (chapter six) exerts a continuing spell. A. M. Ripellino, *Praga magica* (Turin 1973), is enigmatic but worthwhile; not so H. Holzer, *The alchemist . . .* (New
York 1974), or F. Marek, *Severočeské kulturní kapitoly* (Ústí n.L.
1978). F. F. Blok, *Contributions to the history of Isaac Vossius' library*
(Amsterdam–London 1974), has significant information about Rudolfine alchemical manuscripts. Compare J. Červenka in *Acta Comeniana*
xxiv (1970), 21–44; F. Secret in *Bibliothèque d'Humanisme et Renaissance* xxxv (1973), 103–16, 499–531; J. Telle in *Sudhoffs Archiv* lx
(1976), 308 f.—reviewing this book—and in *Euphorion* lxxi (1977),
283–305; and earlier G. Eis in *Südostforschung* vi (1941), 440–62, and
W. Schmitt in *Stifter-Jahrbuch* vii (1962), 177–95. C. Webster in
Health, medicine and mortality in the sixteenth century, ed. Webster
(Cambridge 1979), 301–34, has broader reflections on the Paracelsan
tradition. P. French, *John Dee* (London 1972), is a serviceable biography; while B. L. Sherwin, *Mystical theology and social dissent . . .*
(Rutherford, N.J. 1982), represents the latest study of Rabbi Loew,
and M. E. H. N. Mout examines the Cabalism of Habermann in
Nederlands Archief voor Kerkgeschiedenis N.S. lviii/1 (1977), 163–78.

On the wider intellectual problems of the age of Mannerism and its
legacy (chapters seven and eight) see the important reflections by T.
Klaniczay in *Acta Litteraria Academiae Scientiarum Hungaricae* xiii
(1971), 269–314, and by J. Neumann in *Umění* xxv (1977), 400–48;
xxvi (1978), 303–47 (also summarized in Hořejší (ed.) and *Leids Jaarboek* above). In the *Leids Jaarboek*, 119–48, in his introduction to
Drawings from the Holy Roman Empire 1540–1680, ed. Kaufmann
(Princeton 1982), and in a forthcoming survey of Rudolfine art as a
whole, T. DaC. Kaufmann argues persuasively, though not I think
decisively, for a narrower and more functional use of the term
'Mannerism'. There are analyses of Mannerist aesthetics from a
Central European standpoint by T. Klaniczay, *A manierizmus*
(Budapest 1975), and in *Littérature de la Renaissance*, ed. N. I. Bala-
chov et al. (Budapest 1978), 327–84, and by P. Preiss, *Panoráma
manýrismu* (Prague 1974). For Rudolf and Tintoretto see C. Garas in
Bulletin du Musée hongrois des Beaux-arts xxx (1967), 29–48. The reflections of K. V. Thomas, *Religion and the decline of magic* (London
1971), and C. Webster, *The great instauration* (London 1975), though
English-based, are richly rewarding for the continent also. I should,
finally, have made rather more of the survival of 'Rudolfine' ideas in
the seventeenth century. F. A. Yates, *The Rosicrucian enlightenment*

(London 1972), does so with brio; but see my review in *Historical Journal* xvi (1973), 865–8; and compare B. Vickers in *Journal of Modern History* li (1979), 287–316, and G. Menk, *Die Hohe Schule Herborn in ihrer Frühzeit 1584–1660* (Wiesbaden 1981), the latest contribution to the intellectual history of Germany on the eve of the Thirty Years War.

R.J.W.E.

Oxford, December 1983

CONTENTS

LIST OF PLATES

(at end)

CENTRAL EUROPE ABOUT 1600

Map legend:
▬ Boundary of Holy Roman Empire
▨ Lands of direct rule by Austrian Habsburgs
① Peace of Zsitvatorok 1606
② Battle of the White Mountain 1620

Scale: 0 50 100 200 300 400 km
0 50 100 200 miles

Labels on map:
POLAND
Warsaw
Vistula
Cracow
Breslau (Wrocław,Vratislav)
Brieg
Troppau (Opava)
Olomouc (Olmütz)
Oder
Frankfurt Oder
UPPER LOWER
BRANDENBURG
LUSATIA
Wittenberg
Dresden
SAXONY
Leipzig
UPPER SILESIA LOWER SILESIA
MORAVIA
Brno
Brünn
Nagyszombat (Trnava)
Prague
Trebon
Wittingau
Pilsen
BOHEMIA
Eger (Cheb)
Nuremberg
Krumlov (Krummau)
Passau
Altdorf
Regensburg
Donauworth
BAVARIA
Augsburg
UPPER AUSTRIA
Linz
Vienna
Wien
LOWER AUSTRIA
Wiener Neustadt
Pressburg (Pozsony, Bratislava)
Raab (Györ)
Esztergom (Gran)
Buda (Ofen)
HUNGARY
Pécs (Fünfkirchen)
TRANSYLVANIA
Maros
Danube
OTTOMAN EMPIRE
STYRIA
Graz
Salzburg
Innsbruck
TYROL
CARINTHIA
CARNIOLA
Trent
VENICE
Po
LOMBARDY
TUSCANY
Wolfenbüttel
Cassel
Herborn
Marburg
HESSE
Frankfurt am Main
MAINZ
Cologne
Jülich
CLEVES
Meuse
Trier
Strasbourg
Rhine
PALATINATE
FURTHER AUSTRIA
SWISS CONFEDERATION
SPANISH NETHER-LANDS
UNITED PROVINCES
Elbe
FRANCE
Paris
Seine
Rhône

INTRODUCTION

RUDOLF II OF HABSBURG, Holy Roman Emperor, King of Bohemia and Hungary was without doubt one of the most extraordinary of all European rulers. His personality, attractive and repulsive by turns, has exercised down succeeding centuries a fascination not restricted to his chosen residence of Prague or the extensive Danubian territories where the events of his long reign were mostly played out.

In the Europe of that time his court occupied a central position. The Emperor was the senior sovereign of the continent, and the dignity was not an empty one, even for an age which boasted such diverse and self-willed monarchs as Philip II of Spain, Henry IV of France, Ivan the Terrible, or Elizabeth I. His lands were linked by a nexus of contacts at many social and political levels with all the significant countries of the day. Even the still peripheral England provided a number of important visitors: the diplomats Sidney and Wotton, the poet Westonia and the adventurer Sherley, the Jesuit Campion and the Protestant traveller Moryson, the magicians Dee and Kelley. Moreover, such people were only the famous few; many lesser folk followed in their wake, as the diary of John Dee reveals. Bohemia was not felt to be a land unduly remote, despite Shakespeare's teasing attribution to it of an imaginary sea-coast: when a new Protestant church was built in Prague during the early years of the seventeenth century its greatest subscriber was King James I.

Yet Rudolf remains for all this a strange, fugitive figure. No major biography of him has ever been written; few scholars have attempted a critical appraisal of his role, even in a more limited frame of reference. Thus his wider reputation has fallen largely into the realm of legend: not only the picturesque legend which rather embellishes the facts than distorts them, and may perhaps yield a creative approximation to the truth (such is the dramatist Grillparzer's portrait of Rudolf); but also the negative version, which is a synonym for history's more outdated and ill-considered verdicts.

Posterity has in fact recognized three distinct Rudolfs. The first is the feeble, unstable, and impoverished monarch who began his reign by succeeding to a glamorous political inheritance but ended it a prisoner in his own castle, powerless in the Empire, evicted from Austria and

Hungary, deposed even in Bohemia, where he was forced to endure the coronation tumult of his detested brother. This is a story whose outlines are well-known and documented, especially for the last tragic years: the conflict with Matthias which flared up at the time of peace negotiations with the Turks in 1606; the defection of the Protestant estates in Hungary, Moravia, and the Austrian Duchies followed by the compromise treaty of Lieben in 1608; the forced concession in the next year of the so-called Letter of Majesty, both a guarantee of religious freedoms and a charter of unrest for Bohemia; finally in 1611 the invasion—tacitly approved by the Emperor—of the Passau troops, whose abortive campaign sealed the triumph of Matthias.

The second Rudolf is a great Maecenas, the protector of arts and sciences, of Arcimboldo and Spranger, Kepler and Tycho Brahe. This is a man of another stamp, unyielding in his demands and far-seeing in his commissions, who amassed a collection of artistic treasures unrivalled even in that lavish age. As such he has attracted a devoted specialist literature and his name is assured of an honourable place in the intellectual annals of the period.

The third Rudolf is different again, and seemingly much less edifying. He is a notorious patron of occult learning, who trod the paths of secret knowledge with an obsession bordering on madness. The wizard Emperor has been remembered above all for his alchemy, his links with Kelley or Michael Maier, but the pursuit of magic was also much wider: astrology, Hermetism, Cabala, and plain old-fashioned superstition.

The three aspects thus sketched form points of departure for the present book. Indeed without the existing body of careful scholarship in these fields it could not have been undertaken. At the same time however it attempts, as a first fundamental theme, to draw them together and suggest the ways in which they overlap, as facets of a single problem. Of course some interaction has always been assumed: Rudolf's mental imbalance might be attributed to his occultism and presented as the cause of his political failure; his artistic interests have been associated with a neglect of everyday affairs. Yet the real unity is a deeper one. However hazardous it may be to speak of the philosophy of an age, there was nevertheless an underlying atmosphere, a climate of thought in later sixteenth-century Europe, which was particularly characteristic of the Imperial court in Prague. The manifestations of it were various, sometimes difficult to grasp and even contradictory, but their total picture has a logical pattern befitting an epoch so systematic in its ways. Part of the evidence for this is the universalist striving itself, an effort to preserve the mental and political unity of Christendom, to avoid religious schism, uphold peace at home, and deliver Europe from the Ottoman menace. The Humanists, Protestant or Catholic, were still recognizably a single body of cosmopolitan scholars, just as the artists of Mannerism formed a broad-based international élite. The debates of the age, whether about astronomy or Aristotle, music or magicians, had well-defined rules of play.

Much of that mood is thoroughly unfamiliar to us nowadays, its representatives misunderstood or forgotten. The reason for their neglect is itself important, and forms a second main stress here: the Rudolfine years in Central Europe were the end of an era, a turning-point in development. This holds true in a narrower and a wider sense: on the one hand confessional politics entered a new phase after 1600, urged on by the progress of the Counter-Reformation. The flight into extremism became inexorable and, seven years to the day after Rudolf cowered away in his palace to avoid witnessing the coronation of Matthias, the same building staged a more violent *démarche* when Matthias's own lieutenants in Bohemia were thrown from the window of their Chancery by the enraged estates. On the other hand the decades around 1600 saw a broader cultural change: the decline of Latin Humanism and the rise of Baroque, the sinking of an old world-view and the beginnings of the seventeenth-century intellectual revolution. Rudolf was heavily identified with the traditional cosmology, and this is the greatest adjustment we must make in understanding his period, for the notions to which he and so many of his contemporaries subscribed were in their very essence magical. They believed that the world of men and the world of nature were linked by hidden sources of knowledge, and that the problems of alchemy, astrology, or the Hermetic texts were proper subjects for learned investigation. Research is only now showing how widespread were mystical and occult preoccupations throughout late-Renaissance Europe, even (for example) at the court of Philip II. The enigmatic person of Rudolf stands as an extreme but important case-study of the phenomenon.

The stability of Central Europe, and of Bohemia in particular, was thus being undermined on two levels: by the breakdown of an inherited political harmony which issued in the first total European war, set in motion through that defenestration from the royal palace in Prague; and by the decline of a scheme of mental harmony under attack from narrower empirical scientific ideas. Moreover, these two processes were themselves not independent of each other. Their interplay forms a third thesis in what follows: the clash between practical and intellectual solutions. Of course such matters can easily be oversimplified: realism and idealism always stand in some kind of opposition. But there are moments in history when the upholders of a deep-rooted, theoretical, essentially passive set of precepts are placed over against the exponents of a new, clear-cut activism, and the reign of Rudolf was one of them. The conflict which played itself out in the Habsburg lands during those years was a political reflection of the whole intellectual confrontation between acceptance of nature and domination over it. And while the old cosmology with its magic and symbolism possessed elements which were favourable to a more active view of man's role in the world (we may see them at work in various departments of occultism), it nevertheless held basically to the traditional idea that the highest human purpose was one of contemplation. It taught people to understand a divine scheme of which they formed an integral part and within which they could educate themselves to salvation, rather than to change an objective nature over which they were putative masters.

This study is an attempt at interpretation and not a narrative. It is neither a political history of Central Europe and the Empire under Rudolf—though one is richly needed—nor yet an exhaustive analysis of the larger intellectual problems. I have offered some general exposition of the political issues in the first chapter, and return to the broad cultural questions in the two concluding ones; but between them I have divided the material by topics, moving out from the debate over Rudolf himself to a closer account of his entourage and its relation to the Bohemian background from which it is inseparable. The history of Rudolfine Prague is much more than merely an episode in the evolution of the lands of St. Wenceslas; it is a period when Bohemia, in common with Central Europe as a whole, stood on an international crossroads and took decisions of a lasting momentousness.

1. The Habsburgs, Bohemia, and the Empire

'The Emperor Rudolf was, they say, a most intelligent and sagacious Prince who long maintained a wise peace in the Empire; he was cast in the heroic mould and contemned all vulgar things, loving only the rare and miraculous. His rule was happy, peaceful and secure until the four years before his death. The Spaniard he would never trust, the Pope he disagreed with, the French he viewed with ill-humour . . .'

MELCHIOR GOLDAST (1612)

THE history of the Holy Roman Empire from the Peace of Augsburg to the Defenestration of Prague has traditionally been seen as the uneasy prelude to a holocaust of hitherto unparalleled violence and destruction. The final shipwreck of the Imperial mission, the descent into confessional polemic, the growing anarchy and particularism: this was all systematically narrated by the dedicated historiographers of the last century, for whom history was largely politics animated by the dimension of time, playing itself out endlessly and consistently in a series of neutral facts.

This school laid down a framework for interpretation whose outlines are still clear.[1] The settlement of 1555, which recognized differences of religion within the Empire, but purely in territorial units—the famous clause *cuius regio eius religio*—seemed to no one an enduring solution, though it was in fact followed by the longest period of peace in German history. It left two sources of permanent discontent. On the one hand the so-called ecclesiastical reservation (*geistlicher Vorbehalt*), provided

---

[1] Best are the works of Moriz Ritter, especially *Deutsche Geschichte im Zeitalter der Gegenreformation und des dreissigjährigen Krieges*, i. *1555–86* (Stuttgart 1889), ii. *1586–1618* (Stuttgart 1895), and Anton Gindely, *Rudolf II und seine Zeit 1600–12*, i–ii (Prague 1862–5). There is also a good short sketch by L. von Ranke, 'Zur Reichsgeschichte 1575–1619' in *Zur deutschen Geschichte vom Religionsfrieden bis zum dreissigjährigen Krieg* (Leipzig 1869), who as usual shows himself more subtle and aware of complexities than his 'Rankean' disciples. Two notable old-fashioned biographies throw much light on the later part of the period: J. von Hammer, *Khlesls, des Cardinals . . . Leben*, i–iv (Vienna 1847–51); F. Hurter, *Geschichte Kaiser Ferdinands II und seiner Eltern bis zu dessen Krönung in Frankfurt*, i–xi (Schaffhausen 1850–67). The eleven volumes of the *Briefe und Akten zur Geschichte des dreissigjährigen Krieges* (Munich 1870–1909) are indispensable for detailed political developments in the *Reich*.

that the lands of bishops and abbots who embraced the Protestant faith should be forfeit to the Catholic Church (it was promulgated only by Imperial decree, not by agreement); on the other hand the failure to admit the Reformed religion gave the latter no legal foundation, though its expansion in limited areas was swift and its ideology militant. The first explains much of the increasingly anti-Imperial and independent policies pursued by the leading Protestant princes, Brandenburg, Denmark, Brunswick, even Saxony, whose sights were set on rich bishoprics like Bremen, Münster, Magdeburg, and the rest. The second explains the positive, rebellious quality of Calvinist activity, led by the Palatinate, backed by various smaller principalities (Hesse-Cassel, Nassau, Anhalt, East Friesland, some Imperial cities, etc.) and in close liaison with the insurgent Dutch. At the same time the spirit of Augsburg was thoroughly at variance with that of the Tridentine decrees promulgated in 1563 and the powerful Roman Catholic political revival whose spearhead within the Empire became Bavaria and parts of the Habsburg lands. The threat to peace grew in a series of squabbles of increasing range, none of which could ever be fully resolved, and each of which reduced the field of manœuvre for future negotiation: Aachen, Strasbourg, the notorious *Vierklosterstreit* of the early 1600s, the troubles at Donauwörth during 1606 and 1607. The culmination was complete impasse in the matter of the Cleves–Jülich succession, a problem which loured over the Empire in its immense complexity from the late 1580s, as the mental instability of the last ruler of the duchy, Johann Wilhelm, became clear, and which was not finally settled until well after the Peace of Westphalia.[1]

For the first time 'parties' began to emerge on confessional lines— Lutheran and Calvinist as mutually antagonistic as Protestant and Catholic[2]—in a commonwealth which had no mechanism to cater for them. The various attempts at reform made under the guidance of Maximilian I and Ferdinand I could not bear such a weight of particularism, and their procedures became completely blocked. The financial

---

[1] Ritter, op. cit. ii. 67 ff., 159 ff., 25 ff. There is a comprehensive survey of these disputes as they presented themselves to the Catholic camp by 1582 in *Nuntiaturberichte aus Deutschland 1572–85*, ii, Pt. 3, ed. J. Hansen (Berlin 1894). The best case study is F. Stieve, *Der Ursprung des dreissigjährigen Krieges*, i, *Der Kampf um Donauwörth im Zusammenhange der Reichsgeschichte* (Munich 1875).

[2] See the analysis by K. Lorenz, *Die kirchlich-politische Parteibildung in Deutschland vor Beginn des dreissigjährigen Krieges im Spiegel der konfessionellen Politik* (Munich 1903), and the recent bare narrative of E. W. Zeeden, *Entstehung der Konfessionen. Grundlagen und Formen der Konfessionsbildung im Zeitalter der Glaubenskämpfe* (Munich 1965).

base, so crucial at a time of continuous Turkish pressure periodically erupting into open warfare, collapsed beyond recall.[1] The background to this complicated picture of superficial calm but inexorable rising tensions was a growing lethargy and retreat from practical affairs—an age of occult pursuits, exotic private collections, princely stifling of free endeavour, impractical dreams, and wild social intolerance. Many of the German rulers of the day were either religious bigots or a gallery of curious characters: the alchemist Friedrich of Württemberg, the astrologer Julius of Brunswick, the learned reformer Moritz of Hesse-Cassel, the last decadent Dukes of Cleves, with the prince of the eccentrics Rudolf II immured in his Hradschin castle in Prague.[2]

There is much in this analysis which remains valid; yet it suffers from narrowness of scope. It is at once too parochially German, and too much a projection back before 1618 of positions derived from study of the Thirty Years War itself, positions which themselves are partial. The European roots of that conflict have now been widely recognized; in particular the polarization of forces elsewhere: the formation of confessional camps in France from the time of Francis I,[3] and the international religious fronts, most articulate among the Calvinists, for whom thoroughgoing international co-operation has been postulated, and whose leaders—Mornay, Tschernembl, Anhalt, Žerotín—were the lynch-pins in a wide and secret network of contacts stretching from the Hague and Heidelberg to the castles of the Eastern European nobility.[4] The most powerful extension of these ideas, in conformity with some recent discussion of the early seventeenth century as the crisis of traditional economies, sees the Thirty Years War as an inevitable outcome of conflict between two socio-economic systems: the unsatisfied rising bourgeois estates, whose ethic was commercial and Protestant and whose prototype the United Netherlands, pitted against the absolutist, Catholic,

---

[1] Cf. A. Gindely, *Geschichte der böhmischen Finanzen von 1526 bis 1618* (Vienna 1868).

[2] There is no adequate collective study of the culture of the German courts before 1618, and published material on them is very piecemeal. For a fine novelistic characterization of some of these typical figures see Ricarda Huch, *Der grosse Krieg in Deutschland*, i, *Das Vorspiel 1585–1620* (Leipzig 1914).

[3] R. Nürnberger, *Die Politisierung des französischen Protestantismus* (Tübingen 1948).

[4] The 'international' in A. van Schelven, 'Der Generalstab des politischen Calvinismus in Zentraleuropa zu Beginn des dreissigjährigen Kriegs', in *ARG* 36 (1939), 117–41, though his thesis is tenuous, especially through unfamiliarity with the Central European protagonists Budovec, Peter Vok Rožmberk, and Žerotín. Cf. R. Patry, *Philippe du Plessis-Mornay, un huguenot homme d'état* (Paris 1933); H. Sturmberger, *Georg Erasmus Tschernembl* (Linz 1953); Peter von Chlumecky, *Karl von Zierotin und seine Zeit* (Brünn 1862), a purely political biography on a wide canvas. Gindely, *Rudolf II*, is really a study of the activities of Anhalt, as the author explicitly states.

neofeudal monarchies of the 'centre'—Spain, the Austrian Habsburgs, Poland.[1]

To a large extent the political history of Central Europe in the second half of the sixteenth century has always been written in terms of the war which followed.[2] As such it has frequently suffered from too close association with the official accounts which the different sides in that conflict issued and which became standardized by serving as propaganda: Imperialist-Catholic versus Prussian-Nationalist.[3] Against this the theory of 'crisis' at least has the merit of recognizing a clash of mentalities and providing a broader intellectual frame of reference, whatever weight of interpretative assumption may lie in its labels 'progressive' and 'reactionary'. Recent attempts to reappraise drastically the whole problem, involving in the extreme case denying the existence of a Thirty Years War at all, are certainly exaggerated and rather paradoxical, though some of their changed emphasis is just, especially in their reassessment of cultural conditions.[4]

What seems to be lacking in all these accounts is a feeling for the real character of the forty years before the Defenestration of Prague: every age has features of transition, but none can be understood through them. It was a period of great cosmopolitanism, far more so than any part of the succeeding century; indeed much of the 'extended treatment' which has lately been accorded to the Thirty Years War is more applicable to the Europe of Rudolf, for instance the relevance of Russia which has been canvassed.[5] It was an age whose framework of ideas was still unitary, the last such age which Europe has known, and it can be dangerously confused thinking for historians to separate 'religious' and 'political' issues, as if there were alternatives in the contemporary mind. Con-

---

[1] This is the approach of J. V. Polišenský in many books and articles; most clearly in *Nizozemská politika a Bílá Hora* (Prague 1958), 9–69, with the comparison between Holland and Bohemia as economic flashpoints.

[2] Even Gindely, for whom the diplomacy of the time had a permanent fascination, begins his story only in 1600, as the year when Rudolf became certifiably ill. There are brief treatments of the German lands between 1600 and 1618 by C. V. Wedgwood, *The Thirty Years War* (London 1938, 1957), 11–65, and F. Dickmann, *Der Westfälische Frieden* (Münster 1959), 9–34.

[3] See especially J. V. Polišenský, 'Současný stav bádání o Bílé Hoře', *ČMM* lxx (1951), 1–25.

[4] The 'extreme case' is S. H. Steinberg, *The 'Thirty Years War' and the Conflict for European Hegemony 1600–60* (London 1966), expanding a much earlier article in *History* xxxii (1947), 89–102. Apart from his revised assessment of economic damage Steinberg's narrative is nearer to the traditional version than he allows.

[5] e.g. by O. Vainstein, *Rossiya i Tridtsatiletnyaya Voina* (Moscow 1947). In fact Russia bulked more important at the time of Rudolf's rule from Prague than later; cf. W. Leitsch, *Moskau und die Politik des Kaiserhofes im XVII. Jahrhundert*, ii. *1604–54* (Graz–Cologne 1960).

fessional freedom or unfreedom necessarily found expression in political action, but at the same time there is a clear, overtly religious intention in the political behaviour of the leaders of the Bohemian revolt. It is against this background that the stifling constraints of religious extremism in all directions should be viewed: Kepler's struggle with orthodox Lutheranism, Žerotín's with Calvinism, Bruno's with Tridentine Catholicism. Most of all, this was a period characterized by a deep imbalance between theory and practice; both the pure political and the economic interpretations of it seem too much concerned with the latter at the expense of the former, with social and institutional developments in abstraction from the profound organizational preoccupations which underlay them in the contemporary mind.

The politicians who took decisions in the years after 1555 were of course hardly aware how much they were facing new situations. Yet there was an ever-growing opposition between men who pursued active policies, based on a practical blueprint and activated by the momentum of positive diplomacy, and those whose respect for traditional values was regularly linked with an unthinking belief in the old universal order. On the one hand stood the pressure towards confessional dogmatism, itself a precursor of the modern self-sufficient life of the political party and its ideology; on the other a more passive and intellectual urge to restore the fading harmony of the visible as of the mental world. The contest between these two attitudes was part of the gradual, scarcely perceptible evolution of the new seventeenth-century Europe, and the fate of individuals could not affect its resolution, only its local modifications. But the turning-point was more nearly the years around 1600 than a single hectic act of rebellion in 1618 which was merely the climax of more than a decade of desperate uncertainty.[1] The underlying change was ultimately a decisive factor in the failure of Rudolf's own life; it was also crucial for the whole international role of the Imperial dynasty.

The Habsburgs[2] appear in retrospect to have occupied an anomalous position from the beginning of the religious split: attempting to retain

[1] A recent popular account of the Bohemian war has grasped well the contingent character of leading events, a result of nervous reaction against lethargy and the very weight of the long years of peace: H. Sturmberger, *Aufstand in Böhmen* (Munich–Vienna 1959), 9 and *passim*.

[2] There is an almost complete dearth of writing on the Austrian Habsburgs as a family during this period, at least of interpretative literature. The reader is left with the most general surveys; A. Wandruszka, *Das Haus Habsburg* (Vienna 1962) does make clear the sense of dynastic continuity and 'mission'. For an Englishman's view there is only the classic but pedestrian account of William Coxe: *History of the House of Austria from the foundation of the Monarchy by Rhodolph of Hapsburgh to the Death of Leopold the second* (London 1807); vol. i, Pt. 2 covers 1515–1711.

control over the Empire through reforming centralization and yet, by their identification with the Catholic cause, providing a doctrinaire base for the Counter-Reformation. But during the sixteenth century this was not yet a real antithesis: the Holy Roman Empire was still a unitary concept, from Carniola in the South to Holstein in the North, from Alsace in the West to Bohemia in the East. Its territories were linked by a bond of direct or indirect subordination to the Emperor—between 1438 and 1740 always a Habsburg. Its constitution was so complex as to be largely unfathomable even to its rulers, a rigid hierarchy through Electors, bishops and other ecclesiastics, secular princes of various kinds, and free cities down to the smallest *Reichsritter*, yet at the same time a rich undifferentiated canvas which did not separate the sacred title from the profane; a paradise for the antiquarian hunter, where legal disputes regularly took decades to resolve, yet for all that a living organism where appeal to the highest authority was always possible. It was an amorphous body, in which large areas were not wholly, perhaps not at all, subject to the central power, while the lands most subject—the Habsburgs' own *Erblande*—occupied a special position within the Empire. Some of its disputed territories remained notorious down the centuries: the worst of all was Bohemia, but others were Switzerland, a number of the North Italian fiefs and Istria, the Netherlands, Schleswig (a *casus belli* as late as 1864), and Alsace. The problem was heightened by an administrative reform of the early sixteenth century which introduced ten circles (Kreise); the Austrian and Burgundian lands and Savoy were included, Bohemia and Switzerland were not.[1]

Yet the political *raison d'être* of the Empire the sixteenth century did not call in question; its focus remained the central Habsburg administration, its lines of force still centripetal and not yet centrifugal. Only in 1620 was a separate Austrian Chancery (*Österreichische Hofkanzlei*) distinguished from the *Reichshofkanzlei* whose nominal head was the Archbishop of Mainz, while the highest court of appeal for the whole Empire (as the *Reichskammergericht* became increasingly ponderous through religious deadlock and sheer inanition) was the Habsburg Aulic Council (*Reichshofrat*).[2] The point is also well seen from

---

[1] This complexity is all best appreciated from a map: outstanding is the *Grosser Historischer Weltatlas*, vol. 3 (Munich 1962), page 110 for the *Kreiseinteilung*. See below p. 23.

[2] The standard work on the nature and development of the administration itself has long been T. Fellner, *Die österreichische Zentralverwaltung I (1526–1749)*, vol. i, *Geschichtliche Übersicht* (Vienna 1907), which belies its title for the period before 1618, since the point being made here is that the central organs were not 'Austrian'. See especially 139 ff., 218 ff.

the cosmopolitan composition of the Imperial service in Vienna and Prague.[1]

Underlying the pragmatic convenience of this great realm there remained a dominant spiritual force: the Imperial idea itself. The *Reichsidee* was a fusion of various overlapping medieval notions—the dignity and divinity of the Emperor (*Kaiseridee*), the unity of Christendom, the sanctity of the Imperium. As a political ideal it was a concept which could be reinterpreted by successive generations, even down to the final transformation during the nineteenth century; as a formula for sovereignty its content was continually changing.[2] It was always an ideology of absolutism (in the completest sense of the word, i.e. a single, total polity), but early modern Europe could understand this in two distinct ways: either as the survival of medieval cosmopolitan universalism, or as an expression of the rising doctrine of organized central autocracy which was to be so characteristic of the states of the *ancien régime*. In reality the two overlapped,[3] and it was precisely during the Rudolfine period, which anyway possessed its own obsession with harmony and universality, that the half-apprehended debate between them was joined. As yet some necessary social foundations were lacking for the seventeenth-century development under Ferdinand II and Leopold which foreshadowed the thoroughgoing absolutism of Maria Theresa, and thus sovereignty could still only subsist through moral justification and the support of the traditional polity. There is a parallel in the constitutional corollary to Imperial rule—the evolution of the estates. By the late sixteenth century the Central European nobilities were losing their medieval role as guardians of the exercise of power and being turned into a socio-economic class of powerful landowners whose interests would necessarily conflict with the sovereignty of the monarch. Yet moderate, cultured opinion within their ranks could still respect the moral force of the Imperial idea and support the Emperor as an ideal

[1] This emerges from the study by H. F. Schwarz, *The Imperial Privy Council in the Seventeenth Century* (Cambridge, Mass. 1943), especially in his biographies of the Councillors (Appendix C). See (e.g.) Julius von Braunschweig-Wolfenbüttel or the Prince of Hohenzollern-Hechingen (ibid. s.v.).

[2] On the medieval *Reichsidee* as an enduring influence, an unrealizable ideal, see F. Heer, *Die Tragödie des Heiligen Reiches* (Vienna 1952).

[3] This complexity of old and new notions and their interrelation is well seen by Heinrich Lutz, *Christianitas Afflicta* (Göttingen 1964), Introduction, 15–38. 'Die Politik und Ideenwelt des Kaisers wie seiner französischen Gegner [in the years 1552–6] legt eine übergreifende Betrachtungsweise nahe, welche diese frühneuzeitlichen Komplexe als Phänomene sui generis gegenüber dem Mittelalter wie der Folgezeit abgrenzt . . . mittelalterliches Erbe an Eigenstaatlichkeit und neuerwachten Universalismus — so könnte man die üblichen Gegensatzpaare hier in einer nur scheinbaren Paradoxie vertauschen.' (Ibid. 22.)

dignitary, not simply from personal political calculation.[1] To this extent the Rudolfine *Reichsidee* was quite literally Utopian—in an age of Utopias—but it was still an intellectually founded Utopia. With the final destruction of its ideal during the Thirty Years War it could survive only as a transcendent *literary* vision, the madman's dream of Grimmelshausen's Simplicissimus.[2]

The survival of an old Imperial universalism has been studied mostly in the figure of Charles V, inheritor of the crusading zeal of the Spanish *reconquista*, the cosmopolitanism of his Burgundian ancestors, the breathless unquenchable idealism of his paternal grandfather, Maximilian I. His belief is in a total Christian sovereignty, a sacred mission which transcends *Realpolitik*—or rather subsumes it—and must always remain logically and emotionally prior to the confessional split.[3] Recent research has stressed the continuity of this ideal, and the refusal to consider more limited objectives. Charles created the first 'modern' empire in Spain and its dominions, but this despite himself and his own resolute intention to rule a Christian Europe; his contemporaries were equally unwilling to abandon such a long-cherished dream, and the decades of religious colloquy in the 1530s and 1540s (Augsburg, Ratisbon, etc.) were still filled with a spirit of compromise for the sake of the Imperium.[4] The last years of failure which preceded Charles's abdication in 1556 saw the apparent bankruptcy of the quest, but no alternative to it; a decline in the quality of theoretical thinking, but no resolution of the confusion which Luther's new dimension of politics had brought to both sides.[5] Charles's last aim was to ensure the succession (either immediately or after his brother Ferdinand) of his son Philip in an undivided realm; the project proved abortive, but not without having had strong prospects of success, and not for want of an ideology.[6]

This clash, beginning before the end of Charles's reign and endemic thereafter, between the Spanish and Austrian branches of the Habsburg house is crucial to subsequent developments. It is sometimes latent,

---

[1] Cf. H. Sturmberger, *Kaiser Ferdinand II und das Problem des Absolutismus* (Munich 1957), 3–8, where degrees of practical absolutism are considered, and O. Brunner, *Adeliges Landleben und Europäischer Geist* (Salzburg 1949), especially 23 ff.

[2] P. Rassow, *Forschungen zur Reichsidee im 16. und 17. Jahrhundert* (Cologne 1955), 14 ff.

[3] Ibid. 6 ff.

[4] P. Rassow, *Die Kaiser-Idee Karls V dargestellt an der Politik der Jahre 1528–40* (Berlin 1932); idem, *Die politische Welt Karls V* (Munich n.d. [1946?]), especially Ch. 2.

[5] See the comprehensive study of Lutz, op. cit., who sees how the Calvinists and England first appreciated the new conditions of power in Europe.

[6] Rassow, *Forschungen*, 14 ff., and *Politische Welt*, 34.

never resolved, even in periods of apparent co-operation.[1] In the case of Rudolf II's attitude to Spain—part unthinking acceptance, part violent antipathy—the opposition is fundamental to political activity. With the accession of Philip II in the Spanish lands and Ferdinand in the Empire, together with the new Papal militancy following the Tridentine decrees of 1563, it becomes clear that there are now three contenders for one ideology. Reviving Papal claims to temporal dominion are matched by two Habsburg monarchies, both deriving their authority from an apostolic succession to a 'traditional' Imperium.[2] Bohdan Chudoba has studied the continued Spanish search for a traditional policy as 'one of the many expressions of an age which was frantically seeking to re-establish the lost equilibrium of man'; a just approach, but one which largely ignores the parallel movement, different in emphasis, among the Austrian Habsburgs, and oversimplifies the Spanish cause as the cause of European Catholicism.[3]

From this potential three-sided antagonism follows the ideological importance of the key points of friction within the monolith of Catholic Europe itself—the dispute over the Italian fiefs, the struggle over bishoprics and ecclesiastical presentation, the 'hard' and 'soft' lines over the Netherlands, the squabbles about anti-Turkish offensives. In fine it accounts for the peculiar nature of Austrian Habsburg Catholicism, so suspect both to Rome and to Madrid, and goes far towards explaining its taint of Erastianism and lack of dogmatic conviction.[4]

Another aspect of the problem of Rudolfine sovereignty to which we shall return calls for some preliminary comment here: the dynastic 'mystique' of the house of Habsburg. All the major ruling families of Europe developed during the Renaissance period their characteristic symbolism, which came to represent a kind of apotheosis of their own

[1] As during the reigns of Matthias and Ferdinand II; cf. G. Mecenseffy, 'Habsburger im siebzehnten Jahrhundert', *AÖG* 121 (1951), 1–91.

[2] France must be ignored, although the ideas of Imperium applied there also: one needs to think only of the court mystiques of the last Valois and Marguerite of Navarre. But French foreign policy early evinced a peculiarly *de facto* recognition of religious division quite alien to the Habsburgs.

[3] B. Chudoba, *Spain and the Empire 1519–1643* (Chicago 1952), quotation from page 9. Chudoba's book was originally written for a Czech public, a late fruit of Czech inter-war enthusiasm for Baroque, and for the Spanish role in Central Europe as an expression of it; this edition (*Španělé na Bílé Hoře*, Prague 1945) is more balanced than the later one. He was subjected to severe criticism in Czechoslovakia (e.g. the review by B. Bad'ura and J. V. Polišenský in *ČsČH* iii (1955), 674–9); but the Marxist viewpoint can be an equal and opposite distortion, as in the article by Bad'ura, 'K problému španělské absolútní a universálni Monarchie v 17. století', *ČMM* lxvii (1958), 375–82.

[4] Of course Spanish Catholicism had always an étatist flavour, but its origins were different and its dogma orthodox. The point is complex, but the fiery rebukes of Maximilian's crypto-Lutheranism and Rudolf's inactivity are unthinkable in reverse.

claims to power, and the later sixteenth century with its cult of the emblematic and allusive made full use of such iconography. Classic evidence are the ceremonial masques and pageants of which important case-studies exist for the courts of the Medici in Florence and the Valois in France.[1] Like the rest the Habsburg mystique compounded elements of mission and of mysticism, but its sources were different from those associated with the divine-right theories of Western Europe.[2] It drew above all on the medieval Empire with its roots in the Carolingian Golden Age, and associated the traditions of the *Reich* with those of the Habsburgs themselves, especially with the founder of their power Rudolf I (Holy Roman Emperor 1273–91), in a curious mixture of religious devotion and secular parable, the 'Pietas Austriaca', which stressed the piety of the ruling house as an inspiration to its people.[3] This was supported by a cult of dynastic historiography which reached a climax towards the end of the sixteenth century with the figures of Gerard von Roo, Konrad Dietz, Franz Guilliman, and others.[4]

At the same time the Habsburg house was itself a rigid autocracy, whose head commanded absolute obedience, and whose other members were all equal in their distinctive rank of Archduke. This was the domestic correlative to the outward striving for an undivided realm, and just as fragile—hence the disputes between Rudolf and his close relatives. It meant that the whole weight of tradition rested upon the Emperor himself, and it was here that the mystique was revitalized in the years after 1500 by the irrepressible '*letzter Ritter*', Maximilian I. In Maximilian's commissions to his beloved circle of Humanist artists—among them Dürer and Pirckheimer—are reflected all the dignity and power of the house: the prophecies, the ancestors, the universalist role and the territorial claims, Caesarism and solidarity against the Turk, the Orders of St. George and the Golden Fleece.[5] They are a precise prefiguration of the Rudolfine symbolism, though without some of the latter's intellec-

---

[1] A. M. Nagler, *Theatre Festivals of the Medici 1539–1637* (Yale U.P. 1964, in translation from the German); F. A. Yates, *The French Academies of the sixteenth century* (London 1947), especially Ch. 11.

[2] For instance there is no direct evidence that the Habsburgs practised the king's touch: M. Bloch, *Les Rois Thaumaturges* (Strasbourg 1924), 148–51. But they did institute washing of the feet on the Thursday before Easter from 1528; cf. Zíbrt, *BČH* iii, Nos. 9295 seqq.

[3] Anna Coreth, *Pietas Austriaca, Ursprung und Entwicklung Barocker Frömmigkeit in Österreich* (Vienna 1959).

[4] A. Lhotsky, *Österreichische Historiographie* (Munich 1962), Ch. XI is a summary account; see below, pp. 127 f.

[5] A. Coreth, 'Maximilian I's politische Ideen im Spiegel der Kunst' (Diss. Vienna 1940). His apotheosis was the famous *Ehrenpforte*.

tual underpinning. Rudolf, in any case, knew and revered Maximilian and Charles V; for him the burden of inheritance was that much greater.

The mystique formed a central part of seventeenth-century Baroque absolutism also; indeed those years saw the culmination of its orthodox religious aspects—the endless tracts on the devotion of Leopold I, the Vienna plague column, the bombastic biographies of rulers. Yet with the outbreak of the Thirty Years War the old *Reichsidee* was doomed, not by direct ideological confrontation, but by a growing irrelevance. It was gradually and hesitantly replaced by a limited German nationalism, a new edifice on a pragmatic base, whose spirit grew under the influence of the conflict itself and whose roots lay in practical moderation and national 'German' preoccupations in language and literature.[1] This paralleled the exclusion of Austria from Germany and its establishment as the *Öster-reich*, the Eastern Empire with interests in Italy, the Danube lands, and the Balkans. The international role of the Habsburgs came to be justified as a function of the European balance of power.

The clash between traditional ideals and the practical methods of the new diplomacy of Renaissance Europe is revealed too in the theory which accompanied its political processes, both underlying them and building upon them.[2] Indeed this theory developed at two different levels: the one a commentary on and vindication of the partisans within the new religious camps, the other a more intellectual study of problems in human organization. Such a distinction is itself important, since for all the various and inimical groupings which sprang up in defence of particular religions and national positions, the profounder opposition was between two *kinds* of political thinking. Most of the real theorists of the age of Rudolf still belonged to the broad, undogmatic Humanist world of learning, though in its characteristic late sixteenth-century form with a penchant towards universal and occult solutions.

The war of the pamphleteers emerged most clearly in France, as opposition parties crystallized out in the 1530s, with the weakness of the centre and the decisive break between Calvin and the Erasmian

---

[1] A. Wandruszka, *Reichspatriotismus und Reichspolitik zur Zeit des Prager Friedens von 1635* (Graz–Cologne 1955), who isolates this new tendency among the 'moderates' of 1635. Schwarz (op. cit. 6) sees it in the spontaneous initiative of the Frankfurt *Deputationstag* of 1644, and underlines how it was only then that the view of the *Reich* as a sum of individual interests took over from the *Reich* as the constitutional totality of those ruled by the Kaiser. Cf. the conclusions of F. Dickmann, op. cit. 494–6.

[2] What follows is the merest outline, as it pertains to the present argument. As general works I have used: J. W. Allen, *A history of political thought in the sixteenth century* (third edn. London 1951), and P. Mesnard, *L'Essor de la philosophie politique au XVIe siècle* (second edn. Paris 1952).

moderate Humanists following the so-called *Journée des Placards* of 1534.[1]
These events led under the pressure of increasing persecution to the
tracts of the Huguenot monarchomachs: Beza's *Du Droit des Magistrats*,
Hotman's *Francogallia*, Mornay's *Vindiciae contra Tyrannos*.[2] The
reaction of the French Counter-Reformation was the literature of
the *Ligueurs*, with its rejection of tyranny (Boucher, etc.) and its
justification of the extirpation of heretical rulers in the interest of the
popular will.

The two sides of this argument have much in common: their invoca-
tion of the rights of the people and the nation, yet their strong acceptance
of international sanctions and intense theocratism. The Calvinist line
of reasoning—strongly evident in English writers like Goodman and
Cartwright, and culminating in Althusius[3]—proceeds from implicit
reverence for law and Holy Writ to the *a priori* derivation of a state ruled
by the divine will and a people whose right to resist oppression is vested in
the presbyters or ephors of the Church. The right of intervention which
followed from this (clearest in Mornay) became a passionate blueprint
for international insurrection. For its part, the European Counter-
Reformation was guided by the laxist logic of Jesuits *in partibus infi-
delium*: men like Robert Parsons and Adam Tanner, extremists who
insisted on Papal claims to secular appointments, indeed to the *summa
potestas* over all civil office; men for whom St. Bartholomew's night and
the *coup de main* of Jacques Clément were both good theology and successful politics, and the two inseparably. But all these arguments had
the logic of convinced activism, not of reflection: if all heretics are
tyrants, who is to decide on the nature of heresy? Was Henry IV ab-
solved of his tyranny for being received by the Pope into the Roman
Catholic Church?

Against this the intellectual theorists of all colours are in search of a
no less total solution, yet their analysis is a creature of the mind, an
absolutism removed from everyday realities, and which yields moderation, even relativism in practice. On the Catholic side the neo-scholastic
thinkers were conscious revivers of a medieval theory—concerned to
map out the rights of 'true religion' but not to serve the largest temporal

---

[1] Nürnberger, op. cit., Ch. 1.

[2] Mornay was however a wider figure than this, who embraced also the impassioned
search for a near-mystical toleration; cf. Patry, op. cit., 52 and *passim*. This is his link
with Karel Žerotín.

[3] Johannes Althusius, *Politica methodice digesta* (1603), reprinted from the edition
of 1614 (Cambridge, Mass. 1932) with an introduction by C. J. Friedrich stressing
Althusius's importance. The 'methodic' character of his presentation owed much to
Ramus (ibid. lxi–iii).

claims of the Pope. They transcended the bounds of the Counter-Reformation, most clearly in the case of Juan de Mariana, who came near to saying that the need for religious unity could conceivably be satisfied by a religion other than Catholicism. Mariana has been viewed as a precursor of modern democratic theories, but he stands no closer to these than do the strict, sin-obsessed Calvinists; he is in the tradition of the universal state, but he sees that the sanctions of such a state are ultimately secular, not religious.[1]

What in Mariana was tentative became the firm conclusion of the French party of *politiques* during the 1560s and 1570s. The outcome of the failure of Michel l'Hôpital and the policies of the centre was the scepticism of Montaigne: *agir en chrétien, penser en païen*; but at the same time it brought a more positive attempt to find some intellectual alternative to bloodshed. France fought its religious wars prematurely against a background of ideas that was still late-Renaissance, and these wars gave the impulse to the most important political philosopher of the period, Jean Bodin, as theorist of absolute sovereignty.[2] Bodin's thought, despite its apparent variety, is basically uniform. It is quintessentially a part of its age in its sense of system, its encyclopedic tendency, its pre-occupation with bringing order to all manner of obscure details.[3] A strong believer in astrology and the reality of the spirit world, deeply influenced by Neoplatonic mysticism and the magic of numbers, Bodin searches in his *Republic* for harmony in the political as well as the cosmic world, and proclaims secular sovereignty the only guard against anarchy, his perpetual dread.[4] His theory issues in toleration—for him natural

---

[1] G. Lewy, *Constitutionalism and Statecraft during the Golden Age of Spain: a study of the political philosophy of Juan de Mariana* (Geneva 1960), especially Chs. X and XI.

[2] R. Chauviré, *Jean Bodin, auteur de la 'République'* (Paris 1914) places Bodin in his historical context as *politique* (35 ff., 54, 65 ff.) and considers the strife-torn background to the *Republic* (41 ff., 261–73).

[3] Cf. Jean Bodin, *Methodus ad facilem historiarum cognitionem* (Paris 1566, etc.); idem, *Universae Naturae Theatrum* ... (Lyons 1596, etc.). For his antiquarian obscurity, e.g. *Republic*, Book VI, Ch. 2. The article by E. W. Monter, 'Inflation and Witchcraft: The Case of Jean Bodin' in *Action and Conviction in Early Modern Europe, Essays in Memory of E. H. Harbison* (Princeton 1969) is relevant; despite its title it offers an essay in Bodinist logic rather than the economics of necromancy.

[4] Bodin considers astrology at length—what is true and what is false in the attribution of celestial influences—in his *Republic*, Book IV, Ch. 2. *Les six livres de la République de Iean Bodin Angevin* appeared at Lyons in 1576; I have used the facsimile of the English edition of 1606, ed. E. D. McRae (Cambridge, Mass. 1962). On spirits, see Bodin's *La Démonomanie des sorciers* (Paris 1580 and many later edns.). On Platonic harmony etc., *Republic*, Book IV, Ch. 2, McRae 455 ff. On the nature of sovereignty: ibid. Book I, Ch. 8. It must be perpetual and unaccountable, bound only by divine and natural law; thus Bodin supports hereditary monarchy by primogeniture and an undivided realm; ibid. Book VI, Ch. 5, especially McRae 723 f. and 740–2.

8225164

religion begins to be seen as a generalized form of revelation—but its centre of gravity is not there; rather Bodin conceives the possibility of a single religion accessible to all men, which is to be uniform and state-enforced, as the state enforces its constitution and its education.[1] He allows theoretical constraints on the exercise of sovereignty, but his enthusiasm is for the power of sovereignty itself.

Bodin possesses a typical sixteenth-century blend of pessimism and Utopianism; both were important aspects of the mentality of *fin-de-siècle* Humanism. The Utopian dream belonged to a whole series of projects for general reform characteristic of the age from More to Bacon,[2] but it was in the context of the secular universal mystique that it acquired the status of a political objective (which it never was in either More or Bacon). Evidence for this lies with a crucial group of visionaries and propagandists in the last decades of the century: Postel, Patrizi, Bruno, Campanella. The political programme of these men can only with difficulty be separated from their preoccupation with occultism and magic, chiliasm and pansophic wisdom (thus they will reappear later in this study), but their significance in the present connection is precisely that they actually viewed the state as one aspect of a magical cosmology.

Guillaume Postel (1510–81) was famed in his lifetime as an Orientalist, Cabalist, and mild-mannered mystic prophet tainted with heresy, one of the most learned men of the century.[3] His whole life was a search for *concordia discordantium*, an occult synthesis, a political and religious unity of all humanity (including Jews and non-Europeans), to be achieved through a missionary programme in the fullest tradition of Christian Lullism.[4] This mystic universalism was to be based on a single language. It was to be established through a world empire, embodying Postel's whole metaphysic of order, and in this role were cast first the kingdom of France, later Venice, and at one stage Ferdinand I of Habsburg.[5] The message went largely unheard—though Postel's

[1] Bodin's religion was in practice thoroughly Montaignesque: cf. Chauviré, op. cit. 77–92. His natural religion is an intellectual foundation for toleration, based on the conclusion that all creeds are in fact identical (ibid. 141 ff.). Cf. his attack on atheists, *Republic*, Book VI, Ch. 1 (McRae 644 f.).

[2] On this Utopian literature in general see E. Dermenghem, *Thomas Morus et les Utopistes de la Renaissance* (Paris 1927).

[3] On Postel's life and work see J. Kvačala, 'Wilhelm Postell, seine Geistesart und seine Reformgedanken', *ARG* ix (1911–12), 285–330, xi (1914), 200–27, xv (1918), 157–203; W. J. Bouwsma, *Concordia Mundi* (Cambridge, Mass. 1957).

[4] Bouwsma, op. cit. 101 ff., 213 ff.

[5] Kvačala, op. cit. 305 ff., 205 f. Cf. Dermenghem, op. cit. 195–215. Postel's was 'the most comprehensive justification for French world leadership in the sixteenth century' (Bouwsma, op. cit. 219). For his Viennese stay see Kvačala, op. cit. 224 ff., 157 ff. He also presented his programme at Trent (ibid. 316 ff.).

influence is probably underestimated; Postel himself remained a kind of Catholic, while (significantly) displaying much sympathy for radical, non-denominational Protestants like Servetus and Schwenkfeldt.[1]

Francesco Patrizi (died 1597), a South Slav from Klis in Dalmatia, represented one of the strongest Renaissance assaults on Aristotle; his *magnum opus* is imbued with Neoplatonic light metaphysic and astral correspondences, and had a great influence during the decades around 1600.[2] But his schemes for reform took on political shape also: early Utopianism, backed increasingly by appreciation of the need to enforce uniformity and a stress on obedience to the sovereign power. Patrizi's *Città felice* is intended to show the ruler how to lead his people towards the infinite goodness of God; a desperate need for unity and order brings him—like Campanella—to view the state almost as a creation of archi-tectural symmetry and symbolism.[3]

Like Patrizi, Giordano Bruno (1548–1600) was in Rome during the 1590s, but he was on trial before the Inquisition for his even extremer and more devastating projects of reform (Patrizi was only placed on the Index).[4] Bruno's plan for a Hermetic reform of the universe cannot even be summarized here—it is anyway barely comprehensible—but recent literature has suggested how important in his own mind were its political implications. Fired by his reception abroad, in France and England but especially in Germany, Bruno nevertheless saw the fulfilment of his socio-ethical reformation in Italy, and the documents of his trial in Venice and Rome reveal a single-minded belief in the inspired programme which he was propagating.[5] Bruno envisaged a universal monarchy to achieve total moral redemption, assuring obedience by persuasive magic and exaltation of the 'vital spirits' of its subjects: complete freedom through complete servitude.

The culmination of Italian Renaissance totalitarianism was Tommaso Campanella (1568–1639), a Utopian but deeply political thinker,

---

[1] Ibid. 221 ff., 160 ff. Cf. below, p. 95.

[2] Franciscus Patricius, *Nova de universis Philosophia libris quinquaginta comprehensa... Quibus postremo sunt adjecta Zoroastris oracula CCCXX... Hermetis Trismegisti libelli et fragmenta... Asclepii tres libelli*, i–ii (Venice 1592).

[3] P. M. Arcari, *Il pensiero politico di Francesco Patrizi da Cherso* (Rome 1935), 91 ff., 95 ff., a book with a slight aura of fascism. For the analogy with architecture, especially Palladian, cf. R. Wittkower, *Architectural Principles in the Age of Humanism* (revised edn. London 1962).

[4] On Patrizi's unorthodoxy see T. Gregory in *Medioevo e Rinascimento: studi in onore di Bruno Nardi* (Florence 1957), 387–424.

[5] A Corsano, *Il pensiero di Giordano Bruno nel suo svolgimento storico* (Florence 1940), 265 ff. Cf. F. A. Yates, *Giordano Bruno and the Hermetic Tradition* (London 1964), 338–59; and S. Caramella, 'Ragion di Stato in Giordano Bruno' in *Cristianesimo e ragion di stato... a cura di E. Castelli* (Rome–Milan 1953), 11–20.

perhaps the first to draw the full conclusions from Machiavelli, while at the same time rejecting out of hand the latter's irreligious cast of mind.[1] For Campanella the basis of all political power is nature, but nature in the sense of a unitary animated totality, and thus his theology is natural in that it is potentially common to all men.[2] The essence of all his political action is a millenarianism and sense of impending renewal of the world, which was a lifelong conviction with him and explains some of his more extraordinary behaviour.[3] The apparent contradictions in Campanella's beliefs—the shift in ideal from the Papacy of the *Città del Sole* to the *Spanish Monarchy* and later the apotheosis of France—are redeemed if his whole mission is seen as inspired by a faith in the ethical validity of the *restauratio magna*, his universalist reform. In service of this he was prepared to use all contingent circumstances; it was the foundation of Campanellan *ragione di stato*.[4] Campanella's influence was considerable, though delayed since his books were published only gradually while the heterodox monk was kept in close confinement. His significance here is as the symbol of aspirations around 1600, and as a focal point for the late-Renaissance interaction of metaphysics and politics.[5]

The notorious debate of the sixteenth century was, of course, over Machiavelli; indeed 'debate' is scarcely the *mot juste*, for the widespread revulsion which Machiavelli aroused clouded the real issues and stemmed mainly from the distinction between individual and national morality which he appeared to have drawn.[6] In fact Machiavelli had

---

[1] Campanella's distaste for Machiavelli is analysed by F. Meinecke, *Die Idee der Staatsräson in der neueren Geschichte* (latest edn. Munich 1957), 106–38. Complementing this is the subtle valuation of d'Addio, who sees Campanella as probing beyond *raison d'état* for its metaphysical sanctions: 'C'è, nel Campanella, una valutazione possiamo dire metafisica del Machiavelli considerato in sè e per sè, completamente chiuso in se stesso, e direttamente contrapposto al mondo cattolico come visione universale della vita e dei suoi valori . . .' M. d'Addio, *Il pensiero politico di Gaspare Scioppio* (Milan 1962), 358 ff. (page 375 quoted).

[2] See J. Kvačala, *Thomas Campanella, ein Reformer der ausgehenden Renaissance* (Berlin 1909), 66–130; and L. Blanchet, *Campanella* (Paris 1920), esp. 22 ff.

[3] This emerges from the standard work on his tempestuous career: L. Amabile, *Fra Tommaso Campanella, la sua congiura, i suoi processi e la sua pazzia*, i–iii (Naples 1882), *passim*.

[4] A. Dempf, 'Die Rechtsphilosophie Campanellas und die Staatsraison' in *Cristianesimo e ragion di stato*, 61–70.

[5] For a summary of his influence, notably on the Rosicrucians, see Kvačala, op. cit. 131–51. The *Monarchia di Spagna* was written in 1599–1601, first published in 1620 in German, with a preface by Christoph Besold the friend of Andreae; the *City of the Sun* was written in 1602, first published in Latin at Frankfurt in 1623.

[6] For the debate on the Continent and its low intellectual content see d'Addio, op. cit. 257 ff. Cf. the development in England studied by F. Raab, *The English Face of Machiavelli* (London 1964), 9 and *passim*, who points out the emergence towards the end of the sixteenth century of more restricted notions of politics.

raised basic questions about the nature and use of sovereignty which were increasingly engaging political thinkers.[1] He was obsessed in *The Prince* with the person of the absolute ruler as a vehicle for real national welfare, which was not necessary explicit, or even understood by his subjects. Bodin found no satisfaction in the 'pragmatism' of the Florentine, yet his solution of a secular state which overcomes the disharmonies of dogmatic religion, and in which the citizen somehow finds fulfilment, is not very far from a covert Machiavellism, as contemporary Counter-Reformation and Jesuit opponents realized.[2] Machiavelli's principles— guides to the practical exercise of sovereignty—are akin, so Cassirer observed, to hypothetical imperatives,[3] possible courses of action which yet require a central justification. It was Bodin, Campanella, and the rest who gave a content, intellectual and mystical in various degrees, to this framework.

The turning-point in the argument over political morality came during the years around 1600, when the Machiavellian blueprint was increasingly accepted (if not in name) as a practical guide to a limited, active goal. The initiative passed decisively from theoreticians—for whom politics was philosophy and the state a universalist ideal, whether formulated by moderate Jesuits or moderate Protestants, the reflection of a whole cosmology—to activists, above all the Counter-Reformers. The best representative of their attitude is Gaspar Schoppe (Scioppio), born a Lutheran, leading propagandist of Clement VIII and Paul V in the German lands, architect of the extirpation of heresy not through dogmatic conversion but through *Realpolitik*. In some ways Scioppio is a part of the old world: his deep Humanist interests, his early religious uncertainty, above all his convinced Ramism and his intellectual appreciation of Machiavelli. Yet his inflexible pursuit of the practical implications of the latter through decades of pamphleteering make him the spokesman of a movement which in the years to 1618 and beyond confounded the idea by presenting it with the *fait accompli*.[4]

The relevance of this change to the tense situation in Central Europe is immediate, for it was here during the 1580s and 1590s that the pressure of the new force was increasingly applied. The Papacy, aware of growing divisions within the enemy camp in the German lands and the lethargy

---

[1] Cf. the reappraisals of F. Chabod, *Scritti su Machiavelli* (Turin 1964).

[2] Thus Minuccio Minucci writing to Possevino: M. d'Addio, '"Les six livres de la République" e il pensiero cattolico del Cinquecento' in *Medioevo e Rinascimento*, 129–44. The similarity was urged too by Ribadeneira (d'Addio, *Scioppio*, 317 ff.).

[3] Ernst Cassirer, *The Myth of the State* (Oxford 1946), 154.

[4] D'Addio, *Scioppio*, 2 and *passim*.

of much official Lutheranism, began a calculated assault to recover its old positions.[1] Spain, deadlocked in the Mediterranean with the Turk, frustrated on its desperate Netherlands front, looked to revive its self-assurance by playing a dominant role in the Empire and especially in Bohemia.[2] Both offered a new dynamism to the thrusting and ambitious; what vitiated the speculative theories of the declining century was that practical initiative lay not with universal reform but with tactical advance. Mankind, so Marx opined, sets itself only such problems as it can solve; in the crucial years between 1600 and 1620 the future was with new men setting themselves limited objectives, men for whom the Machiavellian hypothesis needed no larger content and who were prepared to say what the sixteenth century thought unspeakable. The epitome of them was Scioppio, and it was in Prague, in 1598, that Scioppio was received into the body of the Roman Catholic Church.[3]

* * *

The one positive political step taken by Rudolf II was to shift the seat of his government from Vienna to Prague in Bohemia during the first years of his reign, a complicated procedure which occupied the new Emperor's mind from the death of his father Maximilian in 1576, and was not finally completed until 1583. The reasons for this choice were no doubt varied and difficult to evaluate: straightforward practical and strategic considerations weighed (as they did more at the beginning than at the end of Rudolf's life), especially with the Turks raiding the Hungarian *Kisalföld* not 100 miles from the gates of Vienna, together with the Czechs' insistence that their elected ruler should live among them; what is more, the notion of 'capital' was scarcely developed in those days.[4] Yet the decision does dramatize the crucial importance of Bohemia within the Habsburgs' dominions, and it demands a brief summary of the relations at this time between Bohemia and the other lands of their overlordship.

The 'lands of the Bohemian crown' formed in 1576, with their four million or so souls,[5] the most densely populated, richest, and best

---

[1] On Papal activity in the Empire see the works by Stloukal cited below, especially, for a presentation of his general argument, *Papežská politika a císařský dvůr pražský na předělu XVI a XVII věku* (Prague 1925), Ch. 1.

[2] Chudoba, op. cit. 179 ff.

[3] D'Addio, op. cit., 14–16.

[4] The Czech attitude in W. W. Tomek, *Dějepis města Prahy XII* (Prague 1901), 281 ff. *passim*; *SČ* iv. 254 ff. For a Hungarian view that Rudolf's move was just a realistic withdrawal, M. Kárpáthy-Kravjánszky, *Rudolf uralkodásának első tíz éve 1576–1586* (Budapest 1933), 13 and 98 f.

[5] O. Placht, *Lidnatost a společenská skladba českého státu v 16.–18. století* (Prague 1957).

developed region of Central Europe, which meant in practice the one most called on to take the burden of the Turkish wars. They consisted of Bohemia proper, the close-knit topographical unit centred on Prague; Moravia; Upper and Lower Silesia—a patchwork of semi-independent duchies—and the two Lusatias bordering on Saxony. Each of these provinces was administratively and historically distinct and jealous of its local privileges. Silesia spoke predominantly German and maintained a strong commercial tradition, which it had no intention of subordinating to the economy of Bohemia;[1] Lusatia spoke German and Wendish; Moravia acknowledged no common bond with Bohemia beyond a language which differed only in dialect, and prided itself on its own well-administered code of laws and its noted prosperity.[2]

In this uncertainty of relationship, together with strong reliance on tradition and the order which it brings, the Bohemian lands were an epitome of the Empire as a whole. The nature of the legal bond between the two had been debated for centuries and had never needed a decision more: the King of Bohemia was the senior secular Elector, yet took no part in the Imperial government, and was himself not subject to its enactments, just as his subjects were not included in one of the peace-keeping 'Circles'. With the hardening of the religious split, Habsburg control of the Bohemian vote became decisive in purely electoral terms (the other six were equally divided between Catholic and Protestant), and thus the disputed allegiance of the country and the electiveness of its crown became dominant issues. The two protagonists in the debate during the period of the revolt were the legitimist Melchior Goldast, compiler of monumental works on Imperial jurisprudence, and the apologist of the Czech estates Pavel Stránský, whose *Respublica Bohemiae* appeared with Elzevir at Leiden in 1634.[3]

Bohemia was an epitome too of Rudolf's whole inheritance. This embraced the conglomeration of so-called *Erblande*, all largely German-speaking: Austria proper, the Tyrol, Styria, Carinthia, Carniola, and parts of south-west Germany—hereditary lands of widely differing outlook,

---

[1] Fellner, op. cit. 186–90.

[2] O. Odložilík: *Karel st. ze Žerotína* (Prague 1936), 86–90; F. Hrubý, 'Mornay a Žerotín v letech 1611–14' in *Od pravěku k dnešku*, ii (Prague 1930), 43 ff., reproducing a letter by the Pole Ondrzej Rej z Nagłowic.

[3] Goldast (1578–1635) was a colleague—later opponent—of Scioppio and frequently visited Prague. For his life see *ADB* s.v. and the sketch by H. Schecker, *Melchior Goldast von Haiminsfeld* (Bremen 1930). For Stránský I have used the most recent edition: Pavel Stránský, *Český Stát*, ed. Ryba (Prague 1953), 85–104. There is a full bibliography of the problem in Zíbrt, *BČH*, and see especially J. Kalousek, *České státní právo* (Prague 1892), Pt. 1. The order of precedence of Electorates at the time of Rudolf was Mainz, Cologne, Trier, Bohemia, Palatinate, Saxony, Brandenburg.

which after the death of Ferdinand I became in part administered by collateral branches of the family, Ferdinand in the Tyrol and Charles in Styria.[1] To them was added in 1526, as an uneasy counterbalance, the legacy of the last Jagellon king to his Habsburg wife and brother-in-law, the two kingdoms of Bohemia and Hungary.

Yet the real acquisition of these historic crowns did not come about immediately. The presumed death of Lewis II on the field of Mohács left the Habsburgs, it seemed, heirs to the succession, partly by blood right, partly in the interests of collective security. But they had little effective control over Bohemia until after the estates' abortive defiance of 1547; still less in Hungary, where the years to 1550 were ones of utter confusion and a remarkable missing of opportunities on all sides. In this case, as so often, ideology was following the flag. There did emerge, in the later sixteenth century, the widely accepted concept of a 'mission' —or at least a consistent political line of action—which was peculiar to the Austrian Habsburgs as a house, albeit this has often been stoutly denied by modern Czech historians, who have viewed the Habsburg presence as pure exploitation, either racial or economic.[2] It rested in large part on a revival of the crusade against the Turks, a role left almost entirely in abeyance—so far as the Hungarian front was concerned— during the Mediterranean conflicts of Charles V[3] and one which regained symbolic force only with the renewal of war in 1591. The Italian observer Botero observed of Austria: 'Questa Serenissima Casa dunque cominciò ad acquistarsi riputatione, e fama quasi ne' medesimi tempi che la Casa Ottomana, e par fatto da Dio per riparo, e par propugnacolo della Chiesa contra i Turchi, e gli heretici . . .'[4]

At the same time the Habsburg 'mission' was also perforce multi-national: herein lay evidently great weakness, which could, however, have been turned to great strength. The motives of those who elected Ferdinand I to the Bohemian throne were doubtless mixed, heavily tinged by narrow self-interest and disregard for external problems.[5] Yet in the absence of any other suitable candidate they were prepared to entrust

---

[1] Schwarz, op. cit. 1 ff.

[2] Cf. most recently F. Kavka, 'Die Habsburger und der böhmische Staat bis zur Mitte des 18. Jahrhunderts', *Historica* viii (1963), 35–64; and, for a Marxist view of multinationalism as a form of late feudal exploitation, idem, 'K otázce vzniku habsburské Monarchie', *ČsČH* ii (1954), 377–96.

[3] S. Fischer-Galati, *Ottoman Imperialism and German Protestantism 1521–55* (Harvard 1959).

[4] *Le Relationi Universali di Giovanni Botero Benese* (Venice 1596), Pt. 1, 46.

[5] See the various detailed studies by the nineteenth-century historian Antonín Rezek, and most recently J. Janáček, *Doba předbělohorská*, i (*1526–47*) 1 (Prague 1968), 28–56.

the Habsburgs not only with the task of maintaining the frontiers against the infidel, but also with their national sovereignty which was partly limited Czechdom (as it had been personified in George Poděbrad during the previous century), partly a wider unity able to find expression in a supranational monarchy (like that of Charles IV of Luxemburg). The Habsburgs' rights in Bohemia were more than those of simple invitation in a fit of absence of mind;[1] the very subdivisions and heterogeneity of their Imperium challenged them to find a moral sanction for their sovereignty, a task which no member of the family proved capable of fulfilling. Only when backed by the visible power of the Catholic Church in the following century was the authority of the dynasty placed on an incontrovertible political footing; but the very association meant that its universal role, here as in Germany, was forfeit.

The concept of authority in the Eastern European lands during the sixteenth century ran a course parallel to its development in the West. Strong feelings of tradition—as in the historic reverence for the crowns of St. Stephen and St. Wenceslas—brought powerful drives towards a universalist solution. The clearest example of this is perhaps Polish Sarmatism, which drew on a belief in the primordial unity of the Slavs, at least the northern half of them, and in the hands of men like the historian Cromer exercised a considerable cultural influence.[2] But at the same time the pressure of centralization called forth attempts at policies which would be genuinely national, if not necessarily nationalistic: a striving towards some national 'identity' as a base for political action.

In Poland and Hungary this came to be represented by the enemies of Habsburg plans. The problem of the Polish succession bulked very large three times during the period (1572, 1574, 1587) and was eventually decided against the Habsburgs after a passage at arms, but chiefly owing to the astuteness of Jan Zamoyski and his centre party of 'politiki' (so called). Zamoyski's conceptions were thoroughly advanced for his time —he went to the extent of preferring the Turks to the Habsburgs;[3] yet the monarchs he supported were much less of his complexion: Stephen Báthory, a man with private interests strikingly close to those of his

---

[1] Of course they had genealogical rights there too from the time of the Přemysl dynasty, a fact which can easily be overlooked; cf. G. Turba: *Geschichte des Thronfolgerechts in allen habsburgischen Ländern* (Vienna–Leipzig 1903), table, 232–3.

[2] A. Angyal, 'Die osteuropäische Bedeutung des Sarmatismus', *Studia Historica* 53 (Budapest 1963), 501–12; O. Kralik, 'Vliv Kromerův na českou historiografii XVII a XVIII století', *Česko-Polský Sborník* i (Prague 1955), 369–93.

[3] J. Macůrek, *Zápas Polska a Habsburků o přístup k Černému Moři na sklonku 16. století* (Prague 1931).

sworn enemy Rudolf II,[1] and Sigismund Vasa who soon showed strong proclivities towards his erstwhile Habsburg opponents. In divided Hungary the situation was complex. It has been argued that the independent principality of Transylvania was seen by contemporaries as representing the 'real' Hungary, free of either Habsburg or Turkish hegemony, and ancestor of the *kurutz* dream which underlay the policies of Bethlen Gábor, the Rákóczis, Thököly, and the rest.[2] Undoubtedly the opposition to Rudolf even within Western Hungary was considerable,[3] but the ideology of resistance came later, when the Habsburg cause was already fully associated with the logic of the advancing Counter-Reformation. Even in the 1600s the Emperor still had an important body of moderate, largely Protestant support in the Kingdom of Hungary. Only the years from 1604, with their reckless Catholic offensive in Kassa and other towns, accompanied by Rudolf's loss of control over the campaign against the Turks, brought the first polarizing of a Catholic court versus Calvinist country party so familiar later.

In Bohemia this matter of identity was to be the dream of Czech patriots for decades after the White Mountain: not simply of those in exile, but the 'Czech' aspect of the anti-Habsburg manœuvrings of Wallenstein and his henchmen Trčka and Kinsky during the 1630s. Josef Pekař viewed Wallenstein as following the tradition of the national party, the moderate, confessionally uncommitted upholders of Czech honour, and he interpreted this as always an essentially anti-Habsburg position.[4] So, by the seventeenth century, it had become; but the failure of what Albrecht Wallenstein stood for, though it meant the triumph of the Counter-Reformation dogmatism of Ferdinand II, was also the failure of the broad, loyalist politics of Rudolfine Bohemia. The whole *simpliste* thesis of a German-inspired, Catholicizing Habsburg role in Bohemia covers some of the facts—most plausibly the years immediately after 1620—but is quite inadequate to the climate of the sixteenth century. Neither Maximilian II nor Rudolf was opposed to Czechs or

---

[1] Cf. J. Kraushar, *Czary na Dworze Batorego* (Cracow 1888), a superficial work on Báthory's alchemy; T. Csorba, *A humanista Báthory István* (Budapest n.d. [1944]). The subject deserves a full modern treatment.

[2] This is the viewpoint of much of the voluminous Magyar literature on Bethlen, e.g. most recently L. Nagy, *Bethlen Gábor a független Magyarországért* (Budapest 1969); cf. M. Depner, *Das Fürstentum Siebenbürgen im Kampf gegen Habsburg* (Stuttgart 1938), *passim*.

[3] See especially Kárpáthy-Kravjánszky, op. cit. 30 ff., 70 ff., etc., who is, however, inclined to be too credulous towards the reports of the Venetian ambassadors on whom he bases his evidence.

[4] J. Pekař, 'Valdštejn a česká otázka', *ČČH* xl (1934), 1–11; cf. his *Dějiny valdštejnského spiknutí* (first edn. Prague 1895), 35 ff.

Protestants as such, and their culture and administration were a compound of domestic and foreign influences. Before these can be examined we must take a preliminary look at the Bohemian society with which they were involved.

Prague, in the day of Criginger, who depicted it spanning the Vltava on his map of 1568, or of Hogenberg, whose print captures the sprawling metropolis in 1572, was a grandiose and dramatic city, the proud *mater urbium*, as its crest insisted. Its population was not huge, even by contemporary standards, though during the residence of Rudolf it rose to a busy 50,000 or so;[1] its commercial position was to be similarly strengthened by the trappings of Imperial prestige without ever rivalling the financial centres of Southern Germany.[2]

It was rather for its legacy of association that Prague commanded attention, for the physical reminiscences of a past in which it had continuously been the capital of the most powerful state in Central Europe and for a short but glorious period the centre of the most resplendent manifestation of late-medieval Empire, the age of Charles IV of Luxemburg. The marks of uninterrupted tradition lay on its rich town houses and its multitude of churches and towers, above all the Hrad or Hradschin—castle, palaces, cathedral, basilica in one—standing out on its hill against the city, which became so much the earthly paradise or prison of Rudolf that he left it only on the rarest occasions and deposited in it one of the most remarkable art collections the world had seen.

Of course the Habsburgs' presence had been felt here before Rudolf, and they had already added their own commissions to the city; it was the monarchy and its high noble supporters who gradually introduced Renaissance architecture into the country.[3] Ferdinand I's main monument was the exquisite and pure Italianate Belvedere palace built for his queen, Anne of Hungary. His son Ferdinand was made royal lieutenant (*Statthalter*) in Bohemia, and this uncle of Rudolf, later governor of the Tyrol, laid the framework for Rudolf's own occupation by his close cultural links with the local aristocracy. His most remarkable venture was the fantasy summer residence called Hvězda (the Star), a building possibly even designed by him, the first Bohemian essay in a courtly *maniera*. Ferdinand also began with the business of collecting, and his

---

[1] V. Liva, 'Kolik obyvatelů měla Praha před třicetiletou válkou a po ní?', *ČČH* xlii (1936), 344–59.

[2] J. Janáček, *Dějiny obchodu v předbělohorské Praze* (Prague 1955). A slightly later impression of Prague is reproduced in Plate 16.

[3] Z. Wirth, 'Die böhmische Renaissance', *Historica* iii (1958), 87–107, especially 95 ff.; cf. O. Pollak, 'Studien zur Geschichte der Architektur Prags 1520–1600', *Jahrbuch* xxix (1910), 85–170.

own collection, subsequently transferred to Ambras near Innsbruck, ranked as a marvel of the age.[1]

Under Rudolf Prague became once again an international focus, but it had never lacked the tensions and stimulus of its domestic division into Czech and German elements. One of the long-standing approaches to Czech history has been in terms of national and linguistic rivalries, terms strongly influenced by subsequent polemic, and it is intensely difficult to determine what real dualism existed between the two groups. It is certain that the wild attempts to depict Czech existence as a continual struggle from earliest times against foreign pressures are misplaced;[2] they lead anyway to the hopeless impasse of damning the rebels of 1618 as a German-inspired clique and damning the restoration of 1620 as a Catholic Habsburg dictatorship. Stloukal is typical of this mood in construing the whole of sixteenth-century Habsburg policy as a justified urge to centralize, vitiated however by being 'great Austrian' and not guided by Czech national considerations.[3] Clearly there was an internal problem, one which had been largely in abeyance following the Hussite wars, but which returned during the sixteenth century as the economic and cultural strength of the German-speaking minority revived sharply with the help of immigration.[4] Fears for the future of Czech evidently exist in the Rudolfine period, and the *sněm* (parliament) is firm in its insistence on the prerogatives of that language, though necessarily allowing much administrative bilingualism.[5] The difficulties however remained capable of solution during the reign, while always adding a certain piquancy to it, and it is symptomatic that the first really significant linguistic friction dates from 1615, when the *sněm* passed a strongly-worded ordinance to control the threat to Czech, especially among the young. This was soon followed by a virulent polemic along the same lines from Stránský.[6] The correspondence of the great tradi-

---

[1] H. Zimmermann in *Kunstgeschichtliche Characterbilder aus Österreich-Ungarn*, ed. A. Ilg (Vienna 1893), 194–209.

[2] e.g. A. Pražák, *Národ se bránil* (Prague 1945). The view has a long tradition, at least as far back as Palacký; cf. the interesting essay by René Wellek, 'Two traditions in Czech literature' in *Essays on Czech Literature* (The Hague 1963), 17–31.

[3] K. Stloukal, 'Česká otázka v době předbělohorské' in *Doba bělohorská a Albrecht z Valdštejna* (Prague 1934), 7–28, especially 12 f.

[4] This is agreed by both sides. See J. Klik, 'Národnostní poměry v Čechách od válek husitských do bitvy bělohorské', *ČČH* xxvii (1921), 8–62, 289–352 (detailed but rather extreme); W. Wostry, 'Das Deutschtum Böhmens zwischen Husitenzeit und dreissigjährigem Krieg' in *Das Sudetendeutschtum*, ed. Pirchan et al. (Brünn 1937), 295–370: a moderate analysis, considering its date.

[5] Cf. J. B. Novák, 'Jazyková prakse na generálním sněmu 1611' in *Od pravěku k dnešku* ii, 30–8.

[6] The 1615 text is in the *Quellenbuch zur Geschichte der Sudetenländer* i, ed. Weiz-

tional Bohemian families at this time is still conducted mainly in Czech, though capable of turning readily to German and Latin, even to Italian, Spanish, and French as occasion demands.

The real lines of tension in Bohemia under the early Habsburgs were, more than anywhere else in Europe, narrowly religious, and for any understanding of them it is necessary to glance back to the previous century. The Hussite revolt has seemed many things to many people, but certain aspects of it stand beyond dispute. It was a searing national experience which could never be wholly recanted, and which remained a dominant motif in Czech thinking when the initial impetus was lost. Its overt message was religious, but always religion as a commentary on, and inseparable from, the experience of social organization and the validity of different forms of society. The Hussite 'reform' possessed an organizational content—the *Civitas Dei* of Augustine, the ultimately anarchic vision of a self-regulating polity of the elect in God—but it had no major doctrinal one.[1] What is more, it was rooted in medieval conceptions, not least in its debt to esoteric heretical cults.[2] This explains the lack of theological profundity in Czech Protestant debate and polemic, more particularly when it turned into the largely lukewarm Lutheran persuasion of the sixteenth century. It also explains why the Hussite ideal, which was in its original manifestation a vision of the future[3] (though drawing inspiration from a primitive past), a non-doctrinaire alternative to the existing Church and hence 'progressive', had become by the later sixteenth century the retrospective escape of an uncommitted centre from narrow doctrinalism on both sides. Marxist historians have appreciated the vast significance of the Hussite mentality, but have seized only its early moment of 'progressive' ideology and have tended to project this as a continuous slogan for leftist dissent.[4]

The Hussite movement resulted in a decisive break between most of Bohemia and the rest of Europe. If to be Protestant is to be anti-papal, anti-clerical, and fiercely fundamentalist on matters of morality, then the majority of Czechs became Protestants *avant la lettre*; but equally

säcker (Munich 1960), 103–6; Klik, op. cit. 349 ff.; Stránský's tract is reprinted in the new edition of his *Český Stát*, 363–80.

[1] Cf. R. R. Betts, 'Some political views of the early Czech reformers', *Slavonic and East European Review* 31 (1952–3), 20–35.

[2] Czech reformers were loth to admit these connections, but their propaganda was always deeply conservative; cf. Stránský, op. cit. 189 ff.

[3] It had chiliastic aspects too: H. Kaminsky, 'Chiliasm and the Hussite Revolution' in *Church History* xxvi (1957), 43–71.

[4] Cf. especially F. Kavka, *Husitská revoluční tradice* (Prague 1954); and E. Winter, *Die tschechische und slowakische Emigration in Deutschland im 17. und 18. Jahrhundert* (Berlin 1955), 1–8.

the Lutheranism which most of them adopted under the influence of several close associates of Luther between 1520 and 1540 lacked the overt forms of fideism and spirituality which were the renewed contribution of the sixteenth century to religious experience. Thus a majority of the country subscribed to the Confession of Augsburg, and such people became known as 'modernists' (*Neuerer*) or new-Utraquists, to distinguish them from the old-Utraquists, as the traditional Hussites were now called, for whom the chalice for the laity, communion *sub utraque specie*, had been a cardinal slogan.[1] The new-Utraquist position was however without legal or constitutional backing, surviving only on sufferance from the monarchy and through its power within the estates, and its adherents were nominally subject to the so-called 'lower Consistory' which had been grudgingly granted to the Hussites but enjoyed by this time no real independent existence.[2] For ever attempting to consolidate themselves, the Lutherans extracted some concessions from the crown and its mainly Catholic advisers: in 1567 they secured the abolition of the *Compactata*, the agreement which in 1434 had meant a compromise between the Council of Basle and the moderate Hussites but had now become a weapon for conservatism;[3] in 1575 after protracted negotiations at the *sněm* they won the verbal promise of the ailing Maximilian in the name of himself and his son and heir Rudolf that they would be tolerated.[4] Yet the *confessio Bohemica* proclaimed at this time was only superficially a platform for unity among the Protestants. After sixty years of indecisive wrangling the situation was now tenser and more complex than ever; moreover there was no conclusive sign that either the whole Czech population or Czech culture could be rallied to the banner of Lutheranism, despite the observed preponderance of new-Utraquist converts. The leading historian of Czech Protestantism has argued that the spirit of the sixteenth-century movement was in the Hussite tradition and not primarily Lutheran at all.[5] This view, and the

[1] For this new terminology see (e.g.) Z. Winter, *Život církevní v Čechách*, i (Prague 1895), Ch. 3.

[2] Terms are confusing here: the Hussite Consistory was 'lower' by virtue of its relation to its Catholic counterpart. The 'Utraquists' (in Czech 'podobojí') were technically all those legally subject to this Consistory, though the name was less and less applied to the body of the Evangelicals. Curiously, however, the substitution of 'utraquistisch' for 'evangelisch' was the only change in the form of words of the Letter of Majesty which Rudolf managed to extract from the Protestants in 1609 (Gindely, *Rudolf II*, ii. 345).

[3] A. Gindely, *Geschichte der Böhmischen Brüder*, ii (Prague 1868), 41–3.

[4] The standard work on this diet and its consequences is F. Hrejsa, *Česká Konfesse, její vznik, podstata a dějiny* (Prague 1912).

[5] Hrejsa, op. cit., and his article, 'Luterství, Kalvinismus a podobojí na Moravě před Bílou Horou', *ČČH* xliv (1938), 296–326, 474–85.

objections to it, can easily turn into another aspect of the nationality dispute; but there is no denying the general weakness, spiritual and moral, of the Protestant clergy at this time.[1] The German influence was not a creative one so far as Protestant theology was concerned.

A different paradigm is evinced by the sixteenth-century development of the Czech Brethren.[2] These were not a direct foundation of the Hussite wars, but grew up soon afterwards as a limited sect representing the extremist wing of the movement, non-dogmatic, ascetic, and opposed to all civil commitment. Like similar ones elsewhere the community gradually moved from its initial wholly negative valuation of society to a standpoint of greater acceptance, and indeed became increasingly receptive to cultural influences.[3] The most notable achievement of the Brethren was in fact to survive at all: they had never been officially tolerated, and in 1503 and 1508 Mandates were issued against them which were periodically renewed thereafter.[4] Their relations with orthodox Lutherans remained—despite certain politic truces like that of 1575 —scarcely more cordial than those with the Catholics, since the strength and originality of the Brethren lay in their preoccupation with discipline, education, and close-knit organization, and it was this, rather than doctrine, which guaranteed their identity. The point emerged clearly when that identity was called in question: the response was always a self-conscious insistence on independence as such, and apologetics combined with historical justification was the method adopted by the well-known chroniclers of the Brethren.[5] The reign of Rudolf was their great age; the Brethren became arbiters of literary style as well as leaders in education within Bohemia, and yet managed to retain some of the spiritual radicalism of their origins.[6] They moved in fact closest to the Calvinists—although resemblances between the two credos in the years

[1] Gindely, *Böhmische Brüder*, 112: 'In keinem Zeitpunkte der böhmischen Geschichte war der Klerus von so beispiellos geringem Einfluss und nichtssagender Bedeutung wie in diesem.' Cf. E. Denis, *Fin de l'indépendance bohème* (Paris 1890); I have used the—slightly fuller—Czech translation of this famous work: *Konec samostatnosti české*, trans. J. Vančura (Prague 1893), 494 f.

[2] The name they adopted was 'Jednota Bratrská', literally 'Unity of Brethren', but although this is the translation sometimes employed it sounds quite meaningless in English. 'Czech Brethren' is more apposite, particularly since it suggests a link with the later sect of Moravian Brethren, who are in fact a kind of German cousin (in more senses than one).

[3] This is well argued in the best book on the subject: Peter Brock, *The political and social doctrines of the Unity of Czech Brethren in the fifteenth and sixteenth centuries* (The Hague 1957).

[4] Denis, op. cit. 265, 415 f., and *passim*.

[5] Kamil Krofta, *O Bratrském dějepisectví* (Prague 1946), *passim*.

[6] Denis, op. cit. 540 ff.; A. Molnár, *Českobratrská výchova před Komenským* (Prague 1956), 11 f.

before 1618 were disputed then and are still uncertain, mainly because this was for them not the real issue. Theirs was the 'Calvinism' of discipline and pedagogy, the religion of many Ramists and Melanchthonians, and the greatest products of their system were the pessimistic upholder of traditional values, Karel of Žerotín, and the encyclopedic reformer of the mind, Jan Amos Comenius.

The Brethren derived—spiritually and to some extent directly—from the medieval heresies, and they had much in common with the latter's Reformation descendants: Anabaptists, Socinians, Hutterites, and the rest. These sects were in part logical, almost intellectualized extensions of certain fundamentalist tendencies in the movement which Luther began: the extreme reliance on personal revelation and private judgement, the sanctity of lay worship. At the same time they were partly continuations of endemic popular medieval beliefs in the Millennium, Antichrist, and the chosen people. They meant in other words a fusing of the rational—the validity of the intellect in faith—and the apparently irrational; but the paradox is resolved in the context of the later sixteenth century where the intellectualism of (for example) Italian exiles like Fausto Sozzini was conceived in an atmosphere of prophecy, Utopian designs for society, and imminent parousia. The key to such thinking is its rejection of what is *contra rationem* in favour of what is *super rationem*.[1]

The increasingly disorganized political situation in Eastern Europe meant that these areas became the home of many dispossessed enthusiasts, but local tradition was also fundamentally receptive to them and the interaction of causes is significant. In Poland a branch of the Brethren—settled there since the suppressed revolt of the estates in 1547—maintained close contact with Arians of varying kinds,[2] while the Hungarian lands, especially Transylvania, sheltered many sorts of sectarians. But the Bohemian territories were most confused of all, particularly Moravia, where the ancient code of law, strongly defended by moderates of all persuasions, allowed refuge to a multitude of nonconformers.[3] Contemporaries gave the most diverse names to the different groups, and reports of new heresies were frequent until the end of the century.[4] There, toleration of Anabaptists was a basic consequence

---

[1] Cf. S. Kot, *Ideologja polityczna i spoleczna Braci Polskich zwanych Arjanami* (Warsaw 1932; there is also an English translation by E. M. Wilbur, Boston 1957), Introduction and *passim*.

[2] Described in several volumes by Jaroslav Bídlo, *Jednota Bratrská v prvním vyhnanství* (Prague 1900 etc.).

[3] F. Hrubý, 'Die Wiedertäufer in Mähren', *ARG* xxx (1933), 1–36, 170–211; xxxi (1934), 61–102; xxxii (1935), 1–40; cf. Gindely, *Böhmische Brüder*, 19–22.

[4] e.g. Nuncios/Puteo, Prague 17 July 1590.

of a belief in freedom from political interference, and the number of adherents rose to well over 10,000 (it is notable that contemporaries placed them much higher still).[1] Vilém Slavata recalled years later that the reign of Rudolf had brought religious anarchy, unimaginable variety of belief among the Protestant population: 'While he was monarch the inhabitants of this kingdom were for many years not hindered at all in their various religious deviations; each man thought and believed whatever suited him best, so that those who were known in the Bohemian kingdom as Utraquists could really have been called by any name you please.'[2]

The sects' original religious message stood nearer mysticism than dogma; the social beliefs which it involved meant that their attitude to government was wholly negative.[3] Though this tended to alter as the opportunities for political involvement increased—such was the case with the Czech Brethren and the Polish Arians—the positive influence of the Anabaptists was their concentration on the invisibles of salvation and their search for a spiritual reform; in this they have close kinship with the later Rosicrucian movement. A more calculable contribution lies in the relationship between the sectarian communities of the Bohemian lands and wider perspectives of international heresy during the period: they played their role in the interaction between North European mysticism and the heterodox Italian intellectuals who had chosen exile rather than submission to Rome.[4]

The political position of the Catholics in Bohemia during the 150 years after the last Archbishop of Prague, Konrad of Vechta, threw in his hand with the Hussites was a parlous one, despite their strong constitutional guarantees and their wide network of international contacts.[5] The first steps towards retrenchment came after the abortive Protestant revolt of 1547 which gave Ferdinand an opportunity for firm measures against the prerogatives of the estates. Before his death he had set in

---

[1] Hrubý, art. cit. (1933), 3, 196 ff. There is an interesting confession of faith by a Moravian Hutterite, recently reprinted: Peter Rideman, *Account of our Religion, Doctrine and Faith* (first English edn. Bridgnorth 1950). The original was written in German about 1540 and published in 1565.

[2] 'Mohli vlastně slouti quodlibetarii', *Paměti nejvyššího kancléře království českého Viléma Hraběte Slavaty*, ed. J. Jireček (Prague 1866, hereafter 'Slavata'), 36.

[3] 'Governmental authority is appointed and ordained by God as a rod of his anger for the discipline and punishment of the evil and profligate nation . . .', Rideman, op. cit. 102. On their mysticism see Rufus M. Jones: *Spiritual Reformers in the sixteenth and seventeenth centuries* (London 1914), Introduction.

[4] J. K. Zeman, *The Anabaptists and the Czech Brethren in Moravia 1526–1628* (The Hague–Paris 1969); Kot, op. cit. Chs. 1–4 and *passim*. Cf. below, p. 101.

[5] Denis, op. cit. 451 ff. for a convenient summary of what follows.

motion two important forces: in 1561 he achieved the refounding of the archbishopric of Prague; at the same time he began the establishment of a Jesuit academy in Prague, which soon became the spearhead of the Tridentine spirit as a missionary force among the people and an educational influence on the sons of the aristocracy.

The Jesuits were not—as has been argued by apologists—the saviours of the Czech soul; their early years were ones of great hardship in the face of popular mistrust.[1] But equally they were not simply foreign lackeys of the monarchy (though this was notoriously the view of the rebels of 1618).[2] Their strength lay in convinced local Catholics, both as students and as patrons, and they made a conscious attempt to recruit Czech members to the Order. Here too the third arm of the Catholic revival saw its support: the restored nunciature, which established itself in Prague by 1581 after Rudolf's move to Bohemia. The importance of the Central European territories for Papal schemes of unqualified conquest has already been suggested, and it is underlined by an increase in the number of nuncios in this area under Gregory XIII from one to five.[3] The first representative in Prague, Giovanni Francesco Bonomi (1581–4), provides a good example of the line of capable nuncios to the Imperial court whose activity is the most single-minded element in late sixteenth-century diplomacy.[4] Both he and the Jesuits relied in the first instance on the great traditional Catholic families: Rožmberk (Rosenberg), Pernstein, Hradec, Dietrichstein, Lobkovic, and a few others.[5] Moravia and Silesia had their own ecclesiastical organization under the Bishops of Olomouc and Breslau (Vratislav), both with an uninterrupted development but little popular allegiance; the former was a stronghold

---

[1] Valuable information on the everyday activities of the Society of Jesus in Bohemia in its formative stages—particularly 1556–76—is provided by a MS. still in the Clementinum collection: 'Historia Collegii S. J. Pragensis ad S. Clementum ann. 1555–1610', UK, MS. I A I. This was drawn on in part by the standard laudatory historian of the province: J. Schmidl, *Historiae Societatis Jesu Provinciae Bohemiae . . . ab 1555 Pars I–V* (Prague 1747 etc.). Vols. i and ii are relevant. Cf. in general A. Kroess, *Geschichte der böhmischen Provinz der Gesellschaft Jesu*, i, *1556–1619* (Vienna 1910).

[2] In the *Apology* of the estates (Prague 1618) para. 1, for instance, where the resort to force is justified above all against the 'Anstifftung von der, in diesem Königreich allerschädlichsten Jesuitischen Sekt (welcher angetrieb Tichten und Trachten, zu jederzeit am meisten dahin gangen, wie sie nicht allein Ihre Majestät unsern König, sondern auch diesen ganzen Königreich, seine Innwohner und Stände sub utraque Arglistig und betrüglicher Weiss dem Römischen Stuel alss frembder Obrigkeit underwürffig, und demselben in seine Gewalt liefern möchten) . . .'. All the accusations survive in the vituperatively anti-Jesuit work of T. V. Bílek, *Dějiny řádu Tovaryšstva Ježíšova a působení jeho . . .* (Prague 1896), Pt. B. 1.

[3] Stloukal, *Papežská politika*, 61–83.

[4] Idem, 'Počátky nunciatury v Praze', *ČČH* xxxiv (1928), 1–24, 237–79.

[5] The rector of the Jesuit college informed Bonomi in 1582 that about 40 of the noble families could be relied upon for some support (Stloukal, 'Počátky', 9).

of Papal influence in a country almost entirely Protestant and had a steady tradition of able incumbents,[1] the latter was largely in the gift of the Habsburgs themselves.

It is simple and tempting to descry a regular advance of the Catholic Counter-Reformation in the Bohemian lands from the latter years of Ferdinand I's reign: a progress begun by the monarch, then pursued by fervent Catholics and supported by an influential part of the high nobility independently of Maximilian, Rudolf, or Matthias (except for Rudolf's spasms of orthodox zeal), which culminated directly in the happy outcome on the battlefield of the White Mountain. This account is certainly truer to the facts than the naïve old-fashioned view that the Counter-Reformation began only after the defeat of the rebels in 1620[2] (just as the Czech Baroque has its roots in the sixteenth century), but it does violence to the fragility of the Catholic position. There was indeed from the very beginning of Rudolf's reign a plan of campaign— the extent of the problem and suggestions for future policy emerge in a memorandum of the new Archbishop Brus of Mohelnice as early as 1563. But this is still the document of a moderate, exploring the possibilities of a peaceful accommodation with the Protestants in the interests of religious unity.[3] The underlying situation of the Catholics was continuously deteriorating, and providing a steadily less favourable base for militancy.

During the 1580s their resolve seems to have hardened, thanks especially to the efforts of Bonomi and his immediate successors Malaspina, Sega, Puteo, Visconte, and Caetano, and to the apparent favour of the new Emperor. Bonomi submitted to Rudolf in 1584 a plan of campaign aimed at the 'systematic extirpation of heresy in Bohemia',[4] and the policy of reviving the power of the faith was consistently followed: conversions, new seminaries, festivals and ceremonial, education and mission work. The contemporary chronicle lists the annual number of converts and they are rising slowly; it also mentions bequests from the leading families, royal advisers, and ambassadors.[5] Certainly Botero

---

[1] There is a rather vapid history by the nonagenarian Christian d'Elvert, *Zur Geschichte des Erzbistums Olmütz* (Brünn 1895).

[2] Gindely's posthumously published account, for instance, begins only with the political measures after 1620: A. Gindely, *Geschichte der Gegenreformation in Böhmen* (Leipzig 1894).

[3] S. Steinherz, 'Eine Denkschrift des Prager Erzbischofs Anton Brus über die Herstellung der Glaubenseinheit in Böhmen', *MVGDB* xlv (1907), 162–77, reproduces the memorandum.

[4] Stloukal's phrase: 'Počátky', 246 ff.

[5] 'Historia Collegii S.J.': in 1568 there were 81 converts (fo. 8ʳ), in 1597, 120 (fo. 128ᵛ). Large donations are recorded for 1599 (fo. 129ʳ) and other years. But the interest of the

saw a silver lining: 'Onde con applauso e con allegrezza de' buoni, si rinovarono molti riti e usanze Christiane, e si battezzò un buon numero di fanciulli. Accresce la speranza della totale conversione di' Boemi.'[1] But it is difficult to discover how direct the effects appeared at the time, and privately no secret was made of the desperateness of the position.[2] Things worsened distinctly during the 1590s with the tenure of the less competent nuncio Speziano (1592–8). The programme anyway depended very much on the personal influence of a few large magnates, and its realization hung on the fate of individuals, both in the country and at court. One of its staunchest advocates on his extensive lands was George Lobkovic (Jiří Popel z Lobkovic), who founded a seminary and began thorough recatholicization, but this was turned to less than nothing when he fell foul of Rudolf and was imprisoned in 1593 for the crime of *lèse-majesté*.[3] The death in 1592 of the less extreme but devout Vilém Rožmberk was likewise a severe blow.

The activities of the Catholics were also directed against the weakest and most uncertain element in this religious spectrum: the Hussites proper or old-Utraquists, members of the only other grouping whose administration was sanctioned by law. The innovations of the sixteenth century had outflanked their radical origins and their sympathies were now largely Catholic; more particularly they preserved the medieval hankering after a properly constituted clergy and hence sought a union with Rome for purposes of ordination. What the differences were which hindered the complete assimilation of this community are difficult to establish precisely; they varied with the pressures of the moment, but apparently embraced little more than the chalice for the laity, marriage of clergy, child communion, and the honouring of Hus and Jerome of Prague.[4]

Historians have tended to ignore the twilight period of the old-Utraquists—especially after 1562 when Ferdinand appropriated to himself the right to appoint members of their Consistory—dismissing them as a benighted, declining sect riven by internal dissent and condemned

chronicler was of course heavily vested. Similar figures appear in the *Litterae Annuae Societatis Jesu*, published regularly from the 1580s. There is a useful summary of the *modus agendi* in J. Vavra, 'Počátky reformace katolické v Čechách', *Sborník Historického Kroužku* iii (1894), 3–40.

[1] Botero, *Relationi*, Pt. III, 24.

[2] For instance Nuncios/Puteo, Prague 10 Dec. 1587, and his instruction to Visconte in 1589 (ibid. 492 ff.). Cf. Malaspina, Prague 26 Feb. 1585.

[3] For the Lobkovic affair see the documents in *SČ* vii. His Jesuit college in Chomutov was founded in 1591 (ibid. 580–91).

[4] Hrejsa, op. cit. 9.

by utterest mediocrity.[1] There is certainly much truth in this: they had only one important noble advocate in the crucial diet of 1575,[2] while later the extravagant behaviour of Administrator Fabian Rezek, Václav Dačický, and others brought them into worse disrepute and hastened the complete collapse of their moral standards.[3] But they continued to occupy the attentions of the Emperor and Catholic policy-makers, sometimes being consciously used by the latter as a Trojan horse, a means of infiltrating the lines of the Protestants by packing the lower Consistory with crypto-Catholics.[4]

The dogmatic divergences of the old-Utraquists from orthodox Catholicism had shrunk to very little, yet the ideological significance of their continued existence was much greater than has been allowed. Just as the feast day of Jan Hus had now become something almost disowned by the Lutherans and actively opposed by the Catholics,[5] so the Hussite party represented a thread in the domestic tradition which neither of the rival camps adequately embodied. Its failure to maintain itself epitomized the decline of moderate national sentiments; its unwillingness to rejoin Rome the uncompromising nature of reform Catholicism.

It is impossible to give a satisfactory over-all picture of the state of the religious parties in 1576; in particular the figures of allegiance are quite imprecise: Hrejsa's estimate that the Catholics numbered about ten per cent of the population seems a best guess, and a similar figure has been suggested for 1600.[6] What is nevertheless evident is the inability of the Catholics to make significant progress by persuasion at the individual level. Their extremists, we have seen, had a plan of attack. It was ready for implementation through the 1590s, as an intransigently Tridentine manifesto of 1593 shows.[7] The plan was directed at office and

---

[1] Typical views are Denis, op. cit. 535 ff., and Gindely, *Böhmische Brüder, passim.*
[2] Ibid. 110 f.
[3] The case of Rezek, who seems to have toyed with various kinds of Protestantism before announcing with well-simulated contrition that he had really been a Catholic all the time, was widely commented on. Cf. Marek Bydžovský, 'Rudolphus Rex Bohemiae', UK, MS. xvii G 22, fos. 105–7, and the study by J. Matoušek, 'Kurie a boj o Konsistoř pod obojí za administratora Rezka', *ČČH* xxxvii (1931), 16–41, 252–92. Complaints to the *sněm* of the failings of the Consistory were numerous; e.g. *SČ* vi. 300–2, vii. 400 f.
[4] Matoušek, art. cit.; cf. Puteo's instruction for Visconte (Nuncios/Puteo, 488–91).
[5] For the fate of the Hus-day see Denis, op. cit. 482 n. For Catholic opposition to it, e.g. Nuncios/Malaspina: Como to Malaspina, Rome 29 Dec. 1584.
[6] Hrejsa, *Česká Konfesse,* 48, based on the nuncio Delfino; E. Winter, *Tausend Jahre Geisteskampf im Sudetenraum* (first edn. Salzburg 1938), 184. Gindely, *Böhmische Brüder,* is the best existing general summary. Unfortunately one accessible book with a promising title is quite valueless: E. Charvériat, *Les affaires religieuses en Bohême au XVIe siècle* (Paris 1886).
[7] 'Quaedam propositiones ex anno 1593 de fide catholica restauranda', printed in *SČ* viii. 268–72.

office-holders within the Kingdom of Bohemia, and therefore it is necessary to sketch briefly the nature of the administrative body for which it was contending.

The Imperial administration of the Czech lands in the later sixteenth century was more complex than efficient, not least because it was the casual juxtaposition of two quite separate developments: the machinery of the Empire proper which depended mainly on the person of the Emperor himself and was partly, but not entirely, transferred with Rudolf from Vienna to Prague;[1] and the historic Bohemian constitution. The bones of the Imperial organization have been studied with some thoroughness, though the Rudolfine period is notoriously weakly documented and the crucial question of where real power was located remains difficult to resolve. The Bohemian framework is less happily served; despite the monumental series of published records of the national legislative assembly, the *sněm*,[2] there exists no adequate analysis of the chief offices of state which lay, as elsewhere in Europe, somewhere between executive and sinecure appointment, and in their executive capacity were the link between ruler and country. Underlying this is the more serious lack of any comprehensive work on the composition and structure of the high nobility which almost exclusively controlled these offices.[3]

In the course of this book we shall be concentrating on the role of members of the leading families whose place in the country's life was assured by their privileged background. This is not to ignore the cultural and political importance of wider sections of Bohemian society. In the time of Rudolf the nobility was still only differentiated very broadly into lords (*páni*) and knights (*rytíři*);[4] its prosperity was still general and movement within it comparatively free, while the flourishing royal boroughs supported a distinct and educated burgher class. Yet the

[1] For example finance, the *Hofkammer*, remained split between the two (Fellner, op. cit. 81 f.) to the confusion of both jurisdictions.

[2] *SČ = Sněmy České od léta 1526* (Prague 1877–1910); the relevant individual volumes are: iv (1574–6), v (1577–80), vi (1581–5), vii (1586–91), viii (1592–4), ix (1595–9), x (1600–4), xi (1605). The whole series appeared simultaneously in a German version: *Die böhmischen Landtagsverhandlungen und Landtagsbeschlüsse vom Jahre 1526*.

[3] There is of course some material in the standard works. Most recently F. Kavka, *Bílá Hora a české dějiny* (Prague 1962), 27–39 has painted a summary picture. It may be added that the sheer continuity of the Habsburg dynasty and its attendant nobility has made it difficult for historians to place their role in perspective.

[4] Cf. A. Gindely, *Die Entwickelung des böhmischen Adels und der Inkolatsverhältnisse seit dem 16. Jahrhundert* (Prag 1886), Pt. 1. Thus the famous 'Count' Andreas Schlick, most cavalier of the Protestant rebels during the insurrection of 1618–20, possessed only an imperial title. Cf. also the perceptive remarks on the Austrian *Adelswelt* in Brunner, op. cit.

dominant place belonged to the aristocratic ideal and its link with the resplendence of monarchy, just as in Venice it was civic, republican virtues which counted. In Hungary, as is well known, the very concept of the 'nation' was restricted to the nobility and was actively represented in fact only by a highly exclusive group within it. The aristocrats of Bohemia, like their other Central and Eastern European counterparts—the Austrian *Hochadel*, the Magyar *főnemesség*, the highest echelons of the Polish *szlachta*—formed a privileged caste set apart from compatriots by immense wealth, political influence, and a cosmopolitanism of outlook which did not exclude intense patriotism. Although it was not a Bohemian tradition to indulge in the narrow distinctions within the Western peerage, this should not mislead: the domains of the Rožmberks in south Bohemia were as large as many a self-respecting German duchy. Being powerful members of the estates, such men represented the interests of the country when they conflicted with the wishes of the royal house, particularly in financial and military matters. As holders of the highest positions of state they formed part of the court entourage.

Historiography has tended, here as elsewhere, to do the Rudolfine period an injustice by presenting this division of functions as the dichotomy which it only became in the years immediately before the revolt of 1618. There were, of course, always tensions: the court was closely associated with Catholicism and with a pull towards autocracy; the Protestant party in the *sněm* was inclined to assert a somewhat nervous independence, based on the historic sources of the estates' liberties. But the dispute was not simply a long-fought battle between Protestant estates and Catholic centralizing absolutism; under Rudolf it was both more and less than this: less, in that there remained a large body of central opinion which could still support a moderate Imperial policy—there was no trouble over religious issues in the *sněm* between 1585 and 1603;[1] more, in that the crisis went much deeper. Political ideology is the crystallizing into active aims and slogans of complex mental positions; the overt alignment into two camps in Bohemia came only slowly, reluctantly, and without fully reflecting the subtleties of its background.

The best source for the actual holders of court office in these years are the *Hofstaat*s or lists of aulic functionaries, though only a limited number survive. The most complete relate to the years of Rudolf's accession, the two Imperial diets of 1582 and 1594, and his death—the latter three being comprehensive documents from the highest officials of the Empire, Bohemia, and Hungary down to the most menial woodcutters and

---

[1] Gindely, *Böhmische Brüder*, 333.

kitchen staff.[1] There were four senior dignitaries: High Steward (*Oberst-hofmeister*), Chamberlain (*Oberstkämmerer*), Marshal (*Obersthofmarschall*), and Master of the Horse (*Oberststallmeister*), followed by the Presidents of various Imperial organs—the Privy Council, *Hofrat* (Aulic Council), and so forth. The most important among them was the High Steward, who frequently combined this role with the leading position in the Privy Council. In 1576 this was the new king's old preceptor Adam von Dietrichstein.

That same year the representatives of the Bohemian nation included members of most of the greatest families. Senior among them, both in dignity of office and noble pedigree, stood Vilém of Rožmberk, the Burgrave (*Oberstburggraf, nejvyšší purkrabí*).[2] The Burgrave was the right-hand man of the monarch in things Bohemian, with an unspecified competence. After him came various officers of high rank but rather less influence: Ladislav of Lobkovic, the Steward (*nejvyšší hofmistr*), Johann von Waldstein, the Chamberlain (*nejvyšší komorník*), Bohuslav Hasi-štejnský (Hassenstein) of Lobkovic, the Supreme Judge (*Oberstland-richter, nejvyšší zemský sudí*). More important than these in the scope of his powers was Vratislav Pernstein, Rožmberk's close associate, the Chancellor (*Oberstkanzler, nejvyšší kancléř*); his was the only dignity common to all the lands of the Bohemian crown—Moravia for instance had its own Burgrave in the *Hejtman* (*Hauptmann*)—and also the one which controlled the Chancery, the most vital weapon for any future centralization. But it was Zdeněk Lobkovic after 1599 who first made that point clear.

Comparison between the office-holders of 1576 and those of 1612

---

[1] For 1576: J. V. Goehlart, 'Kaisers Rudolf II. Hofstaat und die obersten Behörden', *MVGDB* vii (1869), 112–16; cf. Fellner, op. cit. ii. 191–9. For the diets: Peter Fleisch-man, *Description des aller Durchleuchtigisten, Grossmechtigisten . . . Herrn Rudolphen des andern . . . Erstgehaltenen Reichstag zu Augspurg* (Augsburg 1582); idem, *Kurtze und aigentliche Beschreibung des zu Regenspurg in disem 94. Jar gehaltenen Reichstags* (Regensburg 1594). Both these works are very scarce; the 1594 *Hofstaat* is also given by F. C. Khevenhüller, *Annales Ferdinandei* (Leipzig 1721 etc.), iv. 1210–16. For 1612: 'Aula Rudolphi II Kaisserlicher Hoff Statt Allermassen wie solcher Mit und Nach Absterben dess Allerdurchleuchtigisten . . . Rudolphi des andern . . . hinterlassen worden . . . Michaeln Eckhardt . . . Abgeschrieben im 1612 Jar. zur Gedachtnuss aufzuhalten', printed in *Archiv der Geschichte und Statistik* ii, ed. J. von Riegger (Dresden 1793, hereafter 'Riegger'), 193–262. There is an interesting comparison with the very complete *Hofstaat* of somewhat later date in the printed work, *Status particularis regiminis S. C. Majestatis Ferdinandi II* (anno 1636, Vienna 1637). Gindely, *Rudolf II*, i. 31 ff. gives a list for 1580 based on the Venetian ambassador.

[2] For the following see Gindely, *Böhmische Brüder*, 110 f. His list is for 1575. One ready cause of confusion is that these offices were regularly left unfilled, sometimes for years at a time, when the functions were either not performed at all, or performed by a deputy (as with the Chancellorship in the 1590s).

reveals a significant change in the hereditary balance. During the reign of Rudolf several of the most eminent houses were in the process of atrophy. The last Rožmberks, Vilém and his brother Peter Vok, produced no issue, and their line finished on the death of Peter in 1611.[1] Vratislav Pernstein's only son died in 1597, and the vast but bankrupt Pernstein estates passed into other hands.[2] The lords of Hradec were extinguished in 1596 and thus ended a tradition of faithful service to the Bohemian king.[3] The family of Smiřický survived into the seventeenth century, but it had no real place in the disputes of 1618, though one of its members was a rebel leader during the early stages; much of its rich property passed through a female heir to her husband, Albrecht Wallenstein.[4] In Moravia the ancient house of Boskowitz died out in 1597 and its close cousins of Žerotín were to follow before the end of the Thirty Years War.

It is notoriously difficult to assess the meaning of such changes; the phenomenon of the rise and fall of families is a familiar one (the 'Buddenbrooks paradigm' or whatever we choose to call it), and the notion of 'generation' can be highly dangerous. Moreover some families were better ramified and maintained their dominant position: witness the Lobkovic (despite the fall of Jiří Popel), Dietrichstein, Waldstein, and others. But even here a decisive shift of attitude is taking place: the new protagonists, like Zdeněk Lobkovic, Chancellor from 1599, František Dietrichstein, Bishop of Olomouc from 1598, Karl Liechtenstein, inheritor of the Boskowitz lands and founder of a great fortune, the young Slavata, heir to the lords of Hradec, and his future co-defenestratee Jaroslav Martinic, even the rising Wallenstein—such men breathed a militancy befitting the new century. And it is surely no accident that the older men of an age in decline were so obsessed with their own ill-health;[5] or that there is such a close parallel within the ruling house itself, where not one of the six sons of Maximilian II produced a legitimate heir.

'His passing means a change in this Kingdom', observed the chronicler

---

[1] Cf. A. Rybička, 'Poslední Rožmberkové a jich dědictví', ČČM liv (1880), 85–109, 218–48, 437–57; lv (1881), 38–55, 187–202, 366–75; and see below, pp. 140–3.

[2] J. Křivka, Litomyšlský velkostatek za Pernštejnů (Prague 1959).

[3] The lords of (Jindřichův) Hradec (Páni z Hradce) were confusingly known to the German language as lords of Neuhaus. In fact they were the 'new house', a new branch of the same family tree as the Rožmberks. For their last years see F. Kavka, Zlatý věk růží (České Budějovice 1966), 142–5. Kavka comments on this phenomenon of decline in his Bílá Hora, 58–68 passim.

[4] O. Odložilík, 'Poslední Smiřičtí', in Od pravěku k dnešku ii. 70–87.

[5] Odložilík observes this in his book on Žerotín, 26–9, and in the article, above, on the Smiřický family.

on the death of Vilém Rožmberk in 1592, and the whole narrative has a sense of inevitability.[1] Rožmberk's generation was the last to stand for that kind of moderate national policy whose decline is inseparable from the growing conflict of confessional camps and the assault of the Counter-Reformation which can be followed, in Bohemia as in Hungary and Austria, during the years after 1600. Its religion was generous and broad-minded: when Catholic it aspired to a strong united state rather than papal hagiocratic control. When Protestant it was tolerant both to right and left: Peter Vok Rožmberk left his brother's Jesuits undisturbed after his death, even helping to support them; while the Boskowitz and their relatives the families of Žerotín and Kunovice were the greatest patrons of the Moravian sects.[2] In politics it sought to maintain the influence of the estates, but not without the medieval traditions of kingship which were its concomitant, and its enthusiasm for Spain or the Dutch United Provinces had not yet turned into active fanaticism. In culture it inclined to the accommodating intellectual Humanism of the sixteenth century's last decades. Whether or not its members worked with Rudolf or had personal contact with him, their mentality is made more intelligible through the Emperor, and his through them.

[1] Václav Březan, *Poslední Rožmberkové* (modern edn. by E. Dostál, Prague 1941, hereafter 'Březan'), 167: 'S ním proměnu bralo K(rálovství) Č(eské).' Cf. Václav Budovec's comment on the death of Hradec: 'Desunt nobis viri, et omnia in peius ruunt.' Budovec to Amandus Polanus, 25 Nov. 1596, in *Václava Budovce z Budova korrespondence z let 1579–1619*, ed. J. Glücklich (Prague 1908), No. 14.

[2] *Litterae Annuae S.J.* for 1593 (Florence 1601), 220–3; W. Urban, *Studia z dziejów Antytrynitaryzmu na ziemiach czeskich i słowackich w XVI–XVII wieku* (Cracow 1966), 65 ff.

2. The Politics of Rudolf

'They refuse to swim until the water is up to their mouths, and by then it will be too late . . . In short I think that the Babylonian confusion can scarcely have been as great as this.'

THE ELECTOR ERNST OF COLOGNE (1610)

S U C H was the political background to the accession of Rudolf after the death of his father Maximilian II in Regensburg on 12 October 1576. The old Emperor had been ailing for some time, and his first-born son had already been crowned King of Hungary four years before in Pressburg and King of Bohemia the previous year in Prague, as well as being acknowledged King of the Romans, and hence full heir apparent throughout the *Reich*. What was now to condition developments was the personality of the new twenty-four-year-old ruler. Rudolf has been interpreted —by his contemporaries and by posterity—in widely differing ways: both as one of the most remarkable men of his age and one of the most worthless, as well-meaning and vicious, as devout and sensuous, as bigoted and enlightened, both as sinned against and sinning. But the dominating impression gained from the literature which has grown up around him is a lack of focus and deep misunderstanding, above all a widespread refusal to judge the man from within, from his own intentions and attitudes, rather than as the plaything of conflicting political forces.

This tendency to consider only the exterior has its justifications. Rudolf's expressed viewpoint has hardly survived at all: he wrote very little,[1] and the opinions of his contemporaries can scarcely ever be relied upon as purely objective assessments, even in the terms of the period, coloured as they are by private motives. They are also inclined to be superficial and surprisingly uninformed, even in the case of nuncios'

---

[1] The Habsburgs' correspondence as such—their dealings among themselves, and with foreign rulers and high dignitaries—survives in Vienna (HHSA, Fam. Korr. A & B). Rudolf is scantily represented, and very little of it is personal, or even holograph. There exists one printed collection of Rudolf's letters: *Divi Rudolphi Imperatoris Caesaris Augusti epistolae ineditae, desumptae ex codice manu exarato* (by Bernhardin, Count of Pace, Vienna 1771), but these are mostly official, formal communications, restricted to the years 1589–92.

reports and other ambassadorial relations.[1] In the nature of things the Emperor's contacts with really sympathetic spirits were secretive and went largely unrecorded, while the day-to-day business of government has left comparatively few direct unequivocal marks of his influence.

One very general starting-point emerges immediately from all the evidence: Rudolf was, in the strict sense, extraordinary. Observers noted his dignity, intelligence, and lofty pride, though these were frequently unobtrusive behind an engaging friendliness of manner; they noticed also his strange withdrawal from events, and assigned a significance to it, even if only what was involved in their ascription to him of the word 'melancholy'.[2] Often their strongest emotion was one of fear: Rudolf was never a man to be crossed lightly. They rarely dismissed him simply as weak or lacking in initiative (though later writers have sometimes been less benevolent).[3] Ordinary people rather saw Rudolf's conduct as proceeding from some urge to tap a deeper source of knowledge. Thus the legends grew around him and have become in soberer garb the commonplaces of history. By the end of his life he was famed for his patronage of occult sciences, his unapproachability, his mental imbalance, his mixture of apathy and extreme stubbornness. For a good statement of this view we may turn to the testimony of Daniel Eremita, who visited Prague in the suite of the Tuscan embassy of 1609. Eremita was irritated first of all by the delays before the Emperor would receive even such a high-ranking delegation, and his subsequent description portrays a man whose powers are evidently failing, and who is clinging to the habits and dress of happier times.[4] But he readily admits wisdom and even clarity of vision: 'The Emperor's amazing knowledge of all things, ripe judgement, and skill have made him famous, while his

---

[1] One of the most thorough students of Prague diplomacy in the 1590s has written: 'If however we look more closely at the Venetian relations and dispatches and the correspondence of the nuncios we are surprised how little of the intimate life of the Emperor has penetrated to them, and what a firm barrier he managed to erect against the prying eyes of our informants.' J. Matoušek, *Turecká válka v evropské politice v letech 1592–1594* (Prague 1935), 37.

[2] The term became a vogue word of the period, but it was always related to a definite theory of humours, however curious the conclusion. Thus the nuncio Puteo could write: 'E S. Mtà reputata de complessione colerica et melancolica, della quale si fa giudicio, che sia di mente molto schietta . . .' Nuncios/Puteo, 524. Cf. below, p. 278 n. 4.

[3] Denis comes nearest to dismissing Rudolf completely, suggesting that he was ultimately not a serious man (op. cit. 531 f.). From his very different, and undigested, viewpoint, Coxe takes a similar attitude: op. cit. i. 727.

[4] *Iter Germanicum: Relatio epistolica Danielis Eremitae Belgae de Legatione Magni Hetruriae Ducis ad Rodolphum II* . . . In the copy I have used it is included with the *Status particularis* . . . (above, p. 40 n. 1), 299 ff.

friendliness, steadfastness in religion, and moral integrity have won him popularity; these were the principles of his outstanding and remarkable reign which gained the plaudits of the whole world.' Rudolf has, however, ruined everything by taking up the study of art and nature, with such increasing lack of moderation that he has deserted the affairs of state for alchemists' laboratories, painters' studios, and the workshops of clockmakers. Indeed he has given over his whole palace to such things and is using all his revenues to further them. This has estranged him completely from common humanity: 'Disturbed in his mind by some ailment of melancholy, he has begun to love solitude and shut himself off in his Palace as if behind the bars of a prison.'[1] The result is complete administrative chaos, and the threat that the House of Austria and the Catholic faith will be entirely eliminated.

Such a view, substantiated by other casual observers from the Emperor's later years, has survived in sub-historical writing and belles-lettres until our own day.[2] Since the middle of the last century scholars have begun to reappraise the justice of this verdict, though their research has in fact provided remarkably little positive emendation of the traditional picture. One author who seems to promise much is Anton Gindely; yet Gindely's major work on the political crisis in Germany during the first decade of the seventeenth century is, despite its title, only indirectly about Rudolf. He considers merely the final period of the latter's reign, beginning in 1600 and proceeding from the assumption that the course of events was governed by his illness, and thus by those who took advantage of it.[3] He offers no insight into the mind of the Emperor, since he has already taken a position on his mindlessness. The Bavarian historian Felix Stieve investigated the problem of Rudolf from various angles—though his prime concern was diplomacy—and essayed no real solution. Stieve is convinced of his intelligence and ready grasp of ideas, taking him as a monarch persuaded of a mission in the Spanish mould,

[1] Ibid. 304–6.

[2] Observers like Roderico Alidosi, *Relazione di Germania e della corte di Rodolfo II Imperatore* . . ., ed. C. and G. Campori (Modena 1872), who was in Prague between 1605 and 1607; writers like E. Vehse, *Memoirs of the Court, Aristocracy and Diplomacy of Austria*, trans. F. Demmler (London 1856), i. 230–66. The portrayal of Rudolf and his times in literature is a different story, and a fascinating one, which began with the scurrilous contemporary *roman à clef* by John Barclay entitled *Euphormionis Lusinini Satyricon* (Frankfurt 1623, ii. 201 ff.). Suffice it to say here that it has played an important part in fashioning Czech opinions of him, and it is surely no coincidence that the 'decadent' late nineteenth century saw the greatest interest in that earlier *fin de siècle*: the novels of Zikmund Winter and Josef Svátek for instance, or even the poet Vrchlický.

[3] A. Gindely, *Rudolf II*, especially i. 27 and ii. 330–6.

yet frustrated by indecision and finding release in the timeless world of art; a man of genuine religious conviction and yet generous tolerance.[1]

The contribution of twentieth-century Czech historiography has been severely limited by a tendency to equate the Habsburg presence with Germanizing pressures, and the cosmopolitanism of Rudolf's court with a domineering anti-Czech influence. An interpretation was broached by Novák, who saw clearly Rudolf's involvement in the political world[2]—he dismissed the novelistic view of his carelessness of power—and ascribed the breakdown to his pathological mistrust, brought on by Spanish influence and scheming ministers. But Novák's interest was primarily the final disaster—the invasion of Bohemia by the Passau troops in 1611 —and the malignant designs of Matthias. He saw the tragedy of a well-intentioned and popular ruler whose regime declined into instability and desperate confusion. A much blacker picture was painted by Stloukal, based largely on the reports of the nuncio Spinelli:[3] Rudolf in 1600 was already a madman; his contradictory policies, especially in their rejection of Catholic advice, were the product of a demented mind, and could only issue in catastrophe. A valuable corrective appeared soon after from Matoušek, who doubted the reliability, even the veracity of Spinelli's dispatches, conditioned as they were by a desire for self-exculpation; the nuncio was in disfavour and needed a scapegoat to explain the sudden halt to the Counter-Reformation movement. In wider terms there was no necessity for ascribing Rudolf's actions to mental breakdown; they could be construed in a purely political way, and Matoušek was even prepared to suggest that his whole psychology might not be so inconsistent.[4]

Recent German writing has concentrated on the Emperor as patron of the arts and on his psychological peculiarities. Gertrude von Schwarzenfeld's book—the only attempt at a biography of Rudolf—has no real claim to originality, but is perhaps best in probing the interplay between the artistic and the political in his nature, suggesting the notion of

---

[1] F. Stieve in *ADB* s.v., and reprinted in *Abhandlungen, Vorträge und Reden* (Leipzig 1900), 93–124. This article is the most balanced yet written on Rudolf. Stieve completed enormous labours in his editing of documents for the *Briefe und Akten*, Vols. iv–viii, but these were always orientated primarily towards elucidating the history of the Empire in general and Bavaria in particular.

[2] J. B. Novák, *Rudolf II a jeho pád* (Prague 1935); e.g. 21: 'It would be a great misunderstanding of Rudolf's character and mind if we were to infer that he was unconcerned with the business of ruling.'

[3] K. Stloukal, 'Portrét Rudolfa II z roku 1600', *Od pravěku k dnešku* ii. 1–14.

[4] J. Matoušek, 'K problému osobnosti Rudolfa II', in *Sborník prací věnovaných J. B. Novákovi* (Prague 1932), 343–62.

harmony in his international aspirations and religious outlook and his violent antipathy to 'official' Catholicism.[1]

Existing study of Rudolf has never undertaken a thorough analysis of his mentality, yet to grasp this as a unitary vision of the world would surely allow us to appreciate the interdependence within it of the modes of contemplation and activity, and the way they refracted the various influences which went into the making of his personality. It is doubtful whether Rudolf was in fact ever mad in any serious technical sense; certainly not for longer than brief intervals, as for a time during 1600 or 1606, while much hinges on the meaning which contemporaries attached to words like 'melancholy' and 'possession'.

This immediately raises the question whether Rudolf changed with the passing years. There is no doubt that his strangeness became more marked, especially from 1600. That was the time when, after the abrupt dismissal of Wolf Rumpf and Trautson and the paranoid attack on the Capuchins, it was widely whispered (even in Rome) that he was bewitched.[2] Yet is the Emperor showing more than a heightened unwillingness to adapt or compromise? His apparent volte-face in favour of the Counter-Reformation was not maintained and he was soon hopelessly at odds again with orthodox Catholic opinion. After the turn of the century Rudolf's actions were those of someone torn between the desire for firmness and security and utter mistrust of what surrounded him; the exaggeration of the symptoms was a failure of much more than just the person of the Emperor, while those symptoms had long before been evident to the perceptive.[3] The growing alienation of Rudolf from his

[1] G. von Schwarzenfeld, *Rudolf II, der saturnische Kaiser* (Munich 1961), 73–6, 101–4. In some other respects the book is rather misconceived. A similar view appears in the summary by W. Wostry, 'Rudolf II, der Sonderling in der Prager Burg', *Prager Jahrbuch* 1943, 49–59.

[2] 'Makofski ist der oberste [Kammerdiener], ein ser böser, ja teuflicher Mensch . . . Er gehet mit teuffelskunst umb und meinet jederman, er hab i(hre) Mt. (Majestät) verzaubert.' The Margrave of Ansbach to the Elector Palatine, Ansbach, 24 June 1601; printed in L. von Ranke, *Zur deutschen Geschichte* (Leipzig 1869), Anhang V. 281 ff. The author is otherwise undecided whether Rudolf is really insane or just profoundly melancholic. Cf. *Briefe und Akten*, v. 765 n. 2.

[3] The young Henry Wotton was a good prophet, though a rather superficial judge of such a complex situation, when he wrote in 1591 to Lord Zouche: 'He (Rudolf) now seems rather to bear the title of Emperor for fashion's sake, than authority to command by virtue of it. The Emperor may mend the matter when he will, by yielding every man his conscience at liberty, which either he must do shortly, or peradventure Rodolph the Second will end the Empire after three hundred years continuance in the house of Austria.' Vienna, 17 Apr. 1591, in L. Pearsall Smith, *Life and Letters of Sir Henry Wotton* i (Oxford 1907, hereafter 'Pearsall Smith'), 268. Similarly the agent George Gilpin's description of Rudolf in 1581 foreshadows many of the later observations about his melancholy: *Calendar of State Papers, Foreign, 1581–2* (London 1907), No. 286.

environment after 1600 is a pointer to the changing atmosphere of
Prague. Even in his last year of life the Emperor could be found
by observers to be measured, calm, and reasonable.[1] The difference
was that others had altered their positions much more than he. To call
a man mad is as meaningless as to call him sane; it acquires significance
only when put in the context of intellectual attitudes at the time,
and when the factors which have driven him into abnormality are
examined.

Rudolf's upbringing was strongly conditioned by what may hesitantly
be called the 'collective unconscious' of the House of Habsburg. He was
born in 1552 during the years of dispute over Charles V's universal
inheritance, and as the eldest grandson of Ferdinand I was marked out
at very least for the succession in Hungary and Bohemia and the overlordship of the Austrian lands, perhaps even for eventual rights in
Spain. The burden of such eminence and responsibility is a difficult
subject for study; it is however instructive to compare the feeling of
mission which a little later surrounded another Catholic prince from
Central Europe, a scion of the related house of Wittelsbach. Maximilian
of Bavaria became a close associate of Ferdinand II and proponent of a
peculiarly Germanic Counter-Reformation, but his childhood was spent
in the ancestral and artistic court at Munich, full of the promise of
grandeur as celebrated in contemporary Humanist panegyric.[2] Amid
the complexity of Rudolf's own environment there were three abiding
influences, and these must be briefly isolated, since he was always very
conscious of them: the hereditary background, the 'Spanish humour',
and the court circle of his father Maximilian II.

All the sources are agreed that Rudolf was stiff and dignified in
manner and 'melancholy' in disposition, with moods which could pass
into profound withdrawal. The family history of the Habsburgs affords
numerous examples both of extreme awareness of rank[3] and instability
of temperament. Luxemberger argued, as a psycho-analyst, that schizophrenia was proven in the cases of Joanna the Mad, Don Carlos, the last

---

[1] e.g. the reports printed in *Briefe und Akten*, ix, Nos. 160, 175 (431 f.), 181, 259
(603); cf. ibid. No. 136, the gravamina of the now militant Protestant estates of
Bohemia, accusing Rudolf of having turned against them precisely in 1600.

[2] H. Dotterweich, *Der junge Maximilian: Jugend und Erziehung . . . von 1573 bis
1593* (Munich 1962), 13 ff. and *passim*. In fact Maximilian was far more a late Renaissance Humanist and less a bigot than is often recognized, at least in his earlier years.
He shared Rudolf's interests in art and collecting (he was shown round the Prague
collection as a mark of personal favour by Rudolf in 1593, ibid. 127). He also had links
with Bohemia, even a Czech preceptor (ibid. 44 ff., 90 f.).

[3] Was this unbending humourlessness even a characteristic of the family as such?
Bryce thought so: J. Bryce, *The Holy Roman Empire* (London 1904 edn.), 368 n. 'c'.

Duke of Cleves (a Habsburg through his mother), and presumed in Charles V, Philip II, and Philip III. For good measure he diagnosed Rudolf's mother Maria and his brother Albrecht as schizoid psychopaths.[1] All this is suspect territory for the historian, but there is relevant positive evidence in the case of Rudolf's illegitimate son by Katharina Strada, Don Giulio.[2] This unfortunate was driven to revolting excesses, both homicidal and sexual, and the signs of some schizoid aberration are unmistakable. At the same time Don Giulio reveals in an advanced form certain of his father's own tendencies: the Caesarist illusion, the life of fantasy, the passion for the mechanical, especially clocks; until his confinement and death he was the apple of the Emperor's eye.[3] Another theory which has been advanced claims that Rudolf was a syphilitic from the time of his early illness in 1579–80; but the course of his ailment does not seem to sustain this anyway very limiting interpretation, while it is vitiated by the almost complete absence of any reference from contemporaries to the *morbus gallicus* though they were by then well familiar with its symptoms.[4]

More important as a historical factor was Rudolf's early acquaintance with the atmosphere of the Spanish court, where he and his brother Ernst spent the eight years from 1563 to 1571, not from the willingness of Maximilian, but on the insistence of their uncle Philip II.[5] Observers in Vienna saw the great change in him on his return: stiffness of attitude, pride, and (as they took it) unyielding religious dogmatism.[6] This view of Rudolf has survived unqualified in much casual historical writing.[7]

[1] H. Luxemberger: 'Psychiatrisch-erbbiologisches Gutachten über Don Julio d'Austria', *MVGDB* 70 (1932), 41–54. All this of course was based on very sketchy observation. Somewhat predictably he ascribes inherited schizophrenia also to Rudolf.
[2] There is considerable archive material in Prague: SÚA, SM K 1/148; this was for the most part printed by A. Blaschka in *MVGDB* 70 (1932), 220–55. The case was also studied by Gindely: *Rudolf II*, ii. 336 ff. The story is related in some detail by the contemporary chronicler Václav Březan, 239, 242.
[3] The clocks brought him into debt as he could not pay for them: SÚA, SM K 1/148[11] and /148[21]. Rudolf seems to have planned some major political dignity for Don Giulio; cf. *Briefe und Akten*, v. 816 n. 8.
[4] Kárpáthy-Kravjánszky, op. cit. 59–63. Goldast, writing in 1612, does indeed state as a fact that Rudolf had become diseased through his dissipation, quoting as his authorities the physicians Altmanstedt and Ruland (presumably Martin the Younger), but many of his comments about the court are mere gossip: *Das Prager Tagebuch des Melchior Goldast von Haiminsfeld*, ed. H. Schecker, *Abhandlungen und Vorträge der Bremer Wissenschaftlichen Gesellschaft*, Jg. 5, Heft 4 (1931), 267.
[5] Chudoba, op. cit. 148 ff.
[6] e.g. the Venetian Cortaro in 1574; Fiedler, *Relationen* (*FRA* xxx), 336. Cf. J. Janssen, *Geschichte des deutschen Volks*, iv (Freiburg i. B. 1885), 463 f.
[7] 'But in Rudolf II a product of the Spanish court ascended the throne, and the Counter-Reformation, in a systematic plan of attack, seized one important position after another.' L. Dehio, *The Precarious Balance* (London 1963, original German edn.

The lengthy stay in Spain in close proximity to the royal court certainly worked a profound effect on Rudolf, though direct evidence from the time is scanty, and the education of the Archduke was unexceptional.[1] It was the Spain of high mission, yet also of the Don Carlos episode, of mysticism and *autos-da-fé*, of neo-scholasticism and persecuted illuminists. None of the influences was reflected simply, but the fascination for Rudolf hereafter of things Spanish is manifest: he dressed in Spanish fashion, spoke Spanish formally for preference,[2] and placed great trust in advisers with close Spanish connections. These were preeminently Adam Dietrichstein, who had been Rudolf's major-domo in Spain, a man of high quality, Maximilian's ambassador in Madrid and married to Marguerite de Cardona; Vratislav Pernstein, already mentioned as one of the leading Czech aristocrats, a political moderate whose wife was Maria Manriquez de Lara; and Hans Khevenhüller, Imperial ambassador to Spain from 1573 till 1606, hispaniolated scion of a highly loyal Austrian family and Rudolf's main confidant abroad until his death.[3] Later the undoubted attractiveness for the Emperor of Zdeněk Lobkovic and his circle was due in part to Lobkovic's gifted wife Polyxena, the daughter of Pernstein and Maria Manriquez.

But Rudolf's attitude to Spain was characteristically ambivalent. His experience of it was anyway acting on a natural disposition—the frequent references to his taciturnity for instance bespeak more than just an acquired formality[4]—and led as easily to a revulsion against Spanish pretensions. His refusal to marry the Infanta, and the related problem of the succession to his lands, comes nearest to being a guiding thread through

1948), 44. Both these propositions have their truth; the mistake lies in thinking they are necessarily connected.

[1] E. Mayer-Löwenschwerdt, *Der Aufenthalt der Erzherzöge Rudolf und Ernst in Spanien* (*Akademie der Wissenschaft in Wien, philosophisch-historische Klasse, Sitzungsberichte* 206, Abh. 5, Vienna 1927). There are a few juvenilia in the correspondence (HHSA as above and ÖN MS. 9103), but they are unremarkable.

[2] As at the first audience he gave to the mission of Boisdauphin in 1600: A. Babeau, 'Une ambassade en Allemagne sous Henri IV', *Revue historique* Jan.–Apr. 1896, 39. Cf. Alidosi, op. cit. 6. On the other hand his preferences in writing seem to have been for German.

[3] For general details on these Czech–Spanish marriages see Chudoba, op. cit. 179 ff. Dietrichstein's relations to Maximilian from the Spanish court during the years 1563–8 were published by a later family archivist: H. Koch, *Quellen zur Geschichte des Kaisers Maximilian II* (Leipzig 1857), i. 111–217. The important correspondence of Hans Khevenhüller zu Aichelberg survives through the author's own copies, now in the Stadtarchiv, Nuremberg. Part of it was used for the famous *Annales Ferdinandei* of his nephew, Franz Christoph Khevenhüller. A typescript version is now available in Vienna (HHSA Abt. Spanien, Dipl. Korr. fasc. 8–14) thanks to the devoted labours of Count Georg Khevenhüller-Metsch.

[4] 'Rodolpho di poche parole' as the Venetian Michele calls him (Fiedler, *Relationen* (*FRA* xxx), 284); cf. the nuncio in 1589: Nuncios/Puteo, 483.

the tangle of his political indecisiveness. Moreover he early had the opportunity to imbibe, at his father's court, a quite different atmosphere and set of priorities.

The question of Rudolf's relation to the Humanist circle of Maximilian is an aspect of Habsburg patronage and of a whole cultural policy which will be considered in a later chapter, but something must be said here on his own aptitude to profit from it, and on the mentality of his father. Rudolf's intellectual calibre is no more agreed upon than any other aspect of his personality, and it has even been suggested that his pessimism was the result of realizing his limitations in that direction.[1] This may indeed be to some extent true, but it is an argument rather for considerable self-knowledge; he was clearly obsessed by complexity and the intractability of his world.

So far as the common grounding of a privileged education was concerned, Rudolf was fitted to derive full advantage. He was well-read, well-informed, and infinitely curious. His linguistic powers too were creditable: familiarity with German, Spanish, Italian, Latin, and French, together with some knowledge of Czech. The latter point is an important one, and must remain uncertain, though the king's understanding of the main language of his Bohemian subjects was definitely not great.[2] The failure of successive Habsburgs to learn their tongue brought a storm of protest from Czech nationalist historians, but it was not always true— Ferdinand I spoke it after a fashion and Maximilian knew it excellently —nor was it for want of trying.[3] Anyway their conclusion that this meant unconcern can easily be a false inference. Rudolf saw Bohemia *sub specie universi*, but was nevertheless heavily involved in it; language was not a serious point of dispute between him and the estates.

Rudolf's mental acumen will of course emerge from study of his artistic and collecting credo; but another important factor was his very

---

[1] Mayer-Löwenschwerdt, op. cit. 62 f.

[2] He had a Czech tutor, Sebastian Pechovský z Palatína, from 1571 (J. Svátek, *Obrazy z kulturnich dějin českých* (Prague 1891), 13 ff.), but could not apparently speak or understand the language at his first *sněm* in 1577 (Tomek, *Dějepis*, 271). Alidosi cites it as one of his six languages (*Relazione*), while a correspondent in 1578 reports that Rudolf has been talking with a Muscovite embassy in the 'Slavon tongue': *Calendar of State Papers, Foreign, 1577–8* (London 1901), No. 777.

[3] Svátek, op. cit. 3 ff., 10 ff. Maximilian regularly gave audiences in Czech and addressed the *sněm* in that language (cf. Gindely, *Böhmische Brüder*, 178). According to the Venetian Michele, Maximilian spoke both Czech and Hungarian (Fiedler, *Relationen* (FRA xxx), 279). Michele was a diplomat with great experience of the Empire, so the testimony is worth attention. Curiously enough Rudolf's nineteenth-century namesake (the Archduke of Mayerling) was given as Czech tutor none other than Anton Gindely, and on the grounds that the latter was 'objektiv bei Beurteilung geschichtlicher Tatsachen' (O. von Mitis, *Das Leben des Kronprinzen Rudolf* (Leipzig 1928), 14).

desire for political activity. This has been shown particularly by detailed analysis of his relations with the Bohemian chancery and his role in the catastrophic events of the last years of the reign.[1] His leading German advocate observes it for the period following the 'crisis' of 1599–1600, and the same is true *a fortiori* for earlier years.[2] Even the notorious delays at the Prague court at times arose paradoxically from this intense personal desire to rule. The Emperor insisted on taking his own decisions and would not allow any formal body to follow an independent initiative. Thus the nominal advisory and executive channels, headed by the Privy Council, stagnated while the monarch dealt with his own preferred individual confidants.

Yet all the Emperor's efforts involved him in disaster and brought near-nemesis to his august house. An explanation of the failure can be broached only in terms of certain guiding themes, which a purely chronological approach obscures: the question of the succession and Rudolf's relation to his family; the influence and character of his advisers; and the striving for an international role which proved hopelessly unrealizable. I suggest, as a point of departure, that Rudolf's lines of policy were much closer to those of his father than might initially appear.

The personality of Maximilian II has always been enigmatic (his biographer proclaims it in the title of his book),[3] yet the pattern, wide cultural receptivity and sharp intellect, together with uncertain religious commitment, is not very far removed from that of Rudolf. In the son the whole personality is more hectic, and the religious insecurity more profound, but Maximilian still felt the spirit of an age which believed that the growing tension might be reduced by sensible discussion. Maximilian too, in his much shorter reign, was subject to the pressure of Spanish orthodoxy through his wife Maria, and the problem of his confessional allegiance is central. He was widely considered by both sides to be crypto-Lutheran in sentiment—his court preacher Pfauser was a Protestant and he had many friends of similar inclination in the Empire. But this is only a partial answer and begs the basic question. Maximilian was constantly

---

[1] J. Borovička, 'Počátky kancléřování Zdeňka z Lobkovic' in *Sborník prací věnovaných Dru. Gustavu Friedrichovi* (Prague 1931), 435–55, esp. 444 f., stressing both Rudolf's frequent audiences with Lobkovic and his desire to intervene independently in affairs. This evidence is drawn largely from the Lobkovic 'Manuals' (minutes of discussions and protocols) and 'Calendars' (lists of appointments and meetings) both in the Prague UK.

[2] F. Stieve, *Die Verhandlungen über die Nachfolge Kaisers Rudolf II in den Jahren 1581–1602* (Munich 1879), 109.

[3] Viktor Bibl, *Maximilian II, der rätselhafte Kaiser* (Vienna–Leipzig 1929).

at odds with his Spanish cousins (he really hated them),[1] with the Jesuit henchmen of the Papacy, and the policy-makers of Trent, while sympathetic to the influence of the moderate Melanchthon in Germany; at the same time his decision to uphold the Catholic religion was a political conversion, which his conscience could accept as dictated by the sanctity of secular power.[2] He had designs for large-scale mediation in the Empire, especially in the Netherlands[3] and Bohemia, but was hindered always through fear of Catholic reactions. Rudolph took over all these difficulties, and added one yet more irreconcilable: he stood in the centre of the argument and yet his ideal was a universalist mission, not a compromise.

*   *   *

> Ich hielt die Welt für klug, sie ist es nicht.
> Gemartert vom Gedanken drohnder Zukunft
> Dacht ich die Zeit mit gleicher Furcht bewegt
> Im weisen Zögern sehnd die einzge Rettung.[4]

The popular nineteenth-century view of Rudolf, fed by Grillparzer's famous play about the calamities of his declining years, saw the Emperor as essentially generous and humane, but frustrated by an inability to come to terms with the world. The dramatist's instinct is sound, especially when he depicts the real conflict as lying, not between Rudolf and Matthias—Matthias is just a coarser, less gifted figure in the same mould—but between the two of them and the doctrinaire self-confidence of the rising Ferdinand of Styria. For the old Emperor the future is full of menace and a 'wise hesitation' the only resort against catastrophe.

The clearest evidence of this seemed to come from the whole dilatoriness and irregularity of Rudolf's administration. The papal nuncio is always complaining of the 'tardo moto, con il quale caminano le cose di questa corte'.[5] The nuncio Sega is already speaking by 1586 of total ruin and the same prediction appears from the Bavarian correspondent Sprinzenstein: such is the failure of Rudolf's government that 'Kais. [erlicher] Mt. [Majestät] Regierung in äusserster Gefahr stünde, und da sie nit bald nach guten Leuten trachteten und andere remedi brauchten,

---

[1] Thus the Venetian envoy Cortaro in 1574 who had direct information. Maximilian spoke of Philip's ministers: 'di tanto sdegno, che niuna cosa fa più volontieri, che dir mal di tutti loro . . . et con me n'ha tenuto diverse volte lunghissime ragionamenti, chiamandoli Spagnoleti, quasi volesse inferire, que solo mirino il proprio commodo . . .' Fiedler, *Relationen* (*FRA* xxx), 341.

[2] Bibl, op. cit. 94–105. Bibl sees the Erastianism of this position, but perhaps misses something of its spiritual malaise. Cf. below, p. 84.

[3] Chudoba, op. cit. 134 ff.

[4] Franz Grillparzer, *Ein Bruderzwist in Habsburg*, Act 4.

[5] Nuncios/Puteo, Prague 1 Nov. 1588.

wurde Ihrer Mt. Regiment gewiss müssen brechen, dann es wär kein justitia da.'[1] The Emperor was increasingly difficult to approach; audiences became uncertain—'Dio sa quando l'havera' lamented Fornari in 1603—and might never be granted at all.[2] Many examples could be quoted of his reluctance to receive advisers.[3] At the same time he was more and more unwilling to move from his castle in Prague. After the early years he quit it only for the abortive *Reichstag* of Regensburg in 1594, and when the city was intermittently struck with the plague; on such occasions he would retire to his summer palace at Brandeis or to Pilsen, as in 1599 and 1606. Even these journeys were attended by indecision and delay.[4] Things were growing gradually worse: there was a steady collapse during the 1590s, while after 1600 it began to appear that all serious resolve had failed. The Privy Council, the highest organ for the taking of decisions, was in disarray, and the whole bureaucracy was hindered by lack of directives from above.[5]

There were of course weighty practical considerations which stayed Rudolf's hand: the lack of proper financial backing for any enterprise, especially the struggle against the Turks, and the pressure of that war, from its resumption in the 1590s, on the administrative machine. But these were general problems within the European state structure of the time; more fundamental were the constraints in Rudolf's own personality, and they soon made themselves evident in what became the chronic problem of his marriage and the succession to his lands. The question

[1] Sprinzenstein to William of Bavaria, Ingolstadt, 9 May 1585, printed in *SČ* v. 596–9. Cf. Nuncios/Sega, Prague 17 Oct. 1586: 'Qui non occorre, rebus sic stantibus, di pensar molto più volte, che al sostentare col rappezzare, poichè si vede, che ognuno qui va a questo camino, il quale . . . tende notoriamente col tempo a perdito totale.' But it should be remembered that Sega was never any friend of Rudolf—the latter never confided in him—while Sprinzenstein was also (as Sega himself reveals) in disfavour: Sega, Prague 15 Aug. 1586.

[2] Nuncios/Ferreri: Fornari, Prague 18 Mar. 1603. Fornari was Papal chargé d'affaires between the tours of duty of Spinelli and Ferreri. Cf. Maximilian of Bavaria's emissary Gailkircher in 1600; see *SČ* x, No. 80.

[3] In 1607 for example he summoned Cardinal Dietrichstein for urgent discussions, then kept him waiting over a period of weeks in Prague, and in the end apparently abandoned his original purpose. Nuncios/Caetano, Prague 19 and 26 Nov. 1607.

[4] Especially the departure in 1594; cf. Zeitung aus Prag 26 Apr. 1594, S.A. Třeboň, Historica 5719. The last time Rudolf attended the Hungarian diet at Pozsony (Pressburg) was in 1583.

[5] This is the crucial point. The actual bureaucratic chaos under Rudolf seems to me to have been exaggerated (though it was certainly serious, as declining standards in the day-to-day keeping of books like the Komorní Knihy (Kammerbücher) in the SÚA reveal). But the combination of Rudolf's hesitation with his unwillingness to delegate power hastened a catastrophe. Cf. A. H. Loebl, 'Beiträge zur Geschichte der kaiserlichen Zentralverwaltung im ausgehenden sechzehnten Jahrhundert', *MIÖG* xxvii (1906), 629–77; Matoušek, *Turecká Válka*, 48 and *passim*.

was of central importance: Rudolf's own election as King of the Romans (the heir designate to the Imperial title) had not been automatic,[1] and the Bohemian and Hungarian thrones were even less certain. Long learned wrangles had failed to settle whether the Crown of St. Wenceslas was always elective, or whether it was hereditary in the ruling house, and in that case whether or not by primogeniture.[2] Rudolf's first serious illness in 1578–80, so soon after his accession, immediately brought the matter into the open, and whereas Elizabeth of England made a complete recovery from a dangerous early attack of smallpox, his health was thereafter the subject of continual anxiety. As early as 1581 Charles of Styria was calling for the election of a King of the Romans.[3] But the effect of such pressure was always to bring out the worst in Rudolf, to poison his mind against his relatives and isolate him completely, not only from his family, but from his oldest and closest confidants. Thus it even estranged him from Khevenhüller during the sombre negotiations over the matter in 1592.[4]

The obvious first possibility was of course that Rudolf should marry and have a legitimate successor in his own right, and there was from the outset a ready candidate for his hand in his Spanish cousin the Infanta Isabella, daughter of Philip II. The project for this apparently logical and mutually advantageous match dated from as early as 1568, and opened up the prospect that Rudolf might even acquire all the dominions which Don Carlos had forfeited.[5] At first the young Emperor was clearly tempted by the chance of a large dowry, and the marriage was confidently predicted on all sides; yet by 1582 doubts were creeping in, and thereafter the *Isabellafrage* was continually revived and shelved until the Infanta was finally wedded despairingly to Rudolf's brother Albrecht fifteen years later.[6] No straightforward calculation of benefits

---

[1] H. Moritz, *Die Wahl Rudolfs II, der Reichstag zu Regensburg und die Freistellungsbewegung* (Marburg 1895), Chs. II and III.

[2] For a statement from the Habsburg standpoint: G. Turba, *Geschichte des Thronfolgerechts*, 279–312; for a Czech view of the fundamental laws: Kalousek, op. cit. 206 ff.

[3] Stieve, *Verhandlungen*, 3 ff. Even at this stage concern was not restricted to the Emperor's health: 'Dass die Kränklichkeit und Menschenscheu des jungen Monarchen ein offenes Geheimnis und der Gedanke an einen Regierungswechsel so dringlich geworden war, liess sich jedenfalls nicht mehr rückgängig machen.' F. von Bezold, *Rudolf II und die Heilige Liga* (Munich 1883), 8.

[4] Khevenhüller correspondence, *passim*; F. C. Khevenhüller, *Annales*, iii. 1051–4.

[5] *Fuggerzeitungen*, 7 f. (Madrid 5 Oct. 1568). Rudolf also became Philip's brother-in-law when the latter married (as fourth wife) his elder sister Anna.

[6] For the main details of this story see Stieve, *Verhandlungen*; J. Zöchbauer, *Kaiser Rudolf II and die Nachfolgefrage bis zum Tode des Erzherzogs Ernst* (Urfahr 1899); *Briefe und Akten*, v. 725 ff. and *passim*. Cf. Khevenhüller, *Annales* i. 116 f.; ii. 249 ff., 346 f., 402 ff.; iii. 768–70, 862–4, etc.

could possibly penetrate the mystery of this lack of enthusiasm; Sprinzenstein for instance was quite baffled and could only suggest a little of
the material answer: 'Ihr Mt. werde sich bald entschliessen müssen mit
der Heirat gegen Spania, und könnte niemand wissen, warumb Ihr Mt.
es so lang differierten, ob es Ihr zu thun, dass Sie von Ihrem freien
Leben, wie Sie es bisher gehabt, nit gern wichen oder ob es geschäh,
ein gute Summa Gelds herauszupressen zu Ihrer Unterhaltung.'[1] Plans
were largely suspended during the years 1587–90 while the situation in
Poland engaged all attention, but they were resumed after this, and
reached a climax during Khevenhüller's secretive mission of 1592, the
only time he visited Prague. High hopes were entertained for such
direct intervention by a trusted servant, but the shrewdest observers—
like the Spanish ambassador San Clemente—could already see that
nothing would ever come of the project, and the only result was embitter-
ment on both sides.[2]

The impasse was all of Rudolf's making, though this was not by any
means self-evident to contemporaries, and even so well-informed a man
as the later Venetian ambassador Soranzo could attribute it to Spanish
delays.[3] Rudolf's revulsion against Spain was in the first place parallel
to his father's position: a dislike of its overweening attitude and the
desire for an independent mediatory policy, especially in the Netherlands. To this were added the territorial points of friction in North Italy
and the western borders of the Empire, so important in the literature
of the time.[4] Rudolf certainly looked for the cession to him of Milan, and
probably also part of the Netherlands, together with acknowledgement
of his overlordship of the North Italian fiefs.[5] But the disharmony, in
which politics and religion were intertwined, went much deeper; indeed
we are entitled to say *must* have gone deeper, for the failure of the

[1] Sprinzenstein, see above, p. 54 n. 1.

[2] The Venetians still expected an early marriage; Dolfin to the Doge, Prague 24
Sept. 1591, in Nuncios/Malaspina; cf. Zeitung aus Prag 24 Sept. 1591, S.A. Třeboň,
Historica 5553/8. But something was clearly wrong: 'Herr Hannss Keffenhüller ist im
Werkh sich widerumb nach Spania auf die Raiss fertig zu machen, die Ursach seines
Khomens und so langen Haussen Blaibens, ist bishero inn grossen gehaim gehalten':
Zeitung aus Prag 10 Nov. 1592, S.A. Třeboň, Historica 5594; cf. Matoušek, op. cit.
103 f., 123 ff.; *Briefe und Akten*, iv, Appendix, Nos. 8 and 9 (two letters from San
Clemente to Philip).

[3] Fiedler, *Relationen* (*FRA* xxvi), Soranzo 1614: 'Attribuiva la colpa a Spagnuoli, li
quali per gran pezzo lo tennero in speranza di darle in moglie l'Infanta di Fiandra, che
con grandissima acerbità del suo animo cadi poi nell'Arciduce Alberto suo fratello' (2).

[4] The nuncios' reports are full of them; and cf. Chudoba, op. cit. 144 ff., and
Khevenhüller, *Annales* i. 37 ff.

[5] These were the basis for the Spanish pretensions under Philip III; see G. Turba,
Die Grundlagen der Pragmatischen Sanktion (Vienna 1912), ii, and the literature of the
Oñate-Vertrag of 1617. Cf. Stieve, *Verhandlungen*, 9 ff.

marriage negotiations is itself a prime fact in evidence. The rage and despair with which the Emperor received news of the betrothal of Isabella to Albrecht in 1597 betray the profoundest of frustrations; it was a turning-point in his life. Moreover things were further aggravated the following year when Spanish troops violated Imperial territory by taking up winter quarters in Westphalia.[1]

The same paradigm repeated itself with Rudolf and Marie de' Medici, who was being proposed as a suitable candidate during the 1590s. Links between Prague and Florence were substantial—there was a permanent Tuscan representative at the Imperial court—and contacts flourished in the field of culture. This attempt came to nothing through Rudolf's refusal to commit himself, yet he was again desolated when informed in 1600 that she was to marry Henry IV of France; relations became extremely strained with the French embassy which arrived to announce the news, and he read all kinds of sinister implications into the union.[2] After this there were still persistent rumours of new plans: Margaret, daughter of Charles Emmanuel of Savoy was mentioned, and after her Rudolf's cousin Anne of Tyrol. They grew increasingly far-fetched, even looking to the Protestant camp as the failing Emperor was driven more and more towards a complete rupture with his family; the subject was not dead in 1611. During the very last months of the reign negotiations between Rudolf and the college of Electors, themselves the final make-believe episode in the shadow career of the landless Emperor, were frustrated by his refusal to consider any question of a successor, even as the prelude to a Diet which might somehow restore a semblance of his authority.[3]

Were it not the product of such tragic frustrations Rudolf's attitude to the marriage mart might be accounted droll. 'Yesterday His Majesty ordered me', Hegenmüller informed the trusted Hannewaldt as late as 1608, 'to write that you should make diligent and secret enquiries what sort of nubile princesses, or even high-ranking countesses are available; Lorraine has had some good-looking females in its time and they say that Baden has something Catholic on offer.'[4] The whole story reflects

---

[1] G. Turba, 'Beiträge zur Geschichte der Habsburger aus den letzten Jahren des spanischen Königs Philip II', *AÖG* 86 (1898), 334 ff., 350 ff., based—*inter alia*—on the Khevenhüller correspondence. Cf. *Briefe und Akten*, v, 438 ff.

[2] See Babeau, art. cit. for Boisdauphin's embassy, and cf. the dispatch of Heinrich Haslang to Maximilian of Bavaria, Prague 16 Aug. 1600 (*SČ* x, No. 74), and Rudolf to Maximilian, Prague 13 Sept. 1600 (ibid. No. 78).

[3] Nuncios/Ferreri, Prague 5 and 7 July 1604; /Caetano 16 July and 31 Dec. 1607; Gindely, *Rudolf II*, ii. 314 and *passim*. *Briefe und Akten*, x, esp. Nos. 26, 40, 42, 43, 73, 85.

[4] 'Heri jussit mihi S. Mt. E. Herrl^t zu schreiben, Sie sollen gehaimbe fleissige

not a physical but a mental incapacity. Rudolf was well known for his
illicit liaisons, and he had as mistress for a long time Katharina Strada,
the daughter of his remarkable and favoured court antiquary, Jacopo
Strada; according to the legends he actually married her at a secret ceremony. She certainly bore him several children, none apparently of any
distinction.[1] His penchant for perverse relations and erotica appears
from his artistic commissions: Spranger's voluptuous canvases of
nymphs consorting with old men and so forth; as such it will be mentioned later and belongs to a wider atmosphere of *fin de siècle*. Yet the
chief reason seems to lie with the vicious effect on the Emperor's disposition of constant pressure from advisers and relatives. The process
was cumulative: the dangers while Rudolf remained unmarried were
growing, hence something had to be done to secure the succession; but
no agreement could ever be reached on a candidate, hence Rudolf could
trust no one; this served only to heighten his moroseness and therefore
to hasten family intervention.[2]

Rudolf's sense of majesty involved him centrally in developing the
inherited mystique of his house. Herein lies the crux of his dilemma:
the enormous gulf between the glorious ideal and the sordid, niggardly
reality, thwarted as he was by petty jealousies and rivalries. He would
do nothing that derogated from his rank, and thus any resolution of the
succession question was stillborn: 'Daruf Keiser gefragt: "kan man auch
einen Römischen König ungeschmalert meiner reputation machen?"'[3]
For despite the practical problems of enforcing Habsburg policy, the
Emperor's power within the house was theoretically absolute. Charles V
had originally guaranteed the rights of his brother Ferdinand through an
arrangement of 1522 (the *Erbteilung*), and the latter had established, in
his testament of 1543 and the so-called *Hausordnung* of 1554, that his
lands should be administratively divided among his three sons, but that
the overlordship be reserved to Maximilian. One of Rudolf's first acts of
policy was to ensure that this was seen to have complete validity for him

nachfrag halten, was für nubiles principessae oder auch fürnembe gräfin vorhanden sein:
zu irer zeit hab Lotringen schöne freule gehabt; so soll auch von Baden etwas catholisch
vorhanden sein.' Prague 22 Nov. 1608; *Briefe und Akten*, vi, No. 292.

[1] Alidosi (1607) says there are four sons and four daughters, and gives their names;
Gindely notes six altogether; while Khevenhüller records five: F. C. Khevenhüller,
Conterfet Kupfferstich i (Leipzig 1721), 30. According to other sources Rudolf was still
begetting children to the very end: *Briefe und Akten*, x. 246 n. 3. Cf. above, p. 49 and
below, p. 182.

[2] Cf. the memorial to Rudolf from the councillors Rumpf, Trautson, Hornstein, and
Unverzagt, 12 July 1599, printed in *SČ* ix. 687 ff.; and Tomek, *Dějepis*, 325 ff. on
Ferdinand's concern in 1585.

[3] Undated report (1601) from Prague to the Palatinate, printed in Ranke, op. cit.

also, and he therefore engineered the succession treaty (again an *Erbteilung*) of 1578, by which his brothers rendered him due homage as the senior member of their family.[1] Thus all the intrigues of Rudolf's brothers against him were, strictly speaking, acts of *lèse-majesté*.[2] The extent of the obeisance which this involved can be gauged from a personal 'capitulation' of Maximilian of Tyrol as late as 1600: 'According to the wishes of Y[r] Majesty, and as I did before, I may truly assert that I have never by an inch exceeded the respects due to Y[r] Majesty and would not think to do so, but humbly and completely bow myself before Y[r] Majesty's gracious and sovereign will, to deal with me as may be pleasing.'[3] It was not rare for the Emperor to demand the dismissal of an unwelcome Archducal adviser.

The succession, then, dictated Rudolf's feelings towards his own family. The death of his father left him with a great weight of responsibility, and there was no one to whom he could look for support. No real bond seems to have existed between him and his mother, the sternly Catholic Maria; although Rudolf made some attempts to dissuade her, she returned to Spain in 1581 and thereafter, despite the similarities in mood between mother and son (she was also melancholic), they had little contact.[4] There was equally no sympathy with another partly kindred spirit, Rudolf's uncle Ferdinand of Tyrol. The latter shared with him the pursuit of the artistic, the mania for collecting, the bent towards mechanics,[5] and the Bohemian connection, yet there was no friendship between them and the dominating emotion was one of jealousy.

Nearest of all to Rudolf in character was his childhood companion Ernst, Maximilian's second son. Ernst was also markedly serious in mood, and had a taste in collecting which matched Rudolf's own.[6] Yet he was also apparently an orthodox zealous Catholic, and the favoured

---

[1] For this see Turba, *Thronfolgerecht*, especially 179–99.

[2] Though there were complications: the 1578 treaty was only valid if the Archdukes' salaries were properly paid, and it made no mention of consulting the estates. V. Kratochvíl, 'K poměru císaře Rudolfa II k arciknížete Matyáši', *ČČH* v (1899), 169–76, 216–38. It also took no proper account of a possible interregnum through the interruption of primogeniture.

[3] Maximilian to Rudolf, Neustadt 22 Oct. 1600; HHSA, Fam. Korr. A. 4. 1.

[4] Turba, *Beiträge*, 357 ff. Her court steward was the emblematist Juan de Borja. There is little surviving correspondence between Maria and Rudolf. Her return in 1581 was chronicled by the Venetians: Fiedler, *Relationen* (*FRA* xxx), 381–407.

[5] There is an interesting sketch of Ferdinand by the Venetians Michele and Donato which mentions this: Fiedler, *Relationen* (*FRA* xxx), 359 f. Cf. A. Lhotsky, *Die Geschichte der Sammlungen* i (Vienna 1941), 179–202. Ferdinand also showed an interest in Paracelsus; see K. Sudhoff, *Versuch einer Kritik der Echtheit der Paracelsischen Schriften* (Berlin 1894–9) ii. 13 f.

[6] Lhotsky, op. cit. 213–22.

candidate for the succession until his premature death in 1595.[1] After
the elimination of Ernst the tension moved ineluctably to its climax in
the Emperor's relation with his younger brother Matthias. It is not
sufficient to say that the pathological jealousy which Rudolf felt was
simply transferred, since there has been little more posthumous agreement on the merits of Matthias than on those of Rudolf. While studies
of the Thirty Years War tend to regard him, with his adviser Khlesl, as
the representative of moderation, he was earlier a more militant and
sinister figure. Matthias's first indiscretion however, his attempt to
take over the government of the Netherlands at the request of some local
nobles in 1577, was not far removed from the policy of mediation which
Rudolf himself favoured. It gave rise to an extended exchange of letters
in which the Emperor presses him after a brotherly fashion not to en-
danger the prestige of the house or the Catholic religion, while Matthias
protests his good intentions.[2] Rudolf was embittered, with much justification, that Matthias had acted on private initiative, stealing the wind
from his own sails, and although as late as 1587 we find him still
seeking a reconciliation of his brother with Philip II,[3] there was always
a ground-bass of discontent. From the end of the 1580s they had
little direct contact: their meetings now became either merely formal or
increasingly acrimonious. After 1600, the date of the private Archducal
treaty of Schottwien, Matthias clearly stood in full opposition to the
Emperor, however veiled by asseverations of loyalty, and the latter's
hatred of him grew implacable.[4] Matthias's subsequent actions—his
banding with the Protestant estates and eventual march on Prague—it
seems most logical to consider as motivated largely by territorial ambition. This was the longest frustration of his life, unsatisfied either by
the Netherlands venture or by any other appeals to Rudolf.[5] Once he
had achieved it he had nothing more to contribute.

While rejecting as distasteful any compromise with living members
of his family, Rudolf displayed extreme veneration towards his forebears.
His desire for fitting ceremonial emerged immediately with his first
public act, the funeral of Maximilian II, conducted at vast expense and

---

[1] Not that, in the nature of things, there was ever anything like uniformity on this. But
Sega, for instance, appeared to regard it as almost settled in 1586: Nuncios/Sega xliii ff.
[2] HHSA, Fam. Korr. A. 4. 1. There are holograph letters from Rudolf on 9 Nov.
1577, 3 Jan., 15 Mar., 2 and 28 May, 18 Aug., 21 Oct., 18 Nov. 1588, 16 Jan. and
24 Feb. 1579.
[3] Ibid., Rudolf to Ernst, Prague 16 Aug. 1584 and 14 Apr. 1587.
[4] Cf. Stieve, Verhandlungen 56 ff.
[5] See Kratochvíl, art. cit. There is no full study of Matthias; his ambition and lack
of principle are strongly argued by Novák, op. cit.

in the presence of the whole Imperial nobility. The exequies were first carried out in Vienna on 5 August 1577, where long and precise instructions were prepared of those to be invited, their prescribed dress, station and duties.[1] Then followed the laying to rest in St. Vitus's Cathedral in Prague, a ceremony whose magnificence, as the local chronicler observed, had never before been seen in the city.[2]

The symbolism of the event is difficult to judge; there are not enough studies of the trend to symbolic pageantry in the later sixteenth century to allow serious comparison. The focal point was the *Castrum Doloris*, the decoration which surrounded the coffin of the deceased and was arranged with great elaboration.[3] In this case the *Castrum Doloris* was prepared by the Imperial *Kammerdiener* Hans Popp, who was given 200 thalers for the purpose.[4] This Popp seems to have become a friend of high Catholics as well as an established court favourite; he was ennobled and naturalized in Bohemia with his family by order of the *sněm* in 1598.[5] Great play was made with the various regalia; Bydžovský describes how not only the Bohemian and Hungarian jewels were carried in procession, but also the Imperial insignia: crown, morion (*Sturmhaub*), orb, sceptre, and sword.[6] All had their prescribed place on the *Castrum Doloris*, together with the symbol of that most Habsburg institution, the Knighthood of the Golden Fleece. Twenty-six years later the Emperor showed a similar concern over the mourning arrangements for his mother, adding the characteristic touch that his own presence at the service would be incognito.[7]

[1] SÚA, SM K 1/15: 'Eigentliche Verzaichnuss der beradtschlagten und beschlossnen Ordnung des ganntzen Prozess der vorsteenden Khaiserlichen Exequien und besingkhnus, wie es damit Allenthalben underschidlich zu halten.' There are two copies, the longer extending to 76 pages. The Venetian condolence party comment on the magnificence of Rudolf's suite: Fiedler, *Relationen* (*FRA* xxx), 369–72.

[2] Bydžovský, 11v ff.; the passage begins: 'W tak welikém počtu téměř předních wšeho křesťanstwa knížat, nejjasnější a nejnepřemoženější císař Rudolph mrtwému otci swému slawney, nákladnej a prwe nikdy w králowstwí českém newidanej pohřeb jest učiniti ráčil.'

[3] This can be seen from an interesting drawing of Rudolf's own *Castrum Doloris* in 1612: Heinrich Hiesserle von Chodaw, 'Raiss Buch und Leben . . .' Nat. Mus. MS. vi A 12 fo. 86ʳ. [Plate 15b.]   [4] SÚA, SM K 1/14. Order of 25 Feb. 1577.

[5] *SČ* ix, No. 409 (540–1). Hans Popp was further favoured by being granted in 1596 the right to inherit the castle of Eger, and in 1597 the purchase of Königsberg and Schönbuch: SÚA, Bekennen 1594–9 (Majestalia Vol. 104), fol. 183 ff., 237 f. Magdalena, the wife of Ladislav Lobkovic, who was implicated in the treason trial of 1593, sought the good offices of Popp at court: *SČ* viii, Nos. 213, 250, 251. Cf. *Briefe und Akten* iv, 221 and n. 3. The artist Josef Heintz dedicated a picture to him in the 1590s (J. Zimmer, *Joseph Heintz der Ältere als Maler* (Heidelberg 1967), 304 f.) and he clearly had influence in this cultural circle too, for which he sometimes acted as paymaster; cf. *Jahrbuch* x (1889), Reg. No. 5900; xii (1891), Nos. 8196, 8198, 8241, 8318; xix (1898), No. 16173.   [6] Bydžovský, loc. cit.

[7] *Briefe und Akten*, v. 723 n. 3. In the end—after long delays—he did not attend at all.

Further evidence that Rudolf lavished much attention on the prestige of the dynasty is provided by his reconsecration of the tombs of all the Emperors buried in St. Vitus. In 1590 he had their graves opened and the coffins placed in an elaborate white marble mausoleum at the centre of the Cathedral.[1] This act, along with the matter of the Czech crown discussed below, strongly suggests that the glory of the House of Habsburg was also to be the glory of Prague. At the same time there are parallels with two illustrious members of his family who were not interred in Bohemia: Rudolf's passion for the works of Dürer was surely in part a conscious re-creation of the world of Maximilian I,[2] while there is an equally conscious reminiscence of Charles V in the interesting affair of his contemplated abdication.

Rumours that the Emperor might withdraw entirely from public life circulated as early as 1586,[3] and intermittent suggestions continued thereafter, though most smack just of wishful thinking or uninformed deductions from his mode of living. The possibility only crystallized in Rudolf's relations with his brother Maximilian (the Grand Master of the Teutonic Order), who succeeded Ferdinand as regent of the Tyrol in 1597. Maximilian was himself curiously close to Rudolf in some ways: patron of antiquaries, historians, and artists, dabbler in magic; but this perhaps only increased the friction between him and his sovereign, as Rudolf began to seek direct control over the Tyrol and it came to be mentioned that he might retire to Ferdinand's magic castle of Ambras.[4] Rudolf may have had profound motives for this course of action—he sent one of his favourite artists Roelant Savery specifically to paint in the Alps—and he was clearly thinking also of the pessimistic withdrawal of his ancestor. It was at this time that he commissioned from the sculptor De Vries a bust of himself to form a pair with one of Charles V by Leone Leoni which he had recently acquired for his collection.[5] Charles in his monastic retreat at Yuste indulged some of the obsessions of Rudolf;[6]

[1] Stránský, *Český Stát*, 348; *Paměti Mikuláše Dačického z Heslova*, ed. E. Petrů and E. Pražák (Prague 1955, hereafter 'Dačický'), 254. The Nuremberg Humanist Rittershusius saw the new tombs in Prague in 1589: H. Kunstmann, *Die Nürnberger Universität Altdorf und Böhmen* (Cologne–Graz 1963), 33 ff.

[2] For his Dürer collection see J. Neuwirth, 'Rudolf II als Dürersammler', in *Xenia Austriaca* (Vienna 1893), and below, p. 182.

[3] Nuncios/Sega, Prague 14 and 28 Oct. 1586.

[4] On these negotiations, and what may have lain behind them, see Joseph Hirn, *Erzherzog Maximilian, der Deutschmeister*, i (Innsbruck 1915), 101 ff. and 143–6; and idem, 'Rudolf II und Tyrol', *AÖG* 86 (1899), 255–92. Maximilian's magic is mentioned by Henry Wotton: letters to Zouche, Vienna 19 Dec. 1590 and 9 Jan. 1591, Pearsall Smith, i. 249, 252 and n. On Ambras cf. below, pp. 178 f.

[5] L. O. Larsson, *Adrian de Vries* (Vienna–Munich 1967), 36–8. Cf. below, p. 169.

[6] Mechanical toys, for example. There appears to be little literature worth consider-

the latter too was suffering from an uncontrollable aversion to the world, and seeking how he might bring about one last *coup de théâtre*. But in Rudolf's case the signs were much closer to those of manic depression and there were open hints that suicide might prove the only solution[1]— he seems to have made an attempt on his own life during the crisis of 1600.

*　*　*

It is impossible either to treat the problem of Rudolf's advisers as a self-contained subject or to analyse exhaustively his political entourage. The latter is a complete study in itself, though a fairly unrewarding one, because so confused; names recur almost haphazardly, and the nominal office is often small measure of the influence wielded. I shall try here only to follow through one thread: the Emperor's increasing acceptance of those who appeared independent, for the sake of that independence. He was driven into the hands of men who seemed to oppose large vested foreign interests, especially the Papacy and Spain, and thus with the collapse by 1600 of the traditional policy and its stabilizing force his activities began to lose all weight and consistency. There was perhaps always something of political naïvety in Rudolf's attitude to those around him, though he was far from blind to talent, either administrative, diplomatic, or legal.[2]

The most popular established view sees the Emperor as surrounded by a regiment of underlings—personal valets (*Kammerdiener*), orderlies, and so on, who alone were trusted and alone had regular adit to him; thus for example the famous social historian Janssen.[3] There is some substance in this, above all for the later period, but the distinction between 'servant' and 'official' is blurred, particularly if associated with lower-class and aristocratic origins respectively—some of the powers behind the throne fell into both categories (Rumpf and Barvitius for example). Its most important grain of truth is that Rudolf insisted on the complete obedience of all his ministers: thus they were all in that sense 'servants', and the ones best able to submit to his discipline were those who anyway had no higher aspirations. At the same time the charge of inaccessibility must be modified; some correspondents gave the impression that this was

ing on Charles V's mode of life at Yuste since the two nineteenth-century works: William Stirling (Stirling–Maxwell), *The Cloister Life of the Emperor Charles V* (London, 2nd edn. 1853), and W. Prescott's supplement to Robertson's *Life of Charles V* (London 1857 etc.).

[1] e.g. Nuncios/Ferreri, Prague 4 Apr. 1605.

[2] He was for instance continually concerned with recruiting suitable members for the Aulic Council; see O. von Gschliesser, *Der Reichshofrat* (Vienna 1942), 135–85, *passim*.

[3] J. Janssen, op. cit. v (Freiburg 1886), 242–4 (for the year 1603).

always the case, but it frequently displays only their own inability to gain the Emperor's ear.[1] Rudolf was often aware what kind of advice would be tendered by a certain ambassador or minister, and therefore calling them in audience could be a sign that his mind was already made up. The Jesuit Carrillo had months of waiting in 1597 before the Emperor would ratify a treaty with the Prince of Transylvania which appeared to serve the Habsburg interests well, but events soon proved that Rudolf's suspicions about Sigismund Báthory were not misplaced, nor his evident fears about the future of the Principality exaggerated.[2]

Rudolf's exalted code of majesty would brook no half measures, and he was always tortured by the threat of defection: witness the oath which he extorted from his general in Hungary, Basta.[3] No counsellor was immune from periods of disgrace; nor could any view with equanimity the prospect of the Emperor's displeasure, which was capable of extending to bodily assault.[4] His wrath and enduring rancour, when challenged, were sometimes unassuageable; there were several good instances of this, the best-known that of George (Popel) Lobkovic. Lobkovic was High Steward of Bohemia, a strong supporter of the Catholic religion, a magnate who possessed great power at court and growing connections with Rudolf. His attempts to strengthen that position still further by acquiring the office of Burgrave (made vacant in 1592 by the death of Vilém Rožmberk) finding no echo with the Emperor, he began to work on the Czech estates to insist on his appointment. The conspiracy was discovered before it could get out of hand; Rudolf committed Lobkovic to the dungeons of a royal prison and would hear of no mercy for him until he died there fourteen years later.[5] But this punishment was extreme, and matched the extreme insolence of the crime. Lesser examples of the same presumption could be expiated by thorough self-abasement.[6] Those purged by Rudolf on impulse often did not fall far; Želinský and Milner, the Protestants dismissed in 1599, were soon allowed to reappear

---

[1] This tendency is especially true of the Papal diplomats, and above all the shrewd and calculating nuncio Spinelli; it seems to vitiate some of the conclusions based on Spinelli by Karel Stloukal, op. cit.

[2] E. Veress, *Carrillo Alfonz levelezése és iratai (1591-1618)*, i (Budapest 1906), letters of Sept.–Dec. 1597 and *passim*.

[3] Nuncios/Ferreri, Prague 26 Sept. 1605.

[4] This happened with Rumpf in 1599 (see below), and is alleged on various other occasions. Cf. *Briefe und Akten*, viii. 431, 447 n. 3 (1610).

[5] See above, p. 36. There are also accounts of this affair in *Fuggerzeitungen*, Prague 19 Apr. 1594, and Tomek, op. cit. 353 ff. Lobkovic was involved as a royal creditor; cf. the letter from Rudolf to Lobkovic, 23 Sept. s.a., S.A. Třeboň, Historica 5581.

[6] As by Kinsky in 1586: *Fuggerzeitungen*, Prague 23 Dec. 1586; Tomek, op. cit. 329; Dačický, 248.

at court.[1] On other occasions he wavered hopelessly, and usually regretted it when he finally ordered severe measures—the execution of his favoured general Rusworm in 1605 was a notorious case.[2]

There were throughout the reign two parallel, but not mutually exclusive influences: on the one hand the high Czech aristocratic officials, on the other the Imperial civil servants, mostly (though not entirely) Germanic in their origins. Neither represented at the outset any decisive break with Maximilian; both were sharply interrupted during the crucial years 1599–1600; and the two tended to coalesce later during the mêlée of the last decade. It is simplest to consider separately the two groups of advisers.

At Rudolf's coronation in Prague in 1575 his crown was borne by Vilém, the forty-year-old 'ruler' of the house of Rožmberk.[3] The Rožmberks were the most powerful of that small band of Bohemian magnates who had sided continuously with the Habsburgs and had earned the trust of the dynasty. Next to them stood the Pernsteins from the east of the country, whose greatest figure was Vratislav, the Chancellor; then the lords of Hradec, the South Moravian Dietrichsteins, the Harrachs, and some members of the large family of Lobkovic.[4] It was to these men that Rudolf turned for advice in 1576, and whose influence was to be predominant during the first twenty years of the reign.

Their connections with the ruling family were close. Vilém was in intimate touch with Maximilian while being educated, and accompanied him to Spain in 1551; Philip II wrote to him on the accession of Rudolf urging him to be obedient and helpful to the new monarch.[5] Pernstein knew Maximilian as early as 1545, when he was only fifteen, and then in Spain during the years 1547–50; his Spanish marriage fitted into a pattern of courtly manners and in 1566 he became Chancellor of Bohemia.[6]

[1] Stloukal, *Papežská politika*, 192 ff.; Borovička, *Počátky kancléřování*, 439 and *passim*.
[2] Dačický 296 f. On Rusworm: A. Stauffer, *Hermann Christoph Graf von Rusworm* (Munich 1884); cf. the memoirs of Bassompierre, who was in Prague in 1604: *Mémoires du Mareschal de Bassompierre . . .* (Cologne 1665), i. 88 f. There is a literary account of his end in Huch, op. cit. 49–81, and a novel about him by Miloš Kratochvíl, *Osamělý Rváč* (Prague 1955).
[3] 'Vilém, vladař domu Rožmberského'—this was his official title. The ceremony is recorded in the 'Historie o Korunowání Rudolfa druhýho', S.A. Třeboň, Historica 4930.
[4] The Lobkovic were a very complicated family: one branch (the Hasišteinský) was Protestant; the most important politically (and the one which later became princely) was that of the Popel z Lobkovic, centred on Roudnice, north of Prague, yet even it was 'decentralized' enough to survive the fall of Jiří Popel and prevent his estates falling to the crown. See, in general, Constantin von Wurzbach, *Biographisches Lexikon . . .* xv (Vienna 1866), 310 ff.
[5] Madrid 2 Dec. 1576; S.A. Třeboň, Historica 4975; Březan, 25 ff. and *passim*.
[6] Z. Kalista, *Čechové, kteří tvořili dějiny světa* (Prague 1939), 33 ff.

Jáchym of Hradec, brother-in-law to Rožmberk, was also a great favour-
ite of the Habsburgs. He was accidentally drowned returning from
Vienna to his estates over the Czech border one day in 1565, but his son
Adam (II)—despite heavy drunkenness and a chronic tabetic condition
—enjoyed Rudolf's confidence; he was created Chancellor in 1585 after
Pernstein's death and Burgrave in 1592.[1]

They also had their part in the mystique; at two grand ceremonies in
1585 Rožmberk and Linhart von Harrach, together with Rudolf, Ernst,
and Charles of Styria, received the Golden Fleece, the highest accolade
of Habsburg chivalry. The formalities by which the magnates were
invested differed marginally, but significantly, from those for the Archdukes the previous day; thus they were at once associated with, and
subordinated to the traditions of the dynasty.[2] Their own receptions
were also expansive in the last degree. When Rožmberk married Polyxena, the daughter of Pernstein, as his fourth wife in 1587, it was like a
wedding of royalty, and was indeed attended by Rudolf.[3] The Emperor
and other heads of state regularly visited the Rožmberk capital of Krumlov and Vilém had sets of coins minted, ducats with the legend: Guliel.
Guber. Dom. Rosenberg.[4] Attempts were of course made to intrigue
against him at court, especially through his notorious associations with
alchemists, but this of all things was least likely to succeed; it was no
doubt the closest spiritual bond between him and the Emperor. The
funerals of Vilém in 1592 and Adam of Hradec in 1596 (the others lay
already in their graves: Pernstein in 1582, Dietrichstein in 1590, Harrach
in 1591) were grandiose affairs of state, and made a deep impression on
contemporaries.[5]

With them passed also a spirit of moderation which was not to be seen
again. These families were all convinced Catholics and supporters of the
Jesuits, but their faith, however firm, was not disruptively militant. The
Protestant Dačický observed on Rožmberk's death: 'This lord, although
he was of the Roman religion, judged no other man's faith, and left him
to exercise it in freedom and peace; his symbol was *festina lente*.'[6] Their

---

[1] Kavka, *Zlatý věk růží*, 84 ff., 136 ff.

[2] (Paul Zehendtner von Zehendtgrub): *Ordentliche Beschreibung mit was stattlichen
Ceremonien und Zierlichkeiten die Röm. Kay. May . . . den Orden dess Gulden Fluss in
disem 85 Jahr zu Prag . . . empfangen* (Dillingen 1587). Cf. ÖN, Cod. 7906 [Plate 15a];
Březan, 150; Bydžovsky, fo. 146ʳ; Tomek, op. cit. 324 f.

[3] *Fuggerzeitungen*, Prague 22 Jan. 1587, with a description of the feast.

[4] Březan, 140 f., 146, 151.   [5] e.g. Bydžovský, fos. 234ʳ–235ᵛ; Dačický, 276.

[6] Dačický, 264. Cf. the testimony of Vilém's librarian Březan, who was himself a
Protestant: 'And thus this lord of holy and blessed memory, although practising the
Roman religion from his youth . . . nevertheless never harmed the Evangelicals, but
loved them along with the rest and employed them equally.' Březan, 170 f.

mood was compromising, and also at times overtly fatalistic. In 1574, as the dispute over religion in the *sněm* was reaching a climax, Pernstein wrote to Rožmberk:

Although I cannot take it amiss that they [the supporters of the Augsburg confession] should be zealous and watchful of their affairs, I know it to be a great necessity that we should follow their example and do the same, and that we Catholics, albeit only a small handful, consider in time how to present our own case, so that our Catholic religion should not be further reduced and oppressed, and all of us in this kingdom may be able to live together in love and harmony.

Rožmberk's reply is symptomatic: '. . . That it has come to such a reduction in the number of Catholics in this kingdom is the result of the righteous judgement and wrath of the Lord God for our sins and wickedness; in my opinion it is we and not the Evangelicals who are to blame.'[1]

With this went a strong feeling for legality and inherited tradition, and there is a link here with Karel Žerotín, the leading Moravian magnate, who though in little personal contact with Rudolf—and that little was largely negative—possessed the same sense of historic right. Žerotín exhibited too the same ultimate fatalism: although the most influential member of the Brethren he took no part in the events of 1618–20.[2] The Rožmberks sought increasingly during the sixteenth century to prove their descent from the Roman Orsini (this parallels the far-fetched genealogies of the Habsburgs), while Vilém was engaged in a long dispute —ultimately successful—with the princes of Plauen over which of them took precedence in the Kingdom of Bohemia.[3]

Such identification with the feudal fabric of the country went deeper. The Rožmberks were not narrowly Czech: Vilém's first three marriages were all into ruling German families, the last of them said to have been arranged by Rudolf himself;[4] but they pursued essentially a policy of national solidarity under Habsburg leadership, and that was the aim of their diplomacy, especially of Pernstein, in the Polish question.[5] Not

---

[1] '. . . Že jest pak k takovému zmenšení počet katolických přišel v tomto království, z spravedlivého soudu a rozhněvání pána boha pro hříchy a nepravosti naše to jest se stalo, a takové zmenšení nás a utištění ne konfessionistům příčísti můžeme dle zdání mého.' Ibid. 128 f. (Pernstein's letter of 9 July 1574).

[2] Odložilík, *Karel ze Žerotína*, and see below, pp. 143–5.

[3] B. Rynášová, 'Kdy vznikla fikce o italském původu Vítkovců' in *Sborník prací věnovaných . . . Friedrichovi*, 369–73; Březan, 39 ff., 66 ff. The house of Plauen claimed pride of place by virtue of its Imperial title.

[4] Kavka, *Zlatý věk růží*, 119. For the German 'contamination' of the Rožmberks see Klik, op. cit. 321–3.

[5] Cf. Kalista, op. cit. 41 f.

that they were devoted to their king—the latter could easily make enemies of those who stood closest to him in spirit, and this was never clearer than with the Rožmberks. Rudolf and Peter Vok, the brother of Vilém and last ruler of the house, lived for years in mutual suspicion, yet the two men were of similar temper: eccentric, cultured, mysterious, easily misguided, and in the last resort pathetic. In 1612 the one was to be buried within a few weeks of the other.

The crucial breakthrough in the Bohemian hierarchy came at the turn of the century with the Curial intrigues of Filippo Spinelli. This very capable nuncio succeeded in so working on the Emperor's disposition that he brought him to a positive and uncharacteristically thorough change of course. During the late 1590s, while the Chancellorship was vacant or occupied by fainéant aristocrats, power had become increasingly concentrated in the hands of the Protestant Vice-Chancellor Jan Želinský and his secretary Jan Milner von Mühlhausen (Myllner z Mylhauzu). Both these men were educated and intelligent, and Želinský in particular had managed to win Rudolf's complete confidence through his independent anti-Papal attitude.[1] But on 24 August 1599—the anniversary of St. Bartholomew's!—both were peremptorily dismissed in a regular purge of reliable advisers and confidants which even included the learned Ferdinand Hofmann, President of the Exchequer (*Hofkammer*) for twenty years, loyal servant of the Habsburgs and important link between the Imperial and Bohemian administrations. In their stead came young dogmatic Counter-Reformers, above all Zdeněk Lobkovic, who was appointed Chancellor, and his deputy Jindřich of Písnice, a prototype of the seventeenth-century *arriviste*.[2] The parallel development in Moravia was the election of the militant young František Dietrichstein as Bishop of Olomouc and the attacks which began to be launched on Žerotín.[3]

How do we account for this decisive move of Rudolf towards the Catholic camp? Certainly the new appointments seem to have cheered him up after a period of depression.[4] Stloukal treats it as brilliant diplomacy by Spinelli and leaves unanswered how he was so successful in

---

[1] J. Borovička, 'Pád Želinského', *ČČH* xxviii (1922), 277–304, esp. 284: 'The secret of his influence seems to be explicable in part because he could associate the interests of the Protestants with a buttressing of royal power, which saw in the . . . latest Papal conceptions a limiting of sovereign rights.'

[2] On Písnice and his unscrupulous career see K. Stloukal, 'Jindřich z Písnice', in *Sborník prací věnovaných . . . Novákovi*, 363–80. On Hofmann see below, pp. 153 f.

[3] Odložilík, op. cit., 95–104; cf. below, p. 112.

[4] 'Sa. Caesa Mᵗᵃˢ hilarior multo in hoc itinere quam toto anno Pragaᵉ fuerit, nobis id laetitia(m) spemq. maiore(m) praebet.' Barvitius to Zdeněk Lobkovic, 12 Sept. 1599, marginal note to a letter in German. LRRK, B 209.

persuading Rudolf; others have been driven to suggesting that the nuncio possessed hypnotic powers.[1] It seems to me that a larger explanation is needed: Rudolf was definitely impressed, at least initially, by the force of ideas of the new faction, and perhaps expected from it some dynamic activity to restore his failing authority. It guided his policy fully during the next three years, and in 1602 the Mandate against the Czech Brethren was renewed with fine medieval pageantry to a flourish of trumpets, the high-water mark of Catholicism before 1618, as the Letter of Majesty was to be for the Protestants.[2] These years saw also the hardening of Counter-Reformation censorship controls and the impulse to a new, Jesuit-led Catholic militancy in Upper Hungary which soon provoked the rebellion of István Bocskay.[3]

The men who had now come to power formed what contemporaries called the Spanish party, the 'facción española' or 'Španihelé'.[4] Undoubtedly some of the Spanish elements in their background appealed to the Emperor; but it is important to note that, despite a commonly held view, the group was never by any means all-powerful.[5] Its leader was Lobkovic, a politician of wide interests, strong beliefs, and powerful intellect.[6] His absolutist convictions stemmed at least as much from intellectual dissatisfaction with existing forms of government as from any calculation of personal advantage. Yet when the Catholic autocracy which these men envisaged actually became the order of the day, after 1620, each of them found himself disenchanted: Lobkovic no less than his principal supporters Martinic, Slavata, and Dietrichstein.[7] Rudolf had not, even in 1599, committed himself to it at all unreservedly.

[1] Stloukal, *Papežská politika*, 153–95 for details of the campaign; Schwarzenfeld, op. cit. 154 ff., mostly following Stloukal.

[2] Slavata, 40 ff.; Denis, op. cit. 572. Cf. Žerotín's comment to Heinrich von Eberbach: 'Le bruit commun est que l'empereur y a esté forcé partie par prommesses partie par menaces, et n'y a rien de plus certain comme qu'il a esté fort longtemps a s'y résouldre; enfin on l'y a faict condescendre, si qu'il en a signé sept, lesquels ont esté publiés à son de trompettes et tabourin par la ville de Prague.' Rosice 30 Sept. 1602, in *Dopisy Karla st. z Žerotína 1591–1610*, ed. F. Dvorský (Prague 1904), No. 555.

[3] A. Škárka, 'Ze zápasů nekatolického tisku s protireformací', *ČČH* xlii (1936), 1–55, 286–322, 484–520. For Hungary see B. Hóman and G. Szekfű, *Magyar Történet* iii (Budapest 1935), 357 ff.

[4] Slavata observes that they received this name at the time. Cf. J. Dvorský, 'Španělská Strana v Čechách na počátku 17. století' (Diss. Prague 1960), 4 f.

[5] For the extreme view see (e.g.) J. Lenz, *Kulturní styky českošpanělské v zrcadle dějin* (Prague 1930), 5. The moderate opinion is expressed by Borovička, *Počátky kancléřování*, 444 f.

[6] The only biographical sketch (very brief) is by Kalista, *Čechové*, 71–81. Cf. below, pp. 286–8.

[7] For Lobkovic see Kalista, op. cit. 79–81; for Martinic, Dvorský, diss. cit., 77 ff. and some sad letters in LRRK, B 214. Slavata seems always to have put a certain 'Czechdom' before complete foreign authoritarianism; cf. F. Rachlík, 'Slavatův

In fact the Catholic aristocrat who appears to have wielded most single influence with the Emperor during these years was the Moravian Karl von Liechtenstein, a convert and opportunist with great financial acumen. This expertise undoubtedly endeared him to the sovereign, who also treated with him over certain works of art, but it was probably more than anything else Liechtenstein's ability to seem independent which gained him Rudolf's ear at crucial times.[1] By refusing to be associated with narrowly Papal or Spanish policies he became trusted by Rudolf, who granted him various Church lands in South Moravia to the intense annoyance of Dietrichstein and the Curia, yet at the same time he was always *persona non grata* with the Protestants.[2] The Emperor even sought from him a memorandum on the reform of court administration, which brought forth a document—unique for the period—of a strongly regalistic bias.[3]

Meanwhile Rudolf soon grew disillusioned with his new orientation and recoiled from the orthodox Catholic position so sharply that its whole success was thrown in jeopardy. Only his hated brother Matthias's alliance with the Protestant estates of Hungary, Austria, and Moravia during 1606–8 made him still respond—with bad grace—to the promptings of the Pope and his indefatigable nuncios Ferreri (1604–6) and Caetano (1607–11), the successors of Spinelli. Eventually in July 1609 the Emperor was forced to grant sweeping concessions to the Bohemian Protestants by the celebrated Letter of Majesty, a document which did more violence to his sense of sovereignty than his religious scruples. Lobkovic—characteristically—refused to sign it at all;[4] Liechtenstein—equally characteristically—had already sided with Matthias.

pokus o nezávislost české komory na komoře dvorské z roku 1614', in *Sborník prací věnovaných . . . Novákovi*, 468–85; J. V. Polišenský, 'Viléma Slavaty relace o jednání v příčině knížetství opavského 1614–15', *Slezský Sborník* 51 (11) (1953), 488–98. He was anyway a man of increasingly strange, spiritualist cast of mind: cf. Schwarz, op. cit. 343–7. For Dietrichstein see F. Hrubý, 'První pokusy císaře Ferdinand II o změnu moravské ústavy po Bílé Hoře', in *Sborník prací věnovaných . . . Friedrichovi*, 137–45.

[1] K. Stloukal, 'Karel z Liechtenstein a jeho účast ve vládě Rudolfa II', *ČČH* xviii (1912), 21–37, 153–69, 389–434, esp. 160 ff.; J. Falke, *Geschichte des fürstlichen Hauses Liechtenstein* (Vienna 1877), ii. 127 ff. Liechtenstein lent a large sum of money to Rudolf in 1602: SÚA, Kammer Schulden Buch Sig. 2377, f. 37r; cf. Falke, 138 ff. The Emperor had earlier acquired from him certain *objets d'art* and a book: *Jahrbuch* vii (1888), Reg. Nos. 4621, 4626–8.

[2] Cf. Ansbach's relation of 1601 (Ranke) where he is said to be in league with Maria Manriquez de Lara. On Liechtenstein's long dispute with Rome over the Abbey of Velehrad see Nuncios/Caetano, Prague 7, 16, 23 July 1607, etc.; *Briefe und Akten* v. 548 f. and n.

[3] It is printed in Fellner, op. cit. ii. 368–71; cf. Stloukal, art. cit. above, 389–98.

[4] Gindely, *Rudolf II*, i. 351 f. For the detailed course of events which led to the

The same picture of an old order surviving until 1600, then giving way to increasing confusion is conveyed by the more narrowly Imperial organs of government in Prague. In the first years of the reign the most important court officials were for the greater part older men of pronounced international background, with no strong confessional commitment. Senior among them stood the Imperial Vice-Chancellor Sigmund Viehäuser, Jakob Kurz who succeeded him in that office, and the President of the Privy Council Jan Trautson.[1] But as these persons died (Viehäuser in 1587, Trautson in 1590, Kurz in 1594) real power became centred increasingly on two ministers: Wolfgang Rumpf and the younger Trautson, Paul Sixt. It was the infamous Rumpf—a man by no means so menial, so evil, or so uncultured as he is often portrayed—who was the true *éminence grise*. Through his post of Chamberlain, then High Steward and President of the Privy Council, he came to control most important decisions. As Contarini put it in 1596: 'Al maggiordomo sono aperti tutti i secreti, in mano sua sono tutti i negozi, da lui sono date le udienze, a lui s'indirizzano gli ambasciatori, per mezzo suo si fanno le grazie, a sua instanza si ottiene giustizia. . .'[2] And yet, he continues significantly, 'quello che apporta meraviglia è che l'Imperatore mostra non esser contento di lui'.

Although it became an open secret that Rudolf was not always satisfied with this most ubiquitous of all his advisers, there was nevertheless profound shock when, during a fit of uncontrollable rage in September 1600, he banished both Rumpf and Trautson forever from his court.[3] The causes of this traumatic outburst have never been fully clear, but it seems that Rumpf's close liaison with Spain—he may have been working behind the Emperor's back for several years—together with his pressure for a decision about the succession finally brought the inevitable explosion. The whole episode was accompanied by the most

Majestát see idem, *Geschichte der Ertheilung des böhmischen Majestätsbriefes von 1609* (Prague 1868).

[1] There in fact developed something of a family tradition within the Vice-Chancellorship: Kurz and his immediate successor Freymon were both sons-in-law of Viehäuser's predecessor Weber, and another of Kurz's relatives held the office in the early seventeenth century. All stood very close to the ruling house, though they held their position nominally by the favour of the Elector of Mainz. See L. Gross, *Geschichte der deutschen Reichshofkanzlei* (Vienna 1933), 317 ff.

[2] Alberi, *Relazioni*, i. 6, 248; cf. Schwarz, op. cit. 329 f., and Khevenhüller, *Annales*, ii, 346 f. etc. A catalogue of Rumpf's library, prepared in 1583 and added to in the years succeeding, lists over 1,000 volumes in all fields of learning, with a particularly rich assortment of printed and manuscript music. ÖN, MS. 15286, esp. Nos. 775 seqq.

[3] There is a graphic description in Stloukal, *Portrét*, who hints (with some exaggeration) at the homicidal tendencies underlying the outburst.

severe bout of melancholy which Rudolf ever experienced.[1] His crisis
was one of jealousy, frustration, and religious incertitude, the culmination of a long period of desperate disappointment and superstitious fears
and a sudden revulsion against those who had brought him to it. The
relation of Rudolf to his ministers was one which surprised contemporaries. He was basically a lonely sovereign clinging to counsellors whose
support for him was often more imagined than real, a situation aggravated by the Emperor's ever growing dislike for formal meetings of his
legally constituted advisory bodies. In this way he was easily manipu-
lated by the unscrupulous, but equally their downfall might be very
precipitate. Contarini observes how he could be used: 'I ministri nutri-
scono questa disposizione in Sua Maestà perchè di tal maniera non ha
altre informazione delle cose se non quella che gli vogliono dare.'[2] At
the same time the Venetian was amazed how Rudolf could abuse his
ministers publicly, yet seemed unable to dismiss them.

In this case the change was for the worse. With the departure of Rumpf
and the Marshal Trautson the court administration sank into further
confusion: Liechtenstein became High Steward, after him Friedrich von
Fürstenberg and the weak, but highly favoured Landgrave of Leuchtenberg.[3] Rudolf retired still further from the world; even the venerable
and trusted Spanish ambassador San Clemente did not set eyes on him
for two years, while widespread popular suspicions that the Emperor
had in fact died were not easy to allay.[4] Now the power of underlings
grew more pronounced—men about whom no good could be said by
contemporaries and little by historians. The first were Makofsky and
Franck, then the evil genius Philipp Lang, who was said to have received all correspondence to the Emperor, even from Archdukes or
Electors, and to have controlled all civil and military appointments until
his trial and fall in 1608–9.[5] Certainly it is attested that he recommended

---

[1] Rumpf's Spanish connection is argued for 1592–4 by Matoušek, *Turecká Válka*,
218 ff. and *passim*. Contrast the judgement of Stieve, *Verhandlungen*, 47 ff. and
Briefe und Akten, v. 475 and n., who ascribes the dismissal rather to jealousy
and general dissatisfaction with his handling of affairs. Cf. Ansbach's first relation
(Ranke).

[2] Alberi, *Relazioni*, i. 6, 244. He also notes shrewdly that the Emperor's inaccessibility is only increased by ministers who wish to keep him under their own influence.

[3] Leuchtenberg was President of the *Reichshofrat* (with some intermission) and
Privy Councillor from 1594 till 1609, then *Obersthofmeister* between 1609 and 1611.
The reasons for his high preferment are not altogether clear; cf. Gschliesser, op. cit.
159–65; Schwarz, op. cit. 277–9.

[4] Nuncios/Caetano (Pars III, 2, No. 127): letter of Cardinal Johannes Millinus,
Prague 11 Aug. 1608; *Briefe und Akten*, vi. 94, 401.

[5] F. Hurter, *Philipp Lang, Kammerdiener Rudolfs II, eine Criminal-Geschichte aus
dem Anfang des 17. Jahrhunderts* (Schaffhausen 1851), 27–37, 52–5, etc. Hurter's book

Tilly for the post of field-marshal.[1] After Lang there were others, especially the Silesian Andreas Hannewaldt and the scheming son-in-law of Tycho Brahe, Franz Tengnagel, both agents in the wild plans for the recovery of his lands in which Rudolf was encouraged by his ambitious young cousin Leopold.[2] These intrigues hastened the final catastrophe of early 1611; even then some creatures of the ailing Emperor maintained a shadowy exercise of influence: Martin Hasdal and Kaspar Rutzky, the small-time artists Fröschl and Marquard. Deprived of their protector such servants were powerless: within hours of Rudolf's death several found themselves in detention at the behest of vengeful superiors.[3]

Yet there is still important evidence of 'middle-men', bridging the gap between Rudolf's withdrawn life among his artists and alchemists and his unquenched desire to realize himself in political activity. Foremost among them were two who stood with the Emperor till the very end and were leading patrons of the Prague literary world: Duke Heinrich Julius of Brunswick and Johann Barvitius.[4] Brunswick had originally travelled to Bohemia in an attempt to establish his Protestant claim to the secularized bishopric of Halberstadt, but he became a firm and intimate friend of the Emperor—the last President of his decayed Privy Council—and undertook for him the sordid negotiations surrounding the Passau troops in 1610 and 1611. He built himself a fine house near the castle, and died there only a short while after his sovereign, in 1613.[5] Barvitius, a lawyer of Dutch clerical background,[6] was generally regarded as the closest, and certainly the most permanent, of Rudolf's advisers; he managed always to steer an independent course and favoured the party which Rudolf thought most reliable at the time, though he no doubt drew a Spanish pension too.[7] There were also others: the

is rather wild, but is based on the authentic accounts of Lang's trial, including the questions put to him under torture. (They are in HHSA, Langakten.)

[1] Nuncios/Ferreri, Prague 5 Sept. 1605. Ferreri's statements however sometimes need a slightly cautious interpretation.

[2] Gindely, *Rudolf II*, ii. 38 ff., 55–62, and *passim*. On Hannewaldt's role see Gross, op. cit. 375–8, Schwarz, op. cit. 237–9, and many references in *Briefe und Akten*, *passim*.   [3] *Briefe und Akten*, x, No. 89, 245 n. 5.

[4] On Rudolf's last companions see Gindely, op. cit. ii. 257–8, 310 ff. Brunswick was the patron of men like Hans von Aachen, Adriaen de Vries, and Salamon Frenzelius (cf. below, pp. 148 f., 169 and Larsson, op. cit. 44 f.); Barvitius, of a series of local poets (*Rukověť* (see below, p. 147 n. 1) s.v.).

[5] Gindely, *Rudolf II*, ii. 100 ff., 171 ff.; Dačický, 331; L. Beutin, *Hanse und Reich im handelspolitischen Endkampf gegen England* (Berlin 1929), 65 ff.; *Briefe und Akten*, ix, Nos. 152, 246 and *passim*.

[6] Ansbach calls him 'secretarius, eines tumpfaffen (Dompfaff, i.e. canon) son von Utrecht' (second report from Prague 1601, in Ranke).

[7] Nuncios/Ferreri on Barvitius, Prague 18 Apr. 1605, 5 Jan. 1606. He was associated with Kurz (Matoušek, op. cit. 43 f.) and with Liechtenstein (Stloukal, *Karel z*

mysterious Christoph Lobkovic, variously claimed as a supporter of
Spinelli and a man of Lutheran sentiment, but who was heavily involved
with the Emperor financially and whose intellectual connection with him
seems to have been considerable;[1] the moderate and non-confessional
Rudolf Coraduz, Imperial Vice-Chancellor after the death of Kurz;
Ernst von Mollart, and Wolf Unverzagt, the President of the Aulic
Council.[2] Others more exclusively associated with Rudolf's cultural life
were Matthias Wacker von Wackenfels, Krištof Harant of Polžice,
even Bartholomaeus Spranger, Hans von Aachen, or Johann Kepler.

We must above all not forget how for Rudolf life contained no simple
compartments of business and leisure, or work and play. Although the
lesser servants at the court were acceptable largely because they mirrored
the political whims of the Emperor, many had qualities which Rudolf,
in his isolation, was able to appreciate. Even his orderlies would possess
some gift which he prized: 'Der ander, Franck, ist ein frummer, erlicher
man, und dem Kaiser auch ser angenem, weiln er schöne künst kan, und
sonderlichen die Bemischen edelgestein rein zu machen, das sie den
Orientalischen nicht sehen ungleich.'[3] For him the worlds of art and
of everyday life were inseparable; nor did his commissions to those who
served him draw a fast line between practical and ideal politics.

*   *   *

Rudolfine Prague was in many respects the most cosmopolitan city
in Europe. Politically it attracted great attention, the more so because
the Emperor's own unwillingness to travel meant that a direct approach
to him was necessary on the part of foreign powers, while the Habsburgs
themselves maintained a surprisingly limited diplomatic service abroad:
they had permanent representives only in Madrid, Rome, Constantinople, Venice, and sometimes in Paris.[4] The Papal, Venetian, and Spanish

Liechtenstein, 398); cf. Schwarz, op. cit. 202–4, and Gross, op. cit. 414–18. Barvitius
was mainly responsible for the letters reproduced in Divi Rudolphi . . . Epistolae.

[1] Stloukal, Papežská politika, 174 ff.; Gindely, Böhmische Brüder, 330 ff.; Borovička,
Pád Želinského, 286, 288; SÚA, Kammer Schulden Buch Sig. 2377, fo. 42ʳ; K. Chytil,
Der Prager Venusbrunnen von B. Wurzelbauer (Prague 1902), 10 ff.; Khevenhüller,
Conterfet Kupfferstich, ii (Leipzig 1722), 402. Lobkovic had been with Rudolf in Spain.

[2] Coraduz was thought by the nuncio to favour toleration: Nuncios/Ferreri, Prague
7 Feb. 1605, cf. 20 Dec. 1604; Briefe und Akten, v. 727 n. 3; cf. Gross, op. cit. 322–6.
Mollart seems also to have spoken for sincere religious compromise (cf. Schwarz, op.
cit. s.v.). Unverzagt appears frequently as a close confidant of the Emperor: an obligation
to him for (allegedly) 50,000 ducats from Rudolf ended its life as a polishing rag in one of
Austria's aristocratic households! (J. N. Wilczek, Happy Retrospect (London 1934),
22 f.).

[3] Ansbach, loc. cit.

[4] Matoušek, op. cit. 49 ff. The effective ambassador in Paris until his death in 1592
was the botanist Busbecq; see below, p. 121.

spokesmen in Prague were persons of the first consequence. Enough has already been said of the nuncios, but the Spanish ambassador understandably wielded immense influence—it was only the moderation and ingrained pessimism of the long-time holder of this post, Don Guillén de San Clemente, which avoided a complete rupture with Rudolf—and the Venetians were a focus for various shades of dissident Catholic opinion. In addition to frequent missions from all parts of the Empire, and from Northern Italy, particularly Tuscany and Mantua, there were also French residents (notably Henry IV's envoy, Guillaume Ancel) or embassies extraordinary,[1] and less overt diplomatic activity on behalf of Elizabeth of England. The latter ranged from official policy discussions, like the visit of Christopher Parkins in 1593 or later Stephen Lesieur as representative of the Merchant Adventurers, to thoroughly secretive intrigue, both for and against the Queen.[2]

The most pressing question, however, was still the Turkish menace. The Ottoman Empire after the death of Suleiman the Magnificent and the battle of Lepanto must not be underrated through the easy wisdom of hindsight. Towards the end of the sixteenth century it was entering on a new period of belligerence, spurred on apparently by astrological omens among other things. The deadlock in the Mediterranean and the truce with the Persians concluded in 1590 allowed it to begin its first protracted assault on the Hungarian front for half a century. The fifteen-year war which followed (1591–1606) occupies an insignificant place in Western historiography,[3] but it was very important for Central Europe, and anyway should not be judged only by its consequences, which were indeed small as regards territorial readjustment.

The role of the renewed Turkish offensive as an ideological stimulus was very large, and its effect on public opinion in the Habsburg lands was immediate. The time-honoured bell-ringing and prayers for deliverance were ordered.[4] Popular interest in the Porte, its fearsome strength

---

[1] K. Stloukal, 'Z diplomatických styků mezi Francií a Čechy před Bílou Horou', ČČH xxxii (1926), 473–96, a useful summary. Ancel was in Prague from 1576 to 1592 and from 1599 to 1602, and regarded as very sinister by the nuncio: Nuncios/Caetano, Prague 30 July 1591. For the embassy of Boisdauphin in 1600 see Babeau, art. cit. There were also other agents who settled in Prague, like Desiderio Labbe; on him see J. Dostál in *Sborník prací věnovaných . . . Friedrichovi*, 93–103.

[2] O. Odložilík, 'Cesty z Čech a Moravy do Velké Británie v letech 1563–1620', ČMM 59 (1935), 268 f. and n., 290 f., 297 f., and—in general—241–320 *passim*; J. V. Polišenský, *Anglie a Bílá Hora* (Prague 1949), 42–4, 49–51; Beutin, op. cit., *passim*.

[3] No adequate treatment exists of this war in its European context. A. Loebl, *Zur Geschichte des Türkenkrieges von 1593–1606*, i–ii (Prague 1899, 1904), is a fragment. Cf. J. von Hammer, *Geschichte des Osmanischen Reichs* iv (Pest 1829), for the Ottoman background.

[4] e.g. SČ viii, 14 Jan. 1594 (444–6); ix, 1 June 1596 (291 f.).

and ungodly polity, was served by a great number of writings on all
levels, from the most scabrous news-sheets to sophisticated refutations of
Islam, but the characteristic of almost all of them was strong propaganda
in favour of the house of Habsburg.[1] The efforts of the pamphleteers
coincided with those of the government in their search for a common
anti-Turkish front, whose natural leader was the Emperor in Prague.
For all its dissensions Western Europe was not yet deaf to the claims of
Christendom as a supranational power, and the Holy Roman Empire
could still be persuaded by an energetic financier like the Protestant
Pfennigmeister Zacharias Geizkofler to pay its traditional contribution
towards the cost of a crippingly expensive war.[2] But the countries of the
East were equally important and this was reflected in the contacts between Prague and its potential allies in that direction.[3] Relations with
Poland were close, and it was the pro-Habsburg party there, centred on
the large and influential Zborowski family, which was most insistent on
the need for a new crusade.[4] With the collapse of this faction after 1589,
several of those exiled found new scope for their endeavour in the Czech
lands, among them the indefatigable propagandist and genealogist
Bartolomej Paprocki.[5] Moscow too was becoming better known, though
still little understood; it was Russian policy to humour the Habsburgs
in the hope of a strong offensive against their common enemy the infidel,
and they sent several colourful embassies to Prague, notably that of 1595.
Rudolf responded with the missions to Moscow of Warkotsch in the
early 1590s, Dohna in 1597, and Logau in 1604.[6]

---

[1] J. Polišenský and J. Hrubeš, 'Turecké války, Uherská povstání a veřejné
mínění předbělohorských Čech', *Historický Časopis* vii (1959), 74–104, esp. 96 ff.;
R. J. W. Evans, 'Bohemia, the Emperor and the Porte, 1550–1600', *Oxford Slavonic
Papers*, N.S. iii (1970), 85–106. Cf.—on the pamphlets—K. M. Kertbeny, *A magyar
nemzeti és nemzetközi irodalom könyvészete I: Magyarországra vonatkozó régi német
nyomtatványok* (Budapest 1880).

[2] Cf. F. L. Baumer, 'England, the Turk, and the Common Corps of Christendom'
American Historical Review 50 (1944–5), 26–48; J. Müller, 'Die Verdienste Zacharias
Geizkoflers um die Beschaffung der Geldmittel für den Türkenkrieg Rudolfs II',
MIÖG xxi (1900), 251–304. Geizkofler was assisted by the rising banker Lazarus
Henckel, an Upper Hungarian settled in Vienna; see J. Kallbrunner, 'Lazarus Henckel von
Donnersmarck', *Vierteljahrschrift für Sozial- und Wirtschaftsgeschichte* 24 (1931), 142–56.

[3] There is much more in Bydžovský and other chroniclers on the Turks, Poles,
Russians, and Persians than on simultaneous developments in the West.

[4] These close Czech–Polish contacts are studied by J. Macůrek, *Čechové a Poláci v
druhé polovině XVI století* (Prague 1948), esp. 5–21.

[5] K. Krejčí, *Bartoloměj Paprocki z Hlohol a Paprocké Vůle* (Prague 1946), 49 ff.

[6] Bydžovský, fos. 402 ff.; Tomek, op. cit. 376 f.; Matoušek, op. cit. 244; *Iter Persicum*
(see below, p. 77 n. 5), 71 ff.; cf. Leitsch, op. cit. Ch. 2; H. Übersberger, *Österreich und
Russland seit dem Ende des 15 Jahrhunderts*, i (Vienna 1906), 471–576. On these political
approaches to Moscow and the level of information about the Muscovites cf. also A. V.
Florovski, *Chekhy i Vostochnie Slavyane* (Prague 1947), ii. 357 ff.

To these links were added the grand designs of a series of adventurers mainly from Greek Christendom, who through the century sought to interest Vienna and Prague in the reconquest of the Balkan lands by means of their own, and the Habsburgs' charisma. Best known of them were Jakob Basilikos, the Serb Demetrios, and the heretic Dominican James Palaeologus who became a familiar figure in Prague during the 1560s and had contact with Maximilian II and the Zborowskis; but there were a number of others answering more to the description of professional charlatan.[1] The most extraordinary schemes of all, and those most calculated to attract the fancy of Rudolf, were associated with Shah Abbas of Persia, and his emissary to the West, the wayward Englishman Anthony Sherley.

The original grandiose plan, apparently hatched in the Shah's court, envisaged a European coalition headed by the Emperor which should unite with Persia in a crushing attack on Turkey from two fronts; this was the project brought by Sherley in his spectacular mission of 1600.[2] The embassy reached Prague in October of that year and was greeted with unprecedented ceremonial and enthusiasm by Rudolf, although it occurred during his period of supposedly extreme mental depression following the dismissal of Rumpf.[3] Sherley was certainly an adventurer, and some have interpreted him as motivated solely by mercenary considerations, either his own or those of trading concessions for Elizabethan England. However that may be, his religion, seemingly a kind of wavering Catholicism,[4] answered Rudolf's mood, and the Emperor gave the project his full blessing. He promptly dispatched a return mission via Moscow to the Shah in 1602, led by a loyal Hungarian from Transylvania, István Kakas of Zalánkemény. This enterprise was frustrated since Kakas died before arriving in Ispahan, and his second-in-command Tectander was left to complete the journey and report on it in Prague.[5]

---

[1] e.g. Nuncios/Puteo, Prague 6 Sept. 1588. On Basilikos and Palaeologus see below pp. 108 f.

[2] For the background see Boise Penrose, *The Sherleian Odyssey* (Taunton 1938), 65 ff.; K. Stloukal, 'Projekt mezinárodní ligy všeevropské s Persií z konce XVI. století' in *Z dějin východní Evropy a Slovanstva (Sborník věnovaný J. Bidlovi)* (Prague 1928), 147–55.

[3] Rumpf was banished on 28 Sept.; the Embassy arrived on 20 Oct. For its reception see Franz Babinger, *Sherleiana* (Berlin 1932), 18–22; its cultural importance: O. Kurz, 'Umělecké vztahy mezi Prahou a Persií za Rudolfa II.', *Umění* xiv (1966), 461–87. Cf. also the chronicle of one of the envoys, *Relaciones de Don Juan de Persia* (Valladolid 1604), esp. 148ʳ–152ʳ.

[4] According to the Jesuit Parsons he finally became a convert in Rome: Penrose, op. cit. 110.

[5] Georg Tectander von der Jabel's relation originally appeared in German in 1610. It was republished in French translation in 1877 as *Iter Persicum ou Description du*

But another Persian delegation arrived in 1604, while the following year Rudolf entertained Sherley again in Prague, and then sent him on a specific campaign to Morocco to stir up discontent against Ottoman rule there. Sherley was back in Prague in 1607, when he was raised to the dignity of *eques auratus* and made a Palatine of the Empire, as was later his younger brother Robert, who also entered Persian service.[1] It is clear that Rudolf was attracted by the idealism of the plan, stressing as it did his absolute superiority over all other European princes (this was also the style in which he was addressed by the Muscovite tsar); at the same time it appears from the surviving evidence that his closest adviser Barvitius was implicated.[2] Even in 1610 the Imperial audience with a further Safavid envoy was enough to interrupt the deliberations of the German princes assembled to debate the problems of Jülich and Cleves.[3]

As Ranke observed long ago, Rudolf was determined to play the Emperor: 'In dem Kaiserthum sah man noch die Repräsentation der Einheit der abendländischen Christenheit.... So fasste es auch Rudolf II. auf; es war sein Ehrgeiz, an der Spitze der Christenheit zu stehen...'[4] He desired a complete victory over the Turks or none at all; this explains his remarkably tenacious prosecution of the struggle, then much of his vacillating after 1606 and refusal to sign the compromise, Matthias-inspired treaty of Zsitvatorok. But the whole policy was frustrated throughout by the unwillingness of either Empire, Papacy, or Spain to co-operate with him on his terms and to give support without some guarantee of control.[5] The situation was worse confounded by an arrant military mishandling of the war which is testified to by the leading

Voyage en Perse entrepris en 1602 ... (ed. C. Schafer, Paris 1877). On Kakas see E. Veress, *Zalánkeményi Kakas István* (Budapest 1905).

[1] Nuncios/Ferreri, Prague 19 July and 26 July 1604; /Caetano, Prague 22 Oct. and 19 Nov. 1607; Babinger, op. cit. 31 ff.

[2] Ibid. 37 and n. There is a letter from Logau to Barvitius, Moscow 6 Nov. 1604, about the Persian alliance, printed in the *Iter Persicum* (App. 3), together with private letters from Kakas to Wolf Unverzagt (ibid. App. 1 and 2). Six of Sherley's letters to Rudolf, written in Venice in 1604–5, are printed by Penrose, op. cit. App. c.

[3] *Briefe und Akten*, viii. 230. This envoy's stay seems to have been protracted, but ill-supported financially (cf. ibid. 643 n. 3).

[4] Ranke, op. cit. 182; cf. Schwarzenfeld, op. cit. 199–205.

[5] Cf.—in general—*Briefe und Akten*, v. 241 ff., 713 ff., and *passim*. The Papal attitude emerged in the earliest stages of the war. As Cardinal Aldobrandini, Clement VIII had already gained ample experience of the realities of the Eastern European situation through his activities in Poland. His lack of sympathy is demonstrated by Matoušek, op. cit., *passim*. At a later point in time the desperate need for Spanish help is well evident from the letters of San Clemente to Philip III in 1605: *Correspondencia inedita de Don Guillén de San Clemente ... publicada por El Marqués de Ayerbe* (Zaragoza 1892), 253 ff.

generals during its last phase, Basta and Rusworm, and the squabbles between Italian and German commanders.[1]

The truth was that even within the Empire Rudolf possessed dignity only, and not power.[2] He could never be a substantial Emperor, but only a symbolic one, and the first essential symbol of his sovereignty was the multinational mystique of coronation. We have seen that the opinions of contemporaries differed widely as to the nature of Habsburg claims on the crowns of St. Wenceslas and St. Stephen; foreign observers were apt to conclude that it had become in fact a matter rather of the sovereign's acceptance by the estates than of election.[3] But for the monarchical ideology the *de facto* position was strictly speaking irrelevant; it demanded that the focal-point of sovereignty be an act of coronation, an acceptance in the medieval sense of the mystery of kingship. This tradition was anyway strong in the Bohemian and Hungarian lands: Stránský shows it in his description of the elaborate Czech crowning ceremony, as do Péter Révay and Christoph Lackner when they discuss the age-old symbolism of the crown of the Magyars. It is not without significance that both Révay and Lackner were members of the loyal, pro-Habsburg body of thinking among the Hungarian Protestants, and that the latter had experienced the atmosphere of Mannerist Prague.[4] Rudolf took the significant initiative of creating a personal monument to this cult, and the result was his private *Kaiserkrone*, the resplendent 'house crown' of later generations of Habsburgs.

The Bohemian coronation of Rudolf in the Cathedral of St. Vitus within Prague Castle on 22 September 1575 was a great spectacle, deliberately contrived, as the records show, to dazzle and impress the assembled people.[5] For it the historic Wenceslas crown was used, which

---

[1] Nuncios/Ferreri, Prague 9 Aug. and 16 Aug. 1604; Stauffer, op. cit. Ch. 3.

[2] Cf. Contarini in 1596: 'Giova alla Germania l'Imperio, perche avendo l'Imperatore dignità e non autorità e forze, se non quanto gliene vogliono conferire, non può offendere nè opprimere la libertà.' Alberi, *Relazioni*, i. 6, 240.

[3] Michele (1571) sees Hungary and Bohemia as 'Regni, benche di elettione, però si può dire, che siano come di successione' (Fiedler, *Relationen* (*FRA* xxx), 273). Tron (1576) was even more positive: 'Il regno di Boemia soleva esser elettivo, ma imperatore Ferdinando fece abbruciare i loro privilegi, e ora si procede per successione di maschi.' Alberi, *Relazioni*, i. 6, 198.

[4] Stránský, op. cit. 321–8; Petrus de Révay, *De Sacrae Coronae Regni Hungariae Ortu* . . . (Augsburg 1613); Christophorus Lackner, *Coronae Hungariae Emblematica Descriptio* (Lauingen 1615). Cf. E. Bartoniek, *A magyar királykoronázások története* (Budapest n.d.), 169 f.; E. Angyal, 'Lackner Kristóf és a barock humanizmus kezdetei', *Soproni Szemle* viii (1944), 1–18; and J. L. Kovács, 'Lackner Kristóf Prágában', *Irodalomtörténeti Közlemények* lxxiv (1970), 508–12.

[5] Cf. the document in SÚA, SM K 1/12⁷⁵ which advises the utmost display, to limit the aspirations of estates and nobility. There is a Latin description of the ceremony at SM K 1/12⁸⁶, printed in *SČ* iv. 260 f.; a fuller one in *SČ* iv. 261–8.

occupied an important place in the ceremonial of the later sixteenth century.[1] Rudolf's own crown however, which seems to have been constructed around the year 1602 under the direction of the Dutch goldsmith Hans Vermeyen, took the form of a distinctively 'Habsburg' work of art, and was based—suggestively enough—on the designs by Dürer for the *Ehrenpforte* of Maximilian I.[2] This work, which was wildly admired by contemporaries—the Venetian Soranzo valued it at 500,000 scudi—never formed a part of state regalia (it was described in 1637 as 'ab Imperatore Rudolpho II pro sacra sua persona confecta'), and there have been various conjectures as to its purpose. Karel Chytil seems to argue its 'Czech' character too strongly, since his very useful monograph was partly an attack on the Austrians for retaining it in the Viennese Schatzkammer after 1918; but he well perceived its importance as a supranational symbol of the Habsburg mission, and its place in the development of an iconology of sovereignty within the family.[3] It was clearly a prized object at the court,[4] and was designed to have its place in the rituals surrounding the Emperor as one of the highest fruits of co-operation between the monarch and his artistic circle.

A similar interplay of the political and the spiritual is evident in much else that Rudolf commissioned, and stands out as claiming a central place in the content of Rudolfine art. Just as the crown is decorated with the motifs after nature and set with the Bohemian mountain stones which characterize much that originated in the Prague workshops of that time, so several of the canvases of Spranger and Hans von Aachen, and the sculptures of Adriaen de Vries depict the Emperor's triumphs in Hungary—like the recapture of Raab in 1598—or his eminence as the imagined mediator of Europe. These belong to a later chapter; the present one may be summed up by a comparison which suggests itself and which is not inordinately strained: that between Rudolf and James I of England.

It is remarkable how much of what in isolation was merely perverse falls into place when these two sovereigns are considered together, and if James was the wisest fool in Christendom then Rudolf was perhaps the sanest madman. Both were in the first place educated, self-conscious men, who rebelled against certain features of their upbringing which

---

[1] K. Chytil, *Česká Koruna Králsovská a koruny panovničí do XVII. století* (Prague 1917?), 54 ff.

[2] [Plate 10.] For the details see K. Chytil, *Koruna Rudolfa II* (Prague 1929, trans. of the French original of 1921), the links with Dürer and earlier Habsburg crowns, 5 f. Cf. Lhotsky, op. cit. 255-7.

[3] Chytil, op. cit. [above, n. 2] 4 etc.

[4] It is described by the court jeweller and lapidary Anselm Boethius de Boodt in his *Gemmarum et Lapidum Historia* (Hanau 1609), 8.

were nevertheless formative for them: in the case of James it was the influence of Buchanan and the extreme Scottish forms of Calvinism; with Rudolf the hauteur and narrow-minded intolerance of the Spanish court. Though they were well-meaning and inclined to generosity without calculation, neither could avoid seeming withdrawn and exclusive, while both attracted round them a limited number of sympathetic figures whom they indulged in an, at times, suspicious and secretive fashion: in other words, their patronage was close to esoterism. Their private life was abnormal, dictated by brusque and unaccountable changes of temper, characterized by sexual irregularity and artificially created favourites who reflected only their masters' moods.

There was also much that was similar in their tastes and pastimes, especially the interest in occult studies, the spirit world, and the machine. Heinrich Hiesserle von Chodaw, a Bohemian who visited England in 1607, gives a spirited account of the demonstration by a certain Dutchman before the fascinated James of two *perpetuum mobile* machines, which he describes and illustrates. The incident could easily have taken place in Prague; indeed the same Dutchman was probably a confidant of Rudolf.[1] It is not surprising that the Emperor's great favourite Kepler later received an invitation to come to the court of St. James.[2]

In their political activity both monarchs sought to pursue a middle course, not as a compromise, but as a revulsion against extremist claims which to them were also one-sided; and with both the striving for peace within Christendom appears to have been something possessing almost apodictic force. Comenius records that Rudolf, having achieved harmony in Bohemia by the Letter of Majesty, desired in his declining years to found a 'society of peace', as a defence of freedom of conscience. He divulged his plan to two nobles, both Protestants who had been persecuted for their faith, and it was lack of support for the enterprise among the high nobility at large which led the Emperor to utter his famous curse on the city of Prague and its people.[3] Whatever we may make of this

---

[1] If, as seems very likely, he was Cornelius Drebbel (cf. below, p. 189). Chodaw, 'Raiss Buch und Leben', fos. 48ᵛ–50ʳ. Chodaw later undertook various missions for Rudolf, being involved in the escapade of the Archduke Leopold in Jülich, and with the Passau troops in 1611. In 1609 Rudolf sent James two characteristic gifts: a celestial globe and a clock (*Jahrbuch* xix (1898), Reg. No. 16957). James's patronage of Robert Fludd is relevant here (cf. F. A. Yates, *The Art of Memory* (London 1966), 320 ff. *passim*) and his obsession with demonology and witchcraft.

[2] Via Henry Wotton in 1620: Pearsall Smith, 171 f.

[3] J. A. Komenský, *Historie o těžkých Protivenstvích Církve České* (latest edn. Prague 1952, written 1632, original Latin edn. 1648), 86–8. The account, however consistent with Rudolf's character, sounds more legend than reality, yet Comenius asserts its authenticity: 'All this I who am telling the story heard from the lips of that same Lord

8225164

story (the author vouches for its truth), there are obvious parallels
between the mentality which it reveals and certain forms of mystical
thinking, not least the notion dear to Comenius himself of a 'peaceful
centre', a *Centrum Securitatis*, and a Paradise of the Heart which should
follow after and resolve the Labyrinth of the World.[1]

James and Rudolf each aimed to achieve a European balance of power
by playing off rival forces and casting themselves for the role of international arbiter. This line of policy runs right through James's conciliatory diplomacy during the years 1618–20, which in Protestant eyes
amounted to betrayal, and appears most clearly of all in his pamphlet of
1618, *The Peace-maker or Great Brittaine's Blessing*.[2] Thus considered,
the Catholic Rudolf's continued refusal of a Spanish marriage presents a
strong parallel with the Protestant James's insistence on it for his son the
Prince of Wales. For his part the English king regarded a pacification of
Protestants and Catholics as the necessary prelude to a new united
initiative against the Turk.[3] Both rulers asserted by their political practice that the institution of monarchy was in some sense divine; Rudolf's
stress on the Imperial dignity was a larger claim, but it was James who
was prepared to argue his case publicly. The fruit of his quarrel with
Bellarmin over the demands of national sovereignty was dedicated by
the king to Rudolf, at the head of all the Princes of Europe.[4]

Yet in James ultimately the mystical streak is missing, the real dissatisfaction with the existing world; he is in the last resort a man whose
mentality seems comprehensible, and whose failures are failures of
judgement. What distinguishes Rudolf is not the complete collapse of
his regime—that was after all to be accomplished by James's son—but
his chronically indefinite attitude to the central problem of his age, the

Šmid [Jan Šmid na Kunštátě, one of the two taken into Rudolf's confidence] at his
castle of Kunštát in the year 1626, and at the same time the devout old man, already
over 70, took out of a deep chest the golden chain which Rudolf had made and given to
him as the badge of the society of peace, wiped the tears from his eyes and said: "This
jewel of peace was made by his holiness the emperor with his own holy hands", adding:
"the curse of the God-fearing emperor upon us who were ungrateful to him has now
struck us".' What the episode does not prove about Rudolf, it proves about Comenius's
own highly-charged spiritual sensitivity and credulity. The scene reappears in Act III
of Grillparzer's *Bruderzwist*.

[1] Cf. below, pp. 276 f.
[2] Polišenský, *Anglie a Bílá Hora*, 56–175 *passim*, esp. 66 f. Cf. J. R. Jones, *Britain
and Europe in the seventeenth century* (London 1966), 14 ff.
[3] Cf. Baumer, art. cit. 44 ff.
[4] '*Apologia pro Juramento Fidelitatis Primum quidem anonumos, Nunc vero ab ipso
Auctore Serenissimo ac Potentissimo Principe Jacobo Dei gratia Magnae Britanniae,
Franciae et Hiberniae Rege . . . denuo edita . . . Sacratissimo Caesari Rodulfo II (etc.)
inscripta* (London 1609). Cf. J. W. Allen, op. cit. 247–70.

demands of organized religion. The implications of this were vast for all his policy, especially for his behaviour towards the Empire and the Netherlands. Received religion was Rudolf's Labyrinth, and his attempts to penetrate through it to spiritual security form part of an international pattern in the later sixteenth century.

3. The Religion of Rudolf

'His Majesty has now reached the stage of abandoning God
entirely; he will neither hear nor speak of Him, nor suffer any
sign of Him. Not only does he refuse to attend any sermon,
public service, procession or the like, but he hates and curses
all who participate in them, being never more impatient of God
and every good work than on such holy occasions.'

PROPOSITION OF THE ARCHDUKES IN VIENNA (1606)

MAXIMILIAN II's attitude to the Church was—as we have seen—
profoundly uncertain, and his mature position became one of qualified
Erastianism; yet his attitude to religion was far from indifferent. He was,
as he sometimes brought himself to say, neither Papist nor Lutheran,
but a Christian, and this belief he maintained to his death.[1] There has
been dispute over what passed between Maximilian and his religious
advisers when he lay on his deathbed, but it seems clear that he was
never reconciled to the Catholic Church, though he did not abjure it,
and that he refused the last sacrament, because to receive *sub una
specie* was sinful and to receive *sub utraque* would offend his family.[2]

The same indecision was part of Rudolf also: he was a man addicted
to the mysterious and the miraculous, and his revulsion against dogma
must be viewed in that light. Although in his early years as Emperor he
quite frequently attended services,[3] this later became extremely rare—on
occasion the Pope even complimented him personally when he communicated.[4] After 1600 he appears to have lived in a veritable terror of the
Roman sacraments, and he certainly refused the last rites of the Catholic
Church. 'Not only did His Majesty not confess,' wrote Cardinal Borghese sorrowfully and secretively, 'he did not even display any sign of
contrition.'[5] The Calvinist Melchior Goldast, the last person to view the

---

[1] Bibl, *Maximilian II*, 98.

[2] *Nuntiaturberichte*/Hansen, 169 f.; cf. Hugo Moritz, op. cit. 436-8.

[3] Cf. Puteo's instruction to Visconte: Nuncios/Puteo, 524: 'È pia e zelante della
religione, come comprenderà V.S.Rᵐᵃ. dall'assistenza, che fa frequentemente alli
divini offitii . . .' Against this may however be set the fact that during a six-month stay
in Vienna in 1577 Rudolf never once went to confession: B. Duhr, *Die Jesuiten an den
deutschen Fürstenhöfen des 16. Jahrhunderts* (Freiburg 1901), 17 ff.

[4] As in 1601: Nuncios/Ferreri, lxv n.

[5] Turba, *Beiträge*, 356 f., Borghese's letter, Rome 11 Feb. 1612, in 357 n. Cf. *Briefe
und Akten*, x, Nos. 88 and 89 and 243 n. 3.

body of the Emperor before it was consigned to its vault, confided the same information to his diary.[1]

At the same time, Rudolf and Maximilian were seen by observers as completely distinct personalities. When this point is appreciated, much of the misunderstanding of Rudolf's religious policy can be explained by the expectations which contemporaries had of him. It has frequently been asserted that the first years of his reign at least were ones of eager counter-reforming activity, especially in the Austrian lands; such was clearly the hope of the Catholics and the apprehension of the Protestants.[2] Yet there is little evidence that Rudolf ever played any significant personal part in the persecution of Protestants. The leading figures in Austria were his brother Ernst in Vienna and the North; Ernst's successor there Matthias, guided by the energetic Bishop of Wiener Neustadt, Melchior Khlesl; and somewhat later the young Archduke Ferdinand in Styria. Meanwhile Rudolf restricted himself to strongly-worded promulgations which he seemed curiously unwilling to try to enforce. The Protestant estates were anxious for the future—but this was more an aspect of the pessimistic, even fatalistic tendencies of the old century than the reflection of a real threat to their position; the greatest success of the Austrian Evangelical party was still to come, in 1606–8, and it certainly bore no specific animus against Rudolf himself until that date.[3] The actual results of the Counter-Reformation in Upper and Lower Austria were anyway minimal before the end of the century, as even Papal sources show,[4] while for Bohemia a fanatical Protestant could later write that no positive steps at all were taken by the central authorities before 1602.[5]

The nuncios especially were inclined to expect the Emperor to be a faithful servant of the Curia in Rome and could not comprehend his

[1] Goldast, *Tagebuch*, 261 f., where the testimony of the father confessor is repeated.

[2] e.g. Janssen, op. cit. iv, 465 ff.

[3] V. Bibl, 'Die Religionsreformation Kaiser Rudolfs II. in Österreich', *AÖG* 109 (1921), 377–433, does not appear to justify his title. Other documents presented by Bibl demonstrate how great a role was played by Khlesl's individual initiative: 'Klesls Briefe an Kaiser Rudolfs II. Obersthofmeister Adam Freiherrn von Dietrichstein', *AÖG* 88 (1900), 475–580; 'Klesls Briefe an Herzog Wilhelm V. von Baiern', *MIÖG* xxi (1900), 640–73. Malaspina and Sega record that it is Ernst who is the leading spirit: Nuncios/Malaspina, Prague 1 Oct. 1585, /Sega 22 July 1586. Cf. H. Sturmberger, 'Jakob Andreae und Achaz von Hohenfeld' in *Festschrift Karl Eder* (Innsbruck 1959), 381–94; and Hammer: *Khlesl* [above, p. 5 n. 1] i, *passim*.

[4] Cf. Sega's memorandum in 1586: Nuncios/Sega, 267–75.

[5] Comenius, *Historie*, 83: 'In 1576 the noble Maximilian was torn from this world and was succeeded on the throne by his son Rudolf who, following in his father's footsteps, ruled till the year 1602 without allowing anyone to be acted against for reasons of religion.'

failure to lend unconditional support—hence their strangely distorted reports of him, coupled with their extreme tendency to place the blame on his advisers.[1] When one of the Papal diplomats took an objective view he was forced to admit that Rudolf was a more Catholic figure than any of his immediate predecessors: 'If we cast our minds back dispassionately and give praise where praise is due, there is no doubt that this Emperor, placed between the open enmity of the Turk and the persecutions of the heretics at home, has until now kept them at bay most worthily, achieving much more than was achieved by Charles V, his grandfather's brother, or Ferdinand, his grandfather, or Maximilian II, his father . . .'[2] But Rudolf's Catholicism was subject to a grave spiritual malaise which the years from 1576 could only serve to aggravate. The climax to the first decade following the Council of Trent had been the massacre of St. Bartholomew's Day in Paris, and the aftermath of this was a fever of anxiety throughout Europe about similar plots. The mood in Germany grew tenser, and in Bohemia there were fears among the Protestants both during the protracted negotiations at the diet of 1575 and the vast gathering for Maximilian's funeral in 1577.[3] In 1582 the Empire was so paralysed by terror of a Catholic stroke that it allowed the success of a limited Bavarian action calculated at installing the Wittelsbach candidate Ernst as Archbishop of Cologne.[4] By the end of the century Protestants were willing to believe any reports of Catholic preparations for attack, as is shown by a strange document in the Rožmberk archive;[5] while the links in their own chain of alliances had begun to be forged under the astute management of Christian von Anhalt.

One of the mainsprings of Rudolf's policy was his growing revulsion

---

[1] Cf. Puteo's instruction: Nuncios/Puteo, 524: 'Da molti si crede, che molto più sarebbe pronta et ardente, quando i ministri, nelli quali confida et riposa grandemente, fussero o meno freddi e timidi nella consideratione de rispetti e sospetti o più fervidi et audaci nel portar le esshortationi di N.S.M. e le trattationi delli ministri apostolici.'

[2] Nuncios/Malaspina, 212.

[3] Moritz, op. cit. 4 ff.; Gindely, *Böhmische Brüder*, 165 f.; Bydžovský, fos. 11ᵛ ff. Maximilian's own revulsion against the St. Bartholomew's plot (which he took to be a Spanish–Papal conspiracy) is examined by J. Dostál: 'Ohlas Bartolomějské noci na dvoře Maximiliána II.', *ČČH* xxxvii (1931), 335–49.

[4] Bezold, *Rudolf und die Heilige Liga*, 11 ff.

[5] Třebon, Historica 5916: 'De Sancta Liga'. This reports a solemn alliance of the whole Catholic world—the Pope, the King of Spain, Lorraine, the Imperial Archbishops, Rudolf, the Austrian Archdukes, and Poland—entered into at Ferrara on 12 June 1599 and designed to extirpate heresy totally in the Empire. The eight-page pamphlet outlines the strategy to be followed, and even announces that an 'Antiliga' of Protestant powers has bound itself to resist. The undertaking is to be carried out the following year (1600), and the fantasy therefore presumably forms a contribution to the literature of Armageddon. It is also representative of a widespread feeling: cf. *Briefe und Akten*, v, 574 f. and n. 2, and a similar tract in ÖN, MS. 8880, fos. 54–60ʳ.

against the Papacy. It had straightforward political aspects: there were disputed fiefs, and the Emperor's strong desire for territories in Italy —observed for example by the Venetian Contarini—was probably heightened by their unattainability.[1] The disaffection went much deeper however; Papal activity became increasingly for Rudolf an infringement of regalian privilege. The co-operation between Pope and Emperor which attempted to mediate a settlement of the Hispano-Dutch conflict in the Netherlands[2] could only superficially conceal the fact that Rome's concern was the best maintenance of Curial interests there, Rudolf's the right of sovereign arbitration throughout his territories. Similarly the traditional German–Habsburg position in Italy was much weaker since Charles V for want of a Papal coronation, yet the renewed power of Rome meant that such an act would now necessarily be a gesture of Imperial submissiveness.[3]

A clear rift appeared with the nunciature of Sega in 1586. The Emperor was first of all nettled when his own decree allowing an ecclesiastical visitation of the Church in Bohemia was overruled by the hierarchy which asserted that only a Bull had the necessary competence; and when Sega published the encyclical *In Coena Domini* without his permission he became thoroughly incensed. He was with difficulty persuaded not to press for the recall of Sega, but the incident rankled.[4] Rudolf's relations with Clement VIII were at a low ebb from the start, and difficulties only grew as the Pope achieved diplomatic successes like the conversion of Henry IV in 1593 and the reversion of Ferrara in 1598.[5] After 1600 the Emperor's position appears to have hardened into a paranoid fear of the omnicompetence of the Roman Church; Rudolf still sought absolution (this answered an inner need) but he ordered his confessor to omit the words 'auctoritate apostolica' when administering it.[6] He was more and more alienated from official papal representatives, whether nuncios like Ferreri and Caetano or legates like Cardinal

---

[1] Alberi, *Relazioni*, i. 6, 238: 'Nelle provincie esterne vuol avere giurisdizione, e massime in Italia . . .'

[2] *Nuntiaturberichte*/Hansen, Pt. 2: *Der Pacificationstag zu Köln 1579;* cf. Khevenhüller, *Annales*, i. 98–100.

[3] The suggestion was made at the *Reichstag* of 1582, but Rudolf did not take it up: *Nuntiaturberichte*/Hansen p. 403 and *passim*. Cf. Soranzo in Fiedler, *Relationen (FRA* xxvi), 5 f.

[4] Nuncios/Malaspina, Prague 13 Aug. 1585, /Sega, 22 Apr., 13 May, 3, 10 and 17 June 1586. Characteristically Sega attributed Rudolf's non-cooperation to a fear of the Protestants.

[5] Matoušek, *Turecká Válka*, 92, 231 ff. and *passim*. On Ferrara see Stloukal, *Papežská politika*, 31–6.

[6] Nuncios/Ferreri, Prague 21 Feb. 1605.

Giovanni Millini in 1608, and recalled nostalgically the less fanatical attitude of Speziano during the 1590s.[1]

On the other hand he had no real sympathy with the Protestant camp. He loathed their internal squabbles and their subdivision into ever more sects each asserting its distinct political rights (he especially detested the Czech Brethren in this respect),[2] and he was appalled by their pettiness. That Rudolf was increasingly tempted by Protestant offers emerged soon after the débâcle of 1600, and his dealings with them had become deeply suspicious to the nuncio Ferreri by 1606.[3] The following year he gave a regal welcome to Elector Christian II of Saxony, and even allowed the latter's preacher Polycarp Leyser to hold forth within the precincts of the Hradschin. But the incentive was basically to release himself from dictation by Catholic forces—Christian's visit proved more of a carousal than a political initiative[4]—and the catalysts were certain close advisers who were Protestant, like Julius of Brunswick. The Emperor always feared that they, no less than the Catholics, would claim as a matter of justice what he was prepared to grant them as favour; his sharpest sallies were the result of such pretension, as with the banishment of the Viennese preacher Josua Opitz.[5]

Thus Rudolf was persistently trying to maintain a position which was free of both sides, but in doing so he necessarily offended both. A typical example were the endless negotiations over the bishopric of Strasbourg and its allegiance. Puteo first complains that the Emperor is dragging his feet, despite the urgings of himself and San Clemente that a Ban must be placed on the refractory Protestants there; next he reports that Rudolf has even countermanded existing decrees against them; but later it seems that exorbitant demands by the other party are turning him back to Catholic advice.[6] The same year Rudolf insisted on full court

[1] Cf. the letters of Millini: Nuncios/Caetano (Pars III, 2), esp. Nos. 60 seqq. Rudolf tried to press the nomination of Speziano as Cardinal (ibid. Pars I, introd.; Caetano, Prague 17 June 1607).

[2] e.g. Nuncios/Malaspina, Prague 2 Feb. 1585: '[The Emperor] s'è dichiarata pienamente et virilmente di non volere permettere che nel regno s'annidi questo genere di persone tanto perniciose et per il spirituale et per il politico.' The facts prove of course that this was rather irritation at the Brethren's pretensions than closely calculated intolerance.

[3] 'Va pensando da unirsi con i protestanti, perchè unito con essi stima che si sedariano le ribellioni, et che i cattolici non lo metteriano al ponto di successione.' Nuncios/Ferreri, Prague 26 Dec. 1605. Cf. Stieve, *Verhandlungen*, 76 ff.; Gindely, *Rudolf II, passim*.

[4] 'I. Mt. halten mich so wol', reported the Elector on his departure, 'dass ich auch fast keine Stunde nüchtern zu Prag gelebt.' *Briefe und Akten*, v. 898–900.

[5] G. Mecenseffy, *Geschichte des Protestantismus in Österreich* (Graz–Cologne 1956), 83 f.

[6] Nuncios/Puteo, Prague 11 Oct. 1588, 7 Feb. and 21 Mar. 1589. There was, need-

mourning for the excommunicate Henry of Valois, displaying a—for the nuncio—lamentable insistence on personal decision: 'Et certo, chè S. Mtà in queste cose, che concernono la religione et il peccato, dovria imitare li passati imperatori catholici, che hanno sempre lasciati questi articuli alla determinatione della chiesa et dei pontefici Romani senza volersene fare giudice per se stesso . . .'[1]

The attempt was not an unqualified failure, at least in Bohemia. Despite much special pleading, there is also something genuine in the frequent nostalgia later displayed by both sides for the Rudolfine age, which became to them almost golden in retrospect: Comenius and Stránský said so, even the arch-Catholic Slavata said so, while Žerotín, most moderate of spirits, had a respect for Rudolf, and an affinity with him, although he later took the side of Matthias.[2] Václav Budovec's praise of the Emperor was unqualified in 1598, while as late as 1605 he still regarded him as essentially tolerant.[3]

I have suggested that Rudolf's *political* objections to both confessional camps were underpinned by a *spiritual* uncertainty. Herein lies an important aspect of the problem; for these two threads were interwoven in the same way as the Emperor's physical and mental illnesses were linked. The two great physical crises of his life took place in the years 1578–80 and 1599–1600; both were also to a large extent psychological —the latter almost wholly so—and each bears directly on the present argument. In the first case the major healing influence was the Imperial physician Johannes Crato; in the second the confessor, Johann Pistorius of Nidda. From such fragmentary evidence as survives it cannot now exactly be said how direct was the role of these two men as such, but both their offices clearly assumed a disproportionate significance at Rudolf's court: a whole series of physicians in ordinary ministered no less to the Emperor's alchemical and scientific pursuits than to his bodily health, while the intimate relation of the spiritual adviser to his sovereign gave him extreme powers of persuasion, as shrewd observers realized.[4] At

less to say, no final decision. For the further convolutions of the Strasbourg affair see *Briefe und Akten*, iv. 45 ff., v, 120 ff.

[1] Nuncios/Visconte, Saaz (?) 12 Oct. 1589. Whether this demonstration was due purely to Rudolf's respect for a fellow sovereign who had been assassinated, or to his sense that Henry III's religious leanings were unorthodox in a way rather like his own, is an interesting question.

[2] Comenius, op. cit. 85 (cf. above, p. 85 n. 5); Stránský, op. cit. 237–9; Slavata, 252; Žerotín, *Dopisy*, No. 391: Žerotín to Beza, Rosice 1 Feb. 1599.

[3] '. . . nec in corpora nec in animas nec in facultates subditorum unquam sevire visus et in promissis tum verax tum constans est . . .' Budovec to Beza, Prague 7 Apr. 1598, *Korrespondence*, No. 15; cf. ibid., No. 18.

[4] Nuncios/Caetano, 589: 'Importaria molto, che in quell'offitio fosse adoperata

the same time, both Crato and Pistorius represent the learned interests of the later sixteenth century and its wider mental attitudes which were the solvents of religious orthodoxy: Crato belongs to the world of intellectual eirenism; Pistorius to the world of the magical and occult.

The crisis of 1600 was the more dramatic. It was a culmination of extreme frustration, especially over the plans for marriage, which was undoubtedly exacerbated—though how far is uncertain—by astrological and superstitious fear of the new century. This led to a desperately unstable mood: Rudolf appears to have approved the summoning to Prague of Capuchin monks under the dynamic and proselytizing Lawrence of Brindisi, but then he refused to see them and commanded them to withdraw. He is reliably said to have been turned against them by Tycho Brahe and his scheming Calvinist servant Makofsky; equally clearly he subsequently changed his mind and ordered the Capuchins to remain, though his antipathy towards the Papacy was not hidden for long.[1] Lawrence then proceeded to play an important part in the Turkish campaign of 1601.

The man closest to the Emperor's ear during the whole episode was Pistorius, and it is worth considering what is known about this largely-forgotten person. Johann Pistorius (1546–1608) was a convert, first from Lutheranism to Calvinism, and then—in 1588—to Catholicism, who soon became heavily involved in religious polemic on behalf of his new faith in Germany and Central Europe.[2] He was however equally a scholar who not only published a notable series of historical texts but also edited one of the leading collections of Cabalist writings to be printed during

persona zelante, prudente et grave, nè V.S.R^{ma}. doverà mancare di quei offitii, che potessero giovare a quest'effetto . . .' In the 1590s there was increasing Papal dissatisfaction with the quality of Rudolf's confessors, particularly as his own Catholicism was becoming more suspect. Matoušek, op. cit. 46 f.

[1] Cf. St. Lawrence's own brief account: 'Commentariolum de Rebus Austriae et Bohemiae' in *Omnia Opera*, vol. x, Pars II (Padua 1956), 359 ff., and the article by F. Tischer, 'Uvedení Capucínů do Čech roku 1600' in *Věstník Královské Společnosti Nauk*, 1907. The general literature on St. Lawrence (canonized 1881) is very extensive and mainly hagiographic; cf. Fr. A. Brennan, O.S.F.C., *Life of St. Lawrence of Brindisi* (London 1911), 68 ff. For the Protestant eye-witness account see the second report of Ansbach (Ranke, op. cit.): 'Wenn capuciner kommen sagt i.(hre) Mt.(Majestät) "wie qualen mich die schelme!" Könne keine geistliche noch gebet leiden . . . Kaiser hette selber autori gesagt: "ich weis wol, dass sie mir nach meiner Hoheit trachten; bin inen nicht catholisch genug" . . .'

[2] *ADB* s.v. He engaged in theological disputation with former colleagues like Grynaeus and Osiander and worked closely with Ferdinand of Tyrol, Maximilian of Bavaria, and Rudolf's morganatic cousin Cardinal Andreas, Bishop of Constance (Hirn, *Erzherzog Ferdinand*, 270 f.; *Briefe und Akten*, iv. 29 ff., v. 63 ff., 338 ff.; *Akten der zu Zürich . . . wegen der Religion angestellten Disputation . . . von Herrn J. Pistorius* (n.p. 1603)).

the Renaissance.[1] The nature of Pistorius's involvement in mystical religion after his move to Prague in the 1590s is now difficult to establish —understandably it does not emerge from his dealings with the Papacy[2] —but it may furnish the clue to his influence on Rudolf. Perhaps a contemporary Catholic memorandum was right when it suggested exorcism as the only remedy for the Emperor's ills; there was indeed a spirit of disquiet behind the 'melancholische schwere Perturbationes'.[3]

Pistorius himself told Rome that the disease was simply chronic melancholy: 'Obsessus non est, quod quidam existimant, sed melancholia laborat, quae longi temporis tractu radices nimium egit . . .' Yet it was common knowledge that the complaint was connected with Rudolf's occult activity.[4] The confessor retained his Emperor's trust even during the very lean years of 1604 and 1605 (thereafter the position is less clear). Although the politics of Pistorius were devious and his financial integrity questionable,[5] he stands as a witness that the gulf between Catholic orthodoxy and occult mysticism, Jewish or Christian, was not yet unbridgeable, at least in the privacy of the scholar's study. After all, the saintly Lawrence of Brindisi was himself a man of learning who had dabbled in the Cabala and its number mysticism, maybe in the arts of the artificial memory as well.[6]

[1] *Artis Cabalisticae, hoc est reconditae theologiae et philosophiae scriptorum Tomus I* (Basle 1587); cf. below, p. 237. The whole received picture of Pistorius is very confused: the *ADB* does not even mention his Cabalism, while a text on the theory of the microcosm conventionally attributed to him is by another contemporary of the same name (*Tractatus brevis et utilis de Microcosmo seu de Proportione utriusque mundi* (Paris 1607 etc.)).

[2] Some letters are printed in Nuncios/Ferreri, e.g. Prague 10 and 17 Apr. 1606. Pistorius remained however suspicious to the Jesuits: *Mercure Jesuite*, ii (Geneva 1630), 291–7. At the end of his life he openly recanted his youthful involvement in the practical Cabala, which he now dismissed as Lutheran stupidity, but interestingly made no mention of the learned edition of 1587: J. Pistorius, *Offentliche beweisung, dass die Lutherische zu Regenspurg . . . Año 1601 . . . sich . . . in höchste schand . . . gesetzt. Sampt widerruff wegen der Judischē cabala* (Freiburg 1607), a work apparently written in 1602.

[3] 'Kurzer Discurs, wie der Röm. Kais. Mt. in ihrem itzigen Anliegen vor ihr Person und sonsten zu helfen sein möcht' (October 1600). Printed in *SČ* x. 92–6.

[4] Nuncios/Ferreri, lxiii n. for Pistorius's opinion. The passage from Ansbach, quoted above, p. 90 n. 1, continues: 'Der furnembsten aulicorum meinung sei diese, weil I. Mt. acht jar lang mit der negromantie umbgangen und sonderlich gearbeitet, speculum philosophicum prospectieren zu machen, und noch, dass sie zu weit hinter diese sachen kommen, und von dem bösen feint gleichsam als a furiis also getrieben werde . . .'

[5] On Pistorius's methods—including his ready advocacy of Albrecht's claim to the succession in 1605—v. *Briefe und Akten*, v. 19, 80, 739 ff. For the conflicting evidence thereafter, and the reliable date of his death (19 June 1608), ibid. 824 n. 2, vi, Nos. 74 and 117, pp. 98 and 428 n.

[6] *Opera Omnia*, x. ii. 446–90; cf. F. Secret: 'L'interpretazione della Kabbala nel Rinascimento', *Convivium*, xxiv (1956), 547 ff. Lawrence was reported to have claimed that he could reconstruct the whole Hebrew Testament from memory.

The role of Crato in the first years of Rudolf's reign introduces a different but related intellectual perspective; to investigate it demands some preliminary explanation of the nature of religious peace-making in the later sixteenth century. The importance of moderation and of efforts at confessional reconciliation during the period is only now beginning to be recognized. The reason for this is not far to seek: for the eirenical movement owed its very strength to the heightened confessional tensions which it found so repellent; its significance was not directly as some precursor of democratic tolerance,[1] but as an abstraction, an attitude of mind which found little practical outlet, save in the world of the academic and the artist. It was therefore forced back upon itself, compelled to condemn the extremities of creed as logically and emotionally unworthy, without being able to create a positive platform of its own. Eirenism was essentially an attempt to evade tightening religious antagonisms by calling on intellectual reserves which the practical world would not admit; the mentality of the earlier age of colloquy born out of its time, like the theories of political universalism which tended to accompany it.[2] It was also to a large extent a story of alienation within the Catholic Church, though not of course entirely so; many of its leading spirits— whether Dutch, German, Italian, or whatever—broke with Rome, only to find scant satisfaction among the new Protestant faiths, and to take refuge in an inner religious solution which could be reconciled with external Catholic observances. Others discovered a *modus vivendi* in lukewarm Calvinism.[3]

Friedrich Heer, in a highly stimulating book, has called this movement the 'third force' in sixteenth-century Europe.[4] Heer himself is largely concerned with the first half of the century: he studies the endeavours of Humanism to create a new Pelagian ethic, frustrated by the entrenched powers of the Church and the latent Manichaeism of both Church and the primitive mass of the people.[5] But the concepts with which he is

[1] Hence the use of the word 'eirenism' in this context. Toleration was very rarely conceived as an end in itself in the sixteenth century.

[2] I take the 'age of colloquy' to end with the accession of Philip II and the last session of the Council of Trent. Thereafter attempts at *détente* through discussion were usually stillborn. Dačický (p. 287) describes the abortive colloquy of Ratisbon in 1601 which did not get beyond the earliest *pourparlers* without squabbling, and adds: 'Thus strife and dissent over religion and the church have continued to pass on the spark of hatred from one to another; for the Church of Christ must suffer discord till the end of the world.'

[3] It has recently been well suggested that part of the moderate wing of Calvinism is best seen as the surviving tradition of Erasmus: H. R. Trevor-Roper, *Religion, the Reformation and Social Change* (London 1967), 1–45 *passim*.

[4] F. Heer, *Die dritte Kraft* (Frankfurt 1960).

[5] 'Das Bemühen europäischer Humanisten und Reformer, zwischen 1500 und 1555

working—the 'third ideal', the *Imperium Tertium,* the empire of the spirit, the reconciliation of opposites—are equally applicable, if not more so, to the rarefied, embattled, intellectualized thinkers of subsequent years. They were the articles of faith of many contemporary scholars. Heer's 'Old Europe', the open mind which still seeks to create unity out of extremes of mood and experience, formed the ideal of the universalists and pansophic writers of the Mannerist age, of the Hermetists and adherents of the *prisca theologia.*

One crucial figure in this development was Philip Melanchthon, a man who, though overshadowed during his life by Luther and never reconciled to the split in Christendom, exercised an enormous influence on posterity. Melanchthon was the creator of a natural philosophy which has much in common with the great medieval syntheses and is closer than might be imagined to the neo-scholastic system of Suarez.[1] He was an important theorist on the subjects of logic and method, education, and the interpretation of the world in the light of natural reason.[2] His religious doctrine was one of moderation, underlain by a scholar's ideal of universal brotherhood. That position stood at odds with orthodox Lutheranism of the Flaccian kind, and after the death of Luther the Philippists (as Melanchthon's followers became known) were placed under increasing pressure in Germany which culminated in their expulsion from Wittenberg in the 1570s.[3]

The other mainspring of conciliatory ideas was the revival in religious spirituality which accompanied the Lutheran Reformation, and found its fullest development in the Netherlands and the Rhineland. It began in close association with some forms of Anabaptism and acquired during its evolution different shades of emphasis: at times an active sectarianism like that of the fanatic David Joris, at times a passive semi-quietism in the writings of Denck, Bünderlin, Entfelder, and later Dirck Coornhert.[4] The Southern Netherlands especially contained groups of educated

Europa zu retten vor der drohenden Aufspaltung in die Ghettobildungen der neueren Jahrhunderte, in die Kirchenstaaten, Staatskirchen und Nationalstaaten'; ibid. 7 ff.

[1] As such he fits into Heer's thesis; ibid. 235 ff.

[2] F. Hofmann, 'Philipp Melanchthon und die zentralen Bildungsprobleme des Reformationsjahrhunderts', in *Philipp Melanchthon 1497–1560* (Berlin 1963), 83–109; W. J. Ong, *Ramus: Method and the Decay of Dialogue* (Cambridge, Mass. 1958), 236–9; E. Garin, *L'educazione in Europa, 1400–1600* (Bari 1957), 202–8. Cf. W. Dilthey, *Weltanschauung und Analyse (Gesammelte Schriften,* Vol. ii), 162–202.

[3] G. Zschäbitz, 'Die Auswirkungen der Lehren Philipp Melanchthons auf die fürsten-staatliche Politik in der zweiten Hälfte des 16. Jahrhunderts' in *Philipp Melanchthon . . .,* 190–226.

[4] The best study is R. M. Jones, *Spiritual Reformers,* Chs. II, III, and IV; cf. E. M. Wilbur, *A history of Unitarianism: Socinianism and its antecedents* (Cambridge, Mass. 1946), Chs. IV, XIV.

men, driven into opposition against official Catholicism, who took refuge in a concealed heterodoxy. They formed a cosmopolitan learned world, linked together intimately within the country, having wide contacts throughout Europe, and—this is a vital aspect—centred on the leading printers and publishing houses of the day.

The nodal point of the whole intellectual network was Philip II's typographer royal at Antwerp, Christopher Plantin, who despite his official position has been conclusively shown to have followed the teachings of two different spiritual apostles, Hendrik Niclaes and Hendrik Barrefelt (Hiël), and to have published their works.[1] Niclaes was an enthusiast who founded a community, the so-called 'house of love' (*Huis der Liefde*), devoted to the mystical righteousness of an elect few; Barrefelt preached rather an inner spirituality within the Catholic Church. The juxtaposition suggests that there was little between the two currents; it also suggests that the question of Plantin's 'hypocrisy' is an unreal one: these contacts were evidently ones he wished to keep secret, but he felt no compunctions in the prevailing circumstances, especially since an essential tenet of his clandestine faith was that it represented the true Catholicism which would conquer by persuasion.

The significance of this is immediate: for Plantin was closely in touch with the whole culture of his time, both through the family circle—two of his daughters married the printer Moretus and the orientalist Raphelengien, a granddaughter married the son of Filips Galle the geographer[2] —and by his association with men of letters. Plantin's friends formed an intellectual élite whose visible outlet was the works produced by him, and the correspondence which surrounded publication at the famous sign of the 'Golden Compasses'.[3] Among them were natural scientists and botanists: Clusius, Dodoens, Lobelius; geographers, cartographers, and antiquarians: Galle, Ortelius, Mercator, the De Jodes, Hogenbergs, Hubert Goltzius, Mylius, Gemma Frisius; emblematists: Sambucus, Hadrianus Junius; linguists, Hebrew and Oriental scholars: Kilian, Raphelengien, Lefèvre de la Boderie, Masius. They included also many

---

[1] The evidence was already known in the last century; see C. Clair, *Christopher Plantin* (London 1960), 23–36, 141 ff., who argues that Plantin was probably a heretic from his earliest days, and—most recently—L. Voet, *The Golden Compasses*, i (Antwerp 1969), 21–30. On Niclaes, and Plantin's editions of his works see H. de la Fontaine-Verney, 'De geschriften van Hendrik Niclaes', *Het Boek* 26 (1940–2), 163–211.

[2] Clair, op. cit. 19, 46 f.; J. Denucé, *Oud-Nederlandsche kaartmakers in betrekking met Plantijn* (Antwerp–The Hague 1912), i. 221 f.

[3] A check-list of the works published by Plantin is provided in Léon Degeorge, *La Maison Plantin à Anvers* (third edn. Paris 1886). The fundamental source for the correspondence is the eight-volume edition by the Musée Plantin-Moretus: *Correspondance de Christophe Plantin, publiée par Max Rooses* (Antwerp 1883–1918).

of the leading artists and engravers of the day, several of whom were later to find their way to Prague.[1]

The breadth of these interests is symptomatic, since they exhibit part of the taste of the age: the emblem, the antiquarian and his collecting, the fascination with travel and topography, with the heterogeneous things of the world which possess nevertheless an underlying unity and must be classified. The search for wholeness or union had its religious dimension, and it is evident that Plantin's own heterodoxy was widely shared. Ortelius was implicated in the Niclaes sect, and there was contact, especially when Plantin moved to Leiden, with the circle around Coornhert which included Justus Lipsius; moreover other printers—like Thomas Basson—are known to have held similar mystical beliefs.[2] Most important, the celebrated Antwerp Polyglot Bible of 1572 seems to have reflected this inspiration. Its editor and doctrinal overseer, Arias Montano, was seriously influenced by Barrefelt whom he knew through Plantin, while the distinguished team of scholars involved in its preparation were using it as a mouthpiece for their belief in a broad-based Christian community.[3] They stood in personal touch with Guillaume Postel, who has already been introduced as a prophet of universalism, advocating linguistic and cultural understanding even of the non-European peoples, and speculating on ways to achieve the total redemption of mankind through the 'third force' of reconciliation.[4]

Plantin was a friend too of Justus Lipsius, and published many of his books.[5] Lipsius presents a classic example, perhaps the most famous, of an unsettled intellectual of the time. He moved from Catholicism to various Protestant professions, then in the 1590s back to the Catholic fold again, and his final position was near to a call for monarchical absolutism to curb the squabbles of the sectaries. As a philosopher he evolved the common denominator of all his beliefs and became the greatest late-Renaissance reviver of a Classical stoicism; this amounted to a recognition that the demands of reason were necessarily ineffective

[1] For all this see Clair, op. cit. *passim*; the summary in Voet, op. cit. 362–95; and the two volumes by Jan Denucé (cited above, p. 94 n. 2, and wider than their title suggests). Cf. *Anvers, ville de Plantin et de Rubens* (Paris 1954), 151 ff.

[2] Denucé, op. cit. ii. 51 ff.; Clair, op. cit. 153 f.; cf. J. A. van Dorsten, *Thomas Basson, 1555–1613* (Leiden 1961).

[3] Maurits Sabbe, *De Moretussen en hun kring* (Antwerp 1928), 27–51; B. Rekers, *Benito Arias Montano (1527–98)* (Amsterdam 1961), Chs. III and IV, a detailed study of Montano on the basis of his large correspondence.

[4] On Postel's contacts with Plantin and Ortelius see Bouwsma, op. cit. 27 f.; Kvačala, art. cit. 184 f., 189 f.

[5] 'Plantin devint l'éditeur attitré de Juste Lipse comme Froben l'avait été d'Érasme', *Anvers, ville . . .*, 180.

in practice, hence the educated must take refuge in a private morality, while externally obeying the good sovereign and serving the communal weal.[1] The conclusion, and the mood of pessimistic resignation, harmonized with the age, and they account for Lipsius's extreme popularity and the innumerable editions of his work. They found no less an echo in Eastern Europe—among the cultured aristocrats of Hungary who read the *Libri Politicorum* and the *Monita et Exempla Politica*, as well as the *De Constantia*, for guidance;[2] or among enquiring minds in Bohemia, as Slavata recalled when compiling his memoirs.[3] The Lipsius paradigm reappears in a compatriot of his and another scholar of international reputation: the lawyer Hubert Giffen came into conflict with the official Lutherans at the universities of Strasbourg and Altdorf, was an at least nominal convert to Catholicism, and spent his last years in Prague as adviser to the Aulic Council.[4]

Eirenism was a religious movement, but it possessed direct political implications. The Dutch revolt which left the Southern provinces a cockpit for two extremisms gave rise also to a body of uncommitted middle opinion overlapping with the moderate wings of both confessional parties. Spain came nearest to accepting it under the accommodating government of Requesens (1573–6), the *éminence grise* behind whose decisions appears to have been Arias Montano.[5] Thereafter Philip II renewed his policy of force, but this was never approved by Maximilian or Rudolf. Maximilian always treated with the gravest suspicion any Spanish intrusion in the Empire—even the status of the Low Countries themselves was not entirely certain—while his son resisted Spanish pressure for recruitment in Germany, action against France, designs on the Cleves succession, and so forth.[6]

---

[1] On Lipsius and his stoicism see L. Zanta, *La Renaissance du Stoïcisme au XVIe siècle* (Paris 1914), 151–240; G. Oestreich, 'Justus Lipsius als Theoretiker des neuzeitlichen Machtstaates', *Historische Zeitschrift* 181 (1956), 31–78. Of course Lipsian stoicism was not simply a response to external pressures. It was also rooted in the natural philosophy of the period; see J. Saunders, *Justus Lipsius, the Philosopher of Renaissance Stoicism* (New York 1955), esp. ch. 4.

[2] A. Vargha, *Iustus Lipsius és a magyar szellemi élet* (Budapest 1942); T. Wittman, 'A magyarországi államelméleti tudományosság XVII század eleji alapvetésének németalföldi forrásaihoz: Justus Lipsius', *Filológiai Közlöny* 1957, 53–66.

[3] 'I knew one man of the knightly estate who openly admitted that he did not believe the apostolic article of faith about the resurrection of the dead, and that talk of things to come after death is pure invention; he read only the writings of Seneca, saying that it was just like thinking of the epistles of St. Paul . . .' Slavata, 37.

[4] Nuncios/ Ferreri, Prague 7 July 1604; cf. *ADB* s.v.; Gschliesser, op. cit. 170 f.

[5] Rekers, op. cit. Ch. II.

[6] Cf. Chudoba, op. cit. 134 ff., 157 ff., who mentions the role of Pernstein in this connection. Rudolf, as we have seen, was inclined to regard the Netherlands as part of his own patrimony; cf. above, pp. 53, 56, 87.

Within the Netherlands moderation was channelled into the activities of artists: this is clearest in the symbolism of triumphal entries and pageantry which was associated with the various pacification attempts there from Matthias's adventure onwards.[1] The remarkable 'Valois' tapestries for example (a series of eight, woven in Flanders and now in the Uffizi) were conceived as a symbolic welcome to the Duke of Alençon-Anjou on his arrival in 1582 to fill the role of supposed peacemaker;[2] their probable author, Lucas de Heere, knew Ortelius, Hoefnagel (later called by Rudolf to Prague), and others of that group. There is perhaps a similar background to the Leicester episode of 1586–7, supported as it was by Philip Sidney, his friend the English exile Daniel Rogers, and the Lipsius circle.[3] We may fairly surmise that similar ideas underlay much of the ceremonial for the arrival of Archduke Ernst as governor in 1593; this was certainly lavish, as two accounts testify, and contained at least one elaborate allegory of peace: 'Opposite the court . . . several youths had made a large hill, covered with a blue flower which looked like cornflower. On the hill sat four blacksmiths who were melting down swords, spears and other weapons of all kinds, and making ploughshares of them . . .'[4]

The pageantry of 1593 also included full reference to the glorious traditions of the Habsburgs, but its bias seems to have been directed exclusively towards the Austrian branch of the family, with special honour for Rudolf I.[5] The significance of this would not have been lost in Prague. The links of the Southern provinces with Bohemia were especially close; towards the end of the century we find considerable interaction between the two lands, alike embroiled in acute confessional struggle. Personal contacts were strong, particularly in the artistic and

[1] For the extant evidence of these see *Anvers, ville* . . ., 22 ff. On Matthias: W. Hummelberger, 'Erzherzog Matthias in den Niederlanden', *Jahrbuch* 61 (N.F. 25, 1965), 91–118.

[2] F. A. Yates, *The Valois Tapestries* (London 1959).

[3] Cf. J. A. van Dorsten, *Poets, Patrons and Professors* (Leiden 1962). Rogers also knew de Heere (ibid. 19). The same episode inspired the production of the first English emblem-book, by Geoffrey Whitney in Leiden (ibid. 124 ff.).

[4] Bydžovský, fos. 272ʳ–273ᵛ; Hiesserle von Chodaw, fos. 15 f. and illustrations. Hiesserle was an eye-witness in the train of Ernst, though a somewhat unlettered one. The whole lavish *joyeuse entrée* was conceived by J. B. Houwaerts of Brussels; see J. L. Motley, *History of the United Netherlands from the death of William the Silent to the Twelve-Years Truce* (London 1869), iii. 269–73. Houwaerts had also been associated with Matthias.

[5] Cf. Bydžovský: 'In front of the game preserve a gate had been erected like the heavens, on which sat a man representing, in honour of his grace the Archduke, Emperor Rudolf I, who ruled in the year 1277, very gloriously and with distinction and all majesty.' The others portrayed were Albrecht, Maximilian I, Charles V and the Electors, Ferdinand I, Maximilian II, Rudolf II, and Ernst himself.

scientific worlds which were both substitute and cover for political action; more of this will emerge later when the roles of Clusius and Sambucus, Goltzius, Hoefnagel, and the rest are examined. Rudolf himself turned to Brussels over one matter very dear to his heart: in 1609 he besought Barvitius to arrange for his 'greatest victories' to be depicted in the finest Netherlands tapestries, incorporating designs (*imprese*) of his own invention.[1]

In Bohemia too the teaching of Melanchthon found wide acceptance. Whereas the *Erblande* were often given to a dogmatic Flaccian view of Luther's legacy, the more tolerant strain became characteristic of the best elements in Czech Protestantism.[2] Several of the Bohemian Humanists, notably Collinus who taught Greek at the Charles University, knew Melanchthon personally; he maintained a large correspondence with men like the astronomer Hájek, and his books enjoyed great popularity.[3] He was particularly concerned with the culture and doctrine of the Czech Brethren, while they, as their horizons widened in the 1560s under the shrewd leadership of Jan Blahoslav, came under eirenical influences both from Wittenberg and Heidelberg.[4] Melanchthon's son-in-law, Kaspar Peucer (1524–1602), was himself a Slav (a Wend from Bautzen), and served as a willing intermediary between the Brethren and Germany.[5]

At this point we may return to Crato, because the most important direct connection between such German developments and the court of the Habsburgs was through him and his friends. Their centre was the city of Breslau (now Wrocław) in Silesia, which occupied a cosmopolitan position on the edge of German and Slav worlds. Breslau in the sixteenth century was a thriving and largely autonomous borough, a trading focus receptive to the commerce both of material goods and ideas, and a place whose significance in the Bohemian lands stood second only to that of Prague. Its Reformation had from the first been more mild and Melanchthonian than elsewhere;[6] moreover it prided itself on its high standards

---

[1] *Briefe und Akten*, vii, No. 182 (Report of Vischere, Prague 28 Nov. 1609). Hans von Aachen was also involved in this (ibid. No. 199 (p. 202)).

[2] For Austria cf. Mecenseffy, op. cit. 31 ff., 50 ff., *passim*. This is, of course, oversimplified; yet there seems to have been more intolerance on both sides in the Austrian lands during the period 1570–1600, which may account for Rudolf's evident dislike of them. See also above pp. 30–2.

[3] R. Říčan, 'Melanchthon und die böhmischen Länder', in *Philipp Melanchthon . . .*, 237–60, esp. 244 f.; F. M. Bartoš, *Bojovníci a mučedníci* (Prague 1946), 121–3; G. Loesche, *Luther, Melanchthon und Calvin in Österreich-Ungarn* (Tübingen 1909), 153–67.

[4] Hrejsa, op. cit. 26 ff.; Říčan, art. cit. 252 ff.; Bartoš, op. cit. 118–21.

[5] E. Benz, *Wittenberg und Byzanz* (Marburg 1949), 129–40.

[6] J. F. A. Gillet, *Crato von Crafftheim und seine Freunde*, i–ii (Frankfurt a. M. 1860), i. 151 ff.

of education and civic culture. Crato was born there in 1519, studied in Wittenberg and Leipzig, where he made the intimate acquaintance of both Luther and Melanchthon, then went to continue his medical training in Italy. He became personal physican to Ferdinand I in 1560 and was present at the latter's death. His career now advanced further: he was a great favourite with Maximilian, who ennobled him and would not be separated from him. After 1576 Crato enjoyed the equal favour of Rudolf, but a combination of ill-health and mistrust of the Jesuits caused him to leave Prague in 1581. Soon afterwards he retired to Breslau, with which he had always maintained contact, where he died in 1585.[1]

Crato numbered among his friends a whole series of distinguished patrician families, particularly the Rhedigers (Redinger) and Monaus in Breslau and Camerarius in Leipzig. Another close colleague was his younger contemporary, the theologian Zacharias Ursinus.[2] It was this group which became widely known at the time as crypto-Calvinists, though what was 'cryptic' in their beliefs was much rather their intellectual reservations about confessional extremism than any surreptitious advocacy of narrow Genevan dogma. In the West Crato enjoyed the widest acquaintance with learned Humanists; in particular he was a close friend of the moderate Hubert Languet—the preceptor of Philip Sidney—and Clusius, as is proved by their large correspondence.[3] He must have been instrumental in arranging for many Silesians to be welcomed in Western Europe—Thomas Rhediger for instance was housed by the printer Wechel and travelled with Clusius[4]—as he was certainly responsible for attracting foreigners to the Habsburg court.

Besides being one of the most respected medical men of his age Crato became famous above all in his capacity of companion to three successive Emperors, especially as the close counsellor and religious adviser of Maximilian. Some sense of this emerges from his funeral oration on the latter's death.[5] It is also evident in his intimate relation to the young

[1] The details of his life in Melchior Adam, *Vitae Germanorum Medicorum* (Heidelberg 1620), 261–77 (Adam was himself a Silesian Humanist), and Gillet, i–ii, esp. ii. 1 ff., 206 ff., 248 ff. Cf. Loesche, op. cit. 144 f.

[2] On Ursinus: Gillet, i. 87 ff., 179 ff.; ii. 97 ff.

[3] Ibid. i. 272 ff.; ii. 43 ff. and see below. *Caroli Clusii Atrebatis ad Thomam Redigerum et Joannem Cratonem epistolae*, ed. P. F. X. de Ram (Brussels 1847) contains 28 letters from Clusius to Crato (1561–84, but not in chronological order), as well as letters to Crato from Dodoens, Ortelius, Mercator, and Montano.

[4] Ong, *Ramus*, p. 97 n. 18. The collection cited in the previous note contains twenty letters from Clusius to his pupil Rhediger (1562–71).

[5] *Oratio Funebris de Divo Maxaemiliano II Imperatore Caesare Augusto . . . a Ioanne Cratone a Craftheim, Consiliario et Medico Caesareo . . . scripta* (Frankfurt 1577). His

Rudolf and his beneficent influence on the progress of Bohemian Humanism. Crato had much sympathy with the Czech Brethren, being concerned to bring them out of their isolation and legitimize them. Although his attempt failed on doctrinal grounds, it was not without fruit: it showed the preparedness of the Imperial side for compromise, and had important results at least for education. Crato and Languet were instrumental in bringing the noted teacher and printer Esrom Rüdiger from an intolerant Wittenberg to Moravia in 1574.[1]

Bohemia stood geographically on the periphery of orthodox Protestantism, both Lutheran and Calvinist, but this did not of course mean that Rüdiger's move to the small provincial town of Ivančice (Eibenschütz) was a step into the wilderness. The printing presses of the Czech Brethren there and at nearby Kralice produced in the later sixteenth century a series of scholarly theological texts which culminated in the famous Bible of Kralice, the co-operative work of a whole team of linguistic and doctrinal experts.[2] The essentially non-sectarian character of this enterprise points again to a feature of the Brethren, as of the religious camps in the Czech lands at large: that their lines of dogma were not yet clearly drawn. The long-serving leader of the Brethren in Bohemia was an eirenical, near-mystical figure: Václav Budovec of Budov;[3] their spokesmen in Moravia were the families of Boskowitz and Žerotín, headed by one of the great pupils of Ivančice, Karel Žerotín the Elder. In Silesia these spiritual developments helped to call forth the visions of Jakob Boehme; it is surely no coincidence that the same area saw the most fervent contemporary propagation of the occult theology of Paracelsus.[4] The Christian Humanism of Crato and Ursinus still found an echo in the next generation, in men like David Pareus and Amandus Polanus, though the days of religious accommodation were numbered.

*   *   *

Bohemia stood also at the edge of the orthodox Catholic world, and

other publications seem to have been exclusively medical: a commentary on Galen (*In C. Galeni divinos libros methodi therapeutices*, Basel 1563); a book of opinions edited from the works of Montanus (J. B. Montanus: *Consultationes medicae . . . I. Cratonis . . . opera atque studio correctae*, i–ii, Basel 1583); and a posthumous collection first edited by Scholtzius in the 1590s (*Consiliorum et epistolarum medicinalium . . . Libri*, i–vii).

[1] Gillet, op. cit. ii. 14 ff., 20 ff., 235 ff.; Comenius, op. cit. 80; Hrejsa, op. cit. 39.

[2] M. Daňková, *Bratrské tisky ivančické a kralické (1564–1619)* (Prague 1951), esp. 41 ff.

[3] Budovec, *Circulus Horologi Lunaris et Solaris* (Hanau 1616); cf. Budovec to Kepler, Hradiště nad Jizerou 28 Jan. 1603 (*Korrespondence*, No. 16), etc.

[4] Sudhoff, *Versuch*, ii. Nos. 83–5, 95–6. Cf. below, pp. 200, 281.

the other seat of heresy which had large connections with Central Europe at this time was Italy. The Italian form of the movement showed the same pattern of non-Curial, Catholic protest as can be observed in the Netherlands, though it was much more mystical, frenetic, and temperamental than its Northern counterparts: it led logically to the work of Patrizi, Bruno, Campanella, and De Dominis. Growing out of the reform endeavours of the conciliarists before the middle of the century, the protest against Rome proceeded from an early general evangelism, through a stage of 'Nicodemist' concealment and secret professions of faith, to full diaspora and individual attempts at eirenical solutions.[1]

At first the chief refuge of such heterodoxy was Switzerland, which gathered together men like Lelio Sozzini, Curione, and Occhino who were sympathetic to Philippist influences, maintained contact with other conciliatory Protestant groups, and felt the spirit of the *politiques*.[2] But intolerance elsewhere drove the exiles increasingly into the Habsburg lands where a particularly important meeting-point was Breslau: Crato knew the Sozzini family, Curione, Celsi, and others.[3] Moravia became the home of a number of them, including the Anabaptist and Arian Niccolò Paruta, who was visited by various other heretics and whose house at Slavkov (Austerlitz!) was the last resting-place of Bernardino Occhino.[4] Extremer disciples found ample scope during the second and third generations still further east. Groups of Socinians and Arians were founded in Poland and Transylvania under the dynamic but wild direction of Fausto Sozzini, Ferenc Dávid, and George Biandrata. In theology their severe rationalism blended with growing chiliasm and universalism, though on the practical level their personal relations were frequently riven by internecine squabble. Contact was easy between Moravia and those areas: Palaeologus and Squarcialupi found their way thence to Alba Julia, Buccella and Simonius to Cracow, while the learned Humanist Giovanni Bernardino Bonifacio ended his wanderings as the cynosure of Protestant Danzig.[5]

[1] D. Cantimori, *Prospettive di storia ereticale italiana del Cinquecento* (Bari 1960), 27–35, for an attempt at periodization.

[2] Cantimori, op. cit. 79–81; idem, *Eretici italiani del Cinquecento* (Florence 1939), *passim*. Lelio Sozzini had links with Melanchthon, Maximilian, and Prague: Wilbur, op. cit. 242.

[3] Cantimori, *Eretici*, 140, 268 n., 269, 304, 341 and *passim*.

[4] Ibid. 312, 344; Bartoš, op. cit. 111–13; W. Urban, 'Z dziejów włoskiej emigracji wyznaniowej na Morawach', *Odrodzenie i Reformacja w Polsce* xi (1966), 49–62.

[5] Cantimori, *Eretici*, esp. Chs. XXVII and XXXIV; W. Urban, *Studia z dziejów Antytrynitaryzmu na ziemiach czeskich i słowackich w XVI–XVII wieku* (Cracow 1966), 67 f. and *passim*. Cf. Wilbur, op. cit. Ch. 15 etc.

The aspirations of these men often brought them into contact with the Habsburg court. Jacopo Aconcio for example, known as an apostle of toleration who found no satisfaction with any organized church, worked for Maximilian in Vienna, before continuing his travels to die in England.[1] His correspondence reveals an interest in the illuminist sectarian Isabella Manriquez de Lara, mother-in-law to Vratislav Pernstein, who herself knew many of the exiles.[2] Doctor Simon Simonius of Lucca (1533–1602) was active at the courts of both Stephen Báthory and Rudolf. After falling out with his heterodox friends he was reconverted to Rome in Prague in 1581 and is recorded as one of the Emperor's physicians at the Diet of Augsburg the following year.[3] Similarly the Florentine scholar Giovanni Brutus (1517–92), a person of very considerable erudition, worked for many years in Transylvania and Cracow, but ended his days at least nominally in the Catholic fold as Imperial court historiographer.[4]

There existed two different tendencies in such dealings with Vienna and Prague, the one predominantly mystical, the other humanist: the first is represented most fully by Francesco Pucci, the latter by Andreas Dudith. Pucci provides perhaps the most extraordinary case among all this band of misfits.[5] He was born in Florence in 1543, had a normal education for the priesthood, took the tonsure and devoted himself to religious study. In retrospect Pucci's youthful acceptance of spiritual discipline seems (like Bruno's or Campanella's) to have been the product rather of insecurity than of certitude. Manifestly it was not long sustained: in 1571 he began a series of wanderings around Europe which led him first to France and England, then to the Netherlands, where he made the acquaintance of Lipsius. After that he found his way to Cracow —in late 1583 or 1584—and met there the two English alchemists Dee and Kelley whom he followed in 1585 to Prague. By this time he was already accounted a dangerous heretic, and his own peculiar brand of

---

[1] C. D. O'Malley, *Jacopo Aconcio* (Rome 1955), esp. 10 ff.; cf. Bartos, op. cit. 114–17.

[2] O'Malley, op. cit. 24 and n.; Cantimori, *Eretici*, 248; Chudoba, op. cit. 135.

[3] Botero, *Relationi*, iii. 24; Fleischman (1582), 53; T. Csorba, op. cit. 195–7. Simonius was bitterly attacked for his various apostasies by his compatriot Squarcialupi in a pamphlet issued at Cracow in 1588.

[4] Brutus was an important member of the Central European Humanist circle: witness the five books of his letters published in Cracow in 1583. His historical work was edited, with biographical details, by F. Toldy, *Brutus J. M. . . . Magyar Históriája*, i–iii (Budapest 1863–76).

[5] Much material for the study of Pucci has been collected by L. Firpo and R. Piattoli in *Francesco Pucci, Lettere* (Florence 1955) and *Documenti e Testimonianze* (Florence 1959). The only biography of him is the brief account by Firpo in the latter volume, pp. 8–24.

Pelagianism was being formulated. On a visit to Switzerland he had disputed with Fausto Sozzini, arguing his view of the natural goodness and immortality of man, while his expectation of an imminent judgement day was also evident.[1]

Pucci's initial two years in Prague form a most confused period, during which his personal mysticism and chiliasm first drove him to participate in Dee's seances—the most remarkable of them the *Actio Pucciana*[2]—in the belief that they represented a divine revelation, and then to seek reconciliation in the body of the Catholic Church. He writes thus to his mother in 1585:

But then I heard from the angel most weighty propositions concerning the coming of Antichrist in a short space and received great confirmation of my hopes for an imminent renovation of all things, which God will accomplish through persons authorized by him and adequate to that task. Lamenting therefore my sin I will repair to the ministers of that [Papal] Seat, to give them satisfaction for my offence in the sight of God.[3]

Rome was very suspicious of Pucci—as it was of all Italians in Prague[4]—but the nuncio Sega eventually undertook to hear his full confession and abjuration which took place on 6 March 1587.[5] All this time Pucci was still consorting with Dee and Kelley and visiting them in Třeboň where they were now in Rožmberk employ. He introduced to them the unsettled young ex-Jesuit Christian Francken and apparently made attempts to persuade them also to submit to the Catholic Church.[6] Yet despite his abjuration and a successful appeal that he be allowed to return to Tuscany, Pucci found no peace. He stayed in Prague until 1591—Visconte described him in 1589 as 'homo che è passato quasi per tutte

[1] Pucci, *Lettere*, No. 13, to his brother Giovanni in Florence, Cracow 15 March 1584; he dislikes the Protestant sects and is awaiting the 'vera riforma . . . essendo molto vicino il tempo nel quale deono udirsi queste trombe . . .' Cf. L. Firpo, 'Pucci a Basilea', in *Medioevo e Rinascimento*, 257–95.

[2] The *Actio Pucciana* is reported in John Dee's *True and Faithful Relation* (p. 218 n. 4) and reprinted in Pucci, *Documenti*, No. 101.

[3] 'E allora ho sentiti pur da detto angiolo propositi gravissimi quanto all'Anticristo da venire fra poco tempo e avuto gran confermazione della mia speranza quanto alla prossima rinovazione, che Dio è per fare tosto mediante persone autorizzate da lui e suffizienti a tanta impresa. Però, dolente del mio peccato, sono per ricorrere a ministri di quella Sede, dandoli sodisfazione della offesa fatta a Dio . . .' Pucci, *Lettere*, No. 17, Prague 13 Aug. 1585. The *Actio* took place on 6 August. Cf. his letter to a Dutch friend, François Loockmans, dated 30 August: J. Denucé, *Catalogue des manuscrits de la Musée Plantin-Moretus* (Antwerp 1927), No. 301.

[4] Nuncios/Caetano, instruction for Speziano, 581.

[5] Pucci, *Documenti*, Nos. 113 (Dec. 1586) and 115 (the deed of abjuration).

[6] Ibid. Nos. 106 (report of Dee, 10 and 17 July 1586) and 123 (visit of Pucci and Francken 9–13 July 1587). Cf. Pucci's long appeal to Dee, temporarily exiled at Cassel in Germany, on 18 Aug. 1586 (*Lettere*, No. 22).

le sette de heretici et in Inghilterra'—and then returned to the Netherlands, while keeping in touch with Bohemia.[1] Eventually he began the
journey back to Italy, was arrested in Salzburg, handed over to the
Inquisition, tried as an unregenerate schismatic, and finally executed in
Rome in 1597.

Pucci was engaged in a mystical search for the fundamentals of the
true faith, which should be accessible to all. He seems indeed to have
believed that all men were naturally capable of grasping it, and that they
could be reformed through education, but the need was urgent, since he
apprehended that the new world would begin in 1600, and mankind
must be prepared.[2] Undoubtedly the best insight into his mind is provided by a document now firmly ascribed to him, a treatise on the ideal
form of government, the *Forma d'una republica catholica*.[3] Pucci here
recapitulates the malaise of the religiously uncommitted, repelled by all
received systems of doctrine, and at the same time anticipates Campanella, since his catholic state, like the Dominican's astral one, is founded
on spiritual compulsion and totalitarianism. His 'comune et universale
republica' will embrace men of all countries, who shall henceforward
live as 'foreigners in their own land', but it is clearly only an élite which
will be selected; the corollary of Pucci's apparent religious latitudi-
narianism is the official rewarding of virtue and punishment of vice,
censorship, imposed education, and an enforced observance of the
duties of citizenship.

> Therefore whoever desires to be accepted shall promise to tender obedience
> to our sovereign (who is God) and the senate composed of deputies of our
> colleges, and to be a faithful member of this body, furthering with all diligence
> the benefit of our community, even putting it before his private interest; he
> must be a friend of our friends and enemy of the wretched in so far as they are
> malicious and evil and habituated to vice.[4]

Pucci is an important representative of the late Humanist reformers of
the mind: unstable in personality and repelled by the institutions of the
actual world, he took refuge in a scheme for society on a new foundation,

---

[1] Nuncios/Visconte, Prague 2 Oct. 1589. Pucci's last surviving letter from Prague
was to his brother on 8 Jan. 1591 (*Lettere*, No. 41); he wrote from Salzburg on 5 Jan.
1593 to a friend in Prague (ibid., No. 47). The French resident Ancel writes to Bongars
on 24 Feb. 1592: 'Le pauvre Pucej est à Dieppe et s'y morfond. Vous entendrez bientost
dire qu'il sera passé à Rome pour voir le nouveau Pape.' C. Schultess, *Aus dem Briefwechsel des französischen Philologen und Diplomaten Jacques Bongars* (Hamburg 1905),
183.

[2] There are discussions of Pucci's thought—from different standpoints—in Cantimori, *Prospettive*, 94–6, and Heer, *Dritte Kraft*, 547–53.

[3] This is printed in full by D. Cantimori and E. Feist, *Per la storia degli eretici italiani
del secolo XVI in Europa* (Rome 1937), 171–202, where it is listed as the work of an
anonymous author.   [4] Ibid. 184.

which should provide renewal through education and the dictation of an enlightened 'College'.[1] He wished to guarantee the fulfilment of spiritual wholeness through absolute submission.

Pucci's colleague in Prague, Christian Francken, was himself a curious and interesting (though almost entirely forgotten) figure in the same mould. Born in Brandenburg of Lutheran parents he became a convert to Catholicism and entered the Society of Jesus in Rome; but while a member of its College in Vienna he and a friend Paul Florenus were assailed by doubts and fled the Order, apparently in 1578.[2] After a wandering and unsettled life in Bohemia and Transylvania, during which his views grew markedly extreme and Antitrinitarian, Francken seems to have returned to the Roman faith shortly before his death in 1595, with the blessing of the Prague nuncio Speziano. Although many details of his life and polemical *œuvre* remain obscure, one point is clear: he too was looking for some resolution of spiritual uncertainty. Significantly Francken came strongly under the influence of stoic thought and prepared the first edition in Hungary of the teachings of Epictetus.[3]

The Hungarian Andreas Dudith was a man of very different temper, but he shows similarities of mood and career with Pucci and Francken. He can be claimed at least in part as an Italian heretic, since he was born at Buda of Italian mother—the family of Sbardellato—and Croat father in 1533, during that twilight period for Hungary between the first Turkish assault and the final conquest.[4] From the outset he stood in close connection with the Habsburgs: his uncle Augusto Sbardellato was Bishop of Vác (Waitzen), a councillor and diplomat in the service of Ferdinand I, and the young Dudith assimilated the atmosphere which survived from the erstwhile court of Mary of Hungary, especially through the Queen's Erasmian confessor Henckel, who was his tutor in Breslau

---

[1] 'Dovunque si trova qualche numero di persone della dispositione et affettione detta di sopra si potrà ordinare un collegio, chiamandolo Academia, Compagnia, Fraternità, o con altro simil nome che più accomoda al luogo et costume del paese dove i cittadini vivono.' Ibid. 184 f.

[2] *Collegium Jesuiticum toti orbi Christiano ad recte cognoscendam Iesuitarum religionem utilissimum* (Basle 1580). This tract of self-justification, dedicated to Rudolf II by the two apostates, was immediately translated into English (by William Charke in 1581, as a supplement to his refutation of Edmund Campion) and several times republished. On Francken in general cf. A. Räss, *Die Convertiten seit der Reformation*, iii (Freiburg 1866), 296–307; L. Szczucki in *Odrodzenie i Reformacja w Polsce*, viii (1963), 39–75.

[3] *Epicteti Philosophi Stoici Enchiridion, in quo ingeniosissime docetur, quemadmodum ad animi tranquillitatem, beatitudinemque, praesentis vitae perveniri possit* (Claudiopoli 1585); cf. two letters by Francken in Budapest, Egyetemi Könyvtár, Prae Litterae 150, 161.

[4] For the life of Dudith: Pierre Costil, *André Dudith, humaniste hongrois* (Paris 1935). There is a useful summary from the Polish standpoint by H. Barycz in the *Polski Słownik Biograficzny*, v, s.v.

for some years. The early part of Dudith's life was occupied by study and travel: begun in Breslau, then continued in Vienna and afterwards further afield; he spent several years in Northern Italy and lived in France during 1554–5 and 1557–8, where he made many Humanist contacts.[1] On his return home in 1560 there began a second period, one of high ecclesiastical preferment: Dudith acted as spokesman for Ferdinand at Trent and was raised to the bishopric of Pécs (Fünfkirchen), an office whose dignity was considerable, though his revenues and seat lay in the hands of the Turks.

There were, however, already seeds of dissatisfaction. At Trent Dudith, along with his colleagues the Hungarian Draskovics, the Czech Brus, the Pole Cromer, and others, had defended the Habsburg conciliatory line in sharp opposition to the prevailing ultramontane rigidness which eventually won the day.[2] Then in 1567, while engaged on an Imperial mission to the Polish court, he made a sudden complete break: he married a lady-in-waiting, renounced his Catholicism, and settled in Cracow, a city already famous as a centre of religious heterodoxy which had direct links with Breslau and Prague.[3] Here he became associated in religion with various Arians and Antitrinitarians, and in politics with the powerful pro-Habsburg Zborowski faction—he married one of that family as his second wife.[4] After the failure of this party during the second Polish interregnum of 1574–6, Dudith was forced to flee, and he moved with Rudolf's permission first to Moravia, then in 1579 to Breslau. He lived there quietly, a close friend of Crato and member of his circle, and it was in Breslau that he died in 1589;[5] a monument to him can still be seen there.

Dudith was never a settled member of any Protestant church, but in his later years he seems to have come closest to the moderate persuasion of Breslau. Doctrinally he stood at odds with orthodox Protestantism no less than with the Catholics (as his correspondence with Beza reveals);[6] but he combined dogmatic extremes—he was both anti-trinitarian and anti-adorantist, and had much sympathy for the Hungarian Unitarians[7]

---

[1] Cf. the rather skimpy information in J. Faludi, *André Dudith et les humanistes français* (Szeged 1927). At that time he also visited England, as a secretary to Cardinal Pole (Costil, 72).

[2] Dudith's arguments at Trent appeared as Andreas Dudithius, *Orationes duae . . . in Concilio Tridentino habitae* (Venice 1562 etc.).

[3] Cf. Cantimori, *Eretici*, Ch. XXIX.   [4] Costil, op. cit. 157 f.

[5] Puteo reported to Rome the death of the 'arch-apostate': Nuncios/Puteo, Prague 7 Mar. 1589.

[6] *Epistolae Andreae Dudithii Theodoro Bezae* (1570); appended to *Mini Celsi Senensis, De haereticis capitali supplicio non afficiendis* (n.p. 1584).

[7] For his position on the Trinity see *Epistola Andreae Dudithii . . . ad Iohannem*

—with an outward profession of Lutheranism, a position almost like that of Lipsius on sovereignty and eirenism. He was a friend to many heretics and exiles, particularly in Cracow: he protected Alciati and Squarcialupi, was acquainted with Pucci, and showed continuing interest in the latter's visions.[1]

As a thinker Dudith demonstrated the widest intellectual breadth. The traveller Krafft recalled how, on a visit to Breslau in 1583, he was invited by the 'Edle, hochgelertt und weitt beriembtter herr Andreas Duditcjus, K.M. Ferdinandi, Maximilliani und Ruodolphi gewesner gehaimer Rath' to recount his experiences in the Eastern Mediterranean; he was closely questioned by his host, who displayed special learned interest in the phenomenon of the waterspout.[2] Dudith's Humanist contacts were pre-eminently with the middle opinion of Crato, the Rhedigers, Monaus, Camerarius, and their friends, but he ranged also much wider afield. From his French days he seems to have known the Hebrew scholar Jean Mercier, Joachim Perion (translator of the mystical writer Dionysius the Areopagite), and Hubert Languet. He kept in touch with the Netherlands and England: Plantin, Ortelius, Sidney, and the rest; he corresponded with Lipsius at least during the years 1584–9.[3] Further east his contacts were equally well developed: witness his friendship with Giovanni Brutus, the astronomer Hájek, and the Polish poet Kochanowski.[4] The link with Hájek became particularly close, since both were concerned with the problems of cosmology and astrology, and both were provoked by the comet of 1577, a scientific *cause célèbre* of the day. Dudith's contribution to that debate was published in 1579 and twice reprinted; his line is one of limited acceptance: he retains the scheme of general heavenly causes, while denying that comets, as particulars, can determine human affairs.[5]

Lasicium equitem Polonum (n.p. 1590). Cf. Costil, op. cit. 340 ff., and Cantimori, *Prospettive*, 88–91.

[1] Costil, op. cit. 140, 174, 202 f.; and cf. the letter from Dudith to Hájek of 20 Dec. 1585 in Pucci, *Documenti*, No. 103. Dudith's notions of toleration are discussed in an article by I. Hegedűs in *Irodalomtörténeti Közlemények* 11 (1901), 189–99.

[2] *Reisen und Gefangenschaft Hans Ulrich Kraffts aus der Originalhandschrift*, ed. K. D. Hassler (Stuttgart 1861), 398 ff.

[3] Gillet, op. cit. ii. 303 ff.; Faludi, op. cit. 27 ff.; Costil, op. cit. 146–8, 195 ff., 206 f. and *passim*; Vargha, op. cit. 32–9. Dudith's letters appeared in several collections, e.g. *Pauli Manutii Epistolarum Libri XII* (Leipzig 1669).

[4] For his Polish connections cf. Barycz, loc. cit. On Dudith and Brutus see V. Fraknói, 'Brutus Mihály, Báthory István udvari történetírója', *Századok* 1887, 793–7.

[5] E. Zinner, *Geschichte und Bibliographie der astronomischen Literatur in Deutschland zur Zeit der Renaissance* (Stuttgart 1964), Nos. 2883, 4708; cf. Costil, op. cit. 351 ff. The edition of 1580 (*De Cometis Dissertationes Novae*) contains Dudith's opinion (*De Cometarum Significatione*), addressed to Crato and dated 'ex solitudine mea Pascoviana

In this, as elsewhere, Dudith was a man rooted in tradition, who nevertheless sought reform. He was especially associated with the Habsburgs as a political adviser, and his relations with their supporters the Zborowskis in Poland reveal his willingness to back wider attempts at conciliation, even the recovery of Greek Christendom under Habsburg aegis. That such universalist ideals were by no means dead in the later sixteenth century is proved by such figures as Maximos Margounios[1] in the East and James Palaeologus and Jakob Basilikos in the West. Probably the best-known practical exponent of such a policy was Basilikos, also called Heraclides, who claimed princely Levantine descent, and after much wandering through Europe undertook to effect a 'Reformation' in Moldavia during the years 1561–3. The scheme began with considerable success, attracting the help of certain pronouncedly Utopian persons, but it soon collapsed in disaster and recriminations were heaped upon its instigator.[2] Basilikos was in fact by no means a charlatan and his bad reputation is largely posthumous. In his time he was much admired in Central Europe: he had contact with Melanchthon, and his activities enjoyed, as well as the tacit support of Maximilian II, the full co-operation of the Zborowskis and Albrecht Łaski in Poland.[3]

Palaeologus was a more serious theologian, and his heretical views show considerable similarity to those of Dudith. He was an apostate Dominican monk who, after appearing at the last session of the Council of Trent, fled to Prague and lived there from 1563 to 1571.[4] Here he built up a circle of important friends: Collinus (whom we have already

(Paskov) apud Moravos', 28 Feb. 1579. It also includes the tract of Erastus (*Iudicium de Cometis*) which follows a similar view; a letter from Dudith to Erastus; and another interpretation, by his fellow-heretic Squarcialupi.

[1] Margounios was a Cretan Humanist and oecumenical theorist who had links with South German men of learning and possessed in his library the Hermetic texts in their *Cracow* edition of 1585–90. See D. J. Geanokoplos, *Byzantine East and Latin West* (Oxford 1966), 165–93. He also prepared a Greek translation of Lawrence of Brindisi's essay on the Cabala (cf. above, p. 91 n. 6).

[2] On Basilikos there is the contemporary account, the *Vita Jacobi Despotae* of Johann Sommer (Wittenberg 1587), republished in *Deux Vies de Jacques Basilicos* (publiées par E. Legrand, Paris 1889); cf. (for the best assessment) Benz, *Wittenberg und Byzanz*, 34–58. This Sommer was a youthful collaborator with Basilikos who later became a Transylvanian religious extremist and colleague of Palaeologus; cf. A. Pirnát, *Die Ideologie der Siebenbürger Antitrinitarier in den 1570er Jahren* (Budapest 1961), 17–53.

[3] Benz, loc. cit. The collection by Legrand contains 15 letters which passed between Maximilian and Basilikos, and also two from Melanchthon praising his learning and Christian faith.

[4] For the life of Palaeologus—whose real name was Fra Giacomo of Chios—during these years see G. Rill, 'Jacobus Palaeologus (*c.* 1520–85)', *Mitteilungen des Österreichischen Staatsarchivs*, 16 (1963), 28–86, based on his correspondence with the Habsburgs; and R. Dostálová-Jeništová, 'Jakobus Palaeologus', in *Byzantinische Beiträge*, ed. J. Irmscher (Berlin 1964), 153–75, which adds some Czech material.

noted as a colleague of Melanchthon), Martin Kuthen (whose daughter Palaeologus married), the botanist Matthioli, Crato, Hájek. Palaeologus was held in high esteem, both as Humanist and theologian—some of the Utraquists even wanted him appointed as their bishop—and Maximilian II appears to have been sympathetic towards him, making particular use of his familiarity with Oriental languages.[1] But his tendency to polemic and increasing radicalism forced him to migrate, first to Cracow, where he found the protection of Dudith and became involved with the Zborowskis, and then to Transylvania.[2] Later he returned to Moravia, but Catholicism now regarded him as a highly dangerous heretic and put strong pressure on Rudolf to hand him over to the Papal nuncio. In 1582 the Emperor—who perhaps disliked most of all Palaeologus's own claim to Imperial Greek parentage—allowed him to be sent to Rome, where he was duly executed in 1585.[3]

Palaeologus evidently became more extreme as he grew older, but he appears basically to have aimed at undermining the Ottoman Istanbul by some accommodation with Greek Constantinople, and this project would have held much attraction for Dudith.[4] It appealed to the Habsburgs too, and they were acting in the same spirit by their guarded patronage of moderate Protestant attempts to convert the South Slavs; such was the particular aspiration of the printer Hans von Ungnad and his collaborators in the publication of Slavonic texts, the Slovene Trubar and the Serb Demetrios.[5] The latter actively assisted Basilikos, and the whole movement was conceived as a mission to use the primitive contemporary notions of Panslavism in the service of an oecumenical ideal. In a similar way the Imperial ambassadors to the Porte acted as cover for the celebrated overtures towards Orthodox Christendom made by German eirenical theologians under the leadership of Martin Crusius.[6]

Dudith was an equally important representative of the Habsburg

---

[1] Rill, art. cit. 49 ff., 59 f.; Urban, *Studia*, 44 f.

[2] Rill, art. cit. 74 f., 78–80; Costil, op. cit. 140; Pirnát, op. cit. 54–116. The nature of Palaeologus's extremely interesting religious beliefs and social theories in his last years cannot be considered here.

[3] The seriousness with which the Pope regarded this matter can be gauged from Madruzzo's correspondence during 1582 in *Nuntiaturberichte*/Hansen, 411, 419, 422, 426, 447 f.

[4] Dudith sympathized with the Greek position on the 'filioque'—hence the Catholics compared him to Photius; Costil, op. cit. 340–2.

[5] Benz, op. cit. 59–93, 141 ff.; cf. M. Murko, *Die Bedeutung der Reformation und Gegenreformation für das geistige Leben der Südslawen* (Prague–Heidelberg 1927), 8 ff.

[6] The basic source for this oft-narrated episode is M. Crusius, *Turco-graeciae . . . Libri Octo* (Basle 1584).

religious position in his attitude at the Council of Trent. The attempts of Ferdinand I to persuade that Council in favour of some compromise towards the Protestants are well known. The speeches of Dudith or Draskovics in favour of the chalice and clerical marriage followed on the conciliatory feelers of the 1540s; their standpoint was similar to that of the French group around the Cardinal of Lorraine and Pibrac who embodied the views of the 'politiques' and the Academy, and the spirit of the Colloquy of Poissy.[1] This attitude had a specific reference to the Bohemian context: there the issue of communion in both kinds was still crucial, and timely concessions might yet win over stony Utraquist hearts. Moreover the increasing strain which we have observed between Ferdinand's successors and the papacy created a growing conflict of allegiance for the senior Bohemian clergy, a choice of curial or territorial Church. The widening gap between Prague and Rome has its part in the major Central European ecclesiastical development which was much later to become known as 'Josephinism'.

The first archbishop of the newly reconstituted see of Prague, Anton Brus of Mohelnice, was likewise a member of Ferdinand's Erasmian team of moderate theologians and advisers: his colleagues were Cassander, Witzel, Pflug, Zasius, and Seld.[2] He also worked with Dudith at Trent, where he was clearly disliked by the Roman hierarchy. Brus managed to obtain limited papal sanction during an experimental period for the ordination of Old-Utraquist priests who would be permitted to dispense the chalice to the laity, and he made efforts—albeit vain ones—to come to terms with the lower Consistory.[3] Despite his obvious and widely-acknowledged zeal, neither he nor the Emperor was willing to introduce the Tridentine decrees into Bohemia. In the interests of a true Catholic Church on a national basis Brus remained an adiaphorist over the inessentials of worship and resisted papal pretensions in his diocese.[4]

Under the successor of Brus, Martin Medek, tension became greater, since Medek was a man with the same background (he even grew up in the same Moravian village) and the same attitude.[5] Despite his assurances

---

[1] For the French case see Yates, *French Academies*, 199–235; H. O. Evennett, *The Cardinal of Lorraine and the Council of Trent* (Cambridge 1930), esp. 235–82.

[2] Heer argues strongly the Erasmian legacy in these advisers of Ferdinand: op. cit. 420 ff.

[3] A. Frind, *Die Geschichte der Bischöfe und Erzbischöfe von Prag* (Prague 1873), 182–9 on Brus, who was archbishop from 1561 to 1580; cf. Denis, op. cit. 446 ff. The whole position of Brus at Trent and later is re-examined by F. Kavka and A. Skýbová, *Husitský epilog na Koncilu Tridentském a původní koncepce habsburské rekatolizace Čech* (Prague 1969).

[4] Cf. Winter, *Geisteskampf*, 178.

[5] On Medek (1580–90) see Frind, op. cit. 189–92; cf. Winter, op. cit. 180.

of diligence in the propagation of the faith—witness a diocesan report sent to Sixtus V in 1589[1]—it is significant that the nuncios found Medek most uncooperative, and there were frequent complaints of his laxity. Both Malaspina and Puteo protest that he is weak and ineffective,[2] while Sega (disingenuous about Rudolf as always) is inclined to see him as the worst offender of all: 'I think it certain that there is goodwill both in His Majesty and in the principal Catholics here, and that with the removal of the obstacles I have mentioned we may hope for some improvement in our affairs. If only we had a zealous archbishop I believe we could hope for better things even in the absence of the Emperor.'[3]

On the death of Medek in 1590 the Prague see remained vacant for a period of three years. Despite the lamentations of the Catholics over this situation and the prejudice it did to their religion,[4] Rudolf was long unwilling to act, and for that he had his reasons. From the outset the two main candidates were Zbyněk Berka of Dubá and George Popel Lobkovic;[5] when the former was finally elected he proved an intransigent career Catholic and friend of the nuncios. Berka was the brother of one of the leading anti-Žerotín agitators in Moravia, and he was responsible for much of the Protestant witch-hunting in Prague which culminated in the holding of a long-delayed diocesan synod in 1605 and the archbishop's own reception into the cardinalate before his death the next year.[6] As if resolved to frustrate the Curial camp, Rudolf saw to the election as Berka's successor of his friend and counsellor Karl von Lamberg, who came from a family very loyal to the dynasty and seems to have possessed some of the Emperor's own characteristics: he was ailing, indecisive (he made no report to Rome) and melancholic.[7] In 1611 Lamberg's loyalty to Matthias was in question, but he was anyway too ill to conduct the coronation ceremony and died within a few months of Rudolf. He was followed in office by the low-born and zealous Abbot of Strahov, Jan Lohelius.

    [1] Summarized in J. Schmidlin, *Die kirchlichen Zustände in Deutschland vor dem dreissigjährigen Krieg nach den bischöflichen Diözesanberichten an den Heiligen Stuhl* (Freiburg i. B. 1910), 150 ff. This is a most important source for the state of the Catholic Church during the years 1585–1618 which appears to be almost completely unknown.
    [2] Nuncios/Malaspina: Como to Malaspina, Rome 26 Jan. 1585; /Puteo, Prague 10 Dec. 1587, 2 Feb. 1588.
    [3] Nuncios/Sega, Prague 6 Jan. 1587.
    [4] Nuncios/Visconte and Caetano 1590-2, *passim*; cf. Tomek, op. cit. 345 f.
    [5] Nuncios/Visconte, Prague 6 Feb. 1590.
    [6] Frind, op. cit. 192–5.
    [7] V. Bartůnek, 'Karel z Lamberku, pražský arcibiskup', *Časopis Společnosti Přátel Starožitností*, xliii (1943–5), 174–214. The German form of the name is more appropriate, since Lamberg (1607–12) spoke no Czech. His brother Georg Sigismund von Lamberg was Privy Councillor from 1606 till after 1612 (Riegger, 194).

In contrast to his Prague counterpart the Bishop of Olomouc was traditionally resolutely Curial,[1] partly because his relations with Rome had remained unbroken, partly because of disagreements with the senior Bohemian diocese and the general refusal of Moravia to subordinate itself. There were three notable holders of the office during the period of Maximilian and Rudolf. The first, Vilém Prusinovský (1565–72), was a protégé of the Jesuits and a fearless patron of the Society, which he introduced into Olomouc in 1566, together with a seminary, and to Brno in 1570.[2] He also authorized the calling of a diocesan synod, ignoring the disapproval of Maximilian.

Stanislav Pavlovský, elected in 1579 (after a series of disputed elections and short-lived episcopates), was an even more formidable figure, a strong promoter of the Counter-Reformation in Moravia who worked for the Habsburg candidature in Poland because he conceived it to serve the interests of international Catholicism, a henchman of the Jesuit Possevino and Cardinal Aldobrandini.[3] He nevertheless retained the amity of Rudolf for his part as an anti-Turkish propagandist, and it was the threat of an interruption to that good work on the death of Pavlovský in 1598 which gave weight to Spinelli's crucial nunciature in Prague. Spinelli now sought to impose on the Olomouc Chapter a new Curial candidate, the young and fervent František (Don Francesco) Dietrichstein, despite much local opposition to him in the grounds of his unfamiliarity, his youth, and his foreignness.[4] Rudolf too entertained a cordial mistrust of Dietrichstein: it was the mark of Spinelli's diplomacy that he managed to overcome the Emperor's neurotic fear of papal intervention sufficiently to have Dietrichstein installed, but this occurred at the price of allowing an Imperial nominee, Paul Albert, to succeed in Breslau, where the ruling house was determined to retain control.[5] With Dietrichstein began the indiscriminate attack on national middle opinion which foreshadowed the catastrophe of twenty years later; Dietrichstein and his brother were, with the Berkas, the leaders of intrigue against Žerotín and the greatest patrons of the Moravian Jesuits.[6] In Breslau, on the other hand, the Society had still made no headway and the successor to the

---

[1] Cf. Winter, op. cit. 181 ff.   [2] D'Elvert, op. cit. 48–56.

[3] Ibid. 62–93; Kalista, Čechové, 45–56; Schmidlin, op. cit. 163 ff. (Pavlovský's report of 1590).

[4] Stloukal, Papežská politika, 114–22.

[5] Ibid. 128–40, 143–7. J. Jungnitz, 'Die Bischofswahl des Bonaventura Hahn 1596', ZVGAS 34 (1900), 253–88.

[6] Odložilík, Karel ze Žerotína, 99–101. Some measure of Dietrichstein's efficiency is seen in his reports to Rome; he was one of very few bishops to present them regularly, in 1605, 1608, 1613, and 1617 (Schmidlin, loc. cit.).

short-lived Paul Albert, Johann Sitsch (1600–8), was regularly criticized by later nuncios for his lack of zeal.[1]

The problem of control over the nomination and activities of bishops always forms part of a larger question about the rights which can be exercised by State over Church. This emerges very clearly from the situation in Hungary during the same period. There the issue was aggravated by the presence of a large number of titular bishoprics and sees in Turkish hands. During the sixteenth century a three-cornered struggle developed between Habsburg sovereign, Papacy, and native estates, whose result was an increasing stalemate. Despite the promptings of the Curia most prelates were unwilling to press Tridentine dogmatism, at least before 1600, indeed the cultural horizons of some of them remained far broader; while Rudolf, insisting on his rights of presentation, fearing the challenge of any high ecclesiastical authority, and eternally short of revenue, did not appoint a Primate of Hungary until the last years of his life.[2]

The sensitivity of Rudolf to this contest of forces and his anti-clerical attitude seem to presage in embryo the position of his late eighteenth-century counterpart Joseph II. Josephinism in its religious aspect meant a particular kind of *étatisme*, and one characteristically Habsburg: a movement broadly Catholic but strongly anti-Papal, where the Emperor replaced the Church as a supra-national ideal with the clergy in his service. Yet the history of the notion can be followed back long before the reign of Joseph himself, or even of his mother Maria Theresa. It embraces a line of precursors from the early seventeenth century who were almost all Czech, for Bohemia was the part of the Monarchy which always possessed the strongest animus against the Jesuits and neo-Aristotelians, which retained some measure of national resistance to foreign domination, and which most consistently fostered attempts at intellectual reform within the body of the Church.

---

[1] Nuncios/Ferreri, Prague 24 May 1604; /Caetano: Borghese to Caetano, Rome 23 May 1607 etc. Cf. the documents printed by A. O. Meyer, 'Zur Geschichte der Gegenreformation in Schlesien', *ZVGAS* 38 (1904), 351–61. Roman influence seems generally to have been resisted more successfully in Silesia; in 1589 we hear that Rudolf was insisting on local candidates to fill benefices there (Nuncios/Visconte, Prague 12 Sept. 1589). It was the bishop of Breslau Martin Gerstmann who advised on the exequies of Maximilian II and conducted the service (SÚA, SM K 1/15).

[2] The Hungarian bishops are a recurring theme in the nuncio's reports: e.g. /Puteo, introduction, cxxix–xxxvi. Cf. in general V. Fraknói, *A magyar királyi kegyúri jog Szent Istvántól Mária Teréziáig* (Budapest 1895), 233 ff. The archiepiscopal see of Esztergom (Gran) was vacant from the death of Antal Verancsics in 1573 until the very end of the century; see V. Fraknói, *Magyarország egyházi és politikai összeköttetései a Római Szent-Székkel*, iii (1526–1689), (Budapest 1903) 197 ff., 205 f., 221 f., 259 f.

The first of these precursors was the Capuchin Valerian Magni (1586/7–1661), whose father had been active at Rudolf's court. As a youth Magni came under the influence of Lawrence of Brindisi and Kepler.[1] After the collapse of the estates' revolt in 1620 he sought an inner religious conversion in Bohemia and was wholly opposed to the foreign dictation of Ferdinand II, his confessor Lamormaini, and the Jesuits under Carafa. In this Magni was supported by his friend Ernst von Harrach, Lohelius's successor as archbishop, who defended the independence of the diocesan seminary of priests and the University;[2] but the Capuchin was brought to account by Rome, and he died on his way to stand trial there.

Another figure, significant but neglected, was Magni's follower, the Premonstratensian Abbot of Strahov Hieronymus Hirnhaim (1637–79), who attacked both the religion and the philosophy of the Jesuits and displayed, like Magni, a pronounced anti-Aristotelian sentiment in his writings.[3] In the early eighteenth century the current gained strength through the high-Baroque eccentric Franz Anton von Sporck and his circle, opponents of all ecclesiastical and bureaucratic humbug and searchers after a genuine pietistic reform. Sporck was in touch with Prince Eugene of Savoy and his fellow intellectuals of Jansenist sympathies; he also maintained contact with the early pietists in Germany, many of them in fact Bohemian exiles.[4]

The politico-religious attitude of these men shows a clear analogy with some of the strivings of the Rudolfine period. The essential difference is that during the seventeenth century and much of the eighteenth such an attitude was always associated with a struggle *against* the new Habsburg establishment. For all their worldly pomp and sovereign ceremony the Habsburgs from Matthias to Maria Theresa were in the last analysis the pious House, the Princes of the Church; what linked Rudolf and Joseph in a strange brotherhood was their desire to shift that transcendent mystique to the person of the Emperor. It may not be too far-fetched to isolate two aspects of the process. On one hand the early history of Josephinist ideas embodied the intellectual élitism and universality of the late sixteenth century: Hirnhaim and Magni both sought

---

[1] Eduard Winter, *Der Josefinismus und seine Geschichte* (Brünn–Munich–Vienna 1943), 2 ff.

[2] F. Krásl, *Arnošt Hrabě Harrach, Kardinál sv. Církve Řimské a Kníže Arcibiskup Pražský* (Prague 1886), 158 ff., 267 ff.

[3] C. S. Barach, *Hieronymus Hirnhaim, ein Beitrag zur Geschichte der philosophisch-theologischen Kultur im 17. Jahrhundert* (Vienna 1864); Winter, *Josefinismus*, 7–9.

[4] Winter, op. cit. 10 ff.; cf. idem, *Tschechische und slowakische Emigration*, 232, 258 ff., and in general Heinrich Benedikt, *Franz Anton Graf von Sporck* (Vienna 1923).

to tap stores of knowledge through revelation, and both were sympathetic towards the polymath and pansophist Marcus Marci of Kronland,[1]
while the evolution of their brand of religious 'enlightenment' proceeded
in step with the growth of learned and secret societies. On the other
hand it meant the survival of the national middle way: the politics of
these people were basically a continuation of the tradition of the
'Bohemian party', even of the Old-Utraquists before their final collapse,
indeed a direct legacy of Hus. It was the continuing inherent weakness
of a middle position, its lack of practical backing, which guaranteed the
success of extremer solutions. The large-scale conversions to Rome at
the end of the sixteenth century were, like the readmission of lapsed
apostates, an essential mark of the failure of the centre.

The two aspects, intellectual and political, of this Bohemian tradition
have their wider parallels in the years after 1600. There is the example
of Marc'Antonio De Dominis who abandoned his Dalmatian bishopric
to flee to England in 1616, but whose search for universal salvation
finally drove him back into the arms of Rome. The case of De Dominis
was well-known in Prague.[2] There is also the role of Venice as preserver
of moderate Catholicism against Papal pretensions in the age of Paolo
Sarpi. Venice too was admired by the Czechs and other Central Europeans who visited the Queen of the Adriatic and her celebrated free
university of Padua, although the Venetian republican ideal was a far cry
from the hierarchic, aristocratic culture of the Habsburg lands.[3] To the
latter we must now turn our attention more directly.

[1] Barach, op. cit. 17–28. For a comment on Marci see below p. 289.

[2] Some, like the theologian and logician Jan Opsimathes, knew him personally:
Odložilík, *Cesty z Čech a Moravy*, 313 ff. His Apology appeared in Czech in 1619
(*Ohlasseni a Zprawa* . . . Z. Tobolka and E. Horák, *Knihopis českých a slovenských tisků*,
ii. *1501–1800* (Prague 1939–), No. 2062).

[3] Cf. Cantimori, *Prospettive*, 97–109; F. A. Yates, 'Paolo Sarpi's "History of the
Council of Trent"', *JWCI* vii (1944), 123–43; and the interesting thesis of W. A.
Bouwsma, *Venice and the Defence of Republican Liberty* (Berkeley, California 1968). An
important Czech description of Venice and her constitution appears in the *Putowání*
of Kryštof Harant (below p. 278 n. 3), 14 ff.

4. The Habsburgs, Bohemia, and Humanist Culture

'Frustra, RUDOLPHE, carmina sacrantur tibi:
Nulla inter haec et Caesarum est proportio.
   Vel pauca metra caeteris sunt Regibus
Satis, Tibi uni totus est HELICON parum.
   Ergo, o Poetae inaniis pleni, manum
Hinc abstinete, haec ipsa materies nimis
 Vobisque Apollinique ac Palladi est gravis.'
JOHANN WACKER VON WACKENFELS: ELEGY (1612)

CENTRAL Europe in the late Renaissance sustained a culture broadly receptive to influences from its western and southern neighbours, and creative mainly in its responses to them. The standards of learning displayed by the privileged members of its society and the level of erudition acquired by its scholars were nevertheless not inferior, and they are deserving of much more attention from historians than they have hitherto received. The present chapter is conceived both as an investigation into the kind of influences which were at work in and around Prague during the period, and as a framework for some things which should become clearer after a reading of the two succeeding chapters, where the artistic and occult preoccupations of Rudolf's court will be dealt with more particularly. I shall first sketch separately the progress of Habsburg patronage, then examine the native Bohemian development with special reference to a few leading personalities. This distinction is purely a matter of convenience, since the similarities between the two, occasioned either by direct contact or indirect kinship of ideas, seem to me—*pace* much traditional historiography—far more real and significant than the differences.

The role of the Austrian Habsburgs as patrons of culture and scholarship in the sixteenth century is a curiously unfamiliar one, and it appears never to have been studied directly outside the specialized sphere of art history. Yet, besides all the idolatry or antipathy which their political position may have called forth, the Holy Roman Emperors maintained at their court some of the most notable figures in the intellectual life of the age. The Habsburgs were a cosmopolitan focus for the wide-ranging interests of the time, for collectors, historians, antiquarians, natural philosophers, students of minerals, plants, stones, and the rest; and the endeavours thus focused on the court mirrored the schemes of unity in diversity which so engaged contemporary thinkers. The culmination of the process came, like the seeds of its collapse, with Rudolf II.

The pattern of this development is already to be seen in the lifetime of Emperor Maximilian I, the lion of the South German Humanists, then in that of his granddaughter Mary. Mary was betrothed while still very young to the Jagellon king of Hungary, Lewis; after the latter's death at Mohács in 1526 she retired to Brussels, taking with her the court of Buda and the remains of the Hungarian Humanist tradition which dated from Matthias Corvinus. There she was admired by many scholars, Erasmus among them, while her entourage provided a direct line of contact between the Southern Netherlands and the Austrian lands. Mary of Hungary came strongly under the influence of Jan Henckel, a Melanchthonian intellectual and native of Levoča in Slovakia who was closely connected with Breslau.[1] At the end of her life she shared the abdication of her brother Charles V and withdrew to Spain.

Mary's other brother Ferdinand I was less cultured, certainly during the early unsettled years of his reign over the Austrian lands of the Habsburgs. His activities anyway lie outside the scope of discussion here. But two concerns at least can be isolated which anticipate his grandson Rudolf: his interest in Hebrew studies and his assistance to Czech culture. Guillaume Postel spent part of the 1550s in Vienna, where he was Professor of Oriental Studies at the University,[2] and Ferdinand played an important role in the publication of the Syriac New Testament of another famous Orientalist, Johann Albrecht Widmanstetter.[3] He also employed as court chaplain in Vienna for a period the mysterious adventurer Paul Skalich (1534?–75), who subsequently became a Protestant and later still returned again to the Church of Rome. Skalich, who claimed descent from the ancient family of Scaliger but was in fact a South Slav from Zagreb, enjoyed a notorious and controversial reputation in his day.[4] He has been dismissed as a charlatan, but

---

[1] Ghislaine de Boom, *Marie de Hongrie* (Brussels 1956), esp. 50 ff.

[2] Kvačala, *Postell*, 157 ff., 224 ff.

[3] F. Secret, 'La Tradition du "De Omni Scibili" à la Renaissance', *Convivium* xxiii N.S. (1955), 492–7; idem, 'Guillaume Postel et les courants prophétiques de la Renaissance', *Studi francesi* i (1957), 375–95. Widmanstetter knew Postel; his library, famous for its collection of Cabalistic and Hebraic texts, was acquired on his death in 1557 for the rival court of Munich—see O. Hartig, *Die Gründung der Münchener Hofbibliothek* (Munich 1917), 9 ff., 170 ff.

[4] On Skalich: I. Kukuljević Sakcinski, *Pavao Skalić, Gradjanin Zagrebački* . . .

this seems only partially just; since Skalich, although himself ambitious and largely unoriginal, stood in the tradition of Renaissance pansophy—the search for encyclopedic knowledge of the world through a manipulation of intellectual systems, especially the 'arts' of the Cabala and Lullism. His works, like his religious uncertainty, thus form a link between Italian and German speculations, between Pico della Mirandola and J. H. Alsted; the *Occulta Occultorum Occulta* was originally published at Vienna in 1556; the *Encyclopediae . . . Epistemon* by Oporinus at Basle in 1559 with a dedication to Ferdinand.

An encyclopedia of a rather different kind, though very typical of its time, was Sebastian Münster's enormous *Cosmographia*.[1] Ferdinand was instrumental in having this translated into Czech in 1554 by Zikmund of Puchov, and provided with glosses favourable to his government and family.[2] The Emperor's interest in the Czech language is manifested also by his efforts for the publication in Prague of Matthioli's *Herbal*, the most important natural history of plants since Dioscorides. Pietro Andrea Matthioli was an Italian botanist who moved to Bohemia in 1554 and became Ferdinand's physician and counsellor, as well as standing close to the *Statthalter* Ferdinand; there are two letters from the Emperor to his son granting money to Matthioli for this new version of his work.[3] It was rendered from the original Latin into Czech by Hájek in 1562, and into German by Georg Handsch; both these editions —the *Herbář* and the *Kräuterbuch*—being published by the official printer Jiří Melantrich, the first Bohemian examples of specialized book-production.[4] Matthioli was also consulting physician to the Prague Jesuits, one of the intimate links at that time between them and the court.[5]

Ferdinand's son Maximilian gathered around him a whole collection of learned men, attracted partly from the surrounding Habsburg dominions, partly from further afield. Some of them were leading members of his government, like the historian and cartographer Wolfgang Lazius

(Zagreb 1875), a sketch; L. Mátray, *Régi magyar filozófusok* (Budapest 1961), 9, 210 f. Cf. Secret, 'De Omni Scibili', 493 ff.; and ÖN, MSS. 9471, 9475, 10438.

[1] Cf. G. Strauss, 'A sixteenth-century encyclopedia: Sebastian Münster's Cosmography and its editions', in *From the Renaissance to the Counter-Reformation* (*Essays in honour of Garrett Mattingly*, London 1966), 145–63.

[2] Svátek, *Obrazy z kulturních dějin*, 6 f.; J. V. Polišenský, 'České dějepisectví předbělohorského období a Pražská Akademie', *AUC, Historia Universitatis Carolinae Pragensis*, iv. 2 (1963), 125.

[3] Vienna, 7 Nov. 1559 and 13 Mar. 1561, SÚA, SM S 400/1; cf. V. Maiwald, *Geschichte der Botanik in Böhmen* (Vienna–Leipzig 1904), 20–6. On Matthioli, his importance and his botanical illustrators see A. Arber, *Herbals* (2nd edn. Cambridge 1953), 92–7, 221–6.

[4] F. Rachlík, *Jiří Melantrich Rožďalovický z Aventýnu* (Prague 1930), 67–77.

[5] 'Historia Collegii S. J. Pragensis', fos. 45ʳ, 64ʳ.

or the general Lazarus Schwendi; others were valued more exclusively for their private talents and given purely cultural appointments. A good example of that policy was the Flemish *Hofbibliothekar* Hugo Blotius. With Maximilian and Crato the link between Vienna and the Netherlands first became strong, among scholars as among artists; we have already noticed the way in which religious pressures ran parallel. Lipsius himself sang the praise of this Imperial entourage.[1] Many of its members remained in Vienna and Prague after 1576, thus forming the nucleus also of Rudolf's court: the latter did not spring from nothing, but was rather the climax of a tradition of patronage and owed much to Maximilian's interest, as well as that of the Archduke Ferdinand. Maximilian's circle therefore possesses both its own neglected significance as a chapter in the story of late Humanism, and its relevance in the present context. Among its scholars of international reputation one who may be taken as exemplar is the botanist Clusius.

The revival of botanical studies in the sixteenth century formed one aspect of a changing attitude to the natural world: the urge to classify it, a striving not yet divorced from the sense that it was a world to which men belonged, as members of a consistent chain of influences. Their most distinguished representative was Carolus Clusius (Charles de l'Écluse), a man of Humanist learning and wide intellectual contacts. Clusius was born near Arras in 1526, studied with Melanchthon at Wittenberg, then travelled in France before returning to the Low Countries.[2] He had already begun to move in the circle of Plantin and made the acquaintance of Languet when, in 1561, he was recommended by Crato and Peucer as the mentor of Thomas Rhediger of Breslau. He subsequently lived for several years in the Netherlands—having a number of commissions with Plantin—before being called to Vienna in 1573 as Maximilian's herbalist and plant-collector.[3] The stimulus to this may have come from his senior colleague Busbecq, a long-time servant of the Habsburgs, or from his fellow-countryman Philippe de Monte, the Imperial *Kapellmeister*, who was a close friend.[4] The latter also possessed

---

[1] In his *Taciti Omnia Opera* (Antwerp 1581), 8.

[2] On Clusius's life see F. W. T. Hunger, *Charles de l'Escluse, Nederlandsch Kruid-kundige*, i (The Hague 1927) and his own brief 'Autobiographia' printed in Gyula Istvánffi, *A Clusius-Codex mykológiai méltatása adatokkal Clusius életrajzához* (Budapest 1900), 176 f.

[3] Gillet, op. cit. ii, 43 ff.; Hunger, op. cit. 59 ff.; Clair, op. cit. 117.

[4] G. van Doorslaer, *La Vie et les œuvres de Philippe de Monte* (Brussels 1921), 23 ff., and appendix LXIV–LXXV which contains eleven Italian letters from Monte to Clusius. (These are identical with eleven of those published by P. Bergmans, *Quatorze lettres inédites de Philippe de Monte* (Brussels 1921.)

botanical interests, as is revealed by his letter to Clusius requesting plants for his master, the Vice-Chancellor and leading courtier Jakob Kurz.[1]

Clusius passed the next fifteen years in Vienna—despite complaints that his salary was in arrears after 1576[2]—paying visits to western Hungary, where an enlightened patron Balthasar Batthyány had his castle of Németújvár (Güssing). Batthyány himself indulged wide scientific and alchemical inclinations, and Clusius made other contacts with the Hungarian intelligentsia: Joannes Sambucus, the historian and diplomat Istvánffy, Stephen Beythe, and their friends. He became very absorbed in Hungarian plant life, even its Magyar terminology, on which he did some original work.[3] The twilight of his life he spent in Leiden as curator of the herbal garden there until his death in 1609.

Clusius is the epitome of a cosmopolitan scholar of the time, in both his contacts and his interests. He maintained a large correspondence, most of all with the erudite Joachim Camerarius (the Younger) in Nuremberg, but also with several members of the Prague court and the Landgrave William IV of Hesse-Cassel, as well as his friends in Breslau.[4] His studies belonged essentially to the field of comparative botany, but they led him to a particular pursuit of exotica not far distant from the contemporary mania for collecting, and to an active exploration of nature, as in his ascent of the Ötscher in the Austrian Alps with the astronomer Paul Fabritius (another protégé of Maximilian's) or his searches for plants in Hungary and Bohemia.[5] His religion seems to have been correspondingly moderate and latitudinarian.[6]

Clusius must have found ample enthusiasm for botany in Vienna and Prague: they were the environment of Matthioli and Rembert Dodoens, both in the Imperial service; later too of the Czech Adam Zalužanský.

---

[1] Van Doorslaer, appendix LXXIV: '. . . Signor Curto Vice-cancelliere . . . ha qui comprato un giardino ov'egli fa grandissime fabriche et è tanto invaghito di questo suo giardino che va cercando per tutto d'importo di bei frutti et di bei flori. Pero quanto più posso prego a V.S. di farmi gratia di mandarmi di quelle bulbe che so qu'ella ha et altri sorti di semenze di fiori per metterli al suo giardino.'

[2] *Caroli Clusii . . . Epistolae*: Clusius to Crato, Vienna 29 Jan., 15 Mar., and 12 May 1578.

[3] Istvánffi, op. cit. 184 ff.; cf. J. Ernyey, *Clusius és Báthory István* (Pécs 1935, klny. a *Botanikai Közlemények* XXXII-i évfolyamából). The *Stirpium Nomenclator Pannonius* was first published at Güssing in 1583. I hope shortly to elucidate the role of Batthyány in a separate article.

[4] 195 letters to Camerarius (1573–97) are included in Hunger, op. cit., ii (The Hague 1943). Istvánffi, op. cit. 202–4, gives a catalogue of the letters surviving in the university library at Leiden. The correspondence with Rhediger and Crato was published in *Caroli Clusii . . . Epistolae*.

[5] Maiwald, op. cit. 35.   [6] Hunger, op. cit., i. 326 f.

There also developed, especially in Prague, a growing fashion for contrived gardens. Not only Kurz, but the Rožmberks and Christoph Lobkovic owned favourite gardens in the near vicinity of the royal palace, while on the slopes of the castle stretched the new creations of the Archduke Ferdinand and Rudolf: the Stag's Ditch, the Paradise Garden, and the rest, with their rare and peculiar plants, menageries, and flowers set to represent the personal symbol of the Emperor.[1] The links between the Habsburgs and natural history are evident too from Busbecq, the first purveyor of the tulip to Western Europe, who worked for many years as their diplomatic servant. Ogier Ghislain de Busbecq,[2] a Fleming by birth, was originally sent to Constantinople by Ferdinand I in 1556, a mission which was only crowned with success after many privations, then acted as *écuyer tranchant* to Rudolf and Ernst in Spain. Later he represented Maximilian and Rudolf in Paris, being at first nominally attached to the Archduchess Elizabeth following her marriage with Charles IX. Busbecq was a person of very diverse talents, as emerges from his celebrated *Turkish Letters*, with their observations on plants, customs, religions, languages, and much besides. His own convictions were oecumenical, and he supported the endeavours of the Cardinal of Lorraine.[3] He evidently undertook all kinds of commission for Maximilian and Rudolf in Paris, from the recommending of personnel to dealings in clocks and Hermetic literature.[4] Rudolf was especially favourably disposed towards him: Busbecq's letters to Prague from 1582 to 1585 demonstrate their close contact, as well as being full of valuable information on the French scene and the character of the mystical Henry III; the picture would no doubt be fuller if more of this correspondence had survived.[5]

Another interesting example of the links between West and Central Europe is provided by the travels of Philip Sidney, fêted abroad as the most notable Englishman of his age, the Byron of late Renaissance

[1] Maiwald, op. cit. 50 ff.; J. Svátek, *Ze staré Prahy* (Prague 1899), 126–54.

[2] For Busbecq's life see C. T. Forster and F. H. B. Daniell, *The Life and Letters of Ogier Ghiselin de Busbecq* (London 1881), i; and A. H. Huussen, *Het Leven van Ogier Ghislain de Busbecq* (Leiden 1949), introduction.

[3] Cf. his letter to Maximilian commenting on the death of the Cardinal, Lyons 24 Jan. 1575, in Forster and Daniell, ii, and ibid. i, 341 f.

[4] *Divi Rudolphi Epistolae*, 210; Forster and Daniell, ii: Busbecq, Paris 28 Sept. 1574; *Jahrbuch* vii (1888), Reg. No. 5356.

[5] This correspondence—there are 53 letters from 1582 to 1585 and a further five during 1589–90—was originally published after Busbecq's death and is reproduced in Forster and Daniell, ii. It is not clear why such a long gap exists between 1576 and 1582; Busbecq was undoubtedly in Paris at that time and a letter survives from Rudolf to him: HHSA, Fam. Korr. A. 4 III, 26 Oct. 1580, about the purchase of some Spanish horses.

Humanism. Sidney involved himself in most of the intellectual debates of the period; he was a pupil of the occultist John Dee (whom we shall meet again later) and patron of Giordano Bruno and his follower Alexander Dicson;[1] at the same time he was a student of Ramism—he had known Ramus in Paris and had a Ramist tract dedicated to him in the year of his death.[2] He became heavily implicated in the eirenical movement in the Netherlands during the 1570s and 1580s, a friend of Daniel Rogers and intimate of Lipsius: among the last letters he received was one from Lipsius which condemned religious extremism.[3]

What has been called 'perhaps the most important single influence in Sidney's life' was his friendship with Hubert Languet, and it was this which brought him into contact with both the Breslau circle and Vienna.[4] He travelled to Austria in 1573, spending several months there in the company of Crato, Clusius, Lazarus Schwendi, the Imperial medaller Antonio Abondio, and others. The next year he visited Poland and Moravia, and in 1575 found himself in Prague.[5] Two years later Sidney returned there as official emissary of Elizabeth to offer condolences on the death of Maximilian. Rudolf seems to have lent a sympathetic ear to his pleas on behalf of the Protestants, though there was little personal warmth between the two men, well matched in age. Sidney indeed received the general impression of the Emperor, finding him 'few of wordes, sullein of disposition, very secrete and resolute . . . extreemely Spaniolated'; this may however have been mainly prejudice, based on what he expected to encounter in the person of the new sovereign.[6] Another of Elizabeth's poetic cavaliers and an intimate friend of Sidney was Edward Dyer, who himself appeared in Prague during the late 1580s, a visit directly connected with the work there of Dee.[7] At the same time an Englishman later to be famous as cosmopolitan diplomat

[1] J. Buxton, *Sir Philip Sidney and the English Renaissance* (London 1964), 87; Yates, *Art of Memory*, 263 f., 282–4.

[2] Buxton, op. cit. 44 f.; Ong, *Ramus and Talon Inventory*, No. 733.

[3] Dorsten, *Poets, Patrons and Professors*, 149 f. and *passim*.

[4] Buxton, op. cit. 50–2, etc. The well-known correspondence between the fussing but outstandingly able pedagogue Languet and Sidney was first published in Latin in 1633; much of it appeared in English in an edition by S. A. Pears (London 1845).

[5] R. W. Zandvoort, 'Sidney in Austria', *Wiener Beiträge zur englischen Philologie* lxvi (Vienna 1957), 227–45 (an article based on the Languet–Sidney correspondence); Odložilík, 'Cesty z Čech a Moravy', 245 ff.; Polišenský, *Anglie a Bílá Hora*, 41. Philip's brother Robert was in Prague for about two months during 1580.

[6] Sidney's assessment of Rudolf and report on the state of the Empire are in his letter to Walsingham from Heidelberg, 3 May 1577, in *Works*, ed. A. Feuillerat, vol. 3 (Cambridge 1923), 109–14. From conversations with the Palsgrave he already knew what to expect: Sidney to Walsingham, Heidelberg 22 Mar. 1577 (ibid. 105–8).

[7] R. M. Sargent, *At the Court of Queen Elizabeth; the Life and Lyrics of Sir Edward Dyer* (Oxford 1935), 56 ff., 97 ff. Cf. below, p. 228.

and erudite observer was travelling in the Habsburg lands. The young Henry Wotton received a recommendation from Clusius and spent part of 1591 as guest of the Imperial librarian Blotius in Vienna before proceeding to Bohemia.[1]

Not all these men of learning had their origins in the West; one of the most remarkable of them is the Hungarian Sambucus. Joannes Sambucus (János Zsámboky) was born in 1531 at Nagyszombat (Trnava) and received a broad education both in Germany, studying under Melanchthon and Jan Sturm, and France.[2] He then spent much time in the Netherlands, where a lifelong partnership with Plantin began, and Italy, where he graduated in medicine at Padua; he also became a close associate of Clusius, who dedicated a work to him as early as 1561.[3] Sambucus was an intimate friend of Dudith and Crato; he knew Lipsius and Ortelius, Montano, and the Breslau circle, from his Paris days Ramus and the printer Estienne.[4] From 1564 he occupied the post of court historiographer to Maximilian II and later Rudolf. He was a stout supporter of Habsburg authority, particularly in his funeral oration for Ferdinand, and Stránský took him as an opponent; but his religion was characteristically mild, and some evidence exists that he was accounted a Lutheran.[5]

Sambucus's interests were remarkably far-reaching, but typical of their time. He earned fame as a Classical scholar and editor of texts, many of them published by Plantin, and seems to have devoted special attention to the Greek Church;[6] the wealthy collector Johann Fugger dealt with him for some rare Greek manuscripts.[7] At the same time Sambucus looked back to the flowering of Hungarian Humanism in his

[1] Cf. Wotton's letters from Vienna in Pearsall Smith, op. cit., i. 243 ff. A decade earlier Arthur Throckmorton stayed five weeks with Blotius after passing one winter of his European tour in Prague (A. L. Rowse, *Ralegh and the Throckmortons* (London 1962), 85–9).

[2] There are two brief general biographies of Sambucus: J. Orbán, *Sámboky Jánosról* (Szeged 1916); and E. Bach, *Un humaniste hongrois en France, Jean Sambucus et ses relations littéraires* (Szeged 1932).

[3] Bach, op. cit. 12.

[4] Costil, op. cit. 89; Vargha, op. cit. 41–4; *Abrahami Ortelii . . . Epistolae*, ed. Joannes Hessels (Cambridge 1887, hereafter 'Hessels'), Nos. 13, 62, 89. Cf. Bach, op. cit. 15 ff. There is now an extensive edition of a considerable portion of Sambucus's voluminous correspondence: H. Gerstinger, *Die Briefe des Johannes Sambucus* (Vienna 1968); the most important single addressee is Crato.

[5] J. Sambucus, *In Obitum Imperatoris Ferdinandi I Oratio . . .*; cf. idem, *Oratio Funebris in exequiis Maximiliani II*; Stránský, op. cit. 150; S. Weszprémi, *Succincta Medicorum Hungariae et Transilvaniae Biographia*, iii (Vienna 1787), 383.

[6] e.g. the commentary on Acts by Theophylactus, Archbishop of Bulgaria, 'ex bibliotheca J. Sambuci' (Cologne 1567); *Legatio imperatoris Caesaris Manuelis Comneni Augustissimi ad Armenios* (Basle 1578).

[7] G. Lill, *Hans Fugger und die Kunst* (Leipzig 1908), 28 f.

editions of Janus Pannonius, the cynosure of Matthias Corvinus. This patriotism is evident too in his historiography: he expanded the commentaries on Hungarian history by Bonfini and was a friend of Istvánffy and Brutus; his own diary comprised largely a compilation of the political events of the day.[1] He was deeply interested in medicine—his own training had been medical—and botany (he prepared an edition of Dioscorides); while from the annotations in his copy of Copernicus's *De Revolutionibus* it appears that he accepted the Copernican astronomy.[2]

Sambucus was best-known however as an emblematist. His emblembook was one of the most prized and widely-circulated volumes to come from Plantin's presses and it exercised a large influence, both on other compilers of the same genre, and on the literary world in general, even Shakespeare.[3] For Sambucus the symbolism which underlay the motif of the emblem was not an idle plaything, but a real correspondence. The seriousness with which he approached his material emerges at once from the preface to the *Emblemata*; he seems to have been as conscious as anyone of his time that the emblem was connected with hieroglyphics and the Egyptian mysteries, and that the symbol could possess deeper meaning as an embodiment of the reality of nature. The sources and themes of his emblem work place Sambucus fully in the tradition of Alciati, and show his links with Hadrianus Junius, Ruscelli, and others.[4] They are crucial for any understanding of his life and mentality, exhibiting many of the intellectual assumptions of the period: the power of the image, the underlying didactic message, the obsession with esoteric meaning. It is interesting that one of those who engraved his emblems was Lucas de Heere, the creator of the Valois Tapestries.[5] Sambucus applied the same method of image and text to a work on the history of the medical profession,[6] and an obvious parallel exists here with the

[1] L. Varga, 'Sámboky János Emblémái', *Könyv és Könyvtár* iv (1964), 197, 200. Antonius Bonfinius, *Rerum Ungaricarum decades 4 cum dimidia. His accessere I. Sambuci aliquot appendices et alia: una cum priscorum regum Ungariae decretis . . . Omnia nunc denuo recognita, emendata, et aucta per I. Sambucum* (Frankfurt 1581). The diary is ÖN, MS. 9039. It exists only for the years 1566, 1568, and 1569; part has been edited by Hans Gerstinger, *Aus dem Tagebuch des kaiserlichen Hofhistoriographen Johannes Sambucus* (Vienna 1965).

[2] At least as a hypothesis; see I. Borzsák, 'Ein Copernicus-Exemplar aus der Bibliothek des Joannes Sambucus in Debrecen', *Magyar Könyvszemle* 1965, 133–8.

[3] The *Emblemata* were first published in 1564. They reached Shakespeare through the emblem-book of Geoffrey Whitney; cf. above, p. 97 n. 3, and L. Dézsi, *Magyar irodalmi hatás Shakespeare költészetében* (Budapest 1929, klny. az *Irodalomtörténet*-ből).

[4] Varga, op. cit. 203 ff., 217 ff. Cf. A. Schöne, *Emblematik und Drama im Zeitalter des Barock* (Munich 1964), 36 f.; Volkmann, *Bilderschriften*, 46; and in general below, pp. 269f.

[5] Bach, op. cit. 53 ff.

[6] *Icones veterum ac recentiorum medicum philosophorumque, opera I. Sambuci* (Antwerp

approach of him and his colleagues to the 'inner' meaning of coins, medallions, inscriptions, and the like.

Sambucus's zeal in collecting and his intellectual pursuits joined forces in the books which he acquired. His library became one of the most notable of the age (by far the largest of any Hungarian, it stands comparison with the best in Europe), and its importance is twofold: it affords an insight not only into the interests of Sambucus himself, but also into those of Rudolf his patron, since on the death of the historiographer in 1584 the Emperor and Blotius took the utmost trouble to secure it.[1] It therefore survived as an integral part of the Viennese Hofbibliothek and can be largely reconstructed, thanks to the efficient cataloguing of its volumes begun by Blotius. Sambucus's famous holding of classical manuscripts was also bought by Rudolf, and what remains of it has been described by Gerstinger.[2]

A survey of Sambucus's collection of scientific and occult books thus provides a useful introduction to the kind of literature on which the best minds in Vienna and Prague could draw. He had many of the standard classics on astronomy. As well as Copernicus he possessed the Prutenic tables (88),[3] Ricci on the motions of the spheres (396/3), Schreckenfuchs's commentary on Peuerbach (66) and *Primum Mobile* (67/2), Cardano's Peuerbach commentary in the Basle editions of 1554 (66/2) and 1578 (75), books by Pighius, Dryander, Schöner (the *Tabulae Astronomicae*), Oronce Finé, Gemma Frisius, seven works on the comet of 1577, including that by Hájek, various ephemerides and almanacs, and a number of manuscripts, among them classical and Arabic astronomical writings such as those of Albumazar, Albubalar, Sacrobosco (four printed copies and one manuscript), and Delfini's *Expositiones in Peuerbach* (1895). He also owned much that was primarily astrological: Taisnier's *Astrologiae Judiciariae Isagogica* of 1559 (408/2), Valentin Naboth's *Enarratio Elementorum Astrologiae* (Cologne 1560, 395), Guillaume Postel's *Signorum coelestium vera configuratio* (768), and several copies of Peucer's *Commentarius de Praecipuis Divinationum Generibus* (263, 416, 416/2, 920/5), Nifo's *De verissimis temporum Signis* (2548), and

---

—Plantin—1574); there is a modern facsimile edition prepared by Max Rooses (Antwerp 1901).

[1] P. Lambecius, *Commentariorum de Augustissima Bibliotheca Caesarea Vindobonensi Libri I–VI* (Vienna 1665), i. 40 f., 45 f.

[2] H. Gerstinger, 'Johann Sambucus als Handschriftensammler', in *Festschrift der Nationalbibliothek in Wien* (Vienna 1926), 251–400.

[3] The following survey is based on the catalogue of the library, printed by Pál Gulyás: *Sámboky János Könyvtára* (Budapest 1941), 121–362. The numbers in brackets refer to this classification.

manuscripts like the *Rhetorii de 12 signis zodiaci* (1915) or the astrology of 'Guido' (1874).

Astrology merged into medicine with books like the *Amicus Medicorum* of Joannes Canivetus (1229, 1491) and the *Medicina Astrologica* of Cornelius Schylender (Antwerp 1577) (242/4). Sambucus had much in this field too, including eight works of Paracelsus, with editions by the Paracelsans Dorn, Bodenstein, and Ruland. He possessed a profusion of pharmacopoeias and herbals, including Theophrastus, Estienne, Fuchs, Dodoens, Lobel, Clusius, and eleven copies of Dioscorides. But his collection of natural philosophy and occult studies is Sambucus's most interesting contribution of all. He had Porta's *Magia Naturalis* in the Antwerp edition of 1560 (278), Agrippa's *De Occulta Philosophia* (728), two copies of Cardano's *De Subtilitate* (138, 1446), Finé's edition of Roger Bacon (*De mirabili potestate artis et naturae*) (396/2), Artemidorus on oneiromancy (544), and Taisnier on chiromancy (*Opus mathematicum*, Cologne 1562) (1734/2). He owned a series of the *prisca theologia* and the Neoplatonists; a manuscript entitled *Zoroastreorum et Platonicorum dogmatum anacephaleosis Plethonis* (2612); Plotinus, Porphyry, Proclus, Patrizi; complete editions of, and commentaries on, Plato; and a collection published at Leiden in 1552 of Jamblichus, Porphyry, Proclus, Psellus, Pymander, and Asclepius. Deeper still in the magic art were Scalich's *Occulta* (already mentioned) (1506/3), a manuscript of Heliodorus's *Carmina de mystica philosophia* (2613), Lull's *De Secretis Naturae* (bound with a tract by Albertus Magnus) (221) and his *Clavicula*, republished at Cologne in 1579 (2300). The latter appeared with works by 'Aquinas' and Rupescissa on alchemy; all found their way on to Sambucus's shelves along with similar volumes like Geber's *Summa Perfectionis* (221/2) or a Greek manuscript of Stephanus Alexandrinus (1297/1).

This library cannot in itself provide conclusive proof of anything, but it suggests the breadth of reading of a highly intellectual emblematist—as well as making less surprising Sambucus's mention in his testament of a treasured 'unicorn's horn'![1]—and also indicates the attraction which such a collection would have had for Rudolf. Unfortunately the rest of the Imperial library was too amorphous for any satisfactory deductions to be made as to its contents, though contemporaries were struck by the large number of mystical, Hermetic, and secret books.[2] Anyway most of it remained in Vienna during Rudolf's reign under its custodian

---

[1] G. Magyary-Kossa, *Magyar orvosi emlékek*, iii (Budapest 1931), No. 961.

[2] Daniel Georgius Morhof, *Polyhistor* (Lübeck 1688), i. 89, following Lambecius.

Blotius. But the figure of Sambucus points to two other important learned activities which Rudolf's court took over directly from that of Maximilian: historiography and the cult of the antiquarian.

A growing interest in history during the sixteenth century emerges clearly both from correspondence and from the great number of writings, published and unpublished, which were produced. In the Habsburg lands it was connected with the developing mystique of the origins and privileges of the ruling house and the high aristocracy,[1] though deeper roots lie perhaps in a new attitude towards the meaning of history which evinces close links with the kindred rise of cartography and travel. The Habsburgs became large patrons, and Maximilian's brother Ferdinand of Tyrol was especially active; he supported several historians, notably Gerard van Roo, whom he had originally discovered as a bass in his chapel in Prague and whose monumental history of the dynasty was left uncompleted through death.[2] Despite his strained relations with Rudolf Ferdinand was prepared to recommend this work as a matter of common concern:

Als vor disem mein gewesster Bibliothecarius weiland Gerhard de Roo die Historie unseres fürstlichen Hausses zu beschreiben angefangen, selbiger aber seines unzeittigen Todts Halben nit zu end bringen khünnen, hatt sich mein Hofsecretarius Conrad Diez von Werdenberg hernacher umb die sache angenommen, und nit allein das Lateinisch werkh compliert, und vollendet, sonder auch dasselb wolgewelten unsrem Hauss zu ehrens, in die Teutsche Sprach transferiert.[3]

Ferdinand's successor in Innsbruck, Maximilian III, shared his interest and sponsored the great historical and genealogical labours of Franz Guilliman, who aimed at a vindication of the political universalism of the Habsburgs.[4] Two men who profited from Maximilian's favour in this direction were Pistorius, who borrowed books and manuscripts from him and from Vienna,[5] and—another direct link with Rudolf—the Austrian noble Richard Strein von Schwarzenau (1538–1610). Strein seems to have been an intimate of the Emperor (remains survive of a holograph correspondence between them) and he held a position at the Prague court; he was also an antiquarian who exchanged letters with Maximilian about Habsburg history, and a student of nature who, like

[1] For this tendency see Lhotsky, *Österreichische Historiographie*, Ch. 11; for the development in Bohemia see Polišenský, 'České dějepisectví', 123 ff.; and on the special case of the historians of the Czech Brethren see K. Krofta, *O Bratrském dějepisectví* (Prague 1946).

[2] J. Hirn, *Erzherzog Ferdinand von Tyrol*, i–ii (Innsbruck 1885–8), i. 344 ff.

[3] Ferdinand to Rudolf, Innsbruck 23 Feb. 1592; cf. idem 15 Oct. 1593; HHSA, Fam. Korr. A. 4. I.

[4] Hirn, *Erzherzog Maximilian*, i. 387–418.   [5] Ibid. 376 and n.

Clusius, climbed the Ötscher.[1] Strein's collections enjoyed fame in their day and his castle of Freideck must have been a miniature Hradschin or Ambras; he was no less a bibliophile who bought books for Rudolf and amassed a large library of his own which itself passed to the Habsburgs on his death.[2]

Rudolf employed at different times a number of court historiographers, several of them scholars with wide interests. The only essential presupposition for such favour—which anyway tended to be rather titular than pecuniary—was their acceptance of the role of the dynasty and willingness to propound its virtues. Not all were necessarily close to the Emperor's person: Hungarian holders of the post after the death of Sambucus usually resided in Pressburg (Pozsony) and included the highly cultured Nicholas Istvánffy and Giovanni Brutus as well as the more pedestrian Elias Berger, a convert who displayed impeccable loyalty to the mystique of the House.[3] The leading person in Prague was Jakob Typotius, who had earlier worked at the Swedish court, although born in the Netherlands. Typotius's skill was in fact rather as Humanist orator than chronicler; he soon became a central figure in the Habsburg capital, a member of learned and poetic circles with friends both in the court and at the University.[4] The most important contribution by Typotius was his collaboration in the notable Prague emblem-book entitled *Symbola Divina et Humana*, for which he supplied explanations of symbolism to accompany Sadeler's engravings of popes, emperors, and kings.[5]

The models for the drawings in the *Symbola* were taken 'ex musaeo Octavi de Strada, civis Romani', and they thus provide a direct link with

[1] On Strein: Franz von Khautz, *Versuch einer Geschichte der österreichischen Gelehrten* (Frankfurt–Leipzig 1755), 229–58; K. Grossmann, 'Richard Streun von Schwarzenau', *MIÖG* Ergänzungsband ix (1929), 555–73. Cf. Hirn, *Erzherzog Maximilian*, i. 379–83.

[2] Georgius Calaminus, *Rudolphottocarus* (Strasbourg 1594), a work containing a eulogy of Strein, dedicated to Rudolf II and exhibiting the reverence for his ancestor Rudolf I which has already been mentioned as characteristic of the period; Lambecius, op. cit. i. 48 f. Another Austrian historian and colleague of Strein, Job Hartmann von Enenkel, possessed a still larger library; see Anna von Coreth in *MIÖG* lv (1944), 247–302.

[3] On Berger see V. Frankl (Fraknói), 'Berger Illés magyar királyi hofhistoriográphus', *Századok* 1873, 373–90. Most of his works can be found in the University Library of Budapest. Istvánffy was an interesting and important man who belongs more fully to a different context. On Brutus cf. above, p. 102 n. 4; he was appointed in 1588 (*Jahrbuch* vii (1888), Reg. No. 4592–3).

[4] Polišenský, 'Dějepisectví', 131; R. Schkelenko, 'Die neulateinische Dichtung am Hofe Rudolfs II.', *Prager Jahrbuch* 1943, 98–101.

[5] Vol. i reads: *Symbola Divina et Humana Pontificum, Imperatorum, Regum. Accessit brevis et facilis Isagoge Iacobi Typotii S.C.M. sculptor Egidius Sadeler excu. Pragae 1601.* Vols. ii (1602) and iii (1603) bear slightly different titles. On the death of Typotius the isagoges for vol. iii were devised by Boethius de Boodt. There was a second edition, apud God. Schönwetterum, Francofurti 1652. See also below, pp. 170 f..

one of the most significant families at the court of both Maximilian and Rudolf.[1] Octavio's father Jacopo (1515–88) stood among the most remarkable antiquaries of his age, a shrewd yet cavalier figure as he appears handling a piece of Classical sculpture in the magnificent portrait by Titian.[2] Initially called to Vienna by Ferdinand to be made his court antiquary and keeper of the Imperial treasures, Strada became Maximilian's senior adviser on all artistic matters.[3] He was also richly rewarded by Rudolf, who summoned him to Prague immediately after his accession and entrusted him with commissions of all kinds, not least presumably because it was Strada's daughter who became his mistress. He died in Prague and is buried there in the church of St. Nicholas on the Malá Strana.

Strada was before all else a collector who assembled by dexterous purchases, mostly in Italy, an extraordinary array of coins, medallions, and books (including Arabic and Hebrew texts). On the basis of this he published a series of works calculated to appeal to the Imperial sense of dignity and ancestor-worship, beginning with the *Epitome thesauri antiquitatum*, a history of the Emperors from Julius Caesar to Maximilian II illustrated from coins, which went into three editions with French and German translations. But his interests stretched far wider: he spent many years compiling an enormous eleven-language dictionary which is now lost,[4] and he left a pile of manuscripts dealing not only with antiquities but also with problems of mechanics. Parts of them were eventually published by his grandson in 1617 under the title: *Künstliche Abriss allerhand Wasser- Wind- Ross und Handtmühlen . . .*

Jacopo Strada's son Octavio (1550–1607) succeeded to Rudolf's favour. He too was a learned figure with historical inclinations;[5] in addition to his association with the *Symbola*, he left materials which were collected together after his death as *De Vitis Imperatorum et Caesarum Romanorum*. This appeared at Frankfurt in 1615, followed by a German version, the *Keyser Chronick*, in 1629. Among Octavio's manuscript remains were further projected emblems and genealogies of the Habsburgs.[6]

* * *

[1] On the family of Strada see C. Straka, 'Stradové z Rosbergu', *Památky Archeologické* xxviii (1916), 18–24; J. Svátek, 'Stradové z Rosbergu', in *Obrazy z kulturních dějin českých* (Prague 1891), 103–31.

[2] This picture is now in the Kunsthistorisches Museum, Vienna. It is reproduced by, *inter alios*, Schwarzenfeld, op. cit. 89.

[3] Lhotsky, *Geschichte der Sammlungen*, 160 ff.

[4] Cf. the letter from Strada to Guglielmo of Mantua, Vienna 28 Dec. 1568, in *Jahrbuch* xvi (1895), Reg. No. 13996. This letter also describes his library and coins.

[5] Lhotsky, op. cit. 290–2.   [6] Straka, loc. cit.

Bohemian culture during the years before the battle of the White Mountain has long been one subject in the fierce debate which rages around the meaning of that event for Czech history.[1] The outcome of the battle and the failure of the estates' revolt have been taken in hindsight to be a reflection of the whole state of the country in the preceding period. The only logical justification for such hindsight would be that the course of events during 1618–20 was in fact predetermined, and this indeed formed the basis for the one really consistent line of attack which has been adopted: the thesis—sustained by several nineteenth-century writers and classically expounded by the Frenchman Ernest Denis—that the Protestant defeat was somehow 'inevitable'.

There were two aspects to this assertion. On the one hand the predominantly Protestant Bohemia of the Rudolfine period had sunk into a lethargy and moral decline which made it unable to maintain itself. That was Denis's position; while he did not of course argue that spiritual factors were uniquely the cause of political collapse, he nevertheless saw them as wholly symptomatic.[2] On the other hand the forces of the Counter-Reformation made a positive impact on influential minds, and thus it was ultimately their ideology which carried the Catholic arms to victory in the campaign of 1620. Josef Pekař contended strongly that the Czechs were always largely a plaything of Western forces, hence—echoing nineteenth-century Catholic historians—Hussitism was a discontinuity in development and Habsburg centralization its necessary sequel.[3] The Protestant case has had its staunch advocates: Kamil Krofta argued, in direct opposition to Pekař, that the Czech revolt cut short a healthy evolution of Bohemian society, and that Lutherans, Calvinists, and Brethren—far from losing their way amid internal squabbles as some imagined—were becoming increasingly reconciled.[4] Others have spoken more particularly for the contribution of the Brethren.[5]

---

[1] For the debate among historians cf. most recently Kavka, *Bílá Hora*, Ch. 1.

[2] E. Denis, op. cit. *passim*. His most direct critic, Vlastimil Kybal, took issue with him on his deterministic viewpoint, but agreed that the religious split between king and estates was a crucial development. Kybal thus appears to take the position that the *conflict* was inevitable, but not its outcome. V. Kybal, *Arnošt Denis a Bílá Hora* (Prague 1912), esp. 92–110.

[3] J. Pekař, *Bílá Hora, její příčiny a následky* (Prague 1921); less extreme than his earlier work, *Kniha o Kosti* (Prague 1907), vol. i, *passim*.

[4] K. Krofta, *Duchovní odkaz Husitství* (Prague 1946), *passim*, and esp. 246 f., 262, 272. For an opposing view, e.g. E. Winter, *Geisteskampf*, 190 ff.

[5] e.g. J. B. Čapek, *Duch a odkaz československé reformace* (Prague 1951); A. Molnár, *Českobratrská výchova před Komenským* (Prague 1956), introduction; M. Daňková, op. cit.

These interpretations show above all the complexity of the problem, and here is not the place to discuss them; 1618 and the White Mountain play no immediate part in what follows. But there are certain aspects of the Czech development which stand out and which form the framework of the present analysis. There is first of all the clear 'anomaly' of the Czech position. The beginnings of Humanism in Bohemia fall in the fourteenth century and Prague occupied an important role in the culture of that age, still Catholic and universal.[1] After the Hussite wars the country remained for a time utterly isolated, and the process of reintegration, in the form of a now belated Czech Humanist Renaissance, involved a reconciliation with the predominantly Catholic, or at most Melanchthonian, world of Italy and South Germany, first through the surviving Catholic aristocracy (notably Bohuslav Hasištejnský of Lobkovic and the Rožmberks), then embracing the Old-Utraquists and finally the Brethren. During the sixteenth century all parties were seeking to recapture national identity and in this, as we have seen, Lutheranism enjoyed only a very partial success. The main legacy of Utraquism —the figure of Hus himself—was not forgotten;[2] while to rekindle the popular enthusiasm which the Hussite movement had enjoyed was an aim not only of the Protestants, but equally of the elaborate ceremonial of the Jesuits.

Thus renewed contact with a wider intellectual world came late in Bohemia and was inseparable from religious differences at home. Yet it is important to see that this culture itself remained unitary. No clear distinctions following creed can be observed, at least until 1600, and the same holds broadly true for the court also. The general level of civilization in Prague and elsewhere under Rudolf was high, among both nobles and bourgeoisie;[3] moreover its scope was necessarily international. In the nature of things the Czechs had always needed external contact to extend their mental horizons, and such was never more true than during the later sixteenth century when long isolation had brought a great lowering of domestic educational standards; the Charles University had ceased to play a full role and neither the Jesuit Academy (Clementinum) nor the worthy schools of the Brethren offered an adequate substitute. Thus the pattern which came increasingly to be followed by those who

---

[1] E. Winter, *Frühhumanismus, seine Entwicklung in Böhmen* (Berlin 1964).

[2] For the cult of Hus at this time see Ivo Kořán, 'České řezbářství 1620–1650 a jeho společenské a historické předpoklady' (Diss. Prague n.d.), Exkurs II.

[3] Testimony to this is the high degree of sophistication in domestic *objets d'art* and the anti-sumptuary legislation which attempted to control it. See Z. Winter, 'Přepych uměleckého průmyslu v měšťanských domech XVI věku', *ČČM* lxvii (1893), 46–104.

could afford it was a period, often lasting several years, of foreign travel, incorporating study at various universities. During that time the young nobleman would be accompanied by a preceptor, frequently from a much humbler background. These peregrinations around Europe involved large numbers of Czechs and many of the places they visited are recorded, either in local sources or in university registers and the like abroad.

The most adjacent region was of course the territory of the Empire, and scholars from Bohemia made their way to many of the German universities, especially Heidelberg and Herborn (for those inclined to Calvinism), Wittenberg, Marburg, Frankfurt an der Oder, and (above all) Leipzig.[1] The university most in spirit with Bohemia was Altdorf, near Nuremberg, the brain-child of the Camerarius family and based on the famous progressive *Gymnasium* of Sturm in Strasbourg.[2] Altdorf's links with Prague were to become militantly political by the time of the 1618 revolt, and it gave strong support for the Calvinist candidature of Frederick of the Palatinate, but in its first period (academic privileges were granted by Rudolf II in 1578) the contacts were much broader—not only with Bohemia but also with Blotius in Vienna and the Breslau circle[3]—and embraced wide fields of science, medicine, and the arts.

Next to the Empire came North and Central Italy, which always preserved close relations with Central Europe. Many Italians settled in Prague during Rudolf's time, particularly traders, architects, and artists; and their colony was large enough to support a congregation (1573), a chapel (which still survives), and a hospital.[4] The Czechs who visited Italy were by no means exclusively Catholic; in Siena we find not only Lobkovic (1588), Dietrichstein (1593), and Martinic (1598), but also Protestants like Žerotín and his cousin Ladislav Velen, Liechtenstein and Slavata (not yet converts), Jan Albin Schlick, Zdeněk Brtnický of Valdštejn, Albrecht Jan Smiřický, and Jessenius.[5]

A smaller, but still significant number travelled further west; there

[1] J. V. Šimák, 'Studenti z Čech, Moravy a Slezska na německých universitách v XV–XVIII stoletích', *ČČM* lxxix (1905), 290–7, 419–24; lxxx (1906), 118–23, 300–5, 510–39; F. Menčik, 'Studenti z Čech a Moravy ve Vitemberku od roku 1502 do roku 1602', *ČČM* lxxi (1897), 250–68; in general, and most recent: F. Šmahel and M. Truc, 'Studie k dějinám University Karlovy v letech 1433–1622, iii, Studenti z českých zemí na zahraničních universitách', *AUC, Historia Universitatis Carolinae Pragensis* iv/2 (1963), 37–46.

[2] Kunstmann, *Altdorf und Böhmen*, 1–19. Kunstmann gives a complete list of Czech students registered there (189–226).

[3] Ibid. 39 ff., 121 ff.

[4] Details of their history and activities are given by the nuncio Ferreri in a report to Rome, 14 June 1604 (*Epistolae* (Kristen), No. 59). Cf. A. Cronia, *Čechy v dějinách talské kultury* (Prague 1936), Ch. VI.

[5] Z. Kalista, 'Češi v Sieně 1574–1646', *ČČH* xxxiii (1927), 117–27.

were Czech students at French universities, notably Orleans, and some found their way to England.[1] These were men like Jan Bernart of Přerov, a member of the Brethren, who appeared in Oxford from 1581, Václav Lavín the doctor, recipient of an Oxford B.D., and his pupil Karel Žerotín who attended at Elizabeth's court in 1587.[2] Jan Diviš, Karel's younger brother, had links with the Essex circle, and members of the Smiřický and Valdštejn (Waldstein) families were also in England, especially Zdeněk Brtnický of Valdštejn who travelled under the guidance of Stephen Lesieur. Others to come were Fradelius, the Ramist Opsimathes, and the leader of the estates, Václav Budovec.[3] Contacts with Spain were of a different kind: the fascination of Spanish taste and atmosphere which percolated down from a small, though not exclusive clique of high aristocrats, favoured by the activities of the ambassador San Clemente and the bond of a limited number of influential marriages. In another direction, links with the Netherlands grew and diversified among Bohemian society as a whole, paralleling the development at the Habsburg court. The expanding trade relations brought to Prague figures such as Hans de Witte, later to become famous as Wallenstein's financial adviser.[4]

One result of these travels was the introduction of current foreign literature into the country, but Czech publishing had already begun to build up its own tradition. A cultural touchstone of any Renaissance centre is the quality of its local printers, and the development in Bohemia holds a distinctive place, especially for the publication of Slavonic and Hebrew texts.[5] In Prague several active printing houses existed during the first half of the sixteenth century, particularly those of Mikuláš Konáč (1507–28, with successor to 1547), Bartoloměj Netolický (1530–52), and Pavel Severín (1501–41, with successor to 1553); but leadership was increasingly centred on one family, first under Jiří Melantrich Rožďalovický of Aventýn (1552–80), a pupil of Froben and the Czech Humanist Zikmund Hrubý in Basle,[6] then under his son-in-law Daniel

---

[1] For a conspectus see M. Černá, 'Studenti ze zemí českých na universitě v Orleansu a na některých jiných francouzských universitách', *ČČH* xl (1934), 347–62, 548–64; R. F. Young, 'Bohemian scholars and students at English universities 1347–1750', *English Historical Review* xxxviii (1923), 72–84.

[2] R. F. Young, *Jan Bernart of Přerov (1553–1600)* (London 1928); Odložilík, 'Cesty', 253–7; Polišenský, *Anglie a Bílá Hora*, 48 f.

[3] Odložilík, op. cit. 270 ff.; on Opsimathes cf. above, p. 115 n. 2.

[4] A. Ernstberger, *Hans de Witte, Finanzmann Wallensteins* (Wiesbaden 1954), 11–22. Witte first appeared in Prague as a factor about 1603. Cf. in general Janáček, *Dějiny obchodu*, 95 ff.; Polišenský, *Nizozemská politika, passim*.

[5] J. Dostál in *Co daly naše země Evropě a lidstvu* (Prague 1939), 128–34.

[6] Rachlík, *Jiří Melantrich*, 24 f.

Adam of Veleslavín (1580–1600) and the latter's family. Melantrich took over from Netolický as semi-official printer who enjoyed the benefit of Ferdinand's censorship laws;[1] his publications thus included much governmental material (compare the case of Plantin, who was also succeeded by a son-in-law), besides many Bibles and the usual improving or consolatory religious literature which forms the lowest common denominator in Czech writing of the time.

Despite a few of Melantrich's productions, like the Matthioli *Herbal* of 1562, it was not until Veleslavín assumed control that this level of activity was exceeded. Veleslavín was an intellectual who had worked as professor of history at the Charles University before having to resign because of his marriage; he retained close contact with it and reflected its interests in his public activity.[2] Compilations of history formed a major part of the output of him and his collaborator Jan Kocín (1543–1610): the highly successful *Kalendář Historický* of 1578 (republished in 1590), re-editions and translations of the chronicles of Aeneas Silvius, Martin Kuthen, Eusebius, Cassiodorus, and accounts of the Muscovite and Ottoman Empires.[3] In 1581 Kocín edited Bodin's theoretical work, the *Nova Distributio Iuris Universi*; he was also evidently a Ramist, for he appears in the dedication of the Prague version of Ramus's Greek grammar by the Moravian Jan Opsimathes in 1602.[4] Another large concern of the press was linguistic, and Veleslavín produced a series of dictionaries, both bilingual and polyglot, after the fashion of the time.[5]

Consideration of Veleslavín leads directly to a group of individuals who represented the continuing positive contribution of the celebrated but now decayed and impoverished Charles University. It is indeed not as 'university' that we can appraise this seat of learning during Rudolf's reign, for it was imbued with the 'academy' spirit of the period and an élitism—like the élitism of the court—which its reduced position anyway dictated.[6] Although it numbered only a handful of professors (the worst

---

[1] Rachlík, *Jiří Melantrich*, 32 ff.

[2] M. Kopecký, *Daniel Adam z Veleslavína* (Prague 1962).

[3] For all these see ibid., esp. 20 ff. and 55–60; J. Volf, *Geschichte des Buchdrucks in Böhmen und Mähren bis 1848* (Weimar 1928), 56 ff.

[4] Ong, *Ramus and Talon Inventory*, No. 573. There is no acknowledgement that the work is Ramist, but Ong sees it as directly based on him. Cf. above, p. 133 n. 3.

[5] Kopecký, op. cit. 32 ff. Dictionaries were one by-product of the new international relations; San Clemente's predecessor as ambassador in Prague, Juan de Borja, published a Spanish–Latin–Czech dictionary (Chudoba, *Spain and the Empire*, 160). Cf. below, p. 187 n. 1.

[6] In his *Rudolphus Rex* Bydžovský, who was rector of the University and taught history and mathematics there, always refers to it as the 'Academy' (*Akademie*) or the 'Teaching of Prague' (*Pražské učení*).

constraints on them were lack of finance and the insistence on celibacy) and comparatively few students, there were signs of recovery from the 1570s, embracing at least the work of a small erudite circle.[1]

Throughout the two centuries from 1409 (when most of its German members had defected to Leipzig) the Carolinum remained in a peculiar legal situation, independent both of Church and state control. In this its status was more privileged than that of the rival Jesuit Clementinum, regardless of its academic standards.[2] For many years, especially during the 1570s and 1580s, the Protestant estates sought to gain control of it, supported by some professors like Codicillus.[3] In 1609 they finally succeeded, as a result of their stipulations in the Letter of Majesty of that year, and they maintained their rights through the troubled period to 1618. Historians have generally stated that the University as such was a militantly Protestant organ during the whole time we are considering, but this appears wide of the mark. It is certainly true that it backed the rising of 1618 and its then Rector Jessenius and Pro-rector Fradelius were deeply implicated: the former was executed in 1621, the latter died in exile the same year. But after the events of 1609 the Carolinum became a tool in the hands of the estates and therefore its subsequent decisions are not relevant. Some of its members were appalled at the course of the conflict, among them the classicist, historian, and poet Jan Campanus, who accepted conversion to the Catholic Church before his death in 1622, as also did others of his colleagues.[4] Campanus could countenance the interference of the estates only because of pressing financial need; for their part Jessenius and Fradelius displayed extreme political commitment in the last years before the revolt largely because the other avenues of escape for which their generation had searched seemed all to be closed.

The professors of the Charles University before 1609 were broadly representative both of religious moderation and all the learned interests of the late Renaissance. Marek Bydžovský for example emerges as a mild Catholic opposed to the Jesuits and highly superstitious; Campanus as an uncertain Protestant, like his colleague the grammarian and poet

---

[1] For the condition of the University at this time see W. W. Tomek, *Geschichte der Prager Universität* (Prague 1849), 173 ff.; Z. Winter, *Děje vysokých škol pražských 1409–1622* (Prague 1897), 55 ff.

[2] V. Vaněček, *Kapitoly o právních dějinách Karlovy University* (Prague 1934), esp. 25 ff.

[3] Cf. the memorandum of 10 Feb. 1582, printed in *SČ* vi. 155–65.

[4] O. Odložilík, *Mistr Jan Campanus* (Prague 1938), 37 ff.; cf. the case of Professor Adam Rosacinus of Carlsberg (Z. Tobolka and E. Horák, *Knihopis českých a slovenských tisků*, ii (1501–1800, Prague 1939– , hereafter *Knihopis*), Nos. 14904–5).

Vavřinec Benedikt of Nudožery.[1] The long-time Rector Martin Bacháček, an astronomer and mathematician, was a close friend of the uncommitted Johannes Kepler, who himself toyed for many years with
the offer of a chair at the Carolinum.[2] Kepler's acceptance of Rudolf's
invitation and arrival in Bohemia were—as is well known—a direct consequence of the Archduke Ferdinand's incipient Counter-Reformation
in Graz from 1598, but he was at the same time no orthodox Lutheran.
From his Württemberg background he stood near the mystical eirenism
of men like Valentin Andreae and he held De Dominis in great respect;
later he even became suspected of Catholic sympathies and this brought
him much bitterness. Although deeply fascinated by theological questions, Kepler clearly abstained—in the spirit of Melanchthon—from all
dogmatic wrangles.[3] The only years when he remained free of them
were those which he spent in Prague and which also yielded his period
of greatest creativity.

Kepler's activities form a bridge between University and court, as do
those of other astronomers: not only Tycho Brahe, whose short personal
residence in Prague was the culmination of years of indirect contact
through men like Jakob Kurz,[4] but Bacháček and Tadeáš Hájek, Caspar
Štehlík of Ceňkov (1571–1613), and Bartholomew Scultetus of Görlitz
(1540–1616).[5] A central figure in the intellectual circle of the Carolinum
was Johann Jessenius, a friend of both Kepler and Tycho. Jessenius[6]

[1] J. B. Čapek, 'Příspěvky k životu a dílu Vavřince Benedikta-Nudožerina', *AUC,
Historia Universitatis Carolinae Pragensis* vii/2 (1966), 25 f.

[2] Max Caspar, *Kepler* (English trans. London–New York 1959; original German
edn. 1948), 165 ff.; Bartoš, op. cit. 136–8. Cf. Johann Kepler, *Gesammelte Werke*
(Munich 1938–), xv, Nos. 298, 334, 344.

[3] On Kepler's religion in general see L. Schuster, *Johann Kepler und die grossen
kirchlichen Streitfragen seiner Zeit* (Graz 1888), Pt. III; for De Dominis, ibid. 167 and n.
Apart from the Prague circle he had lifelong Catholic friends like Herwart von Hohen-
burg in Munich and Elector Ernst of Cologne. He also maintained contact with
extreme Protestants like the Arian Martin Crusius; see Ludwik Chmaj, *Bracia Polscy*
(Warsaw 1957), 53–64. Kepler's interest in theology emerges not only in correspondence but also in his scientific work—as with his assumption of Trinitarian patterns
in the universe.

[4] On Brahe: J. L. E. Dreyer, *Tycho Brahe* (Edinburgh 1890), 277–314. In 1591 we
find Kurz, himself described as a great student of astronomy, warmly recommending
Tycho to the Venetian ambassador in Prague: *Jahrbuch* xv (1894), Reg. Nos. 12030–1.

[5] On Hájek see below. Scultetus, who died in Prague, was also a Paracelsan and
dabbler in alchemy. He issued a tract by Isaac of Holland on the philosopher's stone
in Prague in 1572 (Zíbrt, *BČH* iii, No. 10675) and an edition of Paracelsus's *Vom
Ursprung der Pestilenz* three years later. Cf. on Scultetus, Sudhoff, *Versuch*, i, Nos.
151, 167, 216, 219 (esp. 373); on him and Štehlík, *Knihopis*, Nos. 15246–9, 15674–87.

[6] The best work on Jessenius is Friedel Pick, *Johann Jessenius de Magna Jessen, Arzt
und Rektor in Wittenberg und Prag* (Leipzig 1926), who concentrates on the medical
aspects of his career. There is a recent monograph by J. Polišenský, *Jan Jesenský-
Jessenius* (Prague 1965) which is slight, but informative on the Czech background.

came of Slovak stock (he styled himself a 'Hungarian knight'), but was born at Breslau in 1566 and first visited Prague in 1591. After early education amid the enlightened atmosphere of Breslau he studied medicine at Padua between 1588 and 1591 where he was a comrade of Zdeněk Lobkovic, whose departure thence in 1590 he mourned in an elegy.[1] Still at Padua he dedicated his first philosophical tract to Rudolf II;[2] as a reward he was honoured with a degree the following year in Prague and made his first contacts with the Imperial court and its physicians.[3] Jessenius then lived for a number of years at Wittenberg (in the house of Peucer), where he formed an acquaintanceship with Tycho Brahe which led to his intervening on Tycho's behalf in Prague and later helping to heal the rift which grew up between him and Kepler.[4] He gave a major funeral oration on the death of Tycho in 1601.[5] Jessenius worked in Prague almost continuously from 1600 until 1608 and forged close links with Typotius, Bacháček, Zalužanský, Huber, the court doctors (particularly Guarinoni), and later Julius of Brunswick.[6] He was himself appointed *Leibarzt* in 1602.

Jessenius was clearly influenced strongly during his studies in Italy by the Neoplatonist philosophy of Patrizi, and his main philosophical work, the *Zoroaster* of 1593, is closely modelled, even to the title, on him: a farrago of animistic and mystical beliefs and Hermetic learning.[7] His cosmology was partly Copernican, partly geocentric, and later felt decisively the effects of h¹s contact with Tycho;[8] but he was no pure

[1] Polišenský, *Jessenius*, 21.

[2] *De divina humanaque philosophia* (Venice 1591).

[3] Pick, *Jessenius*, 15 f., 23 f.

[4] Ibid. 46, 55 ff.; J. von Hasner, *Tycho Brahe und Johann Kepler in Prag, eine Studie* (Prague 1872), 16 ff.; Caspar, loc. cit. Jessenius's crest and autograph appear in the album of Tycho's son, also called Tycho, during 1599: 'Aspicis aspicior . . . D. Iohan Iessenius à Iessen. Med. et Phil. Witebergae scribebat pingebatque VIII Januarii Juliani Anno MDXCIX', Nat. Mus., MS. VI F 44, fo. 24ʳ. Later the same year the album was signed by Typotius (ibid. fo. 64ʳ).

[5] This oration: *De Vita et Morte Dn. Tycho de Brahe Oratio* is printed in *Tychonis Brahei equitis Dani astronomorum coriphaei Vita authore Petro Gassendo* (The Hague 1655), 224–34; cf. Pick, op. cit. 127–30.

[6] Polišenský, op. cit. 27 ff.; Pick, op. cit. 66 ff., 173 ff.; cf. below, pp. 203 f. and n. 5.

[7] *Zoroaster—Nova, brevis, veraque de Universo Philosophia* (Wittenberg 1593). There was an edition of Patrizi's *Zoroaster* in the same year at Hamburg: *Magia Philosophica hoc est Francisci Patricii summi Philosophi Zoroaster et eius 320 Oracula Chaldaica, Asclepii Dialogus et Philosophia Magna, Hermetis Trismegisti Poemander, Sermo Sacer . . . Jam nunc primum ex Bibliotheca Ranzoviana è tenebris eruta et latine reddita.* This patron was the celebrated Heinrich Rantzau, editor of occult and other texts and friend of Tycho, to whom he later offered hospitality at his castle of Wandsbeck (Dreyer, op. cit. 253 ff.; Morhof, *Polyhistor*, ii. 492).

[8] Cf. Zdeněk Horský, 'Kosmologické názory Jana Jessenia', in *Sborník pro dějiny přírodních věd a techniky* ii (1955), 126–47.

astronomer and his teleological views on the movements of the planets and the primacy of the sun are theocratic and Platonist, showing some similarity with the underlying ideas of Kepler. Jessenius came increasingly to accept astrology, which was anyway a necessary deduction from his belief in correspondences within a threefold universe: elemental, aethereal, and empyrean. His denial of the heavenly spheres and belief in the rotation of the stars accord with Bruno, though whether he read the Nolan philosopher directly remains intriguingly uncertain.

Jessenius was above all a polymath of the late sixteenth-century kind with a firm faith in the unity of knowledge. Not for nothing did he publish in 1596 a volume entitled *Universae philosophiae epitome . . . de divisione, ordine atque usu omnium scientiarum . . . opusculum quadripartitum*, and he prepared—perhaps as a companion to this—a large catch-all of answers to every manner of question which he presented to his protector in Wittenberg, Frederick William the regent of Saxony.[1] At the Carolinum too an important place in the contemporary learned pantheon went to historiography, and several of its members—notably Campanus and his pupils—actively pursued the subject. It was Jessenius who in 1618, with the approval of his colleagues, published Typotius's symbolical work *De Hieroglyphia* and dedicated it to Karel Žerotín.[2] At the same time there were developments in the field of medicine. This was taught both by Jessenius—one of the leading anatomists of the day —and by Adam Huber of Riesenpach, a colleague of the aulic physicians, who translated medical works for Veleslavín and supervised the reedition in 1596 of the Czech version of Matthioli.[3] His friend Adam Zalužanský (1558–1613) is best remembered by an original botanical treatise, his *Methodi Herbarii Libri Tres* (Prague 1592), which sought a systematic study of botany and made important observations on the classification of plants.[4] Zalužanský's concern for method stemmed directly from a reading of Ramus, and he applied similar principles in his lifelong advocacy of university reform, as is revealed by his *Oratio* of 1600.[5] He seems also to have striven for religious union, at least of the Protestant confessions.

Jessenius's younger colleague Peter Fradelius of Štiavnica was likewise a Slovak, who travelled much in Europe, but little definite is known of

[1] 'Iohannis Iessenii a Iessen Illustriss. Sax. Ducum Medici et Professoris Novorum Problematum Centuriae Quatuor . . .', OSzK, Budapest, MS. 799 Quart. Lat.

[2] Polišenský, *Dějepisectví*, 130 f.

[3] Kopecký, op. cit. 68 ff.

[4] Arber, op. cit. 144, 181 f.; Maiwald, op. cit. 29 ff. There is a modern facsimile edition (edidit Carolus Pejml, Pragae 1940).

[5] B. Němec in *Co daly naše země . . .*, 153–6; Bartoš, op. cit. 139–41.

him beyond his own writings. He was born about 1580 and studied in Graz before being forced, like Kepler, to emigrate as a result of the Counter-Reformation there in 1598–9. After a period of uncertainty he was appointed in 1610 professor of logic and rhetoric at Prague on the recommendation of Benedikt and Bacháček, but soon left again to travel for some years (1611–17) as the tutor of two Bohemian noble sons; this took him through Altdorf and Germany to Basle, then to France, England, and the Netherlands.[1] Fradelius was very active as a Latin poet and pursued also serious scientific interests—he certainly knew and read Aldrovandi. But it was his contacts with France which seem to have influenced him most: he was a disciple of Bodin in his attitude to history, and corresponded with de Thou, Scaliger, and Casaubon.[2] It is not clear how much his theory of politics owed to Bodin—Fradelius had visited Duplessis-Mornay—but evidence exists of contemporary sympathy for the French 'politiques' in Bohemia. A manuscript dialogue account of the French religious wars written around 1600, while fanatically anti-Catholic, shows itself very favourable to the spokesman for moderation 'Politicus'.[3] Several of the Prague libraries have copies of Bodin's *Republic* in editions before 1600.

It was precisely this lack of an adequate centre party in the French sense—rightly stressed by Ernest Denis[4]—which prevented the moderate intelligentsia, including many of the personnel of both court and University, from finding a political platform suitable to its cultural cosmopolitanism. The absence of it drove Catholics and Protestants alike into extremism, and its failure was ultimately the failure of Rudolfine society as a whole. The fate of the traditional polity, so intimately linked with the blossoming of late Humanism's intellectual world, is highlighted in the impotence and pessimism of its leaders: on the one hand we see the disaster of Rudolf's declining authority; on the other the inability of the senior spokesmen of the estates to resist mounting intolerance and exclusiveness. Bohemia in the decades immediately before the White Mountain yielded two last great representatives of the middle way, both

---

[1] Polišenský, *Jessenius*, 52–6; idem, 'Politická a literární činnost slovenského humanisty Petra Fradelia ze Štiavnice', *Historický Časopis* ix. (1961), 603–17. Fradelius's printed eulogy of James I which survives in the British Museum (*Prosphonensis ad . . . regem Jacobum I. magnum Magnae Britanniae . . . monarchum* (London 1616), BM C 116 f 1 (4)) has a manuscript letter of dedication with some mention of his travels.
[2] Polišenský, *Dějepisectví*, 131 f. On Fradelius's literary activity cf. *Rukověť* (see below, p. 147 n. 1).
[3] 'Dyalog neb Historyczké Rozmlauwání', UK, MS. XVII D 23.
[4] Denis, op. cit. 130 f.

of them by background and intellect the natural focus of Czech and Moravian Protestant opinion: Peter Vok of Rožmberk and Karel Žerotín.

The last of the Rožmberks, younger brother to the Vilém we have already considered, Peter Vok is one of the most curious figures of the period—he has evidently baffled historians—and yet one of the most typical. He was an eccentric spendthrift of Protestant inclination who fell out periodically with his brother over debts, and permanently with Rudolf over politics, yet displays important similarities with them both. His religious uncertainty seems to have been lifelong: a leaning towards Lutheranism was early noticed and probably gained sustenance by his association with Maximilian II.[1] Later he became a member of the Brethren under the influence of his young wife Kateřina of Ludanice, but his views were always moderate and he sent away his preacher for six years after Rudolf reissued the Mandate against the sect in 1602. Peter reserved his real dislike for the Counter-Reformation and the Society of Jesus (though not to the point of personal intolerance), and believed in religious solutions on a national basis with the affairs of the Church subordinated to political unity.[2] Beside this uncertainty of his went the pessimism and melancholy of the age: his faithful biographer records that he always carried with him a *memento mori*, and even founded a society with a necklet in the shape of a golden skull as its emblem.[3] His wife was of unsound mind, while he suffered in addition (since she bore him no children either) the perpetual awareness that he was the last of his exalted family.

In his politics Peter Vok became involved with militant Protestants of the stamp of Anhalt and Tschernembl, yet he never appears to have been fully committed to them. His court at Krumlov was a meeting-place for influential men of all kinds[4] and he maintained close friendships with Catholics, particularly with Wolf Novohradský of Kolovrat into whose family his beloved nephew Jan Zrinyi married in 1600, a wedding attended by Christoph Lobkovic and Adam Sternberg, and celebrated in verse by the Catholic poet Šimon Lomnický.[5] His lack of

---

[1] Březan, 176–8, 183; Rybička, op. cit. 95 f.

[2] Rybička, op. cit. 218 ff.; O. Hulec, 'Politická činnost Petra Voka z Rožmberka' (Dipl. Práce, Prague n.d.), esp. 10 f. and 14.   [3] Březan, 254.

[4] Březan, *passim*; Rybička, op. cit. 445 f.; Hulec, diss. cit. 24 ff. Cf. H. G. Uflacker, *Christian I von Anhalt und Peter Vok von Rosenberg* (Diss. Munich 1926), who stresses Rožmberk's irresolution.

[5] Březan, 230. Zrínyi died without issue, but was a favourite with Peter Vok, who had wished to make him his heir. Zrínyi's mother was Eva Rožmberk. Cf. Kavka, *Zlatý věk růží*, 131, 154.

commitment is shown also by an unwillingness to accept public office (even when events favoured the Evangelicals), a fact which the diarist Dačický noted on his death.[1] It may likewise be indicated by Rožmberk's possession of two giant manuscripts containing the theological writings of Paracelsus.[2]

Like his brother Vilém, Peter Vok was a highly cultured man and patron of all the arts—in his palace on the Hradschin Tycho Brahe partook of a last fatal banquet during the autumn of 1601. Both also kept themselves extremely well-informed: the Rožmberks had a special service of news-letters, copies of the most topical reports from all over Europe and beyond; in their provenance they overlapped with the celebrated *Fuggerzeitungen* and like them their coverage was markedly pro-Habsburg.[3] Peter Vok's court in the south of Bohemia stood second only to Rudolf's in Prague. He began with the castle of Bechyně and a summer palace at nearby Kratochvíl: both of these he had rebuilt by the best Renaissance architects, decorated according to Mannerist models (the paintings in Kratochvíl were based on designs in German and Dutch manuals), and their gardens organized in the contemporary fashion.[4] On the death of Vilém in 1592 he moved to Krumlov, in the valley of the upper Vltava; then in 1600, forced by debts to cede this castle to the crown, he retired to the small town of Třeboň on the road between Prague and Vienna.[5]

He was accompanied on that journey by 23 large chests containing his library. Peter Vok, like his brother, avidly indulged the passion for collecting books and documents; by the end of his life they had come to total more than 10,000 printed and manuscript volumes.[6] During the years 1602–8 he instructed his servant Václav Březan (himself a man of character and some learning) to catalogue the whole collection, and this catalogue survives in Stockholm.[7] His *ex libris*

---

[1] Dačický, 329.

[2] Sudhoff, *Versuch*, ii, Nos. 88 and 89.

[3] Z. Šimeček, 'L'Amérique au 16ᵉ siècle à la lumière des nouvelles du service de renseignements de la famille des Rožmberk', *Historica* xi (1966), 53–93.

[4] Rybička, op. cit. 104 ff.; Kavka, op. cit. 122 ff.; M. Lejsková-Matyášová, 'K malířské výzdobě rožmberské Kratochvíle', *Umění* xi (1963), 360–70.

[5] Březan, 229 ff.

[6] Rybička, op. cit. 197 f.

[7] 'Biblioteca Rosenbergica, id est consignatio accurata omnium librorum et auctorum ordine alfabetico digestorum illustrissimi principis ac D.D. Petri Vokonis Ursini a Rosenberg . . . Quae biblioteca sumptibus eiusdem illustrissimi D.D. primum in amoena arce Bechinensi colligi coepit, deinde in excellenti castro Crumloviensi aucta et tandem istinc translatione facta in domo inclyta Trebonensi plurimoř codicum duplo ferme amplificata et in recens exstructo capaci atrio collocata est.' Cf. B. Dudík, *Forschungen in Schweden für Mährens Geschichte* (Brünn 1852), 79–82. Březan seems

symbol was apparently designed by the court engraver Sadeler. The Rožmberk library, famous in its day, is now alas sadly dispersed:[1] it passed on the death of Peter Vok to the crown (a notable Habsburg acquisition—Peter had intended it for his school in Soběslav) and was moved to Prague, where it suffered the fate of capture by the marauding Swedes in 1648 as one of their richest prizes. Thus little light can now be thrown on the private studies of the last two Rožmberks, though some manuscripts still remain in Stockholm or Rome which were definitely theirs: among them a Cabalist-mystical work in German which must have belonged to Vilém (*Welt-Spiegel, i.e. Speculum seu Harmonia mundi, oder die vier Monarchien* (1585?)); a Czech translation by Březan in 1604 of medical-alchemical remedies, some by Crato, 'physician-in-ordinary to three Emperors, who wrote this to me as a dear friend while the red sickness was raging among the people in 1580'; and several other tracts of astrology and prophecy.[2]

Peter Vok's closest personal contacts are equally difficult to unravel; he was certainly a less fanatical alchemist than his brother (though much of the evidence for this comes from the sceptical Březan), but he kept intimate touch with the mysterious Dr. Croll, Anhalt's agent in Prague, author of the iatrochemical *Basilica Chymica* (completed in 1608), which included a letter to the writer from Rožmberk. Croll is known to have visited Třeboň in 1607.[3] He died in Prague the following year and his effects fell into the hands of Rudolf. These seem to have included some 'secret matters', but it is far from clear what they were: not necessarily political, since Croll had already been dealing with Rudolf on behalf of Anhalt. Local rumour spoke of a chest of strange and wondrous things—evidently occult literature—which the Emperor desperately wished to acquire.[4] Peter Vok may have been equally curious: among his contacts in Třeboň Croll numbered the court physician Hermann

---

also to have assembled a private library of his own: cf. O. Walde, *Storhetstidens Litterära Krigsbyten*, i–ii (Uppsala 1916–20), i. 319–21. The house where he lived in Třeboň is still pointed out to the visitor.

[1] *Čeští sběratelé knih (In memoriam Josefa Wolfa)* (Prague 1937), 10 f.; Dudík, op. cit. 47–51, 58–60.

[2] Dudík, op. cit. Stockholm: German MSS. No. 2; Czech MSS. No. 17. Cf. Dudík, *Iter Romanum* (Vienna 1855), i. 203: 'Sancti Thomae de Aquino mystica theologia de via purgativa, illuminativa et unitiva . . .'

[3] Hulec, diss. cit. 21 ff.; Rožmberk's letter is dated Třeboň, 31 August 1608 (cf. below, p. 207 and n. 4). Václav Budovec approved of Croll's alchemy: see his *Circulus*, 244.

[4] The date of Croll's death—otherwise a dubious matter—is given in ÖN, MS. 11133, fo. 1r. *Briefe und Akten*, vi. 605 n. 1, 622. Croll's brother Johann was apparently a convert to Catholicism (ibid. 659 n. 1). Hulec seems rather confused about the sequence of events: compare the details on his page 26 with page 32.

Bulderus, and Bulderus—as another source informs us—was an enthusiastic collector of Paracelsan manuscripts.[1]

A further interesting figure in Rožmberk employ was the poet Theobald Höck, who enjoyed a special place in Peter's affections—he earned a mention in his will. Little is certain about Höck's background:[2] he was born in the Palatinate in 1572 and became Peter's German secretary in 1600; his wedding took place at Třeboň in 1611.[3] He is said to have been an eager Protestant, though the evidence is scanty. His book of verses called *Schönes Blumenfeld*, anonymously published in 1601 but only recently rediscovered, shows him as a unique figure in the transition to the German Baroque lyric, a blender of sixteenth-century folk poetry and the beginnings of Baroque ornamentation, heavy with the allusiveness and learning of the late Renaissance.[4] Assuredly Höck's vision went beyond the mere literary conceit: it was he who helped to mediate between Rožmberk and Croll; the latter praises him—along with his master—for their devotion to the true philosophy of nature.

Like Rožmberk in Bohemia, so Karel Žerotín in Moravia was the person in whom the Evangelical party reposed most trust. Educated according to the strictest traditions of the Czech Brethren and devoted to his native land, but much travelled in Europe and acquainted with many of the leaders of international Calvinism—Mornay, Grynaeus, Beza, the Austrian and Hungarian leaders—he seemed an ideal candidate. Yet Žerotín, while detesting the Counter-Reformation and bitterly resenting the apostasy of his adolescent hero Henry IV,[5] could never bring himself to resist it with its own weapons. He remained a restless individual, desperately seeking in the world a harmony and security which could no longer be recovered.

At the heart of his trouble lay a religious uncertainty. Žerotín continually lamented the schism in the established universal Church and, while leaning now, like other members of the Brethren, towards the Calvinists, he was tormented by problems of dogma, especially predestination, and by doubts about the right to rebel against constituted authority. This brought him in the years 1599 and 1600 to a spiritual

---

[1] Sudhoff, *Versuch*, ii, Nos. 54, 55, 95, 127. Croll's comments on Bulderus and Höck are in his Preface to the *Basilica Chymica*.

[2] What little there is can be found in Rybička, op. cit. 190, 370 ff.; and E. von Kamptz, 'Theobald Höck, ein Prager Dichter des Frühbarock', *Prager Jahrbuch* 1943, 83–7. [3] Březan, 247.

[4] Cf. K. Fleischmann, *Theobald Höck und das sprachliche Frühbarock* (Reichenberg 1938, an exceedingly rare book).

[5] Odložilík, *Karel ze Žerotína*, 67–9. *Dopisy Karla ze Žerotína*, ed. Dvorský, Nos. 20, 22, 24, 25, etc.

crisis—compare the Emperor himself. He writes thus to the Hungarian Illésházy:

I see the true catholic Christian religion downtrodden by the enemies of the divine will, Christ's kingdom neglected and the realm of Antichrist growing, the pious followers of pure orthodox doctrine oppressed in many places and impious, arrogant, coarse men raised up, men who have fled God's word, degenerates for the most part, to whom all virtuous living is abhorrent. These men violate our faith, murder the faithful, trespass against law and justice, break underfoot our provincial habits and customs, yet all is tolerated not only with equanimity but with a false sense of security and all manner of foolish hopes.[1]

Žerotín was anyway of a pessimistic cast of mind. Racked by his own ill-health and the early deaths of three wives, he sought consolation in public service and Moravian tradition.[2] He himself wrote tracts on debates and procedure in the Diet, as a guide for those who should follow him, but he expressed dismay at the lack of public spirit among his contemporaries.[3]

Žerotín was one of the most widely read and travelled men of his time. He visited most of the Western countries, speaking and writing several languages fluently. His erudition was Humanist, though tempered by a streak of puritanism; his circle of friends was large and his correspondence enormous. It is significant that he maintained his connections with Catholic families, and even with apostate Protestants. He witnessed with sorrow how his childhood comrade Karl Liechtenstein, who married one of his mother's family, turned to the Roman Church; but while lamenting the circumstances of the conversion he did not break with the man.[4] He remained a close friend of Slavata (Žerotín's stepmother was a Slavata), and in one letter to him even specifically advocated visiting the Papist countries of Italy and Spain: 'All'incontro gli Italiani e Spagnuoli, per la gran prattica che hanno in queste paese et principalmente in corte et per le ragioni dell'imperio et della casa d'Austria, si possono dir come una medesima cosa con noi.'[5] He also managed to admire the vivacious but entirely Spaniolate Polyxena of

---

[1] *Dopisy*/Dvorský, No. 432, Krumlov, 13 Mar. 1600. Cf. Nos. 423, 478, 509, etc.

[2] Odložilík, op. cit. 26–9 and *passim*.

[3] e.g. *Sněm držaný léta 1612* (ze zápisů Karla z Žerotína vydal V. Brandl, Brno 1864), esp. Žerotín's introduction. Cf. Žerotín to Grynaeus, Rosice 2 Feb. 1599: 'Hoc me terret, quod descendentibus nemo succedat, in quo fiduciae quid collocari possit, ita ut appareat, vel finem universi instare, vel periodo harum provinciarum iam discursa adesse ruinam, quam vereor ne nobis vel bellum hoc turpe vel si quae insequatur pax non satis tuta maturet.' (*Dopisy*/Dvorský, No. 392.)

[4] Cf. his letter to Beza, Přerov, 10 Aug. 1599 (ibid. No. 411).

[5] Rosice, 15 Apr. 1598 (ibid. No. 205).

Rožmberk/Lobkovic.[1] Žerotín became a ready confidant of Peter Vok from the early 1590s—he received a lengthy letter from him in 1591.[2] His court in the Renaissance style at Rosice must indeed have been a Moravian equivalent of Třeboň or Krumlov, where he entertained distinguished guests and employed a large personal circle which included several Scots.[3]

Although Žerotín's political career prospered for some years and he rose to be *hejtman* of Moravia, the highest position of state below the Emperor (who ruled the country in the capacity of Margrave), he nevertheless found himself unable to take up a decisive stance during the critical years after 1612. He remained pessimistic about Protestant success, and could not finally approve a revolt against Ferdinand having once duly accepted him as legal successor.[4] Thus he stayed a forlorn figure between two military camps, while his cousin Ladislav Velen became leader of the Moravian Protestants. After 1620 no reprisals were taken against him personally by the victorious regime, but since he refused to change his religion he soon found himself banished as a heretic. He removed with his books and a few friends to the still tolerant Breslau, and died there, in the city of Dudith and Crato, in 1636.

With the death of Žerotín the last embodiment of old-fashioned moderation within the Habsburg lands had disappeared, but this programme had anyway long ceased to be relevant. The culture which had accompanied it lived on after 1612 in some men of both religious persuasions; but its spirit departed from the Habsburg court with the accession of Matthias, as that court departed from Bohemia, and its days had been numbered even before then. Jessenius and the Carolinum turned into more militant channels; even the patient and visionary Budovec, friend of Rožmberk and Žerotín, became intoxicated with the success of Evangelical pressure in 1609. By 1618 Protestants as well as Catholics were mentally prepared for strife and the stage was set for a conflict of material forces which could now suddenly be seen in its essence as Habsburg court versus dissident country.

*   *   *

[1] Cf. his letter to her from Rosice, 24 Aug. 1599 (ibid. No. 403).

[2] This appears in Žerotín's diary for that year, which was published by Arnold Ipolyi in *Rimay János, államiratai és levelezése* (Budapest 1887) (pp. 3–45), 7 ff. This obscure reference—lost in an edition of the works of a man who simply used the unwritten pages of the diary as a copy-book for himself—seems to have become consigned to near oblivion. But at least it proves the links between Žerotín and Rimay, who was in many ways a similar figure in Hungary.

[3] Odložilík, op. cit. 56–62. The names of Alexander Hepburn and Patrick Buchanan appear in the diary for 1591. Another interesting person recorded that year is doctor Simon Simonius of Lucca (Ipolyi/*Rimay*, 31).

[4] Odložilík, op. cit. 141–5, 161 ff.

Under Rudolf things were still quite different; intimate links bound court with country, and it was above all the culture of his time in Bohemia which demonstrated this unity. The quality of openness existing within that intellectual society is now extremely difficult for us to reconstruct. It possessed a basic cosmopolitan freedom so familiar then as to call for little comment, and although of course its background was one of privilege, of noble or royal patron, the dividing-line between protector and protégé could not always be clearly drawn. Moreover the status of scholar and man of letters had begun to appreciate markedly during the course of the sixteenth century.[1] Both the Habsburg lands proper and the Empire as a whole were drawn together by a network of contacts, personal or epistolary, whose nodal points were the chief cities and universities of Central Europe. While Rudolf lived Prague became the greatest focus, though Vienna retained its importance. An easy journey connected the two, and Vienna housed a circle of domestic Humanists as well as Imperial institutions like the court library. The keeper of the latter, Hugo Blotius, who spans almost the entire reign of Rudolf (he was appointed by Maximilian on Busbecq's recommendation in 1575 and died in 1608),[2] was one of the most diligent correspondents of the age and a regular goal for studious travellers en route between Italy and Germany. His letters and albums—still unexploited by historians—reveal a vast acquaintance with contemporary scholars.[3] Under such auspices links between Prague and the Austrian lands grew closer, and the same holds true of relations with Hungary: several of the Carolinum professors were Slovaks by nationality, while a series of other Hungarian intellectuals found their way to Bohemia during the Rudolfine years: Christoph Lackner, János Bocatius, Albert Molnár, Faustus Verancsics, István Csulyák of Miskolc, Jan Filiczky.[4]

[1] Cf. E. Trunz, 'Der deutsche Späthumanismus um 1600 als Standeskultur' (1931), reprinted in *Deutsche Barockforschung*, ed. R. Alewyn (Cologne–Berlin 1965), 147–81, an excellent account of the social background to scholarship in Protestant Germany at the time which is relevant to the general argument of the present section.

[2] Forster and Daniell, op. cit. ii: Busbecq, Paris 7 June 1575; Lambecius, op. cit. iii. 289 f. Blotius was vouched for by Schwendi and the Hungarian Bishop Liszti. Riegger (247) incorrectly reports him as still alive in 1612; in fact he had been succeeded by Sebastian Tengnagel (Lambecius, i. 46). Some of the correspondence surrounding his appointment was printed by J. Chmel, *Die Handschriften der k.k. Hofbibliothek in Wien*, i (Vienna 1840), 185–230.

[3] Especially ÖN, MSS. 9690 and 9707 (albums and lists of friends), 9737 z$^{14-18}$ (correspondence). These sources merit a detailed separate study. To date they have been examined only piecemeal, as by Gerstinger for his Sambucus edition (above, p. 123 n. 4) and by F. Mencsik (1910) and J. von Ernuszt (1943) for other contacts between Blotius and Hungary. The latest *compte-rendu* on Blotius is by F. Unterkircher in *Geschichte der österreichischen Nationalbibliothek* (Vienna 1968), 81–127.

[4] They lie outside the scope of this book, since their activity was not for the most

One characteristic feature of Rudolfine Prague which well illustrates this situation is the literary endeavour of its Humanists. Sixteenth-century learning remained closely associated with classical models and the Latin language, nowhere more so than in Central Europe where the vernaculars were especially underdeveloped. The Latin poem provided a favourite form of expression, not only as artistic vehicle but also—far more widely—as commentary on the intellectual world in which it was conceived. The elegy, satire, epithalamium, and *carmen gratulatorium*, the encomium and oration for funeral, victory, or distinguished guest: such writing covered the whole range of human experience and acted as a kind of common denominator in the network of Humanist friend-ships. At the same time it was consciously erudite, cultivating the learned allusion, the historical, antiquarian, or philological reference, the play on words, the conceit or emblem, the tortuous symbolic processes of Mannerism. It was a *tour de force*, on known models, to a limited and discriminating audience. It was thus also in its essence élitist, even eso-teric, heavily committed to the hierarchy of culture at whose apex sat the philosopher–Emperor and whose gradations were measured by courtly virtue and the privilege of intellect.

Rudolf granted many poets the accolade of *laureatus*, and such a mark of favour did not necessarily imply a court position or even any very definite connection with the Imperial entourage. Reconstruction of their work anyway presents difficulties, since so much verse was casual and soon forgotten, while posterity has never nourished any taste for its possible literary qualities. But study of the situation soon throws up a distinct poetic circle—strongest perhaps in the 1590s—which formed an important stratum in the educated society of Prague. Its members not only wrote fulsome stanzas to their patrons (local aristocrats like Rožm-berk, or Archdukes and dignitaries at court); they also honoured each other, and collaborated on slim volumes or more solid anthologies. If the poetry in these books usually owes little debt to inspiration, it is none the less significant for an understanding of its period, especially since it reveals so immediately the scope and intimacy of late Humanist con-tacts.[1] The exponents of the genre in Prague and Bohemia were—as we

part directly connected with the Rudolfine entourage. One example of their impressions is the *Diarium Apodemicum* of Csulyák (Budapest, OSzK, 656 Oct. Lat.) who studied in Heidelberg and visited both Silesia and Prague; another is the diary of Molnár, pub-lished by L. Dézsi: *Szenczi Molnár Albert naplója* (Budapest 1898). On Filiczky see O. Odložilík in *Sborník prací věnovaných . . . J. B. Novákovi*, 431–42.

[1] The sheer extent of the Latin verse we are here considering is revealed by the already-published volumes of the *Rukověť humanistického básnictví v Čechách a na Moravě* (založili A. Truhlář a K. Hrdina, pokračovali J. Hejnic a J. Martínek), i

should expect—variously Protestant and Catholic, Czech and German. A remarkable number of them came in fact from Silesia—their background the high educational standards and tolerant religion of the local burgherdom of Breslau, Liegnitz, Brieg, Glogau, Wohlau, and other prosperous towns in that province. It is worth dwelling a little on a few such individuals.

A good starting-point is Jakob Monau (1546–1603), the doyen of Breslau Humanism in the last years of the sixteenth century. Monau indulged in one of the favourite practices of his intellectual contemporaries: he chose a suitably pious personal motto or *Symbolum* and kept an album in which his friends could compose verses or epigrams using that *Symbolum* as a theme.[1] Among them are represented many of the great names of the period: Lipsius and Scaliger, William Camden and Theodore Beza, Ortelius and Paul Melissus, Arias Montano and Martin Crusius, Dudith, Sambucus, and Crato. There are also—what especially concerns us here—many representatives of the 'Rudolfine school', and Bohemian figures reappear profusely in two later Silesian collections of *Symbola*: the *Spero Meliora* of Balthasar Exner and the *Domini est Salus* of Caspar Cunrad.[2]

One of the most brilliant of Monau's contributors was Valens Acidalius (b. 1568), a philologist and Classical scholar whose great promise ended prematurely when he died from the plague in 1595. A correspondent of Lipsius and other leading men—some of his stylish letters were published posthumously, after the fashion of the time—Acidalius was a prodigy whose first poems appeared while he was barely in his twenties; his work then found inclusion in many contemporary collections.[3] A companion of his with similar youthful accomplishments was Salamon Frenzelius (1561–1601?), a native of Jauer, who after studying at Strasbourg earned the title of *Poeta Laureatus* in 1584. He settled in Prague and became a regular compiler of gratulatory verse for the dynasty, as well as for the celebrations or publications of his patrons

A–C (Prague 1966), ii Č–J (Prague 1966), iii K–M (Prague 1969, hereafter *Rukovĕt*'), a comprehensive compendium of authors and works which will be indispensable for future research. I shall make no attempt in what follows to give lists of works for individual authors; much can be found in the *Rukovĕt*'.

¹ *Symbolum Jacobi Monawi Ipse Faciat variis variorum auctorum carminibus expressum et decoratum* (Görlitz 1595).

² Balthasar Exner, *Anchora utriusque vitae: hoc est Symbolicum Spero Meliora* . . . (Hanau 1619); *Ad Casparis Cunradi . . . Symbolum Domini est Salus Epigrammatum Centuria*, i–v (Öls 1606–15).

³ *Valentis Acidali Epistolarum Centuria*, i, edita cura Christiani Acidali Fratris (Hanau 1606); *Delitiae Poetarum Germanorum, collectore A.F.G.G[rutero]* (i–vi Frankfurt 1612) (hereafter *Delitiae*), i. 1–150; etc.

and friends. Frenzelius it was who helped the young Jessenius on the latter's first visit to Prague. Much of his output is now extremely scarce, if not entirely lost.[1]

Another who, like Frenzelius, turned into a regular servant of the Emperor was Hieronymus Arconatus (b. 1553). Arconatus studied at Jena and Wittenberg, then travelled widely through Europe and Asia before entering Imperial service. He worked in Vienna and Prague as secretary of the Military Council (*Hofkriegsrat*) and died in 1599. He enjoyed much respect in his lifetime as a scholar and his poetry, including a paean on the recovery of Raab from the Turks in 1598, was published in Vienna and elsewhere.[2] A colleague of Arconatus was George Calaminus (1547–95), author of the Habsburg epic *Rudolphottocarus* and a regular member of Bohemian learned circles. Andreas Calagius of Breslau offered a more local talent, but his many verses are a gloss on the friendships and associations which knit together the Humanist society of Bohemia and Silesia.[3]

The important figure of Caspar Dornavius occupied a more central position. Dornavius (1577–1632) worked for some years in Prague, then travelled as far as England while tutor to Jaroslav Smiřický, son of one of the senior Protestant magnates in the land, before returning to Silesia where he became the greatest influence on the young Martin Opitz. He was a leading pedagogue and educational reformer whose original work covers all the regular forms of oration and dynastic panegyric.[4] At the same time Dornavius compiled highly erudite poetry on various natural and philosophical topics, and was evidently a member of the court circle: his marriage in 1608 to the daughter of a patrician from Görlitz was celebrated by many of them, the list of versifiers on that occasion including Campanus, Adam Huber, Zalužanský, and Kepler.[5]

[1] Some of Frenzelius's work survives in the British Museum: e.g. *Poemata Sacra et Nova* (Strasbourg 1585), his first collection; *Victoria pusilli Christianorum exercitus* . . . (Prague 1588), and *Musa Christiana in Nataliciis Domini Iesu* . . . (Prague 1591), both dedicated to Rudolf. Cf. *Delitiae*, iii. 326–42; *Rukověť*, ii. 164–70.

[2] Hieronymus Arconatus, *Poematum recentiorum volumen* (Vienna 1591); *Carminum . . . farrago* (Vienna 1592), etc. Cf. *Delitiae*, i. 386–94; A. Mayer, *Wiens Buchdruckergeschichte*, i (Vienna 1883), Nos. 822, 826, 878, 881, 895; *Rukověť*, s.v., and J. Martínek in *Listy Filologické* 91 (1968), 303 f.

[3] On Calaminus see above, p. 128 n. 2; Monau, *Symbolum, passim*; M. Adam, *Vitae Germanorum Philosophorum* (Heidelberg 1615), 407–11; H. Slaby, 'Magister Georg Calaminus und sein Freundeskreis', *Historisches Jahrbuch der Stadt Linz* 1958, 73–139; *Andreae Calagii Laurea et . . . Epigrammata* (Breslau 1597), etc.; several poems and collections by Calagius survive in BM 11409 c 36 and 11409 f 35.

[4] Caspar Dornavius, *Rodulphus Habsburgicus panegyrico historico celebratus* (Beuthen n.d.); idem, *Menenius Agrippa* (Hanau 1615); etc. Cf. A. Sellmann, *Caspar Dornau* (Langensalza 1898) and below, p. 187 n. 2.

[5] *Casparis Dornavi et Elisabethae Glyciae Sacrum Nuptiale* (Görlitz 1608). Cf. below,

This list of Silesians could be extended almost indefinitely; only the few have been noted here whose links with Prague seem particularly striking. Others were active mostly in their own province, or elsewhere in the Empire: the brothers Reusner, Martin Mylius, author of the fascinating *Hortus Philosophicus*, the lawyer and historian Hieronymus Treutler, Lawrence Scholtzius, Elias Cüchler, or Tobias Scultetus (1565–1620), Imperial councillor and long-time Prefect of the Silesian and Lusatian Exchequers.[1] It is anyway purely a matter of convenience that they have been singled out initially, for they by no means over-shadowed the rest of the Prague coterie. This included men as diverse as the historian Typotius, the Protestant official Jan Milner, the legist Otto Melander, the philologist Christopher Colerus, the doctor Borbonius, the musician Kryštof Harant, the University professor Campanus, and the zealous Pontanus (to whom we shall return).[2] Most important of them as pure poet was probably George Carolides of Karlsberg (ennobled in 1596), who was born in Prague in 1569 and died there in the same year as the Emperor. A prolific versifier whose work appears in almost every occasional collection of the time, Carolides may well have played a major part in advising which new aspirants deserved Rudolf's approbation.[3] That task also fell to the Imperial almoner, the Dutchman Iacob Chimarrhaeus (1542–1614), himself an active writer and musician.[4]

One of the most interesting personalities of the group was a young English poetess, Elizabeth Jane Weston, internationally celebrated in her day under the name of Westonia as a precocious talent.[5] Westonia was born in 1582 of Catholic family and evidently soon migrated to the continent. She appeared in Bohemia with her mother and brother during the 1590s, settling in Prague in 1598. A collection of her verses was published by Martin Baldhoven—another Silesian—in 1602 and reissued in augmented form four years later.[6] This volume in fact provides the

p. 177 n. 1. On Dornavius's Bohemian connections and allusions to them in his publications see *Rukověť*, s.v., and J. Martínek in *Listy Filologické* 93 (1970), 298.

[1] On Scultetus: *Delitiae*, vi. 34–68; Monau, *Symbolum*, 224 ff.; Exner, *Spero Meliora*, centuria prima, dedication; etc.

[2] The poetic work of Campanus alone would fill several large tomes; see G. J. Dlabacz, 'Biographie des . . . J. Campanus . . . mit einem Verzeichnis seiner bisher entdeckten Schriften', *Königliche böhmische Gesellschaft der Wissenschaften*, Abhandlungen, Band 6 (Prague 1819); and *Rukověť*, i. 254–94.

[3] Kunstmann, op. cit. 43 ff.; *Rukověť*, i. 326–46; *Delitiae*, ii. 185–236; Monau, *Symbolum*, 129 f.

[4] *Rukověť*, s.v.; Exner, *Spero Meliora*, 39; Cunrad, *Symbolum*, i. A2v; etc.

[5] e.g. Márton Szepsi Csombor, *Europica Varietas* in *Összes művei*, ed. S. I. Kovács and P. Kulcsár (Budapest 1968), 208, 521; cf. below, p. 230 n. 1.

[6] *Poemata Elisab. Ioan. Vuestoniae Anglae virginis nobilissimae* . . . (Frankfurt an der

main source for details of Westonia's life and contacts: she dedicates *Carmina* to court officials and her fellow literati, while her own praises are sung by distinguished contemporaries: Melissus, Carolides, Heinsius, Dousa. Various people seem to have lent her support in the Bohemian capital, among them high-ranking dignitaries like Barvitius and the deputy-Chancellor Písnice, but existence was never easy and Westonia did not break off her connections with England: she was a friend of the agent Lesieur and Edward Dyer. In 1603 she married a lawyer at court, Johann Leon, the agent of the Duke of Brunswick, but died in 1612 at the tender age of thirty.[1]

Poetry as such always remained a subsidiary activity—just as the congratulatory stanza formed a necessary adjunct to any kind of academic treatise of the time. Its practitioners were not a group apart: their basic concerns—Latinity, erudition, acceptance of traditional values allied with intellectual curiosity—were both the stock-in-trade of late Humanism and a feature of its mentality. Poets provided the literary dimension of Rudolfine Prague as astronomers, botanists, chemists provided its scientific one. In both fields it would be wrong to see any great divide between 'Imperial' and 'Czech' environments, nor did religious affiliations commonly present a barrier; it is no less misleading to look only at Czech-language writing and publishing in the period than to ignore it altogether. The presses of Veleslavín served both local cultural demands and the wider interests of scholarship; the same holds true of George Nigrin (Černý) who printed many works in Latin, German, and other tongues, or George Dačický, Kepler's publisher Paul Sessius, or Johann Schumann.[2] Moreover the broad horizons evinced by this book trade reflect the concern of many leading figures in public life, Rudolfine ministers as well as domestic politicians. One notable example is the Imperial Vice-Chancellor Coraduz, whose studies embraced history, geography, theology, and natural philosophy. His surviving manuscripts include excerpts from Ficino and Montano, Vitruvius and Widmanstetter, Riccio and Reinhold.[3]

Oder 1602); *Parthenicon Elisabethae Ioannae Westoniae virginis nobilissimae . . . Libri III* (Prague n.d. [1606]).

[1] There are various articles on Westonia: some add interesting details, e.g. A. Rebhahn, 'E. J. Weston, eine vergessene Dichterin des 16. Jahrhunderts', *MVGDB* xxxii (1894), 305–16; I. Patzak, 'Eine Prager Dichterin im Zeitalter Rudolfs II', in *Prager Jahrbuch* 1943; B. Ryba, 'Westoniana', *Listy Filologické* lvi (1929), 14–28. See also J. Martínek in *Listy Filologické* 93 (1970), 302.

[2] For brief details of these printers see Volf, op. cit. Much research remains to be completed before the balance of their activities can be drawn up.

[3] ÖN, MSS. 9138, 9547, 9549, 9581, 9676, 10546, 10707[16a–20a].

Like the poets, the natural scientists were operating basically within an accepted scheme of things, a hierarchy of values and an essential unity of endeavour, though in their work there breathes a more vital sense of inquiry and a heightened intellectual initiative. One of their leaders was the Imperial physician Tadeáš Hájek who has already been mentioned as a friend of Crato, Dudith, and Sidney, and the colleague of Matthioli who translated his renowned *Herbal*. Hájek, or Hagecius (1525–1600) came from a prosperous Prague family and served as doctor to three Habsburgs; he occupied a central position at Rudolf's court and maintained wide contacts outside the country—his three sons studied in England.[1] He was concerned in most of the important astronomical and medical debates of the day; his place both in the legend and the reality of its alchemy is assured; and he produced several more orthodox medical works, as well as one—appropriate to Bohemia—on brewing techniques.[2]

Hájek knew or corresponded with many of the astronomers of his time, among them Rheticus and Brahe, and his presence was one of the factors which induced Tycho to settle in Prague from 1599.[3] He took an active part in cosmological polemic: a treatise called *Dialexis* on the new star of 1572 forms perhaps his most significant work, and he was widely consulted about the comet of 1577. Yet Hájek's attitudes remained deeply superstitious and for all his interest in the Copernican hypothesis he was ultimately more concerned with the role of celestial events as portents and as manifestations of an organic universe.[4] In this sense his observations proceeded from the same preconceptions as those of his contemporaries Digges, Maestlin, Dee, or even Tycho. Recent discovery of Hájek's annotations to a copy of Carelli's *Ephemerides* throws further light on his belief in astral influences and his methods of casting horoscopes; he also edited a tract of pure astrology.[5]

The year of Hájek's death (1600) was also that during which Johann Kepler arrived in Prague, and Kepler was shortly afterwards appointed

---

[1] Odložilík, 'Cesty', 245.

[2] O. Zachar, 'Rudolf II a alchymisté', *ČČM* 87 (1913), 250, and below, pp. 203 f.; Maiwald, op. cit. 47.

[3] Lynn Thorndike, *History of Magic and Experimental Science*, vols. v and vi (Columbia U.P. 1941), v. 415 f., vi. 84 n.; Dreyer, *Brahe*, 131 ff.; Hasner, op. cit. 6 ff.

[4] *Dialexis de novae et prius incognitae stellae apparitione . . . per Thaddaeum Hagecium ab Hayck* (Frankfurt 1574, republished in facsimile, ed. Z. Horský, Prague 1967); Thorndike, op. cit. vi. 72, 79, 381, 474, Ch. XXXII *passim*; *Knihopis*, No. 2864.

[5] Ivo Kořán, 'Kniha Efemerid z biblioteky Tadeáše Hájka z Hájku' in *Sborník pro dějiny přírodních věd a techniky* vi. 221–7. *Astrologica Opuscula Antiqua*: [1] *Fragmentum Astrologicum, incerto autore* [2] *Liber Regum de Significationibus Planetarum* [3] *Hermetis Astrologi Antiquissimi . . . Liber* (Prague 1564); cf. Zíbrt, *BČH*, iii, No. 11029 who mentions a re-edition in 1598, apparently under Rudolf's aegis.

Imperial astronomer in succession to Tycho. The twelve years of his residence there proved the most productive of his life; during them he moved to definitive statement of his three provocative laws on the motions of the heavenly bodies. The *Astronomia Nova* was published at Prague in 1609 with a dedication to the Emperor. For all the far-reaching implications of that treatise, however, Kepler remained in his way typical of the Rudolfine environment and not so very different from a scholar like Hájek. His complex personality has never been adequately explained, yet clearly Kepler's whole scientific attitude was profoundly imbued with presumptions of universal harmony and an astrological world-view of cosmic powers and influences. This rested partly on Pythagorean traditions—very striking in the early *Mysterium Cosmographicum*—partly on other occult beliefs; his view of the metaphysical properties of light stands close to the Neoplatonism of Patrizi.[1] There is also the Utopian element represented by the *Somnium*, a curious little visionary tale of life on the moon which Kepler wrote in 1609.[2] Above all his astronomical reform was far rather an *a priori* attempt to justify certain postulates about a divinely-ordered and harmonious universe than any simple manipulation of Tycho's compendious observations.[3]

Kepler's patrons and friends in Prague included, besides the Emperor, Rožmberk and Budovec, Jessenius and Bacháček, Barvitius and Pistorius. Closest of all stood two of its foremost intellectual figures: Baron Hofmann and J. M. Wacker von Wackenfels. Ferdinand Hofmann von Grünpichl und Strechau (1540–1607), who acted as intermediary between Tycho and Kepler in the troubled year of 1600 and to whom the latter dedicated his *De Stella Cygni*,[4] was a wealthy nobleman of Styrian origin. His family, although staunchly Protestant, took pride in its loyalty to the dynasty (Ferdinand I was his godfather). From his youth Hofmann had been familiar with the Bohemian environment—part of his education was with Peter Vok Rožmberk at Krumlov[5]—and later as President of the *Hofkammer* he bought estates there and settled permanently. He became well-known among literary and artistic circles as

---

[1] R. Haase, 'Keplers Weltharmonik und das naturwissenschaftliche Denken', *Antaios* v (1964), 225–56; W. Pauli, 'The Influence of archetypal ideas on the scientific theories of Kepler', in C. G. Jung and W. Pauli, *The Interpretation of Nature and the Psyche* (Eng. trans. London 1955), esp. 159 ff.

[2] *Somnium sive Astronomia Lunaris* (first published 1634, English trans. ed. J. Lear, Berkeley, Cal. 1965; another trans. ed. E. Rosen, Madison 1967).

[3] A. Koestler, *The Sleepwalkers* (London 1959), 225–422; A. Koyré, *La Révolution Astronomique* (Paris 1961), 119–458.

[4] Kepler, *Gesammelte Werke*, i. 292–311; xiv, Nos. 155, 156, 157, 160.

[5] Březan, 173 ff.

a man of learning and moderation—Campanus and the rest mourned his death in a volume of characteristic verses.[1] Hofmann's great glory however was his library: among its 4000 volumes and more were incorporated not only a very important earlier collection (that of the Humanist Hieronymus Münzer) but all his own acquisitions from the learned literature of the time, suitably bound and ornamented with a personal *super libros*. The library with its manuscripts survived almost intact into the present century, but has now been dispersed and any adequate reconstruction of it presents grave problems.[2] Enough is known however to illustrate Hofmann's wide interests: theology of all kinds, including an amazing range of bibles; geography, travel, and antiquities; medicine and natural science; books in Czech, Hebrew, and Arabic. Specifically occult books are also represented: he bought for example the Cracow edition of the Hermetic texts, works by Della Porta, and Thurneysser's *Magna Alchemia*. Hofmann certainly moved in the Emperor's most intimate company; access to both his sovereign and the business of state was easy from his town house beneath the Hradschin. He became the possessor of two important manuscripts by Octavio Strada—the one containing designs, the other symbols—both of which bear Rudolf's own arms.[3]

Johann Matthias Wacker settled in Prague only at the very end of the century, but he had already spent long years in the Imperial service. He was by origin a Swabian, born at Constance in 1550[4]—thus a near-contemporary of Rudolf; after studying law at Strasbourg and Geneva he found his way to Vienna, where he was welcomed by the Crato–Languet circle. Through them he was recommended as tutor to Nicholas III Rhediger (the nephew of Thomas) in 1576. This proved the prelude

---

[1] *Rukověť*, ii. 328; cf. below, p. 166.

[2] The library formed a central part of the Dietrichstein (later Dietrichstein-Mensdorff-Pouilly) family collection at Nikolsburg/Mikulov; see in general M. Trantírek, *Dějiny mikulovské dietrichsteinské knihovny* (Mikulov 1963), 13 ff. In the 1930s this was put up for sale, and the catalogues offer a source for precise identification of the most important volumes which bear Hofmann's *super libros*: H. Gilhofer and H. Ranschburg, *Bibliothek Fürst Dietrichstein Schloss Nikolsburg; Versteigerung Luzern 21–2.11.1933* (Cat. No. XI), *Versteigerung Luzern 25–6.6.1934* (Cat. No. XIII), *Versteigerung Wien 25.2–1.3.1934* (Cat. No. XLI). A less comprehensive contemporary catalogue also survives in Brno: V. Dokoupil, *Soupis rukopisů mikulovské dietrichsteinské knihovny* (Brno 1954), Sig. Mk 48.

[3] Ibid. Sig. Mk. 4: Libro de dissegni per far Vasella di Argento et Oro . . . di Ottavio Strada, Cittadino Romano et Gentilhuomo della Casa di Rodolpho II (this MS. was published in Vienna in 1869 as *Entwürfe für Prachtgefässe . . .*); Sig. Mk 51: Simbola Romanorum Imperatorum . . . per Octavium de Strada.

[4] There is nothing adequate on the life of Wacker; for such details as are known, mostly on the first part of his life, see the old article by Theodor Lindner: 'Johann Matthäus Wacker von Wackenfels', *ZVGAS* viii (1868), 319–51.

to Wacker's career; he travelled with his charge through France, Germany, and Italy before returning to Breslau, where he became a lively member of its intellectual community. From that time date his friendships with Dudith, Monau, Clusius, and Sidney, whom he was later to call 'magnus quondam amicus meus'.[1]

While at Breslau Wacker was made a councillor to the Silesian Exchequer (Schlesischer Kammerrat) and Imperial representative to the diet there (Krafft describes its meeting in 1583);[2] he was also entrusted with missions to Poland and enjoyed the friendship of the educated and Habsburg-sponsored Bishop of Breslau Andreas Jerinus. After the death of Jerinus in 1596 Wacker played a large part in securing the eventual election of a successor approved by Rudolf, even arguing the Imperial case in Rome.[3] He was ennobled in 1594 as 'von Wackenfels' and moved to live in Prague continuously from 1599.

Wacker became a convert to the Roman Catholic Church in 1592, for reasons over which we are left to speculate—at all events the change in allegiance led to no break with his Protestant friends.[4] It seems to have been the influence of Wacker (and perhaps of that other convert Pistorius) which turned Gaspar Scioppio towards the Roman Church after his period of uncertainty in 1597. The latter was a member of his mission to Rome the following year,[5] as was Simon Simonius, another prominent ex-Protestant whom we have already encountered in this narrative. Little record exists of Wacker's actual relations with the Emperor (the same holds true for so much of Rudolf's personal intercourse), but he was still serving him in 1611 and took part in the last political intrigues of that year. As a general adviser Wacker carried weight until the very end, besides being a long-time member of the Aulic Council.[6] After 1612 he remained in Prague—his house (like Hofmann's) stood just below the castle on the Malá Strana—but he died in 1619 in Vienna, having just been forced to flee there by the pressure of untoward events.

---

[1] Ibid. 321 ff.; Gillet, op. cit. ii. 88 ff.; Costil, op. cit. 199; Hessels, Nos. 166, 242, 274; *Caroli Clusii Epistolae*, Clusius to Crato 19 Dec. 1576; Monau, *Symbolum*, 31 f. The reference to Sidney is Wacker's marginal note in his copy of Bruno's *Spaccio della Bestia Trionfante*, opposite the dedication of the book: Epistola explicatoria . . . cavaliero Signor Philippo Sidneo (UK, Sig. XII J 237). Wacker also wrote to Sidney in England (Buxton, op. cit. 83).

[2] Krafft, op. cit. 401. The date in question may have been 1584. In 1617 Wacker claimed to have been in Imperial service for 36 years (Loebl, 'Beiträge', 664).

[3] Lindner, art. cit. 326 ff. Jerinus was an acquaintance of Lipsius. Cf. Jungnitz, 'Bonaventura Hahn', 258 ff., 272 ff.

[4] Lindner, art. cit. 330 f.   [5] D'Addio, *Scioppio*, 14–19.

[6] Lindner, art. cit. 344–7; Beutin, op. cit. 55 ff.; *Briefe und Akten*, viii. 709 n. 1; Gschliesser, op. cit. 167–9. Wacker is named as an Imperial creditor for the sum of 2000 Schock Groschen in 1607: SÚA, Bekennen, Majestalia Vol. 109.

The appeal of Wacker to Rudolf seems easily explained, for his interests fit perfectly the late Humanist paradigm. He was a man of the widest talents, with a gift for languages, and a poet in the classicizing style. His library contained all kinds of books, including Neoplatonic texts, Paracelsan writings, and demonologies;[1] he was also, as we shall see, a patron of Bruno. From the years of permanent residence in Prague Wacker's most important association was with the fellow-Swabian Kepler, who dedicated to him several of his works and records (a very human touch) how he first received news about Galileo's discovery of the moons of Jupiter from the excited shouts of Wacker as he drew up in his coach.[2] Wacker's politics were evidently strongly Imperial; they were also tinged with Utopianism. Kepler dedicated his own *Somnium* to him, while from Wacker's correspondence with Jakob Monau it emerges that he himself prepared a book on Utopia (he speaks of his 'Skiagraphiae Utopianae').[3] We know nothing about its text, but it included a map with the names of imaginary cities (three of them to be called after Wacker, Monau, and Ortelius). The volume must actually have been published by Ortelius, as his nephew later acknowledged receiving twelve copies of it in London.[4]

I have argued that until 1600 no unbridgeable rift existed between religious or social factions in Bohemia, and that the culture of the Rudolfine age was an expression of that essential unity. Wacker provides an excellent example of its learned profile. Yet all the confessional moderation of Wacker (it may even look like indifference) should not obscure the fact that he became a convert to the Church of Rome. With this we immediately touch the root of the crisis of the late sixteenth century. For there is unmistakable mounting evidence of the intellectual attractiveness of Catholicism at this time, and the fact is highlighted by the rising number of such conversions in Prague. A whole list of important cases could be cited during the years around 1600, from Francken, Simonius, and Pistorius, through Wacker and Scioppio, Acidalius, Colerus, and Melander, to Karl Liechtenstein and Vilém Slavata.[5] What

---

[1] Lindner, art. cit. 332–4; cf. *Delitiae*, vi. 1057–65. Polišenský, *Jessenius*, 17 f.

[2] Kepler, *Gesammelte Werke*, iv. 288 f. He also wrote epigrams on the death of Wacker's brilliant nine-year-old daughter (ibid. 96 f.).

[3] Hessels, No. 274: (Wacker to Monau, Nysa 1 Aug. 1595).

[4] Ibid. Nos. 286 (Ortelius to his nephew, Antwerp 23 Mar. 1596) and 294 (nephew to Ortelius, London Oct. 1596).

[5] Most of these people are discussed elsewhere in the text. On the scholar and poet Christopher Colerus see Nuncios/Ferreri (Kristen), Prague 5 July 1604 (No. 79); on his colleague Otto Melander, R. Schkelenko, 'Die neulateinische Dichtung am Hofe Rudolfs II', *Prager Jahrbuch* (1943), 99 f. Cf. Räss, *Convertiten*, ii. 488–507 (on Pistorius); iii. 264–8 (Acidalius); iii. 395–443 (Scioppio).

makes for significance is anyway not the total of persons involved—that would be a statistic impossible of accurate computation—but their eminence. However we may weigh the motives which underlay each individual decision, the phenomenon remains a central one, for nothing contributed more to the self-confidence of the Catholic camp after 1600, and hence to its powerful psychological advantage, than the vigour of some of these converts. By the next generation the phenomenon was unmistakable: compare for instance the education of the young 'Baroque cavalier' Humprecht Jan Czernin with that of his counterpart Karel Bruntálský of Vrbno, failing scion of the Žerotín family and grandson of Karel.[1]

Material factors of course always obtained in this process, but their role should not be exaggerated, especially for the period of Rudolf's reign when thoroughgoing Catholicism was restricted to a small embattled minority. Rather the existing state of culture and intellectual inquiry itself encouraged the trend. The very society of educated Bohemia in the day of Rudolf and Wacker, Rožmberk and Žerotín, gave birth to a climate of opinion which would encompass its own overthrow. Even those who later, often after conversion, led the vanguard of the Catholic reform had belonged to it: Lobkovic was a patron of poets and artists; Slavata, in his Protestant youth, lived as a protégé of Adam of Hradec and married his daughter Otýlia;[2] Karl Liechtenstein, the governor of Bohemia after 1620, had been a schoolfriend of Karel Žerotín in Moravia. When the problem is presented in these terms it can be seen to have two aspects. On one hand stand the positive qualities of the 'Counter-Reformation' which enabled it to plunge Central Europe into turmoil within twenty years of the new century and emerge triumphantly with a position of commanding dominance; on the other stand the forces of continuity, those ways in which the new attitudes grew organically out of the world of late Humanism. The mentality of the Counter-Reformation is not directly a concern of the present study—though we shall return to the question of how it could capitalize so effectively on the weaknesses of the older intellectual universe. But we should never overlook how close a personal interplay lay between the genesis of one and the decline of the other. Before 1600 the tensions were still often latent only.

This can be observed among the early Jesuits, whose attitudes were themselves by no means so opposed to the currents of sixteenth-century

---

[1] Z. Kalista, *Mládí Humprechta Jan Černína z Chudenic, zrození barokního kavalíra* (Prague 1932); A. Haas, *Karel Bruntálský z Vrbna* (Prague 1947).

[2] Kavka, *Zlatý věk růží*, 145. On Lobkovic see below, pp. 286–8.

Humanist or Mannerist thought as might be imagined. It was rather one of the Society's chief aims to woo them. The Jesuit zeal for educational reform provided a spur to the work of Zalužanský, Dornavius, and Comenius; in Prague it revealed itself in the energetic instruction given by members of the first priestly generation, notably the English exile Edmund Campion who taught there with great success between 1573 and 1579. Campion's lectures on Aristotle, Porphyry, and others survive almost verbatim in the notes of his pupils.[1]

The Jesuits were concerned to win popular support—hence their use of the Czech language in sermons and tracts;[2] hence also their elaborate displays of ceremonial, drama, and pageantry which at times rivalled those of the dynasty (the two may not always have been independent).[3] There are contemporary records of the effects of this ostentation. The Society's own chronicler thus reports the success of a play on an old Czech theme in 1567:

The tragedy of St. Wenceslas recently composed in Bohemian metres by Brother Nicholas Salius was performed on the tenth day of the month and pleased everyone greatly, most of all the Czechs. Many said that the Jesuits are now at last really earning their bread and accommodating themselves to the Bohemian situation. For the preparation of it, as of the comedy and disputation, the council of the Old Town of Prague willingly provided us with many carpets, military banners and all manner of other objects, and this may be accounted no small mark of favour towards our Order from such important men of the city.[4]

In their Fellowships and Sodalities, moreover, the Jesuits came close to the ideal of the learned or secret society; the first to appear in Prague were the Marian Fellowships of 1574 and 1575 which had Campion as spiritual adviser and enjoyed the patronage of Rudolf. This aspect of Jesuit activity was clearly the most congenial to the withdrawn monarch, and on the basis of it, at least, they entertained high hopes of his piety.[5]

The early Czech Jesuits produced one striking intellectual pupil: the writer and bibliophile Jiří Barthold Pontan of Breitenberg (Pontanus), a man much more significant than the extremely scanty literature about

---

[1] APH, MSS. M XLII, M LXV (both later belonged to Pontanus). There are also eulogies of Campion in the 'Historia Collegii S.J. . . . .' (e.g. fo. 126v), and copies of letters by him to the novices in Brno.

[2] J. Vašica, České literární baroko (Prague 1938), 177 ff.

[3] As for example with the arrival of Maximilian in Prague in 1562: 'Historia', fos. 58–9.

[4] Ibid. fo. 5v.

[5] Ibid. fos. 12r, 112v; Vašica, op. cit. 151–60. Cf. the chronicler's favourable report on Rudolf at the time of his accession: 'Historia', fos. 113 ff.

him would suggest. Pontanus (1550?–1614) was a Catholic patriot, closely involved with the reforming efforts of Jesuit society and the Premonstratensians, both in Bohemia and Moravia, and advocate of the vernacular language and the cult of early national saints. He was a friend and companion of Zdeněk Lobkovic, a canon of St. Vitus, and Vicar-General under Archbishop Medek from 1586.[1] Pontanus also associated with a circle of Counter-reforming propagandists and littérateurs who wrote in an idiom already nearer the Baroque than the Renaissance in its spiritual fervour and concern for the reality of death. These men were grouped around Lohelius, the Abbot of Strahov, and Pavlovský, Bishop of Olomouc, and they included Catholics of diverse talents like the poet Šimon Lomnický, intimate of the Rožmberk and Hradec families, and the physician Sinapius (Hořčický).[2]

Yet at the same time Pontanus remained—as befitted an almost exact contemporary of the Emperor—a typical Rudolfine character. He was a very familiar person at court—the Emperor granted him a patent of nobility in 1588—and a well-known poet in the circle of Westonia, Campanus, Borbonius, Carolides, and Arconatus.[3] Typotius too was his colleague; he possessed a manuscript copy of a long Latin poem by the historiographer—*Encomii Divini Libri III*.[4] His friend Sinapius likewise found favour with Rudolf and is remembered as the creator of an elixir which could supposedly cure the Imperial ailments.[5] Pontanus the author stands fully in the emblematic world of the late sixteenth century: he prepared numerous volumes of allusive and convoluted verse, orations on the Turkish war and histories, dithyrambs to the ruling house, as well as scientific work like an edition in 1601 of the *De Proprietatibus Rerum* by Bartholomaeus Anglicus.[6] His extant manuscript writings include, beside scribbled Latin elegies, *carmina gratulatoria*, and so forth,

---

[1] Frind, op. cit. 192; Bauschek MS. (below, p. 286 n. 3) p. 24.

[2] Vašica, op. cit. 13 f.; V. Bitnar, *Postavy a problémy českého baroku literárního* Prague 1939), 87–111. On Lomnický cf. *Knihopis*, Nos. 4934–84.

[3] *Rukověť*', s.v. 'Jiří Bartholdus' (i. 137–67), listing his Latin works; Westonia, *Parthenicon*, i, B7v; etc. Arconatus dedicated to him a copy of Borbonius's *Caesarum Romanorum Tesseradecades* (Leipzig 1595): Arch. Lib., K c 604. Pontanus presented to Arconatus a copy of some of his own highly allusive poems: BM 11409 f 16, 1–4.

[4] APH, MS. M 122; Pontanus has inscribed it and written underneath 'Labor Typotii'. The text appears to contain only two books.

[5] B. Balbín, *Bohemia Docta* (Prague 1777), i. 124 f.; Maiwald, op. cit. 34 f.; K. Pejml in *Co daly naše země*, 150. Hořčický, whose name means 'mustard' in Czech, was thus given the Humanist sobriquet 'Sinapius'. His 'hořčičná voda' was presumably extremely piquant. Cf. below, p. 239.

[6] Maiwald, op. cit. 35. Pontanus wrote a number of his works in German; see R. Wolkan, *Böhmens Anteil an der deutschen Literatur des 16. Jahrhunderts*, i (Prague 1890), Nos. 359, 378, 379, 394.

notes on Aristotelian physics and logic, and various vocabulary compilations, among them a *Rottwelsche Grammatik* of thieves' or gypsies' cant.[1]

It is best of all his large library which shows how far Pontanus's breadth of interest exceeded that of any pure disciple of the Council of Trent.[2] We cannot now be precise about the contents of his collection—its vicissitudes have been too great—but a study of the surviving library of the Archbishops of Prague reveals many volumes autographed by him and others to which he must have had access. It therefore also throws light, albeit less directly, on the reading matter of the Chapter of St. Vitus.

Pontanus possessed many historical works: editions of Eyczinger, Peucer's *Chronici*, Reusner's *Rerum Turcicarum Narratio* (Frankfurt 1603), van Roo's *Annales* (Innsbruck 1592), Typotius's *Orationes Turcicae*, and so forth; and a variety of medical ones: Cardano's *Contrariantium medicorum libri II* and his *Somniorum Synesiorum Libri*, works by Paracelsus, the iatrochemist Toxites, Rudolf's Paracelsan *Leibarzt* Martin Ruland (N c 17), Rupescissa's *De Quinta Essentia* in a Basle edition bound with a Lullist tract (N c 45), and the writings of Villanova. He owned editions of Melanchthon, including an ethical treatise which he annotated in Latin and Greek (O c 324), and an anti-Aristotelian tract by the Ramist Renemannus (O c 288). In natural philosophy, including the less orthodox kinds, he was equally well-versed: he had Bodin's *Universi Naturae Theatrum* (Leiden 1596), J. B. Porta on human physiognomy (Hanau 1593)—the library preserves also his *Magia Naturalis* in the Frankfurt printing of 1591—he bought Boethius de Boodt's book on gems and magic stones and Croll's *Basilica Chymica*; he possessed a volume of 'Lullist' and German alchemical works (V c 20), the *Disputatio de metallo et lapide* by the Jesuit Hagelius, published at Ingolstadt in 1588, and a *Theatrum Chemicum* of 1602 (V c 26). Among his works on spirits were a copy of Bodin's *Daemonomania* (Frankfurt 1590) and at the same time the more sceptical Johann Wier's *De praestigiis daemonum incantationibus* in its 1583 edition.

Pontanus evidently acquired such books on a large scale; one of his copies of the astrological writings of Junctinus had belonged to the Czech astronomer Codicillus, as is revealed by its inscription (V b 79) (he also

[1] APH, M 149/1–2, M 152, M 153.
[2] The library has the merit that most of its volumes, perhaps all, were inscribed by Pontanus. Unfortunately it is impossible to reassemble it, since much is now housed in the larger collections at Strahov and the Charles University, and the search would be too laborious. Conclusions here are founded solely on the evidence of the Archbishops' Library. Reference numbers in brackets are to the latter.

owned the *Speculum Astrologiae* of 1573). His most important capture
was the library of the leading court architect Bonifaz Wolmut, who died
in 1579. This consisted primarily of major works on astronomy and
astrology which show well the interests of a trusted Habsburg adviser.[1]
Wolmut arranged at his own expense German translations of Cardanus
and Ptolemy, and left versions of Peuerbach, Regiomontanus, and Münster as well as more popular astrological and genethliac tracts.

The collection made by Pontanus was clearly a major but characteristic scholar's library of Rudolfine Bohemia, and`the concerns which
predominate in it could be demonstrated again and again if more study
of this kind of evidence were possible. We find the same texts in monasteries like Strahov as in the houses of private patrons like Ferdinand
Hofmann or Rudolf Coraduz, whose many thousands of books were
later taken into Habsburg possession.[2] They are witnesses to the breadth
and quality of Bohemian culture during the period, but they also argue
a common set of attitudes and a uniform body of intellectual opinion.
They belong to a culture in which science and art, experiment and
speculation were still homogeneous. A closer analysis of Rudolfine art
and magic should now help to illuminate the nature of this unity and the
key issues with which contemporary thinkers were engaged.

[1] I. Kořán, 'Knihovna architekta Bonifáce Wolmuta', *Umění* viii (1960), 522–7.

[2] Lambecius, op. cit. i. 65. The richest of the surviving monastic libraries in
Bohemia, that of the Premonstratensian monks at Strahov, with whom Pontanus
lived in close contact and which now contains a fair part of his own collection, is
excellently provided with books for this period. Some of them—they are mostly un-
annotated—must have fallen to the monastery by confiscation after 1620, but they reflect a keen local interest in some of the key thinkers of Rudolf's time. Strahov has for
instance a considerable series of Bodin's works: the *République* in its editions of 1577
and 1593–6 (Lyons), 1586 (Paris), 1591 (Frankfurt), and several of the Ober-Ursel
printings; his *Universi Naturae Theatrum* in four different editions (Frankfurt 1596 and
1597, Leiden 1596, Hanau 1605); his *Daemonomania* in its 1586 and 1590 printings;
his *Exetasis de Magicis Actionibus*; and three copies of the Prague edition of his *Nova
Distributio Iuris Universi* (1581). There are also various of the occult scientific works of
J. B. Porta: three early editions of his *Magia Naturalis*; three more between 1593 and
1606 of a book on the secret meanings of letters of the alphabet; and four of his *Physio-
gnomonia*. As another example: the late sixteenth-century interest in the alchemical and
magical writings of Paracelsus is well represented by a range of editions between 1567
and the end of the century.

5. Rudolf and the Fine Arts

'Whoever so desires nowadays has only to go to Prague (if he
can), to the greatest art patron in the world at the present time,
the Roman Emperor Rudolf the Second; there he may see at the
Imperial residence, and elsewhere in the collections of other
great art-lovers, a remarkable number of outstanding and
precious, curious, unusual, and priceless works.'

KAREL VAN MANDER (1604)

HISTORY has dealt harshly with Rudolf in its assessment of his politics.
In a different regard his memory is better served: it is generally agreed—
though there is room for wrangling within this position—that he was an
exceptional patron of the arts. Mander's contemporary verdict has just
been quoted[1] and, thanks in part to his own valuable observations, for
Mander maintained a close friendship with Rudolf's leading painter
Spranger and lived in Vienna, the subject has been quite well treated
by later writers.

I shall restrict attention here as far as possible to the purely 'artistic'
circle with which the Emperor surrounded himself, and defer till the
next chapter the more occult and magical interests of the court. That
distinction is somewhat artificial, partly because the same personalities
might be involved in both, partly (and more significantly) because the
same intellectual background was common to both. Thus, as a single
example, the passion for glyptics—the cutting and engraving of gems—
was in one respect a love of rare and exotic artistic material, in another
the opportunity for a conscious display of skill, in a third the reflection
of a belief in talismans and the astral powers of stones. The art of
Rudolfine Prague was essentially a revelation of mystery,[2] whether
through the medium of canvas, or the manipulation of stones, or the
alchemical and Cabalist 'arts'. No difference in kind obtained between
all these manifestations: they were all intellectual in the sense that they

---

[1] Karel van Mander, *Het Schilderboeck waer in Voor eerst de leerlustighe Iueght den
grondt der Edel Vry SCHILDERCONST in Verscheyden deelen Wort voorghedraghen*
(Haarlem 1604, hereafter 'Mander'); quotation from the 'Voor-reden, op den grondt
der edel vry Schilder-Const'.

[2] This is observed by the basically hostile critic Neumann: J. Neumann, *Obrazárna
pražského Hradu* (Prague 1964), 15.

sought a solution to problems lying beyond rational activity and every-day experience.

At the same time they were, within a definition to which we shall return, 'Mannerist'. Prague formed one of the leading centres in the late phase of that controversial movement, whose outward characteristics were a uniform style of courtly elegance and a highly artificial mode of expression. Hocke sees Prague as the most important representative of such contrived anti-Classicism. Würtenberger points to the Imperial court as the last great bastion of European Mannerism. Hauser regards Spranger, especially when popularized by his engraver friend Goltzius, as the arbiter of cosmopolitan taste in painting during the two final decades of the sixteenth century.[1] The main features of this Mannerism as they stand revealed in Rudolf's artists may be briefly enumerated.

It was in the first place international and far-reaching. Not all those commissioned by Rudolf ever actually resided in Prague, though he usually sought to attract them (examples are Jacopo Bassano, Giovanni da Bologna, Christoph Schwarz, and Hans Rottenhammer),[2] while the ones who did come had often a colourful background behind them. Moreover, existing works of art were purchased from all over Europe. It was secondly a culmination of the whole post-Renaissance process of developing *maniera*: panache and self-conscious artistry, and great virtuosity, particularly in the applied arts. Difficult poses, theatrical arrangements, striking contrasts are deliberately chosen, sometimes with notable aesthetic success; Shearman proclaims the highest regard for the stylistic achievement of the sculptor Bologna and his Prague pupil Adriaen de Vries.[3]

Rudolfine Mannerism further based itself more or less consciously on both the art-theory of the North Italian school and the academic mentality of the later sixteenth century. Contacts between Florence, Milan, Venice, and Prague were close; many of the court artists were either Italian by birth or had trained there for some years, and one of the most famous, Arcimboldo, was a good friend of the critic Paolo Lomazzo. The real theoretician of the Prague school was the Dutchman Karel van Mander, a Northern European equivalent of Vasari: painter, art

[1] G. R. Hocke, 144–8; F. Würtenberger, 23 f., 42 f.; A. Hauser, i. 252 f.; cf. J. Shearman, 28. For full titles of these works and further discussion see below, pp. 256 (with nn. 1, 4) ff.; p. 259 n. 3.

[2] Karel Chytil, *Umění v Praze za Rudolfa II* (Prague 1904, also published in German as *Die Kunst in Prag zur Zeit Rudolfs II*), 32 ff.; A. Ilg, 'Giovanni da Bologna und seine Beziehungen zum kaiserlichen Hofe' in *Jahrbuch* iv (1886), 38–51.

[3] Shearman, 28, 86 ff.

historian, critic, pedagogue, and pupil of Lucas de Heere.[1] Mander, with his colleagues Goltzius and Cornelisz, founded in Haarlem one of the earliest academies of art (1583),[2] and the spirit of this must have been felt in Prague, not only by way of Mander's links with Spranger, but also through Goltzius, who was another of Spranger's intimates. Hendrik Goltzius enjoyed enormous fame in his day as painter, drawer, and above all engraver; his prints were widely copied as models of Mannerist technique.[3] He had worked with Dirck Coornhert and there is evidence that he shared the latter's unorthodox religious beliefs; at the same time he was a man of culture, acquainted with Lipsius and Jan de Witt. His art made great play with allusion: one of his pictures for example clearly represents an allegory of alchemy, a study to which Goltzius became addicted.[4] It is doubtful, however, whether an academy existed in any precise or explicit sense in Prague. Morhof does not mention one and although Sandrart, who was personally familiar with the city and forms a valuable witness, employs the word, it seems more probable that he is being anachronistic.[5]

Finally the Prague Mannerists enjoyed as direct patron the sovereign himself, and their choice of subject-matter reflects Rudolf's own inclinations. The Emperor employed and encouraged them personally, approved and criticized their work, on occasions even participating in their

---

[1] On Mander (1548–1606) in general see H. Floerke's edition of the *Schilderboeck* i–ii (Munich 1906); N. Pevsner, *Academies of Art, Past and Present* (Cambridge 1940), 80–2. The main purpose of the *Schilderboeck* was instruction of the young, as its title proclaims (p. 162 n. 1, above).

[2] 'Verarmt setzte er [Mander] sich hin mit den seinigen zu Schiff, und reiste also Holland zu, in die alte Stadt Harlem allda er wol empfangen und mit allen nöhtigen Mobilien versehen wurde, erhielte auch gleich Arbeit genug, und mahlte noch eine Sündfluht, wodurch er sich bey dem *Golzio* und Cornelischen bekant gemacht, die daraufhin unter ihnen dreyen eine Academie nach dem Leben zu zeichnen, davon Carl ihnen die Italiänische Manier gewiesen, angestellt.' Sandrart (see below, n. 5), fo. 277[r].

[3] Ibid. 276–8. In the National Museum of Budapest there is a book of drawings after Goltzius compiled in the 1590s which appears to have come from Prague: OSzK, 514 Fol. Ger.

[4] Mander, fo. 282a–b; E. K. Reznicek, *Hendrik Goltzius als Zeichner* (Utrecht 1961), 3 and n.; O. Hirschmann, *Hendrik Goltzius als Maler* (The Hague 1916), 21 f., 53 ff.

[5] Morhof, *Polyhistor*, i: he treats learned Academies in Chapter 14. Joachim von Sandrart, *Der Teutschen Academie Zweyter Teil; von der alt und neu-berühmten Egyptischen, Griechischen, Römischen, Italiänischen, Hoch und Niederteutschen Bau- Bild- und Mahlerey-Künstlern Lob und Leben* (Nuremberg 1675, hereafter 'Sandrart'). He mentions a 'universal Academy of the Arts' in Prague: '. . . Johannes Fischer, der sich durch sonderbars wolersonnene Arbeit allda sehr berühmt gemacht, und weil ihn sein kluger Geist durch innerlichen Trieb immer zu höehern Künsten anreizte, begab sich aus seinem Vatterland auf die damalige universale Künsten-Academie Prag, da er einen guten Grund in der Mahlkunst geleget, auf welchen er hernach in Italien und andern Ländern einen beständigen Bau gesetzt.' (fo. 322.)

activities.[1] Thus their iconography is a vital clue to his state of mind, though it can never provide conclusive evidence. This emerges most clearly in the works whose content was overtly political: the apotheosis of Rudolf, the glorification of the Habsburgs and their splendour; but it also appears in motifs which were typical of Rudolf and the late sixteenth century in general: the new observation of nature, the large play with allusion, the tendency towards eroticism and unnatural 'decadent' themes, above all the employment of symbol as a means of communication. It is the more necessary to consider this aspect of the artists' achievement since circumstantial details of their relations with the Emperor are scarce, beyond what can be derived from surviving *Hofstaats* and administrative records, especially those—all too typical— dealing with arrears of pay.[2] We must likewise regret that so little has come to light on the precise content of the court spectacles which occupied such a central place in the presentation of the Imperial mystique.

The chief master of Rudolf's ceremonial and one of his most trusted friends was Giuseppe Arcimboldo (1527–93).[3] Arcimboldo provides another example of a long-standing servant of the Habsburgs who before joining Rudolf had been a faithful retainer to his father Maximilian, and in this case had left his native Milan at the original invitation of Ferdinand I in 1562.[4] His contemporary fame was great, not solely for the grotesque paintings which are now remembered, but as a leading contributor to Imperial prestige. He won favour 'non tanto nella pittora ma anco altre si in molte altre inventioni come de' torniamenti, giostre, giuoche, apparecchi di nozze e di coronatione . . .' Thus the Milanese historian Morigia, who knew him, and who continues by recalling a special occasion 'quando Carlo Arciduca d'Austria tolse moglie'. Lomazzo also mentions this wedding, which took place at Graz in 1571, and regrets that he cannot do justice to the symbolism of the pageantry, but

[1] Cf. Alidosi, *Relazione*, 6: [Every day Rudolf] 'va a veder dipingere, dipingendo ancor lui proprio alcuna volta, et va a veder lavorar gli orefici, maestri d'orioli, ed intagliatori de pietre . . .'

[2] There are numerous examples in the Kammer Schulden Buch (SÚA), some of which dragged on long after Rudolf's death. Most of these archive sources were printed as supplements (Register) to the original series of the Vienna *Jahrbuch*; see Notes on Sources, IV.

[3] More recent literature exists on Arcimboldo than on any other person considered in this chapter. Most comprehensive is Sven Alfons, *Giuseppe Arcimboldi* (*Tidskrift för Konstvetenskap* xxxi, Malmö 1957). There are also monographs by B. Geiger, *I dipinti ghiribizzosi di Giuseppe Arcimboldi* (Florence 1954), and F. C. Legrand and E. Sluys, *Arcimboldo et les Arcimboldesques* (Aalter 1955), as well as a brief biography in Czech: P. Preiss, *Giuseppe Arcimboldo* (Prague 1967).

[4] For this and Arcimboldo's family background see Paolo Morigia, *Historia dell'Antichità di Milano* (Venice 1592), 566 f.

that would require a whole volume.[1] It seems to have been an occasion for displaying the magnificence of the House, and each of its Archdukes portrayed one of the various parts of Europe. Among them were, so we learn from another source, Rudolf and Ernst, newly returned from Spain;[2] thus a first contact was made between Arcimboldo and the future Emperor.

Unfortunately very little is known about the activity of Arcimboldo as organizer of Rudolf's court entertainments, but a series of drawings for festive dresses and costumes survives from the year 1585,[3] and there are also designs of his for some kind of decoration at the house of Ferdinand Hofmann.[4] His favour with the Emperor is, however, clear, and he was ennobled and rewarded with the title of Count Palatine. More evidence remains of Rudolf's relations with his other most favoured artist, Bartholomaeus Spranger. Spranger came to Prague from his original home in Antwerp after a protracted period in Italy, mostly in Rome, and five years at Vienna, where he was sent with his compatriot Hans de Monte on the recommendation of another countryman, Giovanni Bologna.[5] In Vienna he worked with Monte (a man about whom very little is known) on a triumphal arch for the arrival of Rudolf in the city in 1577, and on the building known as the 'New Work' in the *Fasangarten*. This latter must have been a remarkable piece of Mannerist design, combining 'curieuse Architectüre' and fantastically decorated towers with irregular beds of flowers and various water 'inventions'; it attracted the attention of every traveller to Vienna, and in 1591 we find Henry Wotton trying fruitlessly to acquire a *model* of it for his friend Lord Zouche.[6] The triumphal arch was also impressive and can be imagined from Mander's description of it (he was an eye-witness): it brought together the architecture of Monte and the painting of Spranger, standing higher than the highest houses around it, and depicting members of the Habsburg family with allegorical figures of virtues and

    [1] Ibid.; G. P. Lomazzo, *Idea del Tempio della Pittura* (Milan 1590), 155.
    [2] H. von Zwiedinek in *Mitteilungen des historischen Vereins für Steiermark* xlvii (1899), 193–213, esp. 204.
    [3] Geiger, op. cit. Ch. VI; Alfons, op. cit. 111–6. The drawings are illustrated in Preiss, op. cit. nos. 12–47.
    [4] Alfons, op. cit. 117–20.
    [5] For the details of Spranger's life see Mander, fos. 268a–274b, and Ernst Diez, 'Der Hofmaler Bartholomäus Spranger', *Jahrbuch* xxviii (1909), 93–151.
    [6] Pearsall Smith, op. cit. i: Clusius to Wotton, Frankfurt 20 Nov. 1590; Wotton to Zouche, Vienna 19 Feb. and 21 April 1591. Cf. *Die Reisen des Samuel Kiechel* (Stuttgart 1866), 141–4; L. Chatenay, *Vie de Jacques Esprinchard* (Paris 1957), 157; K. Oberhuber, 'Die stilistische Entwicklung im Werk Bartholomäus Sprangers' (Diss. Vienna 1958), 74 ff. The *Neugebäude* is now destroyed; see Ilg, art. cit. 45 f., and eundem, 'Das Neugebäude bei Wien', *Jahrbuch* xvi (1895), 81–121.

mythological characters 'alles seer conslich en uytnemende gheeslich ghedaen'.[1] By the early 1580s Spranger had grown quite indispensable to Rudolf, who would spend days watching his work and engaging him in private conversation.[2] He became thoroughly a part of his Bohemian environment; he died in Prague in 1611 and even drew up his will in Czech.[3]

With Spranger we stand at the centre of Rudolf's artistic world: his whole *œuvre* reflects the friendship and stimulus of the Emperor. Like the majority of his colleagues he came from the Low Countries[4] (not for nothing did the sack of Antwerp coincide with the beginning of Rudolf's reign), and although we cannot know for certain it seems probable that his religion was a confused and undogmatic Catholicism. Spranger's style offers a complex study in itself,[5] but characteristic Mannerist motifs are most evident: a sense of conscious virtuosity, irregular composition, dramatic devices, allusiveness—extending at times to the unreal atmosphere of a Bellange drawing[6]—and intellectuality. Here we are most concerned with the latter aspects, the problem of Rudolfine iconography.

The completest series of Spranger's paintings which survives is a group of highly erotic, mythological canvases, depicting primarily the amorous adventures of stylized, contorted couples who are usually—like Hercules and Omphale, or Vulcan and Maia—ill-suited in age and appearance.[7] This preoccupation with suggestive, even indecent subjects is typical of Rudolf and the last two decades of the sixteenth century; it also represents a feature of later Mannerist art to which some critics

---

[1] Mander, fo. 272a; Oberhuber, diss. cit. 90 f. The only other description of this arch, a monumental work constructed within a month, appears to be by the nuncio Giovanni Delfino in a letter to Cardinal Como of 20 July 1577. Delfino implies that the symbolism was both visual and verbal: 'Si vedevano molti quadri di chiaroscuro con i loro motti e significati quali non intrarò a scrivere . . . V'erano a mano destra dell'arco la statua dell'Imperatore Massimiliano finta di marmori che haveva sotto i piedi un gran globo celeste et sopra queste parole: Sub pedibus videt astra, et poi la giustizia e prudenza et della mano sinistra la statua dell'Imperatore con un globo terrestre sotto i piedi et di sopra questo motto: Sed hic terrena gubernat, et dopo seguivano le statue della fortezza e della temperanza. Sotto al cielo dell'arco d'una banda erano tali parole . . .' Quoted (more fully) in M. Vaes, 'Le séjour de Carel van Mander en Italie', in *Hommage à Dom Ursmer Berlière* (Brussels 1931), 239 n. 5.

[2] Cf. the evidence of Krafft, op. cit. 390, and Mander, fo. 273a.

[3] Diez, op. cit. 147–51, where it is reprinted.

[4] Cf. M. Wünsch, 'Die Niederländer am Hofe Rudolfs II', *Prager Jahrbuch* 1943, 60–4.

[5] See the work by Oberhuber, which, however, deliberately abstains from any wider problems.

[6] Cf. the engraving of Goltzius after Spranger, *The Judgement of Midas*, illustrated in Diez, fig. 27 and pl. XXIII.

[7] Ibid. 117–25, with illustrations of most of them.

have drawn attention.[1] The Swiss Josef Heintz (1564–1609) was another of Rudolf's favourite artists (he was sent abroad on a number of commissions) who excelled in voluptuous subjects: Leda and the Swan, the Rape of Proserpine, and so forth.[2] As such paintings mirror the uncertain personal relationships of the Emperor, so there are other allegories by Spranger inspired directly by his political role. Their details vary, but the content is always similar: an apotheosis of the ruler as conqueror or Maecenas, with strong suggestions of astrological and alchemical symbolism. Since none of these works has been adequately studied from our point of view, it is only possible to make a provisional assessment of them; some in fact have only recently been rediscovered, like the *Allegory of Loyalty conquering Fate* painted in 1607.[3]

The only other dated work by Spranger is his *Allegory of the Virtues of Rudolf II* (1592).[4] This seems to depict Rudolf as the defender of Christian truth against the infidel, and thus belongs with further paintings by court artists based on the anti-Turkish mystique, like Spranger's own *Bellona blowing the Horn of War*. *Bellona* survives only in an engraving by Jan Müller[5] while several of the astrological canvases are also lost. Pictures like the *Triumph of Wisdom over Ignorance* and *Fama leading the Arts to Olympus*[6] were most likely conceived with an occult programme, the Emperor as the Hermes of the true Arts. They reflect a whole mythology of Imperial virtue which dissolved the constraints of limited finance, two-edged counsels, and empty panegyric in a pantheon of subtle divinities: the sagacity of Minerva, the swiftness of Mercury, or the infinite power of Fortuna.

Besides Spranger two others at the court were pre-eminent in this kind of subject, the painter Hans von Aachen and the sculptor Adriaen de Vries. Aachen worked in Italy and Munich after leaving his Rhenish homeland, then migrated to Prague where Rudolf had been trying to attract him for some years.[7] Of all the Emperor's artists, Aachen perhaps stood closest to him in spirit; he became one of Rudolf's leading personal agents: for example he was sent to the Tyrol where he was involved in

[1] e.g. Hocke, op. cit. 179–205; N. Pevsner, 'Gegenreformation und Manierismus', *Repertorium für Kunstwissenschaft* 46 (1925), 257 f.

[2] [Plate 6.] Sandrart, 286; B. Haendcke in *Jahrbuch* xv (1894), 45–59. There is a recent comprehensive study of Heintz by Jürgen Zimmer, op. cit., including a descriptive catalogue of all his known work.

[3] J. Burián, 'Sprangerova Alegorie z roku 1607', *Umění* vii (1959), 54–6; Neumann, *Obrazárna*, Cat. No. 59.

[4] [Plate 2.]

[5] Diez, op. cit. fig. 26.

[6] [Plate 3.] The latter exists as an engraving by Müller (ibid., fig. 25).

[7] R. A. Peltzer in *Jahrbuch* xxx (1911), 59–182; Mander, fo. 290a–b.

a contretemps with Philipp Lang, and we find him on business in Dresden in 1607. At the same time he was evidently an intimate friend of Julius of Brunswick.[1] Several of Aachen's canvases depict the victory of Truth and Art over war and confusion: the *Triumph of Truth* (now in Munich),[2] the *Allegory of Rudolf as Augustus* (Rudolf had also borrowed from his Imperial ancestor the device of a fish-tailed goat),[3] and a painting which Mander describes—Peace as a naked woman treading underfoot the weapons of war.[4] Others represent direct glorifications of military success, like the portrait of Adolf von Schwarzenberg as the victor of Raab, the Hungarian fortress whose reconquest in 1598 provided the greatest feat of arms during Rudolf's reign. More works by Aachen are still coming to light.[5]

De Vries (1545–1626), pupil of Bologna, first achieved fame as a creator of decorative fountains in Augsburg, but he was employed at least irregularly by Rudolf from 1593 and later settled permanently in Prague.[6] He was a friend of Spranger and Aachen and evidently co-operated with them on some monumental commissions, as well as producing smaller-scale work, such as wax models, which survives only in engravings. His most beautiful pieces are pure Mannerist ornamental mythology (like the *Mercury and Psyche* now in the Louvre), but he made two heroic busts (in 1603 and 1607) which are among the most familiar portraits of Rudolf: full-faced, dignified, noble, yet more than a little dissipated.[7] De Vries also produced reliefs, and his *Allegory of the Turkish Wars* is the best example of this kind of apotheosis, inspired no

[1] Rudolf to Maximilian III, Prague 21 July 1603, HHSA, Fam. Korr. A. 4. I; Hurter, *Philipp Lang*, Beilage 1; SÚA, KK 1794 (Patente und Mandata 1600–22); *Briefe und Akten*, vii. 411 n. 2, viii. 95, 479 n. 1, 506 n. 1 (508), 643 n. 3. Under the heading *Kämmerer* (Chamberlain) in the *Hofstaat* of 1612 appears the following note: 'Ihro fürstlicher Gnaden [Julius of Brunswick] haben diesse Besoldung [as Kämmerer] dem Hansen von Ach, Kammermahler, einzunehmen übergeben und geschenkt.' Riegger, 245. Cf. Lhotsky, *Sammlungen*, 263 f.

[2] Illustrated in Schwarzenfeld, op. cit. 96/7.

[3] It is depicted in the *Symbola* (see above, p. 128 n. 5) as Habsburg hieroglyphic No. XXXVIII. The painting, now in Nuremberg, is illustrated in Schwarzenfeld, op. cit. 192/3.

[4] Mander, fo. 273a: '. . . een naeckte schoon Vrouw met een lieflijcke schoon Tronie, welcke beteyckent de Vrede met de Olijftack, en heeft den krijgh oft krijgh-tuygh onder voetens: by haer comt d'overvloedicheyt en de Consten, Pictura, en ander bewijsende, dat door Vrede voorspert en de Consten bloeyen.'

[5] [Plate 8a.] Neumann, op. cit., Cat. Nos. 1 and 2; idem, 'Aachenovo zvěstování Panny Marie', *Umění* iv (1956), 119–32.

[6] Conrad Buchwald, *Adriaen de Vries* (Leipzig 1899), for what is known of his life. There is a new monograph by Lars Olof Larsson, *Adrian de Vries* (Vienna–Munich 1967), which provides a definitive account, with complete catalogue, of Vries's work.

[7] Buchwald, op. cit. 42–5; Larsson, op. cit. 36–8, 47 f.; both busts are now in Vienna. [Cf. Plate 5.]

doubt by the reconquest of Raab which figures prominently on it. Another follows Spranger's lead in presenting the Emperor as patron of the Liberal Arts throughout Bohemia.[1]

In close contact with the painters themselves and their royal patron stood the engravers. These men were becoming increasingly the link between artists and their public; like the best of the printers they lived within the world of ideas of those whose work they made accessible and were on occasion original creators themselves. They might be of local importance like the Jan Müller who reproduced much work by Spranger (and artists of a similar hue), or of international reputation like Goltzius, whose engravings after Spranger dictated the mannered taste of the 1590s. Goltzius, who in common with others of his kind was also a painter, never resided in Prague, but he had close links there, and Rudolf showed himself anxious to acquire any available canvases of his.[2]

The leading engraver in Prague was Aegidius Sadeler (died in 1629), most important member of a family of artists, who after working with his uncles Johann and Raphael in Munich and Rome was summoned by Rudolf and became intimately associated with the court circle, especially Spranger. He produced portraits of many major figures of state and visiting foreign dignitaries, and prepared plates for book illustrations.[3] Sandrart, who was his apprentice in the 1620s, regarded him as the pride of German engraving.[4] Sadeler evidently played a central role in Prague life; he also produced the illustrations for the *Symbola Divina et Humana*, the emblem-book already mentioned in which he collaborated with Octavio Strada, Typotius, and Boodt. This work, which presented a long series of Emperors, Popes, and monarchs with appropriate devices, mottoes, or rebuses to accompany them, laid conscious stress on the underlying symbolism and its connection with the Egyptian hieroglyphic mysteries.[5] It was not only extremely popular, influencing poets of the German Baroque such as Gryphius;[6] it was also

---

[1] [Plate 4.] See Larsson, op. cit. 39–42, 49 f., for more detailed iconographical interpretation.

[2] Cf. the letter from Johann Tilman to the Count of Lippe, printed by Hirschmann, op. cit. 35–7; and above, p. 164 n. 3.

[3] Édouard Fétis, *Les Artistes belges à l'étranger*, i (Brussels 1857), 67–83.

[4] Sandrart, 355–7. 'Sadeler blieb allein daselbst [i.e. in Prague] . . . massen ich ihn Anno 1622 gesehen, als ich noch ein junger Mensch expresse seiner Wissenschaft halber von Nürnberg zu ihme nach Prag verreist . . . [und] weil ich bey demselben zu verbleiben gesinnet gewesen, für einen Lehrling angeboten, der mich dann freundlich empfangen, und mir alles, was er gehabt, oder gekönnt, gezeiget.' (Ibid. 356.)

[5] This is evident from the whole layout of the volumes, and their emblems are explicitly termed 'hieroglyphics'. Cf. Volkmann, op. cit. 58 f.

[6] Schöne, op. cit., Introduction.

one climax of the great vogue for that kind of book during Rudolf's reign. Beginning with Sambucus and Hadrianus Junius the tide swelled in the German lands to include the *Empresas Morales* of Juan de Borja, Spanish ambassador in Prague, and the well-known collections of Joachim Camerarius, Reusner, and others.[1]

The culmination of the *Symbola* is Rudolf himself: sixteen separate emblems are devoted to him, and they include his personal motto ADSIT, interpreted by Typotius first in the anti-Turkish ideology: 'Adiuvante Domino Superavit Imperatorem Turcarum'; then in the more neutral spirit of the *Pietas Austriaca*: 'Divinum enim *adsit* auxilium, ubi humanum deficit nos, necesse est.' Others depict him as an eagle, a lion against the Ottomans, a symbol of the virtues which lead to heaven. The whole collection is deliberately more than just a picture-book or diversion: 'Utere fruere, non contemplare modo. Nam si paullò penitius introspexeris, videbis non tam oculos quam animam pasci, quod magnis illis viris propositum est . . .'[2]

One further feature of some of Spranger's paintings—his *Odysseus and Circe* for instance, or *Mars and Venus*[3]—is the precise and vivid portrayal of animals, which moreover have a more than purely decorative function. This leads us to another important aspect of the art of Mannerist Prague: its observation of nature. The late sixteenth century saw the beginnings of the 'realist' landscapes soon to become so familiar among the Dutch school; their origins were closely linked with the new study of topography, drawings of towns, book-illustrations, especially botanical and zoological, and allied fields.[4] Such work was characterized by an at times minute fidelity in reproducing the natural world, and has been christened by one Austrian scholar—basing himself partly on the evidence of Rudolfine artists—the 'naturalistic' or 'rustic' style.[5]

In this development Prague occupied an important place, yet the evaluation of it is far from straightforward. For the artists in Prague

[1] *Empresas Morales a . . . Don Phelipe nuestro Señor dirigidas por Don Ivan de Borja de su Consejo y su Embaxador cercala M. Caesarea del Emperador Rudolpho II* (Praga, por Iorge Nigrin, 1581), etc. The sheer profusion of this literature is indicated by Mario Praz, *Studies in Seventeenth-century Imagery* (2nd edn. Rome 1964) ii, *Catalogue*. Something of the taste appeared in England from the 1580s, when Geoffrey Whitney published his *Choice of Emblemes*; see Rosemary Freeman, *English Emblem Books* (London 1948). Cf. above, p. 97 n. 3, and below, p. 269 n. 1.

[2] From the Preface to the Reader by Sadeler. [Cf. Plate 13.]

[3] Diez, fig. 21 and pl. XX.

[4] Of course this is to abstract from the purely art-historical development which cannot be entered into here; but cf. W. Stechow, *Dutch Landscape Painting of the Seventeenth Century* (London 1966), esp. p. 18 (on C. J. Visscher) and 34 f. (on Goltzius).

[5] E. Kris, 'Der Stil "Rustique"', *Jahrbuch* N.F. i (1926), 137–208.

combined a direct approach to nature with a thoroughgoing symbolism which was directly linked to their theories of the macrocosm and of occult and astral influences. It is surely significant that Sadeler's engravings for the *Symbola* also include a variety of emblematic creatures, all of them carefully reproduced. As with alchemy or the lore of gems, which we shall examine further below, such a view of nature is not 'naturalistic' but rather the reverse: it is the intuition of magical properties.

The rustic style emerges very clearly in the work of Georg Hoefnagel (1542?–1600), 'Inventor Hieroglyphicus et Allegoricus', an educated man, poet, traveller, and friend of Ortelius, who on leaving his native Antwerp after the Spanish terror in 1576 worked for the Fuggers and the Dukes of Bavaria before passing into the service of Ferdinand of Tyrol and then of Rudolf.[1] Hoefnagel became celebrated for his drawings of towns (many of them appeared in the *Civitates Orbis Terrarum* of Braun and Hogenberg), and national dresses and customs;[2] this background suggests a person of broadly eirenical disposition. Under the Habsburgs he developed further his graphic techniques: for Ferdinand he prepared a Missal to Plantin's published text, richly decorated with all kinds of flowers, fruit, insects, and animals;[3] for Rudolf he drew several 'animal books' which Mander mentions: 'een van alle viervoetighe Dieren, den anderen van de cruypende, den derden van de vliegende en den vierden van de swemmende oft Visschen'.[4] The models were exhibits in the Imperial collection, and typically it was the exotic species on which he concentrated. In Prague he produced his masterwork, the illustrations to a calligraphy primer by the Hungarian George Bocskay which had been written at the behest of Maximilian II twenty years earlier. Complementing Bocskay's beautifully constructed scrolls and serifs, Hoefnagel's art teems with emblematic subjects from living creatures through religious themes to the dynastic *Imprese* of his Habsburg master.[5] His son Jakob followed him as Imperial *Kammermaler*: Jakob seems also to have copied many items in Rudolf's museum, while another son Jan illustrated a volume called *Diversae Insectarum Volatiliumque Icones*, published in 1630.[6]

[1] For biographical details see Eduard Chmelarz, 'Georg und Jakob Hoefnagel', in *Jahrbuch* xvii (1896), 275–90. Mander gives the date of his birth as 1543, Fétis as 1545.

[2] Mander, fo. 262b; Fétis, op. cit. 97 ff. [Cf. Plate 16.]

[3] Chmelarz, art. cit. 281 ff. There is now a minute analysis of the symbolism which Hoefnagel employed in his work by Th. A. G. Wilberg Vignau-Schuurman, *Die emblematischen Elemente im Werke Joris Hoefnagels*, i–ii (Leiden 1969).

[4] Mander, fo. 263a.

[5] [Plate 8b.] Vienna, Kunsthistorisches Museum, Sammlung für Plastik und Kunstgewerbe, Inv.-Nr. 975; Vignau-Schuurman, op. cit., *passim*.

[6] Chmelarz, art. cit. 287–90; Fétis, op. cit. 117. Jakob was still at court in 1612 when

One of the younger Hoefnagel's colleagues at Prague was the still-life and landscape artist Roelant Savery (1576–1639) who entered the Emperor's service in 1604.[1] Like Hoefnagel, Savery was a specialist in the precise representation of nature, especially its less familiar creatures, and deviations from normality. That no doubt accounts in part for his popularity with Rudolf. Yet the roots of his inspiration went deeper: his flower-pieces, some of the earliest known, are arranged symmetrically and reflect close observation, but they possess an intellectual meaning beyond their value as diversion, just as do the drawings in the *Symbola*.[2] This is clearer in Savery's landscapes, which combine the figures of animals and birds in a fantastic ensemble, almost a prefiguration of Douanier Rousseau. Many of the settings are Alpine, and it is known that Rudolf sent Savery to study the mountains of the Tyrol as subjects for his work;[3] they suggest a close sympathy between the artist and the Emperor, who had himself an unfulfilled yearning for the Tyrol which these paintings may have partly satisfied.

The dual role of Mannerist art, its serious metaphysical purpose behind a diverting exterior, which we can observe in artists like Sadeler and Savery, appears most forcibly in the paintings of Arcimboldo, the grotesque 'composed heads' which have so intrigued historians of art and are still so enigmatic. Are these pictures amusements, essays in social satire, as one critic has suggested?[4] In part they undoubtedly are: we have already noted Arcimboldo as chief of revels at the Habsburg court, and it has been established that several at least of them are portraits of specific people, particularly one which depicts Rudolf himself as the gardener's god Vertumnus.[5] But at the same time they possess a deeper meaning. They belong to the Mannerist tradition in their grotesqueness (having antecedents, for example, in the work of Rosso[6] or some Dutch still-life), in their anti-Classical pose, in their conscious medievalism of motif;[7] above all they are Mannerist in embodying a system of natural correspondences.

he appears as *Contrafetter* (Portraitist) (Riegger, 249). He later took the side of the Protestants in the rebellion (Polišenský, *Nizozemská politika*, 162 f., 193, 201, 205 ff. *passim*).

[1] Fétis, op. cit. ii (Brussels 1865), 88–103.

[2] [Plate 9, a and b.] On Savery's still lifes see I. Bergström, *Dutch Still-Life Painting in the Seventeenth Century* (Eng. trans. London 1956), 89 ff. Cf. below, p. 268 n. 4.

[3] Sandrart, fo. 305.

[4] Geiger, op. cit. esp. Ch. III.

[5] [Plate 1.] Alfons, op. cit. 134–9; cf. Lomazzo, *Tempio*, 154, describing a compound portrait of the Vice-Chancellor—whom Alfons identifies as Johann Zasius (ibid. 56, 59). [6] Cf. the masks by Rosso illustrated in Shearman, op. cit. 153.

[7] Hocke, op. cit. 153.

The nearest to a 'key' to Arcimboldo comes from his contemporary Comanini, who explains one of his pictures, a head composed entirely of animals, as relating the attributes of each animal to the relevant human seat of each attribute; as the elephant and the cheek both signify modesty.[1] Thus the framework within which Arcimboldo operated supposed a scheme of interrelations, including the notion of the microcosm and theories of the elements, which was both teleological and endowed with moral significance. His paintings are *concętti*, in the sixteenth-century sense of the term, but they also employ illusion in the service of symbolism; they hover with permanent uncertainty between the realms of pure Idea and pure sensibility. As such Arcimboldo's own profoundest symbol within the circle of Rudolf's initiates was precisely the god Vertumnus, who represented the Emperor, but at the same time connoted the very essence of impersonation: transformation—in fact the mask of that courtly pageantry in which the age excelled.

The same interplay of natural and artificial, immediate experience and deeper significance, is evident in the applied art and smaller-scale creations of the Rudolfine period. Such activity—objects in gold, silver, glass, enamel, and the rest—achieved a special importance at the court, and earned fame far beyond it, for reasons which are not altogether clear.[2] Inspiration perhaps stemmed most of all, besides the local traditions which encouraged it, from the personal and tangible nature of this work and the very intractability of the materials used, affording as it did great opportunities for Mannerist virtuosity.[3] Here too, moreover, occult properties were also involved. However that may be, the same kind of iconographical programme as appears in painting and sculpture can often be recognized, and Rudolf himself certainly played an active part in furthering the art.

[1] G. Comanini, *Il Figino* (Mantua 1591), 32, 46 ff. On the role of this essentially medieval approach to physiognomy in Renaissance art see P. Meller, 'Physiognomical theory in Renaissance heroic portraits', in *The Renaissance and Mannerism, Studies in Western Art* (Princeton 1963), 53–69. It is worth observing that while Arcimboldo was in Prague his colleague Hájek republished a popular treatise he had written on the astrological principles of physiognomy: Thaddaei Hagecii ab Hagek ... *Aphorismorum Metoposcopicorum libellus unus* (Frankfurt 1584).

[2] The best general treatment is in Lhotsky, op. cit. 245–61.

[3] Cf. the shrewd observation by Kris: 'Andererseits hat die Glyptik wohl darum in jenem virtuosenhaften Milieu Bewunderung gefunden, weil eben hier ein Schnittpunkt zwischen den "bonae artes" und den "artes mechanicae" lag, ein Schnittpunkt, der sich einem Zeitalter doppelt empfahl, dessen Intellektualismus nicht zuletzt die Überwindung der Schwierigkeit als Eigenwert empfand.' E. Kris, *Meister und Meisterwerke der Steinschneidekunst in der italienischen Renaissance* (Vienna 1929), i, 6. As far as local tradition was concerned the passion of Charles IV of Luxemburg for precious stones may be recalled.

The 'naturalistic' figures for instance reappear on the work of the Jamnitzer family, especially Wenzel Jamnitzer of Nuremberg (1508-85), who probably never lived in Prague but was in close contact with Archduke Ferdinand and Rudolf,[1] and Anton Schweinberger (in Prague 1587-1603) whose jug made of Seychelle-nut forms one of the masterworks of the period, decorated with plants and creatures both real and mythical.[2] Similar scenes, often incorporating exotic and grotesque animals, appear on crystalware articles made at the turn of the century, and on the gemstones produced mostly by Italian masters.[3] A related genre was the construction of tableaux, mostly landscapes, out of mosaics of stone, the so-called *commessi in pietra dura*. The centre for this was Florence, but Rudolf showed great interest and attracted to Prague Giovanni and Cosimo Castrucci who prepared a whole series of views, mostly idealized like Savery's paintings, but two of them depicting the city of Prague. The *commessi* were prized extremely highly—in 1619 their valuation amounted to half the total of all the applied art in Rudolf's collection.[4]

The finest achievement of Imperial design under Rudolf was undoubtedly the crown, already described, now attributed to Hans Vermeyen who was celebrated in his time as a goldsmith.[5] But other *invenzioni* can be isolated which were evidently inspired by the monarch, such as the silver and gold work of Paulus van Vianen (in Prague 1603-12), an artist closely associated with Rudolf—perhaps also in his religion—and a friend of Aachen and Julius of Brunswick.[6] One of the most notable of them is the *Triumphal Jug*, formerly ascribed to Vianen, now linked with the name of Christoph Jamnitzer, and completed about 1609.[7] This vessel has four panels depicting Time, Truth, Death, and Fame, and follows a programme of considerable, but hitherto unexplained complexity. Truth is represented by four painters: Leonardo, Titian, Dürer, and Aachen (the latter two are particularly significant), while the linking of motifs on the other reliefs suggests an occult source,

---

[1] Cf. his inkwell: E. Kris, *Goldschmiedearbeiten des Mittelalters, der Renaissance und des Barocks*, i (Vienna 1932), No. 44, pl. 31, in Ambras; some of the weight of Kris's argument in 'Der Stil "Rustique"' rests on Jamnitzer.

[2] [Plate 11.] Kris, *Goldschmiedearbeiten*, No. 79.

[3] Kris, *Steinschneidekunst*, 97 ff. and *passim*.

[4] See E. Neumann, 'Florentiner Mosaik aus Prag', *Jahrbuch* N.F. 53 (1957), 157-202, with illustrations of most of these pieces.   [5] Cf. above p. 80 and n. 2.

[6] H. Modern, 'Paulus van Vianen', *Jahrbuch* xv (1894), 60-102, esp. 67 f. Sandrart says Vianen was held in Rome by the Inquisition and only released at Rudolf's insistence to go to Prague: Sandrart, fo. 341.

[7] [Plate 12.] Kris, *Goldschmiedearbeiten*, No. 88. Modern (art. cit. 77 ff.) still regarded Vianen as the maker.

perhaps the *Occulta Philosophia* of Agrippa of Nettesheim or some compilation based on that celebrated text. Another jug by Jamnitzer offers a simpler version of the same style and shows Amor being borne onwards in triumph.[1]

Further opportunity for the development of the mystique lay in the field of coins and medallions. What the Strada family pursued from an antiquarian standpoint was realized in metal by skilled craftsmen, especially by Antonio Abondio (in Prague from 1580) and his son Alessandro.[2] Antonio served the Habsburgs for more than thirty years, both as artist and agent; his many portraits of the dynasty include a series of original designs for the famous thalers minted in Upper Hungary. Alessandro married Aachen's widow and is remembered as a friend by Sandrart, writing in 1665, who recalls his fame both for his medals and his figures in wax.[3] Like the Hoefnagels, the Abondios and similar craftsmen at the court must generally have been working from models and materials which formed part of the extraordinary and fabled Imperial collection.

Parallel with Rudolf's patronage of the artists around him went his zeal in collecting paintings and *objets d'art* of all kinds, both antique and contemporary. Various judgements have been passed on this activity: it has been regarded as greed divorced from aesthetic taste, or as a passion animated by high connoisseur's standards. Even viewed from a modern standpoint the latter verdict seems a fairer one; Rudolf made great efforts to secure the Isenheim altar-piece of Grünewald and Holbein's altar in Freiburg, as well as seeking out famous classical antiquities.[4] But this debate misses the point. More significant is the habit of collecting itself, which reached a remarkable climax in the later sixteenth century. It represented indeed a first stage towards the modern permanent collection of works of art, but for the contemporary mind its meaning was also much wider, and we must look to the latter in explaining the catholic—even over-catholic—principles of Rudolf.[5] For him the assembling of many and various items reflected the essential variety in the

[1] Kris, op. cit. No. 87, pl. 58–60.

[2] [Plate 15c.] Lhotsky, op. cit. 260 f.; T. Gerevich, 'Antonio Abondio', in *Dr. Gróf Klebelsberg Kunó emlékkönyve* (Budapest 1925), 463–97.

[3] Sandrart, Vorrede and fo. 341.

[4] See Kurz, *Umělecké vztahy*, 477 ff.; Lhotsky, op. cit. 242 ff.; cf. *Jahrbuch* vii (1888), Reg. No. 4618, 4622, 4625.

[5] Valuable hints to an understanding of this mood (though not in a specifically 'Mannerist' mould) were provided by Julius von Schlosser, *Die Kunst- und Wunderkammern der Spätrenaissance* (Leipzig 1908), esp. 90 ff.

world, which could nevertheless be converted into unity by a mind which brought them together and divined their internal relations one with another. Once again we see the analogy from microcosm to macrocosm and the search for a 'key' to the harmony of the created universe; in other words we see an aspect of the pansophic striving.

The very words used by contemporaries to describe the phenomenon are worthy of note: they spoke of the Rudolfine *Kunst- und Wunderkammer*, cabinet of arts and curiosities, implying that whatever the physical dimensions of the collection, its underlying idea was to present much in a limited space, an encyclopedia of the visible world. With this went a deliberate parallelism between nature and art: for there was also a mental world, governed by the *disegno interno* of the Mannerists, which would reproduce the divine creative purpose for material things; hence the task of Hoefnagel and others to imitate the multiplicity of forms which the Emperor observed around him. Clearest epitome of that tendency were the so-called *Kunstschränke* (cabinets of virtù) which were designed as incapsulations of the world and its mysteries, full of marvels and allusive carving in marquetry or intaglio. The most famous was the cabinet made in the early seventeenth century for Duke Philip of Pomerania and exhaustively described by Hainhofer, but others came from Eger in Bohemia and their inlay work was often in mosaic like that of the Prague workshops.[1]

It should not be forgotten too that Rudolf collected the animate as well as the inanimate, and his gardens, stables, and menageries bore witness to this. Observers marvelled at the profusion of strange plants and creatures which could be seen around the Hradschin,[2] and the contemporary curiosity was not an idle one. Alongside the artists who depicted the ideal forms of originals in the Imperial menagerie or aviary —Savery is the most distinguished—and the architects who, like Heintz, designed fitting accommodation for them,[3] can be set the Humanists who wrote erudite poems on the same subjects. There is a long series of such verses in Dornavius's *Amphitheatrum Sapientiae Socraticae Joco-Seriae*.[4]

---

[1] *Des Augsburger Patriciers Philipp Hainhofer Beziehungen zum Herzog Philipp II von Pommern-Stettin*, ed. O. Doering (Vienna 1894, hereafter 'Hainhofer'), 289–348; *Barock in Böhmen*, ed. K. M. Swoboda (Munich 1964), 280 f.; Neumann, *Florentiner Mosaik*, 190.

[2] e.g. *Hans Georg Ernstingers Raisbuch*, ed. P. A. E. Walther (Stuttgart 1877), 100; and Chatenay, *Esprinchard*, 168 f.

[3] On Heintz's work for the royal stables see J. Zimmer, 'Iosephus Heinzius, Architectus cum Antiquis Comparandus', *Umění* xvii (1969), 217–43.

[4] Caspar Dornavius, *Amphitheatrum Sapientiae Socraticae Joco-Seriae . . .*, i–ii (Hanau 1619); an anthology.

Animals and birds, like plants, had their virtues, and zoology stands with botany in this period as an expression of learned interest which was directed ultimately towards the divine cosmological mysteries. The widespread legend that the Emperor's last illness was betokened by the deaths of his pet lion and two ravens belongs to an environment which was not only profoundly superstitious but aware of a set of correspondences and a harmony underlying phenomena.[1]

Rudolf used his collection for private contemplation; he was very secretive about it and few accounts survive of its contents. One of those who did penetrate it was Krafft, and the achievement occasioned his travelling companions much surprise: 'Alls Ichs bestettigte dem sey, Also sagtten Ire G(naden): Wolan, krafft, Ir mögtt euch dössen Riemen, Ir haptt gesehen, so vil Grafen und herren nitt kan zu tail werden.' Another was the wandering Humanist Jacques Esprinchard of La Rochelle, who brought an introduction to Spranger and Hans von Aachen. A third was the lawyer Melchior Goldast, who had himself shown around immediately after Rudolf's death in 1612.[2] Unfortunately none of them was sufficiently a connoisseur to take much advantage of his opportunity. Yet although few contemporaries managed to see its treasures the Rudolfine *Kunstkammer* was widely regarded as one of the miracles of the age. Like the Emperor's alchemy and his intellectual patronage, it stood to other European courts—Munich or Dresden for example—in the relation of *primus inter pares*: the typical late Humanist preoccupation in its classic form.

The preoccupation was also one which Rudolf shared with his family; both his father and brothers indulged the taste, and for his uncle Ferdinand it likewise became a passion. Ferdinand's monument was the celebrated Ambras collection, which began during his Statthalter-ship in Prague and was then transferred to the castle of that name near Innsbruck. Ambras contained everything: paintings, furniture, stones and cameos, suits of armour and weapons, coins and inscriptions, classical relics, curious and exotic objects of all kinds.[3] Rudolf was pre-

---

[1] Contemporaries attributed this prophecy to Rudolf himself (e.g. *Briefe und Akten*, x. 246 and n. 2); there seems no reason why they should not have been correct. The legend is repeated by—among others—Khevenhüller, *Conterfet Kupfferstich*, i. 31, who appends a Latin poem on the same subject.

[2] Krafft, op. cit. 390; he was shown around by Spranger in 1584. Chatenay, *Esprin-chard*, 168 f.; Esprinchard was a mild Huguenot with wide antiquarian, geographical, and botanical interests. Goldast, *Tagebuch*, 264.

[3] The inventory of Ambras drawn up on Ferdinand's death in 1596 is reprinted in *Jahrbuch* vii (1888), Reg. pp. ccxxvi–cccxi. Cf. Schlosser, op. cit. 35–72; Hirn, *Erz-herzog Ferdinand*, ii. 21–49.

dictably extremely jealous of Ambras; he saw himself alone as custodian of the treasures of his House, and considered himself entitled by right to claim it after the death of Ferdinand in 1596.[1] It probably entered into his plans for abdication to the Tyrol in the early years of the seventeenth century. He also had a long struggle with his brothers over some other inherited items of doubtful provenance, particularly the *Achatschale*, a supposedly Byzantine agate shell, and the *Ainkhürn*, a magic horn from a unicorn.[2]

Reconstruction of the contents of Rudolf's collection is made extremely difficult both by the lack of witnesses who penetrated the 'Spanish rooms' of the Hrad to see it, and by its bizarre subsequent history. Although partly transferred to Vienna by Matthias and his successors, partly sold off or pillaged during the Thirty Years War, enough of it remained through the seventeenth century to excite the notice of travellers.[3] Following a series of auctions during the Enlightenment and further transfers to Austria in the nineteenth century it was believed that the whole collection had been dispersed, until the remarkable discovery during the last decade that over seventy paintings and pieces of sculpture (including several well-known works presumed lost) still survived *in situ*.[4] They are, however, just a remnant of the total, whose largest part is now stored in Vienna's Kunsthistorisches Museum, while fragments found their way to the galleries and museums of all Europe.

Several inventories of the Prague collection have long been known, but none of them contemporary, though we learn—via Skála—that it was valued in 1612 at seventeen million gold pieces.[5] The most interesting are the 'Liechtenstein' inventory of 1621,[6] and that compiled by Dionysio Miseroni in 1650,[7] but both present merely garbled and uncomprehending

---

[1] The point is made by Lhotsky, op. cit. 239 f.; cf. Rudolf to Maximilian III, 14 Feb. 1603 (draft): 'Alss ist mein freundt brüderlich begern an E(ure) L(iebe) Sie wollen die sachen nachsinnen . . . (um) obgedachtes Ombras abzutretten, und mir Ir guetachten hieruber zukommen lassen . . .' HHSA, Fam. Korr. A. 4. I.

[2] *Jahrbuch* xv (1894), Reg. Nos. 12155, 12270; cf. Lhotsky, 240 f.; Schwarzenfeld, op. cit. 46–8.

[3] e.g. William Crowne in 1636 (Francis C. Springell, *Connoisseur and Diplomat* (London 1963), 71 f.) and Charles Patin in the 1670s: *Relations historiques et curieuses . . .* (Amsterdam 1695), 222.

[4] The story is told in Neumann, *Obrazárna*, 7–14, 19–51. The old masters were not, as some reports had it, 'discovered in a cellar', but had rather been overpainted, mutilated, or rendered unrecognizable by age and false cataloguing.

[5] J. Svátek, *Culturhistorische Bilder aus Böhmen* (Prague 1879), 234, 235 and n.

[6] 'Inventarium aller derjenigen sachen, so nach der victori in ihrer majestät schaz- und kunstcamer zue Praag seind gefunden und auf ihrer mayestät und ihrer fürstlich gnaden von Lichtenstein bevelch seind den 6. decembris anno 1621 inventirt worden, wie volgt . . .', printed in *Jahrbuch* xxv (1905), Reg. pp. xx–li, with index supplied.

[7] 'Specification der ienigen Sachen, welche bei dem auf der löbl. Böhm. Camer

itemizations, while nevertheless showing the scale of the *Kunstkammer* as it must have been in its entirety. In the 1930s a list prepared by the Protestant estates was discovered—or more correctly rediscovered, since it was known that the dissidents had drawn up a catalogue of the fabled Rudolfine treasures in 1619 before selling off some of them to finance their armies.[1] This is an important document, but inferior as a source to that of two years later. Most recently an inventory for 1607–11 has come to light: written probably by the miniaturist Daniel Fröschl, it will yield new information about the applied art which to contemporaries evidently represented the heart of the collection.[2] The absence from both it and the 1619 list of any paintings is to some extent made good by a catalogue of the pictures which passed after Rudolf's death from his gallery to that of Albrecht and Isabella in Brussels.[3]

What emerges clearly from all these sources is the fact that the contents of Rudolf's collection were international; they derived—in addition to the products of the Prague *ateliers*—both from gifts and from purchase.[4] Thus Rudolf received many Oriental treasures as presents;[5] we also find him thanking European courts, not excluding Protestants like Christian von Anhalt, for artistic works which they have sent him. He had constant dealings with the rich South German towns Augsburg and Nuremberg, which sent gifts to the Emperor as well as negotiating purchases for him.[6] He was in close touch too with the great commercial families of Fugger and Welser, now enjoying the fruits of their wealth by offering munificent patronage to the arts; he stayed with Hans Fugger—collec-

beschehene gnadige Verordnung, den 29 Julij An° 650 gehaltenen Inventar, in der Kays. Schaz und Kunst Camer befunden, und wie hernach folget, beschrieben worden.' SÚA, SM S 21/7.

    [1] J. Morávek, *Nově objevený inventář rudolfinských sbírek na Hradě pražském* (Prague 1937).
    [2] E. Neumann, 'Das Inventar der rudolphinischen Kunstkammer von 1607/11', in *Queen Christina of Sweden, Documents and Studies* (*Analecta Reginensia*, i, Stockholm 1966), 262–5. Dr. Neumann, of the Kunsthistorisches Museum in Vienna, is preparing the document for publication.
    [3] M. de Maeyer, *Albrecht en Isabella en de Schilderkunst* (Brussels 1955), 316–19. This catalogue was prepared by two Rudolfine artists, Jeremias Gunther and Hans von Pettl, and is dated Prague 6 Sept. 1615. On the extent to which Rudolf's paintings were forthwith portioned out among members of his family cf. K. Garas, 'Zur Geschichte der Kunstsammlungen Rudolfs II', *Umění* xviii (1970), 134–40.
    [4] See in general J. Morávek in *Co daly naše země . . .*, 143–5.
    [5] There is a long list of Turkish and Indian items in Morávek, *Inventář*, 19 ff.; cf. Kurz, art. cit. Some of it of course came as booty from the Ottoman wars.
    [6] Lhotsky, op. cit. 270–4; Rudolf's correspondence, *passim*. The collected edicts on artistic matters of the town of Nuremberg unfortunately contain exclusively legal procedures, but there are many references to Prague: *Nürnberger Ratsverlässe über Kunst und Künstler*, ii. *1571–1618* (Vienna–Leipzig 1904).

tor, bibliophile, and employer of Sustris, Dietrich, and Alexander Colin
—during the Augsburg *Reichstag* of 1582.[1]

Much light is thrown on the artistic connections between Prague and
Germany by the letters of the much-travelled correspondent Philip
Hainhofer. Hainhofer knew about cultural circles in the Bohemian
capital, being a friend for instance of Fradelius.[2] He was himself a considerable collector and some of his possessions attracted the covetous
gaze of Rudolf; he notes on one occasion that his woodcut of Charles the
Bold and a reversible ring with a face on it (evidently in the style of
Arcimboldo) are being sought by the Emperor.[3] Hainhofer, however, was
unwilling to offer anything to Prague on loan, even his album. In this
he was well advised; Rudolf had a reputation for acquiring whatever
caught his fancy with a sovereign disregard for payment or restoration.
He was energetic in summoning to court those with whom he wished to
bargain, and sending out agents on clandestine missions. Much money
was expended on servants 'welche die Kay. Maytt. in dero aigenen sachen
verschiekhen' and among them were numbered some of his favourites
like Aachen and Octavio Strada. In 1595 as important a politician as
Rudolf Coraduz spent weeks in Rome negotiating for paintings with
various Italian notables.[4]

The Emperor was served too by personal contacts abroad, especially
by Khevenhüller in Madrid whose correspondence with Rudolf contains
many records of *objets d'art* acquired: not only celebrated pictures, but
bezoar stones, emeralds, and other treasures from the far-flung Spanish
empire.[5] Khevenhüller was among those commissioned to secure important items from the legacy of Cardinal Granvelle when this came
on offer in Burgundy. The Cardinal, who had been a great patron of
culture, died in 1586 and some of his paintings were sold off forthwith.[6]
The rest of the collection was dispersed around 1607. It seems more than

---

[1] G. Lill, *Hans Fugger und die Kunst* (Leipzig 1908), 35 ff. and *passim*; cf. *Jahrbuch*
xix (1898), Reg. Nos. 16160, 16266.

[2] Hainhofer; *Rukověť*, ii. 154–6. A 'Melchior Hainhofer' was *Hofkammerrat* from
1 Feb. 1610 (Riegger, 197; *Briefe und Akten*, viii. 709 n. 1).

[3] Hainhofer, 94.

[4] Coraduz's letters on this subject are in *Jahrbuch* xv (1904), Reg. Nos. 12219, 12246,
12250, 12262, 12266.

[5] Some of Rudolf's agents are listed by Chytil, *Umění*, 28–32. On Khevenhüller see
above, p. 50 n. 3; cf. *Jahrbuch* vii (1888), Reg. No. 4634; xiii (1892), Nos. 9165, 9167,
9244, 9251, 9256; xv (1894), Nos. 12153, 12257, 12412, 12426, 12431, 12494; xix
(1898), Nos. 16215, 16232, 16267–71, 16273–5, 16621; and next note below.

[6] M. van Durme, *El Cardenal Granvela* (Barcelona 1957), 287 ff.; Lhotsky, op. cit.
283 f. The negotiations with Rudolf showed two spurts of urgency, during 1586–8
and again in 1600; cf. *Jahrbuch* xiii (1892), Reg. Nos. 9465, 9485, 9504, 9509, 9583,
9590; vii (1888), Nos. 4648, 4656; xv (1894), Nos. 12521, 12526.

coincidence that in the very same year we hear of a marriage between
Rudolf's natural daughter Caroline and one of Granvelle's heirs, his
great-nephew François Thomas Perrenot, Count of Cantecroy.[1] A short
time earlier the young man's uncle had been acting for the Emperor
in Venice, entrusted by him with the purchase of 'res quasdam nobis
curiosas'.[2]

Such documents as survive show how personal was this art policy to
Rudolf. When he heard of a notable work, a rare gem, a manuscript, or
some object of superstition which interested him, he spared no pains to
secure it. Thus the collection which he assembled reflected exactly, not
simply his taste—the matter was not so narrowly aesthetic as that—but
his mentality. We have already observed his passion for the canvases of
Albrecht Dürer. His reasons for valuing them were no doubt various:
emulation of Maximilian I must have played its part, together with the
Emperor's sympathy for the symbolism in Dürer's work, not only in its
service to the mystique, but also through its wider occult and magical
significance. The gallery of Dürers became both famous and legendary:
it was well known that Rudolf had organized the transportation of the
Rosenkranzfest (a painting full of Habsburg symbolism) across the Alps
from Venice, with four bearers to hold it upright.[3] He acquired pictures
from the artist's native town of Nuremberg, from Augsburg, from the
Granvelle collection, and elsewhere.[4] Moreover he employed a number
of his lesser court artists to imitate the style of Dürer, especially the
miniaturist Fröschl who was also an exponent of flower and bird minia-
tures, his antiquary after the death of Octavio Strada, and one of his most
intimate servants till the end.[5]

The Emperor's other preferred master was Pieter Breughel.
With him, as with the Dürer of the *Rosenkranzfest* or the *Massacre
of the Ten Thousand*, it has been suggested that Rudolf was attracted
by a combination of monumentality and precise observation of

---

[1] Nuncios/Caetano, Prague 24 Sept. 1607, 14 Jan., 2 and 18 Feb. 1608; *Briefe und
Akten*, vi, No. 59. The wedding was celebrated early in 1608, though Alidosi (*Relazione*),
writing in 1607, regards the pair as already married. François Thomas Perrenot de
Granvelle was the grandson of the Cardinal's younger brother Thomas.

[2] *Jahrbuch* xix (1898), Reg. No. 16534; letter of Rudolf to François Perrenot de
Granvelle, Prague 28 Feb. 1605; cf. *Briefe und Akten*, v. 822 n. 2.

[3] Mander, fo. 209a; Hainhofer, 59 f. and *passim*; Lhotsky, op. cit. 279 f.; F. X.
Harlas, *Rudolf II, milovník umění a sběratel* (Prague 1917?), 52 ff.

[4] e.g. Rudolf to the Augsburgers, 20 Sept. 1604, thanking them for an *Adam and Eve*
by Dürer and a Pordenone: HHSA, Fam. Korr. A. 4. II; *Jahrbuch* xix (1898), Reg.
Nos. 16608–9, 16617–18, 16749–50. Cf. above, p. 181 n. 6.

[5] K. Chytil, *Umění a umělci na dvoře Rudolfa II* (Prague 1921), 12; Hainhofer, 12;
Lhotsky, op. cit. 293; Gindely, *Rudolf II*, ii. 313; *Briefe und Akten*, x, No. 75, 176 n.
and 184 n.

detail.[1] Certainly the joining of a spiritually or metaphysically conceived whole with a 'realism' of detail is characteristic of intellectual Mannerism and typical of the Prague school. We may fairly surmise too that the allegory in Breughel, especially in so far as it represented an attack on established religion, was particularly appealing. Mander cites nine specific works of Breughel which can be identified in Rudolf's collection, and adds that there are several more in Prague.[2] The painter's family was also clearly welcome. Both Jan (Velvet) Breughel and Pieter II visited Prague; Hainhofer counted the former, with Paul Bril, as the finest living landscape artist in Europe.[3]

In one respect the artists at Rudolf's court represented a close-knit and esoteric circle, a cultural élite; but this does not mean that they were wholly isolated from the country of their adoption. Here again it must be stressed, as with religion and politics, that there existed no absolute gap; the development of Bohemian art in the period was not divorced from that of Western Europe as refracted through the entourage of the Emperor. Some of the important points of interaction must now be considered.

Debates over the nature of the influence of Rudolf's court on native Czech art will never be adequately resolved, especially when attention stays concentrated on painting, where the domestic tradition was least creative. There an old-fashioned guild structure, coupled with restrictive commissions from ecclesiastical and bourgeois donors, maintained a mediocre level of achievement,[4] while Rudolf was always, as we have observed, loth to allow Spranger and his associates to work for others. But this formed no hard-and-fast rule; Spranger in fact painted a number of works for friends in Prague like the goldsmith Müller or the printer Peterle, and for the Church.[5] Meanwhile other forces were making for closer contact. The patronage of high aristocrats, especially the Rožmberks, Lobkovic, and Brunswick, encouraged local groups of artists in a mannered courtly style;[6] connoisseurs in Prague could trade with royal

---

[1] J. Neumann notes the all-embracing quality of the large-scale work of both artists: *Obrazárna*, 15.

[2] See K. Mádl, 'Obrazárna a umělci Rudolfa II v Praze', *Památky Archeologické* xxii (1906–8), 178 f.

[3] Chytil, op. cit. 12 f.; J. Neumann, 'Kleine Beiträge zur rudolfinischen Kunst und ihre Auswirkungen', *Umění* xviii (1970), 151–4; Hainhofer, 15.

[4] Karel Chytil, *Malířstvo pražské 15. a 16. věku* (Prague 1906); Z. Winter, *Český průmysl a obchod v 16. věku* (Prague 1913), ii. 491 ff.

[5] See J. Pešina, 'Skupinový portrét v českém renesančním malířství', *Umění* ii (1954), 290.

[6] The Lobkovic were the leading patrons of a school of portraiture in the style of Antonis Mor, Sancho Coello, and Sustris; cf. *Československá vlastivěda* viii (Prague 1935), 108 ff.

artists—an engraving by Sadeler shows the 'market' in the main hall of the castle, and there was a flourishing exchange of art materials—while they also acquired considerable collections of foreign masters: Kaspar Loselius left ninety pictures, Sixt of Ottersdorf sixty-six, and so forth.[1] A number of Prague collectors were interested in Dürer, and Hainhofer's friend Ferdinand Matthioli, son of the herbalist Pietro Andrea, offers an important example of this taste.[2] The guild system itself was raised to a higher plane: several of Rudolf's artists became members of it, Spranger from 1584 till his death; while, more significantly, the Emperor decreed in 1595 that it should receive a privileged status.[3] Thus it was effectively reconstituted as an Academy, and a vindication was given to the new creative role of the visual arts.

Czech art, like Bohemian culture in general, had suffered from the blight of the Hussite wars, and the notion of its 'Renaissance' in the sixteenth century is rather a portmanteau expression for the gradual assimilation of Italian, and then increasingly of Dutch models.[4] But the negative evidence which it represents, the very resistance to change, is of importance, for here the Mannerist retrospection and conscious antiquarianism became grafted on to real survivals of medieval motifs. On the one hand, as was to be expected, the foreign influences at the Habsburg court were reflected in domestic production, and that to a very significant degree;[5] on the other hand local modifications of Gothic and Renaissance entered as a formative element into the Rudolfine style.

This is clearest in architecture. It has been said that Rudolf possessed no interest in building, perhaps because the medium was too 'solid' and impersonal for him.[6] The observation is at best a half-truth: certainly no uniform 'court' style emerged and there was no wave of palace building by the Emperor. But he continued to favour the architects of his father and Ferdinand of Tyrol, especially the erudite Bonifaz Wolmut until his death in 1579, the naturalized Italian Ulrich Avostalis de Sala,

---

[1] Z. Winter, *Český průmysl*, 524 ff.; cf. eundem, 'Život v pražském Ungeltě roku 1597', *ČČM* lxxiii (1899). [Plate 14.]

[2] Harlas, op. cit. 38; Hainhofer, 100, 156 f. and *passim*. Matthioli, born in Prague in 1561, later settled in Augsburg. His portrait was painted by Josef Heintz (Zimmer, op. cit. 326 f.).

[3] The text is given in Chytil, *Malířstvo*, 310 ff.

[4] Cf. Wirth, *Böhmische Renaissance*, 105–7 and *passim*.

[5] Z. Winter, *Průmysl*, 522 ff.; K. V. Herain, *České malířství od doby rudolfinské do smrti Reinerovy* (Prague 1915), 5–25. But this matter is still disputed; some standard accounts reduce the influence almost to vanishing point (e.g. *Československá vlastivěda*, viii. 111), while in some genres there is admittedly little evidence of it.

[6] Chytil, *Umění v Praze*, 30; Harlas, op. cit. 20; O. Schürer, *Prag—Kultur, Kunst, Geschichte* (Vienna–Leipzig 1930), 137.

who became so settled in Prague for over forty years (he died in 1597) that he even wrote at times in Czech,[1] and the Innsbruck-based Alexander Colin who was employed on the new mausoleum in St. Vitus. They worked in a style which combined late Renaissance features like the Palladian façade of the royal tennis court (*míčovna*) with strong echoes of Gothic.[2]

Elsewhere in Prague the same blending of old and new appears. The aristocratic Renaissance in architecture proceeded with growing momentum during the later sixteenth century, following Italian models, especially Serlio, with Dutch decorative motifs.[3] Vilém Rožmberk, a zealous builder, bought a palace adjoining his own on the Hradschin in 1573 and had it turned by Avostalis into an arcaded garden after the fashion of Serlio (his friend Strada published Serlio's seventh book on architecture in 1575). This was later bought by Rudolf in 1600 and incorporated into his own Imperial residence.[4] Italian influence was prominent in church building, regardless of faith: the Protestant St. Salvator was sufficiently Italianate to be acceptable to the Catholics who took it over after 1620, and the same went for wooden decoration within churches.[5] St. Salvator also retained many of the features of the *Spätgotik*, as did several other Prague churches built or reconstructed during this time: Holy Trinity and St. Thomas on the Malá Strana, St. Václav in the New Town. The latter appears to have been financed by Rudolf II, and the most extraordinary example of them all is the votive chapel of St. Roch on Strahov, founded by the Emperor and raised during the early years of the seventeenth century in a perfectly Gothic idiom.[6]

Rudolf was very concerned with his surroundings as an ensemble, for his palaces in their setting of gardens with fountains, show-cases of curious animals and birds, remarkable plants bizarrely arranged, stables for his favourite horses, and so forth. He attracted to Prague, as both designer of the new 'Spanish' wing (which housed his collections) and expert in perspective work and the disposition of fountains, Hans Vredemann de Vries who through his artistic manuals was one of the foremost

<hr />

[1] e.g. his suggestions and opinions in SÚA, SM S 21/4 (Hofbauamt).

[2] *Barock in Böhmen*, 16 f.

[3] See in general Pollak in *Jahrbuch*, art. cit.

[4] A. Kubíček, 'Rožmberský palác na pražském Hradě', *Umění* i (1953), 308–18; J. Krčálová, 'Palác Pánů z Rožmberka', ibid. xviii (1970), 469–83.

[5] Kořán, 'České řezbářství', 22, discussing the pulpit of 1613 in St. Stephen's in the New Town.

[6] V. Kotrba, 'Die nachgotische Baukunst Böhmens zur Zeit Rudolfs II', *Umění* xviii (1970), 298–330, esp. 318. The chapel survives and has recently been repaired. Cf. in general E. Šamánková, *Architektura české renesance* (Prague 1961), Ch. 5; B. Knox, *The Architecture of Prague and Bohemia* (London 1965), 37, 42.

popularizers of Mannerist models. Vries, equally famous as a constructor of triumphal arches, worked for some years in the Bohemian capital with his son Pauwels.[1] The Emperor's most favoured country seat was the castle of Brandeis on the Elbe (about twelve miles from Prague), and he spent much money on improvements to it and its gardens. There too he commissioned artistic compositions to suit his particular taste.[2]

Everywhere in late sixteenth-century Europe this cult of the sovereign residence included a new passion for fountains and water-inventions of all kinds which involved the royal exchequer in considerable expense.[3] Besides reflecting the refined fancy of the day and occupying men like Vredemann de Vries or Wurzelbauer, Adriaen de Vries or the Jamnitzers especially to ensure their artistic success, such effects possessed another important aspect: they were a branch of the vogue for mechanics and automata so characteristic of the period. The fashion revealed itself in a growing intellectual concern for developments in crafts and technology and a new enthusiasm for the artisan.[4] Some of the landmarks in this process are well known—the *Diverse et Artificiose Machine* of Ramelli, for instance, published in Paris in 1588; what needs to be recognized more fully is the extent of interest among educated and serious men, and its sources. For although the movement had certain obvious links with the 'progressive' trends from which experimental science was to spring —and Francis Bacon owed much to his understanding of sixteenth-century artisanship[5]—it belongs as much to the Mannerist spirit we have been examining. It provided an opportunity for ingenuity and *invenzione* and the triumph of artifice; at the same time it had a deeper symbolic purpose, since a mechanism was in a real sense 'alive', as the world was alive, and could be used to harness the magical properties of nature. Evidence also exists that the machine, conceived as a plaything, was seen to offer scope for the workings of chance and could therefore even possess a mantic or prophetic significance.[6]

---

[1] Mander, fos. 266b–267a; cf. Mádl, art. cit. 184 f., and *Jahrbuch* xii (1891), Reg. No. 8317.

[2] J. V. Prašek, 'Zámek Brandýs nad Labem, oblíbené sídlo Rudolfa II', *ČČM* lxxx (1906), 246 ff. Adriaen de Vries constructed a relief altar-piece at Brandeis after a design by Dürer (Larsson, op. cit. 35).

[3] e.g. a report by Avostalis on the maintenance of 'die unterschiedlichen Rörwasser darauff Jarliches mit Unterhalt und ausbesserung der Rören nit wenig unkosten unnd Muhe verlauffet', 3 Feb. 1593; SÚA, SM S 21/4$^{236-8}$. Cf. Chytil, *Prager Venusbrunnen*, 7 ff.

[4] Cf. Thorndike, op. cit. v, Ch. XXVII.

[5] P. Rossi, *Francesco Bacone*, 23–48.

[6] e.g. the *lusus globulorum* described by E. Neumann in H. von Bertele and E. Neumann, 'Der kaiserliche Kammeruhrmacher Christoph Margraf und die Erfindung der Kugellaufuhr', *Jahrbuch* N.F. 59 (1963), 90–3.

Many among Rudolf's entourage were involved in these pursuits. Jacopo and Octavio Strada produced a series of mechanical drawings, like a more notable scientist, the Hungarian bishop Faustus Verancsics (*c.* 1550–1617), who spent much time in Prague and was a friend of Campanella and de Dominis.[1] Verancsics's *Machinae Novae*, published in Venice shortly before his death, contains all kinds of ingenious designs for clocks, pumps, and fountains, as well as more Utopian schemes like men in flight. The Emperor himself apparently excogitated a kind of mechanical chart for travellers, actuated from beneath by a compass, and briefly described by Caspar Dornavius in an Oration which praises the present flourishing state of arts and sciences.[2] Arcimboldo was well known for his inventions and Lomazzo makes explicit how close they came in the minds of his contemporaries to mystification: 'In ogni cosa egli fù d'acutissimo ingegno, onde ritrovò arteficii di passar fiumi espeditamente, ove non fossero ponti ne si havessero navi, e fù inventor di cifre che non si potevano intendere senza il suo stromento.'[3] The fruits of those studies are evident in some of his portraits which embody collections of instruments.[4] Kepler too had an interest in water-machines: during 1603–4 he ordered some device of this kind to be made for him in Augsburg and it seems after much testing to have proved successful; a little later he was in correspondence with a Prince of Anhalt over the best design for a water-pump.[5] His chief helper in the work was apparently the brilliant inventor Jost Burgi, whom Kepler described in one of his astronomical treatises as 'S. C. Majest. Automatopoeus; qui licet expers linguarum, rerum tamen Mathematicarum scientia et speculatione multos earum Professores facile superat'.[6]

---

[1] L. Tóth, 'Verancsics Faustus csanádi püspök es emlékiratai V. Pál Pápához a magyar katholikus egyház állapotáról', in *Jahrbuch des Graf Klebelsberg Kuno Instituts für ungarische Geschichtsforschung in Wien* (Budapest 1933), 155–211. Verancsics was also a lexicographer, author of a five-language dictionary published at Venice in 1595 and reissued in Prague in 1605.

[2] Caspar Dornavius, *Felicitas Seculi: hoc est Oratio qua probatur artes liberales et mechanicas nostra aetate cultiores esse, quam multis retro seculis* (Beuthen n.d.), D 2: 'Laudabimusne aliud instrumentum, quod mappam in plano chartaceo, adspiciente eo, qui pedes iter facit, describit? In superiore nempe illius parte vitrum exstet, sub quo tota mappa solitariis punctis notetur; quae non ab acu magnetica perforantur: sed ab orbiculo, sub charta latitante, quae cum alio illi adjuncto, magnes in hanc illamque partem agitet. Invenit hoc opus olim ingeniosissimus Caesar Rudolphus II in cujus Regia . . . thesaurus servabatur selectissimarum rerum, quà naturae miraculo, quà artis divinitate elaboratarum.'

[3] Lomazzo, op. cit. 155.   [4] e.g. Alfons, op. cit. 89 ff.

[5] Kepler, *Gesammelte Werke* xiv, 448; xv, 12; various letters from Ludwig von Dietrichstein in Graz to Kepler: ibid. xv, Nos. 291, 295, 303, 329, 384; Kepler to Anhalt, Prague n.d. [1607]: *Werke* xvi, No. 436.

[6] Johannes Kepler, *De Stella Nova* (Prague 1606), in *Gesammelte Werke* i, 307.

Burgi (1552?–c. 1620) was evidently a many-sided figure (he has a claim to be considered the discoverer of logarithms and he certainly produced mathematical instruments),[1] but he is remembered primarily as a clockmaker, and it is perhaps the clock which offers the central symbol in this whole pursuit of the mechanism. The clock has often been regarded—most recently by Cipolla—as an element in the progressive development of modern technological civilization,[2] but that is surely to oversimplify the case. In the symbolism of Mannerism and some aspects of the Baroque it plays a characteristic role rather as illuminating the fallibility of reason and immediate experience.[3] Time was not yet a taskmaster unquestioningly accepted to be the quantitative standard against which all events should be measured, but a subjective datum whose relation to the world of appearance remained problematic. The passion for clocks we have observed in Rudolf's son Don Giulio; his father was celebrated as a collector of timepieces, which he acquired both by gift and purchase.

The Emperor also employed several clockmakers: Georg Schneeberger, Georg Roll of Augsburg, Martin Schmidt, Christoph Margraf, and above all Burgi.[4] Burgi had worked for many years at the court of the astronomer Landgrave William IV of Hesse-Cassel, then after keeping contact with Rudolf throughout the 1590s he finally took up a post at Prague in 1604 and was still there in 1612.[5] During that time he produced clocks of all kinds, some of which have survived, and their importance is twofold: not only do they embody technical refinements (they were the first ever to allow the measurement of seconds), but they are masterpieces of Mannerist decoration and programming. The greatest of them, the planet-clock now in Vienna, represents the heavens according to both Copernican and Ptolemaic systems and is covered with complicated allusive scenes worked in gold, both mythical and astrological.[6] Burgi's colleague Christoph Margraf (in Prague 1584–c. 1604)

[1] Cf. Levinus Hulsius, *Dritter Tractat der mechanischen Instrumente* (Frankfurt 1604–5), on the proportional circle: 'dieser Zirckel wirdt bey M. Jobst Burgi, so sie selbst macht, und bey mir Levino Hulsio zu kauff gefunden ...'

[2] Carlo M. Cipolla, *Clocks and Culture 1300–1700* (London 1967); Cipolla makes two passing mentions of Burgi.

[3] Cf. Hocke, op. cit. 79 ff.; Angyal, op. cit. 100.

[4] Chytil, *Umění v Praze*, 46.

[5] Riegger, 251; the details (such as are known) of Burgi's life are in C. Alhard von Drach, 'Jost Burgi', *Jahrbuch* xv (1894), 15–45.

[6] H. von Bertele, 'Jost Burgis Beitrag zur Formenentwicklung der Uhren', *Jahrbuch* N.F. 51 (1955), 169–88, esp. 180 f. Johannes Kepler designed a drinking-cup for Friedrich of Württemberg in the 1590s as an epitome of his astronomy (Koestler, op. cit. 268 ff.).

is now established as the inventor of the so-called rolling-ball clock, and he too created several works with characteristic Rudolfine decoration.[1]

The perfection of clockwork could come very near to the striving after perpetual motion, and Rudolf was not behindhand in that popular quest either. He lent support to a number of mysterious figures who claimed to have discovered it.[2] The principal of them were Erasmus Habermel,[3] a man who seems also to have constructed artificial fountains, and the extraordinary Dutchman Cornelius Drebbel, whom Rudolf sought to attract from the court of James I and who became associated with the Emperor's last desperate political ventures.[4] Drebbel's name has since passed into complete obscurity, but he was celebrated in his day as an inventor and the reputation was not unfounded.[5] He had been apprentice to Goltzius as engraver and map-maker in Haarlem, but the lure of machines and automata seems to have been irresistible. Drebbel was widely mistrusted—by Kepler among others[6]—but he actually constructed a whole series of working models, including more than one *perpetuum mobile*. Of course these had their scientific explanation— they were in fact apparently a kind of air-barometer whose motions derived ultimately from changes in atmospheric pressure—but the boundary between the rational and the magical was not clearly defined, especially since some sort of clock mechanism was attached. It hardly comes as a surprise that James entrusted him with preparing spectacular effects for his court masques; nor is it remarkable that Rudolf also employed him as alchemist and he was believed to have the secret of transmutation. Drebbel belongs thoroughly in the spirit of Rudolfine natural science: his two tracts—one on the Elements, a second on the Quintessence—are commonplaces of the old cosmology, inextricably linked with the esoteric tradition and the theory of the philosophical arcanum.[7]

---

[1] Bertele and Neumann, art. cit. 39–98.

[2] e.g. his letter to William of Bavaria, Prague 9 June 1603, asking that one Hans Oberer who 'mir mit underschidlichen inventionen, firnemlich aber den mottum perpetuum betreffendt, dienen wolte' be sent to him. HHSA, Fam. Korr. A. 4. II. This same Oberer had in fact been recommended to Rudolf long before by Wilhelm zu Öttingen: *Jahrbuch* vii (1888), Reg. No. 4602, letter of 29 Jan. 1592.

[3] Lhotsky, *Geschichte der Sammlungen*, i. 275.

[4] On Drebbel: F. M. Jaeger, *Cornelis Drebbel en zijne Tijdgenooten* (Groningen 1922). Drebbel was certainly in Prague by 1610. Cf. Gindely, *Rudolf II*, ii. 313.

[5] Morhof describes him as 'Magister rerum naturalium et artificialium insignis, quique multis magni Arcani Philosophici Possessor fuit habitus': *Polyhistor*, ii. 362, 383.

[6] Kepler to August von Anhalt, the letter cited, above p. 187 n. 5. Anhalt had asked him his opinion of Drebbel, Krossen 10 July 1607 (*Werke*, xvi, No. 435).

[7] *Tractatus Duo: De Natura Elementorum . . . De Quinta Essentia . . . editi curā Joachimi Morsi* (Hamburg 1621). There were various other editions, and most contain also Drebbel's brief dedication of his *perpetuum mobile* to James I. This machine is

Another invention of the time, attributed to Arcimboldo and perhaps to Drebbel also, was a 'perspective lute' which affected to establish a relation between musical tones and colours, allowing the use of some kind of coloured notation.[1] Further links can be found at Rudolf's court between mechanics and music: the organist and composer Hans Leo Hassler for example attracted the Emperor's attention by experimenting with new automatic instruments.[2] The two activities had a deeper common bond: music was also practical, yet offered immediate contact with cosmic forces. There existed throughout the period a whole metaphysical theory along these lines which we cannot enter into here—it emerges most clearly in Kepler's *Harmonices Mundi* of 1619 (a work dedicated to James I). One aspect of it was the doctrine of affects, or aural stimulus, which made music an important part of ceremonial and courtly symbolism, and thus of the 'stagecraft' techniques of Arcimboldo and the rest.[3] An interesting and curious extension of the theory was the use made of music by alchemists, as helping the favourable atmosphere necessary to the work of transmutation. Michael Maier employs a set of primitive canons in one of his books, the *Atalanta Fugiens*.[4]

Music in Prague had been strong since the days of Ferdinand of Tyrol, and it was the occupation of a circle closely linked with the rest of the artists at court—Hans von Aachen married the daughter of Lassus, Philippe de Monte was a friend of Clusius, Dodoens, the poetess Westonia, and the painter Pieter Stevens[5]—yet not separated from its Bohemian background. The Habsburg *Hofkapelle* formed the largest of a number of aristocratic chapels (next to it came that of the Rožmberks), employing by the end of the sixteenth century more than sixty instrumentalists and cantors.[6] They included a proportion of local

described, illustrated, and praised by Thomas Tymme in his *Dialogue Philosophicall Wherein Nature's Secret Closet is Opened* . . . (London 1612), 60–3.

[1] See the note by Lionello Levi, based on Comanini, in Geiger, op. cit. 89–94.

[2] *Musik in Geschichte und Gegenwart* (hereafter *MGG*) v (1956), 1805 f.; *Jahrbuch* xix (1898), Reg. No. 16211; cf. Harlas, op. cit. 60.

[3] Cf. D. P. Walker, 'Musical Humanism in the Sixteenth Century and early Seventeenth Century', *The Music Review* ii (1941), 1–13, 111–21, 220–7, 288–308, iii (1942), 55–71, esp. 9: 'For Baïf, Tyard, Galilei or Mersenne this [the linking of words and music] was only the first step towards the recreation of an art which should arouse and control passions, inculcate and preserve virtue, even cure disease and ensure the stability of the state'; idem, 'Kepler's Celestial Music', *JWCI* 30 (1967), 228–50; and below, p. 271.

[4] Some examples are illustrated in J. Read, *Prelude to Chemistry* (London 1936), 281–8. The Rožmberk alchemist Bavor Rodovský was also a musician: Zíbrt, *BČH*, iii, No. 9604.   [5] Doorslaer, *Philippe de Monte*, 23 ff. and App. LII.

[6] The fullest lists of personnel are given by A. Smijers, 'Die kaiserliche Hofmusikkapelle von 1543–1619', *Studien zur Musikwissenschaft* vi (1919), 139 ff., supplementing the information in L. von Köchel, *Die kaiserliche Hof-Musikkapelle in Wien von 1543–1867* (Vienna 1869), who anyway ignores the fact that Rudolf's chapel was in Prague.

musicians, as well as those attracted from abroad: Netherlanders inevitably, like de Monte, Karl Luython, and Jacob de Kerle, but also Frenchmen like the poet-composer Jacques Regnart and Germans like the organist Valerian Otto and the Protestant Hassler brothers, Hans Leo (1564–1612) and Jakob (1569–1622).[1] Rudolf's senior musician was de Monte (1521–1603), who had originally been summoned by Maximilian II in 1568 and was one of the best-known polyphonists of the day. The dedications of his large *œuvre* include some of the leading court figures— Rudolf himself, Rumpf, Kurz, Medek; they also reveal his interest in Pythagorean theories of music.[2] Another established personality was the Spanish monk Mattheo Flecha (1530?–1604) who likewise came to the *Hofkapelle* in the 1560s, and was created titular abbot of Tihany in Hungary by Rudolf before returning to Catalonia in 1599. Flecha published various works—both music and poetry—with the printer George Nigrin in Prague, as did Jacobus Gallus or Handl (1550–91), a South Slav composer of some significance who appeared in Bohemia during the 1570s and later joined the Emperor's retinue.[3]

The most important Czech representative of this brand of courtly polyphony was a noble whose music has only recently been rediscovered, Kryštof Harant of Polžice (1564–1621). Harant was an outstanding figure of the time: the son of an unassuming Catholic country squire (*rytíř*) loyal to the Habsburgs, he received his education at the court of Archduke Ferdinand in Innsbruck under the historian van Roo and the composers Utendal and Regnart.[4] After extensive travels he became one of Rudolf's retainers—his official position from 1601 was chamberlain—winning the complete trust of the Emperor, who ennobled him and treated him as an intimate confidant.[5] Harant was a man of erudition,

Cf. G. L. Pazaurek, 'Beiträge zur Geschichte der Musik in Böhmen', *MVGDB* xxxi (1893), 280–93. On the Rožmberks: F. Mareš, 'Rožmberská kapela', *ČČM* lxviii (1894), 209–34.

[1] Many archival details were collected by Smijers, loc. cit. and *Studien zur Musikwissenschaft* vii (1920), 102–42, viii (1921), 176–206. Fullest musicological information is in *MGG* s.vv.

[2] Doorslaer, op. cit., esp. Apps. IV, VII, VIII, XIV, XVII, XVIII.

[3] Smijers, art. cit. (1920), 135 f.; *MGG* iv (1955), 296–9; Fleischman (1594), fo. k ii^r. Flecha would repay some further study: he travelled as chaplain to the Empress Maria, then became confessor to the Archduchess Elizabeth (widow of Charles IX of France), on whose death he issued a volume of verse: *Obra nuevamente echa . . . de la muerte y miseria humana . . .* (Prague 1593). On Gallus see *MGG* iv. 1329–34.

[4] Z. Nejedlý, *Kryštof Harant z Polžic* (Prague 1921), 13 ff. On his music cf. R. Quoika in *Die Musikforschung* vii (1954), 414–29, and *Československý hudební slovník* i (Prague 1963), 403 f.

[5] Alidosi observes that 'Arant' is one of the three persons who attend the Emperor when he dines (op. cit. 6 and 8). Harant was still a *Kämmerer* in 1612 (Riegger, 243).

an artist and poet, and a musician, both composer and performer. His political career shows similarities with that of Wacker, but it was to end very differently, since Harant left the Habsburg service, apparently after a visit to Spain in 1615, and became a leader of the Protestants during the revolt; he was one of those executed in 1621 as part of the reprisals which followed. Harant's religious position has never been clear.[1] He was presumably a Protestant at the end of his life (Comenius regards him as a typical martyr for the cause),[2] but his family and background were Catholic and there are strong Catholic overtones in his religious music, while the reports of his travels suggest an oecumenical belief in the essential unity of all religions. Thus he appears a good example of the uncommitted intellectual, to whom the atmosphere at Rudolf's court was congenial but the pro-Spanish and pro-Papal attitudes of his successors were not.

With the death of Rudolf his musical circle dispersed. The same is largely true of the many craftsmen and artists in the applied fields. Here lay the closest links between Rudolfine masters and local developments, and the Mannerism of the former found a more lasting domestic echo than elsewhere.[3] Besides the work of goldsmiths and silversmiths there were major achievements in the realm of glass-cutting and glyptics, and all owed much to the ready local supplies of raw materials. The records show a large number of men, their names sometimes Czech, sometimes German, sometimes Italian, whose business was to search for stones, gems, and precious metals, or to act as middlemen in the trade both within the borders of Bohemia and beyond. One such was Peter Schiebel, who received a patent in 1602 'to look for precious stones in the regions of Moravia, Silesia, and Glatz'; another was Philip Holbein, who had a pass 'zu hiereinführung in Behem vor die Kay: Maitt: allerley schöne sachen von Edelgestain, Goldt: und Silberwerck';[4] others were both prospectors, buyers, and cutters, like Matthias Krätz, a leading member of the *atelier*.[5] The Hasslers and Ferdinand Matthioli were likewise involved in the mineral trade.[6] It is equally clear that these undertakings proceeded at the direct instigation of the Emperor himself, forming part of his general interest in metals, minerals, and their exploitation which found expression too in alchemy.

[1] For this see J. B. Čapek, 'Osobnost a dílo Krištofa Haranta', in *Zprávy Bertrámky* 1964, 1–8, which inclines towards the Protestant side.

[2] Comenius, *Historie o Protivenstvích*, 133 f.

[3] Chytil, *Umění*, 48 ff.; *Vlastivěda*, 111–13.

[4] SÚA, KK 1794 (Patente und Mandata 1600–22).

[5] On Krätz and others see Lhotsky, *Geschichte der Sammlungen*, i. 248 ff.; and cf. *Jahrbuch* vii (1888), Reg. Nos. 4650, 4658, 4667–8, 4671, 4674, 4679.

[6] *H. L. Hassler, Leben und Werk* (Ausstellung Nürnberg–Augsburg 1964).

The finest workers in stone were the Milanese, and Rudolf began by sending Bohemian jewels to be cut there by the families of Masnago, Sarachi, and Miseroni.[1] The last-named he attracted to Prague; its leading members Ottavio (in Prague 1588–1624) and his son Dionysio brought off triumphs of Mannerist virtuosity in semi-precious stones and rock-crystal, as well as carrying out Imperial commissions for series of portraits and the like. Drinking vessels with 'naturalistic' ornamentation apparently formed one of their specialities. The family became established in the city—Miseronis were hereditary keepers of the Imperial treasury during the seventeenth century—and closely attached to the Habsburg court.[2] But this genre did not advance after the death of Rudolf. Enthusiasm turned rather to another offshoot of the art of the court, the cutting of glass, and Sandrart was correct to stress Rudolf's part in the revival of this craft: 'So ist auch bey höchst-gedachten Käysers *Rudolphi* Regierung, die Kunst des Glasschneidens wieder von neuem erfunden, und an den Tag gebracht worden, und haben Ihre Majestat den *Authorn* und Erfindern Caspar Lehmann stattlich *recompensirt*.'[3] Lehmann, who came to Prague in 1603 and was a great friend of Aachen and Vianen, in fact received a privilege for glass-cutting in 1609; this monopoly position then passed to his pupil Georg Schwanhardt and the latter's family.[4]

I have dwelt on the interrelations between the international and the local in the courtly society of Prague, partly because to do otherwise would suggest an unreal dichotomy, partly because the characteristics of Czech cultural development throw important light on the problem of Mannerism we have been considering. The crucial question in interpreting the period from an art-historical standpoint is the demarcation drawn between late Mannerism and the origins of the Baroque. Whatever the Baroque may have signified in general, in Bohemia it was always positively associated with the strivings of the Counter-Reformation, and this has meant that it has popularly been regarded as beginning only after 1620.[5] Since, however, the revival of Catholic sentiment can be dated at least twenty years earlier, there is equally clear evidence of the Baroque before the White Mountain in some of the pompous and ostentatious art of orthodox Catholic patrons, as in the church of

---

[1] Kris, *Steinschneidekunst*, 84 ff., 104 n., 111 ff., 138.

[2] O. J. Blažíček and L. Neubert, *Škréta's family portrait of Dionysio Miseroni* (London 1964), an introduction to the fine painting of Miseroni and his family by Škréta dating from the 1650s; B. Bukovinská, 'Anmerkungen zur Persönlichkeit Ottavio Miseronis', *Umění* xviii (1970), 185–98; H. Klapsia, 'Dionysio Miseroni', *Jahrbuch* N.F. xiii (1944), 301–58.

[3] Sandrart, 345.   [4] Ibid. 346; *Barock in Böhmen*, 278 f.

[5] Cf. typically V.-L. Tapié, *The Age of Grandeur* (Eng. trans., London 1960), 197 ff.

St. James in the Old Town, or the rebuilding of Litomyšl for Maria Manriquez de Lara, or the poetry of the Jesuits,[1] or perhaps the Matthias gateway in the royal castle.[2] Against this the court art of Rudolf or Peter Vok Rožmberk remained self-conscious, involved, and allusive. We can find survivals of it well beyond 1612: the Miseroni family, the work of Adriaen de Vries and the alchemist G. B. Pieroni for Wallenstein in the 1620s,[3] the provincial Mannerism of Bartholomaeus Strobel, or Matouš Radouš and his school.[4]

The situation was, however, not simply a matter of parallel developments, for the one epithet 'Baroque' covers a complex set of phenomena whose relation to what had gone before was by no means exclusively negative. Just as some elements of intellectual Humanism remained even in such a Baroque hero as Zdeněk Lobkovic or a militant priest like Pontanus, so the artistic forms which dominated Bohemia after 1620 subsumed aspects of the Mannerist heritage of Rudolf's court. This appears evident not only in individual artists,[5] but in aspects of iconography and decoration, even of style. There are, for example, buildings dating from the seventeenth and eighteenth centuries in a consciously Gothic idiom;[6] there are cases of symbolism (like the Sternberg castle of Troya) very similar to the apotheoses of Rudolf;[7] there are connections between late Renaissance mysticism and the cult of saints and pilgrimage.[8]

---

[1] Vašica, op. cit. 13 f. and *passim*; Bitnar, op. cit. 183 ff. and *passim*.

[2] This portal, after Scamozzi, completed in 1615, can be interpreted either as Renaissance survival or as proto-Baroque. The latter conveys better its spirit, since it marked the withdrawal of the Habsburg House from direct habitation of the Hrad, and with it one of the key postulates for the revolt of 1618.

[3] Z. Wirth, 'Valdštejn a současné umění', in *Doba bělohorská a Albrecht z Valdštejna*, 173–92. Wallenstein also had plans for an 'ideal' city, elaborated and landscaped in his North Bohemian capital of Jičín (ibid. 187 ff.). That his architect and designer Pieroni was also an alchemist appears from the latter's conversations with Matthias von Brandau: M. E. von Brandau, *Warhaffte Beschreibung von der Universal-Medicin*, 18. Pieroni equally enjoyed the friendship of Kepler and Galileo (e.g. Galileo, *Opere* (Florence 1890–1909) xiii, 333–4; xiv, 61–2, 323–4; xvi, 188–90, 300 ff., etc.).

[4] J. Neumann, *Malířství XVII století v Čechách* (Prague 1951), 67–9; and idem, *Kleine Beiträge . . .*, 154 ff.

[5] The greatest Czech seventeenth-century painter, Karel Škréta, was the son of a loyal servant of the Habsburgs—his father was one of Rudolf's book-keepers, whose salary was never properly paid (there was a debt still owing in 1654: SÚA, Sig. 2377, fo. 98ʳ)—and owed his early inspiration to court models. See Pešina, art. cit. 291; J. Neumann, 'K italským začátkům Karla Škréty', *Umění* iii (1955), 308–29.

[6] See Angyal, op. cit. 19 ff. The leading architect in this style was Santini-Aichel; cf. Knox, op. cit. 131–41.

[7] *Barock in Böhmen*, 197 f.

[8] The two were reassociated early in the seventeenth century: Hiesserle, before leaving on his journey to Western Europe in 1607, visited the holy cell of Svatý Jan pod Skalou near Prague, and relates how many others were doing the same (Raiss Buch fo. 40ᵛ). Cf. the complex symbolism of the Marian cult: Angyal, op. cit. 26 ff.

If this be allowed, then the full nature of the Bohemian Baroque lay neither in a pure identification with aristocratic Catholicism on the model of Tapié, nor—as J. Neumann has argued—in the attempts of the oppressed classes to represent their ideology of social 'realism'.[1] Its origins were in fact closely intertwined with the spiritual and mystical forces so dear to Rudolf. Yet the latter had ultimately a quite different orthodoxy, to which we must now turn: they acknowledged the orthodoxy of a magical universe, and expressed it in their obsession with the occult.

[1] Tapié, op. cit. *passim*; Neumann, *Malířství*, esp. 13–22.

6. Rudolf and the Occult Arts

'His Majesty is interested only in wizards, alchymists, kabbalists and the like, sparing no expense to find all kinds of treasures, learn secrets and use scandalous ways of harming his enemies . . . He also has a whole library of magic books. He strives all the time to eliminate God completely so that he may in future serve a different master.'

PROPOSITION OF THE ARCHDUKES IN VIENNA (1606)

A SENSE of secrecy and mystery surrounded all Rudolf's private contacts in his fastness on the castle hill of Prague. One Venetian observer summed it up thus: 'He delights in hearing secrets about things both natural and artificial, and whoever is able to deal in such matters will always find the ear of the Emperor ready.'[1] We have already noticed Rudolf's increasing withdrawal from the world around him, as well as the marked unwillingness to share his collection with outsiders. But this tendency to stand at a distance from practical affairs was not simply a trait of the Emperor's character; it also formed an integral part of his mentality.

The occult striving was in essence an attempt to penetrate beyond the world of experience to the reality which underlay it, and as such it paralleled or overlapped with the artistic use of symbol and emblem. At the same time it belonged in a central way to the whole apprehension of nature during Rudolf's age, for the 'natural philosophers' of the period were men who studied the forces at work in the world around them, not as discretely observed patterns of cause and effect, but as motive spirits acting through a divine scheme of correspondences. Thus their experiments, alchemical and physical, far from following any process of free induction, were predicated on a complete aprioristic scheme of things. Their practical activity was coupled with some higher insight into the laws which governed it, and both involved a denial of the merely discursive reason. This pursuit of practical demonstration guided by intuition is fundamental to the philosophy of Paracelsus which was so

[1] Contarini in Albéri, *Relazioni*, 245.

vastly influential in the later sixteenth century.[1] It also provides a key to other famous writers on the mysteries of nature: Agrippa, Cardanus, above all the Neapolitan J. B. Porta, the most voluminous and perhaps the most widely read of them all. Porta, a friend of the young Campanella, presided over a distinct esoteric circle—the self-styled *Accademia Curiosorum Hominum*—whose members engaged in the speculations of the time and were enthusiastic collectors.[2] In 1597 we learn that Porta himself was working on the judicial astrology of Ptolemy, his brother on the quadrature of the circle.[3] It is hardly surprising that Rudolf became interested and sought more than once to attract Porta to Prague.[4]

The object of such a philosophy was not only to describe the hidden forces of nature but also to control them, since the initiate who understood their powers could also apply his knowledge.[5] This pursuit was magic, yet—as its exponents never ceased explaining—the magic was 'natural' and not 'black', for the inspiration which made it possible was divine, not diabolical. Occult undertakings were inseparable from a religious standpoint close to the mysticism of some sixteenth-century heterodoxy, and the occult rejection of a rational approach to the world often stood in alliance with a spiritual rejection of both brands of established religion: the Protestant and the Roman Catholic. That held especially true in the German lands, where the Renaissance magical tradition from Trithemius, Agrippa, and Paracelsus was steeped in Neoplatonism and intimately linked with the mystical experience of men like Valentine Weigel.[6] Common to both was the ideal of a 'sacred harmony', as the title of a Prague manuscript of 1598 proclaims.[7]

---

[1] Cf. the argument of the important article by Walter Pagel, 'Religious motives in the medical biology of the seventeenth century', *Bulletin of the Institute of the History of Medicine*, iii. 4 (1935), 97–128, 213–31, 265–312.

[2] Blanchet, *Campanella*, 22; M. Ornstein, *The Role of Scientific Societies in the Seventeenth Century* (new edn. London 1963), 73 f. Porta's group was also called the *Academia Secretorum Naturae*.

[3] Hessels, No. 309 (letter from Ortelius's nephew, 18 Oct. 1597).

[4] D'Addio, op. cit. 57. Rudolf's miniaturist Hoefnagel acted as a go-between for Porta and Ortelius: Hessels, No. 147.

[5] 'I due temi: potenza dominatrice delle forze della natura e potenza reformatrice degli uomini attraverso il sapere, convergono sotto il segno della magia e dell'astrologia. Nel punto indicato dagli astri come momento di una grande crisi, l'uomo sapiente sposa habilmente le forze, le combina per ottenere l'opera voluta.' E. Garin, *Medioevo e Rinascimento*, 176.

[6] W. E. Peuckert, *Pansophie*, esp. 127 ff. on Agrippa, 185 ff. on Paracelsus, 290–310 on Weigel. Weigel's works were not published until the seventeenth century, but they circulated widely in manuscript. A collection of his sermons for instance survives in Prague: Nat. Mus., MS. XIII G 13; they were written down during the years 1574–88.

[7] APH, MS. F 23/1–2.

Rudolf's own religion clearly had a markedly spiritist hue. This revealed itself in a negative way in his belief that he was bewitched, a prey to the forces of evil: 'I know that I am dead and damned; I am a man possessed by the devil.'[1] His concern, however, also appeared in a more active form. It is known that he sought works on Christian mysticism: he ordered a copy to be made of the *Liber de laudibus sanctae crucis* by Hrabanus Maurus from the Fulda manuscript, and his interest in the remarkable *Codex Giganteus*—a vast scriptural, chronological, and scientific compilation—led him to secure it for his collection.[2] Both these works were borrowed from monasteries and seem (characteristically) never to have been returned. The same is true of a third manuscript, the most precious among all those acquired by the Emperor, the so-called *Codex Argenteus* which contained Bishop Ulfilas's Gothic translation of the Gospels.[3] It is an intriguing question whether Rudolf sought this text for its philological, or purely its exotic and mystificatory value. His library certainly included the Hermetic *Pymander* in its Cracow edition of 1585 by the Minorite friar Hannibal Rosseli.[4] At the other end of the scale he was full of superstition: he possessed the medieval catch-all of credulity, the *Picatrix*, vade-mecum of the necromancers—it was used by one of his underlings, allegedly at the Imperial behest, to cast an evil spell on Matthias.[5] Moreover a little remains (it is admittedly very little) of a collection of narrowly magical items: mandrake roots in the form of homunculi, a bell to summon the spirits, and so forth.[6]

Rudolf's occultism is thus difficult to study. On the one hand it belonged to a whole late-Renaissance tradition whose frame of reference was a complete cosmology, and it is impossible to isolate particular aspects of that tradition without falsely suggesting discontinuities in the scheme of relations which sustained it. On the other hand the material evidence

[1] Nuncios/Ferreri, Prague 4 Apr. 1605, quoting a remark from Rudolf to Philipp Lang. Ferreri presumably had it on hearsay, but such outbursts were often attributed to the Emperor.

[2] J. von Schlosser, 'Eine Fulder Miniaturhandschrift der k.k. Hofbibliothek', *Jahrbuch* xiii (1892), esp. 29 f.; the *Liber de laudibus* is full of number mysticism and other symbolism. Dudík, *Forschungen*, 207-35; the *Codex Giganteus* was brought from the Bohemian monastery of Broumov.

[3] Dudík, *Forschungen*, 315-17; this treasure came from the Abbey of Werden in the Rhineland. Cf. O. von Friesen and A. Grape, *Om Codex Argenteus, dess tid, hem och öden* (Uppsala 1928), 131 ff.

[4] Walde, *Litterära krigsbyten*, 322.

[5] On the *Picatrix*: *Briefe und Akten*, ix, No. 218. Cf. ÖN, MS. 5580, fo. 49ʳ.

[6] G. von Schwarzenfeld, 'Magica aus der Zeit Rudolfs II', *Antaios* iv (1963), 478-81, and *Rudolf II*, 84. As Kurz rightly stresses (*Umělecké vztahy*, 474) there is little surviving evidence for Rudolf's court of this purely primitive superstition; little, to put it in other words, which could not be backed by some shade of serious contemporary opinion.

of his contacts is slight and the records in surviving correspondence are usually abrupt, mysterious, and uninformative. We may best approach the subject by turning to a body of men famous both among contemporaries and posterity, the Rudolfine alchemists.[1]

Alchemy was the greatest passion of the age in Central Europe. Like the pursuit of magic in general it embraced at one and the same time a direct attitude to nature—the adept was the classic hopeful experimenter —and a metaphysical speculation which rested on total assumptions about the secret powers and interactions of substances. 'Alchimia', wrote Hoghelande, a worker well known in Prague, 'sedem sibi constituerit in capacitate intellectus et in demonstratione experimentali';[2] the divinely-illuminated intellect was setting itself to work upon divinely-ordained nature. This dual justification emerges clearly in the central process of the alchemists, the *magnum opus* of transmutation: for transmutation could either be explained as a deduction from the principle of a uniform, undifferentiated matter which took the quality of one substance or another depending on the 'spirit' with which it was informed, or inferred from the practical evidence of metallurgy like smelting of ores and decomposition.

The search for the stone was of course an ancient pastime, but it reached a climax in the half century after 1570. Before that time the characteristic symbolic positions of the late Renaissance had not yet been arrived at; after it came a parting of the ways between the practical and spiritual aspects of alchemy which paralleled the Galilean revolution in physical science. One main ingredient in the distinctive quality of the period was the contribution of the Paracelsans. Paracelsus himself had died in 1541 but greater interest in his blend of mystic philosophy with practical medicine and chemistry, which drew on alchemical, astrological, and Neoplatonic sources, came with the renewed publication of his work by a group of German disciples in the 1560s and 1570s: Bodenstein, Toxites, Suchten, and the precursor of Boehme, Gerhard Dorn.[3] The followers of Paracelsus played 'out a role—nowadays more justly appreciated—in the history of experimental science, especially in the realm of pharmaceutics; but their whole activity rested on the view that the universe itself formed a body whose alterations were ultimately

[1] The adventures of alchemists at the Prague court appear in all the eighteenth- and nineteenth-century histories of the subject—Murr, Lenglet du Fresnoy, Schmieder, etc. For a later view see K. Kiesewetter, *Geschichte des Occultismus* ii (Leipzig 1895), 93–102.

[2] *De Alchemiae Difficultatibus Theobaldi de Hoghelande Mittelburgensis Liber* (Cologne 1594), A 4ᵛ.

[3] For these men see Peuckert, op. cit. 260–9, 285–9; cf. Thorndike, op. cit. v, Ch. XXIX.

chemical in character. They were positive reformers over a wide range of matters, but in the name of an occult world-harmony.[1] The influence of this iatrochemistry (as the Paracelsan teaching came to be called) bulked large in Bohemia, both through the authentic writings of the master and through others which were attributed to him. His works were translated into Czech, and Paracelsan learning is clear in many who lived at Prague or who had contacts there: the Rulands, Maier, Croll, Thurneysser, Khunrath, Johann Hartmann, Sinapius, Daniel Sennert of Breslau. Indeed the greatest collector of Paracelsan manuscripts was a Silesian, Johann Montanus of Strigau, and the first full published edition of the texts (Basle 1589–90) rested heavily on Silesian sources.[2]

Alchemy then was an inference from a vitalistic cosmology, from doctrines of influences, harmonies, signatures, and the rest, and this is frequently made explicit in its literature. 'De Signatura; von der Geburt und Beziehung aller Wesen,' proclaims one manuscript: 'Wie alle Wesen aus einem einigen mysterio erstanden . . . und wie guttes in böses und böses in guttes verwandelt werde.'[3] Equally such writers insisted on the religious content of their art, even to the extent of apparent blasphemy. One of the texts best known to the sixteenth-century initiate was the 'alchemical mass' written by Nicholas Melchior of Szeben in Transylvania (Melchior Cibiniensis) which had allegedly been presented to his patron Ladislas II Jagellon, King of Bohemia and Hungary; we find this reproduced—both in print and manuscript—by several writers associated with Prague, among them Benedikt Figulus, Barnaud, Rodovský, and Maier.[4] The extensive work of Karl Jung on the symbols used by the alchemists led him to postulate that the pursuit of the philosophers' stone was an unconscious quest for the divine archetype which mirrored the striving, on a conscious plane, of revealed religion.[5]

[1] Cf. A. G. Debus, *The Chemical Dream of the Renaissance* (Cambridge 1968).

[2] Sudhoff, *Versuch* i, Nos. 48, 83, 89, 151, 170, 182, 216–25 and a; ii, Nos. 83–5 and 129; below, p. 281 n. 5. Cf. Kiesewetter, *Geschichte des Occultismus* i (Leipzig 1909), 127–42; Thorndike, op. cit. vii, Ch. VII, 203–17.

[3] Nostitz MS. c 2. Chapter 1 begins: 'Auss der Signatur kan man alles erkennen. den der geist der in der Signatur lieget, offenbaret sich aus der Essentz, durch das principium . . . durch das Wort, wird er kundbar: und kan seines gleichen geist in einem andern menschen erwäcken, das diese Signatur im andern auch offenbar wird, und wird also ein Wille, ein geist, ein Verstand . . .'

[4] Benedictus Figulus, *Thesaurinella Olympica aurea tripartita* . . . (Frankfurt n.d. [1608]), a work dedicated to Rudolf II; Nicolas Barnaud, *Commentariolum in Aenigmaticum quoddam Epitaphium* . . . (Leiden 1597), 37 ff.; Nat. Mus., MS. III G 12: 'Msse o kamene ffilo. od knieze Mikulasse sloziena'; M. Maier, *Symbola Aureae Mensae Duodecim Nationum* (Frankfurt 1617) includes Melchior in his gallery of celebrated alchemists. Cf. L. Szathmáry, *Magyar alkémisták* (Budapest 1928), 250 ff.

[5] C. G. Jung, *Psychologie und Alchemie* (2nd edn. Zurich 1952), 41: 'Die Alchemie

Whatever the fuller psychological and metaphysical implications of his conclusion, it offers a profound insight into the mentality of the age of Jakob Boehme.

The alchemists sought not only the regeneration of metals through the stone, but also the moral and spiritual rebirth of mankind. In this sense alchemy is inseparable from the conceptual framework of Boehme's 'system' (which essentially describes a *process* of realization, paralleling the 'labyrinthine' pursuit of truth through a protracted work of transmutation)[1] as it is inseparable from the Rosicrucian writings or the spiritualistic reform of John Dee. It could be embodied in the meaningful symbol or emblem—indeed the mystic message of the alchemist might be communicated entirely through a real symbolism, as is shown by the works of Maier or the beautiful emblem-book of a late representative of Rudolfine Prague, Daniel Stoltzius von Stolzenberg, whose title betrays at least some of its purpose: 'A Chemical Pleasure-Garden, decorated with handsome figures cut in copper, illustrated with poetic paintings and explanations, so that it may not only serve to refresh the eyes and the spirit but arouse at the same time a very deep contemplation of natural things . . .'[2]

Of course these last remarks present an extreme case for alchemy: an interpretation of what the quest involved and how it can be evaluated in the context of Mannerist symbolism. In fact the normal practitioner was an elusive figure, who committed few of his thoughts to paper and has left little documented trace of his existence. Alchemical tracts were typically very standardized, handwritten, often anonymous, highly allusive and secretive, composed by men who wandered through Europe (they regularly earned the name 'cosmopolitan') either asserting their

nämlich bildet etwas wie eine Unterströmung zu dem die Oberfläche beherrschenden Christentum. Sie verhält sich zu diesem wie ein Traum zum Bewusstsein, und wie dieser die Konflikte des Bewusstseins kompensiert, so bestrebt sich jene, die Lücken, welche die Gegensatzspannung des Christentums offengelassen hat, auszufüllen.'

[1] For the *magnum opus* as a process cf. Read, op. cit. 130 ff.

[2] '*Chymisches Lustgärtlein Mit schönen in Kupffer geschnittenen Figuren gezieret, auch mit Poetischen Gemälden illustrirt und erleutert. Also dass es nicht allein Augen und Gemüt erquicket, sondern zugleich eine sehr tieffe Betrachtung der natürlichen dinge erwecket . . . Beschrieben von M. Daniele Stoltzio de Stoltzenberg Boh. der Medicin Candidato.*' This work, which was published by Jennis in Frankfurt in 1624 and employs some plates derived from Maier, has a preface by another Bohemian, Daniel Meissner of Komotau (Chomutov). There is a modern facsimile edition (by F. Weinhardt, Darmstadt 1964). Very little is known about Stoltzius, though he published an *Oratio de bellorum ex astris praedicatione* in Prague in 1618. He apparently studied and practised alchemy in England during the early 1620s and produced other books on the subject: see V. Krůta in *Acta Comeniana* 17 (1958), 127 f. Later he worked as a doctor in Danzig and had some contact with Comenius in the 1630s (cf. M. Blekastad, *Comenius* (Oslo 1969), 267 f.).

claims to the sympathetic hearer or defending themselves against their opponents as representatives of the 'genuine' traditions of the art.

This difficulty hinders any account of the Prague alchemists under Rudolf. From their day to ours the subject has been obscured by a cloud of unsubstantiated hearsay, reproduced more or less mechanically by a succession of historians. Much of it was widely believed at the time, or very soon afterwards, while other stories seem to have been embellished at a later period.[1] In their attempts to interpret this extraordinary farrago of received information about the Englishmen Dee and Kelley, the Pole Sędiwoj, the Italian Bragadino, the German Güstenhofer, and the rest some modern writers have been led to accept most of the facts and criticize the mentality (the most entertaining nonsense in that direction came from an American),[2] some to essay a different explanation of the facts (Svátek saw it in Rudolf's desperate need for gold to fill his empty coffers),[3] others still to reconsider the facts themselves. From the latter standpoint a Czech historian, Otakar Zachar, adopted the most significant approach: he concluded that Rudolf's contacts with adepts were much fewer than had been imagined, and that most of those with whom the Emperor did deal were not real alchemists at all.[4] These were valuable correctives, but Zachar's positivistic, rational view carried him too far; he was for instance mistaken, as we shall see, in regarding Dee as a political agent of Elizabeth I.[5] He erred too in defining 'alchemy' so narrowly that he reduced the pursuit of it to a collection of charlatans whose activity in Prague, even their very existence, remained unproven.

We are not concerned here with charlatans, those timeless figures who had no interest in the work of transmutation beyond hope of financial gain. Some of the most notorious personalities of the time may have fallen into this class, like the 'Count Bragadino' who enjoyed a meteoric career in Venice at the end of the 1580s, then reappeared in South Germany and perhaps visited Prague,[6] while several of the men who

[1] A number first appeared in print with D. G. Morhof, *De metallorum transmutatione ad Joelum Langelottum Epistola* (Hamburg 1673). Some survive even in Schwarzenfeld, *Rudolf II*—for instance the claim that Rudolf patronized 'about 200 alchemists', many of them from Venice (p. 70).

[2] H. C. Bolton, *The Follies of Science at the Court of Rudolf II* (Milwaukee 1904): 'It is evident from the events recorded in this and in preceding chapters that in the time of Rudolf's reign belief in "the subtill Science of Holy Alkemy" [*sic*] was practically universal among all classes of people' (p. 129).

[3] J. Svátek, *Culturhistorische Bilder*, 63 ff.

[4] O. Zachar, 'Rudolf II a alchymisté', *ČČM* 86 (1912), 417–24; 87 (1913), 148–55, 243–57.   [5] Ibid. 154 f.

[6] The affair of Bragadino, who was at length put to death by the Duke of Bavaria in 1591, is exhaustively analysed from all available sources by I. Striedinger, *Der Goldmacher Marco Bragadino* (Munich 1923). There is no record that the 'count' ever

definitely sought employment with Rudolf and Vilém Rožmberk appear to have been mere adventurers. Examples are the brothers Antonelli, whose tenure of the Imperial favour in 1604 was certainly startling, but also startlingly brief.[1] Nor is this the place to enter into the complexities of the ephemeral alchemical literature to be found in Bohemian archives, which is indeed more heavily concentrated during the years around 1600, both in manuscripts and printed texts, but makes an equally timeless appeal to the authority of Geber, Villanova, Rupescissa, etc., or the writings spuriously attributed to Aquinas, Lull, Albertus Magnus, and various kings and emperors.[2]

Behind the legends and against the background of impostors and simpletons there were at Rudolf's court significant representatives of alchemy in its widest sense, and several of them lived as members of the Emperor's permanent establishment in the capacity of court physician (*Leibarzt*). The relations between the sovereign and his doctors cannot now be properly reconstructed; it is not even clear how many persons held this official position at any one time, while some evidently wielded a much greater influence than others. Likewise we cannot say for certain how far they formed a conscious, closed circle, but it seems probable that there was a tendency in that direction: the popular imagination considered them an élite, and that accords well both with the academic mentality of the age and the esoteric character of alchemical and occult activities.[3]

The roll of Rudolf's physicians begins with the erudite Crato, whose position we have already examined, and the link with Breslau was retained on his retirement by Peter Monau, brother of Jakob, whom Crato recommended to the post in 1580.[4] Others inherited from Maximilian II were the learned Platonist Julius Alexandrinus, Dodoens the botanist, Hájek the astronomer, and Bartholomew Guarinoni.[5] Hájek

visited Bohemia, though his portrait was certainly painted by the later Imperial artist Hans von Aachen (ibid. 90 f.).

[1] Nuncios/Ferreri, Prague 26 July 1604.

[2] It is interesting that the alchemists, like the Ramists and some natural philosophers, frequently represented themselves as attempting to restore the 'true' Aristotle whose teaching had become distorted. But their 'Aristotle' was a mystic sage, the author of the *Secret of Secrets* and the counsellor of Alexander the Great. Cf. below, p. 254.

[3] Hippolytus Guarinoni speaks of a Prague medical academy in the work mentioned below (p. 204 n. 6), *passim*. Cf. the fantasies of Bolton, op. cit. 108 ff.

[4] Gillet, op. cit. ii. 215. Peter Monau, who died young in 1588, was another Silesian Humanist; he has an entry in Jakob's *Symbola*, 25 f. A number of his letters were included by Scholtzius in his edition of Crato's *Consiliorum et Epistolarum Medicinalium Libri*.

[5] On Alexandrinus see Khautz, *Versuch einer Geschichte . . .*, 204–28; he died in 1590, apparently still in the Habsburg service. Dodoens and Guarinoni are mentioned in the *Hofstaat* of 1576 (Goehlart, art. cit.). Hájek's links with the dynasty stretched

may well have acted as a senior alchemical adviser to Rudolf (the legend has it so);[1] certainly he was favoured by the Emperor (being ennobled in 1595)[2] and his house was used for the work, as several witnesses relate.[3] Guarinoni (1534–1616), by origin a Veronese, remained in Prague until at least 1604, though he seems to have become increasingly jealous of his fellow-countryman Dr. Octavian Rovereto, and by 1607 the latter was firmly installed as Rudolf's favourite.[4] He is not to be confused with another member of the family, Christopher Guarinoni, a medical and philosophical author who was apparently also in Bohemia at some stage during these years.[5] Hippolytus Guarinoni (1571–1654), the son of Bartholomew, was brought up in Prague and educated with the Jesuits there; he produced a massive medico-philosophical tome which, while including a nominal attack on alchemy, in fact only inveighs against the debased science and irreligion of the quacks. The work is full of fantasies, spirits, and miracles, and its central message is a chiliastic appeal for the moral regeneration of mankind.[6]

Another leading family of doctors in the service of Rudolf were the Rulands, father and son—both were christened Martin, which makes separation of them extremely difficult. The family had Bavarian origins,

back to his collaboration with Ferdinand I, but his official position is difficult to determine. The same holds true for later medical men attached to the Carolinum, like Jessenius and Adam Huber von Riesenpach.

[1] e.g. Svátek, op. cit. 66.

[2] A. Bauer, *Die Adelsdocumente österreichischer Alchymisten* (Vienna 1893), 45–7.

[3] *Historiae aliquot transmutationis metallicae ab Ewaldo de Hoghelande conscriptae* . . . (Cologne 1604), 28; Barnaud, *Commentariolum*, 10 f., 18 f. Cf. the remarks by Dee, *True and Faithful Relation* (see below, p. 218 n. 4), 212, that Hájek's study was decorated with writings 'and very many *Hieroglyphical* Notes *Philosophical* in Birds, Fishes, Flowers, Fruits, Leaves and Six Vessels, as for the Philosopher's works'. All three writers note that Hájek's son Simon was involved (ibid. 235); cf. Ancel to Bongars, Prague 2 Jan. and 25 Apr. 1592 in C. Schultess, *Aus dem Briefwechsel des französischen Philologen und Diplomaten Jacques Bongars* (Hamburg 1905), 183, 185.

[4] Nuncios/Ferreri, Prague 3 May 1604; cf. Aldobrandini to Ferreri, Rome 27 Mar., 26 June 1604; Alidosi, 6, 9.

[5] The kinship, and indeed identification of these two Guarinonis offers something of a puzzle. The *Universal Lexikon* of J. H. Zedler, s.v., gives Christopher's death as occurring in 1601, and relates that he became Imperial physician in Prague and founded an Academy there (a possible confusion with Bartholomew). The *Biographisches Lexikon der hervorragenden Ärzte aller Zeiten und Völker* (republished Munich–Berlin 1962), ii. 878, follows this, but places Christopher's death in 1654 (an obvious confusion with Hippolytus). He was a friend of Crato, but the only evidence I have found for any sojourn in Prague—or at least at the court—is that of Fleischman's 1594 *Hofstaat*, where both Christopher and Bartholomew appear (fo. J ii[r]).

[6] [Hippolytus Guarinoni], *Die Grewel der Verwüstung Menschlichen Geschlechts* . . . *Neben vor- mit- und nachgehenden | so wol Natürlichen | als Christlich- und Politischen darwider streitbaren Mitteln* . . . (Ingolstadt im 1610 Jar), dedication to Rudolf II. The book is in fact nearly unreadable: over 1,300 pages of deeply felt but almost incomprehensibly convoluted German.

but became well established from the later sixteenth century at Pressburg in Hungary.[1] The father (died 1602) was a noted Paracelsan who besides medical works compiled several dictionaries and involved himself in theological debate.[2] His son (died 1611) was a doctor at Regensburg in the 1590s, but later moved to Prague and signed himself 'Phil[osophiae] et Med[icinae] D[octor] & Caesar[eae] Maiest[atis] Personae S[uae] Sac[ratissimae] Medicus et a cubiculo chymiatrus'; his favour with the Emperor is clear, for his patent of nobility survives, dated 1608.[3] This son continued and edited the elder Ruland's work,[4] and there are some iatrochemical publications which he presumably prepared alone. At the same time he was a thorough-going alchemist: in 1606 he issued a tract called *Lapidis Philosophici Vera Conficiendi Ratio*, following it a year later with a defence of the historic Art, dedicated to Rudolf's sinister adviser Andreas Hannewaldt. Just before his death he completed a regular *Lexicon* of alchemy, a mine (as it were) of information about everything from the elixir of life to the treatment of metallic ores, which was subsequently translated into English.[5] Martin Ruland the Younger must have been a considerable polemicist, both on this subject[6] and in related fields: he took a major part in the protracted debate over one of the local miracles of the age, a Silesian boy born with a golden tooth.[7] The extent of the Rulands' library of occult and spiritual works emerges from a treatise on damnation and the places of hell, written with their co-operation.[8]

The most mysterious of the court physicians was Michael Maier (1568–1622), an enthusiastic Paracelsan, alchemist, and reformer who served Rudolf during the years before 1612, then moved to Holland and Germany, and apparently paid more than one visit to England where he had friends in Robert Fludd and King James's doctor, Sir William

---

[1] Szathmáry, op. cit. 274 ff.; Weszprémi, *Centuria*, i. 158–60.

[2] *Testimonia S. Patrum, Quibus explicatur quaestio, an Mali et Indigni sumant verum corpus et sanguinem Christi in Eucharistia per M. Rolandum Frisingensem* (Tübingen 1561). Cf. T. Swoboda, 'Alchemisten und Paracelsisten in Prag', *Prager Jahrbuch* 1943, 65–9—a slight article.

[3] Bauer, op. cit. 51 f.

[4] e.g. the later editions of his *Curationum empiricarum . . . centuria* (Basle 1581, etc.).

[5] Martin Ruland, *Progymnasmata Alchemiae sive Problemata Chymica* (Frankfurt 1607); *Lexicon Alchemiae sive Dictionarium Alchemistarum* (Frankfurt 1612). The *Lexicon* is dedicated to Julius of Brunswick and dated Prague, 10 Apr. 1611.

[6] e.g. *Alexicacus Chymiatricus . . . adversus Oberndorfferum* (Frankfurt 1611) and his letter to Kepler (Kepler, *Gesammelte Werke* xv, No. 411) written in 1607.

[7] This event occurred in 1593 and was first described by a professor from Helmstedt. Ruland's contributions were: *Nova, et . . . inaudita historia de Aureo Dente . . .* (Frankfurt 1595) and *Demonstratio iuditii de Aureo Dente* (Frankfurt 1597).

[8] *De Inferno seu cacodaemonum, damnatorumque domicilio . . . Tractatus . . . nunc recens ex bibliotheca Clariss. Viri Doct. M. Rulando depromptus ac . . . desperati Mundi gratia editus* [by Philip Haylbrunner] (1594).

Paddy.[1] Between 1614 and 1620 Maier produced a series of remarkable emblematic works on alchemical subjects, and all were published in the Rhineland, either at Oppenheim with the brothers De Bry or at Frankfurt with Lucas Jennis. Little is known of Maier's life beyond what he himself reveals in the prefaces to these books and it is far from clear why all appeared almost simultaneously, for the labour of inventing and preparing them must have occupied him through his Prague years and earlier.

Maier's books won considerable renown in the seventeenth century and have several times been noted by modern historians of science.[2] They represent a climax of the movement which combined close observation and analysis of the material world with a background of occult explanations: in his best creations, like the *Symbola Aureae Mensae* of 1617 or the *Atalanta Fugiens* of 1618, Maier seems even to argue that the underlying reality of symbols is alchemical, indeed that the processes of alchemy offer a progressive revelation of truth. His thoughts are obscure, being presented characteristically in the form of emblem and explication; but they are by no means crude: he drew on a wide reading both of classical and alchemical literature as well as being capable of considerable poetic invention.[3] Maier's approach—intellectual yet practical, arcane, esoteric, and profound—must have made great appeal to Rudolf, especially in the Emperor's last years; we know that he was raised to the dignity of Count Palatine and employed as a private secretary.

Maier indubitably belonged to Rudolf's circle; he was also, on the basis of his published work, the most inventive and original of the alchemists. But several other doctors whose relations with the Emperor himself are more obscure nevertheless form typical representatives of his environment. They include the irascible Italian religious émigré Simon Simonius, the Jesuit physician Sinapius/Hořčický, ennobled in 1608 with the predicate of Tepenec,[4] and another Czech, Matthias Borbonius. Borbonius seems never to have been a *Leibarzt*, though he earned the early favour of Rudolf by producing a poetic-emblematic volume calculated to appeal to his taste for Caesarism mixed with antiquarianism, while he enjoyed the friendship of Maier and a number of

[1] For available details of Maier's life see J. B. Craven, *Count Michael Maier* (Kirkwall 1910), 1–11. An early letter of his to Rantzau is in ÖN, MS. 9737^m, fos. 27–30.
[2] Cf. Read, op. cit. 212–54.
[3] H. M. E. de Jong, *Michael Maiers Atalanta Fugiens: Bronnen van een alchemistisch Emblemenboek* (Proefschrift, Utrecht 1965); and eadem, 'Michael Maier's Atalanta Fugiens, Commentary on emblem XLVIII', *Janus* lii. 2 (1965), 83–112. Some of Maier's poems are reproduced in Dornavius, *Amphitheatrum*.
[4] Cf. above, pp. 102, 159.

the court poets.[1] Borbonius was probably the most sought-after physician in Prague during the first years of the new century (among his patients was Polyxena Lobkovic),[2] and his alchemical interests emerge from a correspondence with the adept Johann Hartmann (1568–1631), Maier's successor as doctor to Moritz of Hesse-Cassel, a ruler whose intellectual inclinations matched Rudolf's own.[3]

Among the numerous professional contacts of Borbonius were several alchemists, notably Croll and Lavín. Oswald Croll, whose political intrigues we have already encountered, appeared intermittently in Prague and may have been semi-officially attached to the court. His *Basilica Chymica* (1609), which contains engravings by Aegidius Sadeler and poems from Paul Melissus and Westonia, is enthusiastically Paracelsan and filled with all manner of symbolism.[4] Appended to it is a treatise on signatures (dedicated to Peter Vok of Rožmberk) which includes the mention of some herbs received by Croll from Rudolf's estate at Brandeis.[5] Václav Lavín must have been a familiar figure in Prague before his death in 1600, both as physician and practising alchemist, but he also travelled much abroad, had studied in England, and probably maintained connections with Joachim Camerarius in Nuremberg.[6] Outside Bohemia this Borbonius circle kept special links with Vienna—for instance with the alchemist and Paracelsan William Aragosius who had served the last Valois monarchs[7]—and with Moravia. There the senior doctor was Tomáš Jordán (1539–85), who entertained Philip Sidney during his visit to Brno and was a friend of Clusius, Dudith, and Crato.[8] Borbonius, Croll, and Lavín had all worked in

[1] *Caesarum monarchiae romanae tesseradecades* (Leipzig 1595); this earned Borbonius a patent of nobility in 1596. See G. Gellner, *Životopis lékaře Borbonia a výklad jeho deníků* (Prague 1938), 11–13, 39, 94; Kunstmann, op. cit. 51–4.

[2] Gellner, op. cit. 97 ff. It was Zdeněk Lobkovic who later acquired his large library (cf. below, p. 287 n. 1).

[3] This is printed by Gellner, op. cit. 92 ff.

[4] *Osualdi Crollii . . . Basilica Chymica continens Philosophicam propriā laborum experientiā confirmatam descriptionem et usum Remediorum Chymicorum Selectissimorum è Lumine Gratiae et Naturae Desumptorum. . .*

[5] *Tractatus de Signaturis Internis Rerum*, Preface 4; the dedication is dated Prague, 10 Sept. 1608.

[6] See Gellner, op. cit. 21 and n.; Kunstmann, op. cit. 56 ff.; above, p. 133. Lavín was accepted into the Bohemian knighthood in 1590 (*SČ* vii, No. 489). His single known alchemical writing appeared as part of a collection at Marburg in 1612: *Cheiragogia Heliana de Auro Philosophico . . . accessit Tractatus Venceslai Lavinii Moravi De Coelo Terrestri* (Marpurgi Cattorum 1612). [7] Gellner, op. cit. 53 and n.

[8] G. Gellner, 'Tomáš Jordán', *ČMM* 60 (1936), 85–140, 315–34, esp. 95 f. Sidney to Jordán, Prague 2 Mar. 1575 in *Works* (Feuillerat), iii. 102. There are letters from Dudith to Jordán in Scholtz's collection of *Epistolae Philosophicae . . .* published at Hanau in 1610; another in *Materiały do dziejów Reformacji w Krakowie*, ed. R. Żelewski (Cracow 1962?), 99. Cf. from the Hungarian side—Jordán was a native of Kolozsvár—

Moravia and all knew the Žerotín family. Lavín was a personal friend, preceptor, and correspondent of Karel Žerotín and a relative of the latter's private physician between 1600 and 1606, Matyáš Timín. Timín later joined Peter Vok Rožmberk, and it seems that the role of the intelligent *Leibarzt* in such leading aristocratic entourages must have paralleled his role at the court of the Emperor.[1]

Outside the ranks of the professional doctors stood a further twilight assemblage of practising alchemists whose traces appear and disappear abruptly in the records of both the Imperial and the city administration. Some of these are reasonably well-documented historical personalities, like the Dutchman Ewald Hoghelande, who wrote a number of 'textbooks' in an effort to make the art accessible and also a description of various attested transmutations, among them Bohemian ones, to which he attached a life of Ramon Lull.[2] The Frenchman Nicolas Barnaud, a character about whom singularly little is known,[3] definitely lived in Prague for some years during the 1590s. Barnaud compiled a number of alchemical tracts, most of them simply editions of classic initiates' texts like those by the English friar George Ripley. He also worked actively as a Huguenot pamphleteer and was presumably a refugee for religious reasons when treading the wandering paths of the adept.[4] Certainly he was a familiar figure both to the French resident in Prague, Guillaume Ancel, and to Henry of Navarre's representative in Germany, Jacques Bongars. It is striking how closely those learned Humanists and diplomats followed Barnaud's experiments, and the evidence of his Bohemian contacts suggests that he was something more than the fly-by-night magician of recurring legend.[5]

Weszprémi, *Centuria*, i. 74–6; G. Magyary-Kossa, *Magyar orvosi emlékek*, ii (Budapest 1929), 117–21.

[1] Odložilík, *Karel ze Žerotína*, 40 and letters in the diary of Žerotín (Ipolyi/*Rimay*); Gellner, *Borbonius*, 71 and n. Croll mentions Timín in his Dedication to Rožmberk (loc. cit.). Cf. Karel st. ze Žerotína, *Listy psané jazykem českým*, i–iii, ed. V. Brandl (Brno 1870–2), i, No. 23; ii, No. 219 (on Lavín); ii, No. 309; iii, Nos. 786, 812, 831, 863 (on Timín).

[2] e.g. the *De Alchemiae Difficultatibus* (above, p. 199 n. 2). *Historiae aliquot transmutationis* (above, p. 204 n. 3).

[3] J. Ferguson, *Bibliotheca Chemica* (Glasgow 1906), i. 73 f. communicates scarcely anything about Barnaud beyond his published works of which he gives a list.

[4] e.g. N. Barnaud, *Quadriga Aurifera* (Leiden 1599). Barnaud's Huguenot writings —like the *Cabinet du Roy de France* (n.p. 1581)—were all published either anonymously or under a pseudonym, and his authorship of them does not seem unequivocally demonstrated. But the attribution is a contemporary one and circumstantially strong, while Barnaud clearly had a penchant for the use of aliases.

[5] Ancel to Bongars, Prague 25 Apr., 1, 8, 15, and 29 Aug., 8 Sept. 1592, in Schultess, op. cit. 185, etc. Part of the *Quadriga Aurifera* is dedicated to Barnaud's patron Ancel. Cf. above, p. 204 n. 3; below, p. 213 n. 8, p. 217 n. 4, and p. 283 n. 1.

Other personages from this underworld remain yet more elusive and their names and backgrounds are hopelessly confused, though we need not be utterly sceptical about their existence. According to a traditional story, for instance, one of Rudolf's chief associates in his secret laboratory was the converted Jew Mardochaeus de Delle, who wrote down versified details of all the experiments performed (with illustrations by the courtier Hans Marquard) in a book which later vanished.[1] He is also credited— but as 'Martinus de Delle'—with a short occult text published only towards the end of the seventeenth century.[2] Whatever wè may make of this there survives in Prague a manuscript commentary on Paracelsus by one 'Mardochaeus de Nelle Judaeus': it claims to be based on an original source given to the writer by Toxites (the iatrochemist) at the '*Reichstag* of Maximilian II'.[3] The claim may look suspicious, but the tract is clearly buttressed by the actual chemical observations of the author and his son, carried out in the 1570s. 'Delle' then was indeed an alchemist, though his real name, it appears, was Nelle.

No testimony remains to the supposed dealings of the Emperor with Philip Güstenhofer of Strasbourg, with Alexander Seton, the possessor of a powder capable of projection, with Count Bragadino, or the 'Johann Müller von Müllenfels' who received a patent of nobility in 1603.[4] While some of Rudolf's correspondence turns on such men, like a report in 1609 about the 'artist with the arcanum of copper, Christoph Ulrich',[5] few alchemical manuscripts seem to be extant which owe their direct inspiration to him, and one of these—now at Wolfenbüttel—was very likely written in Augsburg.[6] None of them offers any special features,

[1] This appears first in Morhof; see (e.g.) Karl Christian Schmieder, *Geschichte der Alchemie* (Halle 1832), 301 and *passim*.

[2] Martinus de Delle, *Discursus de Universali*, in Ali Puli, *Centrum Naturae Concentratum . . .*, ed. J. O. Helbig (Heidelberg 1682), reprinted in *Quadratum Alchymisticum das ist Vier auserlesene rare Tractätgen vom Stein der Weisen* (Hamburg 1705). Cf. Ferguson, op. cit. i. 204.

[3] Strahov, D. G. iv. 40: 'De Cementis et Gradationibus Theophrasti Mardochaei de Nelle Judaei . . .' It begins: 'Diser Judt Mardochaeus Nelle ist kein kindt in Chimicis gewesen(!), dan er fundamentaliter auf die fixation aller Specierum / ohne welche nichts fruchtbarliches verrichtet wird / gangen ist.' Another copy of this manuscript is noted by Sudhoff, *Versuch* ii, No. 152. Toxites was indeed in some kind of contact with Maximilian II (cf. ibid. i, No. 118).   [4] Bauer, op. cit. 47–51.

[5] SÚA, SM A 72/1¹⁶, 7 Nov. 1609. The report describes the alchemist's preparations and materials, and his experiments till now (one test yielded 21 lbs. of copper). It then goes on to consider other practitioners: 'Berichten darbei, das der Herzog [of Savoy] ainen Mantuaner namens Cesar Rinara und anderer Alchymistischen Khunst, deren Er dem Herzog Jarlich 60 Cronen lifern und jezt 4 Jar bey Ime sitzt zu ainem Marchesen gemacht . . .'

[6] 'Libri VII experimentorum magicorum Hermetis Trismegisti. Et sunt secreta magica rerum Aegypti . . . Ex thesauro Rodolphi II Romanorum imperatorum dignissimi.' I have not consulted this MS. It is listed in O. Heinemann, *Die Handschriften*

though that in Rome—another translation of Ripley's 'Book of Keys'—
was compiled by Nicolaus Maius, whom we know from further sources to
have been an *Appellationsrat*, prefect of the mines at Joachimsthal, and a
member of poetic circles in Prague.[1] Another is a straightforward series
of recipes written in 1596 by Johann Herman Reising of Breslau, who
describes himself as 'His Majesty's *Hofmedicus*'.[2] The most curious is the
Speculum Alchemiae in Vienna by 'Odoardus Scotus', a mystic-alchemical
tract, dedicated to Rudolf and fairly unremarkable in itself, but
interesting for an introductory panegyric to the House of Habsburg as
guardians of the sacred mystery of transmutation.[3] The author claims to
have received great reward from Rudolf: 'Ob hanc ipsam . . . Occultam
sapientiam, olim mihi à Deo datam, hodie in te translatam, Rudolphus
II Caesarum Maximus me Officiis Supremis, honoribus maximis,
decoravit.'[4] Scotus is another unidentified, fleeting figure—his Christian
name seems most often to be recorded as Alessandro and his origins as
Italian, though he is also reported to have appeared in Germany.[5]
Zachar denied his existence altogether, and confusion could certainly
arise with the medieval 'wizard' Michael Scot, but he earns a mention
in Hoghelande as a man who could turn copper into gold or lapis lazuli
into silver, and he is noted both by Dačický and by Bydžovský, who says
he spent much time in Prague.[6]

... *zu Wolfenbüttel*, II Abth. Pt. 4 (Wolfenbüttel 1900), 351 (No. 3338). One alchemical
collection now in Leiden (MS. Voss. Chym. 4° 31B) has a tradition linking it with
Rudolf and some annotations in a hand akin to his; another (MS. Voss. Chym.
Oct. 3) bears his arms, but contains only a very primitive farrago of recipes. There
is an anonymous MS. dedicated to Rudolf in Budapest (OSzK, MS. 9 Duod. Ger.)
but it has no visible connection with Prague.

[1] Dudík, *Iter Romanum*, 228 (Sig. 1381). This may originally have belonged to the
Rožmberk collection. It begins with a dedication to Rudolf, an appeal for the Emperor
to maintain his patronage of the good arts. On Maius cf. Westonia, *Parthenicon*, i,
B3ʳ-5ᵛ, etc.; he also contributed a poem to Croll's *Basilica Chymica*. A little alchemical
tract published in Latin and German in 1647 claims to be taken from a manuscript of
Maius's: *Fratris Ferrarii Tractatus Chemicus . . . ex MS exemplari Dn. Nicolai Maii . . .
Rudolfi secundi . . . quondam Consiliarii* (Geismar 1647), and *Chymische Abhandlung
für den Pabst * * ** (ibid.). This was apparently edited by L. Combach (1590–1657),
another *Leibarzt* to Moritz of Hesse-Cassel. Maius also knew John Dee: Bodleian
Library, MS. Ashmole 488, fo. 125ʳ.

[2] Vienna ÖN, MS. 11450: 'Alchymistische Kunststücke, in gutter Ordnungk Auf
das Intent der Chymicorum mit grosser muhe zusammen getragen'. Another adept,
Johannes von Kitlitz, recommends himself to Rudolf in ÖN, MS. 11259.

[3] Odoardus Scotus, 'Speculum alchemiae in IV libris', Vienna, ÖN, MS. 11404.
It is beautifully written on both sides of a single strip of vellum, elaborately folded. Cf.
Figulus's dedication of his *Thesaurinella Olympica* (above, p. 200 n. 4), 6 f.

[4] Scotus, fo. 6.   [5] Cf. Schmieder, op. cit. 309 f.

[6] Zachar, op. cit. 244 f.; Hoghelande, *Historiae aliquot transmutationis*, 13 ff.;
Dačický, 262; Bydžovský, fo. 73ᵛ under year 1583: 'Hieronymus Scotus Placentinus
čarodějník (kterýž také v Praze drahně času byl)'.

The most interesting of these characters is one who was mysterious but by no means peripheral, the Pole Michael Sędiwoj or Sendivogius (1556–*post* 1630). Sędiwoj has acquired a reputation for quackery and there are indeed strong suspicions of duplicity in his relations with the gullible Czech nobleman Kořálek of Těšín which led to his trial and brief imprisonment in 1599;[1] yet in other respects Sędiwoj presents a typical intellectual attitude of the period. He became celebrated among his contemporaries, not simply the public at large but also his fellow alchemists, and he is the most recent of the twelve 'sophic apostles' as they appear in one of Maier's works which was later reproduced by Stoltzius.[2] His several tracts on alchemy, the best-known the *Novum Lumen Chymicum* of 1604, were published anonymously (though sometimes prefaced with an obvious anagram of his name) between 1604 and 1614 and regularly reprinted. No less a figure than Isaac Newton read them thoroughly.[3]

Sędiwoj seems to have lived in Prague intermittently during the 1590s and he evidently formed a centre of controversy, for he was thrown in prison more than once. Rudolf must have known him at this time— though evidence is scanty—since he appealed to the Emperor to be released from custody in 1597, and he was well acquainted with some of the doctors: Borbonius, Lavín, Maier, and Johann Hartmann.[4] He returned to Bohemia at various times thereafter, and there exists a word-for-word Czech translation in manuscript of his *De Lapide*, prepared about 1604–5 and bound in another Czech text, a version of a work attributed to Trithemius of Sponheim.[5] After 1612 it becomes difficult to follow Sędiwoj's movements; he was in Vienna in 1617, then in Silesia and Poland. Of his last years nothing appears to be known, but there is a series of letters written by him from Cracow to Zdeněk Lobkovic in the 1620s whose confidentiality and recollection of past

---

[1] R. Bugaj, *W poszukiwaniu kamienia filozoficznego; O Michale Sędiwoju najsłynniejszym alchemiku polskim* (Warsaw 1957), 119 ff. Bugaj has consulted Czech sources, but his biography is credulous and confused. Sędiwoj and Kořálek were in touch with Lavín.

[2] The *Symbola Aureae Mensae*; cf. Read, op. cit. 222–8.

[3] Bugaj, 231 ff. One anagram was 'Author sum qui Divi Leschi Genus Amo'. The *Novum Lumen Chymicum et naturae fonte et manuali experientiae depromptum et in duodecim Tractatus divisum* (1604 etc., underlining mine) was often held to be the secret wisdom of the Scot Alexander Seton, transmitted to Sędiwoj in 1603 (this story is repeated in Bugaj, op. cit. 135–59). Newton's copy of it with marginal notes is now in the British Museum (c. 112. aa. 3(i)).

[4] HHSA, Fam. Korr. A. 4. III: Prague 10 Feb. 1597. Gellner, op. cit. 94; Bugaj, op. cit. 119 ff., 217 f. Cf. his letter to Hans Popp in HHSA, Langakten, 8. fo. 58.

[5] Nat. Mus., MS. III H 20. The work by Trithemius was supposedly presented to the Emperor Maximilian I.

services suggest that the Chancellor had been a good patron to him.[1]

This correspondence has a political nature, and Sędiwoj's political allegiance is noteworthy. The alchemists as a class of men were inclined to pursue a cult of esoterism which required the sponsorship of some elevated patron, and thus their identification of Rudolf with the new Hermes Trismegistus provided an occult representation of the mystique of absolutism by divine right. Sędiwoj passed his early career in Cracow, and he established contact there with Paracelsan circles, but the largest influence on him was Mikołaj Wolski, a leading noble and supporter of the Polish claims of the Habsburgs.[2] Besides being personally acquainted with the latter, Wolski was a friend of the Zborowskis, Łaski (the patron of John Dee), and Barnaud (part of whose *Triga Chemica* of 1599 is dedicated to him), and it seems clear that there existed an intimate connection between the Habsburg party in Poland and the occult arts. From the 1570s, then more especially after the death of Báthory—also some kind of initiate—and the triumph of Zamoyski, such people were forced into exile, and that may explain Sędiwoj's first association with Prague.

Second only to the Imperial palace as a famous centre of alchemy in late sixteenth-century Bohemia was the court of Vilém Rožmberk. Rožmberk employed adepts both at his residence which adjoined Rudolf's on the Hradschin in Prague, and in his domains further south whose focal point was Krumlov. He too attracted the cosmopolitans from far afield to seek his favour,[3] but once again the records which survive cannot back all the imprecise hearsay. It is unfortunate that our chronicler Březan was a rather orthodox, strait-laced soul and showed himself singularly reticent about alchemy, for which he had no sympathy. He did however leave a considerable list of names of those active with his master during the 1570s: among them Nicholas Reusberger, who claimed discovery of the *perpetuum mobile*;[4] Christoph von Hirschberg, whom Březan regards as a complete charlatan, but who worked with Vilém for a long time under contract and was still active in 1592;[5] and Claudius Syrrus, another who

---

[1] LRRK, B 221[134 seqq.]: 'M Sendivogius de Skorsko, Regis Poloniae Secretarius'. Brandau (op. cit. 15 ff.) writing about 1630, says Sędiwoj is still alive in Cracow and has married the wife of a successful French alchemist who died in Prague. The latter—if the story is true—could perhaps have been Barnaud.

[2] Bugaj, op. cit. 90 ff.

[3] See Svátek, op. cit. 54 f.

[4] Březan, 137. Reusberger appears in Vilém's correspondence as the 'Rensperg' who offered his services in 1570–1; S. A. Třeboň, RAR 25 (Briefe 1528–96, Natürliche und Geheime Wissenschaften, hereafter 'RAR 25').

[5] Březan, 137 and 166 f. His contract with Rožmberk and Peter Hlavsa of Liboslav dated 18 Jan. 1574 is in RAR 25.

operated under definite 'conditions of employment'. An extant manuscript bears witness to the latter's stay in South Bohemia.[1] Others appear
in Rožmberk's correspondence: Anton von Ebersbach, a Cabalist and
magician;[2] Serranus, who had connections with the Rhedigers in Breslau;[3] Jakob Faber, Martin Faber, and many more.

Rožmberk also accumulated a sizeable collection of alchemical manuscripts: from apocalyptic and philosophical tracts on the soul of the
world and the Cabala to the merest scraps of recipes.[4] His chief servant
in this was the most important Czech writer on alchemy, Bavor
Rodovský of Hustiřany. Rodovský,[5] who worked with Daniel Prandtner
in the Prague laboratory and whose interests also embraced prophecy,
astronomy, and machines, produced for the most part translations of
foreign texts, including Paracelsus, in beautifully careful manuscript.
His *Philosophical Lectures*, *Hermetic Philosophy*, and *Book of the Perfect
Chymical Art* (now in Leiden) are collections of traditional alchemical
wisdom, translated during the 1570s and 1580s.[6] His *Secrets of Aristotle*
—based on one of the banal mystic–political sets of precepts popularly
attributed to Aristotle—was dedicated to Vilém in 1574, and the previous
year Rodovský had written to his patron from prison in Prague to announce his vernacular rendering of Paracelsus.[7]

Two practitioners of greater international fame were associated with
Rožmberk in his last years. One of them, Nicolas Barnaud, we have
already met;[8] the other was Heinrich Khunrath of Leipzig who, as

[1] Březan, 137; Leiden, Univ. Lib., MS. Voss. Chym. 4° 34. Syrrus stated his
conditions to Vilém (letter from Prague, 9 Jan. 1577, in RAR 25): 'De perfectione
magisterii Claudius nihil promittit: sed Artem et laborem certo astipulatur: Perfec-
tionem autem Alt. Deo committit: si negotium itaque non succedat ut dictus Claudius
non habeatur pro impostore aut reputetur . . .'

[2] RAR 25: letters of 11 Aug. 1588, 8 July 1592.

[3] Ibid.: undated letter including various magic and astrological lists, and material
to be provided by his friend 'Nicolaus Rudiger' in Breslau.

[4] These manuscripts are also collected in RAR 25; almost all are undated, so the
presumption must be that they belonged to Vilém (most are of later sixteenth-century
origin). Some are serious, like an 'Apocalypsis Spiritus Secreti' or a 'Clavicula Raymundi Lullii . . . (Dieses Büchlein nennen wir unsern Schlüssel denn ohn dieses gegen-
wertige Buch khan niemand verstehen, was wir in den anderen Büchen geschrieben
haben(!))'; some are more homely: 'Ein Aurum potabile quod humanum Corpus ad
multos Annos tingirn unnd veriungern thuet', etc.

[5] Cf. O. Zachar, *O alchymii a českých alchymistech* (Prague 1911?), 171–225.

[6] Řeci filosofské, Nat. Mus., MS III g 12; 'Wohermesowe ffilozoffigi To gest o
Poženhnanem Kamenii ffilozowskem Wysocze Urozeneho Pana Pana Bernharda Hrabete
z Marku a zterwiz Gedna Knizka', Nat. Mus., MS. IV c 20; Leiden, Univ. Lib., MS.
Voss. Chym. Fol. 3.

[7] 'Secreta Aristotelis, Kniha Lidskeych Cztnosti a mnoheych Nauczeni kterak se
Kralowe Knižata y Pani w swem panowani Opatrowati . . . magi ku Pocztiwosti', UK,
MS. XVII G 11; letter of 6 Feb. 1573 (in Czech) in RAR 25.

[8] Barnaud seems to have joined Rožmberk in 1591 and settled temporarily on one

Březan records, became Vilém's court physician on 15 December 1591.[1] Khunrath (1560–1605) must have been among the most extraordinary characters of his time; certainly his occult works—which form the only real source of information about him—rank with the most grandiose even of that magniloquent age. He was the author of a series of books published during the 1590s and 1600s which led up to a magnum opus, the *Amphitheatrum Sapientiae Aeternae Christiano-Kabalisticum*, first printed in 1595, then revised and reissued posthumously.[2] For the modern reader they present an incomprehensible jumble of arcane theosophy and Cabalistic incantation, the *Amphitheatrum* being prefaced with remarkable illustrations of a kind of sophic Utopia, the whole symbolic landscape of the occultists. It would require a special study to investigate the philosophy of Khunrath and the serious purpose which undoubtedly underlay his work, but that does not belong here since his relation to Bohemia seems to have been a more or less casual one and he cannot long have attended the ailing Vilém Rožmberk. It was anyway as practising alchemist that he earned renown in his day—one of the pictures in the *Amphitheatrum* shows him in his laboratory, surrounded by the paraphernalia of the mage. This reputation was established by 1589 when Khunrath met John Dee in Bremen and perhaps forged the link with Rožmberk which was to take him to Bohemia.[3] Rudolf gave Khunrath a comprehensive privilege in 1598 to protect from plagiarism all his books 'tam scripta quam picta, Medicinalia, Chymica, Cabalistica

of his estates: *Commentariolum*, 10 f.; Ancel to Bongars, Prague 8 Sept. 1592, in Schultess, 196.

[1] Březan, 165. The only book definitely published by Khunrath in these years is known to me through a single casual reference in Wolkan, *Böhmens Anteil* iii (Prague 1894), 453 and n. Wolkan, who possessed a copy of it, quotes its title as: *Zebelis Regis et Sapientis Arabum Vetustissimi . . . Zebelis des Weisen und sehr Alten Arabischen Königs, von Bedeutungen und ausslegungen etlicher Zufälle, welche den Menschen ungewöhnlich unverhofft oder unversehen zu wiederfahren, und geschwind zu begegnen pflegen, nach unterschiedlichem Lauff des Monden, durch die zwölff himlischen Zeichen, sehr fleissige Auffmerckungen. Ex bibl. Henrici Khunrathi . . . Wilhelmi a Rosis . . . Medici Ordinarii, Pragae tum commorantis* (Prague–Peterle 1592).

[2] There is much that is obscure, both about Khunrath's movements and the publication of his works. The first edition of the *Amphitheatrum* is of extreme rarity (listed in D. I. Duveen, *Bibliotheca Alchemica et Chemica* (London 1949), s.v.); that produced at Hanau in 1609 is probably the second, though Ferguson lists a number of other issues which possibly preceded it, beginning with a Prague one of 1598 (*Bibliotheca Chemica*, s.v.). The Hanau edition was prepared (by Erasmus Wolfart) because of the book's great scarcity (see the anon. 'Judicium und Bericht . . .' in Khunrath, *De Igne Magorum Philosophorumque* (Strasbourg 1608)), and seems to have been a response to widespread learned interest. The same uncertainty surrounds other texts of Khunrath's; Duveen and Ferguson list the *Warhafftiger Bericht vom philosophischen ATHANOR* only in a 1603 edition, but I have consulted one printed at Magdeburg in 1599 (Budapest, Univ. Lib., D C 122).

[3] Dee, *Private Diary* (below, p. 218 n. 3), 31; cf. Bodleian, Ashmole 488, fo. 130ᵛ.

pleraque alia secretiora'. The content of such volumes can scarcely have left the Emperor unmoved.

An enterprise which brought together Rudolf and Rožmberk was the search for precious stones and metals. We have already seen that the hunt for jewels belonged inseparably to artistic life at the court, and in the same way developments in mining were not distinct from the experiments of the alchemists.[1] Mining techniques in the later sixteenth century owed much to the classic pioneering work of the German George Agricola, and two leading representatives of his influence in Central Europe were Thurneysser and Lazarus Ercker.[2] Leonhard Thurneysser (1530–96) was a kind of Paracelsus-figure—botanist, Cabalist, alchemist, and wandering scholar[3]—who clearly saw himself, like Khunrath, as embodying a magical tradition reserved to initiates, yet had wide practical experience of metallurgy and prospected for ores in the Habsburg lands. This emerges at times from his books, which are diffuse and arcane but not lacking in all merit: we find sections on Bohemian and Hungarian mining in the *Magna Alchemia* or on the properties of the Danube and its tributaries in the *Ten Books on Mineral and Metallic Waters*.[4] Thurneysser served Maximilian II for a period, but his connections with Rudolfine Prague are unclear. Ercker on the other hand, whose treatise on assaying and smelting methods—first published there in 1574—represents a landmark in the history of the subject, was Rudolf's main adviser on the exploitation of minerals and served the Habsburgs for 29 years until his death in 1591,[5] as well as corresponding with Rožmberk on alchemical matters.[6]

Both Rudolf and Rožmberk took an active part in furthering mining enterprises: a new town was founded with the name of Kaiser Rudolfs Stadt (Rudolfov)[7] and the Emperor granted many privileges in connection with exploration, including several to Vilém.[8] The most important

---

[1] Cf. Read, op. cit. 74 ff.   [2] Cf. Zachar, *Rudolf a alchymisté*, 252 ff.

[3] For Thurneysser's life see *ADB*, s.v. His botanical studies are contained in the *Historia sive descriptio plantarum omnium* (Berlin 1578).

[4] L. Thurneysser von Thurn, *Magna Alchimia* (Berlin 1583), *passim*; idem, *Zehen Bücher von . . . Mineralischen und Mettalischen Wassern* (Strasbourg 1612), Book 5. On his interest in Hungary cf. Szathmáry, op. cit. 319–22, and Magyary-Kossa, op. cit. iii, No. 848.

[5] SÚA, Majestalia Vol. 104 (Bekennen 1594–9), fo. 106, approving an allowance for Ercker's widow. Ercker's book, *Beschreibung Allerfurnemisten Mineralischen Ertzt unnd Bergkwercks arten* (Prague 1574), was republished at Frankfurt in 1580, then again in 1598 as a second edition revised by the author himself.

[6] Cf. his undated letter to Vilém in RAR 25.

[7] SÚA, Majestalia Vol. 100 (Bekennen 1583–9), fos. 147–9, Privilegium of 30 Dec. 1583. Dee visited this town in 1588 (*Private Diary*, 30, Bodleian, Ashmole 488, fo. 121ᵛ).

[8] e.g. SÚA, Majestalia Vol. 100, Privilegium of 1586.

existing centre was Joachimsthal (Jáchymov), famous for its resources of silver which were massively exploited during the sixteenth century, and the prefect of mines there counted as an influential personage. The post was held towards the end of Rudolf's life by Nicolaus Maius; earlier the Emperor had conferred it on a more controversial alchemist, Sebald Schwaertzer, who fled to the court in Prague during 1592 under suspicion of having poisoned two successive Electors of Saxony. Schwaertzer was widely credited with the secret of transmutation, but he was no mere charlatan; he well illustrates the interlinking of occult and practical in the field of metallurgy.[1] At a lower level this can be seen too with such men as the self-styled 'distiller-royal' Christopher Thoman.[2]

Meanwhile Rožmberk and his colleagues Adam of Hradec, Václav Vřesovic (a person of considerable learning), Peter Hlavsa of Liboslav, and Carolus Widman of Augsburg were busy with various projects, and there are reports about the progress of the work, as in a memorandum by Daniel Prandtner on the exploitation of their 'Bergwerk' for the preparation of the stone, the universal remedy, and 'die ander Haimbligkeit, wie auss dem goldt das Erdtrich gemacht wirdt'.[3] Their interests were not restricted to south Bohemia but extended to the rich metalliferous hills of the north. One of Rožmberk's laboratories operated in the castle of Reichenstein in Silesia, whence he received reports on esoteric and alchemical matters from Jonas Freudenberg, Lorenz Schmalzer, and Melchior Hornung;[4] it is in Reichenstein that Mardochaeus de Nelle claimed to have experimented with his Paracelsan remedies.

In all this work we find a strong link between search and research, between observation, collection, and theory. Rudolf's chief lapidary was one of his doctors, Anselm Boethius de Boodt, an emblematist and herbalist who co-operated in the Prague *Symbola*.[5] Boodt's *Gemmarum*

---

[1] Ancel to Bongars, Prague 29 Aug. 1592 in Schultess, 195; Ferguson, *Bibliotheca Chemica* ii, 350 f. On Maius cf. above, p. 210 n. 1.

[2] *Krátká Správa. O Mocy a působitedlném užitku pravé a dobře přistrogené Aureae Aquae Sanitatis . . . kteráž . . . nagde se Umne Krystoffa Thomana měsstěnina v Kremži. Od geho Milosti Cýsařské z obzwlásstnej milosti na to Privilegium a Swobodau obdarowaného Dystillatora. Nyni se nacházý na Králowským Paláce w Praze* (Prague 1598) in Tobolka, *Knihopis*, No. 16184.

[3] Undated German report in RAR 25. Vřesovic's library later passed to the Caroline University; see J. A. Hanslick, *Geschichte und Beschreibung der Prager Universitäts-Bibliothek* (Prague 1851), 74–6. It contained for instance works by Postel and Skalich (205, 363). Cf. the tract written for him by Syrrus in Prague, Nat. Mus., MS. XI E 35.

[4] Letters of 22 Aug. 1582, 4 Apr. 1585, and others in RAR 25; cf. *Schlesiens Bergbau und Hüttenwesen (1529–1740), Urkunden und Akten*, ed. K. Wutke (Breslau 1901), Nos. 787, 790, 794. Reichenstein was sold by Peter Vok in 1600 (ibid. No. 811).

[5] Apart from his *Gemmarum et Lapidum Historia* he also produced a *Symbola varia Diversorum Principum . . . totius Italiae, cum facili isagoge D. Anselmi de Boot Brugensis*

et Lapidum Historia, first published in 1609, has been called 'the most important lapidary of the seventeenth century'[1] and went into several editions. The book offers a complete reclassification of stones, with sections on their origins, their properties—both benevolent and evil—their virtues and powers. While it is no treatise on mystification, the extent of its credulity and belief in the unseen forces which inhere in natural objects reflects the attitude towards minerals of Rudolf's whole court. The Emperor is praised by Boodt as a lover of stones 'not simply in order that he may thereby augment his dignity and majesty . . . but so that in them the excellence of God may be contemplated, the ineffable might of Him Who is seen to press the beauty of the whole world into such exiguous bodies and include in them the powers of all other created things . . .'[2] One prize exhibit of the Rudolfine collection was the celebrated Gemma Augustea, plundered from Paris in 1591 and bought by the Imperial agent David von Brüssel; to it various kinds of magic properties were ascribed.[3]

Boodt was himself engaged in transmutations,[4] and the same pattern appears in his curious Venetian contemporary Agostino Riccio, jeweller, writer on stones and their lore (he knew of the work being carried out in Prague), natural scientist, and student of the artificial memory.[5] An important Czech servant of Rudolf as stonecutter and geologist, Šimon Tadeáš Budeck of Lešin,[6] turns out to be identical with the author of a fascinating alchemical manuscript now in Vienna. In it Budeck describes his official position as 'His Majesty's prospector for treasures, metals, precious stones, and *all hidden secrets in the whole of nature*, appointed with full powers throughout the Crown of Bohemia'.[7] The treatise is partly derivative (including a translation into Czech of 'Paracelsus'), partly a record of his own observations and experiments, witnessed by

(Amsterdam 1686), and *Florum herbarum ac fructuum selectiorum icones, et vires pleraeque; hactenus ignotae* (also published posthumously, in 1640).

[1] Joan Evans, *Magical Jewels of the Middle Ages and the Renaissance* (Oxford 1922), 152 f., where the 1636 edition is, however, taken as *editio princeps*. Cf. Thorndike, op. cit. vi. 318–24.   [2] *Gemmarum et Lapidum Historia* (Hanau 1609), dedication, 7.
[3] Kris, *Steinschneidekunst*, 137; R. Chadraba, 'Die "Gemma Augustaea" und die rudolfinische Allegorie', *Umění* xviii (1970), 289–97.
[4] According to Hoghelande, *Historiae aliquot transmutationis*, 27, and Barnaud, *Commentariolum*, 11–13.
[5] Kris, op. cit. 103 n., 138 n.; F. A. Yates, 'The Ciceronian Art of Memory', in *Medioevo e Rinascimento*, 899; Rossi, *Clavis Universalis*, App. V.
[6] Svátek, *Obrazy z kulturních dějin českých*, 81 ff.
[7] Vienna, ÖN, MS. 11133, fo. 24ʳ; a tract called 'Ars Artium et Scientia Scientiarum . . . a me M. Simone Thaddaeo Budeccio à Leschino et Falcmberga S.C.M. Thesauroru, Metalloru, Lapidu preciosoru et omnium in universa natura secretò abditoru cum plenaria potentia per totu Regnu Boemiae ordinato Inquisitore ab anno 1604 . . .'

such distinguished men as Kryštof Harant.[1] One of the main areas for Budeck's investigations was the Krkonoše or Giant Mountains (Riesengebirge) in the north-east of the country; it is no coincidence that the late sixteenth century saw both the closer exploration of this region from the scientific point of view and the growth of a large body of tenacious folk-legend.[2] For the contemporary mind they represented two sides of the same coin.

*   *   *

A further link between Rudolf and Rožmberk was one which we must now consider separately and which leads far beyond the bounds of alchemy narrowly defined: the Bohemian careers of John Dee and Edward Kelley. These two Englishmen were among the most famous and best documented personalities of their age, and the years which they spent in or around Bohemia (1583–9)—the years of their partnership and the climax of Dee's career—are illuminated by two of Dee's own writings: the so-called *Private Diary*, which was edited in the nineteenth century from an Oxford manuscript;[3] and the extraordinary *True and Faithful Relation*, which must surely stand as one of the most precious of all accounts describing spiritual experience.[4] First of all we must sketch the background to their arrival on the continent.

Dee, who was born in 1527, was one of the most learned men of the sixteenth century. A leading mathematician, astronomer, and bibliophile, he gathered together perhaps the best scientific library in Europe;[5] he was a spokesman for geographical exploration,[6] a correspondent of Ortelius, teacher of Philip Sidney, and friend of Daniel Rogers.[7] His real reputation, however, lay in the occult sciences: he acted as a kind of court

---

[1] Vienna, ÖN, MS. 11133, fo. 4ᵛ.

[2] Cf. Zíbrt, *BČH* iii. 10813–989.

[3] *The Private Diary of Dr. John Dee and the Catalogue of his Library of Manuscripts*, edited by J. O. Halliwell (London 1842, hereafter *Private Diary*). This brief record covers the years 1577–83, late 1586 to 1598, and 1600–1. The portion of it with which we are most concerned—that relating to the later 1580s—was transcribed from marginal notes to Giovanni Antonio Magini's *Ephemerides Coelestium Motuum* (Venice 1582) in the copy Bodleian Library, Ashmole 488. The printed text has some misreadings of names and the occasional small omission.

[4] *A True and Faithful Relation of what passed for many years between Dr. John Dee . . . and some spirits tending (had it succeeded) to a General Alteration of most States and kingdoms in the World . . . Out of the original copy . . . with a Preface by Meric Casaubon* (London 1659, hereafter *T.F.R.*). It treats mostly the years 1583–6, but with considerable gaps of time.

[5] F. R. Johnson, *Astronomical Thought in Renaissance England* (Baltimore 1937), 134 ff.

[6] F. A. Yates, 'Queen Elizabeth as Astraea' (see below, p. 275 n. 1), 46 ff., who points out how this was underpinned in Dee's mind by a belief in universal imperial 'mission'.

[7] e.g. his letter to Ortelius, Mortlake 16 Jan. 1577, in Hessels, No. 67.

astrologer to Elizabeth I, and the surviving catalogue of his library shows the wealth of arcane literature which it contained.[1] Dee's broad metaphysical position was characteristic of an intellectual of his time: he believed in the theory of the microcosm, in hidden forces underlying the visible world, in cosmic harmony.[2] His views led him (like Bruno) to advanced astronomical speculations. At the same time he believed (with Bruno) that access to these mysteries could be achieved through such things as symbols, intellectual 'keys', and combinations. In a letter to Cecil he described his delight at finding a copy of Trithemius's *Steganographia* (a treatise on ciphers and secret writing),[3] and he was a great disciple of Roger Bacon, for whom he wrote an *Apologia* and whose writings on the mysteries of nature he annotated.[4]

All this combined in Dee with an intense spiritualism. Kiesewetter's analysis of both him and Kelley as mediums is probably conceived too much according to later theories of occultism,[5] but there is no doubt that Dee felt the spirit world to be a full reality. Whatever the origin of the messages which it communicated to him, Dee believed them unwaveringly, and when set against the contemporary mood of intellectual striving the schemes of universal reform and regeneration which he derived from his seances grow much more comprehensible.

Dee came increasingly to see himself as the prophet of an occult revelation, and the man on whom he initially pinned his aspirations was the Polish magnate Albrecht Łaski. Łaski (1536–1605), the Palatine of Sieradz, a vast landowner and strong though unorthodox Catholic, was

---

[1] Cf. the catalogue of manuscripts appended to the *Private Diary*. The catalogue of Dee's whole library (main copies: British Museum, Harleian MS. 1879; Trinity College, Cambridge, MS. O iv 20) remains unpublished.

[2] See Dee's Preface to Billingsley's Euclid: *The Elements of the Geometrie of the most ancient Philosopher Euclide of Megara . . . translated into the Englishe toung by H. Billingsley . . . With a very fruitfull Praeface made by M. I. Dee* (London 1570). The significance of this *Preface* as a major statement of the Platonic tradition in Renaissance natural philosophy is now becoming better appreciated. The unpublished thesis of I. R. F. Calder, 'John Dee studied as an English Neoplatonist' (Diss. London 1951), contains a wealth of valuable information.

[3] This was printed by R. W. Gray, 'Letter of Dr. John Dee to Sir William Cecil (1562–3)', in the *Miscellany of the Philobiblon Society*, Vol. I (London 1854). Dee calls the *Steganographia* 'a boke . . . so nedefull and commodious, as in humanye knowledg none can be meeter or more behovefull'.

[4] In his *Monas* Dee mentions his own manuscript 'Speculum Unitatis sive Apologia pro R. B. Anglo'; see C. H. Josten, 'Translation of John Dee's "Monas Hieroglyphica"', *Ambix* 12 (1964), 123. *Epistolae Fratris Rogerii Baconis De Secretis Operibus Artis et Naturae . . . Opera Johannis Dee . . . Nunc verò a quodam veritatis amatore . . . cum notis quibusdam partim ipsius Johannis Dee partim edentis* (Hamburg 1618). There was much Bacon in Dee's library: *Private Diary*, Catalogue, Nos. 16, 17, 19, 20, 21, 22, 23, 26, 27, 41, 56, 61, 81, 96, 196.

[5] K. Kiesewetter, *John Dee, ein Spiritist des 16. Jahrhunderts* (Leipzig 1893), *passim*.

heavily involved both with the pro-Habsburg activities of the Zborowski faction and adventurers like Basilikos, and in occult or magical speculations of all kinds.[1] He was a great patron of alchemists and financed the first edition of an important work by Paracelsus.[2] Łaski has traditionally been seen as a superficial and prodigal aristocrat who even espoused alchemy merely to restore his finances and was taken in by Dee's promises of worldly fame; but while evidence exists that he was wanton and ambitious, there must have been deeper springs to his character.[3] The very circumstances of his visit to England in 1583 and the lavish but serious reception which he was given by such as Sir Philip Sidney and the Earl of Leicester would seem to argue that conclusion. During this visit Łaski met Dee and his new assistant Kelley, and later a stay in Oxford was arranged for him which inspired the celebrated disputation between members of the University and Giordano Bruno.[4] Dee and Kelley entered Łaski's service when he left England, and the three travelled together to Poland.

There the seances which are so exhaustively described in the *Relation* continued, both on Łaski's estates and in nearby Cracow. While Kelley mediated the promptings of the spirits to his master and patron, Dee made contact with members of the University (to whom he left a valuable Greek manuscript)[5] and others in the city who shared his interests,

[1] Łaski is a man who deserves some serious study and has apparently received very little (the sketch by A. Kraushar, *Olbrecht Łaski, wizerunek historiczny* (Warsaw 1882), is not a work of scholarship). His family was traditionally Catholic, though it produced one notable Protestant theologian (Johannes à Lasko). His Catholic fervour emerges (e.g.) from *Materiały do dziejów Reformacji* (ed. Żelewski), 33, 36, 50, 60, 64 f.; his support for Maximilian II from *Étienne Batory, Roi de Pologne, Prince de Transylvanie* (Cracow 1935), 86, 99 f., 104; his association with Basilikos is mentioned in Sommer, *Vita Jacobi Despotae*.

[2] *Archidoxae Philosophiae Theophrasti Paracelsi . . . Libri X Nunc primum studio et diligentia Adami Schröteri . . . in Latinum translati. Marginalibus annotationibus . . . per Ioannem Gregorium Macrum . . . adiectis* (Cracow 1569), dedicated to Łaski. Macro was his personal physician at the time: Magyary-Kossa, op. cit. iii, No. 907. Cf. Szathmáry, op. cit. 361–3.

[3] For the standard account see Weszprémi, *Centuria*, i. 92 f. Łaski's viciousness emerges from his attack on the town of Késmárk in 1584; cf. the letter from Rudolf II to Pál Máriássy, Prague 16 Apr. 1585 in B. Iványi, *A Márkusfalvi Máriássy család levéltára* (Lőcse 1917), 116; and Kárpáthy-Kravjánszky, op. cit., Doct. No. 120 (Prague 5 June 1584).

[4] D. W. Singer, *Giordano Bruno, His Life and Thought* (New York 1950), 28–35; *Private Diary*, 20; Yates, *Bruno*, 206–11; S. Kot, 'Anglo-Polonica, angielskie źródła rękopiśmienne do dziejów stosunków kulturalnych Polski z Anglją', *Nauka Polska* xx (1935), 74–8.

[5] *Private Diary*, Catalogue No. 47, where the date of donation is given as 28 July 1584; *Katalog rękopisów Biblioteky Universiteta Jagiełłonskiego*, ed. W. Wisłocki (Cracow 1877–81), No. 620, which records the donation by 'Ioannes Dee, Anglus, philosophiae christianae et mathematicarum artium studiosus' on 24 Nov. 1584. The item in question was a fifteenth-century Greek translation of Boethius.

like the Hermetist Hannibal Rosseli, compiler over the succeeding few years of a gigantic edition of the *Pymander*. Dee seems at this time to have been highly obsessed with number mysticism and Cabalistic manipulations.[1] At the beginning of August 1584 he and Kelley left Poland and proceeded to Prague, where Dee sought Rudolf as a vehicle for the same mystic reform which he had preached to Łaski.

This was not his first contact with the Habsburgs, as Dee himself made clear in a supplication to the Emperor. He had already in 1563, during his earlier travels through Europe, visited Maximilian II at Pressburg and dedicated to him the most complex, recondite, and embracing of all his works, the *Monas Hieroglyphica*, which behind an enormously difficult astral and alchemical symbolism was some kind of attempt at the rediscovery of truth through a universal spiritual transmutation.[2] Dee had thus entrusted the esoteric wisdom to Maximilian twenty years before and he now simply transferred the role to the latter's son.

The genuineness of his conviction is borne out by the hand-written entries in Dee's own copy of a prognostic almanac prepared by the Czech astrologer Cyprian Leowitz and published—under the patronage of Maximilian—in 1564. The book contained a series of prophecies about events to be expected from 1564 to 1584; Dee evidently bought it at the time, and it is striking how he has underlined especially those passages connected with Habsburg or Bohemian history.[3] Leowitz himself forecast some sudden violent change to coincide with the new trigon which would enter the heavens in 1584, and he was very probably a personal acquaintance of Dee's. Besides being well known to his contemporaries in England and abroad he was the author of a tract on the casting of horoscopes to which Dee had appended one of his first published works in 1558.[4] Further links already existing between the English scholar

---

[1] *T.F.R.* 75 ff., 397 (Rosseli).

[2] The *Monas* was published with Silvius at Antwerp in 1564. Cf. the translation by Josten, op. cit. and his introduction, 99 ff., and Dee's letter to Rudolf, Prague 17 Aug. 1584 (*T.F.R.* 218).

[3] *De Coniunctionibus Magnis Insignioribus superiorum planetarum, Solis defectionibus et Cometis, in quarta Monarchia, cum eorundem effectuum historica expositione . . . Auctore Cypriano Leovitio à Leonicia* (Lauingen 1564), copy now in University Library, Cambridge, R*5 21(E), signed 'Joannes Dee 1564'.

[4] Cyprian Leovitius, *Brevis et perspicua ratio iudicandi genituras . . . Adiectus est praeterea Libellus de Praestantioribus quibusdam Naturae virtutibus Ioanne Dee Lond. Authore* (London 1558). Leowitz published a series of astrological volumes in the second half of the century which were widely read, and he was on good terms with men like Melanchthon and the Humanist Hieronymus Wolf, the Fuggers and the Rožmberks. Cf. also D. C. Allen, *The Star-Crossed Renaissance* (New York 1966), 73 f.

and Central Europe may only be hinted at: Dee had certainly known
Maximilian's Paracelsan physician and herbalist Bartholomaeus Carrichter, while in 1578 he met the mysterious Thurneysser, probably
at Frankfurt on the Oder.[1]

In examining Dee's relations with Rudolf's court and subsequently
with Rožmberk we can enlist the help of the *Relation* only up to a certain
point. It is still extremely comprehensive on the subject of individual
seances, which were becoming more and more weighed down with the
prophetic utterances of the 'Archangels' Úriel and Gabriel; but large
gaps exist in the sequence of events (as between October 1584 and
January 1585), while the *Private Diary* was renewed only during 1586
and is anyway very fragmentary. The story, as these documents appear
to tell it, runs roughly as follows.[2] Dee and Kelley stayed in the Old
Town of Prague with Hájek and sought access to the Emperor through
the Spanish ambassador San Clemente, who was friendly to them, and
the aulic councillor (later Imperial Vice-Chancellor) Kurz, who was not;
Dee talked with Rudolf only once, and then a Catholic intrigue turned
the Emperor against him. With at least two interruptions in Cracow,
Dee and Kelley stayed in Prague until 1586, continuing their seances,
some of which involved the heretic Francesco Pucci. Finally, a decree
of banishment inspired by Rudolf's Catholic advisers forced them to
flee to Germany, but having gained the protection of Rožmberk they
lived on his lands in Třeboň until 1589 amid growing personal tension
between the two, after which Dee returned to England while Kelley
moved to Prague.

This narrative is of course authentic in its essentials, but it is some
way from being complete, and we must look at the other protagonists
a little more carefully. Hájek's role as a thoroughly respectable occultist
has already been noted. San Clemente too was evidently well-disposed
towards Dee, who wrote several grandiloquent letters to him (three are
quoted in the *Relation*)[3] and also dined with him regularly. The ambassador was not just a good listener, since Dee relates that he claimed

---

[1] Bodleian, MS. Ashmole 1788, fos. 134–5, transcript of a letter from Carrichter to Dee
—'amico et familiari meo plurimum dilecto'—dated Vienna 24 Dec. 1564; Carrichter,
who died in 1574, compiled a series of occult texts, notably the *Kräuterbuch*, which was
several times reprinted. The meeting with Thurneysser is noted in MS. Ashmole 487
(Stadius, *Ephemerides*, ad 15 Dec. 1578, wrongly transcribed in *Private Diary*, 5) and
was perhaps devoted primarily to a discussion of Queen Elizabeth's health.

[2] C. Fell-Smith, *John Dee* (London 1909), 144–200, an unsatisfactory biography,
weakest on the Prague period and unsympathetic to Dee's magical and astrological
interests.

[3] *T.F.R.*, 225 (letter of 24 Aug. 1584), 248 (letter of 28 Sept. 1584, also in the *Correspondencia . . . de San Clemente*, 215–18), 257 (letter of 31 Dec. 1584).

direct descent from Ramon Lull, and he was definitely an expert on his supposed forebear—Hoghelande drew on him for information about the Catalan philosopher.[1] In 1585 San Clemente acted as one of the patrons at the christening of Dee's son Michael in St. Vitus's Cathedral; the others were Rudolf's minister Wolf Rumpf and the Spanish wife of Adam Dietrichstein, Marguerite de Cardona.[2]

It is on the other hand not clear that Jakob Kurz, who as we have seen became one of the Emperor's closest advisers during this period, showed himself ill-affected towards Dee. On their first meeting, arranged by Rudolf, Kurz says that he has heard much about him;[3] that should not surprise us, since Kurz was a man of broad and ready education, but they spent six hours together while Dee explained his purpose, which suggests they had much to discuss, especially because a little later Kurz took the initiative of paying Dee a visit and was shown various occult books.[4] He is also reported to have engineered for Dee a doctorate of medicine from the University.[5] These dealings occurred during the summer of 1584 before the Englishmen's first 'withdrawal' to Cracow. Thereafter no mention is made of Kurz or of further meetings with Rudolf, but the sources are almost totally silent about the whole of 1585 and become helpful again only for the episode of banishment which did not take place until the end of May 1586, a full two years after Dee and Kelley's appearance in Prague.[6] It would be false to infer from this that they necessarily remained out of touch with the court.

Indeed the evidence of the nuncio Sega argues that they were important and dangerous adversaries: 'Giovanni Dii et . . . suo compagno sono *in questa corte* buon pezo fa, et vanno a camino di farsi autori d'una nuova superstitione, per non dire heresia, *sono noti all'imperatore et a tutta la corte.*'[7] It was Sega, his predecessor Malaspina, and the Curialist George Lobkovic who encompassed Dee's expulsion,[8] and Dee made himself reprehensible to orthodox Catholicism precisely because his message was both *relevant* and *meaningful* to his Prague audience. The machinations of nuncios and Imperial confessor appear more clearly still since the

---

[1] Ibid. **245**. Hoghelande's life of Lull, appended to the *Historiae aliquot transmutationis*, was communicated to him by San Clemente.

[2] *T.F.R.*, 382.

[3] Ibid. **239** f.   [4] Ibid. **247**.

[5] C. H. Josten, 'An Unknown Chapter in the Life of John Dee', *JWCI* 28 (1965), 229.

[6] *T.F.R.*, 426 ff.

[7] Nuncios/Sega, Prague 29 Apr. 1586 (my italics).

[8] See Březan, 153; L. Firpo, 'John Dee, scienziato, negromante e avventuriero', *Rinascimento* iii (1952), 60–2.

rediscovery of a manuscript which describes one of the last of the Prague seances.[1]

Dee was, it must be stressed, no hole-and-corner adventurer. He had a European reputation which stretched as far as Moscow (the Tsar made attempts to attract him to Russia in 1586),[2] and even Březan, so scathing about the alchemists, called him a 'learned man' suffering persecution from the Catholics.[3] The Lutheran leader Budovec, no friend of magicians, but whose religious views were tinged with mysticism, knew Dee personally. In a later recollection he gives a revealing insight into both the latter's erudition and some of the content of his message: 'A learned and renowned Englishman whose name was Doctor De: [sic] came to Prague to see the Emperor Rudolf II and was at first well received by him; he predicted that a miraculous reformation would presently come about in the Christian world and would prove the ruin not only of the city of Constantinople but of Rome also. These predictions he did not cease to spread among the populace.'[4] According to Budovec the nuncio so stirred up Rudolf against Dee that he ordered him to leave Prague within a day. Evidently this was a sudden and unpredictable impulse of the Emperor, since the two Englishmen had already spent so long in the city and were so well known. The most likely explanation is that Catholic insinuations acted on one of his abrupt moods, as they did later in the case of Želinský and Milner.

A crucial aspect of the matter is the problem of Dee's religious sympathies and his relations with Pucci. Dee has been interpreted as orthodox Protestant or as equally pronounced Catholic,[5] but it is surely clear from the *Relation* that he believed in some kind of mystic universal revelation, and in a spiritual Christianity which accepted no doctrinal limitations. That came close to the chiliasm of Pucci, whom Dee seems initially to have met in Cracow,[6] and they were indeed commonly linked together, especially by Papal supporters. Yet this was precisely the

---

[1] Josten, 'Unknown Chapter', *passim*—Dee's account of the proceedings of 10 Apr. 1586.

[2] *Private Diary*, 22; cf. N. A. Figurovski, 'The Alchemist and Physician Arthur Dee', *Ambix* 13 (1965-6), 35–51, on the relations with Moscow of Dee and his son Arthur.

[3] Březan, 153 f. Ferdinand of Tyrol wished to know more about him in 1586: Ferdinand to Rožmberk, Innsbruck 14 June 1586, in *SČ* vii, No. 8.

[4] Budovec, *Circulus horologi Lunaris*, 245.

[5] e.g. by Kiesewetter, *John Dee*, 59. The best existing treatment of the Dee–Pucci relation is by Firpo, art. cit.

[6] An astrological note by Dee on the Polish wife of a Florentine named Montelupi ends: 'Hanc notam recepi Cracoviae a° 1585 July 12 per F. Pucci', Bodleian, MS. Ashmole 488, front leaf.

moment when Pucci began meditating his ultimately disastrous return
to the Roman Catholic fold, and he apparently regarded Dee's message
as an inspiration from that quarter. Thus while the nuncio saw the
Englishmen as tarred with the same brush of heresy as Pucci and his
friend Christian Francken, Dee and Kelley took Pucci increasingly for
a Roman agent. Since the latter was anyway a man difficult to handle—
he is one of very few whom Dee obviously dislikes on a personal level—
there could be no real co-operation between them, although the Italian
later reappeared a number of times as a fairly unwelcome guest at Třeboň.[1]

Pucci is not the only link with the second period of Dee and Kelley's
stay in Bohemia, that which began on their return from Germany in
August 1586 to the protection of Rožmberk at Třeboň.[2] There is other
evidence of continuity: Łaski paid several visits to Třeboň,[3] while both
Dee and his assistant undertook a number of private and secretive journeys which must have included Prague. These are obscure episodes—
one of them took the pair to the castle of Reichenstein[4]—and it seems
likely that renewed contact was established with the court and the
Emperor. Rudolf perhaps appreciated that he had misjudged Dee
(certainly renewed Catholic attacks on Rožmberk for his patronage of
occultists failed to move him) and he was well aware of the further activities of the Englishmen. At Třeboň the seances continued, sometimes
in the presence of Rožmberk;[5] but here the fame of the learned Doctor
and his collaborator was above all as alchemists. The place of the philosopher's stone in Dee's metaphysical scheme is made clear at a point in
the spiritualist actions in Prague when he believes himself enjoined by
the angel Uriel to tell the Emperor that he possesses the secret of transmutation.[6] For him alchemy offered just one way of communicating the
truths which he felt bound to deliver; its processes represented simply
an aspect of his whole occult striving, the material demonstration of a
superior power. From a Bohemian standpoint his fame as a practising
alchemist was overshadowed by that of his enigmatic colleague Kelley.

Edward Kelley is usually numbered in the ranks of the professional
rogues, a thorough charlatan enjoying at most some sadly abused talents

---

[1] *Private Diary*, 23 (1587), 26 (1588).
[2] *T.F.R.* 425, Dee to Rožmberk, Prague 26 May 1586, seeking his protection. The
first entries from Třeboň are on 435 ff., where the year is erroneously given as 1589.
[3] *Private Diary*, 22, 23, 27 = Bodleian, Ashmole 488, fos. 94ᵛ, 99ᵛ, 100ʳ, 114ᵛ, 116ᵛ.
The identification of 'Illustrissimus' with Łaski seems justified.
[4] *T.F.R.* 28 (in the second order of pagination); Bodleian, Ashmole 488, fo. 95ʳ,
which lists the stages on their route.
[5] *T.F.R.* 444 ff.; this record breaks off during 1587.
[6] Ibid. 240, 243 (seances of 21 and 22 Sept. 1584).

as ventriloquist or conjurer.[1] The accusations seem based on a fair, though exaggerated, assessment of his character, but they, like some of the details of his biography, are incomplete. His performances at the seances suggest at very least thorough familiarity with the technical procedures of occultism, while his transmutations and alchemical recipes were frequently described and copied, not only in seventeenth-century publications,[2] but in Bohemian manuscripts of the period. These typically bear a note like: 'this was used by Edoardus Gelleus, the English alchemist',[3] or 'Alia purificatio . . . Vom Engelender zue Wittgenaw H. Edu. Keleo 1588',[4] and found their way also to neighbouring regions like Hungary, where one practitioner claims to be reiterating the true wisdom of St. Dunstan as rediscovered by Kelley and passed on through Rudolf.[5] The Bohemian adept Matthias Erbinäus von Brandau, a grateful pupil, insists that he has seen Kelley's tincture and recalls that the Englishman could manufacture the *Mercurius Solis* in no more than a quarter of an hour.[6]

In 1589 Kelley left Dee and returned to Prague, where he was fêted by the Emperor, accepted as a citizen of Bohemia (the while purporting to be a member of the Irish knighthood),[7] and granted a patent of Imperial nobility.[8] The transition from Rožmberk's to Rudolf's employ did not, however, take place overnight; an intimate letter from the Emperor to Vilém, whose only dating is '27 October', requests—in friendly terms— that 'Eduardus' be temporarily released from his service there to come to Prague and supervise a great alchemical work which is in progress.[9] Rudolf will not detain him ('will in nit langer aufhalten, als er selbst begern wird'), but the operation is a difficult one which needs expert assistance: 'das Hoechststuck darzu mangelt, der mercurius solis, an dem die sach nit kan verfertigt werden, halt derhalben für guet das der Eduard derselbst hieher khamb, disem manglen zu helffen'.

    [1] See J. Svátek, *Obrazy*, 135–59; thus also the literature which concentrates on Dee, e.g. Firpo, op. cit. 38 ff.
    [2] Like Ashmole's *Theatrum Chemicum Britannicum* (London 1652), 324–33, or Hoghelande's *Historiae aliquot transmutationis*, 28. Transmutations by Kelley were cited by Gassendi, Libavius, and others; cf. Schmieder, op. cit. 304 f., 308.
    [3] Nat. Mus., III H 20, at end of section beginning: 'Spis o dwau wečnegch a neuhasytedlnegch hořigcych čiasnych swětlech'.
    [4] Strahov, MS. DD V 34, fo. 45 and *passim*; Wittgenaw = Wittingau, the German name for Třeboň.
    [5] Budapest, National Museum, OSzK 239 Quart. Ger. 48ʳ: 'Herrn Ioanni Tustani [*sic*] process . . .'
    [6] Brandau, *Warhaffte Beschreibung*, 13, 79, 92. Brandau was writing about 1630.
    [7] *SČ* vii, No. 412 (1589): 'Eduard Kelley, born an Englishman, of the knightly kin and house called Imaymi in the county of Conaghaku in the kingdom of Ireland.'
    [8] Bauer, op. cit. 44.
    [9] Rudolf to Vilém of Rožmberk, Prag den 27 October s.a., holograph, in LRRK, B 3/1, No. 59. It begins: 'Es hat mir der Heiden die Prob geleisten . . .'

It would be instructive to know the year of this letter; at all events Kelley stood in high favour with the Emperor at least during 1589 and 1590.[1] His success provokes one interesting speculation: was Kelley himself the 'Odoardus Scotus' of the Vienna manuscript already described? His background was obscure and surrounded by legends, and he was widely believed to be Scottish or Irish, while another tract circulated and printed in the seventeenth century claimed his personal authorship: it was supposed to have been sent by him to Rudolf from prison in 1596.[2] There are two separate questions here: whether Kelley and the so-called 'Scotto' were one and the same; and whether Kelley wrote the treatise. In the first case the evidence of Bydžovský and Dačický suggests that two distinct persons really existed (unless one were perhaps a confused version of Dee?); but in the second, the very relation of the Englishman to Rudolf at this time argues that Kelley may have been the author, or at least the inspirer, of the manuscript.

In May 1591 the situation was rudely disturbed, and Kelley was suddenly ordered to be detained in Prague at his sovereign's pleasure.[3] It was widely thought that the trickery of this 'Cacochymicus' had now received its just reward. But the subsequent story of his imprisonment is confused, like most information about his life.[4] Kelley was certainly transferred to the royal stronghold of Křivoklát (Pürglitz) and apparently held in other castles as well; there he is said to have made several attempts to escape, in one of which he broke a leg (though he may in fact have been a cripple anyway).[5] No proof exists that he remained continuously in royal disfavour, and Dee at least thought at one stage that he had been pardoned.[6] Even the date of his death is not clear: Dee recorded in 1595 'the newes that Sir Edward Kelley was slayne'; yet he was definitely alive in 1597 at the castle of Most, and Borbonius thought he was still active in 1598.[7]

[1] Březan, 164.

[2] This was published in *Drey Vortreffliche und noch nie im Druck gewesene Chymische Bücher als* ... (3) *Des Weltberühmten Engelländers Edoardi Kellaei ausführlicher Tractat dem Kayser Rudolpho zugeschrieben* ... (Hamburg 1670, reprinted 1691). It is a straightforward alchemical work, with a modest introduction from Kelley. Cf. Bodleian, Ashmole MS. 1420, fos. 89–94.

[3] Březan, 164 f.; Nuncios/Visconte, Prague 7 May 1591; Žerotín's diary (Ipolyi/Rimay), 7 f.; Fuggerzeitungen for 1591 (ÖN, MS. 8964), *passim*; J. Strype, *Annals of the Reformation*, iii (London 1728), App. No. lxxiv.

[4] Kelley's biography falls into three periods: before 1583, for which no sober details exist; 1583–8, reasonably documented thanks to Dee; and 1588–97(?). Much of the received story derives from Morhof, *De Transmutatione*, 152–8; cf. Schmieder, op. cit. 302–7.

[5] Sega already in 1586 speaks of 'Giovanni Dee et il Zoppo suo compagno': Nuncios/Sega, Prague 29 Apr.   [6] *Private Diary*, 46, 47 (1593).

[7] Ibid. 54; Nat. Mus., MS. VI D 17, a copy of the German translation of the basic Bohemian 'constitution', has the colophon: 'Diss Buch der Landtsordenung ist dem

Meanwhile Kelley's reputation did not diminish among practising alchemists. One widely-believed explanation of his confinement was Rudolf's own desire to prise from him the secrets of the philosophers' stone. Some continued to visit him in prison—Oswald Croll went to Most, apparently in the hope of some enlightenment over the *Secretum solutionis*.[1] Nor was Kelley ignored in England. Sir Edward Dyer, a friend of Dee since the 1570s, took a great interest in him, pressing long and vainly for his return, while even Lord Burghley besought the errant knight to give Her Majesty's court the benefit of his talents. Dyer spent several months in Prague learning the mysteries of the Art and was only spared the full force of Rudolf's displeasure over this rivalry through diplomatic overtures from Queen Elizabeth.[2] The fabled accounts of Kelley's transmutations lingered on into the new century: Elias Ashmole was to receive the substance of his information from Dee's son Arthur (Dyer's godson), who had been involved with them at Třeboň and Prague in his youth and who still remembered—decades later—playing childish games with the 'Plates of Gold made by Projection'.[3]

By the time of Kelley's demise Dee had settled down to a life of retirement in England, yet his five years spent in Bohemia remain as the central chapter of his life. His 'mission' to Prague is a complex story, parts of it still largely obscure, but it was conceived on a grand scale; Dee sought a world reform by harnessing ancient spiritual powers and working through occult and magical forces. The legends surrounding him and Kelley are muddled and far-fetched, but they contain a grain of truth, as the intimations of the spirits contain some genuine evidence of Dee's own mental condition. Irrationality, even superstition, was not merely a cover for action or a cloudiness of perception: it formed a vital component of contemporary intellectual activity. The very worst misunderstanding—of Dee and Kelley no less than of Rudolf—consists in underrating its role.

While Dee and Kelley were working in Třebon, another yet more controversial magician and prophet made a mercurial appearance on the

---

Gestrengen Edlen Ernnesten Ritter unndt Herrn Edwardo Kelleo von Imanij undt auff New Lüben, Röm: Khaj: Maj: Rath von mir Caspar Littman auffm Brüxer Schloss den 22 Maj Anno 1597 aussgeschrieben undt vollendet' (Brüx = Most); Gellner, *Borbonius*, 92.

[1] Brandau, op. cit. 89.
[2] Sargent, 97–122 (cf. above, p. 122); Bodleian, Ashmole MS. 1420, fos. 271–327. On Burghley: Strype, *Annals*, iii, App. No. lxxiii; iv (London 1738), Nos. ii and iii; cf. Ashmole MS. 1788, fo. 159ʳ.
[3] C. H. Josten, *Elias Ashmole* (Oxford 1966), ii. 662 f.; iv. 1312 f., 1757.

Bohemian stage: Giordano Bruno. Bruno of course created a whole metaphysical edifice now barely comprehensible to the modern reader, but it is important to see that this was rooted in the universalist and mystical tendencies of the occult revival of the late sixteenth century.[1] He was an emblematist, a philosopher whose works hang heavy with visual and literary symbolism, a Hermetist, Cabalist, and Lullist, a mage communicating the secret traditions of the world of hidden spiritual powers, a Catholic at odds with the Roman Church, a wandering 'adept' seeking a 'transmutation' of the human condition. Recent research has shown how ambitious were his plans for a universal reform, as they found exposition in books, public lectures, and disputations during the decade after his first appearance at Paris in 1582.

Bruno was perhaps the most original thinker of the second half of the sixteenth century, but what concerns us here is the way his ideas were interpreted and the nature of his audience. After extended stays in France and England—including his dramatic visit to Oxford staged in honour of Albrecht Łaski's presence—Bruno moved to Germany, and at Wittenberg in 1587–8 he wrote several works based on Lullist and medieval memory techniques which recapitulate the themes he had already developed.[2] Early in 1588 he came to Prague and lived there for some months before continuing his journeyings to Switzerland and back into Germany, finally making a fateful return to Italy on the invitation of the Venetian nobleman Giovanni Mocenigo in 1591. Throughout these travels his personality and publications excited much interest, and it has even been suggested that he founded a secret sect of 'Brunonians' ('Giordanisti') among those in Germany who accepted his message.[3] Certainly there is something of the master in one of his disciples, Lambert Schenckel, who originated from the Netherlands (he was at one time tutor to the grandchildren of Plantin),[4] sympathized with Lipsius, and compiled various treatises on the artificial memory which were popular in Germany from the 1590s.[5] We have no means of knowing whether Schenckel found his way to Rudolfine Prague, but it is very probable,

---

[1] This is the burden of the book by Dr. Frances Yates, *Giordano Bruno and the Hermetic Tradition.*

[2] Yates, *Art of Memory*, 287–93; Singer, *Bruno*, 140–4.

[3] Yates, *Art of Memory*, 299–307.

[4] Sabbe, *De Moretussen* . . ., 10. Several of Schenckel's works were published by Plantin; he also wrote a poem on the occasion of the latter's death: Voet, op. cit. 122.

[5] Rossi, *Clavis Universalis*, 128 n. Schenckel was read by Descartes and Leibniz (ibid. 154 ff., 253). After his *De Memoria* (Douai 1595) came his best-known work, *Gazophylacium artis memoriae*, first published at Strasbourg in 1610. He also edited excerpts from Lipsius's *De Constantia* (Paris 1606 and n.p. 1615).

for he was definitely in the city a little later and published a volume of
verse there which contains several poems in admiration of the already
deceased Westonia.[1] One of his pupils was a Silesian, Martin Sommer,
who—like Schenckel himself—toured Central Europe giving instruction
in memory techniques and demonstrations of his own prowess.[2]

The reasons for Bruno's decision to visit Prague are unknown. Probably he made contact in Wittenberg with Czechs, as he definitely did
with Hungarians and Silesians; Valens Acidalius took an interest in him,
as did the young Magyar nobleman Mihály Forgách (both of them later
studied in Italy), while Dornavius makes an oblique and cryptic reference
to him in his *Amphitheatrum*.[3] Doubtless too Bruno knew of the proclivities of Rudolf, and his esoteric philosophy was naturally attracted
to a sovereign Hermes Trismegistus who might implement his reform.[4]
In Paris he had become acquainted with the mathematician and inventor
Fabricio Mordente, but the two subsequently fell out when Bruno reinterpreted some of Mordente's ideas to suit his own higher prophetic
purposes. Bruno had no time for the discursive reason and in Prague he
took the opportunity to make his position plain again with a small book
which he entitled *160 Articles against the Mathematicians* and had published by the Czech printer George Daczicenus (Dačický). This volume
is now exceedingly rare and possesses a twofold interest: on the one hand
it is a further shot in the campaign against Mordente, who had by that
time taken a post in the Imperial service; on the other it includes a fulsome dedication to Rudolf which rehearses the whole Brunonian philosophy of a single true universal religion rooted in the occult tradition,
and the salvation of mankind through the intuitions of an intellectual
élite.[5] In Prague Bruno continued too with his Lullist and Hermetic

[1] Lambertus Schenckelius, *Jovinianus Imperator* (Prague 1617), 63–72. This work is
dedicated to Baltazar Zuñiga, San Clemente's successor as Spanish ambassador.

[2] In 1619 Sommer published an abridged version of the *Gazophylacium*: *Gazophylacium artis memoriae . . . per L. Schenckel, nunc vero ipsius permissu a Martino Sommero,
Silesio, in diversis Germaniae academiis traditum et illustratum* (Venice 1619). Cf. the
German edition of this by J. L. Klüber: *Compendium der Mnemonik oder Erinnerungs-
wissenschaft* (Erlangen 1804).

[3] Acidalius, *Epistolarum Centuria*, Nos. 2, 3, etc. On Forgách, cf. E. Koltay-Kastner,
'Amici, nemici e studiosi di Giordano Bruno in Ungheria', *Rivista di Filosofia* xlii
(1951), iii. 9–12; and E. Veress, *A Páduai Egyetem magyarországi tanulóinak anya-
könyve es iratai* (Budapest 1915), 94, 98 f. C. Dornavius, *Amphitheatrum*, dedication:
'Citantur de caetero nonnulla; in quae nequidem inquirendum mihi censui: puto
praeconium Diaboli; quale Wittembergae Bruno Nolanus recitasse dicetur . . .'

[4] 'Apud Aegyptios primum, successu verò temporum apud Persas atque Romanos
. . . usu venit ut de sapientibus fierent Reges, et de Regibus essent Sacerdotes; unde
scientia, potestate et authoritate insignes meritò dicerentur Trismegisti . . .', Bruno's
Preface to *De Monade, Numero et Figura Liber* (Frankfurt 1591).

[5] *Articuli centum et sexaginta adversus hujus tempestatis mathematicos atque philosophos*

studies and completed one text which he had begun in Wittenberg, the *De specierum scrutinio et lampade combinatoria Raymundi Lulli*, printed during 1588 by George Nigrin, perhaps the most important of the city's specialized publishers.[1]

Bruno was one of the closest sixteenth-century students of the Lullist 'art', in its revived form as a logic which was held to reflect the articulations of the deeper, occult reality of the world, and the cities in which he moved—Paris, London, Prague, Wittenberg, Frankfurt—formed the centres of this kind of conceptual and mnemonic system-building.[2] Significantly his Prague volume on the combinatory art was dedicated to San Clemente, whose interest in Lull must thus have been well known. What can be determined of Bruno's other contacts there reinforces the impression that court circles were heavily involved in such pursuits— Rudolf personally granted the philosopher a sum of 300 thalers.[3] That certainly holds true of Julius of Brunswick, who was not yet in Prague when Bruno visited it but met the Nolan at his own university of Helmstedt in 1589.[4] There Bruno delivered a memorial oration to Brunswick's father (who had died the same year) and later he dedicated to Julius himself two of his last published works, the *De Monade* and *De Triplici Minimo et Mensura* which appeared at Frankfurt in 1591. Brunswick was a man of great learning: a littérateur, bibliophile, and scientist, he studied at the feet of a leading Melanchthonian and had a knowledge of Hebrew.[5] Like Rudolf, Bodin, and King James I he combined broad intellectual horizons with a deep belief in the reality of spirits, and he was one of the foremost persecutors of witches in his day.[6] His closeness to the Emperor during Rudolf's last years has already been remarked upon; it is possible that the Rudolfine alchemical manuscript now in his old capital of Wolfenbüttel once belonged to his own fine collection. Brunswick knew Tycho Brahe, who seems also to have owned Bruno's

---

(Prague 1588). Only three copies were known in 1956; see J. Hayward, 'The location of copies of the first editions of Giordano Bruno', *The Book Collector* 5 (1956), No. 21. Cf. V. Salvestrini and L. Firpo, *Bibliografia di Giordano Bruno* (Florence 1958), No. xx; V. Spampanato, *Vita di Giordano Bruno* (Messina 1921), 429; Yates, *Bruno*, 294–7, 313–15.

[1] Singer, op. cit. 144 f.; Salvestrini and Firpo, op. cit. No. xix. Part of this was just the reprint of a Wittenberg text (ibid. No. xv).

[2] Cf. Rossi, op. cit. 113; T. and J. Carreras y Artau, *Historia de la filosofía española* ii (Madrid 1943), 225–31.   [3] Spampanato, op. cit. 431, 703.

[4] Singer, op. cit. 146 f.; Yates, *Bruno*, 316 f.

[5] For a general sketch of Brunswick's talents (mainly political): Schwarz, op. cit. 204–8. His teacher was Johann Caselius (Heer, op. cit. 238).

[6] A. Rhamm, *Hexenglaube und Hexenprozesse vornähmlich in den braunschweigischen Landen* (Wolfenbüttel 1882), 75–8.

works; a copy of one of the Wittenberg texts, the *Camoeracensis Acrotismus*, bears a personal dedication to him from the author.[1]

Another Bohemian friend of Bruno was Johann Wacker. Wacker possessed the *Spaccio de la Bestia Trionfante*,[2] one of the most grandiose expositions of the astrological reform, as well as the treatise on the infinite universe, published in Venice in 1584.[3] His celebrated library must have contained further volumes as well since Scioppio, who moved in Wacker's immediate circle during the late 1590s, mentions reading several works by Bruno while resident in Prague.[4]

The most interesting Czech Brunonian is a nobleman whose roots, like Wacker's, lay in Silesia: Hans von Nostitz. The Nostitz were a widespread family with a highly complicated genealogy,[5] and the branch to which Hans belonged had a tradition of loyal service to the Habsburgs. Although Hans himself seems to have remained a Protestant and was active mainly in his home territory of Liegnitz and Brieg near Breslau, his brother-in-law Otto (1574–1639) became Vice-Chancellor of Bohemia after the White Mountain and was both aulic and privy councillor,[6] while his two sons—both converts to Catholicism—likewise rose high in Habsburg office.[7]

Little is known about Hans von Nostitz except what he himself records, though a series of elegies and tributes by various local poets on the occasion of his death in 1619 reveal at least that he was a great patron of the arts.[8] Born in 1562, he undertook during his young manhood the kind of travels which were usual among the Bohemian aristocracy; in 1582 he was in Paris and later he visited England.[9] After this he apparently settled down in Silesia, serving the Duke of Liegnitz and filling

[1] UK, Sig. XV K 22: 'insigni et famosi Dm. ill^mo et excell° D. Tichoni Dani insignit benevolentia et obsequis au(tor).' In 1605 Brunswick recommended to Rudolf another mathematician and astronomer, Johann Krabbe: *Jahrbuch* xix (1898), Reg. No. 16531.

[2] The edition published in Paris in 1584: UK, Sig. XII J 237. The inscription is crossed out, but the name 'Wacker' is decipherable.

[3] *De l'infinito Universo et Mondi*: UK, Sig. XII J 238. The inscription has again been largely expunged.

[4] D'Addio, op. cit. 28.

[5] On its individual members (the name was also spelt 'Nosticz') see V. Boetticher, *Geschichte des oberlausitzischen Adels* ii (Oberlössnitz bei Dresden 1913), s.v.

[6] Ibid. s.v., and Schwarz, op. cit. 316.

[7] The elder, Otto (1608–64), *Freiherr* and privy councillor, was known for his learning and his library; the younger, Johann Hartwig (1610–83), became Bohemian Chancellor on the death of Slavata in 1652: Schwarz, op. cit. 313–15.

[8] *Musae Lacrumantes super immaturum, sed beatum Obitum Dn. Ioannis à Nosticz* (n.p. 1619); *Arae Exsequales . . . Generosi et Magnifici Viri J. à N.* (n.p. 1619); *Super decessu luctuosissimi Viri I. à N. . . . Threnodiae* (Liegnitz 1619); *Viri Magnifici . . . J. à N. . . . Vexillum Sepulcrale* (n.p. n.d.); *Memoria . . . Dn. I à N.* (Liegnitz n.d.).

[9] 'cum . . . exteras Galliae, Angliaeque terras haud obiter perlustrando, juveniles annos exegisset . . .' *Vexillum Sepulcrale* (see previous note).

diverse local offices, though there is a manuscript in his name which suggests that he also travelled to Constantinople, and he clearly showed an interest in the history and customs of the Turks and Persians.[1]

One event has particular relevance here: while in France Nostitz had attended the courses of Giordano Bruno. In his introduction to the work on logic and memory which he wrote many years later he recalls that formative experience: 'I can still remember how, thirty-three years since, Iordanus Brunus of Nola first demonstrated his magnificent Lullian and Mnemological arts in Paris and drew many disciples to him privately. Finding myself at that time in the same city for the purpose of travel (*peregrinatio*) and other forms of study, I too more than once joined his audience to hear what this marvellous art might be.'[2] Initially, he continues, he found Ramism simpler and more intelligible, but his enthusiasm for the subject did not wane and he read widely the literature which was available to him on his return home. In 1586 he began an album (*Stammbuch*) which contains, beyond the usual entries from friends, many emblems—including some on the Rudolfine ADSIT—and symbols, some gematria, and letter-combinations; all these he sought increasingly to apply in the preparation of more broadly valid logical categories.[3] As his study of Lullism revived he evidently had access to the books necessary for pursuing it, and Nostitz records how he quite modified his first unfavourable opinion on 'Lull himself and his disciples and interpreters Bernhard de Lavinheta, the Syntax in the magical arts of Martin Sebaldus, Valerian de Valeriis, and the book of Iordanus Brunus which once I had rejected'.[4]

Nostitz's idea was to make the mysteries of Bruno and Lull more accessible, and in this he was working on the lines of a more famous contemporary, the polymath J. H. Alsted. The latter's *Clavis Artis Lullianae* of 1609 represented an attempt to reconcile the 'sects of logicians', Aristotelians and reformers, whose differing approaches did violence to

[1] Nostitz, MS. a 28. This contains a copy of privileges from the principalities of Schweidnitz and Jauer, and then several casual writings, including a description of Constantinople (fos. 65^r–71^v), a narrative of the Turkish–Persian war, and a genealogical account of the Shahs of Persia, dated Constantinople 13 Aug. 1587 (fos. 75^r–89^v).

[2] *Artificium Aristotelico-Lullio-Rameum In quo per Artem Intelligendi LOGICAM Artem Agendi PRACTICAM Artis Loquendi partem eam, quae agit de Inventione, TOPICAM Methodo et Terminis Aristotelico-Rameis Circulis Modo Lulliano inclusis, Via et ratio, plura quam centies mille Attributa vel Argumenta de quovis themate inveniendi, cum ipso quotidiano usu conveniens, ostenditur.* [For Iohannes à Nosticz] . . . *elaboratum à Conrado Bergio Colberg.* (Bregae 1615); Introduction to the reader. This work is mentioned in recent literature but regarded as lost; cf. Singer, op. cit. 19 f.; Rossi, op. cit. 114 n. I have used the copy in the library of Strahov (Sig. E L XIV 37).

[3] Strahov, Sig. D B V 12 Stammbuch: 'Joachimus à Nosticz an. 1586'.

[4] *Artificium*, loc. cit.

the true harmony of knowledge. Alsted too had drunk deep at the sources of occult wisdom and his next work, the *Systema Mnemonicum Duplex* of 1610, was a monument to what he saw as the genuine tradition of memory theory, championed most recently by Bruno and Schenckel. He was also well known in Bohemia: the *Systema* was dedicated to a Czech nobleman, Jiří of Hodice, while it and another work of the same year express their author's debt to Karel Žerotín in Moravia.[1] Two years later Alsted published his *Artificium Perorandi*, an esoteric tract on rhetoric derived from a manuscript of Bruno's written in Wittenberg, and presented it to a Polish patron, Abraham Wysocki;[2] Another figure who belongs in this picture is the eclectic logician from Danzig, Bartholomew Keckermann (1571–1609), a man widely respected in his day and the compiler of a large number of systematic treatises. Keckermann had connections with Central Europe—with Wysocki for example—and he was much admired, though with certain reservations, by Alsted, who prepared a posthumous edition of his works.

Like Keckermann and Alsted, whose writings he consulted,[3] Nostitz sought to resolve the apparently disparate principles of Lull, Ramus, and Aristotle. He evidently had willing local helpers, for he quotes several logical 'systems' of persons known to him: Johann Hockelshoven of Breslau, Nicholas Vigelius, Hieronymus Treutler, and one, Tobias Scultetus, who seems also to have ordered his library according to some pre-ordained scheme. A certain Gregor Martinus, who was tutor to Nostitz's sons in 1611, elaborated not only a metaphysical theory of classes but also a curious logical analysis of travel—its methods, types, causes, places, and the rest.[4]

Nostitz aimed then to fuse the traditional Aristotelian models with the brevity of Ramus and the wheels of Lullism. The finished product appeared in the album during 1614 and was published the following year at Brieg as his *Artificium Aristotelico-Lullio-Rameum*, with a drawing of the whole 'artifice' by a Breslau engraver. Nostitz left the working out of

---

[1] J. H. Alsted, *Panacea Philosophica* (Herborn 1610), his first encyclopedic work. Cf. below, p. 283.

[2] *Artificium Perorandi traditum a Iordano Bruno Nolano, Communicatum a Johan-Henrico Alstedio* (Frankfurt 1612); cf. Salvestrini and Firpo, op. cit. No. xxvii.

[3] Nostitz mentions the *Clavis Artis Lullianae* in his introduction to the *Artificium*. One of the few surviving copies of the *Artificium Perorandi*, now in Wrocław (Breslau) and bound with Alsted's *Panacea Philosophica*, came from the library in Nostitz's town of Brieg. See A. Nowicki, 'Early editions of Giordano Bruno in Poland', *The Book Collector* 13 (1964), 342–5.

[4] Stammbuch (there are no page references); one of the illustrations is 'Eiusdem Dñi Thobiae Sculteti . . . Bibliothecae dispositio'. Martinus appears as physician to the Duke of Wohlau in one of the Nostitz funeral elegies.

the scheme to another of his sons' tutors, Conrad Berg from Pomerania, who in a preface freely admits to understanding less of it than his master but is nevertheless convinced of the value of the enterprise.[1] It seems more than likely that the book and its contents were in fact discussed over a period of years by a number of men about whom it would be valuable to know more, and who may also—like various members of the Scultetus family—have concerned themselves with Paracelsan medicine and the Rosicrucians. They were at the same time active figures in the educated society of their day: Treutler and Tobias Scultetus wrote poetry of that Humanist kind which has already been considered at an earlier point in this narrative, while Nostitz himself was well known in such circles; he appears in several of the verse collections of the period, like the *Symbola* of Jakob Monau.[2]

Nostitz died four years later amid the rebellion of his fellow-estates, which must have rudely disturbed intellectual life in Silesia, albeit less radically than in neighbouring Bohemia. There, one of the politicians who gained most from the Catholic triumph was his brother-in-law Otto, and the latter had plenty of opportunity to add to his already large library by seizing the books of some of the insurgents (among them perhaps Jessenius). This makes it impossible, despite a personal autograph, to be sure whether Otto's books and manuscripts which remain in the family library in Prague were acquired before or after 1621.[3] But his interest in occult works likewise stands out clearly. He had manuscripts on mystical religion ('darinnen das Reich der Natur und das Buch der gnaden erkleirt wird');[4] on alchemy, including a copy of the *Lumen Chymicum* of Sędiwoj, and the lore of signatures; prophecy; and a holograph medical tract by Crato.[5] Most significant of all, he owned a large bound volume which included several of the foremost works on the artificial memory: Schenckel's *Gazophylacium*, Alsted's *Trigae Canonicae*, Marafioti's *De Arte Reminiscentiae*, a re-edition of Peter Ravenna

---

[1] 'Aristotelica carere, circulis quibus copia et memoria adiuvetur: Ramum doctrinae plenitudine: Lullium terminorum accuratione et methodo naturali destitui. Fieri posse aliquid Aristotelico-Lullio-Rameum, si ita inventis eorum utamur: ut Aristotelica Rameā brevitate per circulos Lullianos adumbrentur.'

[2] Monau, *Symbolum*, 27, 266 ff. Cf. above, pp. 147–50. Another probable member of this group is Adam Bruxius, a Silesian writer on the artificial memory, whose most important work, *Simonides Redivivus* (Leipzig 1610), contains poems by Caspar Cunrad and an approving mention of the alchemist Hartmann.

[3] There is anyway no adequate catalogue of printed works—only a handwritten German list of volumes alphabetically by authors. The MSS. are detailed in a work by J. V. Šimák (see note on sources).

[4] Nostitz, MS. e 18: 'De Mysterio Magno'.

[5] Nostitz, MSS. b 17; c 2; b 39; b 20.

and others, together with a work by Bruno and a tract on magical gems.[1] In Otto von Nostitz the Rudolfine mentality was still strong; but like other members of the younger Catholic generation he had insured himself against its passive implications by embracing the intemperate orthodoxy of Ferdinand II.

Parallel with the Hermetic and occult strivings of the last decades of the sixteenth century went a revival and popularizing of the Cabala, both within and outside the ghettos of those European cities where the Jews formed an organic part of the social framework. In its widest terms the 'Cabala' is the mystical religion of the Jews, based on a number of visionary writings the most famous of which, the *Zohar*, was produced in thirteenth-century Spain. Its essential aspects are a philosophy of the creation of the world—the doctrine of the Sefiroth, or divine emanations; a mystique of numbers and letters including the art known as gematria; and an apocalyptic message, expressing the characteristically Jewish view of earthly Messianism.[2]

In the period we are considering there are three possible definitions— overlapping but distinct—of 'Cabalism'. The first may be briefly dismissed: the whole magical tradition of the Renaissance incorporated elements which were either consciously or unconsciously 'kabbalistic'. Thus the cosmology of Neoplatonism has much in common with the belief in mediation through the Sefiroth, while the combining of letters and numbers belongs equally to the legacy of Pythagoreanism and the medieval mystics. In this sense John Dee was a Cabalist (the *True and Faithful Relation* is full of such magic) and so were many more who shared his mentality. Some of the writing of Khunrath or Thurneysser falls into the same category, as do the equally arcane 'mathetic' manipulations of Bruno. The other definitions are more significant and must be treated separately: one is the so-called Christian Cabala, the second the practising Cabala of the Jews themselves.

In the broad resurgence of enthusiasm for Hebrew studies during the Renaissance period Germany and the surrounding lands had a high importance, from the acrimonious debate between the Humanist philo-

---

[1] Nostitz, Sig. cg 270. On these memory treatises see Rossi, *Clavis Universalis*, 127 n. The volume on gems bears the title *Veterum sophorum sigilla et Imagines Magicae sive Sculpturae Lapidum et Gemmarum secundum Nomen Dei Tetragrammaton, cum Signatura Planetarum et iuxta certos coeli tractus et constellationes, ad stupendos et mirandos effectus producendos* (n.p. 1612).

[2] See in general, from the Jewish side, G. G. Scholem, *Major Trends in Jewish Mysticism* (London 1955), *passim*; from the Christian side, J. L. Blau, *The Christian Interpretation of the Cabala in the Renaissance* (New York 1944), 7 ff.

semite Reuchlin and his adversary Pfefferkorn,[1] through the followers of Melanchthon and beyond. The depth of contemporary interest in the Jewish mystics is only now becoming better appraised;[2] the occult tradition deriving from Agrippa and Paracelsus incorporated major borrowings from their teaching, and there were individual specialists like Skalich and Widmanstetter, Postel and La Boderie. The culmination of this movement was the work of Pistorius, Rudolf's confessor, who published in Basle in 1587 the first volume of what was planned as a full compendium of Cabalistic texts, embracing the best of Hebrew wisdom together with leading commentaries on it by Christian scholars. It included works by Paul Ricci, perhaps the greatest of the Christian Cabalists, and Reuchlin; various writings of converted Jews; and the visionary *Sepher Iezira*, the Book of Creation.[3] Only after producing it did Pistorius take up his appointment in Prague, and no more of the projected series ever appeared, yet the available evidence does not suggest any complete renegation.[4] Advocacy of the Cabala could, after all, be combined with acceptance of the Catholic religion, as various Renaissance figures demonstrated; it was only Tridentine conformity which gradually rendered it disreputable. After his conversion Pistorius clearly came under pressure from that flank, as well as from representatives of his earlier Protestantism like the chemist Andreas Libavius who censured both him and John Dee in 1595.[5]

Other indications exist of an enthusiasm inside Bohemia for this secret philosophy. Johann Habermann of Eger (1516–90), who became well known in neighbouring Saxony under the name of Avenarius as a Lutheran theologian,[6] was also a student of Hebrew and produced grammars in that language. His last work appears, from the copy which survives in Prague, to have been a far less orthodox undertaking: under the title *Biblia Arcano-Magica Mosaica* it claims to be a rediscovery of the secret divine revelation to Moses which, having passed via Solomon and Alexander the Great to Greece, Venice, and finally Naumburg in Saxony, is now (1591) printed in Wittenberg for the first time.[7] Most of

[1] Blau, op. cit. 41 ff.; F. Secret, *Les Kabbalistes chrétiens de la Renaissance* (Paris 1964), Ch. IV.

[2] Cf. F. Secret, *Le Zohar chez les Kabbalistes chrétiens de la Renaissance* (Paris 1958), 4–25, a critique in part of the somewhat superficial work by Blau cited above.

[3] *Artis Cabalisticae: hoc est, reconditae theologiae et philosophiae, scriptorum Tomus I . . . ex J. Pistorii . . . bibliotheca* (Basle 1587). On the place of Pistorius in sixteenth-century Cabalism see Secret, *Kabbalistes chrétiens*, 279 f.

[4] See above, pp. 90 f.

[5] Secret, *Kabbalistes chrétiens*, 280; Josten, *Dee's Monas*, 96 f.

[6] See *ADB*, s.v.

[7] Johann Habermann, 'Biblia Arcano-Magica Mosaica', Nat. Mus., MS. XI G 7.

the text consists of crude Hebrew characters, seemingly drawn freehand. A Prague manuscript dated 1595 contains a translation into Czech by Ioannes Polentarius of the *Sepher Raziel*, the Book of Raziel 'which is called the book of powers and mysteries, and here are seven treatises in the seven arts and the seven powers'.[1] This too purports to embody the wisdom of Solomon and is a farrago of number mysticism, astrological influences, and manipulations of letters and names. Its title clearly suggests a Spanish medieval original; 'Raziel' was a pseudonym of Abraham Abulafia, whose prophetic Cabala sought to achieve a state of ecstasy through precisely these methods.[2]

There are signs of an interest in Cabalist literature at the court. Julius of Brunswick possessed a copy of the *Cabalistarum Dogmata* of Pico,[3] while the Vice-Chancellor Coraduz, a bibliophile and friend of alchemy, studied Hebrew and even wrote out for himself the mystical *Sepher Iezira*.[4] The Emperor himself was on the search for such books. Friedrich of Württemberg, also a great patron of the occult arts, mentions one in 1600: 'Was E. Röm. Kaj. Majt. mir underm Dato Pilsen, den 13 Aprilis nachst verschinen, eines Hebraischen Buchs halben, so ich bei handen haben soll . . . zugeschrieben, das hab ich an gestern mit gebüerender underthanigster Reverentz empfangen.'[5] Another reference to a 'casket with secret writings' may well reflect the study of ciphers which formed an especial part of Jewish mysticism;[6] and here as elsewhere we must regret that so little of Rudolf's private correspondence survives.

The preoccupation with codes and hidden languages was a growing feature of late Renaissance occultism and it fascinated a variety of enthusiasts in Prague, Arcimboldo, Drebbel, and Dee among them. It might, on the lowest level, be little more than primitive magic or esoterism—so it appears with a man like Thurneysser—and a manuscript incomprehensible to contemporaries like the *Codex Argenteus* may easily have been valued for superstitious reasons. The same perhaps applies to the most perplexing of all documents associated with Rudolf: a cryptic hand-written and hand-illustrated text, attributed on no known

---

[1] UK, MS. XVII F 25.

[2] See Scholem, *Major Trends*, Ch. IV. I have not discovered any printed Cabalistic text under this name, though there presumably is one.

[3] Arch. Lib., Sig. W a 15; the dedication runs: 'A Serenissimi Augusti Ducis Brunsvicens. Lunaeburgq. Domini mei clementissimē manu librum hunc donae accepi: Johannes Saubertus.'

[4] Lambecius, *Commentarius*, i. 65 f. On his alchemy cf. Zíbrt: *BČH* iii, No. 10772.

[5] HHSA, Fam. Korr. A. 4. I.

[6] Ibid. III: 'gelbes Trühelein mit geheimen Schrifften', Rudolf to Mollart, 3 May 1605.

authority to Roger Bacon, which was apparently bought by the Emperor and then passed on to his physician Sinapius.[1] But cipher could also make a positive contribution to the problem of building up a consistent world-picture (the *code* of nature as the age of Rudolf understood it) and in this sense study of it anticipated the universal languages of the next century: Comenius, Bisterfeld, Leibniz, and the rest. Its classic text was a work heavy with Cabalist symbolism and the more sought after because it was not printed until 1606: the *Steganographia* of the Abbot Trithemius. Trithemius had originally offered his compilations on artificial writing to Maximilian I and the manuscript of the *Steganographia* in the Imperial library was eagerly sought by the young Henry Wotton for his friend Lord Zouche in 1591.[2] About the same time we find it being copied too —along with the magical *Picatrix*—in the Liechtenstein town of Eisgrub (Lednice) in south Moravia.[3]

Alongside the new concern shown by gentiles for the Hebrew religious mysteries went a parallel and largely independent revival of interest anong the Jews. With the dispersion of the Sephardic Jewry after 1492 by order of Ferdinand and Isabella, their Cabala became increasingly imbued with intellectual reflection on the significance of this fresh diaspora and a heightened sense of the imminence of an apocalyptic judgement. The movement issued in the so-called Lurianic Cabala of Isaac Luria (1534–72) and Moses Cordovero (1522–70) which grew up in Palestine and began to be propagated in Europe during the late sixteenth century.[4] Its principles display some notable similarities with contemporary Christian thinking: the belief in imminent reform and restoration of primal harmony through moral and spiritual regeneration; the attempt to popularize an esoteric doctrine (in other words the imposition through education of an élitist culture); the theory of prayer as a creative faculty in man, similar to the magical Neoplatonist world of atmospheres and the Hermetic astrology.

With the persecution of Jews in the West their communities in Central

---

[1] W. M. Vojnich in W. R. Newbold, *The Cipher of Roger Bacon* (Philadelphia–London 1928), 29–43. The MS. later passed to Marcus Marci, and it is he who mentions that its author is believed to be Bacon. In the absence of any warranty for this identification it must remain merely speculation that Rudolf could have acquired the MS. from Dee, whose interest in Bacon was well known (cf. above, p. 219 n. 4), or even that Dee may have written it himself. Attempts to decipher the MS. have so far proved vain, and the intrinsic fascination of the text, with its curious and unique drawings, remains.

[2] Lambecius, *Commentarius*, ii. 462 ff., 805 ff., 988; Wotton's letters of 15 Jan., 17 and 21 Apr. 1591 in Pearsall Smith, op. cit. i. 253 f., 266, 269 f.

[3] Dudík, *Iter Romanum*, i. 229 (Sig. 1344).

[4] This, and what immediately follows, is of course drastically simplified. See Scholem, *Major Trends*, Ch. 7.

Europe assumed an even greater importance, and among them Prague occupied a leading place. Here the first Hebrew book was printed in 1512,[1] and the ghetto, which stood self-contained right in the centre of the city, prospered both economically and culturally. Despite the occasional threats of banishment, the Habsburgs proved broadly accommodating towards the Jews, and their own chronicler is loud in the praise of the sovereigns.[2] The Jews were in fact a central part of the system of Imperial finance; their wealthiest citizen, Mordechai Meizl, who died in 1601, was by far the richest man in Prague and maintained very close contact with the court and the nobility. He received a special trading privilege from Rudolf in 1592 and the Imperial favour later passed to Jakob Bassevi, subsequently to become famous as the financial adviser of Wallenstein.[3]

The blossoming of Jewish intellectual life at the end of the century was based on a renewed study of the Cabala. Prague, like Cracow, early grew acquainted with Lurianic thinking; Cordovero circulated in the 1591 (Cracow) edition of his main work, the *Pardes Rimmonim*, while his disciple Isaac Ashkenazi was read in manuscript.[4] One representative of this scholarship was Sabbatai Horowitz, member of an established Prague family, whose introduction to Cordovero's system was published in 1612.[5] A commentary on the *Zohar* appeared at almost the same time.[6]

The greatest figure in the movement was Judah Loew ben Bezalel, one of the most celebrated rabbis of the Renaissance. Loew, born probably in 1520, spent a large part of his life in Prague; he taught there from 1573 and worked as chief rabbi from 1597 until his death in 1609. He was a man of vast learning and a prolific author.[7] His philosophical writings are mostly concerned to justify the irrational and the supernatural in traditional Jewish teaching.[8] He challenges the rationalism

[1] *The Prague Ghetto in the Renaissance Period*, ed. O. Muneles (Prague 1965), 67.

[2] David Gans, *Zemach David*, Pt. II, German trans. by M. Grünwald (Prague 1890), 23 f., 88, 111 f., 121 f.

[3] Janáček, *Dějiny obchodu*, 69 f., 329; *Prague Ghetto*, 46 ff.; cf. *Jahrbuch* xii (1891), Reg. No. 8257. Meizl was noted for his beneficence to the Jewish community and he founded their unique town-hall, built by an Italian.

[4] *Prague Ghetto*, 89. The first edition of the *Pardes Rimmonim* appears to have been in 1586 in Venice.

[5] Ibid. 89 f.; O. Muneles, *Bibliografický přehled židovské Prahy* (Prague 1952), No. 92; S. Schechter, *Studies in Judaism* ii (1908), 260. Another work of Horowitz appeared in Prague in 1616 (Muneles, No. 102).

[6] By Jissaker Ber ben Moshe Petahja; Muneles, *Přehled*, Nos. 79–82.

[7] For his life see F. Thieberger, *The Great Rabbi Loew of Prague* (London 1954–5), 8 ff.; some writers insist on 1512 as the year of Loew's birth, despite the intrinsic unlikeliness of such longevity. His works are listed in Muneles, op. cit. Nos. 17, 19, 20, 23, 24, 32, 35, 38, 45, 46, 49, 50, 52.

[8] For this exposition I rely on Thieberger, op. cit. 45–75; Rabbi ben Zion Bokser,

of the school of Maimonides and the benighted educational methods of
the time in favour of a higher exegesis of scripture which proceeds from
the divine illumination of the intellect. Loew's was the characteristic
Cabalist and Hermetic striving for harmony, set in something of the
ecstasy of the mystic,[1] and his thought accepted the same cosmology of
divinely-moved powers and influences. He was a master of the manipulations of numbers and letters typical of the practical Cabala.[2] At the
same time he believed in the reform and perfection of mankind through
new principles of education and in the recovery of true harmony through
the imminent end of the world as he knew it.[3]

What is the relevance of the world of Loew to the world of Rudolf?
Both men have been well served by legend, and Loew's great notoriety
is as the supposed magus or Faust who created a 'golem', an artificial
servant similar to the 'homunculus' of the alchemists.[4] The legends
further insist that the Emperor was deeply involved in Jewish mysticism.
Unfortunately we only possess evidence of a single meeting between the
two, but the chronicler relates that on this occasion (in 1592) Rudolf
summoned the rabbi and they had a long and secretive conversation.[5]
There are pointers to some contact between Jewish and gentile thinkers:
merchants like Meizl dealt very regularly with the court and some of
Rudolf's closest servants were converted Jews, like Philipp Lang,
Kühbach, or the mysterious 'Nelle'. Dee suggests at one point that
Rudolf is being influenced against him by the Jews, though it is difficult
to guess what he had in mind.[6] A more material example of the international links of the Prague ghetto is the figure of Joachim Gans or
Gaunse who worked in England as metallurgist and mining expert during the 1580s.[7]

Ultimately the arguments for such an interpenetration of ideas remain
a matter of speculation. There are striking similarities between the development of Jewish thought and Christian in the period here under

From the World of the Cabbalah (London 1957), 59 ff.; and most recently A. Neher, _Le
Puits de l'exil: La théologie dialectique du Maharal de Prague_ (Paris 1966), who stresses
particularly the encyclopedic, mystical, and messianic striving which underlay Loew's
reformist position.

[1] Scholem regards him as a direct precursor of Hasidism; _Major Trends_, 339.
[2] See Bokser, op. cit. 119–22.
[3] Ibid. 133 ff., 171 ff.; cf. Scholem, op. cit. 308.
[4] On Loew and the golem see G. G. Scholem, _On the Kabbalah and its Symbolism_
(English edn. London 1965), Ch. 5.
[5] David Gans, _Zemach David_, Pt. I, in _Chronologia sacra-profana a mundi conditu ad
annum M 5352 vel Christi 1592, dicta Germen Davidis. Auctore R. David Ganz . . . per
G. H. Vorstium_ (Leiden 1644), 159.   [6] _T.F.R._ 382.
[7] M. Donald, _Elizabethan Copper_ (London 1955), 208 ff., 299.

investigation. Loew's theories issued, like those of Comenius, in a universal educational reform tinged with chiliasm. The Cabala of Horowitz and other Safedists has elements which were later elaborated by Jakob Boehme, and it is entirely possible that the Lusatian mystic absorbed the influence during visits to Bohemia, just as he must have learnt somewhere the alchemy of which his philosophy is full.[1] A further hint is the growing interest among educated Jews in Christian learning. David Gans (1541–1613), presumably a relative of Joachim, was the first Jew to compile a chronicle which embraced gentile history, and this was published in Prague in 1592.[2] Gans also worked as an astronomer—he was a friend and associate of Tycho Brahe—and he possessed wide scientific horizons; towards the end of his life he prepared some kind of encyclopedia of the sciences, part of which appeared in 1613, though much remained in manuscript.[3] Another product of such pansophic activity was a massive ten-volume encyclopedia published during the 1590s by Mordechai Jaffe (1530–1613), a scholar 'great and excellent in wisdom' as Gans observes.[4]

It is no doubt impossible to establish fully what real links were forged and what influences received in these fields. Prejudice was anyway too great to allow much open contact, and the best sources for the historian are in Hebrew. But Cabalism, however pursued, was always one of the most universal of disciplines; like alchemy or the Hermetic philosophy, it formed an aspect of that combination of secret teaching and aspiration to reform which we must now seek to evaluate more broadly.

[1] On Boehme's Cabala cf. R. T. Llewellyn, 'Jakob Boehmes Kosmogonie in ihrer Beziehung zur Kabbala', *Antaios* v (1964), 237–50.

[2] Muneles, op. cit. No. 31. It is partly accessible to the non-Hebraist in translations (neither complete) by Vorstius into Latin (above, p. 241 n. 5) and Grünwald into German (p. 240 n. 2).

[3] *Prague Ghetto*, 85 f. and ill. Nos. 48–52; J. Alter, 'Gans und Delmedigo', *Rozpravy Československé Akademie Věd*, Year 68, No. 11 (Prague 1957); Muneles, op. cit. Nos. 28, 33, 34, 42, 51, 59, 75.

[4] Gans/Vorstius, 159 f.

7. Prague Mannerism and the Magic Universe

'Il est plus aisé de dire des choses nouvelles que de concilier
celles qui ont été dites.'

VAUVENARGUES: RÉFLEXIONS ET MAXIMES, I

THE last chapter has attempted some account of the occult interests of
the Emperor Rudolf II and his entourage. Further research would reveal
more of the intimate links between those strivings after secret knowledge
and the general intellectual currents of the sixteenth century, in relation
to which Rudolf stands only as an extreme case, not an exception. This
wider context we must now seek to clarify. For it is important to see that
the whole mentality of occultism—in its broadest sense—belongs in-
tegrally within the cosmology of late Renaissance Europe. It was not
merely a primitive simplification or a sub-scientific distortion. The age
of Rudolf still acknowledged a world-order, albeit one so vast in its
dimensions that it could only with difficulty be grasped as a totality.
Court Humanism and art were the expression, even the revelation, of
this massive inherited intellectual edifice.

As a method of approach, let us return to a thread which has already
been emphasized in the learning, art, and scientific endeavour of Rudolfine Prague: its characteristic observation of nature. For all the artificiality and conscious learning which the products of the period display,
there is no shortage of real practical investigation, even a closeness to
the natural world which is scarcely equalled elsewhere. Minerals, stones,
and plants come to command a reverence in themselves, and this is
reflected in the diligence with which men seek them in the countryside,
as in the closeness with which they are copied or used as artistic models.
Precise fidelity to animate and inanimate objects is a facet of the art of
the late sixteenth century which seems to grow in significance the more
one studies it. In the present connection we may recall the canvases of
Spranger, Savery, or Arcimboldo, the metal and stone compositions of
Vianen and Miseroni, the cameos and mosaics of the Prague workshops.
The genre is just as lively in the field of literature; there is a respect for

the complexity and perfection of a flower or animal which is often based on real observation. The Breslau Humanist Lawrence Scholtz, a doctor and friend of the Monaus, kept a garden which was the admiration of his learned colleagues and a regular subject for their poetic attentions.[1] One of them, Dornavius, later compiled a major anthology of verses which was intended to cover the whole gamut of created things. Another, Martin Mylius, wrote a philosophical treatise about gardens and their contents, beginning with the planting of Eden and proceeding to a close analysis of the species to be seen in his native Silesia. A third, Caspar Schwenckfeldt, produced startlingly comprehensive volumes on the flora and fauna of the same province, dedicating one of them to his patron Hans von Nostitz.[2]

Such bestiaries and herbals paralleled the actual collections of the day, above all those of the Emperor and leading courtiers, which were drawn on for creative inspiration and illustrated by local artists. The collections were themselves based on all the preliminary exploration and field-work necessary to secure the specimens they contained. They were one product of the new fascination for travel, with its detailed study of different regions from a variety of standpoints: topography, ethnography, archaeology, customs, and so on. There are few more objective records of the sixteenth century than the maps of Ortelius's *Theatrum* (to which Sambucus and others were contributors) or the townscapes in Braun and Hogenberg's *Civitates Orbis Terrarum*, among them those by Georg Hoefnagel.

No less precise were the findings of scholars like Clusius or Zalužanský, as they drew together the botanical evidence of their own tours and observations. Other scientific work too rested on such practical foundations: Ercker and his successors in the royal mines, worthily analysing the processes of metallurgy; Boethius de Boodt, examining each new acquisition among the precious stones of the Imperial *Schatzkammer*; the anatomical investigations of Jessenius; the experimenters and inventors who surrounded the monarch or importuned him from further

---

[1] e.g. A. Calagius, *Hortus Doct. Laurentii Scholzii* (Breslau 1602), and Wacker's stanza in Adam, *Vitae Medicorum*, 365. Scholtz edited two important medical works which reveal his contacts with Crato, Dudith, and the rest: *Consiliorum Medicinalium . . . Liber Singulus* (Hanau 1609); *Epistolarum Philosophicarum, Medicinalium ac Chymicarum . . . Volumen* (Hanau 1610).

[2] C. Dornavius, *Amphitheatrum Sapientiae Socraticae . . .*; M. Mylius, *Hortus Philosophicus* (Görlitz 1597). Mylius makes due reference to Scholtz's garden (16). C. Schwenckfeldt, *Stirpium et Fossilium Silesiae Catalogus* (Leipzig 1600); *Therio-Tropheum Silesiae, in quo Animalium . . . vis et usus . . . perstringuntur* (Liegnitz 1603); the former much indebted to Scholtz.

afield; even the more reputable alchemists who were serious students of pharmacology. These men were capable of genuine inductive research; indeed they relied on it and gloried that the wonders of nature might be thus discovered. The same years saw Kepler's laborious work in Prague on the movements of the planets, which continued and emended the minutely detailed astronomical tables of Tycho and brought its definitive result in the *Tabulae Rudolphinae*. Kepler also applied himself continually to the problems of optics and carried out experiments with light, a subject which obsessed no less the glass-makers and mirror-grinders, alchemists like Maier, and philosophers like Jessenius.

Yet we should beware of mistaking this vision for the kind of neutral objectivity which is associated with the methods of modern natural science. Still less was it any naïve acceptance of the evidence of the senses. Its 'modernity' is in fact only superficial, and its 'realism' nearer to a medieval notion than to any subsequent definition. For the apperception of nature during the late Renaissance was always posited on a unitary scheme of things, whose processes could indeed be studied discretely, but whose totality was a given and universal world order.

The cosmology of the sixteenth century was a tightly-knit coherent system of aprioristic correspondences. The study of nature and man which followed from it must be set against a background where all science, despite its compartments of psychology, medicine, botany, metallurgy, and the rest, was intimately linked with the whole cosmic hierarchy. Psychology studied the soul and the body and the effects of one on the other; the soul, with its division into vegetable, sensible, and rational, paralleled in microcosm the division of the macrocosm into mineral, animal, and spiritual; the body was a little world made cunningly of the same elements which formed the world beyond it, its humours influenced by sympathetic natural forces outside.[1] Medicine called on countervailing sympathies and antipathies in the natural world to balance the disharmonies of the human frame. Botany dealt with the lore of plants, their 'signatures', or contractions of cosmic forces, and their benign or malignant powers;[2] just as mineralogy considered stones in their symbolical and magical aspects, like talismans drawing down and storing astral influences;[3] while metallurgy studied metals and their properties, and transmutation was a neither more nor less inexplicable phenomenon than the smelting of ore. These are examples drawn at

[1] There is a good summary in J. B. Bamborough, *The Little World of Man* (London 1952).
[2] Cf. A. Arber, *Herbals* (2nd edn. Cambridge 1953), Ch. IV *passim*.
[3] Joan Evans, *Magical Jewels*, esp. Ch. VIII.

random; yet if their selection is random, the evidence is not, since each field incapsulates the whole, extracts from it and contributes to it, each provides a branch for the unified *arbor scientiae*. The principles are recurrent: the argument from microcosm to macrocosm and back again, the interaction and identification on various levels, the sense of a primeval harmony and a pre-existent equilibrium, the unbroken continuity of created things.[1]

Thus the seeker after truth paid in his practical activity a necessary and fitting debt to the world of appearances, but his field labour was in vain if it was not guided by some inner illumination of a universal purpose. Of course the ultimate author of this purpose was God, and the presence of the hand of the Creator manifest in nature was the highest justification for its study. There is a beautiful statement of the theme in Sir Walter Raleigh's *History of the World*:

> By his owne word, and by this visible world, is God perceived of men, which is also the understood language of the Almightie, vouchsafed to all his creatures, whose Hieroglyphical Characters are the unnumbered Starres, the Sunne, and Moone, written on these large volumes of the firmament: written also on the earth and the seas, by the letters of all those living creatures, and plants, which inhabit and reside therein.[2]

Few can have made this assumption more explicit than the pastor of Joachimsthal, Johann Mathesius, a friend of Luther, whose compelling sermons were full of parables and homilies suggested by the mining activity of his parish. Mathesius's *Sarepta* provides both a powerful series of analogies between the material and spiritual worlds, and a handbook to the contemporary mining industry in Central Europe almost as valuable as that of his colleague George Agricola.[3]

The same divine purpose is recognized in the workings of light by Boodt, who sees it operating through the reflective powers of gemstones,[4] or by Kepler in his apostrophe to the celestial order which surrounds

---

[1] For the underlying assumption of continuity cf. the classic work by A. O. Lovejoy, *The Great Chain of Being* (New York 1936), Ch. IV.

[2] *History of the World* (London 1614), i. 2.

[3] The *Sarepta* was first published in 1571. On Mathesius see G. Loesche, *Johann Mathesius, ein Lebens- und Sittenbild aus der Reformationswelt*, i–ii (Gotha 1895); E. Göpfert, *Die Bergmannssprache in der Sarepta des Johann Mathesius* (Strassburg 1902); and Wolkan, *Böhmens Anteil*, i, *passim*, and iii. 423 ff.

[4] 'Haec lucis dignitas, praestantia, ac excellentia, qua Deus Opt. Max. se intelligi voluit, etiam quodammodo in gemmis apparet. Nam dum plures gemmae homini adhibentur, etiamsi conspici possint, lucis tamen receptione, variaque illius reflectione aspicientium oculos ita replent, illuminant, radiisque perstringunt, ut iis occupata et impedita visus acies, gestantis faciem et corpus quodammodo inconspicuum faciat.' *Gemmarum et Lapidum Historia*, 5 f.

the sun, or by the more overtly Neoplatonist Patrizi and Jessenius. But it is not conceived as a separate category of investigation. Rather the Creator is approached through the harmony of His universe; everything must have its appointed place in that scheme, and this is the logic behind the great new search to classify animate and inanimate things, to view birds and beasts, plants, stones, and the rest in a systematic fashion. The collecting mania of the period was thus not idle curiosity, but an attempt to organize diverse objects in a way which would reflect their original disposition, their place in the chain of creation. One presentation of the idea is revealed by the *Kunstkammer* of the Dukes of Bavaria, as described by S. Quicheberg in his *Theatrum Sapientiae* of 1565; the serious purpose behind the Rudolfine collection is equally evident from its inventory of 1607–11.[1]

An intimation of order was fundamental to such attitudes. Yet it was not simply a framework passively received from the Middle Ages; it was also one capable of dynamic adjustment and rethinking, without transcending the bounds of its own *a priori*, indeed in part anti-empirical presuppositions. This is perhaps clearest in the realm of pure astronomy; it is very evident that the period we are here considering (say 1550–1600) saw a profound break with traditional cosmology; but what kind of revolution was involved? It is now common ground that Copernicus's was a mental reconstruction which adjusted one metaphysic and almost accidentally turned it into another.[2] The more vital and devastating hypothesis—as Johnson has well shown[3]—was that of the infinity, even plurality of the universe, which was most eloquently and completely sustained by the cosmopolitan genius of Giordano Bruno. Yet Bruno's reform proceeds ultimately from principles, part-Platonic, part-Hermetic, which derive from within the system, and are thus an extreme stage of intellectual speculation aimed at revolution through the powers of the mind.[4] The first cosmological publication of the young Johannes Kepler, his *Mysterium Cosmographicum* of 1597, was intended as a new justification of the principles of Pythagorean harmony and the regular solids of Euclid.

In this context, then, the Humanist and artistic activity of the later sixteenth century played itself out, an unbroken natural hierarchy

[1] Cf. E. Neumann, *Inventar* (see p. 180 n. 2); G. Händler, *Fürstliche Mäzene und Sammler in Deutschland 1500–1620* (Strasbourg 1933), and above, pp. 176–8.
[2] On Copernicus's revaluation see A. Koyré, op. cit. 15–115; earlier E. A. Burtt, *The Metaphysical Foundations of Modern Physical Science* (2nd edn., London 1932), 23 ff.
[3] F. R. Johnson, *Astronomical Thought in Renaissance England* (Baltimore 1937), esp. Ch. IV.
[4] Yates, *Giordano Bruno*, 205 ff. and *passim*; cf. Lovejoy, 116–21.

paralleling the courtly gradations of its social background. But now, far more than in earlier generations, such activity was coming to be seen as something positive and worthy in itself. Thinking and debating were still carried on inside the existing conceptual system, but they were now increasingly dynamic, autonomous, and conscious. At the same time the greater valuation placed on the active, practical life as such had raised the status of the whole common-sense world of objects. The result was a heightened awareness of the antithesis between the *observation* of appearance and the *intuition* of an underlying reality. This antithesis was resolved for the Renaissance through the role of magic and the occult.

The central position of magical thinking in the Renaissance is now reasonably familiar, at least to specialists, though it awaits fuller evaluation.[1] Magic, it has been well said, involves not creation but summons, and the great argument about it in the Renaissance was whether what it summoned was good or evil, white or black, divine or diabolical. In other words its power was also responsibility. At best, therefore, Renaissance magic meant the beneficial revelation through non-natural means of a supernatural reality. Both the end and the means were deeply rooted in the spiritual Neoplatonism of Marsilio Ficino, as D. P. Walker has shown, and the sixteenth-century debate generally took this as its starting-point.[2] Just as the sensible world is a network of internal relations, so the celestial world—man's intimate link with the divine—is susceptible of an immediate intuition; here is the factor common to the whole tradition, a current underlying the apparently harmonious rationality of Erasmian Humanism and coming to the surface as a characteristic speculative attitude. It manifested itself as Neoplatonist or Pythagorean revival, as Cabalism, as Hermetism;[3] it was present in the arcane theorizing of Paracelsans and alchemists. All these forms of occult activity, with their very various notions of direct or progressive revelation, were in some way destructive of straightforward discursive thought

[1] Cf. E. Garin, 'Magia ed astrologia nella cultura del Rinascimento', in *Medioevo e Rinascimento* (Bari 1954), 150–169.

[2] D. P. Walker, *Spiritual and Demonic Magic from Ficino to Campanella* (London 1958); and cf. the interesting but arcane work by Peuckert on sophisticated white magic versus residual black magic in Germany: W.-E. Peuckert, *Pansophie* (2nd impression, Berlin 1956), esp. 94–184.

[3] On Neoplatonism in the Renaissance there is no synthetic study. Most stimulating are various works by E. Garin, Ernst Cassirer: *Individuum und Cosmos in der Philosophie der Renaissance* (Leipzig 1927 and English trans.), and idem, *Das Erkenntnisproblem* (Berlin 1906), Vol. i. On Cabalism, most recent and best is F. Secret, *Kabbalistes chrétiens*; for a first orientation in Renaissance Hermetism: Yates, *Giordano Bruno*, 1–61, and Garin, 'Nota sul Ermetismo', in *La cultura filosofica del Rinascimento italiano* (Florence 1961), 142–54.

in favour of what is unreasoned, and positively unamenable to reason; hence the often-remarked, typical sixteenth-century preoccupation with the concept of fortune and systems involving chance, especially astrology.[1] One of the most elaborate manuscripts presented to Rudolf II was an extensive treatise on geomancy (divination by random dots on a sheet of paper),[2] and many similar examples could be quoted.

At the same time it needs stressing that this intuitional vision was not regarded as contingent. It was an artistic insight into truth, which can be communicated and which is power. The magus invoked a higher world which could change the natural one; Francis Bacon was the first to take the crucial step of formulating this anew as the creation of a different purely *physical* world, and thus initiating a basic tenet of modern scientific thinking.[3] Astrology had the great paradox that while it could be on the one hand an abject surrender to determinism (in the context of the *fin de siècle* it frequently was, particularly in Bohemia), it gave on the other hand a possible lever to greater freedom of action—as the artist's muse was free—by using flexibility within the whole cosmological system to overcome or justify limited rigidities. Thus the horoscope might be said to determine character by the rules of judicial astrology (this, with the closely associated theory of humours, was the contemporary approach to a psychology of 'types'), but it also elevated the individual into participation in the motive powers of the universe and could equally be a principle of emancipation.[4]

The great disputes over astrology, like those over astronomy, were in fact conducted to a large extent with common terms of reference.[5] There is another parallel in the argument over witchcraft. The persecutory craze against witches likewise reached its height in the half century after

---

[1] E. Garin, 'Considerazione sulla magia', in *Medioevo e Rinascimento*, 170–91; cf. the general thesis of J. Huizinga, *Homo Ludens* (English edn. London 1949).

[2] ÖN, MS. 11414: 'Divo Rudolpho II . . non minus Almae Minervae quam Adrasteiae Antistiti haecce Reconditae Philosophiae Monumenta Philippus Knodius a Schlammerstorf . . . DDD' (1589).

[3] Bacon's debt to sixteenth-century magic, and at the same time his rejection of the magus as a mystic figure are argued by Paolo Rossi, *Francesco Bacone, dalla magia alla scienza* (Bari 1957). The period around 1600 has been seen as an important one for the revival of the cult of the magus: e.g. G. F. Hartlaub, *Das Unerklärliche* (Stuttgart 1951), 195–228.

[4] This was the principle behind Bruno's—very obscure—plans for Hermetic reform; cf. Yates, op. cit. The Lullist 'art' was also, in one sense, a cosmological 'manipulation': F.A. Yates, 'The art of Ramon Lull', *JWCI* xvii (1954), 115–73.

[5] The astrological debate in Europe reached a climax between 1550 and 1600; see D. C. Allen, *The Star-Crossed Renaissance*, Ch. 2. Cf. the inspiring passage on Fate and Fortune in Raleigh's *History*, 14–17, 19–22. On the subject in general: F. J. Boll and C. Bezold, *Sternglaube und Sterndeutung* (fourth edn. by Gundel, Leipzig 1931).

1550, and even those who doubted the seriousness of the accusations, or objected to the barbarous procedures and punishments employed by the courts, rarely denied the reality of some form of possession, still less the existence of spirits at all.[1] The Dalmatian savant George Raguseus, who poured scorn on multifarious forms of divination and prediction, showed himself nevertheless very familiar with the subject and not averse to some other kinds of occult influence.[2] In a similar way many of those who attacked alchemy rather despised it for the shortcomings of its practitioners than impugned the ideas which sustained it. The premises of debate were anyway themselves confused; the two most celebrated repudiations of Renaissance magic came from men who were deeply wedded to its use, Pico della Mirandola and Cornelius Agrippa of Nettesheim.[3]

Even the anathemas of the Churches, especially of Catholics like the Jesuit Martin del Rio, were not unequivocal nor did they proceed from a radically different position. This can be seen, for instance, in the interpretation of miracles: it was obviously not consistent with Christian teaching to account for them as merely some harnessing of supernatural powers—they must involve the suspension of otherwise immutable laws —yet they had something in common with the beneficent procedures of 'white magic'. The strongest resistance to occult studies came nevertheless from established religion. Magic—in its widest sense—sought an active justification of man's intellect and provided its own scope for an improvement in the human condition. It asserted the responsibility of the individual, both as thinker and performer. Moreover, it propounded its own rituals, and an exclusiveness which centred on the figure of the *mage*, that adept, prophet, or operator so familiar from the history of alchemy and astrology. Hence although the truths which it mediated were claimed to be a part of the divine revelation, they necessarily appeared as a rival metaphysic.

Whereas the occult thus proved irreconcilable in the long run with orthodox Christianity, and was—as we have already seen—associated with the irregular reform and reconciliation attempts of the later sixteenth

---

[1] Cf. H. R. Trevor-Roper, 'The European Witch-craze in the sixteenth and early seventeenth centuries', in *Religion, the Reformation and Social Change* (London 1967), esp. 177 ff.

[2] Georgius Raguseus, *Epistolarum Mathematicarum seu de Divinatione Libri Duo* (Paris 1623).

[3] G. Pico della Mirandola, *Disputationes adversus Astrologiam Divinatricem* (written 1493-4); H. C. Agrippa of Nettesheim, *De Incertitudine et Vanitate Scientiarum* (Antwerp 1530). Cf.—on the latter—C. G. Nauert, *Agrippa and the Crisis of Renaissance Thought* (Urbana 1965), and—in general—Walker, *Spiritual and Demonic Magic, passim*.

century, it came for the same reasons ever closer to another move-ment from which it had initially been further distanced: Renaissance Humanism. The two developments were not separate, since Humanism, which had begun as a severely rational and anti-speculative current, critical, literary, and classicizing, was forced by religious schism to an increased awareness of larger problems. The crisis of the Church was, however, only one cause of a growing philosophical self-consciousness within Humanism—if that designation can still be applied to the scholarship of the sixteenth century. Another was the influence of Greek and Hebrew traditions, especially the legacy of Plato, and a broadening of the whole base of learned inquiry, which in one of its aspects meant the readmit-tance of some scholastic notions. More than this: discoveries, economic pressures, political separatism, and constant warfare were calling the old world-view into question in a thousand practical ways.

The response was not a wholesale intellectual denial, least of all from erudite individuals, each studying a field which was—as it were—only one room within a large mansion. Rather the very fragility of an in-herited cosmology, which sustained the great edifice of secular learning as well as theology, inspired the conscious advocacy of it so characteristic of the late Renaissance and found logical expression in a flowering of oc-cult science. From this follows much of the mentality of the period. We should hesitate to exaggerate its malaise (as some have done), but there is an unmistakable spiritual insecurity, issuing in a desperate search for certainty and completeness. Much of the distinctive mood of later sixteenth-century Europe becomes evident when this striving for har-mony is set against the confessional and political rifts which were gradually and unwillingly being acknowledged as an accomplished fact.

Thus the outstanding intellectual challenge of the age was given, and it is worth recapitulation: if all real things are pre-ordained in a divine objective scheme, how can one classify the distinct phenomena of con-templation and natural inquiry? The matter was the more urgent as widening geographical and astronomical horizons, collections, and archaeological investigations were sowing a new diversity. Again we see the antithesis: men are fascinated by appearance—there was for example a regular cult of the exotic and peculiar, evidenced not only by Rudolf's oriental treasures but in such books as the *Histoire véritable* (1610) and *Palais des Curieux* (1612) of Béroalde de Verville. Yet they are only content to accept it as part of a universal system; they are wedded to a conceptual discipline which unifies the seemingly unrelated. Theirs was the first great age of travel and its adjuncts: cartography, chorography, descriptions of places and countries; travel not simply to the New World but to the heart of the Old—Persia, Constantinople, Egypt, Palestine. Its purpose was empirical observation, but on another level it involved also the search for valid principles and a real unitary rationale of what was observed. Such travel was in the last analysis an intellectual quest, and its symbol was the labyrinth, the pursuit of completeness through partiality. The labyrinth played an important role in Mannerist art, just as did the whole topic of *Concordia discors*, harmony out of apparent disharmony.[1]

It is against this background that the craving for universal knowledge, pansophy, should be seen. The idea that the key to full understanding lay in man's mental disciplines, especially in their hitherto unexploited powers, was at one with an occultist view of the world. It found expression in the Hermetic doctrines made accessible by Ficino and Pico, with their stress on the primeval unity of all mankind; in the related study of the Cabala, whose starting-point was a cosmogonic revelation; in the 'art' of Ramon Lull and allied techniques aimed at perfecting the capacity of the mind and memory.[2] Another aspect of it was the striving after complete experience: Spiess's *Faustbuch*, the first published version of the famous legend, appeared in 1587 and found many successors, Marlowe among them. The vogue was intimately linked with magic and its high priests like Cornelius Agrippa or Trithemius of Sponheim, who perhaps served in the popular imagination as originals for the wizard Faust.[3]

Pansophy was neither a meaningless obsession with variety of things, nor a barren constructing of artificial systems, but an attempt to systematize the variety. The encyclopedic mentality as such can easily be dismissed out of hand: 'Indiscriminate pursuit of universal knowledge is scarcely better than a romantic obsession . . . It is only in the childhood of thought, when knowledge appears undifferentiated and each fresh piece of information seems significant just because it is fresh that

---

[1] Hocke, *Welt* als *Labyrinth*, esp. 98–104; cf. W. H. Matthews, *Mazes and Labyrinths* (London 1922), 100 ff., 193 ff., a rambling survey, but containing some interesting ideas.

[2] On Hermetism and Cabalism see above, p. 248 n. 3; on sixteenth-century Lullism, T. and J. Carreras y Artau, *Historia de la filosofia española*, Tomo II (Madrid 1943), 216 ff.; P. Rossi, 'The Legacy of Ramon Lull in 16th century thought', *Mediaeval and Renaissance Studies* v (1961), 182–213; and idem, *Clavis Universalis: arti mnemoniche e logica combinatoria da Lullo a Leibniz* (Milan–Naples 1960), 41 ff.

[3] Peuckert, *Pansophie*, 326 ff. and *passim*. Cf. E. M. Butler, *The Fortunes of Faust* (Cambridge 1952), 3 ff. On Agrippa's place in the occult tradition cf. the gigantic new edition of his *De Occulta Philosophia*, prepared by K. Nowotny (Graz 1967).

universal knowledge can appear to satisfy the philosophic passion.'[1] But a different ideal inspired the encyclopedic works which are so much a feature of the years from 1550: Gesner's *Bibliotheca Universalis* (1545–55), Zwinger's *Theatrum Vitae Humanae* (1565), and their successors, an unbroken line leading in Central Europe to the early pansophic writings of Comenius. Many of the best thinkers of the late Renaissance, especially in the Empire, were possessed by the notion of a logical key to reality; to this end they amended and interwove existing systems, not as eclecticism but as synthesis, and avowedly metaphysical, in that they aimed at a coherence which would be truth. The central importance of Ramism between 1580 and 1620—not as something exclusive or final, but as a debate about method—is now clear;[2] so is the application of memory techniques as 'real' place systems, and the integration of them with the Lullist art by Bruno, Alsted, and their circles.[3] But the interest was much wider and involved all kinds of permutations of Aristotelianism, Melanchthonian logic, Ramism, Lullism.[4]

Part of this pansophy was pure retrospection, a reversion to the universal scheme of the high Middle Ages. There was a new willingness to indulge, not the quibbles, but the speculations of the schoolmen, and it was directed above all towards secret and unorthodox currents of thought. Protestants and Catholics now consciously harked back to the unsullied teachings of an age of greater spirituality. Neo-scholasticism, especially in its Scotist aspects, was by no means simply an offspring of the Spanish Counter-Reformation, of Suarez and the school at Salamanca; and the revitalized religious orders carried with them in their international mission many other medieval doctrines beyond Aristotelian–Thomist canons. Good evidence of this is the strong revival of mnemotechnics and the study of the artificial memory among the Dominicans,[5] or the cult of prophecy—above all the predictions of the twelfth-century Abbot Joachim of Fiore—which penetrated into the Society of Jesus no less than into the visions of Postel and Campanella.[6] The great magicians

---

[1] Michael Oakeshott, *Experience and its Modes* (Cambridge 1933), 1.

[2] W. J. Ong, *Ramus: Method and the Decay of Dialogue* (Cambridge, Mass. 1958), Ch. XI; idem, *Ramus and Talon Inventory* (Cambridge, Mass. 1958), *passim*; W. S. Howell, *Logic and Rhetoric in England 1450–1600* (New York 1961), 7 ff., 173 ff.

[3] Rossi, *Clavis Universalis*, 109 ff.; Rossi also considers how far Ramus went in this direction (ibid. 135–42); cf. C. Vasoli, 'Umanesimo e simbologia nei primi scritti Lulliani e mnemotechnici del Bruno', in *Umanesimo e simbolismo . . . a cura di E. Castelli* (Padua 1958), 251–304.

[4] Ong, *Inventory, passim*; cf. above, pp. 231–5.   [5] Yates, *Art of Memory*, 105–28.

[6] On Joachite prophecies in the confessional age: H. Grundmann, *Studien über Joachim von Floris* (Leipzig–Berlin 1927), esp. Exkurs I; M. Reeves, 'The Abbot Joachim and the Society of Jesus', *Mediaeval and Renaissance Studies* v (1961), 163–81;

of the Middle Ages were rediscovered: Lull, who was valued both as a universal logician and a revealer of occult truths; Roger Bacon, admired in the years around 1600 by men such as John Dee;[1] Michael Scot, and the rest. To them, as to more sober figures like Albertus Magnus and even Aquinas, were attributed vast numbers of alchemical textbooks—manuscript and printed—which served the needs of that very extensive passion, though alchemy also had a more private gallery of celebrated forebears: Geber and Avicenna, Villanova and Rupescissa.[2] Developments in sixteenth-century Cabalism are relevant here on two counts: on the one hand Christian interest in the *Zohar* and the other inspirational texts was partly dictated by their message of Jewish secular messianism and the realization of prophecies; on the other there are the revivals within the Hebrew community itself, the Lurianic Cabala and the new anagogy of Rabbi Loew in Prague.[3]

The return to medieval models was one facet of a general appeal to authority which lay at the root of the contemporary belief in a divine scheme knowable only through revelation. If popular wisdom is seen as superficial, and the evidence of the senses as fallible, there follows a need for properly illuminated guidance. Of course such a notion of authority was nothing new: traditional Catholic teaching invoked the infallibility of Holy Church, the Protestants that of Holy Scripture. But with the blossoming of natural philosophy in the sixteenth century the term acquired intensified meaning: for it was now—as Neoplatonists, Hermetists, Cabalists all proclaimed—the mediation of the learned intellect which could yield knowledge of God's truths. Hence the role of the mage, the alchemical or astrological initiate, the correctly-attuned contemplator of nature's mysteries. Hence also the atmosphere of secrecy and mystique which attached to their study, the hesitation about communication, and the exclusiveness of the message conveyed. These further major derivations from the magical world-view we have been considering are best pursued by reference to the other category of

---

and—more generally—eadem, *The Influence of Prophecy in the Later Middle Ages* (Oxford 1969). The Joachite manuscripts are listed by F. Russo, *Bibliographia Gioachimita* (Florence 1954); cf. F. Secret, 'Guillaume Postel et les courants prophétiques de la Renaissance', *Studi Francesi* i (1957), 375–95.

[1] Cf. above, p. 219 n. 4, and the series of spurious Bacon texts which were issued during that time: *De mirabili potestate artis et naturae libellus* (Basel 1593); *De arte chymica scripta* (Frankfurt 1603); *Specula mathematica: in qua de specierum multiplicatione . . . agitur* (Frankfurt 1614), and others.

[2] See John Read, *Prelude to Chemistry* (London 1936), 45 ff.

[3] Cf. above, pp. 236–42.

privileged performer which the Rudolfine age recognized: for beside
the Humanist scholar it also enthroned the Mannerist artist.

*   *   *

In an earlier chapter I have already endeavoured to point out the
significance of Rudolf II's devotion to the arts. That devotion not only
throws light on the character of the sovereign patron himself, but reveals
a vast change in the status of artistic activity. Everywhere we find a new
confidence and pride in creative achievement, while the Holy Roman
Emperor himself encourages it by invitation, persuasion, and advice, by
patents of nobility, guild privileges, and financial inducement. The
flattery of talent by princely authority, so powerfully evoked by Charles
V's gesture in modestly picking up the brush of his servant Titian, was
carried a stage further at the court of his grandson.

This development was not caused simply by some Renaissance liberation of the individual as such. Rather it was connected with the wide
intellectual problem of the age, for the sixteenth-century artist could be
respected as a man whose powers were not only distinctive, but literally
supernatural. What was at stake was not his individuality but his role as
communicator, and thus his muse was not subordinate to any other way
of investigating the world. The painter's vision and the poet's insight
overlapped with the experiments of the scientist and the speculations of
the philosopher. Therefore it was not surprising to a contemporary that
one person should embrace several of these disciplines; no clear line of
division could be drawn.

The artist had become a privileged member of society, conscious of
the worth and responsibility of his position. With the change in his
conditions of work went a new style: the courtly and self-possessed style
which for half a century now has generally been called 'Mannerism'.
The concept of Mannerism, although originally a term limited to particular features of painting in the period, has become so important, and so
widely applied both within the fine arts and beyond them, that we must
devote some attention to it here. The thorny problems to which its use has
given rise are in part definitional; the extended and fruitful debate about
Mannerism since the 1920s has failed to produce any broadly accepted
conclusions. This was, however, always inevitable, since the topic has
been from the first closely linked to wider interpretations of sixteenth-
century culture, and thus firmly harnessed to the varying presuppositions
from which they themselves proceeded. A short excursus is necessary to
take some account of the issues and to establish, not what 'Mannerism'

should signify in general, but what aspects of the style are relevant to the present context.

The study of Mannerism[1] began with some individual problems in the history of Italian painting, primarily those surrounding the breakdown of the High Renaissance in the years between 1510 and 1530. Its specific conclusions were then soon made broader and modified in the light of further analysis. One whole literature has seen a mood from the early sixteenth century which rejected the classicism of the Renaissance— partly in the restricted sense of its veneration for antiquity, partly in the larger perfection and timeless untroubled repose which High Renaissance art had embodied.[2] Thus Mannerism became immediately an expression of negativity, of conscious resistance to any general law or symmetry, a denial of facility in art. By extension it also became an aesthetic constant, a thread running through the *corso* and *ricorso* of art history, a turbulent disharmony always threatening the embattled islands of classical certainty and calm. This is no place to examine the fuller implications of such an approach:[3] its stress on the inadequacy of the Renaissance synthesis when subjected to explicit questionings is proper and relevant; its concern with irrationality, disproportion, caprice can easily lead to exaggeration.[4] It can also lead into inconsistency: some of the roots of Mannerism lie deep in Classical Antiquity, but they were the conscious response to a contemporary situation rather than the working-out of a timeless style.

A second fairly well-defined school of thought has followed the lead given by the Viennese Czech Max Dvořák who in a famous essay canonized Greco and Tintoretto as the arch-Mannerists for the spirituality of their art.[5] They represent a spiritualizing of the phenomenon, an other-

---

[1] There is by now a large literature on Mannerism as an artistic phenomenon. The best *compte rendu* is by E. Battisti, 'Sfortune del Manierismo', in *Rinascimento e Barocco* (n.p. 1960), 216–37. Good illustrated surveys of the movement are A. Hauser, *Mannerism* (London 1965), Vol. i, Pt. 2 and Vol. ii (illustrations), and Franzsepp Würtenberger, *Der Manierismus* (Vienna 1962). The catalogue of the 1955 exhibition, *De Triomf van het Manierisme* (Amsterdam 1955), is also useful.

[2] The classic text is W. Friedländer, 'Die Entstehung des antiklassischen Stils in der italienischen Malerei um 1520', *Repertorium für Kunstwissenschaft* 46 (1925), subsequently elaborated by Friedländer and others. See esp. E. Battisti, *L'Antirinascimento* (Milan 1962). For a brief interpretation of Mannerist architecture in these terms see N. Pevsner, 'The Architecture of Mannerism', in *The Mint*, ed. G. Grigson (London 1946), 116–37.

[3] See E. R. Curtius, *Europäische Literatur und lateinisches Mittelalter* (Berne 1948), 277–305 (there is also an English translation (1953)).

[4] For an extreme view see some of the arguments of Hocke, *Die Welt als Labyrinth*, or E. Wüsten, *Die Architektur des Manierismus in England* (Leipzig 1951).

[5] M. Dvořák, 'Über Greco und den Manierismus', in *Kunstgeschichte als Geistesgeschichte* (Munich 1924), 261–76.

worldliness with an almost ascetic disregard for immediate appearance; hence a view of the powerfully Godly, or at least numinous, which shows direct parallels with the mystical upsurge in the religious revival of the sixteenth century, especially of Spain and France, and a strong kinship of feeling with the high Middle Ages. This is a thoroughly fruitful line of inquiry: that the age could not be satisfied by received doctrine and that it drew creative inspiration from a deep religious impulse are beyond question. Yet it remains by itself a one-sided interpretation, which allows little individuality to the particular strivings of the late sixteenth century. The drawings of Jacques Bellange,[1] for example, belong to a pattern of impractical, almost Utopian visions, and are paralleled elsewhere in the nervous years after 1600. To isolate them in their spirituality alone can be dangerously close to attempting a history of the ineffable, while to associate them directly with the Counter-Reformation is oversimplification.[2]

The third major approach to Mannerism has been the conception of it as an international movement. Any definition of the term involves problems of chronology and extent, and some treatments are inclined to localize—either distinct 'Mannerisms' in restricted environments, or individual artists with whom the *maniera* was rather fantasy, exoticism, or pure eccentricity: Pellegrino Tibaldi, Lelio Orsi, Arcimboldo, Caron, and others. At the same time there was evidently a process of broadening as the years passed, from the beginnings in Rome and Florence, through the second generation in Italy and the Fontainebleau circle around François I, to the international court Mannerism after 1550, with its centres in Prague, Munich, Madrid, Brussels, and their lesser epigones. It is in fact the international rather than national aspects of the development which are more significant—the latter were often simply arrests in receptivity, very strong traditional influences like the Spanish *plateresco* or the Antwerp Mannerism of the 1520s. One important theory has seen the reception of the Renaissance north of the Alps as really an acceptance of it in its 'Mannerist' aspects, which were most in conformity with native culture;[3] though there is a danger here of ignoring the positive contribution of the north and undervaluing the continuing anti-Classical current within Italy, which itself forms a whole chapter in any history of

---

[1] On Bellange (court painter to the Duke of Lorraine between 1600 and 1616) see F.-G. Pariset in *Studies in Western Art* iii (Princeton 1963), 118–26.

[2] This was done in the important essay by Nikolaus Pevsner, 'Gegenreformation und Manierismus', *Repertorium für Kunstwissenschaft* 46 (1925), 243–62.

[3] Denis Hay, *The Italian Renaissance in its Historical Background* (Cambridge 1961), Ch. 7. Cf. the book by O. Benesch referred to below, p. 271 n. 2.

European Mannerism.[1] However that may be, the international style of the later sixteenth century, *maniera* as a formula for living, became a common denominator of culture and courtly society.

This universalist element in the movement has encouraged a number of recent scholars to draw together the various threads of earlier research and to argue a 'maximum case' for Mannerism, especially by placing its concerns in a still wider framework of European intellectual history. The most far-reaching attempt at a complete resolution of the mind of the sixteenth century is by Arnold Hauser: a grandiose but abstract analysis of men alienated from society and from themselves. 'Mannerism is . . . an expression of the unrest, anxiety and bewilderment generated by the process of alienation of the individual from society and the reification of the whole cultural process. The alienation of the individual does not in this case exclude the creation of true works of art; on the contrary, it leads to the most profoundly self-revelatory creations.'[2]

For Hauser, then, the style and its conventions are a reflection of social crisis and psychological disturbance. An approach equally Germanic but more uniformly argued from the standpoint of *Geistesgeschichte* is that of Gustav René Hocke, who in two ingenious books has studied Mannerism as the parent of modern surrealism in its philosophy of the irrational, as a mode of revelation of the Absolute in its secret and symbolic manifestations.[3] Hocke is heavily committed to belief in a recurrence of 'timeless' Mannerisms, and his learning tends to be exhibited in large canvases of diverse facts which do not isolate sufficiently the historical points of conflict which bear on his thesis. But he has observed how many different elements are relevant to the problem —pansophy, grotesques, labyrinths, chiliasm, to select at random—and how none of them can be adequately evaluated in isolation. He has also been alone in stressing the important position occupied by the many-sided court of Rudolf in Prague (beyond the customary casual references to painters like Spranger, Heintz, and Aachen). Hocke's view of the modernity of Mannerist art—its close spiritual affinity to recent non-representational and symbolist currents—must be received with caution; but no less caution is necessary before we reject it in favour of some more traditional account of the sixteenth century which may in fact be equally foreign to its nature.

Briefer and more balanced than Hauser or Hocke is the synthesis by

[1] Battisti, *L'Antirinascimento*, Introduction.
[2] A. Hauser, op. cit. Quotation from 111.
[3] G. R. Hocke, *Die Welt als Labyrinth* (Hamburg 1957), and idem, *Manierismus in der Literatur* (Hamburg 1959).

Franzsepp Würtenberger,[1] who concentrates on Mannerism in the fine arts, presenting it as an elevated manifestation of broad European intellectual developments. The same kind of task is undertaken, from a different starting-point, by the literary critic Hiram Haydn in his pioneering work entitled *The Counter-Renaissance*.[2] Haydn sees the need for a clarification of some basic terminology. To him the crucial distinction is between an age which perceives the artistic ideal within the actual world (Classical acceptance) and one which pursues it in some other dimension: the idyll of a Golden Age, the discovery of Platonic reality, mystical fulfilment (all these are Romantic search). The whole sixteenth-century reaction—what he characterizes as Counter-Renaissance—was a form of inability to accept the fragile Classical construct of unquestioning human affirmation, which does not recognize the profoundest problems. Under the impact of doubt the High Renaissance collapsed into various forms of faith-through-scepticism which rejected the validity of what is immediately given and consequently eschewed 'mere' imitation of reality. Here Haydn suggests further that artistic 'Naturalism' may best be seen as an admission that the ideal is divorced from the actual, but which nevertheless limits itself to concern for the actual: an attitude which is thus predicated on the Romantic consciousness of imperfection, but takes the further step of accepting the incongruities of this world. Thus the scope of analysis is widened: the seventeenth-century Newtonian synthesis rebuilt a world of reason which had been lost since the Renaissance, but it founded it on a base of empirical science, not theology. Mannerism, by extension, remains valid as a historical category, while now appearing equally as transition (the period was after all very conscious of profound changes), without our having to resort to any immutable laws of aesthetics.

Such attempts, however provisional, to impose some total interpretation have inevitably provoked a reaction. Few critics are now driven to the complete denial of Mannerism as such, but a growing number have questioned the usefulness of a concept so widely and loosely applied. Thus there has of late been outlined a 'minimum case', which retains the term, and even its general purview, but suppresses its claims to philosophical consideration. The most recent and outstanding example is the book on Mannerism by John Shearman,[3] which achieves, within these

---

[1] F. Würtenberger, op. cit.

[2] (New York 1951); his general thesis emerges in the early chapters of the book.

[3] J. Shearman, *Mannerism* (London 1967). Cf. the important articles: J. Shearman, 'Maniera as an aesthetic Ideal', in *The Renaissance and Mannerism, Studies in Western Art* ii (Princeton 1963), 200–11; and C. H. Smyth, 'Mannerism and Maniera', ibid. 174–99.

prescribed limits, an acceptable definition of its field and a satisfactory analysis of it. Shearman's is a verdict in the classic tradition of pure art-history which stresses the observable and the intrinsic; as such his results cannot move beyond the initial presuppositions, but a summary of his conclusions provides solid ground as a point of departure for wider discussion.

For Shearman the characteristics of Mannerism are essentially stylistic; indeed they are the triumph of style, style for style's sake, an increasing delight in artistic virtuosity, a self-confident overcoming of difficulties, an approach which is clearly artificial in that it is self-conscious and lacks directness, yet which equally rejects adhesion to rules and acknowledges some sort of immediacy of expression as proof of artistic genius. The stock contemporary vocabulary is evidence: the notion of *maniera* in Vasari as the touchstone of acceptability, with its corollary of disdain for a simple natural vision; the cult of *sprezzatura*, cultured contempt for the ungraceful; the *virtù* attached to a complete resolution of self-imposed *difficultà*.[1] This development is rooted in the critical years between Michelangelo's Sistine Ceiling and the rise of the second Mannerist generation (roughly 1510–30), but is not seen as a tortured and crisis-ridden denial of the High Renaissance, rather as a continuation of it in the direction of greater elegance and artistic emancipation.[2] Its relation to what preceded it is logical and organic; its connection with the Baroque more complex; in part the movements are parallel, even interdependent, yet Mannerism lacks the other's emotional drive and dynamic unity, and is in a sense the avoidance of Baroque implications within the Renaissance. It is an art which sterilizes passion, ritualizes movement. It can thus be linked to a whole series of phenomena which conform to the same broad contemporary pattern: *Bembismo* and Ciceronianism; rhetoric and its influence on the literary conceit; the embracing of variety which is then given a static, formal unity, as in the madrigal; the indulgence of convention at the expense of emotional weight, as in the pastoral novel, or of *meraviglia* without practical relevance, as in the passion for *intermezzi*.[3]

Such an approach is very valuable and salutary; it appreciates the impossibility of bringing under one umbrella all the diverse manifestations which clamour to be called 'Mannerist', and rejects the notion that the creative minds of the sixteenth century were eternally plagued by anxiety or obsessed by spirituality. At the same time it is a positive contribution to our understanding of the courtly culture of the late

---

[1] Shearman, *Mannerism*, esp. 81 ff.   [2] Ibid. 22 ff.
[3] Ibid. 91 ff. and *passim*.

Renaissance. The affected and conscious artistry, with its appeal to the connoisseur; the pastoral conventions and the cult of the madrigal; the delight in marvels, both of nature and human industry; the quest for *multum in parvo*: all these were typical of the Rudolfine circle, as of the entourages of the Tuscan Dukes or the Valois Kings.

Yet there is more to be said about the matter than this deliberately restrained viewpoint would suggest. Later sixteenth-century art, of all kinds, does have other common features which go well beyond the refined *maniera* and the virtues of sophistication. Its creators were not concerned with style alone, just as the grounds of their creativity cannot be identified with the social or economic context in which they worked. We must also draw on the results of iconographical inquiry; the apparent primacy of form at this period involves (and obscures) an ideative content which originated independently of it—in fact in the limiting case it is content expressing itself in form. The Mannerist age was above all one of intellectual concern: of return to first principles, including the fundamentals of religious commitment. Its self-awareness stands revealed in its thoroughgoing critical mentality; increasingly through the century this was an attack on superficial, naïve, obvious views, a sense of the problematical in life. Yet it was at the same time positive; Mannerist art manuals for instance are full of models to be imitated by the reader, but their artificiality is a complete rejection of Renaissance 'imitation', the assumption that nature can be mindlessly copied. The new respect for the artist was a recognition of his power, and hence his intellectual responsibility, in possessing private subjective access to great cosmic secrets; while Mannerist expression—its conceits, its imagery, its fantasy —was often a deliberate attempt to communicate profound insights. Certainly this mood became more striking in the latter half of the century, especially north of the Alps, and some of its particularly important features take us a long way from Mannerism's Italian beginnings. Yet it is not just terminological convenience which keeps the whole movement together; there is also an inner logic, and this comes closest to overt expression in Mannerism's analysis of itself, its theory of criticism.

Renaissance theory—most clearly expounded by Alberti for fifteenth-century Florence—had seen the function of art in obedience to nature; it recognized an objective world of appearance and a creative subject, but found no problem in this, since it believed that fixed and scientific rules could be derived to govern artistic activity.[1] Beauty lay in

[1] The basic study is Erwin Panofsky's brilliant excursus, *Idea, ein Beitrag zur Begriffsgeschichte der älteren Kunsttheorie* (Berlin, 2nd edn. 1960): 'Naiv, wie diese

symmetry and proportion, in selecting from nature according to precise precepts, never in going beyond it. As Panofsky observes, it is a paradox that the age which revived serious study of Plato's epistemology and Neoplatonic mysticism in the Florentine Academy of Ficino, was nevertheless satisfied by an artistic canon shallower and less fully argued than the Middle Ages had known. Only in the latter half of the *Cinquecento* did the implications of this formulation come to be appreciated, as people began to realize that a deeper problem—the very justification of the artist—had been posed and only superficially resolved. Even Vasari, in some respects a Mannerist paragon, is deeply rooted in Renaissance beliefs; he asks the metaphysical question, but answers it still in functional terms: the artistic idea is the product *a posteriori* of experience and its realization is purely naturalistic. Vasari was the culmination of the earlier phase of Mannerism which concentrated on the practice of elegance and skill—his slogan was *grazia*—without coming to grips with the issues which had been raised by the Renaissance, and not less by its own self-conscious vaunting of the artist.[1]

What was characteristic of the later Mannerists was not a rejection of rules—the sixteenth century is the golden age of the manual and the iconographical model—but a new awareness that there were conceptual difficulties to be faced and that rules must be justified if they are to be the guarantors of real creative freedom. 'The fundamental novelty about all this' (again I follow Panofsky) 'is not that antitheses *exist*, but that they begin to be *observed*, or at least felt as such. Where the purpose of theory had earlier been to provide a practical basis for artistic creation, now it was called on to give it theoretical backing.'[2] Imitation is no longer an uncomplicated copying of nature, because the artist must now be true to an inner image which moulds experience, and also because nature itself is not a simple objective datum.[3] What the Renaissance had used

neue Disziplin die beiden Forderungen der Richtigkeit und der Schönheit aufstellte, glaubte sie auch die Wege zu ihrer Erfüllung bahnen und weisen zu können: die formale und objektive Richtigkeit schien ihr gewährleistet, sobald der Künstler auf der einen Seite die Gesetze der Perspektive, auf der anderen die Gesetze der Anatomie, der psychologischen und physiologischen Bewegungslehre und der Physiognomik beachtete' (26).

[1] Ibid. 34 ff.; A. Blunt, *Artistic Theory in Italy 1450–1600* (Oxford 1940), 86–102. On Vasari as Mannerist in his art-history see Julius von Schlosser, *Die Kunstliteratur* (Vienna 1924), Book V.

[2] Panofsky, op. cit. 44–6. 'Das grundsätzlich neue an allem diesen besteht nicht sowohl darin, dass derartige Gegensätze *vorhanden* sind, als vielmehr darin, dass sie als solche *bemerkt* oder wenigstens deutlich gefühlt zu werden beginnen . . . War es früher das Ziel der Kunstlehre gewesen, das künstlerische Schaffen *praktisch* zu *fundamentieren*, so muss sie nunmehr versuchen, es *theoretisch* zu *legitimieren*.'

[3] On both these points see E. Battisti, 'Il concetto d'imitazione nel Cinquecento

as a practical guide for constructing works of harmony and beauty was now seen in its metaphysical context and reintegrated with the traditional currents of philosophical speculation, especially Neoplatonism.[1] The crucial step was taken of questioning whether the Idea in the mind of the artist is in any way abstracted from nature, and of regarding it rather as the expression of an *inner* vision, a transcendent reality which only he can capture. It was against this position that battle was joined by the earliest theoretical opponents of Mannerism; the seventeenth-century voices of academic Classicism (Bellori was the loudest of them, but his views were adumbrated much earlier) condemned the Mannerists for ignoring nature and raising up an artificial and fantastical world of their own.[2] This criticism was always misplaced: the responsibility of the Mannerist artist to his reality was complete, his model parallel, but anterior, to the model of nature; his rules mental, not observational, but equally rigid and academic.[3] Mannerist iconography thus became a representation of reality, its image the substance and power of that reality, an essential revelation which was also symbolical since the whole universe could be grasped as a series of correspondences.[4] It was a mythology because the world was mythological.

The two leading spokesman for this viewpoint are Federigo Zuccaro and Paolo Lomazzo.[5] Their approaches are far from identical, but both are clearly anti-rational, supernatural, and in the last analysis mystical. Zuccaro was the proponent at the turn of the century of a reform in the Academies of painting, a pedagogue and prime mover in the founding

italiano', in *Rinascimento e Barocco*, 175–215: 'Questo richiamo alla natura [by some North Italian writers], a ben considerare, è altrettanto mitologico che l'opposta teoria dell'idea manieristica' (199). Cf. also J. Białostocki, 'The Renaissance concept of Nature and Antiquity', in *The Renaissance and Mannerism, Studies in Western Art* ii, 19–30.

[1] On the deeper meaning in Renaissance theories of proportion cf. R. Wittkower, *Architectural Principles in the Age of Humanism* (London 1949, revised edn. 1962). The Mannerist art manual was the logical culmination of many iconographical currents within the Renaissance, which themselves continued medieval traditions. Cf. J. Seznec, *La Survivance des dieux antiques* (London 1940, English translation 1953), *passim*.

[2] D. Mahon, *Studies in Seicento Art and Theory* (London 1947). Of course on another front Bellori was defending an ideal, albeit a non-transcendent one, against the indiscriminate realism of Caravaggio.

[3] Blunt (op. cit. 137 ff.) observes this link between the most anti-rational Mannerists and the Bolognese school.

[4] On the definition of symbol and allegory see H. G. Gadamer, 'Symbol und Allegorie', in *Umanesimo e simbolismo* . . . On the symbolic versus the 'representational', and the intimate links of the former with Renaissance traditions of Neoplatonism and magic, there is the important essay by E. H. Gombrich, 'Icones Symbolicae: the visual image in neo-Platonic thought', *JWCI* x (1947), 163–92.

[5] For them see Schlosser's compendium, *Die Kunstliteratur*, Book VI, Pt. 2, which also treats some less well known figures: Armenini, Danti, Dolce, Comanini. Cf. Panofsky, op. cit. 49 ff.; Blunt, op. cit. 137 ff.

of the Accademia di San Luca in Rome; Lomazzo was a Milanese, the pupil of Gaudenzio Ferrari. Both were well known to Rudolf in Prague: the Emperor made strenuous efforts through Khevenhüller to commission paintings from Zuccaro, or at least obtain copies of his canvases.[1] With Lomazzo he must have been in direct contact—perhaps through their common friend Arcimboldo—since he received from him for his collection a number of works by Leonardo da Vinci.[2]

Zuccaro writes as the theoretician of an art based on the 'inner idea', the *disegno interno*, which he defines precisely and to which he ascribes universal significance:

By *disegno interno* I mean the conception which is formed in our mind so that we can know something and operate from outside in conformity with the thing understood. Thus we painters, when we want to draw or paint a suitable story . . . first form in our minds the best conception we can of it. At the same time, in using this term of *disegno interno* I do not mean only the conception within the mind of the painter, but also that which any intellect at all may form.[3]

The *disegno* has three forms, descending from the divine through the angelic to the human; God's creation of the world according to His *Disegno* is the absolute guarantee of the artist's own power.[4] This power is exerted through the human *disegno interno*, which divides into the speculative (essentially what later art philosophy was to call *Kunstwollen*) and the practical, and the latter into moral—which governs virtuous behaviour—and artificial. The last guides practical artistic endeavour, but Zuccaro insists that even here the Idea in the intellect is still prior to the execution: 'Ogni atto poi esterno operatico ha origine dall'atto interno dell'intelletto pratico. Dunque il Disegno nell'intelletto non pure ajuta l'artifice ad operare, ma è causa dell'arte istessa.'[5] He is very clear that art 'imitates nature' only in the sense that it applies to experience a process of creativity which is parallel to creativity within the world of experience and is unintelligible except as part of a cosmic series of correspondences.[6]

---

[1] *Jahrbuch* xiii (1892), Reg. Nos. 9409, 9514, 9583, 9590, 9592.

[2] A. Mazenta, *Le memorie su Leonardo da Vinci*, ed. L. Gramatica (Milan 1919), 35: 'De più studiosi d'imitarlo [Leonardo] fu Giovanni Paolo Lomazzo, detto il Brutto. Questi accolse molte sue pittore, disegni e scritture: ne arrichì le gallerie e Museo di Ridolfo secondo Imperatore.' Cf. Preiss, op. cit. 21 f.

[3] *L'Idea de' Pittori, Scultori ed Architetti del Cavalier Federigo Zuccaro* (Turin 1607 is the original edition; I have used the Rome edition of 1768), 6 f.

[4] 'Ora perchè il Mondo non è stato fatto a caso, ma fatto da Dio per l'intelletto agente, è necessario che nella mente di Dio fosse la forma, alla cui similitudine fu fatto il Mondo.' Ibid. 13.

[5] Ibid. 26.

[6] Ibid. 27 ff.

The atmosphere of Lomazzo's tract is quite different: his is a Neo-platonic vindication of the status of painting, filled with arcane astrology and number mysticism.[1] But he is equally convinced of the primacy of the Idea and its derivation from God. Lomazzo is obsessed with the problem of beauty (which Zuccaro scarcely raises) and resolves it as the reflection of divine symmetry and perfection in a full-blown Neoplatonic metaphysic of light.[2] For him painting is harmony and truth,[3] and his obscure description of a 'temple of painting' which somehow incapsu-lates a complete mystical cosmology is largely the familiar variety-versus-unity opposition presented as one element in a higher synthesis. For him, as for Zuccaro, the artist can reproduce eternal, supernatural forms. Both their treatises are strong revivals of old currents of thinking—Zuccaro resolutely medieval in his Aristotelianism, Lomazzo standing in the broad tradition of Renaissance Neoplatonism;[4] and any apparent differ-ence in source is outweighed by the close similarity of conclusion. Both are essentially authoritarian affirmations of the speculative faculty in man.

The literary criticism of the late Renaissance is an involved subject, and little agreement exists even on its precise terms of reference. What is relevant here is again only to summarize some of the preoccupations in the writing of the sixteenth century which were so much a part of it that they can with difficulty be disengaged. Let us consider the English case: the belief in the organic wholeness of the universe and the con-cordance of its members was a commonplace of Elizabethan thinking.[5] It not only provided the poet with an inexhaustible store of images, but also guaranteed his status as an interpreter—however humble—of the divine work of art. Here as elsewhere it was precisely the breakdown of this secure harmony in face of a new naturalism and a particularizing pursuit of the empirical during the earlier seventeenth century which threw the unquestioned axioms into sharp relief and aroused conscious defence of them. The effect on literature was deeply disturbing—the mystical escape of the Metaphysical poets is a clear example—and has

---

[1] *Idea del Tempio della Pittura di Giovanni Paolo Lomazzo, Pittore* (Milan 1590). Its very starting-point is Hermetic: 'E però con grandissimo ragione diceva Trismegisto, che con la pittura era nata la religione' (23).

[2] Cf. ibid. 83: 'E prima habbiamo da sapere che la bellezza non è altro che una certa gratia vivace e spirituale la qual per il raggio divino prima s'infonde ne gl'Angeli in cui si vedono le figure di qualunque sfera che si chiamano in loro essemplari e Idee . . .' Panofsky notes the debt of this to Ficino, op. cit. 55.

[3] Lomazzo, op. cit. 30 f.

[4] Blunt observes the medieval influences on Lomazzo: op. cit. 144. His borrowings from Renaissance magic, especially Ficino and Agrippa, are noted by R. Klein, 'La forme et l'intelligible', in *Umanesimo e simbolismo . . .*, 103–21.

[5] See E. M. W. Tillyard, *The Elizabethan World Picture* (London 1963).

been remarked upon by a number of students of the period.[1] Donne's telling lines are well known:

> 'Tis all in peeces, all coherence gone
> All just supply, and all Relation . . .

A sense of decadence and decay pervaded literature at this time, and brought forth pessimistic debates about theodicy and the immanence of evil.[2]

On a deeper level, the very fact that the 'Metaphysicals' were so called, that their philosophical profundity had become so unnatural, so apparently speculative and unscientific, is evidence of how much had vanished by their time. Progress *towards* perfection may have been an ideal accessible to later minds; since the end of the Renaissance there has been no further possibility of self-association with existing cosmic perfection. The universe as an animate macrocosm allows identifications, correspondences which are not mere 'analogy', and this is a vital clue to the nature of Mannerist thought. 'What once seemed "identicals" seem to the modern world only "similars". Here is one profound change in our cosmological thinking: metaphor, based on what man believed *truth*, inscribed by God in the nature of the universe, has given way to simile.'[3]

This reality of metaphor, paralleling the reality of the visual symbol, throws light on the crux of literary 'artificiality': the *maniera* or conceit, and the relevance to it of an 'imitation' which does not simply copy. As Rosamund Tuve has shown, imagery in the sixteenth century was commonly seen as functional with regard to various generalized realities, form fusing with content on the different levels of those realities; thus there is no gulf between 'artificial' and 'natural', rather a right poetic invention for a certain content. 'The poet who imitates not the visible world, but the intelligible as manifested in the visible, will not consider that the use of artifice to emphasize form makes imagery less true to nature.'[4] This concept of decorum is part of the writer's moral responsibility; he must order his material according to coherence and ultimate

---

[1] As well as H. Haydn, op. cit., see M. H. Nicolson, *The Breaking of the Circle* (Evanston, Ill. 1950); Victor Harris, *All Coherence Gone* (Chicago 1949); C. M. Coffin, *John Donne and the New Philosophy* (New York 1938).

[2] Cf. Harris, op. cit., esp. Ch. 2, on the Goodman–Hakewill controversy. Goodman was a believer in the inevitable corruption of the universe.

[3] Nicolson, op. cit. xxi.

[4] R. Tuve, *Elizabethan and Metaphysical Imagery* (Chicago 1947), quotation from 36. Cf. 37: 'The task of imposing form was not assumed to be easy, but neither was it assumed to set the poet in opposition to "nature", the mother of forms within the poet's mind as without it.'

significance.[1] Further the whole tenor of such a poetic is didactic: there are valid universal messages to be conveyed and the artist is—consciously—a hierophant, an implicit but widely acknowledged legislator of the world.

One forthright exponent of the viewpoint must suffice as example— Philip Sidney, that cynosure of the Humanists:

> For if it be, as I affirme, that no learning is so good, as that which teacheth and moveth to vertue, and that none can both teach and move thereto so much as Poesie, then is the conclusion manifest; that incke and paper cannot be to a more profitable purpose employed . . . I conjure you all . . . to beleeve with me, that there are many mysteries contained in Poetrie, which of purpose were written darkly, least by prophane wits it should be abused.[2]

*   *   *

Sidney is making explicit an assumption which was so widely held as to be little vaunted, like the theory of correspondences or the notion of the microcosm. We are back with the appeal to a hidden or universal authority and the deduction from it of an educative programme. Through this it is possible to see how closely the movement somewhat awkwardly called 'Mannerism' was tied to the intellectual world of the late Humanists. It was itself a reflection of the magic universe; indeed the Mannerist idea of art as the creation, or perhaps re-creation, of its own reality meant that in a certain sense art *was* magic.

Mannerism too was cleft by the antithesis between apparent and real. There is an intellectual world which is true: it is revealed by the *disegno interno*, by poetic insight, by spiritual perception, by conscious learning. But sensible forms are eternally uncertain: they are partial, lacking order and harmony, and can confuse, even completely mislead the observer. Hence much of the oddness of the style: its deliberate asymmetries and sometimes grotesque figures, its tendency to exaggerate and distort. A good example is the art of Parmigianino, especially a painting like his famous *Self-Portrait in a Convex Mirror* which found its way into the Imperial collection in Prague.[3] There is evidence that Rudolf valued Parmigianino highly, as he did the Parmesan's teacher Correggio, and spared no pains to acquire their works.[4]

---

[1] The question had an important logical dimension—the role of Ramism in late Renaissance imagery—which cannot be entered into here.

[2] Philip Sidney, *Defence of Poesie*, in *Collected Works*, ed. Feuillerat (Cambridge 1923), iii. 28, 45.

[3] It was left to Rudolf by Alessandro Vitoria in 1608. *Jahrbuch* xix (1898), Reg. No. 16836; cf. S. J. Freedberg, *Parmigianino* (Harvard 1950), 104–6, 201 f.

[4] He spent years negotiating—through the indefatigable Khevenhüller—to buy Parmigianino's *Amor* and various Correggios from the collection of Antonio Perez,

Another instance, in a different vein, is provided by the Emperor's great favourite, Pieter Breughel the Elder. We now know that such canvases as the *Combat between Carnival and Lent* (also in Rudolf's gallery) were intended to depict not only the folly of human ways, but the particular monstrousness of the confessional strife between Protestant and Catholic.[1] Similarly the harshness of the religious wars in France gave rise to the mystical, withdrawn art of the Valois court painter Antoine Caron, while the comparative stability, but intense otherworldliness of Philip II's Spain helped to call forth the heavily mannered, spiritually charged works of the young El Greco.[2] Greco stands for the miraculous beliefs of the Catholic revival, as does the Venetian Tintoretto, another artist whom Rudolf admired.[3]

These are figures drawn at a venture; the phenomenon which they represent is, however, a broad and important one. They are men who have taken flight from the repugnant world of appearance, with its conflicts and contradictions, into a kingdom of the mind; men whose repressed ideals are given expression in the intellectual sphere of the artistic *symbol*. The depth and complexity of late Renaissance iconography are by now a familiar matter, thanks mainly to the illuminating research of the Warburg–Saxl school. The subject still requires clarification and extension, while its role as an integral part in the culture of the age needs further underlining. Even the 'Mannerist' landscapes of Breughel, of the Frankenthal painters, or Roelant Savery and his colleagues in Prague, are rarely so simple as may appear on first inspection, and the same is true of the early experimenters in still life.[4]

eventually with success. See *Jahrbuch* xiii (1892), Reg. Nos. 9409, 9419–20, 9433, 9436, 9514; xv (1894), Nos. 12495, 12504, 12542, 12599; xix (1898), Nos. 16224–7, 16231, 16433; cf. Freedberg, op. cit. 88 f., 184–6. The provenance of works by these artists remains, however, a little obscure. The *Amor* was long thought to be by Correggio.

[1] C. G. Stridbeck, 'Breughel's "Combat between Carnival and Lent"', *JWCI* xix (1956), 96–109.

[2] J. Ehrmann, *Antoine Caron* (Geneva–Lille 1955); A. Blunt, 'El Greco's "Dream of Philip II"', *JWCI* iii (1939–40), 58–69.

[3] He was well represented in the Prague collection. Khevenhüller bequeathed the Emperor two paintings by Tintoretto on his death in 1606: *Jahrbuch* xix (1898), Reg. Nos. 16998–9.

[4] I. Bergström, *Dutch Still-life Painting in the Seventeenth Century* (London 1956), Introduction, sees the early still life as a disguised symbol developing from motifs in religious art. C. Sterling, *La Nature morte de l'antiquité à nos jours* (Paris 1952) connects it rather with Renaissance marquetry, which itself had its successors in the inlaid cabinets of the Mannerists. On Savery see above, p. 173 and cf. the articles by J. Šíp in *Sborník Prací Filosofické Fakulty Brněnské University Řada Uměnovědná* 8 (1964), 165–9; *Jahrbuch* 65 (N.F. xxix, 1969), 29–38; and *Umění* xviii (1970), 276–83. Another Prague landscapist on whom recent work has been done is Pieter Stevens; see A. Zwollo in *Jahrbuch* 64 (N.F. xxviii, 1968), 119–80; eundem in *Umění* xviii (1970), 246–78; and H. G. Franz, ibid. 230 ff.

Artistic symbolism in the sixteenth century was of course in part a mere drawing on the accepted manuals which provided models largely from classical antiquity, now stripped of some of their more bizarre medieval metamorphoses; in part too it was an elaboration of standard Christian ideas. But at the same time symbolism became increasingly 'overt', in the sense that the artist felt himself more self-consciously part of the secret tradition; the premises which underlay his activity came closer to those which underlay magic. A powerful influence here was the philosophy of Neoplatonism, with its stress on the power of contemplation, and especially of visual communication.

On the widest scale this commitment of the Mannerist mind to intellectual compensation for practical disharmony can be seen in the passion for the emblematic conceit. The study of emblem books in their historical context is a recent one, but their vast importance at that time was observed by Herder, and attempts to catalogue the contemporary literature have now abundantly borne out the point.[1] Their significance was European, in east no less than west; their writers—Alciati, Ruscelli, Giovio, Sambucus, Junius, and the rest—were household names. The emblem reflected in various ways the mentality of the period: its origins were rooted in the esoteric tradition of hieroglyphics;[2] it was a method of moral instruction through the power of word and image; it possessed a hidden message; above all it was a true symbol, that is, it meant more than it said and its meaning was a revelation, a discovery, not an artistic invention.[3]

These themes were often made explicit. Sambucus's Preface to his *Emblemata* is one example; another is the learned syncretic logician Nicolaus Taurellus of Altdorf, a man well known in Central Europe, who explains that he is using the emblem form as a vehicle for philosophical and moral lessons.[4] It is only through symbols, he stresses, that nature's truths may be made patent; thus the link is drawn between the emblem and the whole magical–Hermetic doctrine of hieroglyphics. It

[1] See the catalogue by Mario Praz, op. cit. and the colossal check-list of favourite emblematic themes by A. Henkel and A. Schöne, *Emblemata. Handbuch zur Sinnbildkunst des XVI und XVII Jahrhunderts* (Stuttgart 1967). Cf. A. Schöne, *Emblematik und Drama im Zeitalter des Barock* (Munich 1964), whence a quotation from Herder (17), and R. J. Clements, *Picta Poesis* (Rome 1960).

[2] L. Volkmann, op. cit. 41 ff.; cf. G. Boas (ed.), *The Hieroglyphics of Horapollo* (New York 1950), on a classic text which was reprinted thirty times in the century between 1505 and 1605.

[3] Schöne, op. cit. 21 f., 29 ff. Cf. Gombrich, art. cit.

[4] *Emblemata Physico-Ethica hoc est Naturae Morum moderatricis picta praecepta à Nicolao Taurello* (Nuremberg 1595). Many of his dedications are to Poles and Czechs, the more so in the second edition of the work (1602).

should not surprise us that some emblematists had an interest in alchemy; the connection is overt in the writings of Michael Maier, whose *Arcana Arcanissima* is an erudite and very speculative treatise on the real meaning of the ancient gods and myths.[1] Maier stood, as we have already seen, at the mystical end of the Rudolfine spectrum, but even an apparently much more orthodox artist like Georg Hoefnagel received an Imperial privilege to protect some of his drawings 'quae praeter elegantiam picturae plerumque hieroglyphicam quandam ac mysticam interpretationem aut moralem habeant'.[2]

Emblems were the visual representation of abstract thought and could be interpreted at various levels: literal, figurative, allegorical, anagogical. For these higher symbolic planes to be generally intelligible it was necessary that they should be explained. Jacopo Zucchi thought understanding of his obscure fresco cycle in the Palazzo Rucellai in Rome so important that he wrote a commentary which evidently only a learned fellow-initiate could appreciate. What was required, though, was that his message should be communicated, since its subject-matter was taken to be scientifically valid.[3] Here we are immediately in the presence of an attitude which is plainly didactic—emblematists like Taurellus again and again acknowledge such a purpose in their work—but whose conception of education is severely hierarchic.

The sixteenth-century recognition of the artist's status thus had two aspects: there are precise models to be followed, insights to be revealed; yet these are at the same time inaccessible to the ordinary untrained layman. In other words, art has a definite relation to its public (it is the reverse of uncommitted), but stands in a privileged position above it. With this development went a growing academism of mentality. Academies of painters were founded, first in Italy, then in northern Europe, with narrowly-defined rules and regulations.[4] Alongside them the universities experienced a change in character: those which already existed turned into much more exclusive, aristocratic institutions under the firm patronage of secular rulers, while new ones were founded, especially in Germany, having this direct aim in view: Herborn, Helm-

---

[1] M. Maier, *Arcana Arcanissima, hoc est Hieroglyphica Aegypto-Graeca* (n.p. 1614).

[2] *Jahrbuch* xiii (1892), Reg. No. 9677, Prague 1 Apr. 1590. On Hoefnagel's debt to the emblem books cf. Wilberg Vignau-Schuurman, op. cit. i. 262 ff. and *passim*.

[3] Fritz Saxl, *Antike Götter in der Spätrenaissance* (Leipzig–Berlin 1927), where the commentary is reprinted (37–111); it was published as *Discorso sopra gli Dei de' Gentili e loro Imprese* (Rome 1602).

[4] N. Pevsner, *Academies of Art Past and Present* (Cambridge 1940) provides a detailed study of individual academies and their seventeenth-century successors. Cf. above, pp. 163 f.

stedt, Jena, Dillingen. We may see further parallels on the one hand in the artistic support for the new absolute monarchies: the courtly symbolism of masque and triumphal entry; on the other hand in the cult of secret societies around the end of the century: the groups of alchemists, Lullist cells, and Rosicrucian 'fraternities'.

In such ways the pursuit of the arts was allotted its place in the hierarchy of powers, as were the workings of the Humanist scholar. There can be no doubt that the notion of a universal order was an important constituent within the kind of Mannerism which is revealed by Rudolfine Prague. The sense of a total scheme runs through some of its most characteristic activities: the linking of word and image in the emblem books; the blending of forms in courtly pageant or palace design; the close contacts between painting, applied skills, and literary circles; the cabinet of *virtù*, that Mannerist approach to a *Gesamtkunstwerk*. The artist both owed and contributed much to the occult sciences during this period. We have seen that they regularly dictated his subject-matter; but they could be equally vital for the execution of his task. In Ficino's Neoplatonism and beyond through the sixteenth century the means of magic were inseparable from its end, the form of the incantation from its content. Thus it was necessary to have the right astrological signs not only for an alchemical experiment or a royal birth, but also for artistic creation. This is seen most clearly in the doctrine of affects, the need to ensure beneficial influences as an atmosphere in which the magical work could be achieved—a credo, traceable back to Plotinus and earlier, which gained widespread popularity in the Renaissance. It underlay much of the theory and practice of music at the time, and became a dominant agent in the ritual court mystique, as Miss Yates has shown in her study on the last Valois monarchs, striving for a new mission in the twilight of their political power.[1]

To this context belongs the far-reaching attempt of Otto Benesch—himself a pupil of Max Dvořák—to pursue the correspondences between different art genres as reflections of a unitary conceptual pattern dictated by a cosmology. 'The creative mind at a given historical moment thinks in certain forms which are the same in arts and sciences.'[2] Thus Tintoretto's *Paradiso* reflects Bruno's notion of infinite space, Breughel's

[1] Yates, *French Academies*, esp. Ch. 3. The best study of the theory of musical affects is D. P. Walker, 'Musical Humanism in the sixteenth century and early seventeenth century', *The Music Review* ii (1941), 1–13, 111–21, 220–7, 288–308, iii (1942), 55–71; and idem, 'Orpheus the theologian and Renaissance Platonism', *JWCI* xvi (1953), 100–20. Cf. above, p. 190.

[2] O. Benesch, *The Art of the Renaissance in Northern Europe* (second edn. London 1965). Quotation from 145.

canvases the pessimistic view of the world as uncontrollable, undifferentiated mechanism.[1] Kepler displays a unity of artistic and scientific impulse: he is both fantastical—his ellipse a Mannerist intuition of space—and mathematical; his cosmic harmony is matched in music, his studies with light in the chiaroscuro of Elsheimer and the philosophy of Boehme.[2] Benesch may overstate his case, but his approach to a definition of Mannerism as pure spirituality of the whole and precise observation of individual parts recalls the deep antithesis which was so much a feature of the period: at once a direct perception of things (metals, emblem subjects, animals, sitters for portraits, and the rest) at the empirical level, and an intuition on a different plane.

In its retrospection too art paralleled modes of intellectual inquiry. The survival of medieval motifs through the Renaissance and into the Baroque is a familiar story; it occupies an important place in the cultural development of Europe north of the Alps and the less advanced Slav realms.[3] Some have suggested that it can provide the basis for an interpretation of Mannerism which seeks this style in the compromise between Mediterranean High Renaissance forms and persistent traditions of art and social ordering evolved elsewhere by the courts of the fifteenth century. What is more significant is the extent to which such retrospection became a conscious medievalism. The sixteenth century was in a sense the first fully historical age; where the Renaissance had revived antique types because they possessed eternal validity, the years that followed introduced a historical dimension and a message of history, whether in Vasari, or Baronius, or Sarpi. The 'ancients' and 'moderns' were not yet in dispute, but guide-lines were being laid down within which their debate could have meaning.

For the fine arts it is particularly difficult to distinguish the conscious and unconscious aspects of this historicity—the extent to which it was real revivalism as against the passive continuance of late-Gothic elements.[4] The truth is perhaps that the one influenced the other, creating a climate for retrospection, as the grandeur of the Prague of the Luxembourgs, with its great monuments of the Parler school commissioned by Charles IV, was the setting for the medievalizing symbolism of the Rudolfine court. Where the tension was most severe, the revival was most obviously a construct; in the Netherlands it appears as Breughel's picture of the universe, rooted in the work of Hieronymus

[1] Ibid. 148 f., 102 ff.   [2] Ibid. 157 ff.
[3] Cf. Angyal, *Slawische Barockwelt*, Ch. II.
[4] See above, pp. 184 f. Cf. in general V. Kotrba, art. cit., and the English case-study: Kenneth Clark, *The Gothic Revival* (second edn. London 1950), 13 ff.

Bosch and late medieval moralizing;[1] in France as the increasingly mystic art associated with the last Valois, Marguérite of Navarre, and the court of Lorraine: the slender deeply-felt figures of Pilon or Bellange, the apocalyptic intensity of Duvet, the preciosity of Niccolò dell'Abbate.[2]

The continuing influence of the Middle Ages was thus not merely formal or residual. The pre-Renaissance world was conceived in various ways to be the embodiment of a universal order, and—I have suggested —the notion of a pattern of natural things is a central feature both in Mannerist art and in the writings of philosopher or poet. Its importance, moreover, did not stop there: the pattern played itself out, *pari passu*, in human institutions. Here too the appointed scheme was paramount:

> For that infinite wisdom of GOD, which hath distinguished his Angells by degrees, which hath given greater and lesse light and beautie to Heavenly bodies, which hath made differences betweene beasts and birds, created the Eagle and the flie, the Cedar and the Shrub, and among stones given the fairest tincture to the Rubie, and the quickest light to the Diamond, hath also ordained Kings, Dukes or Leaders of the People, Magistrates, Iudges and other degrees among men.[3]

This famous passage by Raleigh is evidently only an undefined blue-print—the author himself proceeds to a list of many rulers who have grievously abused their divine mission; but it draws clearly the link between intellectual and social systems: every truth about the one was also relevant to the other, and every valid insight into the body of nature pointed a moral for the body politic.

The 'Renaissance' state of the later sixteenth century could easily be fitted into this scheme, and its gradations answered well the requirements of 'degree'. In Central Europe especially the hierarchy of powers associated with the Emperor and his government was mirrored at various levels in wider forms of exclusiveness, privilege, and aristocratic dominance. That political, social, and economic background was a close formative influence on artists and thinkers: Rudolf's court circle grew out of the whole state of cultural development in the Habsburg lands. Yet the programmes of Mannerism and late Humanism no more took it as given and final than they accepted the character of the visible world of nature. For neither was better than the imperfect copy of a true underlying harmony whose revelation would need a thoroughgoing plan of reform, both intellectual and political.

Reforming activity could, however, never go further towards a direct,

---

[1] Benesch, *Renaissance in Northern Europe*, 102 ff.
[2] Ibid. 122 ff.   [3] Raleigh, *History*, Preface.

empirical solution of problems than its own premises allowed. The widespread commitment to a magical universe in the later sixteenth century was an acceptance of practical limitations; it sought rather to reveal facts in their true nature than to change them. And whereas a crucial step had been taken from the medieval position which separated entirely the processes of contemplation from those of involvement in the everyday world, the task of the reformer was still primarily to alter men's notions. He was a propagator, a communicator, a mediator of *a priori* and superior knowledge. Just as a fundamental issue in Mannerism was the 'model' and its relation to the real, just as pansophy looked for some intellectual framework with which to apperceive the real, taking the individual datum to be incoherent without that framework, so the reformer was instilling a new mental discipline. His weapons too were symbols, his ultimate panacea education and self-knowledge.

This movement showed itself in a number of ways: among the religious eirenists (whose moderate programme was so widely subscribed to in learned circles), the mystics and Hermetists, *politiques* and neo-stoics, the Utopians, pansophists, Paracelsans, and chiliasts. All its manifestations ended in practical failure. But the failure was more than simply the inevitable collapse of unrealizable ideals. Rather it was rooted in a major reaction against some of the cardinal presuppositions of sixteenth-century educated Europe. It therefore throws light on a great particular failure— itself the delicate combination of a fatalism about action and a striving for ideal solutions—the catastrophic policies of Rudolf II. Thus in analysing a little further the impulse to reform, we shall be returning to the first thread of the present book.

8. Epilogue

In earlier chapters we have seen something of the increasingly authoritarian quality of later sixteenth-century thought. It was universalist and academic. It gave support to the traditional social order in its courtly form, more specifically to the notion of the Renaissance prince, and laid a Humanist stress on the virtuous exercise of power and patronage. This was not the issue of political absolutism as such, at least in the way that succeeding centuries were to debate the question: the plenary administrative and legislative powers of centralized monarchy. The late Renaissance reformer was less concerned with matters of pragmatic sovereignty (here he was outflanked by the practical statecraft of the Jesuits and Calvinists), and he did not necessarily take sides in the constitutional conflict between ruler and estates; rather he sought to justify some absolute system by reference to the universal background in which he believed. Within the total scheme all political groups—estates among them—had their appointed place.

An important item on this agenda was provided by the mystical and occult aspects of sovereignty. The apotheosis of ruling families was accomplished in verse and image, ceremonial masque and heroic portrait; one level in the interpretation of symbol and emblem was regularly political. The seriousness of the preoccupation can be seen not only in Rudolfine Prague, but in Elizabethan England, where the queen was surrounded by a similar mass of allegorical apostrophizing from scholars like Dee and poets like Spenser.[1] Both the unmarried Emperor and the Virgin Queen were widely regarded as figures prophetic of significant change in their own day, as symbols of a lost equilibrium when they were dead. Such a myth of kingship did not imply great visible power or personal exclusiveness: members of the Habsburg family were far more accessible than most modern public figures; frequently they would take meals or amuse themselves quite openly, and their lives were not always acted out amid the *hauteur* of official protocol.[2] Even Rudolf could be conspicuously at ease with friends of high or low degree, direct and ac-

---

[1] F. A. Yates, 'Queen Elizabeth as Astraea', *JWCI* x (1947), 27–82; Tillyard, op. cit. 17, 109, 128. Cf. above, pp. 147 ff.

[2] Cf. the observations of Wotton (in his letter to Zouche of 20 Nov. 1590) and Moryson: Pearsall Smith, op. cit. i. 244 and n. 6.

commodating with those who sought audience. But conversely the myth
would only function when the hierarchy which underpinned it was
secure; Rudolf's gradual self-immurement in the Hradschin was his own
recognition of its breakdown.

The monarch then, especially the Christian Emperor, could be seen
as a symbol of universality and order. Beside this secular paradigm went
an even more important spiritual one: for the idea of reform was still
posited on the theological concept of salvation. Whereas man's sin had
brought chaos into the world, his redemption—as microcosm—would
entail the restoration of harmony in the macrocosm of nature. But that
harmony had never been destroyed in the underlying divine scheme,
hence—as a corollary—the contemplation of the latter by the human
intellect was a religious obligation.[1] Thus viewed, the pansophic striving
became a way to salvation, while the historical dimension of occult
studies was the art of prophecy. The years around 1600—most of all
those immediately preceding the turn of the century—were among the
classic ages of chiliasm, and the pursuit of the millennium runs through
much apparently sober confessional debate in the period. The promised
salvation was to some extent conceived physically: an extreme position
was the cult of the elixir of life so dear to many Paracelsans;[2] but its
essence was a spiritual change, and here the full measure of the age's
didacticism becomes manifest. It was education which must accomplish
this spiritual purpose in man; learning was his moral duty, and he should
apply his unique faculty of free will to make correct use of its lessons.

An excellent representative of these views is Jan Comenius, whose
early pansophic tract called *Theatrum Universitatis Rerum* is full of the
salvationist thesis.[3] In 1623, when the victory of Ferdinand over the
forces of Bohemian Protestantism was just sealed, Comenius completed
in Czech one of his most important and characteristic works and dedicated
it to his friend, patron, and fellow sufferer, Karel Žerotín. He gave it the
title: *The Labyrinth of the World and the Paradise of the Heart*, and this
conscious antithesis goes immediately to the root of the problem which
he was trying to describe. One half of the book is a bitter allegory of the
human condition: the futility and meaninglessness of man's institutions,
ideals, and endeavours, as depicted with repugnance by a spiritual

---

[1] The point is well made in Tillyard, op. cit. 29 ff. and *passim*.

[2] Examples are an elegant MS. of the work, attributed to Raymond Lull, *De Con-
servatione Vitae Humanae*, presented to Maximilian II by a certain Camillus Sachetus
in 1572, now Budapest OSzK 582 Oct. Lat.; and a typical fruit of the Bacon revival—
R. Bacon, *Libellus de retardandis senectutis accidentibus* (Oxford 1590).

[3] This work, dating from 1614 and the years following but unpublished until recent
times, survives as a MS. in Prague, Nat. Mus. III E 34.

pilgrim; the remainder presents more briefly a complete contrast: the ineffable wisdom and perfection of God and the security of divine peace.

Although the *Labyrinth of the World* dates from after 1620, the work and its author are fully representative of the currents of thought which we have been studying; Comenius was a late inheritor of the Rudolfine mood. This is true of the sources of the book in a narrow sense:[1] the idea of the 'labyrinth' was a prevalent one at the time, and others viewed it, like Comenius, in eschatological terms, with connotations of pilgrimage and alienation. His obsession with prophecy and chiliastic beliefs was a survival from the years around 1600 (there is also much of Žerotín's passive melancholy), and the vision of an inner paradise, a centre of security, finds close parallels in the symbolism of alchemy and the religious mystics, even Václav Budovec.[2] It shows links too with Neoplatonist doctrines of emanation, especially with the metaphysical position of Cusanus, whom Comenius read and greatly admired.[3] His nearest literary model was the Lutheran mystic Valentin Andreae, whose Utopian political dream 'Christianopolis' he adapted, and there were also Bohemian anticipations of this theme.[4]

On a wider view the preoccupations of Comenius, as he withdrew through the writings of the 1620s into a realm of intellectual consolation, were typical of the age which the Thirty Years War was destroying. His own disgust with the sordid world around him was experienced by many who lived in the Prague of Rudolf. There was a widespread feeling of mistrust, a climate of violence and intrigue.[5]

[1] On these sources see D. Čiževsky, 'Comenius's "Labyrinth of the World"', *Harvard Slavic Studies* i (Cambridge, Mass. 1953), 83–135; J. B. Čapek, 'K otázkám kořenů stavby a funkce "labyrinthu" Komenského', *Acta Comeniana* xxii (1964), 255–71; S. Souček, 'K výtahu K. B. Skrbenského z neznámého dílu spisu Komenského', *ČČH* xxxi (1925), 337–56.

[2] One of Comenius's works almost contemporary with the *Labyrinth* was called *Centrum Securitatis* (1625). Cf. above, p. 100 n. 3, and Croll, *Basilica Chymica*, Preface, 3: 'Cum Pater noster coelestis, nos omnes affluenter suis donis praeveniens, SOL sit, omnibus aequaliter lucens (sine respectu enim et invidiâ Bonis et Malis, Gratis et Ingratis suam communicat lucem) meritò hunc, cuius filii esse debemus, imitari tenemur: iique omnium maximè, quos suâ gratiosâ misericordiâ, è tenebroso Laborum Errorumque Labyrintho et circumferentiâ ad manifestam Quietis et Veritatis semitam ac centrum deduxit.'

[3] See Jan Patočka, *Aristoteles, jeho předchudci a dědicové* (Prague 1964), 329–41, esp. 332 ff.

[4] The *Reipublicae Christianopolitanae Descriptio* was first published in 1619. There is a modern translation and analysis by F. E. Held (New York 1916). Cf. Čiževsky, op. cit. 91 ff.

[5] The decline in public morality was readily associated with the new *arriviste* courtiers, particularly those from abroad. Cf. the picaresque novel by Niklas Ulenhart, published in 1617: M. Weiss, 'Niklas Ulenhart, ein Darsteller des Alt-Prager Volkslebens', in *Prager Jahrbuch* 1943, 93–7.

Es ist kein Freundtschafft mehr auff Erdt
Ein Mensch dess andern Teufel

wrote Theobald Höck in 1601.[1] This mood is reflected in Hippolytus Guarinoni's book published in 1609: for him the current miserable state of mankind, even its short span of life, is a direct result of its godlessness. Guarinoni laments the passing of so many traditional aristocratic families (we may recall the Rožmberk, Hradec, Pernstein) and urges regeneration in face of the impending judgement-day. The motif of the labyrinth found its way into contemporary art and design—the manual of gardens by Vredemann de Vries is full of it.[2] There is the same concern in the travel literature of the day with its pronounced religious undertones; in Central Europe this genre was particularly widespread and the greatest Czech traveller, Harant, was also one of the leading domestic figures at Rudolf's court.[3] The state of pessimism—the contemporary condition of melancholy[4]—was felt most of all in the decade of the 1590s, when the pamphleteer Paprocki attempted deliberately to revive the spirit of his patrons by entertainment,[5] as in their own way the Jesuits were also seeking to do.

At the root of this malaise was the astrological debate, with its twin poles of fatalism and occult reform. Obsession with the lowest forms of astral science—judicial astrology, horoscopes, predictions—was characteristic of the later sixteenth century (almanacs were produced by all the leading 'astronomers' of the Carolinum: Hájek, Codicillus, Adam Huber, Bacháček, Zalužanský),[6] and the years before 1600 witnessed a great increase in prophecies of imminent doom or revelation. Some saw the point of decision as 1588, when the world would again enter the conjunction of the fiery trigon for the first time in 800 years and the second time since the birth of Christ;[7] others as 1597, which was a powerful magic number;[8] others as 1599 or 1600 itself. In 1591 the Venetian

---

[1] Quoted by L. W. Forster, *The Temper of Seventeenth-century German Literature* (London 1952), 16.

[2] Jan Vredemann de Vries, *Hortorum Viridiarumque Formae* (Antwerp 1583); cf. Matthews, op. cit. 100–9 and figs. 72–4.

[3] Harant's *Putowání aneb Cesta z Králowstwí Czeského ... do Země Swaté ... a dále do Egypta* (Prague 1608) is full of curious and exotic information, exhibiting the author's extensive learning. Cf. my article cited above, p. 76 n. 1.

[4] See Bamborough, op. cit. 95 ff. for a discussion of the meaning of this term.

[5] Krejčí, *Paprocki*, 56–8.

[6] František Palacký, 'O pranostikách a kalendářích českých zwláště w 16. století', *ČČM* 1829, 33–64.

[7] W.-E. Peuckert, *Die Rosenkreutzer, zur Geschichte einer Reformation* (Jena 1928), 8 ff.; E. Zinner, *Bibliographie der astronomischen Literatur*, 18 ff.

[8] Peuckert, op. cit. 40 ff. A MS. in the Strahov library which appears to have been written by one of the monks treats 1597 as a year even more dangerous than 1588

Gregor Jordanus, a physician and cosmographer to the Emperor, issued a book of Joachimite and Brigittine prophecies in Latin and German, and his was only one echo of the continuing interest in those medieval oracles.[1] The remarkable occurrences in the heavens, the novae of 1572 and 1604 and the comet of 1577, provoked more specialist astronomical opinion. Dudith, Hájek, Codicillus, Paul Fabritius, Kepler, and Tycho joined the fray of speculation, along with less distinguished stargazers like Johann Rasch of Vienna, who offered the prophecies of Daniel as an interpretation.[2] To this was added the confusion over the introduction of the Gregorian Calendar from 1583, which not only aggravated in a very practical way the existing religious split, but was also fraught with astrological problems. Both Kepler and Tycho supported the reform, though many Protestant academics—including Kepler's teacher Maestlin—opposed it, and Rudolf seems to have hesitated in acceptance.[3]

Rudolf himself was highly superstitious by nature: his horoscope had been cast by Nostradamus,[4] and he was disposed to act on all kinds of irrational suggestions. It is likely that part of his 'crisis' in 1600 was due to fears that he would die before the age of 50, like his father, perhaps at the hands of a second Jacques Clément, the assassin of an equally hesitant and introspective monarch, Henry III of Valois.[5] Contemporaries definitely thought that he was under the influence of a prophecy (attributed even to Tycho Brahe) that he would be intrigued against by members of his own family, and his attitude to the Capuchins may well have been similarly conditioned. The same kinds of tensions, aggravated by political conflict and buttressed by apocalyptic intimations, were widespread in Bohemia and elsewhere in the Habsburg lands.[6]

because of the conjunction in it of the magical numbers 9 and 7; by the same reasoning the author attaches great significance to '63', though he makes no mention of the Council of Trent, whose decrees were promulgated in that year. Strahov, AM XIV 18.

[1] *Prophetiae seu Vaticinia XIIII Tabellis expressa* (n.p. 1591). A German version appeared at Augsburg in 1592. Jordanus is represented in Exner's Album for 1598 as Rudolf II's 'Medicus et Cosmographus' in Prague (*Spero Meliora*, 58). Two other brief astrological compendia by him—one dedicated to the Emperor—survive in Vienna: ÖN, MSS. 10581, 10597. Cf. above, p. 253 n. 6.

[2] J. Rasch, *Von dem newen Stern . . . unnd von den Cometen des 77 und 81 Jars* (Munich n.d.); idem, *Drey greuliche weissagung Daniels des Propheten . . .* (Munich n.d.).

[3] Zinner, op. cit. 25–8; *SČ* vi, *passim*; Janssen, op. cit. iv. 473 ff.; L. Schuster, op. cit. Part I.

[4] *Mih. Nostradami gerechnete und gestellte Nativität principi Rudolpho Imp. Maximiliani filio* (1564)—Zíbrt, *BČH* iii, No. 9807, quoting Dudík, *Forschungen in Schweden*, 115, 287.

[5] See the second relation of Ansbach in 1601 (Ranke, op. cit.). The Emperor had apparently earlier survived an attempt on his life by a Flemish priest: Henry Wotton to Zouche, Vienna 9 Jan. 1591; Pearsall Smith, op. cit. i. 251. Cf. his reaction to the assassination of Henry IV in 1610: *Briefe und Akten* viii, 275 n. 1.

[6] Cf. Peuckert, op. cit. 33 ff.; Kavka, *Bílá Hora*, 47, 51 f.; Kopecký, *Veleslavín*, 51 f.

One of those who wrote on the new star of 1604 was Johannes Kepler, and he connected it with the fiery trigon of A.D. 1.[1] He recalls observing it in Prague with Jost Burgi and Franz Tengnagel, the son-in-law of Tycho. Neither Kepler nor Tycho was 'opposed' to astrology (the question thus presented is meaningless). Both accepted a possible interplay between the separate elements of a unified cosmology; thus ample evidence can be found that they shared the fashion for astral interpretations, and Tycho had a library of such works which he annotated freely.[2] But this astrology was not held to eliminate free will: it left room for a reform within the existing recognized system; indeed it demanded one, since the determining factor in it was the power of the human intellect to react to certain cosmic configurations.[3] The same notions appear in lesser astronomer contemporaries; Nicholas Raimarus Ursus, mathematician to the Emperor and Tycho's deadly rival (the latter accused him, probably correctly, of plagiarism), linked some fairly unremarkable arithmetical achievements with a penchant for the mysterious—he knew John Dee—and a conviction that the end of the world was nigh.[4] The Paduan Giovanni Antonio Magini (1555–1617), respected correspondent of Tycho and Kepler, was a famed caster of horoscopes, stout defender of astrological methods, dabbler in alchemy, and purveyor of concave mirrors to the Imperial court in Prague.[5]

The culmination of the mood of prophecy and chiliasm around 1600 was what became known as the 'Rosicrucian movement'. The relevant

[1] J. Kepler, *De Stella Nova* (Sessius, Prague 1606) with a dedication to Rudolf II. Cf. Max Caspar, *Kepler* (Stuttgart 1948, English translation London–New York 1959), 154–7.

[2] F. J. Studnička, *Bericht über die astrologischen Studien des Reformators der beobachtenden Astronomie, Tycho Brahe* (Prague 1901).

[3] Cf. Koestler, op. cit. 242 ff.; Caspar, op. cit. 178 ff.; Pauli, op. cit. 180 ff.

[4] Ursus's cosmological hypotheses appeared as *Fundamentum Astronomicum . . .* (Strasbourg 1588) and were then defended against Tycho's fulminations in a book published in Prague, *De Astronomicis Hypothesibus, seu Systemate mundano tractatus . . .* (1597). In the same year he presented to the Emperor a mathematical work of considerable triviality, introduced with some arcane Platonic verbiage: 'Tractatiuncula von der Allerkunstreichesten und Sinnreichesten Regel Cossa, oder Algebra', Vienna, ÖN, MS. 10943. After Ursus's death there appeared a thin tract by him, allegedly written in 1596, whose title is a full description of the contents: *Chronologische gewisse und unwiderlegliche Beweisung auss heiliger Göttlicher Schrifft und Heiligen Vättern dass die Welt vergehen und der Jüngste Tag kommen werd innerhalb 77 Jaren* (Nuremberg 1606).

[5] Magini's letters to and from astronomer contemporaries were published by A. Favaro: *Carteggio inedito . . . con G. A. Magini* (Bologna 1886), who also gives a useful account of his life and works. Apart from his important *Ephemerides Coelestium Motuum* (Venice 1582) which contains sections on astrological methods, Magini wrote a firm justification of the art: *De astrologica ratione, ac usu dierum Criticorum seu Decretorum* (Frankfurt 1608). Magini's relations with Rudolf and Barvitius appear from the Dedication to *Tabulae primi mobilis quas directionum vulgo dicunt* (Venice 1604) and *Jahrbuch* xix (1898), Reg. Nos. 16939, 16963; cf. Favaro, op. cit. 163–71. The Emperor clearly valued his talents, though payment for services rendered was slow.

issue here is not the mystery of whether a Rosicrucian brotherhood ever had any physical existence—it seems very unlikely that it did—but the *message* which the various Rosicrucian tracts proclaimed and which aroused widespread interest even among the apparently orthodox: the call of an intellectual élite for a universal reform of society, couched in the language of the alchemical transmutation or the 'rebirth' of the mystics, and claimed as a rediscovery of secret stores of knowledge.[1] The most imaginative of these writings, the *Chymical Wedding of Christian Rosenkreutz*, was composed, on his own admission, by Valentin Andreae,[2] and the latter's circle of friends included a number who embraced the mystic and occult approach to knowledge: the Cabalist and Hermetist Besold, translator of Boccalini's *Ragguagli*; Adami, the admirer of Campanella; Wilhelm Wense, and others.[3] A leading defender of Rosicrucian ideas was Michael Maier[4] and there seem to have been other direct links with Bohemian and Silesian circles, like the Paracelsan Johann Montanus of Strigau who was looking for reform in the 1590s.[5] The religious–alchemical language of the Rosicrucian 'confession of faith' is very close in spirit to the beliefs of the iatrochemists and related Hermetic and occult reformers: Bruno, Dee, Khunrath, Boehme, Fludd. The whole Paracelsan call for a new attitude to education and scientific method, represented on the more serious level by a Robert Fludd or a Michael Maier, easily blended into the vaticinations of lesser operators like Benedikt Figulus.[6]

[1] The external history of the 'movement' is chronicled in Peuckert, *Rosenkreutzer*, 59 ff., 116 ff., and P. Arnold, *Histoire des Rose-Croix et les origines de la franc-maçonnerie* (Paris 1955), 23 ff. Individuals were certainly persecuted as Rosicrucians (e.g. Peuckert, 169 ff.) but there is no evidence that the 'Fraternity' claimed by the first tract had any substantial existence.

[2] It was written in 1604, though not published until 1616. See Peuckert, *Rosen-kreutzer*, 89–116, who takes Andreae to be the author of the *Fama Fraternitatis* and the *Confessio* also; Arnold, op. cit., sees the other tracts as written jointly by him and his friends. Both deny that the writings were intended as satire.

[3] Arnold, op. cit. 54 ff. The anti-Spanish *Ragguagli* were printed with the first edition of the *Fama Fraternitatis*; see L. Firpo, *Traduzioni dei Ragguagli di Traiano Boccalini* (Florence 1965).

[4] e.g. his *Verum Inventum* (Frankfurt 1619) and cf. Morhof, *Polyhistor*, Pt. I, 131 ff.; Arnold, op. cit. 139–41.

[5] Above, p. 200 n. 2; Peuckert, *Pansophie*, 468 f.; *Epistolae Fratris Rogerii Baconis*, Dedication. This man, also known as Johann Scultetus, lived from 1531 to 1604 (J. H. Cunrad, *Silesia Togata* (Liegnitz 1706), 281) and is credited by Brandau with the discovery of a rejuvenating elixir (op. cit. 35). He may thus be identical with the 'Jakob Montanus of Königsberg' to whom Figulus ascribes a recipe for the *aurum potabile* (B. Figulus, *Pandora Magnalium Naturalium Aurea et Benedicta* (Strasbourg 1608)). Montanus was also famous for the discovery of a local nostrum, the 'sigillated earth' of Strigau; cf. Schwenckfeldt, *Stirpium et Fossilium Catalogus*, Bk. 3, 395–7.

[6] e.g. Figulus, *Thesaurinella Olympica*, dedication; idem, *Rosarium Novum Olympicum et Benedictum* (Basle 1608), dedication. Cf. Debus, *Chemical Dream*, passim.

The *Chymical Wedding* was published in 1616 by Zetzner at Strasbourg, then again the following year by Lucas Jennis at Frankfurt, and the role played in the spreading of such esoteric literature by a number of Rhineland printers is surely highly significant. These men were, like other engravers and publishers we have considered, not only active in business but also initiates. The publishing house of Lazarus Zetzner issued a series of well-known but unorthodox texts, among them a large collection of Lullist works (including Bruno's commentaries on Lull),[1] a number of Paracelsan writings, and various tracts of alchemy, the largest a six-volume *Theatrum Chymicum.* Jennis produced a *Musaeum Hermeticum* and a great many alchemical texts, including the emblems of Stoltzius and some of those of Maier. He was linked by marriage with the family of de Bry in Oppenheim, famous for its emblematic and topographical books, which published many of the works of Maier and the English Hermetist Fludd.[2] John Theodore de Bry's son-in-law was Matthias Merian, celebrated both as engraver and printer, not least of esoteric subjects, who worked for a time with Jacques Callot. Merian was certainly known in Prague, since the Czech artist Václav Hollár became apprenticed to him in 1627, having presumably left Bohemia for religious reasons.[3]

At the same time there were re-editions of further important occult works of the Middle Ages and Renaissance: Roger Bacon, Bruno, Lavinheta, and the first appearance in print of mystical writings by Paracelsus and Weigel, while these same German presses were being widely used to propagate the great debate over principles of logic linked with the name of Ramus.[4] Another publishing dynasty which settled in the Rhineland and was closely associated with such currents in Central Europe was that of the Wechels: Andreas, the Humanist friend of Ramus, Crato, and Sidney, his son John (printer of books by Dee and Bruno), his sons-in-law Jean Aubri and Claude Marne, and their descendants through the early decades of the next century.[5] We may compare

---

[1] Cf. Carreras y Artau, op. cit. ii. 237–9.

[2] Cf. Yates, *Art of Memory*, 322, 325. On Jennis see E. Trenczak, 'Lucas Jennis als Verleger alchemistischer Bildertraktate', *Gutenberg-Jahrbuch* 1965, 324–37.

[3] E. Dostál, *Hollár* (Prague 1924), 13 ff. This was the same Wenceslaus Hollar who later joined the Earl of Arundel and lived most of his life in England. His religious position has never been clear; he came from a family traditionally loyal to the Habsburgs and Catholic, and was associated with the court party in England.

[4] Ong, *Ramus and Talon Inventory*, passim.

[5] J. Benzing, *Die Buchdrucker des 16. und 17. Jahrhunderts im deutschen Sprachgebiet* (Wiesbaden 1963), 119 f. gives brief details. I hope to examine in a separate article the importance of this family, especially Aubri, for the intellectual life of Central Europe. Works like Croll's *Basilica Chymica* and Kepler's *Astronomiae Pars Optica* appeared on its presses.

their activity with that of Dutchmen like Plantin's son-in-law Raphelengien, or Thomas Basson, publisher of Nicolas Barnaud and similar alchemists as well as Ramist and occult literature.[1]

A central figure in all this endeavour was J. H. Alsted, the leading professor at the Academy of Herborn, where one of his most attentive pupils was Comenius, and friend—as we have seen—of Žerotín and other Eastern Europeans.[2] Alsted edited several Lullist works, among them the Lavinheta commentary, because he saw the 'Art' as a possible key to the pansophic striving which informs all his teaching and appears most clearly in his seven-volume Encyclopedia of human knowledge.[3] Pansophy presupposed, for him and his contemporaries, the belief that the heterogeneous objects of appearance, the Labyrinth of the World, could be understood through a higher faculty of the intellect as a complete and unitary system. At the same time it was a framework for reform, since the revelation of this system, the real nature of the universe, was a principle which could liberate mankind from its present toils and raise it to participation in the divine order. Alsted was a chiliast no less than Comenius.[4] Thus the *a priori* truths known to the pansophic initiate needed to be communicated through education, and the reform plan of Alsted was a plea for a new universal education, to be guided by an erudite academy.

In this formulation we should recognize not only the programme of Comenius, as presented most clearly in his *Pansophiae Prodromus* (1639) —one of the fruits of a collaboration with the English Utopian Samuel Hartlib—but that of several other prophets of total education, notably Wolfgang Ratke (Ratichius), who presented a scheme for universal reform to the Emperor in 1612.[5] Comenius aimed at imparting to the young a comprehensive account of knowledge through the 'key' of

[1] Raphelengien published Barnaud's *Triga Chemica* and *Quadriga Aurifera* (1599), Basson his *Commentariolum* (1597), *De Occulta Philosophia*, and *Tractatulus Chemicus* (1601). On Raphelengien cf. Voet, op. cit. 147 ff.; on Basson cf. Yates, *Art of Memory*, 285, and above, p. 95 n. 2.

[2] A. Heyberger, *Jean Amos Comenius* (Paris 1928), 19 ff. and, most recently, M. Blekastad, *Comenius* (Oslo 1969), 21 ff. Comenius studied at Herborn from 1611 to 1613, together with other Czechs; cf. J. Vávra, 'Štambuch Bratra Matouše Tita krajana a spolužáka Komenského v Herbornu 1611-12', *ČČM* 81 (1907), 64-9. Alsted later fled to Transylvania during the Thirty Years War.

[3] This was published at Herborn in 1630 but begun much earlier. Cf. Carreras y Artau, op. cit. 239-49.

[4] e.g. his *Diatribe de mille annis apocalypticis* (Frankfurt 1627). Cf. Rossi, *Clavis Universalis*, 179-84.

[5] Cf. G. H. Turnbull, *Samuel Hartlib, a sketch of his life and his relations to J. A. Comenius* (London 1920), 26-41; G. Rioux, *L'Œuvre pédagogique de Wolfgangus Ratichius, 1571-1635* (Paris 1963), 17 ff.

correspondences between words and the things they represent, and in a process of progressive realization from childhood to manhood. His pedagogy, which reached a final form in the *Magna Didactica* and the *Orbis Sensualium Pictus*, was 'totalitarian' in its metaphysical insistence on the need for an education towards universal salvation (*pampaedia*);[1] to view it as democratic or egalitarian *per se* is to misconstrue the sources of Comenius's inspiration and his debt to the occult tradition.

At the centre of Comenius's scheme stood an Academy of Wisdom, an educational élite, and this too was an offspring of the whole movement towards esoteric societies, which embraced artists, alchemists, 'Rosicrucians', Paracelsans, and the rest. In the German lands it gave rise to secretive Academies which were founded out of opposition to the prevailing superficial orthodoxy of the universities, like the heavily symbolical *Fruchtbringende Gesellschaft* of 1617, whose leading spirits were the eirenists Ludwig of Anhalt-Köthen and Matthias Bernegger,[2] or the *Collegium Philosophicum* founded in Rostock by Joachim Jungius. Jungius, one of the most learned pansophists of the seventeenth century, was a friend of Andreae, Comenius, and Ratke, and his Rostock society owed much to the ideals of the Christianopolis.[3] A colleague and pupil of his, the alchemist Joachim Morsius, moved in similar circles: he knew Maier and Fludd, Alsted and Andreae, Arndt and Boehme, Hartlib and Bernegger, de Dominis and Cornelius Drebbel.[4] Such Academies, like the earlier one around Della Porta in Naples, were dedicated to philosophical and occult studies outside the constraints of established religion and the universities, and were strongly tinged with the mood of confessional reconciliation.

Among the educational reformers we have returned to a central concern of the age of Rudolf: the belief in a single universal authority and the total, all-embracing conception of society. It went with a faith in the moral power of ideas and a reaction, often avowedly retrospective, against vacuous late scholasticism and shallow Humanism. A line of anti-Renaissance thinking in the field of pedagogy can be traced from Melanchthon and Montaigne to Campanella, Alsted, and Comenius;[5] it

---

[1] K. Schaller, *PAN, Untersuchungen zur Comenius-Terminologie* (The Hague 1958). The *Magna Didactica* was first published in Amsterdam in 1657, the *Orbis Sensualium Pictus* in Nuremberg the following year; both had been begun much earlier.

[2] L. Keller, *Comenius und die Akademien* (Berlin 1895).

[3] Ornstein, op. cit. 167–9. Cf. G. E. Guhrauer, *Joachim Jungius und sein Zeitalter* (Stuttgart 1850).

[4] H. Schneider, *Joachim Morsius und sein Kreis* (Lübeck 1929), 17 ff. and *passim*.

[5] This is the argument of the later chapters of Garin, *Educazione*.

parallels the attack on existing standards in logic by Sturm, Ramus, and the Lullists, or the visual and verbal conceits of the Mannerists.

* * *

These late figures like Comenius and Alsted may seem to have taken us a long way from the courtly atmosphere of the later sixteenth century. Yet they belong here because their importance is precisely as survivals of that earlier intellectual climate, preservers of a pattern of thought which was gradually being superseded. The final breakdown of the Renaissance and the dispersal of its ideas was a complex process, but two aspects of the same development may helpfully be distinguished: on the one hand some of the heritage of intellectual Humanism was organically embodied in succeeding movements, though never again as a central theme; on the other hand there were increasing signs that a thorough reaction was taking place against the very principles on which it had stood.

In Central Europe the half-century after 1600 brought almost complete triumph to the Catholic camp, to an offensive begun by the Papacy and its agents, then directed increasingly by the Habsburg dynasty itself. It is therefore within the body of revitalized Catholicism that one must search for evidence of earlier traditions, for signs indeed that those very traditions somehow contributed to the prosperity of the Catholic cause. The whole notion of a European *Counter*-Reformation must be treated with great reserve, even in Bohemia, which was one of the first nineteenth-century breeding-grounds for the idea.[1] In the present context it is not the expression's dangerous connotations of forced alteration from above which are significant, but the attractiveness of conversion, both to those who had become Protestant and those who—like so many intellectual figures of the sixteenth century—had inwardly rebelled against all the new orthodoxies: of Rome, Wittenberg, or Geneva.

Thus alongside the representatives of a new conformity and the spirit of the Council of Trent we still find exemplars of old concerns and continuity; the two could easily be combined within the same person. Alongside nuncios like Spinelli or Ferreri, Jesuits like Carrillo in Transylvania[2] or Scherer in Austria, bishops like Martin Brenner or František Dietrichstein, there stand influential and loyal servants of the Church whose debt to the world of Humanism was still overwhelming. The prelate Pontanus is one who has already been analysed; the Spanish ambassador in Prague San Clemente is another. An example from the

[1] H. O. Evennett, *The Spirit of the Counter-Reformation* (Cambridge, 1968), 5.
[2] Veress, *Carrillo*; L. Szilas, *Der Jesuit Alfonso Carrillo in Siebenbürgen 1591–1599* (Rome 1966). Carrillo must rank as one of the most capable of all Papal diplomats of his period.

rising generation of aristocrats is the Chancellor, Zdeněk Vojtěch Lobkovic.

Lobkovic was the spearhead of the Catholic revival in Bohemia from 1600 and thus his wider historical significance seems relatively uncomplicated. But that is to mistake the profounder roots of his politics: he became a convinced activist, yet his background is the uncertainty of the 1590s; his sure faith in the Roman Church needs to be explained, just as does the inability of the older Rudolf and his contemporaries to find satisfaction. Lobkovic combined his deep faith with deep learning; evidence of it can be found in his diaries, which are filled, besides the everyday notes on appointments, with religious texts, quotations from the Czech and German Bibles, Classical mottoes and aphorisms, mostly in Latin, but also in Spanish and occasionally German.[1] His belief in the saving grace of the Catholic Church shines through these lines, but his great concern about salvation no less: 'Peccantem me quotidie et non me penitentem timor mortis conturbat me. Quia in Inferno nulla est Redemptio, miserere mei Deus et salva me. Deus in nomine tuo salvum me fac et in Virtute tua libera me. Quia in Inferno nulla est Redemptio. Miserere mei Deus et salva me . . .' Lobkovic's education was in the pattern of late Renaissance Humanism and he maintained its passion for correspondence. He wrote and received letters on a grand scale and many are preserved, though unfortunately the best survivals are for the years after 1620.[2]

Zdeněk Lobkovic was born in 1568 and studied much abroad, especially in Italy, where he read law at Perugia. Little is known about the quality of this education but there is one passing reference by his family biographer which suggests that it may not have been altogether straightforward: he appears to have learnt the techniques of the artificial memory.[3] On his return to Bohemia progress was rapid: he was aulic councillor in 1591, went with Rudolf to the Regensburg Diet of 1594, and stayed with Khevenhüller in Madrid the following year. From 1599 he was Chancellor; in 1603 he married Polyxena, the widow of Vilém

---

[1] Lobkovické Kalendáře, UK, MS. VII Ad 118. The diaries which Lobkovic used were printed either in German or Czech; they date from the years after 1600.

[2] The letters are in S.A., Litoměřice-Žitenice, LRRK: letters to Zdeněk B 209–31, to Polyxena B 232–9. The internal correspondence of the family is separate: e.g. Zdeněk's letters to his wife (there are not many) D 162, fos. 1–169; Polyxena's to Zdeněk D 165, fos. 1–175.

[3] Bauschek, MS. Life of Zdenko, S.A., Litoměřice-Žitenice Sign. VI E G 34, p. 2: 'Noch in demselben Jahre (1587) gieng er nach Cingoli(?), wo er die Kunst des Lokalgedächtnisses lernte, unfehlbar unter Joanninus Cingulanus Picenus memoriae magister, dessen Tod er auf dem 8ten December 1596 angemerkt hat.'

Rožmberk and daughter of Vratislav von Pernstein and Maria Manriquez de Lara.

Zdeněk and Polyxena enjoyed the intellectual respect of contemporaries as diverse as Žerotín, Pontanus, and Jessenius, but the fullest proof of their interests is their large library. They combined the existing collection of the Lobkovic (Zdeněk acquired that of Jiří Popel after the latter's death in prison in 1607) with the books of the last Pernsteins and on this foundation the Lobkovic library became the largest among all those of the Bohemian aristocracy.[1] There are now problems in reconstructing it,[2] though Chudoba has made attempts for the political literature on the basis of the particular and unmistakable bindings which Zdeněk used and the *ex libris* symbol which Polyxena seems to have adopted.[3] Beyond this we are left with the surmise that editions for the period 1590–1620 are most likely to have been acquired by Zdeněk and his wife.

The breadth of Lobkovic's political reading is most striking: he had not only the whole range of Catholic literature—Suarez, Aquinas, Juan de Salazar, Juan de la Puente, Diego de Rojas, Mariana, Bellarmin, Ribadeneira—but much more that was distinctly unorthodox. There were four editions of Machiavelli, all containing his *Prince*; Patrizi's *De Regno* in its 1578 edition, as well as a Spanish translation of 1591; Bodin's *Republic* in Italian translation (and two other copies survive in the library); Beza's *Droit des Magistrats* in a 1594 binding; the *Vindiciae contra Tyrannos*; much Lipsius; Boccalini's *Ragguagli di Parnasso*; and works by Erasmus, Luther, and Melanchthon. Zdeněk bought one edition of Melanchthon's *Ethics* in Prague in 1589.[4]

Further afield his library must have embraced many emblem books[5] and works on natural magic—there are various editions of J. B. Porta dating from the 1590s and later. It was also rich in books on medicine and alchemy: there are several copies of the works of Martin Ruland between 1590 and 1610, much of Cardanus, including his very rare *Somniorum synesiorum . . . Libri 4* (Basle 1562), Croll's *Basilica Chymica* (1609, 1611, and four later editions), the writings of Rupescissa and other

---

[1] *Čeští sběratelé* . . . (above, p. 142 n. 1), 13–18.

[2] The library itself is at the moment of writing (1971) still inaccessible, having been evacuated from the Lobkovic castle of Roudnice in the years after 1945. The multi-volume MS. catalogue is available in the manuscript department of the UK. Zdeněk hardly ever annotated or inscribed his books.

[3] B. Chudoba, *Roudnická politika (zastoupení renesanční politické vědy v knihovně českého státníka na rozhraní XVI a XVII století)* (Prague 1933).

[4] Ibid. 7 (the *Ethicae Doctrinae Elementa*).

[5] Ibid. 21 n. and catalogue in UK: Alciati, Ruscelli, Camerarius, etc.

'artists', and no less than thirty-eight separate editions of Paracelsus, either before 1620 or undated. Much more of interest in this collection might emerge on fuller investigation; it has for instance four copies of Ramus's *Dialectics* between 1561 and 1606.

Zdeněk and Polyxena Lobkovic stand on both sides of the great divide: friends of the Jesuit College, the nuncios, and the Italian community in Prague, yet intimates of the old Emperor and patrons of traditional culture; convinced supporters of the Habsburg power, yet respecters of local custom. Their backing for the Counter-Reformation was perhaps the most important single political cause of its success (witness Zdeněk's refusal to sign the Letter of Majesty in 1609). For them, as for others, the intellectual superiority of Catholicism was related to its universal values, its symbolic content, its sense of hierarchy and mystery. Such things belonged in the world of Rudolf, but they were now increasingly grafted on to a new orthodoxy, just as the proselyte brings with him parts of a former background while becoming a more than thorough apostle for his adopted faith.

The same gradual process can be seen reflected in the development of art from Mannerism to Baroque: the latter more direct and uniform, but exhausting itself in the human drama as such, seeking only a religious, not a metaphysical fulfilment. Both doctrine and emotion now became popularized in a way which had always been foreign to the religious and philosophical debates of the sixteenth century. It is a kind of paradox that the universal Church reasserted itself in Central Europe on the ruins of a universal culture, and the men who did most to achieve the one were often those who least understood the other. The Pope's representatives in Prague, for all their diligence and ability, never displayed any comprehension of the personality of Rudolf, let alone sympathy for his interests.

In fact the very strength of those interests—the influence of late Humanism—and the society which sustained them delayed the Catholic revival in the Habsburg lands. At the same time they long moderated the views of the Protestants. The latter too moved progressively towards extremer positions after 1600 (the paradigm is well seen in a person like Jessenius) while retaining important aspects of the old mentality. Alchemy continued to hold its place, even among such leaders of the Bohemian revolt as Fels, Ladislav Velen Žerotín, and Christian von Anhalt,[1] while the role of chiliasm in their activities is worth a serious

---

[1] On Fels: Zíbrt, *BČH* iii, No. 10754. Anhalt was the leading patron of Oswald Croll. On Žerotín: F. Hrubý, *Ladislav Velen z Žerotína* (Prague 1930), 27 ff. Cf. the

study. One current of German Lutheranism kept a concern for eirenism until the end of the century, from the Heidelberg professor Pareus (significantly a native of Frankenstein in Silesia), through syncretists like Calixtus and Molanus to Leibniz.

Yet for all the tenacity of individual elements, the magical world-view was met by unmistakable rejection as the seventeenth century proceeded. The organic assimilation of its ideas became far outweighed by official denials of them. In Central Europe this trend was at work in the years after 1600; it was then strongly accelerated by the political blows of 1618–20 and the necessity for a militant simplification of ideas. The generation after the White Mountain was one of fighting ideologies. The intellectual reformers found themselves driven into the ranks of the heterodox: whether within the Protestant sects where mystical and Utopian solutions became identified with doctrinal and social exclusiveness,[1] or in Catholic groups which resisted the influence of the Jesuits and the dead hand of confessionalism. Among the Czechs there were representatives in exile, like Comenius or the strange Cabalist Christian Knorr von Rosenroth, son of a Silesian clergyman,[2] and at home, most notably Valerian Magni, the pious sceptic Hirnhaim, and his teacher Jan Marcus Marci (1595–1667). The last stands as a distinguished but characteristic figure within the old scientific framework: a professor of medicine whose philosophy was full of Neoplatonic theories of light, occult forces, and innate, archetypal ideas; again the combination of mystical assumptions with exact observation, even the fascination with mechanics.[3]

Such men were condemned to obscurity not only for standing outside the new orthodoxies of politics, but for resisting the new philosophy of the seventeenth century. Their traditional cosmology was basically a magical one; its symbolism drew on a series of possible objective correlatives; its self-consciousness was directed towards an inner illumination

tract ed. Dominicus Gnosius, *Hermetis Trismegisti Tractatus vero Aureus, De Lapidis Philosophici secreto* (Leipzig 1610), dedicated to Žerotín, but not mentioned by Hrubý.

[1] Cf. J. B. Neveux, *Vie spirituelle et vie sociale entre Rhin et Baltique au XVIIe siècle* (Paris 1967), 504 ff. and *passim*.

[2] K. Salecker, *Christian Knorr von Rosenroth* (Leipzig 1931).

[3] On Hirnhaim see above, p. 114 and Pagel, op. cit. 123–8. Marci's major works were the *Idearum Operatricum Idea* (Prague 1635) and the *Philosophia Vetus Restituta, omnia in omnibus* (Prague 1662). See the short biography of him by J. Vinař, *Jan Marcus Marci z Kronlandu* (Prague 1934); Pagel, op. cit. 224–31; J. Marek, 'Některé názory Jana Marka Marci' in *Sborník pro dějiny přírodních věd a techniky* v (1960), 210–24; B. Baumann, *Filosofické názory Jana Marka Marci* (Prague 1957). Marci's direct links with the Rudolfine tradition are shown by his possession of the 'Bacon manuscript' (cf. above p. 239 n. 1.).

which found expression in its notions of criticism; its natural philosophy
sought the justification of innate truths. While many intermediate
positions were possible, the *essence* of their attitude was quite opposed
to that which developed into the mechanistic view of science, and the
watershed in this opposition is formed by the writings of Descartes,
Bacon, and Galileo. It was Descartes who rejected as a fantasy picture
his predecessors' symbolic reproduction of the world: the memory key
of Schenckel,[1] the mixture of rational and supernatural in Comenius,[2]
the occult revelation of the Rosicrucians.[3] Bacon attacked the notion of
the mage or adept controlling esoteric forces, and although there is still
much of the late Renaissance in him, especially his Utopian dreams of an
ideal erudite society and his view of man's place in nature, he introduced
a new, limited, rational approach to scientific activity.[4] Galileo—Magini's
great rival—eschewed the magical book of nature and substituted for it
the mechanical and statistical, abandoning the qualitative pattern of
correspondences and influences for a quantitative search, the synthetic
epistemology for an analytic.[5] In this he was representative of a new
conception of the world as mechanism, which involved both denying the
animist assumptions of the sixteenth-century natural philosophers and
abdicating from metaphysical speculation about the first principles of
the universe.[6] It was a world-view increasingly exhausted in the interpretation of empirical evidence.

It was also a world-view bound by the laws of causality, and here too
an important change was taking place. The older thinkers possessed no
clear modern notion of causation and hence no feeling for the 'causal
definition' which Cassirer takes to be a crucial presupposition of the
Enlightenment.[7] Thus events could not be considered discretely, and
even those branches of investigation which laid stress on isolating observable changes in nature—alchemy is an example—needed other,
non-observable guiding principles, empirical details blending with metaphysical scheme. Nor was there any strong sense of temporality:
arguments could, as it were, move both ways, and resolution (the illation

---

[1] Yates, *Art of Memory*, 373 f.; cf. above, pp. 229 f.

[2] Cf. J. Tvrdý, 'Komenský a Descartes', *Acta Comeniana* 18 (1959), 1–15.

[3] Arnold, op. cit. 273–99. On Descartes' attitude to symbolism in general see
H. Gouhier, 'Le refus du symbolisme dans l'humanisme cartésien', in *Umanesimo e
simbolismo*, 65–74.

[4] Rossi, *Francesco Bacone, passim*.

[5] E. Garin, *Cultura filosofica*, 451–65; cf. Burtt, op. cit. 64. On Magini see above
p. 280 n. 5.

[6] Cf. the argument of Robert Lenoble, *Mersenne ou la naissance du mécanisme*
(Paris 1943).

[7] E. Cassirer, *Die Philosophie der Aufklärung* (Tübingen 1932), 24 ff.

from effect to cause) was conceptually quite legitimate. Calvinists appeared to be predestined to heaven or hell by divine prescience; but they just as readily used evidence of being in a state of grace as if this could influence the divine judgement. In a similar way Machiavelli's fortune favoured the brave, in that his heroes were seen as somehow capable of acting upon their own destiny, so that history became a record of strong men dominating weak men, not by direct force but because the former alone took a hand in the determining processes. And Bruno's Hermetic reform or the manipulations of applied Lullism show the same intertwining of liberty and bondage. For the young Kepler mathematical harmonies are the formal cause of observed astronomical facts,[1] and this kind of interaction between visible and invisible worlds explains the deep contemporary interest in the working of chance and astrological fate.

The debate was ultimately one about both freedom and cognition. The Renaissance position assumed a greater or lesser degree of human unfreedom in the practical sphere—hence its distance from the average post-Baconian scientific viewpoint—but the corollary was a stress on the powers of the intellect, as the Neoplatonists from Ficino and Pico saw salvation in contemplation.[2] The latter was not necessarily a purely contingent freedom, but rather a power of intellectual insight into a reality which was taken to be pre-ordained and necessary. From it flowed again the fundamental concern of that age with an unseen realm, its combination of a direct view of nature with some 'deeper' principle, its self-consciousness and awareness of the fragility of the sensuous world.

There existed of course—the point may be stressed once again—no precise dividing-line between the old philosophy and the new; indeed the survivals of the former were recognizable by their virulent attack on the material and narrowly rational preoccupations of seventeenth-century contemporaries. In England this is seen among the Cambridge Platonists[3] or occultists like Fludd and Ashmole; in Germany in the pansophic mood which lasted till Leibniz or the mysticism of the Lusatian Jakob Boehme. Some of the old currents were moreover important bridges to the future as well as relics of the past; whereas official Calvinism set its face more firmly against magic and imagery than any other orthodoxy, it was among the English Puritans that the practical and artisan elements

---

[1] Cf. Burtt, op. cit. 52 ff.

[2] Cf. the article by Charles Trinkaus, 'The Problem of Free-Will in the Renaissance and Reformation', in *Journal of the History of Ideas*, x (1949), 51–62.

[3] E. Cassirer, *The Platonic Renaissance in England* (1932; English translation London 1953).

of the Renaissance tradition found fullest expression.[1] Equally there can
be no exact parallelism between the collapse of the existing political
order in the turmoil of religious war and the decline of Mannerism in
favour of Baroque, that prop to the rising absolute monarchies.

Yet it is useful to show some model of the old system, even if opposition to it was never clear-cut and co-ordinated on all fronts; and here
lies the prime relevance of the Rudolfine age in Central Europe. It
provides the key to a wider perspective. Nowhere do we see more clearly
the various strands which made up the intellectual fabric of the years
before 1600 than in Prague, around the greatest personification of
traditional order. The triumph after 1600 of the political activists and
the culture of the Roman Baroque indeed carried with it elements of
that visionary universal mentality which was superseded. But the weight
of intellectual Humanism was not there: its ideal and its reform were
retrospective and self-conscious; the vocabulary it contributed to the
new century proved little more than an epitaph.

[1] C. Webster, 'Macaria: Samuel Hartlib and the Great Reformation' in *Acta
Comeniana* 26 (1970), 147–64.

NOTES ON SOURCES AND
ABBREVIATIONS

THE nature of the contemporary materials consulted while this book was being prepared may well be unfamiliar to the reader. I therefore append a brief excursus on the most important Central European sources and on some of the main printed collections of documents.

I. ARCHIVES

1. *Prague: Státní Ústřední Archiv* (SÚA)

The archives of—*inter alia*—the Habsburg administration in Bohemia, housed mainly in the building known as the Central Archive of the Ministry of the Interior (Ústřední Archiv Ministerstva Vnitra). The basic guide is Z. Šamberger, *Průvodce po ÚAMV v Praze* (Prague 1952). The multifarious records for the sixteenth and seventeenth centuries comprise minute-books, registers, accounts and lists of debts, privileges, mandates, and other official documents in German, Czech, or Latin. They are grouped in various series, while a large bulk of miscellaneous material has been brought together in the so-called Stará Manipulace (SM). The existing indexes (*elenchi*) are often primitive, though modern archivists have begun to rectify the situation. Removals at different times to and from Vienna have complicated the provenance of some of this matter.

2. *Prague: Archiv Pražského Hradu* (APH)

This is the document and manuscript collection of the Cathedral Chapter. It corresponds to the Archbishops' Library mentioned below but is now separated from it, being stored in the basement of the Presidential residence which forms part of the third court of the castle. There is a good catalogue by J. Patera and A. Podlaha, *Soupis rukopisů knihovny Metropolitní Kapitoly pražské* i (Sigs. A–E), ii (Sigs. F–P) (Prague 1910–22). The material is mostly ecclesiastical, with a strong bias to the medieval period.

3. *Vienna: Haus- Hof- und Staatsarchiv* (HHSA)

The most important source I have consulted here is the correspondence of Rudolf and his relatives within the Habsburg house. Most of it is collected in the *Familienkorrespondenz*, though some of the *Familienakten* also relate to the persons of the Emperors and contain much other court business. Some political documents on the Rudolfine period can be found in the manuscript department of the archives; cf. C. von Böhm, *Die Handschriften des Haus- Hof- und Staatsarchivs* (Vienna 1873).

4. *Litoměřice: State Archive* (S.A. Litoměřice)

This is the home of the family archives of the Lobkovic, which, after several centuries in the castle of Roudnice on the Elbe and a peripatetic spell following the last war, are now mostly located at *Žitenice*, a sub-department of the main building. The family correspondence (LRRK) forms one vast division within the whole (Oddělení III); the parts of it relevant to Zdeněk and Polyxena Lobkovic are indicated above, p. 286 n. 2.

5. *Třeboň: State Archive* (S.A. Třeboň)

The former castle and archives of the Schwarzenbergs, and before them of the Rožmberks. The most important subdivisions of the archive for present purposes are the family collection of the Rožmberks (RAR), whose section 25 contains an assorted batch of letters and writings on occult subjects, and the so-called 'Historica', a long series of documents, separately numbered, which throw valuable light on political history. They are well catalogued and cross-indexed on typed cards.

II. LIBRARIES

1. *Prague: Universitní Knihovna* (UK)

The library and manuscript collection of the combined Caroline–Jesuit University, now also the State Library of Czechoslovakia. The manuscripts are catalogued in three main series, Latin, Czech, and German, but the last only reaches to the year 1550: *Catalogus Codicum Manu Scriptorum Latinorum*, by J. Truhlář, i–ii (Prague 1905–6); *Katalog českých rukopisů c.k. veřejné a universitní knihovny pražské*, by J. Truhlář (Prague 1906); *Katalog der deutschen Handschriften* . . . i (Prague 1909). The printed books and their history are discussed most fully by J. Hanslick (see bibliography). Their classification is at times confusing. The extremely rich Lobkovic library, mentioned in the text and laid up at present in a castle north-west of Prague, has its author-catalogue deposited in the UK.

2. *Prague: National Museum* (Nat. Mus.)

The museum has a rich legacy of manuscripts in several languages. They are listed by F. M. Bartoš, *Soupis rukopisů Národního Musea v Praze* i–ii (Prague 1926), a work whose value would be much enhanced if it were provided with an index.

3. *Prague: Strahov Library* (Strahov)

This, the richest of all Bohemian monastic treasures, occupies its magnificent rooms in what has now become the Czech Literary Museum (Památník Národního Písemnictví). Manuscripts and printed books are not distinguished and share the same handwritten catalogue, alphabetical in loose-leaf folders. Strahov acquired a great deal of rare heretical literature of all kinds after 1620, and much interesting material must still be lying there awaiting a chance find.

4. *Prague: Archbishops' Library* (Arch. Lib.)

The library of the Primates of Bohemia, traditionally stored in the Cathedral of St. Vitus, was removed during the last century to the rear of a house in the square outside the castle precincts (Hradčanské Náměstí). There is no librarian, though the Cathedral Chapter still has the administration of it. The only catalogue is a comprehensive but handwritten three-volume one, arranged according to subjects and evidently compiled by some late nineteenth-century scribe.

5. *Prague: Nostitz Library* (Nostitz)

Now renamed the Library of Josef Dobrovský, this is still housed in its seventeenth-century surroundings, though accessible only on one morning of every week and supervised by the National Museum. Its manuscripts are described by J. V. Šimák, *Rukopisy majorátní knihovny Hrabat z Nostitz a Rhienecka v Praze* (Prague 1910). Printed works are indexed only in an old hand-catalogue on cards available in the library itself.

6. *Vienna: Österreichische Nationalbibliothek* (ÖN)

The library and manuscript collection of the Habsburg court, with many later additions. The Western manuscripts have a comprehensive general catalogue: *Tabulae codicum manu scriptorum, praeter Graecos et Orientales, in Bibliotheca Palatina Vindobonensi asservatorum* i–x (Vienna 1864–99). This is now being complemented by the description of more recent accessions: *Katalog der abendländischen Handschriften der österreichischen National- bibliothek*, Series nova (Vienna 1965–). A fuller account of some selected codices is provided by J. Chmel (see bibliography).

7. *Budapest: Országos Széchenyi Könyvtár* (OSzK)

The library of the Hungarian National Museum. Its manuscript collection contains some matter of general Central European interest but there is no printed catalogue, except of medieval works.

III. CONTEMPORARY OBSERVERS

1. *Papal nuncios*

The regular weekly dispatches of nuncios to their superiors in the Holy See make Papal diplomacy the best documented of all the politics of the period, and they are valuable for much other information on personalities and activities of all kinds. They are, however, not free of special pleading and even misrepresentation, and their lines must frequently be read between. Since Prague was one of the pivots of Papal policy at this time a mass of evidence survives, both individual letters and some longer memoranda. Rudolfine material has been printed in three series:

(a) *Nuntiaturberichte aus Deutschland 1585–92*, published by the Görres-Gesellschaft: ii, *Die Nuntiatur am Kaiserhofe*:

    1. *Germanico Malaspina und Filippo Sega 1585–7*, ed. R. Reichenberger (Paderborn 1895).

   2. *Antonio Puteo in Prag 1587–9*, ed. J. Schweizer (Paderborn 1912).
   3. *Alfonso Visconte 1589–91, Camillo Caetano 1591–2*, ed. J. Schweizer (Paderborn 1919).

(b) *Nuntiaturberichte aus Deutschland*, published by the Prussian historical institute in Rome:

   Die Prager Nuntiatur des Giovanni Stefano Ferreri und die Wiener Nuntiatur des Giacomo Serra 1603–6 i–ii, ed. A. O. Meyer (Berlin 1911–13).

(c) *Epistulae et Acta Nuntiorum Apostolicorum apud Imperatorem (1592–1628)*:

   III. *Epistulae et Acta Johannis Stephani Ferrerii 1604–7*, Pars I, 1, ed. Z. Kristen (Prague 1944, only covers Jan.–July 1604).
   IV. *Antonii Caetani Epistulae et Acta 1607–11*, Partes I–III, ed. M. Linhartová (Prague 1932–46, only covers the years 1607–8).

One further volume is tangential to the present purposes (*Nuntiaturberichte*, ed. Hansen, listed in bibliography), while unpublished matter from the years 1592–1603 is incorporated in cited works by Borovička, Matoušek, and Stloukal.

2. *Venetian ambassadors*

The *relazioni* or detailed final reports of Venetian diplomats at the various courts of Europe are a basic source for the early modern period, though their interest is usually narrowly political and they are often rather superficial or lacking in balance. Most of them were printed, either at Venice in a great series edited during the last century by E. Albéri, or in supplementary volumes covering Germany and Austria. Their evidence is disappointing for the Habsburg lands at this time, but three volumes are relevant:

E. Albéri (ed.), *Le relazioni degli ambasciatori veneti . . .* (Florence 1839–63), Series 1, No. 6.
J. Fiedler (ed.), *Relationen Venetianischer Botschafter über Deutschland und Österreich, Fontes Rerum Austriacarum (FRA)* Vol. xxvi (Vienna 1866); Vol. xxx (Vienna 1870).

3. *Briefe und Akten zur Geschichte des dreissigjährigen Krieges*

A major series of documents covering especially the last part of Rudolf's reign. The *Briefe und Akten* were collected by a succession of Bavarian scholars during the decades before 1914, a monument to the fascination for historians around 1900 of politics around 1600. The centre of their attention was always rather Wittelsbach affairs than Habsburg. The full titles of individual volumes are:

   I. M. Ritter, *Die Gründung der Union 1598–1608* (Munich 1870).
   II. —— *Die Union und Heinrich IV 1607–9* (Munich 1874).
   III. —— *Der Jülicher Erbfolgekrieg* (Munich 1877).
   IV. F. Stieve, *Die Politik Baierns 1591–1607*, Part 1 (Munich 1878).
   .V —— *Die Politik Baierns 1591–1607*, Part 2 (Munich 1883).

VI. F. Stieve, *Vom Reichstag 1608 bis zur Gründung der Liga* (Munich 1895).
VII. —— and K. Mayr, *Von der Abreise Erzherzog Leopolds nach Jülich bis zu den Werbungen Herzog Maximilians von Bayern im März 1610* (Munich 1905).
VIII. —— —— *Von den Rüstungen Herzog Maximilians von Bayern bis zum Aufbruch der Passauer* (Munich 1908).
IX. A. Chroust, *Vom Einfall des Passauer Kriegsvolks bis zum Nürnberger Kurfürstentag* (Munich 1903).
X. —— *Der Ausgang der Regierung Rudolfs II und die Anfänge des Kaisers Matthias* (Munich 1906).

4. *News-letters*

The *Fuggerzeitungen*—eye-witness reports copied out for the Fugger family in Bavaria, especially for Rudolf's friend Philip Eduard—offer much information on events in Central Europe, though the quality of the informants is extremely variable. See in general J. Kleinpaul, *Die Fuggerzeitungen 1568–1605* (Leipzig 1920). The news-letters were acquired by Ferdinand III in the 1650s for the Imperial library and shipped down the Danube to Vienna without serious mishap. They now form MSS. Nos. 8949–75 of the ÖN, carefully arranged by years. Those relating to the Habsburg lands (primarily Prague) are listed by J. Chmel, op. cit. i, Nos. XXI–XLVII. No satisfactory printed selection exists, though some of the more sensational were edited by V. Klarwill, *The Fugger News-Letters* (London 1924). Another important collection of contemporary news-letters is that of the Rožmberks, now in the series 'Historica' at Třeboň.

IV. JAHRBUCH

The *Jahrbuch der kunsthistorischen Sammlungen des allerhöchsten Kaiserhauses* was founded in Vienna in 1883 and reflected the very high standard of art-historical scholarship which obtained in Austria at the time. In 1926 it was renamed the *Jahrbuch der Kunsthistorischen Sammlungen in Wien*, and this new series (Neue Folge) is cited as N.F., first with its own numbering, then from 1954 reverting to the original sequence. The old *Jahrbuch* had a long succession of appendices (Register = Reg.) which printed archival sources dealing with artistic matters. Some of them are quoted in the present book and they are a vast storehouse of information for anyone interested in the subject. Those relating directly or indirectly to Rudolf are as follows:

VII (1888) pp. xv–lxvii: documents from the Archiv des Innern (1586–1612).
,, pp. xci–ccxxvi: documents from the Hofbibliothek.

X (1889) pp. i–xix: documents from the Hofbibliothek (1596–1614).
,, pp. xx–lxii: documents from the Nuremberg Archives (–1612).

XII (1891) pp. i–xc: documents from the Statthalterei-Archiv (now SÚA) in Prague (1529–1600).

XIII (1892) pp. xxvi–clxxiv: documents from the HHSA (–1590).

XV (1894)   pp. i–xlviii: documents from the Reichsfinanzarchiv (1569–1618).

    ,,   pp. xlix–clxxix: documents from the HHSA (–1600).

XIX (1898)   pp. i–cxvi: documents from the HHSA (1601–11).

XX (1899)   pp. xlix–cxxii: documents from the HHSA (1619: Inventory).

XXIX (1910–11) pp. i–xlvi: documents from the Hofbibliothek: Hofzahlamtsrechnungen (1606–37).

XXX (1911–12)   pp. i–xxxiii: documents from the Statthalterei-Archiv in Prague (1601–17).

V. OTHER ABBREVIATIONS

ADB	*Allgemeine Deutsche Biographie*
AÖG	*Archiv für Österreichische Geschichte*
ARG	*Archiv für Reformationsgeschichte*
AUC	*Acta Universitatis Carolinae*
BČH	*Bibliografie České Historie*, see Zíbrt in bibliography
BM	British Museum, London
ČČH/ČsČH	*Český Časopis Historický*, continued 1953 as *Československý Časopis Historický*
ČČM	*Časopis Českého Muzea*
ČMM	*Časopis Matice Moravské*
JWCI	*Journal of the Warburg and Courtauld Institutes*
MGG	*Die Musik in Geschichte und Gegenwart* (Kassel 1949–68)
MIÖG	*Mitteilungen des Instituts für Österreichische Geschichtsforschung*
MVGDB	*Mitteilungen des Vereins für Geschichte der Deutschen in Böhmen*
SČ	*Sněmy České*, see p. 38 n. 2
T.F.R.	*True and Faithful Relation*, see p. 218 n. 4
ZVGAS	*Zeitschrift des Vereins für Geschichte und Altertum Schlesiens*

SELECT BIBLIOGRAPHY

THE following list contains primarily those works to which repeated reference is made. In particular the writings of contemporary authors who are studied in the text will not normally be entered again here. Some of the wordier early titles which are well descriptive of contents appear more fully in footnotes. *Festschriften* and *Sborníky* are shown under the name of the dedicatee.

ACIDALIUS, VALENS, *Epistolarum Centuria I* (Hanau 1606)

ADAMUS, MELCHIOR, *Vitae Germanorum Philosophorum* (Heidelberg 1615)

—— *Vitae Germanorum Medicorum* (Heidelberg 1620)

d'ADDIO, MARIO, *Il pensiero politico di Gaspare Scioppio* (Milan 1962)

ALBÉRI, E., *Relazioni*, see Notes on Sources, III. 2 (p. 296)

ALFONS, S., *Giuseppe Arcimboldo* (Malmö 1957)

ALIDOSI, RODERICO, *Relazione di Germania e della corte di Rodolfo II Imperatore* ed. C. and G. Campori (Modena 1872)

ALLEN, D. C., *The star-crossed Renaissance* (2nd edn. New York 1966)

ALLEN, J. W., *A history of political thought in the sixteenth century* (3rd edn. London 1951)

ANGYAL, ANDREAS, *Die slawische Barockwelt* (Leipzig 1961)

Anvers, ville de Plantin et de Rubens (Paris 1954)

ARBER, AGNES, *Herbals* (2nd edn. Cambridge 1953)

ARNOLD, PAUL, *Histoire des Rose-Croix et les origines de la franc-maçonnerie* (Paris 1955)

BABEAU, A., 'Une ambassade en Allemagne sous Henri IV', *Revue Historique* 60 (1896), 28–49

BABINGER, FRANZ, *Sherleiana* (Berlin 1932)

BACH, E., *Un humaniste hongrois en France, Jean Sambucus* (Szeged 1932)

BAMBOROUGH, J. B., *The little world of man* (London 1952)

BARACH, C. S., *Hieronymus Hirnhaim* (Vienna 1864)

BARNAUD, NICOLAS, *Commentariolum in Aenigmaticum quoddam Epitaphium . . .* (Leiden 1597)

Barock in Böhmen, ed. K. M. Swoboda (Munich 1964)

BARTOŠ, F. M., *Bojovníci a mučedníci* (Prague 1946)

BATTISTI, E., *L'Antirinascimento* (Milan 1962)

—— *Rinascimento e Barocco* (n.p. 1960)

BAUER, A., *Die Adelsdocumente österreichischer Alchymisten* (Vienna 1893)

BAUMER, F. L., 'England, the Turk and the common corps of Christendom', *American Historical Review* 50 (1944–5), 26–48

BENESCH, OTTO, *The art of the Renaissance in Northern Europe* (2nd edn. London 1965)

BENZ, ERNST, *Wittenberg und Byzanz* (Marburg a.d. Lahn 1949)

BERGSTRÖM, I., *Dutch still-life painting in the seventeenth century* (London 1956)

BEUTIN, L., *Hanse und Reich im handelspolitischen Endkampf gegen England* (Berlin 1929)

BEZOLD, F. VON, *Rudolf II und die heilige Liga* (Munich 1883)

BIBL, V., *Maximilian II, der rätselhafte Kaiser* (Vienna–Leipzig 1929)

—— 'Die Religionsreformation Kaiser Rudolfs II. in Oberösterreich', *AÖG* 109 (1921), 377–433

BITNAR, V., *Postavy a problémy českého baroku literárního* (Prague 1939)

BLANCHET, LÉON, *Campanella* (Paris 1920)

BLAU, J. L., *The Christian interpretation of the Cabala in the Renaissance* (New York 1944)

BLUNT, ANTHONY, *Artistic theory in Italy 1450–1600* (Oxford 1940)

BOKSER, RABBI BEN ZION, *From the world of the Cabbalah* (London 1957)

BOODT, A. BOETHIUS DE, *Gemmarum et Lapidum Historia* (Hanau 1609)

BOROVIČKA, J., 'Pád Želinského', *ČČH* xxviii (1922), 277–304

—— 'Počátky kancléřování Zdeňka z Lobkovic', *Friedrichův Sborník*, 435–55

BOTERO, GIOVANNI, *Relationi Universali* (Venice 1596)

BOUWSMA, W. J., *Concordia Mundi, the career and thought of Guillaume Postel* (Cambridge, Mass. 1957)

BRANDAU, M. ERBINAEUS VON, *Warhaffte Beschreibung von der Universal-Medicin* . . . (Leipzig 1689)

BŘEZAN, VÁCLAV, *Poslední Rožmberkové*, ed. J. Dostál (Prague 1941)

Briefe und Akten, see Notes on Sources, III. 3 (pp. 296–7)

BRUNNER, O., *Adeliges Landleben und europäischer Geist* (Salzburg 1949)

BUCHWALD, C., *Adriaen de Vries* (Leipzig 1899)

BUDOVEC, VÁCLAV, *Circulus horologi Lunaris et Solaris* (Hanau 1616)

—— *Korrespondence z let 1579–1619*, ed. J. Glücklich (Prague 1908)

BUGAJ, R., *W poszukiwaniu kamienia filozoficznego* (Warsaw 1957)

BURTT, E. A., *The metaphysical foundations of modern physical science* (London 1932)

BUXTON, J., *Sir Philip Sidney and the English Renaissance* (London 1964)

BYDŽOVSKÝ, M., see p. 37 n. 3.

Calendar of State Papers, Foreign Series, of the Reign of Queen Elizabeth, xi–xx (London 1880–1921)

CANTIMORI, D., *Per la storia degli eretici italiani del secolo XVI* (Rome 1937)

—— *Eretici italiani del Cinquecento* (Florence 1939)

—— *Prospettive di storia ereticali italiani* (Bari 1960)

ČAPEK, J. B., 'Příspěvky k životu a dílu Vavřince Benedikta-Nudožerina', *AUC* vii 2 (1962), 7–32

CARRERAS Y ARTAU, T. and J., *Historia de la filosofía española*, ii (Madrid 1943)

CASPAR, MAX, *Kepler* (London–New York 1959)

Československá vlastivěda, viii (*Umění*) (Prague 1935)

CHATENAY, L., *Vie de Jacques Esprinchard* (Paris 1957)

CHAUVIRÉ, R., *Jean Bodin* (Paris 1914)

CHLUMECKY, PETER VON, *Karl von Zierotin und seine Zeit* (Brünn 1862)

BIBLIOGRAPHY 301

CHMEL, J., *Die Handschriften der k.k. Hofbibliothek in Wien* i–ii (Vienna 1840–1)

CHUDOBA, B., *Spain and the Empire* (Chicago 1952)

CHYTIL, K., *Der Prager Venusbrunnen von B. Wurzelbauer* (Prague 1902)

—— *Umění v Praze za Rudolfa II* (Prague 1904)

—— *Malířstvo pražské XV a XVI věku* (Prague 1906)

—— *Koruna Rudolfa II* (Prague 1929)

CLAIR, COLIN, *Christopher Plantin* (London 1960)

Caroli Clusii . . . Epistolae, ed. P. F. X. de Ram (Brussels 1847)

Co daly naše země Evropě a lidstvu (Prague 1939)

COMENIUS (KOMENSKÝ), J. A., *Labyrint Světa a Ráj Srdce* (written 1623, new edn. Prague 1958)

—— *Historie o těžkých protivenstvích církve české* (written 1655, new edn. Prague 1952)

CORETH, ANNA, *Pietas Austriaca* (Vienna 1959)

COSTIL, P., *André Dudith, humaniste hongrois* (Paris 1935)

COXE, WILLIAM, *History of the House of Austria*, i. 2 (London 1807)

CRAVEN, J. B., *Count Michael Maier* (Kirkwall 1910)

Cristianesimo e ragion di stato . . . a cura di E. Castelli (Rome–Milan 1952–3)

CROLL, OSWALD, *Basilica Chymica . . .* (Frankfurt 1609); see p. 207 n. 4

CUNRAD, CASPAR, *Symbolum Domini est Salus Epigrammatum Centuria* i–v (Öls 1606–15)

DAČICKÝ Z HESLOVA, MIKULÁŠ, *Paměti*, ed. E. Petrů and E. Pražák (Prague 1955)

DAŇKOVÁ, M., *Bratrské tisky ivančické a kralické* (Prague 1951)

DEBUS, A. G., *The chemical dream of the Renaissance* (Cambridge 1968)

DEE, JOHN, *True and Faithful Relation* (London 1659); see p. 218 n. 4

—— *Private Diary*, ed. J. O. Halliwell (London, 1842)

—— *Monas Hieroglyphica* (Antwerp 1564); English translation by C. H. Josten in *Ambix* 12 (1964), 84–221

—— *Epistolae Fràtris Rogerii Baconis*, operā Johannis Dee (Hamburg 1618)

Delitiae Poetarum Germanorum, collectore A.F.G.G. (Frankfurt 1612)

DENIS, ERNEST, *Konec samostatnosti české*, trans. J. Vančura (Prague 1893)

DENUCÉ, JAN, *Oud-Nederlandsche kaartmakers in betrekking met Plantijn* i–ii (Antwerp–The Hague 1912)

DERMENGHEM, E., *Thomas Morus et les utopistes de la Renaissance* (Paris 1927)

DICKMANN, F., *Der westfälische Frieden* (Münster 1959)

DIEZ, E., 'Der Hofmaler Bartholomäus Spranger', *Jahrbuch* xxviii (1909), 93–151

Doba bělohorská a Albrecht z Valdštejna, see Valdštejn

DOORSLAER, G. VAN, *La vie et les œuvres de Philippe de Monte* (Brussels 1921)

DORNAVIUS, CASPAR, *Amphitheatrum Sapientiae Socraticae Joco-Seriae* i–ii (Hanau 1619)

DREYER, J. L. E., *Tycho Brahe* (Edinburgh 1890)

DUDÍK, BEDA, *Forschungen in Schweden für Mährens Geschichte* (Brünn 1852)

—— *Iter Romanum* i–ii (Vienna 1855)

DVOŘÁK, MAX, *Kunstgeschichte als Geistesgeschichte* (Munich 1924)

d'Elvert, C. *Zur Geschichte des Erzbistums Olmütz* (Brünn 1895)

Eremita, Daniel, *Iter Germanicum, Relatio epistolica* (Vienna 1637)

Evans, Joan, *Magical jewels of the Middle Ages and the Renaissance* (Oxford 1922)

Exner, Balthasar, *Anchora utriusque vitae: hoc est Symbolicum Spero Meliora . . .* (Hanau 1619)

Falke, J., *Geschichte des fürstlichen Hauses Liechtenstein*, ii (Vienna 1877)

Faludi, J., *André Dudith et les humanistes français* (Szeged 1927)

Fellner, Thomas, *Die österreichische Zentralverwaltung*, i (Vienna 1907)

Ferguson, J., *Bibliotheca Chemica* i–ii (Glasgow 1906)

Fétis, E., *Les artistes belges à l'étranger* i–ii (Brussels 1857–65)

Fiedler, J., *Relationen . . .*, see Notes on Sources, iii. 2 (p. 296)

Firpo, L., 'John Dee, scienziato', *Rinascimento* iii (1952), 25–84; see also Pucci, Francesco, and Salvestrini, V.

Fleischman, Peter, *Description des . . . Herrn Rudolphen . . . Erstgehaltenen Reichstag* (Augsburg 1582)

—— *Kurtze und aigentliche Beschreibung des . . . Reichstags* (Regensburg 1594)

Forster, C. T., and Daniell, F. H. B., *The life and letters of Ogier Ghiselin de Busbecq* i–ii (London 1881)

Freedberg, S. J., *Parmigianino* (Harvard 1950)

Friedrich, G.: *Sborník prací věnovaných Dru Gustavu Friedrichovi* (Prague 1931)

Frind, A., *Die Geschichte der Bischöfe und Erzbischöfe von Prag* (Prague 1873)

Fuggerzeitungen, see Notes on Sources, iii. 4 (p. 297)

Gans, David, *Zemach David* (Prague 1592); see pp. 240 n. 2, 241 n. 5, 242 n. 2

Garin, E., *Medioevo e Rinascimento* (Bari 1954)

—— *La cultura filosofica del Rinascimento italiano* (Florence 1961)

—— *L'educazione in Europa, 1400–1600* (Bari 1957)

Geiger, B., *I dipinti ghiribizzosi di Giuseppe Arcimboldi* (Florence 1954)

Gellner, G., *Životopis lékaře Borbonia a výklad jeho deníků* (Prague 1938)

—— 'Tomáš Jordán', *ČMM* 60 (1936), 85–140, 315–54

Gerstinger, Hans, *Die Briefe des Johannes Sambucus/Zsámboky* (Vienna 1968)

Gillet, J. F. A., *Crato von Crafftheim und seine Freunde* i–ii (Frankfurt am M. 1860)

Gindely, A., *Rudolf II und seine Zeit* i–ii (Prague 1862–5)

—— *Geschichte der Böhmischen Brüder* i–ii (Prague 1868)

Goehlart, J. V., 'Kaisers Rudolf II Hofstaat', *MVGDB* vii (1869), 112–16

Goldast, Melchior, *Tagebuch*, ed. H. Schecker, in *Abhandlungen und Vorträge der Bremer Wissenschaftlichen Gesellschaft*, Jg. 5, Heft 4 (1931)

Gombrich, E. H., 'Icones Symbolicae', *JWCI* x (1947), 163–92

Gross, L., *Die Geschichte der deutschen Reichshofkanzlei von 1559 bis 1806* (Vienna 1933)

Gschliesser, O. von, *Der Reichshofrat 1559–1806* (Vienna 1942)

Guarinoni, Hippolytus, *Die Grewel der Verwüstung menschlichen Geschlechts* (Ingolstadt 1610); see p. 204 n. 6

Gulyás, Pál, *Sámboky János Könyvtára* (Budapest 1941)

HAINHOFER, P., *Des Augsburger Patriciers Philipp Hainhofer . . . Correspondenzen aus den Jahren 1610–19* (Vienna 1894)

HANSLICK, J. A., *Geschichte und Beschreibung der Prager Universitäts-Bibliothek* (Prague 1851)

HARANT, KRYŠTOF, *Putowání . . . do Země Swaté* (Prague 1608)

HARLAS, F. X., *Rudolf II, milovník umění a sběratel* (Prague 1917?)

HARRIS, V., *All coherence gone* (Chicago 1949)

HASNER, J. VON, *Tycho Brahe und Johann Kepler in Prag, eine Studie* (Prague 1872)

HAUSER, ARNOLD, *Mannerism* i–ii (London 1965)

HAYDN, H., *The Counter-Renaissance* (New York 1951)

HEER, FRIEDRICH, *Die dritte Kraft* (Frankfurt 1960)

HERAIN, K. V., *České malířství od doby rudolfinské* (Prague 1915)

HESSELS, J. H. (ed.), *Abrahami Ortelii . . . Epistulae* (Cambridge 1887)

HIRN, J., *Erzherzog Ferdinand II von Tyrol* i–ii (Innsbruck 1885–8)

—— *Erzherzog Maximilian, der Deutschmeister* i–ii (Innsbruck 1915–36)

HIRSCHMANN, O., *Hendrik Goltzius als Maler* (The Hague 1916)

Historia Collegii S.J., see p. 34 n. 1

HOCKE, G. R., *Die Welt als Labyrinth* (Hamburg 1957)

—— *Manierismus in der Literatur* (Hamburg 1959)

HOGHELANDE, EWALD DE, *De Alchemiae Difficultatibus* (Cologne 1594)

—— *Historiae aliquot transmutationis metallicae . . .* (Cologne 1604)

HREJSA, F., *Česká Konfesse* (Prague 1912)

HRUBÝ, FRANTIŠEK, *Ladislav Velen z Žerotína* (Prague 1930)

HUNGER, F. W. T., *Charles de l'Escluse, Nederlandsch Kruidkundige* i–ii (The Hague 1927–43)

HURTER, FRIEDRICH, *Philipp Lang* (Schaffhausen 1851)

IPOLYI, A. (ed.), *Rimay János államiratai és levelezése* (Budapest 1887)

ISTVÁNFFI, G., *A Clusius-Códex mykológiai méltatása* (Budapest 1900)

Iter Persicum . . . (by Georg Tectander), see p. 77 n. 5

JANÁČEK, J., *Dějiny obchodu v předbělohorské Praze* (Prague 1955)

JANSSEN, JOHANNES, *Geschichte des deutschen Volkes seit dem Ausgang des Mittelalters* i–viii (Freiburg i. B. 1881–94)

JOHNSON, F. R., *Astronomical thought in Renaissance England* (Baltimore 1937)

JONES, R. M., *Spiritual reformers in the sixteenth and seventeenth centuries* (London 1914)

JOSTEN, C. H., 'An unknown chapter in the life of John Dee', *JWCI* 28 (1965), 223–57; see also Dee, John

JUNG, C. G., *Psychologie und Alchemie* (2nd edn. Zurich 1952)

—— and PAULI, W., *The interpretation of nature and the psyche*, Eng. trans. (London 1955)

JUNGNITZ, J., 'Die Bischofswahl des Bonaventura Hahn', *ZVGAS* 34 (1900), 253–88

KALISTA, ZDENĚK, *Mládí Humprechta Jan Černína z Chudenic, zrození barokního kavalíra* (Prague 1932)

—— *Čechové, kteří tvořili dějiny světa* (Prague 1939)

KÁRPÁTHY-KRAVJÁNSZKY, M., *Rudolf uralkodásának első tíz éve* (Budapest 1933)
KAVKA, FRANTIŠEK, *Bílá Hora a české dějiny* (Prague 1962)
—— *Zlatý věk růží* (České Budějovice 1966)
KEPLER, JOHANNES, *Gesammelte Werke*, ed. W. van Dyck and M. Caspar (Munich 1938–)
KHAUTZ, F. C. F. VON, *Versuch einer Geschichte der österreichischen Gelehrten* (Frankfurt–Leipzig 1755)
KHEVENHÜLLER, FRANZ CHRISTOPH, *Annales Ferdinandei* i–xii (Leipzig 1721–6); and cf. p. 50 n. 3 above
—— *Conterfet Kupfferstich* i–ii (Leipzig 1721–2)
KIESEWETTER, K., *Geschichte des Occultismus* i–ii (Leipzig 1895–1909)
KLIK, J., 'Národnostní poměry v Čechách od válek husitských do bitvy bělohorské', *ČČH* xxvii (1921), 8–62, 289–352
Knihopis, see Tobolka, Z.
KNOX, BRIAN, *The architecture of Prague and Bohemia* (London 1965)
KOESTLER, A., *The sleepwalkers* (London 1959)
KOPECKÝ, M., *Daniel Adam z Veleslavína* (Prague 1962)
KOŘÁN, IVO, 'České řezbářství 1620–50 a jeho společenské a historické předpoklady' (Diss. Prague n.d.)
KOT, S., *Ideologja polityczna i społeczna Braci Polskich zwanych Arjanami* (Warsaw 1932)
KOTRBA, V., 'Die nachgotische Baukunst Böhmens zur Zeit Rudolfs II', *Umění* 18 (1970), 298–330
KOYRÉ, A., *La révolution astronomique* (Paris 1961)
KRAFFT, HANS ULRICH, *Reisen und Gefangenschaft*, ed. K. D. Hassler (Stuttgart 1861)
KRATOCHVÍL, V., 'K poměru císaře Rudolfa II k arciknížete Matyáši', *ČČH* v (1899), 169–76, 216–38
KREJČÍ, K., *Bartoloměj Paprocki z Hlohol* (Prague 1946)
KRIS, E., *Meister und Meisterwerke der Steinschneidekunst in der italienischen Renaissance* i–ii (Vienna 1929)
—— *Goldschmiedearbeiten des Mittelalters, der Renaissance und des Barocks*, i (Vienna 1932)
—— 'Der Stil "rustique"', *Jahrbuch* N.F. 1 (1926), 137–208
KUNSTMANN, H., *Die Nürnberger Universität Altdorf und Böhmen* (Cologne–Graz 1963)
KURZ, OTTO, 'Umělecké vztahy mezi Prahou a Persií za Rudolfa II', *Umění* xiv (1966), 461–87
KVAČALA, JAN, *Thomas Campanella* (Berlin 1909)
—— 'Wilhelm Postell', *ARG* ix (1911–12), 285–330, xi (1914), 200–27, xv (1918), 157–203
LAMBECIUS, P., *Commentariorum de Augustissima Bibliotheca Caesarea Vindobonensi Libri I–VIII* (Vienna 1665–79)
LARSSON, L. O., *Adrian de Vries* (Vienna–Munich 1967)
S. Laurentii a Brundusio Opera Omnia, x, Pars II (Padua 1956)
LEITSCH, WALTER, *Moskau und die Politik des Kaiserhofes im XVII Jahrhundert*, i (Graz–Cologne 1960)

LHOTSKY, ALFONS, *Die Geschichte der Sammlungen* i–ii (Vienna 1941–5)
—— *Österreichische Historiographie* (Munich 1962)
LILL, G., *Hans Fugger und die Kunst* (Leipzig 1908)
LINDNER, T., 'Johann Matthäus Wacker von Wackenfels', *ZVGAS* viii (1868), 319–51
LOEBL, A. H., 'Beiträge zur Geschichte der kaiserlichen Zentralverwaltung im ausgehenden sechzehnten Jahrhundert', *MIÖG* xxvii (1906), 629–77
LOESCHE, G., *Luther, Melanchthon und Calvin in Österreich-Ungarn* (Tübingen 1909)
LOMAZZO, PAOLO, *Idea del Tempio della Pittura* (Milan 1590)
LORENZ, K., *Die kirchlich-politische Parteibildung in Deutschland vor Beginn des dreissigjährigen Krieges* (Munich 1903)
MACŮREK, J., *Zápas Polska a Habsburků o přístup k Černému Moři na sklonku 16. století* (Prague 1931)
MÁDL, K., 'Obrazárna a umělci Rudolfa II v Praze', *Památky Archeologické* xxii (1906–8), 171–90
MAGYARY-KOSSA, G., *Magyar orvosi emlékek* i–iv (Budapest 1929–40)
MAIWALD, V., *Geschichte der Botanik in Böhmen* (Vienna–Leipzig 1904)
MANDER, KAREL VAN, *Het Schilderboeck* (Haarlem 1604); see p. 162 n. 1
Materiały do dziejów Reformacji w Krakowie, ed. R. Żelewski (Cracow 1962?)
MATOUŠEK, J., *Turecká válka v evropské politice v letech 1592–4* (Prague 1935)
—— 'K problému osobnosti Rudolfa II', *Novákův Sborník*, 343–62
MATTHEWS, W. H., *Mazes and labyrinths* (London 1922)
MAYER-LÖWENSCHWERDT, E., *Der Aufenthalt der Erzherzöge Rudolf und Ernst in Spanien 1564–71* (Vienna 1927)
MECENSEFFY, G., *Geschichte des Protestantismus in Österreich* (Graz–Cologne 1956)
Medioevo e Rinascimento, see Nardi, B.
MELANCHTHON: *Philipp Melanchthon 1497–1560*, i (Berlin 1963)
MODERN, H., 'Paulus van Vianen', *Jahrbuch* xv (1894), 60–102
MONAU, JACOB, *Symbolum Ipse Faciat variis variorum auctorum carminibus expressum* . . . (Gorlitz 1595)
MORÁVEK, J., *Nově objevený inventář rudolfinských sbírek na Hradě pražském* (Prague 1937)
MORHOF, D. G., *Polyhistor* (Lübeck 1688)
—— *De metallorum transmutatione . . . Epistola* (Hamburg 1673)
MORITZ, H., *Die Wahl Rudolfs II, der Reichstag zu Regensburg und die Frei-stellungsbewegung* (Marburg 1895)
MUNELES, O., *Bibliografický přehled židovské Prahy* (Prague 1952)
—— (ed.), *The Prague Ghetto in the Renaissance period* (Prague 1965)
NARDI, B.: *Medioevo e Rinascimento, studi in onore di Bruno Nardi* i–ii (Florence 1957?)
NEUMANN, ERWIN, 'Florentiner Mosaik aus Prag', *Jahrbuch* N.F. 53 (1957), 157–202
NEUMANN, JAROMÍR, *Malířství XVII století v Čechách* (Prague 1951)
—— *Obrazárna pražského Hradu* (Prague 1964)
NICOLSON, M. H., *The breaking of the circle* (Evanston 1950)

NOSTITZ, JOHANN VON, *Artificium Aristotelico-Lullio-Rameum* (Brieg 1615); see p. 233 n. 2

NOVÁK, J. B., *Rudolf II a jeho pád* (Prague 1935)

—— *Sborník prací věnovaných J. B. Novákovi* (Prague 1932)

Nuncios, see Notes on Sources, III. 1 (pp. 295–6)

Nuntiaturberichte aus Deutschland 1572–85, ii, ed. J. Hansen (Berlin 1894)

NÜRNBERGER, R., *Die Politisierung des französischen Protestantismus* (Tübingen 1948)

OBERHUBER, K., 'Die stilistische Entwicklung im Werk Bartholomäus Sprangers' (Diss. Vienna 1958)

ODLOŽILÍK, O., *Karel starší ze Žerotína* (Prague 1936)

—— 'Cesty z Čech a Moravy do Velké Britanie v letech 1563–1620', *ČMM* 59 (1935), 241–320

Od pravěku k dnešku, see Pekař, J.

ONG, W. J., *Ramus: method and the decay of dialogue* (Cambridge, Mass. 1958)

—— *Ramus and Talon inventory* (Cambridge, Mass. 1958)

ORNSTEIN, M., *The rôle of scientific societies in the seventeenth century* (2nd edn. London 1963)

PAGEL, W., 'Religious motives in the medical biology of the 17th century', *Bulletin of the Institute of the History of Medicine* iii (1935), 97–128, 213–31, 265–312

PANOFSKY, ERWIN, *Idea* (2nd edn. Berlin 1960)

PATRY, R., *Philippe du Plessis-Mornay, un huguenot homme d'état* (Paris 1933)

PEARSALL SMITH, L., *Life and letters of Sir Henry Wotton*, i (Oxford 1907)

PEKAŘ, J., *Bílá Hora* (Prague 1921)

—— *Od pravěku k dnešku, Sborník prací k šedesátým narozeninám Josefa Pekaře* i–ii (Prague 1930)

PELTZER, R. A., 'Hans von Aachen', *Jahrbuch* xxx (1911), 59–182

PENROSE, BOISE, *The Sherleian Odyssey* (Taunton 1938)

PEŠINA, J., 'Skupinový portrét v českém renesančním malířství', *Umění* ii (1954), 269–95

PEUCKERT, W.-E., *Die Rosenkreutzer, zur Geschichte einer Reformation* (Jena 1928)

—— *Pansophie* i–ii (Berlin 1956–67)

PEVSNER, NICOLAUS, *Academies of art, past and present* (Cambridge 1940)

—— 'Gegenreformation und Manierismus', *Repertorium für Kunstwissenschaft* 46 (1925), 243–62

PICK, F., *Johann Jessenius de Magna Jessen* (Leipzig 1926)

PIRNÁT, A., *Die Ideologie der Siebenbürger Antitrinitarier in den 1570er Jahren* (Budapest 1961)

POLIŠENSKÝ, J. V., *Anglie a Bílá Hora* (Prague 1949)

—— *Nizozemská politika a Bílá Hora* (Prague 1958)

—— 'České dějepisectví předbělohorského období a Pražská Akademie', *AUC* iv. 2 (1963), 115–37

—— *Jan Jesenský-Jessenius* (Prague 1965)

POLLAK, O., 'Studien zur Geschichte der Architektur Prags', *Jahrbuch* xxix (1910), 85–170

Prague Ghetto, see Muneles, O.

PRAZ, MARIO, *Studies in seventeenth-century imagery* (2nd edn. Rome 1964)

PREISS, P., *Giuseppe Arcimboldo* (Prague 1967)

PUCCI, FRANCESCO, *Lettere, documenti e testimonianze* i–ii, ed. L. Firpo and R. Piattoli (Florence 1955–9)

RACHLÍK, F., *Jiří Melantrich Rožďalovický z Aventýnu* (Prague 1930)

RALEIGH, SIR WALTER, *History of the World* (London 1614)

RANKE, L. VON, *Zur deutschen Geschichte vom Religionsfrieden bis zum dreissig-jährigen Krieg* (Leipzig 1869)

RÄSS, A., *Die Convertiten seit der Reformation*, ii–iv (Freiburg i. B. 1866)

RASSOW, P., *Die Kaiser-Idee Karls V* (Berlin 1932)

—— *Die politische Welt Karls V* (Munich 1946?)

READ, JOHN, *Prelude to chemistry* (London 1936)

REKERS, B., *Benito Arias Montano 1527–98* (Amsterdam 1961)

The Renaissance and Mannerism, Studies in Western Art, ii (Princeton 1963)

Retorica e Barocco . . . a cura di E. Castelli (Rome 1954–5)

REZNICEK, E. K. J., *Hendrik Goltzius als Zeichner* (Utrecht 1961)

RIDEMAN, PETER, *Account of our Religion, Doctrine and Faith* (Brünn 1565, Eng. trans. Bridgnorth 1950)

RIEGGER, J. VON (ed.), 'Aula Rudolphi II . . .', *Archiv der Geschichte und Statistik*, ii (Dresden 1793), 193–262; see p. 40 n. 1

RILL, G., 'Jacobus Palaeologus', *Mitteilungen des österreichischen Staatsarchivs* 16 (1963), 28–86

RITTER, MORIZ, *Deutsche Geschichte im Zeitalter der Gegenreformation und des dreissigjährigen Krieges* i–iii (Stuttgart 1889–95); see also *Briefe und Akten*

ROSSI, PAOLO, *Francesco Bacone, dalla magia alla scienza* (Bari 1957)

—— *Clavis Universalis, arti mnemoniche e logica combinatoria da Lullo a Leibniz* (Milan–Naples 1960)

Divi Rudolphi Imperatoris . . . epistolae ineditae, ed. B. de Pace (Vienna 1771)

Rukovět' humanistického básnictví v Čechách a na Moravě, see p. 147 n. 1

RYBIČKA, A., 'Poslední Rožmberkové a jich dědictví', *ČČM* liv (1880), 85–109, 218–48, 437–57; lv (1881), 38–55, 187–202, 366–75

SABBE, M., *De Moretussen en hun Kring* (Antwerp 1928)

SALVESTRINI, V., and FIRPO, L., *Bibliografia di Giordano Bruno* (Florence 1958)

SAN CLEMENTE, GUILLÉN DE, *Correspondencia inedita*, ed. Marqués de Ayerbe (Zaragoza 1892)

SANDRART, JOACHIM VON, *Der Teutschen Academie Zweyter Teil* (Nuremberg 1675); see p. 164 n. 5

SARGENT, R. M., *At the court of Queen Elizabeth, the life and lyrics of Sir Edward Dyer* (Oxford 1935)

SAXL, FRITZ, *Antike Götter in der Spätrenaissance* (Leipzig 1927)

SCHLOSSER, J. VON, *Die Kunst- und Wunderkammern der Spätrenaissance* (Leipzig 1908)

—— *Die Kunstliteratur* (Vienna 1924)

SCHMIDLIN, J., *Die kirchlichen Zustände in Deutschland vor dem dreissigjährigen Krieg* (Freiburg i. B. 1910)

SCHMIEDER, K. C., *Geschichte der Alchemie* (Halle 1832)

SCHOLEM, G. G., *Major trends in Jewish mysticism* (London 1955)

—— *On the Kabbalah and its symbolism* (London 1965)

SCHÖNE, A., *Emblematik und Drama im Zeitalter des Barock* (Munich 1964)

SCHULTESS, C., *Aus dem Briefwechsel des französischen Philologen und Diplomaten Jacques Bongars* (Hamburg 1905)

SCHUSTER, L., *Johann Kepler und die grossen kirchlichen Streitfragen seiner Zeit* (Graz 1888)

SCHWARZ, H. F., *The Imperial Privy Council in the seventeenth century* (Cambridge, Mass. 1943)

SCHWARZENFELD, G. VON, *Rudolf II, der saturnische Kaiser* (Munich 1961)

SECRET, F., *Le Zohar chez les Kabbalistes chrétiens de la Renaissance* (Paris 1958)

—— *Les Kabbalistes chrétiens de la Renaissance* (Paris 1964)

—— 'L'interpretazione della Kabbala nel Rinascimento', *Convivium* xxiv N.S. (1956), 541–52

SHEARMAN, JOHN, *Mannerism* (London, 1967)

SIDNEY, SIR PHILIP, *Works*, iii, ed. Feuillerat (Cambridge 1923)

SINGER, D. W., *Giordano Bruno, his life and thought* (New York 1950)

SLAVATA, VILÉM, *Paměti*, ed. J. Jireček (Prague 1866)

SMIJERS, A., 'Die kaiserliche Hofmusik-Kapelle von 1543–1619', *Studien zur Musikwissenschaft* vi (1919), 139–86, vii (1920), 102–42, viii (1921), 176–206

SOMMER, JOHANN, *Vita Jacobi Despotae* (Wittenberg 1587)

STAUFFER, A., *Hermann Christoph Graf von Ruszworm* (Munich 1884)

STERLING, C., *La nature morte de l'antiquité à nos jours* (Paris 1952)

STIEVE, FELIX, *Die Verhandlungen über die Nachfolge Kaisers Rudolf II in den Jahren 1581–1602* (Munich 1879)

—— *Abhandlungen, Vorträge und Reden* (Leipzig 1900); see also *Briefe und Akten*

STLOUKAL, K., *Papežská politika a císařský dvůr pražský na předělu XVI a XVII věku* (Prague 1925)

—— 'Karel z Liechtenstein', *ČČH* xviii (1912), 21–37, 153–69, 389–434

—— 'Počátky nunciatury v Praze', *ČČH* xxxiv (1928), 1–24, 237–79

—— 'Portrét Rudolfa II z roku 1600', *Pekařův Sborník*, ii. 1–14

STRÁNSKÝ, PAVEL, *Český Stát*, ed. B. Ryba (Prague 1953)

STURMBERGER, HANS, *Kaiser Ferdinand II und das Problem des Absolutismus* (Munich 1957)

SUDHOFF, K., *Versuch einer Kritik der Echtheit der Paracelsischen Schriften* i–ii (Berlin 1894–9)

SVÁTEK, J., *Culturhistorische Bilder aus Böhmen* (Vienna 1879)

—— *Obrazy z kulturních dějin českých* (Prague 1891) (N.B. These two books are not identical)

Symbola Divina et Humana . . . (Prague 1601–3); see p. 128 n. 5

SZATHMÁRY, L., *Magyar alkémisták* (Budapest 1928)

TAPIÉ, V.-L., *The age of grandeur* (London 1960)

THIEBERGER, F., *The great Rabbi Loew of Prague* (London 1954–5)

THORNDIKE, LYNN, *History of magic and experimental science*, v–vii (New York 1941–58)

TILLYARD, E. M. W., *The Elizabethan world picture* (London 1963)

TOBOLKA, Z., and HORÁK, E., *Knihopis českých a slovenských tisků*, ii– (Prague 1939–)

TOMEK, W. W., *Dějepis města Prahy*, xii (Prague 1901)

TREVOR-ROPER, H. R., *Religion, the Reformation and social change* (London 1967)

TRUNZ, E., 'Der deutsche Späthumanismus um 1600 als Standeskultur', reprinted in *Deutsche Barockforschung*, ed. R. Alewyn (Cologne–Berlin 1965), 147–81

TURBA, GUSTAV, *Geschichte des Thronfolgerechts in allen habsburgischen Ländern* (Vienna–Leipzig 1903)

—— 'Beiträge zur Geschichte der Habsburger aus den letzten Jahren des spanischen Königs Philip II', *AÖG* 86 (1898), 313–452

TUVE, R., *Elizabethan and Metaphysical imagery* (Chicago 1947)

Umanesimo e simbolismo . . . a cura di E. Castelli (Padua 1958)

URBAN, WACŁAV, *Studia z dziejów Antytrynitaryzmu na ziemiach czeskich i słowackich w XVI–XVII wieku* (Cracow 1966)

VALDŠTEJN: *Doba bělohorská a Albrecht z Valdštejna*, ed. J. Prokeš (Prague 1934)

VARGA, L., 'Sámboky János emblémái', *Könyv és Könyvtár* iv (1964), 193–226

VARGHA, A., *Iustus Lipsius és a magyar szellemi élet* (Budapest 1942)

VAŠICA, JOSEF, *České literární baroko* (Prague 1938)

VERESS, E., *Carrillo Alfonz Jezsuita Atya levelezése és iratai* (Budapest 1906)

VOET, L., *The golden compasses*, i (Antwerp 1969)

VOLF, J., *Geschichte des Buchdrucks in Böhmen und Mähren bis 1848* (Weimar 1928)

VOLKMANN, L., *Bilderschriften der Renaissance* (2nd edn. Leipzig 1962)

WALDE, O., *Storhetstidens litterära krigsbyten* i–ii (Uppsala 1916–20)

WALKER, D. P., *Spiritual and demonic magic from Ficino to Campanella* (London 1958)

—— 'Musical Humanism in the sixteenth century and early seventeenth century', *The Music Review* ii (1941), 1–13, 111–21, 220–7, 228–308; iii (1942), 55–71

WELLEK, RENÉ, *Essays on Czech literature* (The Hague 1963)

WESTONIA, ELISABETH JOAN, *Parthenicon* (Prague 1606)

WESZPRÉMI, S., *Succincta Medicorum Hungariae et Transilvaniae Biographia*, Centuriae i–iii (Leipzig–Vienna 1774–87)

WILBERG VIGNAU-SCHUURMAN, TH. A. G., *Die emblematischen Elemente im Werke Joris Hoefnagels* i–ii (Leiden 1969)

WILBUR, E. M., *A history of Unitarianism, Socinianism and its antecedents* (Cambridge, Mass. 1946)

WINTER, EDUARD, *Der Josefinismus und seine Geschichte* (Brünn–Vienna 1943)

—— *Tausend Jahre Geisteskampf im Sudetenraum* (2nd edn. Munich 1955)

—— *Die tschechische und slowakische Emigration in Deutschland im 17. und 18. Jahrhundert* (Berlin 1955)

WINTER, Z., *Děje vysokých škol pražských 1409–1622* (Prague 1897)
—— *Český průmysl a obchod v XVI věku* (Prague 1913)
WIRTH, Z., 'Die böhmische Renaissance', *Historica* iii (1958), 87–107
WITTKOWER, R., *Architectural principles in the Age of Humanism* (3rd edn. London 1962)
WOLKAN, R., *Böhmens Anteil an der deutschen Literatur des 16. Jahrhunderts* i–iii (Prague 1890–4)
WÜRTENBERGER, F., *Der Manierismus* (Vienna 1962, Eng. trans. New York 1963)
YATES, FRANCES A., *The French Academies of the sixteenth century* (London 1947)
—— *Giordano Bruno and the hermetic tradition* (London 1964)
—— *The art of memory* (London 1966)
—— 'Queen Elizabeth as Astraea', *JWCI* x (1947), 27–82
ZACHAR, O., *O alchymii a českých alchymistech* (Prague 1911?)
—— 'Rudolf II a alchymisté', *ČČM* 86 (1912), 417–24; 87 (1913), 148–55, 243–57
ZANTA, L., *La renaissance du stoïcisme au XVIᵉ siècle* (Paris 1914)
ŽEROTÍN, KAREL, *Listy psané jazykem českým* i–iii, ed. V. Brandl (Brno 1870–2)
—— *Dopisy 1591–1610*, ed. F. Dvorský (Prague 1904)
ZÍBRT, Č., *Bibliografie české historie* i–v (Prague 1900–11)
ZIMMER, J., *Joseph Heintz der Ältere als Maler* (Heidelberg 1967)
ZINNER, E., *Geschichte und Bibliographie der astronomischen Literatur in Deutschland zur Zeit der Renaissance* (2nd edn. Stuttgart 1964)
ZUCCARO, FEDERIGO, *L'Idea de' Pittori, Scultori ed Architetti* (Turin 1607)

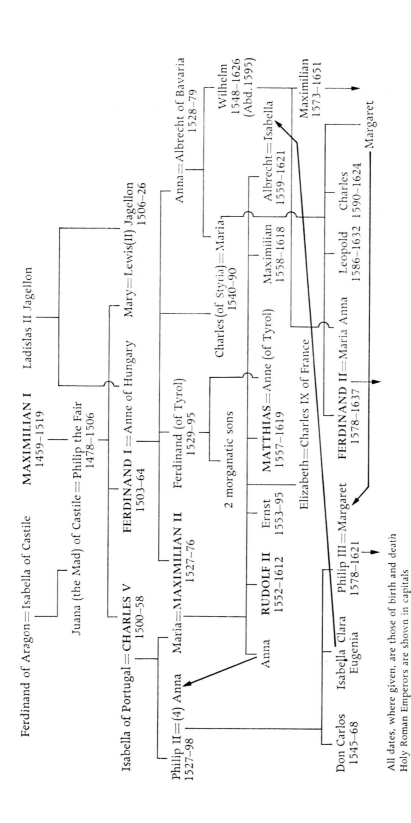

THE HOUSE OF HABSBURG IN THE 16TH CENTURY

Ferdinand of Aragon = Isabella of Castile

MAXIMILIAN I
1459–1519

Ladislas II Jagellon

Juana (the Mad) of Castile = Philip the Fair
1478–1506

Mary = Lewis (II) Jagellon
1506–26

Isabella of Portugal = CHARLES V
1500–58

FERDINAND I = Anne of Hungary
1503–64

Anna = Albrecht of Bavaria
1528–79

Wilhelm
1548–1626
(Abd. 1595)

Philip II = (4) Anna
1527–98

Maria = MAXIMILIAN II
1527–76

Ferdinand (of Tyrol)
1529–95

2 morganatic sons

Charles (of Styria) = Maria
1540–90

Albrecht = Isabella
1559–1621

Maximilian
1573–1651

Anna

RUDOLF II
1552–1612

Ernst
1553–95

MATTHIAS = Anne (of Tyrol)
1557–1619

Maximilian
1558–1618

Leopold
1586–1632

Charles
1590–1624

Don Carlos
1545–68

Isabella Clara
Eugenia

Philip III = Margaret
1578–1621

Elizabeth = Charles IX of France

FERDINAND II = Maria Anna
1578–1637

Margaret

All dates, where given, are those of birth and death
Holy Roman Emperors are shown in capitals

INDEX

1. Giuseppe Arcimboldo: *Rudolf II as Vertumnus*

In Roman mythology Vertumnus was the god of the changing seasons, hence also of flowers and fruits. This extraordinary creation, a late work of the artist's, apparently gave great satisfaction to its subject.

2. Bartholomaeus Spranger: *Allegory of the Virtues of Rudolf II*

An allegory of war, with the virtuous as victor—a pious hope, as the inscription suggests. Bellona with lance and statuette sits on a globe, surrounded by Athene, Bacchus, Venus and Amor, and figures which symbolize Hungary and the Croatian river Sava (right foreground, with boar).

3. Bartholomaeus Spranger: *The Triumph of Wisdom*

Another very stylized work. The provocative figure of Athene treads down ignorance, which has the ears of an ass. Around her are gathered Bellona and the nine Muses, prominent among them Urania (with celestial globe) and Geometria (with compasses).

4. Adriaen de Vries: *Rudolf II as Patron of the Arts*

A subtle and complicated scene. The Emperor, at once general and peacemaker, turns to greet the liberal and plastic arts. The latter three—architecture (with instruments), sculpture (with hammer and statuette), and painting—stand closest to him. Among the other representations note the river-god and lion in the left foreground: symbols of the Vltava and Bohemia.

5. Adriaen de Vries: *Rudolf II, with the head of a Lion*

This relief, less well known than the busts by the same artist, displays to good effect the association of Rudolf with Hercules, as also the parallel (carried to the lengths of physiognomical accuracy) between the Emperor's place among men and the lion's among animals.

6. Josef Heintz: *Venus and Adonis*

A typical scene of erotic mythology from the Rudolfine atelier.

7. Hans von Aachen: *Rudolf II* (print by Aegidius Sadeler)

Here again we find the linked ideas of Humanist virtue and military victory. Note the fish-tailed goat and the eagle above the motto 'ADSIT'. Widely circulated, this became one of the most familiar portraits of Rudolf, with his laurel wreath, idealized armour, and decoration of the Golden Fleece.

8a. (above) Hans von Aachen: *The Liberation of Hungary*

A small but characteristic testimony to the iconographical stimulus of the Turkish War. The background scene depicts the storming of the Danubian fortress of Raab in 1598 by Imperial troops under Schwarzenberg. Ironically it was the aftermath of the First World War which brought the painting from Vienna to Budapest.

8b. Georg Hoefnagel: *Miniature from George Bocskay's book of calligraphy*

The page shown contains embellishment to a sample text. The artist's tiny view of Prague castle may be compared with that reproduced in the *Civitates Orbis Terrarum* (Plate 16 below).

9a. Roelant Savery: *Paradise* (detail)

A splendid example of Savery's distinctive art, not the less appropriate here for being painted a few years after Rudolf's death. It was formerly in the Nostitz gallery.

9b. Roelant Savery: *Orpheus with Beasts and Birds*

Savery painted at least twenty variations on this theme. Here as usual the figure of Orpheus with his lute is pure staffage, though the artist was clearly attracted by his connotations of Christian, and perhaps also Neoplatonist, symbolism.

10. Jan Vermeyen: *Crown of Rudolf II* (*Austrian Hauskrone*)

Despite the magnificence of this object little is known about its construction. Its side-panels depict the three coronations of Rudolf: Imperial, Hungarian, and Bohemian, and a symbolic representation of Victory, with the usual imagery and decoration. Later Emperors employed the crown on certain state occasions, though its place in the Habsburg regalia was never fully clarified.

11. Anton Schweinberger: *Jug of Seychelle-Nut*

The decoration presents variations on classical aquatic themes. The nut itself is of a very exotic kind, and it seems that Rudolf bought this specimen from the Dutch admiral Wolfer Hermanszen, who had received it from the Prince of Bantam (W. Java).

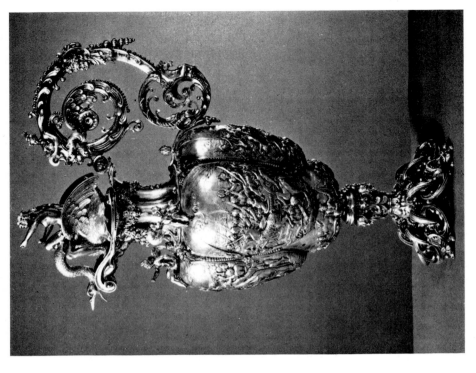

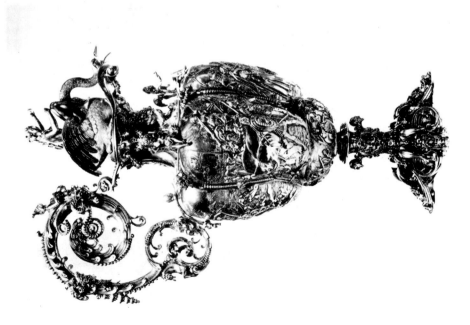

12. Christoph Jamnitzer: *Triumphal Jug*

A highly original, and thoroughly non-functional, masterwork of Mannerism. The two panels illustrated depict (left) the Triumph of Fame, behind whose elephant-drawn wagon stand celebrated artists and literati; and (right) the Triumph of Truth, with the figures of martyrs and a prominent unicorn.

13. Aegidius Sadeler: Rudolfine *imprese* from the *Symbola Divina et Humana*
These examples of personal emblems are typical of the contemporary taste.

14. Aegidius Sadeler: *The Vladislav Hall of Prague Castle in 1607*

A colourful scene under Benedict Rejt's great late-Gothic vault in the main reception room of the Hradschin, a space almost unchanged to the present day. The busy trading is observed by some Persian visitors (in centre), and the print bears a dedication from the engraver to the Chief Justice Christoph Lobkovic, who had a special knowledge of Eastern affairs. The quaint little figure standing by an upper window at the back of the hall could just possibly be the Emperor himself.

15a. *Investiture of the Order of the Golden Fleece in Prague, 1585*

The Archduke Ferdinand presents Rudolf with the chain of the Order, while Ernst and Charles of Styria look on. The doggerel beneath provides a predictable pious commentary.

15b. *Castrum Doloris of Rudolf II, 1612*

A primitive view of the Emperor's elaborate lying-in-state, to accompany the narrative of Heinrich Hiesserle von Chodaw.

15c. Antonio Abondio: *Medallion of Rudolf II* (obverse and reverse)

A portrait of the young Rudolf, but the features strikingly resemble those shown later by Vries and others. The reverse has a simple imperial motif.

16. Georg Hoefnagel: *View of Prague, c. 1590*

Above we see the Hradschin (Ratzin!) in all its embattled isolation and crowned by the Cathedral of St. Vitus. Below Hoefnagel gives a general view of the city from the hill of Letná: on the far side of the Vltava lie the Old and New Towns; to the right is the Malá Strana (Kleinseite) straggling up the hill towards the Hradschin, which now appears from a different angle.